The Inquisition in the Spanish Dependencies

Sicily - Naples - Sardinia - Milan - The Canaries - Mexico - Peru - New Granada

Henry Charles Lea

Alpha Editions

This Edition Published in 2020

ISBN: 9789354219665

Design and Setting By
Alpha Editions
www.alphaedis.com
Email – info@alphaedis.com

As per information held with us this book is in Public Domain.
This book is a reproduction of an important historical work. Alpha Editions
uses the best technology to reproduce historical work in the same manner
it was first published to preserve its original nature. Any marks or number
seen are left intentionally to preserve its true form.

PREFACE.

THE scope of my History of the Spanish Inquisition precluded a detailed investigation into the careers of individual tribunals. Such an investigation, however, is not without interest, especially with respect to the outlying ones, which were subjected to varying influences and reacted in varying ways on the peoples among whom they were established. Moreover, in some cases, this affords us an inside view of inquisitorial life, of the characters of those to whom were confided the awful irresponsible powers of the Holy Office and of the abuse of those powers by officials whom distance removed from the immediate supervision of the central authority, suggesting a capacity for evil even greater than that manifested in the Peninsula.

This is especially the case with the tribunals of the American Colonies, of which, thanks to the unwearied researches of Don José Toribio Medina, of Santiago de Chile, a fairly complete and minute account can be given, based on the confidential correspondence of the local officials with the Supreme Council and the reports of the *visitadores* or inspectors, who were occasionally sent in the vain expectation of reducing them to order. While thus in the colonial tribunals we see the Inquisition at its worst, as a portion of the governmental system, we can realize how potent was its influence in contributing to the failure of Spanish colonial policy, by preventing orderly and settled administration and by exciting disaffection which the Council of Indies more than once warned the crown would lead to the loss of its transatlantic empire. It is perhaps not too much to say that these revelations moreover go far to explain the influences which so long retarded the political and industrial development of the emancipated colonies, for it was an evil inheritance weighing heavily on successive generations.

I have not attempted to include the fateful career of the Inquisition in the Netherlands, for this cannot be written until the completion of

Professor Paul Fredericq's monumental "Corpus Documentorum Inquisitionis hæreticæ pravitatis Neerlandicæ," the earlier volumes of which have thrown so much light on the repression of heresy in the Low Countries up to the dawn of the Reformation.

It is scarce necessary for me to make special acknowledgement to Señor Medina in all that relates to the American tribunals, for this is sufficiently attested by the constant reference to his works. With regard to Mexico I am under particular obligation to David Fergusson Esq. for the use of collections made by him during long residence in that Republic and also to the late General Don Vicente Riva Palacio for the communication of a number of interesting documents. To the late Doctor Paz Soldan of Lima my thanks are also due for copies made in the archives of Peru prior to their dispersion in 1881.

PHILADELPHIA, OCTOBER, 1907.

CONTENTS.

CHAPTER I—SICILY.

	PAGE
The Old Inquisition in Sicily	1
The Spanish Inquisition introduced in 1487	2
Expulsion of Jews in 1492	3
Tardy Organization of the Tribunal	5
It gradually becomes efficient	7
Financial Mismanagement	9
Popular Disaffection	10
Increasing Activity	12
Complaints of Sicilian Parliament	13
Death of King Ferdinand—Tumult of 1516	14
Re-establishment in 1519	17
Efforts to reform Abuses	18
Renewed Complaints of the Parliament	21
Charles V suspends the Temporal Jurisdiction in 1535	22
Dread of Protestantism—Jurisdiction restored in 1546	24
Official Immunity—Case of the Duke of Terranova	25
Renewed Activity—Popular Hostility	26
Enormous Increase in Number of Familiars	27
Abuse of official Immunity	28
Attempt at Reform in the Concordia of 1595	31
Increased Aggressiveness of the Tribunal	33
Collisions with the Secular Authority	34
Quarrels with the Bishops	35
Continued Strife—Concordia of 1635	37
Activity during the Seventeenth Century	38
The Inquisition under Austrian Rule—Auto de Fe of 1724—Pragmatic Sanction of 1732	40
Reconquest of Sicily by Spain in 1734—The Inquisition placed under the Holy See—Its Exuberance repressed by Carlos III	42
Suppressed by Ferdinando III in 1782	43

MALTA.

A Dependency of the Sicilian Tribunal	44
Charles V in 1530 grants the Island to the Knights of St. John	45

Episcopal Inquisition under Bishop Cubelles 45
The Tribunal passes under Papal Control 46

Chapter II—Naples.

The Old Inquisition in Naples—The Jews 49
Refugees from Spain 50
Spanish Conquest in 1503—Capitulation excludes the Spanish
    Inquisition 52
Julius II revives the Papal Inquisition 53
Ferdinand proposes to introduce the Spanish Inquisition in 1504 53
Neapolitan Organization—the *Piazze* or *Seggi* 54
Activity of the Papal Inquisition—Its Subordination to the Royal
    Power 55
Ferdinand, in 1509, arranges to introduce the Spanish Inquisition . 56
Popular Opposition becomes uncontrollable 58
Ferdinand abandons the Attempt 62
His fruitless efforts to stimulate Persecution 63
Inertness of the Papal Inquisition 65
Banishment of Jews in 1540 66
Protestantism in Naples—Juan de Valdés—Bernardino Ochino . 67
Organization of Roman Inquisition in 1542—Charles V orders its
    Introduction in Naples 70
Tentative Efforts create popular Excitement 71
The Tumult of 1547—its Suppression 73
Punishment of the Leaders 76
Recrudescence of Persecution—The Roman Inquisition tacitly
    introduced 78
The Calabrian Waldenses—Their Extermination 79
The Apulian Waldenses 85
Intermingling of Jurisdictions 86
Philip II promises the *Via Ordinaria* 87
The Roman Inquisition under Cover of the Episcopal . . . 87
The Accused sent to Rome for Trial and Punishment . . . 88
The Exequatur of the Viceroy is a Condition precedent . . . 89
Gradual Encroachment—A Commissioner of the Roman Inqui-
    sition established in Naples 92
He assumes to be an Inquisitor—Rome in 1628 denies the Neces-
    sity of the Viceregal Exequatur—Quarrels over it . . 94
The Roman Inquisition virtually established in Naples . . . 96
Popular dissatisfaction—Demand for the *Via Ordinaria* . . . 96
Commissioner Piazza banished in 1671 99

CONTENTS xi

PAGE

Outbreak in 1691—Commissioner Giberti ejected 99
Carlos II prohibits the residence of Commissioners—Permanent
 Deputation to oppose the Inquisition 100
The Roman Inquisition in 1695 publishes an Edict of Denunciation 101
The Episcopal Inquisition disregards the *Via Ordinaria*—Struggles under the Austrian Domination 102
Accession of Charles of Spain—*Atto di fede* of 1746 104
Episcopal Inquisition suppressed—Archbishop Spinelli forced
 to resign 105
Continued Vigilance of the Deputati until 1764 107

CHAPTER III—SARDINIA.

The Spanish Inquisition introduced in 1492 109
Conflicts with the Authorities 110
Productive Confiscations 112
Decadent condition of the tribunal 114
Charles V endeavors to reanimate it—Its chronic Poverty . . 115
Interference of the Bishops 117
Multiplication of Officials 117
Quarrels with the Secular Authorities 118
The Inquisition disappears under the House of Savoy . . . 119

CHAPTER IV—MILAN.

The Old and the reorganized Roman Inquisition 121
Energy of Fra Michele Ghislieri (Pius V) 122
Inefficiency of the Inquisition 123
Cardinal Borromeo's persecuting Zeal 124
Philip II proposes to introduce the Spanish Inquisition . . . 125
Popular Resistance—General Opposition of Italian Bishops . . 126
Philip II abandons the Project 128
Political and Commercial Questions affecting Lombardy—Intercourse with Heretics 129
Cardinal Borromeo stimulates Persecution 131
His Mission to Mantua 133
The Roman Inquisition perfected—Its Struggle to exclude Swiss
 Heresy 135
It is suppressed by Maria Theresa in 1775 137

xii   CONTENTS

Chapter V—The Canaries.

	PAGE
Importance of the Islands as a Commercial Centre	139
Episcopal Inquisition by Bishop Muros, in 1499	140
Tribunal established in 1505—It is dependent on Seville	140
Its Activity until 1534	141
It becomes dormant and is suspended	144
It is reorganized in 1567 and rendered independent of Seville	145
Activity of Inquisitor Diego Ortiz de Fúnez	147
Visitation of Doctor Bravo de Zayas in 1570	148
Visitation of Claudio de la Cueva in 1590—Abuses	150
Prosecution of escaped Negro and Moorish Slaves	152
Prosecution of English and Dutch Sailors	153
Number of Relaxations	155
Finances—Early Poverty—Wealth from Confiscations	156
Prosecution of Judaizers	158
Moorish and Negro Slaves—Renegades	159
Trivial Cases	161
Mysticism—*Beatas revelanderas*	162
Solicitation in the Confessional	163
Sorcery and Superstitions	165
Foreign Heretics—Sailors and Merchants	167
Treaties with England in 1604 and with Holland in 1609	171
Precarious Position of Foreign Merchants	173
Censorship	176
Examination of Houses of Foreign Residents	177
Irreverent religious Objects	178
Visitas de Navíos	179
Quarrels with the Authorities, secular and ecclesiastical	180
Popular hostility—Opposition to Sanbenitos in Churches	188
Suppression in 1813	189
Final Extinction in 1820	190

Chapter VI—Mexico.

Propagation of the Faith the Object of the Conquest	191
Organization of the Colonial Church	192
Attempts to exclude New Christians	193
Episcopal Inquisition	195
Establishment of a Tribunal proposed—Dread of Protestantism	199
Inquisitors sent out in 1570	200
Tribunal installed, November 4, 1571	202

CONTENTS

	PAGE
Distance renders it partially Independent	203
Commencement of Activity—The first auto de fe, February 28, 1574	204
Autos of 1575, 1576, 1577, 1578, 1579, 1590, 1596, and 1601	207
Persecution of Judaizers	208
Indians not subject to Inquisition	209
Finances—Temporary royal Subvention—The Tribunal expected to be self-supporting	212
Its early Poverty	213
It claims Indian Repartimientos	215
It refuses to render Account of its Receipts	216
It obtains a Grant of Canonries in 1627	216
Fruitless Efforts to make it account for the Confiscations	217
Large Remittances made to the Suprema from the Autos of 1646, 1648 and 1649	219
Efforts to make it forego and refund the royal Subvention	219
Misrepresentations of the Confiscations and Remittances	223
Comparative Inaction in the first Half of the Seventeenth Century	226
Efficacy of the Edict of Faith	227
Growth of Judaism—Active Persecution commences in 1642	229
Autos de Fe of 1646, 1648 and 1649	230
Auto de Fe of 1659	234
Cases of William Lamport and Joseph Bruñon de Vertiz	236
Inertia during the Rest of the Century	240
Solicitation in the Confessional	241
Temporal Jurisdiction—Immunity of Officials entitled to the Fuero	245
Familiars—Commissioners—Abuse of their Privileges	247
Concordia of 1610	251
Competencias	252
Concordia of 1633	254
Abusive Use of Power by Commissioners	256
Quarrels with Bishops—Case of Bishop Palafox	257
Case of Doctor Juan de la Camara	259
Exemption from Military Service	263
Censorship—Irreverent Use of Sacred Symbols—*Visitas de Navios*	264
Repression under the Bourbon Dynasty	267
Decadence of the Tribunal	269
Political Activity caused by the Revolution—Censorship	272
Prosecution of Miguel Hidalgo	276
Suppression in 1813	288
Re-establishment in 1815	290
Prosecution of José María Morelos	292

	PAGE
Extinction in 1820	297
Persistent Intolerance	298

THE PHILIPPINES.

Included in the District of the Mexican Tribunal	299
A Commissioner established there—His Powers	300
Solicitation—Military Deserters.	302
Trivial Results	304
Censorship	306
Conflicts with the Authorities	308
Audacity of the Commissioners	310
Commissioner Paternina imprisons Governor Salcedo and rules the Colony	311
Records burnt in 1763	317
Episcopal Inquisition in China	317

CHAPTER VII—PERU.

Deplorable Condition of the Colony	319
Episcopal Inquisition—Its Activity	321
Case of Francisco de Aguirre	322
The Bishops seek to maintain their Jurisdiction	325
The Tribunal established January 29, 1570	326
The first Auto de Fe, November 15, 1573	328
Organization and Powers—Exemption of Indians	329
Supervision over Foreigners	332
Extent of Territory—Commissioners and their Abuses	333
New Granada detached in 1611—Other Divisions proposed	337
Finances—Initial Poverty—Speedy Growth of Confiscations	342
Fruitless Efforts to withdraw the Royal Subvention	344
Suppression of Prebends for the Benefit of the Tribunal	346
Enormous Confiscations in the Auto de Fe of 1639	347
Other Sources of Income.	349
Increased Expenses exceed the Revenues	350
Malversations and Embezzlements in the Eighteenth Century	351
Financial Condition at Suppression in 1813	354
Abusive use of arbitrary Power	355
Scandalous conduct of Inquisitor Ulloa	355
Visitation of Juan Ruiz de Prado	357
His charges against Cerezuela and Ulloa	358
Ulloa's Visitation of the District	360

Abusive use of arbitrary Power:
    Inquisitor Ordoñez y Flores 362
    Inquisitors Gaitan and Mañozca 363
    Inquisitors Calderon and Unda 366
    Visitation of Antonio de Arenaza 367
Paralysis of the Tribunal—Purchase of Offices 372
Quarrels with the Viceroys 373
    Humiliation of Viceroy del Villar 374
    Complaints of succeeding Viceroys 380
Conflicts of Jurisdictions 382
Limitation of the Temporal Jurisdiction by Fernando VI . . 386
Quarrels of Inquisitor Amusquíbar with Archbishop Barroeta . 389
Activity of the Tribunal—Bigamy, Blasphemy, Sorcery . . . 390
    Propositions 392
    Solicitation in the Confessional 393
    Mystic Impostors—Maria Pizarro 396
        Angela Carranza 400
    Quietism—The Jesuit Ulloa and his Disciples 406
    Protestantism—English Prisoners of War 412
    Judaism 419
        Portuguese Immigration through Brazil and Buenos
           Ayres 421
        Case of Francisco Maldonado de Silva 423
        The *Complicidad Grande*—Auto de Fe of 1639 . . . 425
        Decline of Judaism—Case of Doña Ana de Castro . . 433
Punishments 437
    Arbitrary Inconsistency—Case of François Moyen . . . 439
Censorship 444
    Morals and Politics 446
Decadence and Suppression 447
Re-establishment and Extinction 449
Work accomplished 451

Chapter VIII—New Granada.

Settlement of New Granada 453
Commissioners appointed by Tribunal of Lima 454
Demand for an Independent Tribunal 455
Extent of District—Attempt to include Florida 457
Tribunal established in 1610 at Cartagena 460
Early Operations 461
    Sorcery and Witchcraft—Blasphemy 462
    Judaism 466

	PAGE
Inertia—Sack of Cartagena in 1697	467
Decadence	468
Censorship—The Copernican System	470
Quarrels with the Authorities	473
Arbitrary Control exercised by Inquisitor Mañozca	473
Incessant Broils—Inquisitor Vélez de Asas y Argos—Fiscal Juan Ortiz	476
Visitation of Dr. Martin Real in 1643—Its Failure	480
Internal Dissensions and external Quarrels	483
Visitation of Pedro Medina Rico in 1648—Death of Inquisitor Pereira and Secretary Uriarte	485
Internal and external Quarrels continue	488
Degradation of the Tribunal	489
Quarrel with Bishop Benavides y Piedrola—Inquisitor Valera	491
Humiliation of Governor Ceballos	498
Decadence after the Sack of 1697	499
Finances—The Royal Subvention	500
Wealth accruing from Confiscations	501
Quarrels over the Subvention	502
Asserted Distress of the Tribunal	505
The Revolutionary Junta banishes the Tribunal in 1810	506
It takes Refuge in Santa Marta and Puertobelo	508
It returns to Cartagena in 1815	508
It is extinguished by the United States of Colombia in 1821	510
Influence of the Inquisition on the Spanish Colonies	511

APPENDIX OF DOCUMENTS 517

THE INQUISITION

IN THE

SPANISH DEPENDENCIES.

CHAPTER I.

SICILY.

The island of Sicily, in the fifteenth century, was a portion of the dominions of Aragon. Like the rest of the possessions of that crown, it had enjoyed the benefits of the old papal Inquisition under the conduct of the Dominicans, but, as elsewhere, towards the close of the Middle Ages, the institution had become nearly dormant, and at most was employed occasionally to wring money from the Jews. An effort to galvanize it, however, was made, in 1451, by the Inquisitor Fra Enrico Lugardi, who produced a fictitious decree, purporting to have been issued in 1224, by the Emperor Frederic II, granting to the inquisitors a third of the confiscations, together with yearly contributions from Jews and infidels; this was confirmed by King Alfonso of Naples, and again, in 1477, by Ferdinand and Isabella.[1] When, in 1484, the Spanish Inquisition was extended to Aragon, Ferdinand did not at first seek to carry its blessings to his insular possessions. February 12, 1481, he had appointed Filippo de' Barbari, one of his confessors, as inquisitor of Sicily, Malta, Gozo and Pantelaria, who apparently did nothing to further the cause of the faith, for Sixtus IV, in

---

[1] Páramo de Origine S. Officii S. Inquisitionis, pp. 197–99.—Ripoll Bullar. Ord. Fr. Prædic., III, 510.—La Mantia, L'Inquisizione in Sicilia, pp. 16–18 (Torino, 1886).

letters of February 23, 1483, to Isabella, complained of the prevalence in the island of the same heresies that pervaded Spain; to repress these he had issued sundry bulls, which had proved inoperative in consequence of the opposition of the royal officials, to his no little grief. Seeing the zeal displayed in Spain, he prayed and exhorted that it should be extended to Sicily and that the necessary royal favor be exhibited to the measures which he had taken and might take in the future.[1] There is no evidence that this produced any effect, and the institution seems to have remained inert until, about 1487, Torquemada, as Inquisitor-general of Aragon, appointed Fray Antonio de la Peña as inquisitor who, on August 18th of that year, celebrated the first auto de fe, in which Eulalia Tamarit, apparently a refugee from Saragossa, was burnt. It seems that a Dominican, named Giacomo Roda, had been exercising the functions under a commission from the General of his Order, who subsequently instructed the provincial, Giacomo Manso, to dismiss him. In 1488 la Peña left Sicily, appointing Manso to act during his absence, when Roda reasserted himself and it required a brief from Innocent VIII, February 7, 1489, to make him desist. In fact, at this time there seems to have been some confusion between the claims of the papal and Spanish Inquisitions, for we hear of another Dominican inquisitor, Pietro Ranzano, Bishop of Lucera, to whom the senate of Palermo, on January 19, 1488, took the customary oath of obedience.[2]

In Sicily, as in Spain, the objects of the principal labors of the Holy Office were the converts from Judaism. The Jews were numerous and rich and, although popular hatred was perhaps not so active as in Spain, it was sufficiently vigorous, in 1474, to bring

---

[1] Pirri, Sicilia Sacra, p. 910 (Panormi, 1733).—Llorente, Hist. crít. de la Inquisicion de España, Append. No. III.

[2] La Mantia, op. cit., pp. 20-1.—Franchina, Breve Rapporto del Tribunale della SS. Inquisizione in Sicilia, pp. 23, 108–16 (Palermo, 1744).

If we may believe an inscription of 1631, Ranzano had been inquisitor in 1482.—Jo. Mariæ Bertini Sacratissima Inquisitionis Rosa Virginea, I, 385 (Panormi, 1662). He died in 1492.

about a massacre, under the pretext that they were endeavoring to undermine the Catholic faith by argument. The viceroy, Lope Ximenes de Urrea, hanged six of the leaders of the movement, in the hope of suppressing it but, undeterred by this, the populace, in many places, sacked the Juderías and put the inmates to the sword; five hundred thus were slain in Noto, six hundred in Modica and, for several years, the Jews were in constant fear of massacre, in spite of royal and vice-regal edicts.[1] The number of victims in these troubles indicates how considerable was the Jewish population; indeed, in 1450, they petitioned that, in the assessment of a donation to King Alfonso of 10,000 florins they might be reckoned as a tenth of the population, a favor which was refused and, when in 1491, the Jews were banished from Provence, a large portion of them flocked to Sicily, attracted by the favorable conditions which had long been accorded there to the race.[2]

The edict of expulsion from Spain, in 1492, was operative in Sicily, under conditions even more repulsively cruel. It was published June 18th, and the day of departure was fixed at September 18th, under pain of death and confiscation. At once all their valuables were seized, in a house to house investigation, and inventories were made of their other possessions. They were required, within the three months, not only to collect what was due to them and to pay their debts, but also to indemnify the king for their special tributes by capitalizing the annual aggregate, on a basis of four per cent. interest. On August 13th an order was issued to license each to take a suit of common clothes, a mattress, a pair of worn sheets, a coverlet, three *tari* in money (equivalent to half a florin), and a few provisions for the journey. Reduced

---

[1] Zurita, Añales de Aragon, Lib. xix, cap. xiv.—Giov. di Giovanni, L'Ebraismo della Sicilia, pp. 190-1 (Palermo, 1748).

[2] Giovanni, pp. 21, 96.

Isidor Loeb considers the ordinary computations to be grossly exaggerated and, from the statistics of several places, assumes the total to have been not more than from twenty to thirty thousand.—Revue des Etudes Juives, 1887, p. 172.

to despair, the Jews of Palermo petitioned to be allowed to retain money enough to pay their passages; that the rich could leave their property on deposit, and that poor debtors might be discharged from prison a month in advance. This drew from the viceroy an edict allowing the rich to take twice as much as the poor, except in the matter of clothes. Not only their mattresses were to be searched for money and jewels, but even the cavities of their bodies, for which examiners of both sexes were appointed. A payment of fifty thousand florins to the king procured a postponement of three months, until December 18th, and during the interval the composition for their tributes was agreed upon, at a hundred thousand more, on payment of which they were to be allowed to take what was left of their inventoried goods, but all precious metals and jewels were required to be turned into merchandise. There was delay in collecting these sums, causing a further postponement of departure until January 12, 1493.[1] As the object of the measure was the salvation of souls, the alternative of conversion was offered, to which the Jews were urged by a proclamation of Torquemada and by promises from the bishops and the viceroy. Ferdinand, however, was not disposed thus to forego the opportunity of despoiling his Jewish subjects, and issued an order requiring them to purchase the privilege of baptism with the surrender of forty-five per cent. of their property, which must have brought him in a considerable sum for, in spite of it, the rigorous terms imposed upon the exiles drove many into the Christian fold.[2]

These compulsory Christians, always suspected, and generally with reason, of secretly cherishing their ancient faith, furnished a larger and more lucrative field for inquisitorial operations, but

---

[1] Giovanni, p. 210.—This *celeste benefizio*, as the pious author terms it, proved so destructive to the commercial prosperity of the island that, in 1695, the Jews were invited to return, under certain rigorous restrictions. As they manifested no readiness to avail themselves of the permission, the invitation was repeated in a more attractive form in 1727 and, this proving unavailing, still further inducements were offered in 1740. Even this, however, did not produce the desired effect and the edict was revoked in 1747.—Ibidem, pp. 239–42.

[2] Giovanni, pp. 233–5

there seems to have been no immediate haste to cultivate it, and there is no trace of increased inquisitorial activity during the remaining years of the century. In December, 1497, Micer Sancho Marin, inquisitor of Sardinia, was ordered to transfer himself to Sicily; he was in no haste to obey and, on March 11, 1498, Ferdinand wrote to him angrily that he was doing no good where he was and was much wanted in his new post, wherefore he was commanded summarily to go there and leave all the effects of the Sardinian tribunal for his successor. Short as was his career in Sicily, he managed to disorganize the Inquisition and to incur general detestation. Before the year was out, Ferdinand ordered him home and, on January 20, 1499, he sent for all the other officials to return. To get back, Marin borrowed three hundred ounces,[1] without making provision for repayment; to settle this and other debts and to pay for the homeward voyage of the officials, Ferdinand ordered his viceroy to give to the receiver of confiscations, who was practically the treasurer, eight hundred ducats, with a significant order to see that the parties were not maltreated, which indicates the feelings popularly entertained for them. The eight hundred ducats apparently were not easily raised, for correspondence continued during the rest of the year as to the payment of debts and salaries; Pedro de Urrea, the receiver, fell into disgrace and Ferdinand, in August, sent the notary, Ximeno Mayoral, to make copies of all the papers in the tribunal, in order to be able to straighten out matters.[2] Apparently the officials had been intent solely upon their own gains, allowing the affairs of the tribunal to fall into complete confusion, and had confined their operations to selling pardons and exemptions for, when the auditor examining Urrea's accounts asked for certificates of all who were condemned or penanced during his tenure of office, Ferdinand epigrammatically replied that, as there were none condemned or penanced, no certificates were required. It is true that there is mention of a certain Iñigo de Medina as having died

---

[1] The Sicilian *onza* was nearly equivalent to $2\frac{3}{10}$ ducats.
[2] Archivo general de Simancas, Consejo de la Inquisicion, Libro 1.

in prison, but he had not been arrested as a heretic and his sequestrated property was ordered to be returned to his widow.[1]

Evidently the Sicilian Inquisition thus far had been a failure and thorough reorganization was necessary. It was for this that Ferdinand had recalled the officials and, after an interval of some months, he proceeded to replace them. A letter of July 27, 1500, to Montoro, Bishop of Cefalù, announced his appointment as inquisitor, together with that of the bearer, Doctor Giovanni Sgalambro as his colleague, with whom were sent Diego de Obregon as receiver, and Martin de Vallejo as alguazil, the rest of the officials being left for his selection. At the same time the viceroy was instructed to show them all favor, to lodge them in some suitable building and to advance to Obregon 780 gold ducats for salaries, the sum to be repaid out of the expected confiscations.[2] The Sicilian tribunal, however, was doomed to be unlucky. Ferdinand speedily discovered that Sgalambro was utterly unfit for the position and, on November 6th, we find him writing in hot haste to Inquisitor-general Deza that, after it had had so unfortunate a beginning, Sgalambro's incumbency would destroy it; he had sent to Valencia to stop his departure, but too late, and now he instructs Deza to select some good jurist for the place, as soon as possible, and before some evil is wrought in Sicily.[3] This eager-

---

[1] Archivo de Simancas, Inquisicion, Libro 2, fol. 23, 24.

[2] Under the same date Obregon was ordered to pay salaries as follows:

Doctor Johan Sgalambro, inquisitor	6000	sueldos jaquenses.
Martin de Vallejo, alguazil	6000	" "
Johan Crespo, portero	500	" "
A notario del secreto ⎫ To be appointed by the ⎧	2500	" "
A notario de los secuestros ⎬ inquisitors ⎨	2500	" "
A fiscal ⎭ ⎩	2500	" "
Diego de Obregon, receiver	6000	" "

—Archivo de Simancas, *ubi sup.*

Although no salary is here provided for the Bishop of Cefalù, it does not follow that bishops were expected to serve gratuitously. When Pedro de Belorado was sent to Sicily as Archbishop of Messina and inquisitor, Obregon was ordered, Sept. 10, 1501, to pay him the same salary as that of Sgalambro whom he replaced. —Ibidem.

The *sueldo* was one-twentieth of the *libra*, which was nearly equivalent to the Castilian ducat.

[3] Archivo de Simancas, Inquisicion, Lib. 1.

ness, however, speedily subsided and Sgalambro was allowed to retain his office for a year. On November 8th, Montoro and he issued an edict requiring the surrender of all official papers by those formerly connected with the tribunal; also one prohibiting all *Conversos*, or baptized Jews, from leaving the island without special licence, under pain of excommunication, confiscation and arbitrary penalties, and offering to informers ten per cent. of the confiscations. In December, the viceroy and all public officials took the customary oath of obedience and the inquisitors issued an Edict of Grace, promising relief from death and confiscation to all heretics who would, within fifteen days, come forward and confess fully as to themselves and their associates. This was accompanied with an Edict of Faith, ordering all cognizant of heresy to denounce it within fifteen days, threatening those who omitted to do so with prosecution for fautorship of heresy and promising secrecy for informers. This latter edict apparently brought in few denunciations, for it was repeated on January 14, 1501, and, at the same time, was published a decree of the inquisitor-general, announcing the disabilities of the descendants of those convicted of heresy. That these proceedings were as yet a novelty in Sicily is apparent from a monition issued by the inquisitors to the president of the states of the *Camera reginale* not to impede in those districts the publication of the edicts.[1]

Evidently the Inquisition was rapidly becoming organized for work, but it still lacked a fixed habitation for, on August 22d, Ferdinand wrote to his viceroy that a house was necessary for it and, as the one occupied by Mosen Johan Chilestro, the royal carver, was suitable, it was to be taken for the purpose; he had no recollection that it had been given to the latter except for life but, if the heirs could prove a gift in perpetuity, they should be paid a suitable rent. Apparently the labors of the tribunal were beginning to promise results in the long-expected confiscations, for a letter of September 4th empowers the receiver Obregon to compound a suit against Johan de San Martin, for property

---

[1] La Mantia, pp. 23, 25, 26, 28.

derived through his brother and father, for five thousand florins and more if it could be obtained. It would seem, however, that as yet the status and privileges of the officials were not clearly recognized in Sicily, for a letter of September 10th to the viceroy urges him to see that the inquisitors enjoy the immunities and exemptions conceded to them by the Holy See and that the officials are as well treated as in the rest of the Spanish dominions.[1]

At length a successor was found for Sgalambro in the person of Pedro de Belorado, an old Spanish inquisitor, now Archbishop-elect of Messina, to whom Obregon was ordered, September 30th, to pay the same salary.[2] The people had not even yet become accustomed to the arbitrary methods of the Holy Office, for the earliest act by which Belorado makes himself known to us is his excommunication of the magistrates and judges of the town of Catania as impeders of the Inquisition, because they had prevented the alguazil Martin de Vallejo from removing from their city certain New Christians whom he had arrested. Vallejo had vindicated his office by imposing on the spot a fine of a thousand ducats on the offenders, and this Belorado confirmed. In 1502 we find him issuing fresh Edicts of Grace and of Faith and, in 1503, Deza empowered him and Montoro to act either independently or conjointly.[3] It would seem that the governor of the districts of the Camera reginale was still recalcitrant, for a letter from Ferdinand, August 13, 1504, orders him to favor the operations of the tribunal, "for our officials have naught to do but what we ourself do, which is to obey the Holy Office."[4]

There is not much evidence of activity at this period, but an auto de fe was celebrated, August 11, 1506, in which was burnt

---

[1] Archivo de Simancas, Inquisicion, Lib. 1.
[2] Ibidem. Sgalambro managed to regain the royal favor, for a letter of Ferdinand, April 23, 1506, gratifies him with the Cistercian abbey of S. Maria di Terrana, burdened, however, with a pension of eighty ducats to the official chronicler, Luca de Marinis, better known as L. Marinæus Siculus.—Pirri Sicilia Sacra, I, 670.
[3] La Mantia, pp. 27, 28.
[4] Parecer de Martin Real (MSS. of Bodleian Library, Arch Seld., 130).

Olivieri de Mauro, a renegade Christian.[1] Probably this was followed by others, of which the records have not reached us, but the troubles of the tribunal were not yet over and, in 1509, it was practically suspended for awhile, for the Bishop of Cefalù was transferred to Naples, as we shall see hereafter; Belorado died, the receiver Obregon was in Spain, and the other officials apparently dispersed, as there was no money to pay their salaries. At length a successor was found in Doctor Alonso Bernal, whose appointment Ferdinand announced to the viceroy, January 19, 1510, but he was in no haste to assume the duties for, on April 2d Ferdinand was obliged to furnish him with sixty ducats to expedite his departure from Valencia. Obregon accompanied him and, as the whole staff of the tribunal had disappeared, he was empowered to fill their places and regulate their salaries, which were to be paid out of three hundred ducats to be advanced by the royal treasurer and to be repaid out of the first proceeds of the expected confiscations.[2] The need of money was doubtless an incentive to active work. Bernal lost no time in getting the tribunal into shape and, by August 27th, we hear of his having many prisoners, for whose safe-keeping he had spent fifty ducats in arranging a gaol.[3] The result of this industry manifested itself in an auto de fe, celebrated June 6, 1511, in which eight persons were burnt.[4]

He was speedily furnished with a colleague, for royal letters of June 18th and 24th inform us of the appointment of a second inquisitor, in the person of Doctor Diego de Bonilla, promoted from the position of fiscal, to whom Obregon was ordered to pay a salary of 6000 sueldos, while the new fiscal, Leonardo Vázquez de Cepeda was to receive 2000 and the notary, Pedro de Barahona the same. It was one thing, however, to grant salaries and quite another to get them paid, in the habitual mismanagement of inquisitorial business. From a letter of September 17th we learn that Obregon

---

[1] La Mantia, p. 28.
[2] Archivo de Simancas, Inquisicion, Lib. 3, fol. 51, 52, 77, 81, 82, 83.
[3] Ibidem, fol. 127.
[4] La Mantia, p. 29.

had left Sicily in the fleet, placing as his substitute his son, a boy of 15 or 16. The salaries had fallen greatly in arrears and the boy declared that he had no funds save twenty ounces, while Inquisitor Bernal asserted that he had imposed fines and pecuniary penances to the amount of thirteen hundred ducats, besides considerable confiscations, which should be ample to meet all salaries and expenses, whereupon Ferdinand ordered the viceroy to investigate the accounts and discover where the money had gone.[1]

These were not the only difficulties which the tribunal had to encounter. Accustomed as the people had been for centuries to the existence of the Inquisition, the Spanish institution was a very different affair, not only as to activity and severity but still more from the privileges and immunities claimed and enforced by its officials and their servants and familiars, especially their exemption from taxes and import dues and their *fuero* or right to the jurisdiction of the Inquisition, whether as plaintiffs or defendants, giving rise to perpetual irritation through the oppression and injustice thus rendered possible. These innovations were not admitted without resistance, which Ferdinand sought to repress by a letter of September 10, 1508, ordering Belorado to see that his officials were as well treated in these respects as elsewhere in the Spanish dominions. This received scant obedience for, on November 14, 1509, he wrote to the *stratico* of Palermo expressing extreme displeasure on learning that he had arrested a scrivener of the tribunal and had deprived other officials of their arms; in future he must maintain their privileges and exemptions and show them every favor and protection.[2] Yet Ferdinand knew that the troubles arose from the over-weening pretensions of the tribunal and its officials for, in a letter of July 30, 1510, to Bernal he attributed them to the exorbitant invasions of the royal jurisdiction by the inquisitors and their appointment of men of evil

---

[1] Archivo de Simancas, Inquisicion, Lib. 3, fol. 134, 148, 153.
[2] Portocarrero, Sobre la Competencia en Mallorca, n. 38 (Madrid, 1624).—Archivo de Simancas, Inquisicion, Lib. 3, fol. 30.

life who caused scandal and infamy. Bernal must bear in mind that, in Sicily, the prerogatives of the crown were greater than elsewhere; whenever he had to take action in matters unconnected with heresy he must consult the viceroy or advocate fiscal, so as to avoid prejudice to the royal pre-eminence; he must also furnish to the viceroy a list of officials, servants and familiars, the latter not to exceed ten in number.[1]

Inquisitors, especially of distant tribunals, were not accustomed to pay much heed to instructions inculcating moderation in the exercise of their powers and the Sicilians were indisposed to submission. We learn from a royal letter of December 25, 1510, that the jurats objected to taking the customary oath of obedience to inquisitors and that the local authorities persisted in levying taxes on the officials.[2] Relations were strained and disaffection grew until there was an explosion on St. Bernard's day, August 20, 1511, when the people rose with demands that the privileges of the officials should be curtailed—a rising which cost, it is said, the lives of a thousand Spanish soldiers.[3] Neither this warning nor Ferdinand's exhortations abated the pretensions of the Holy Office. A letter of the viceroy, Hugo de Moncada, September 6, 1512, relates that when some troops pursued a band of robbers and arrested them in the country-house of an inquisitor, where they had sought refuge, the latter threatened the captain and his men with excommunication if the prisoners were not released and then claimed jurisdiction to try them, on the ground of the place of their capture.[4] This was by no means an isolated case

---

[1] Archivo de Simancas, Inquisicion, Lib. 3, fol. 116. In December, however, Ferdinand increased the number of familiars to twenty in each large city.—Ibidem, fol. 135.

[2] Ibidem, fol. 127.

[3] Parecer de Martin Real, *ubi sup.* Possibly this is too absolute an attribution of the troubles of 1511 to the Inquisition, though Doctor Real, as an official of the tribunal, ought to be good authority, even though not a contemporary. Fazelli, who was a boy at the time, says (De Rebus Siculis, Decad. II, Lib. ix, cap. 11) that it was occasioned by the outrages committed by the unpaid and starving Spanish troops.

[4] Llorente, Añales de la Inquisicion, II, 26.

for soon afterwards two other flagrant examples of similar character evoked from Ferdinand, October 25th, an order to rescind their action, coupled with an expression of extreme displeasure at their thus affording protection to malefactors on one pretext or another. Their behavior in the custom-house to evade the payment of duties was a further subject of animadversion and he warned them sternly to avoid in future creating such scandals.[1]

This somewhat exuberant zeal in asserting their privileges was accompanied with corresponding activity in the performance of their regular duties. In 1513 there were three autos de fe celebrated, in which the burnings aggregated thirty-nine, a large portion being of those who had been previously reconciled and had relapsed, thus indicating the increased vigilance of the tribunal.[2] A further evidence of this was the arrival, in September, 1513, at Naples, of four hundred fugitives, including a number of priests and friars, to escape the rigor of the inquisitors, who they said were endeavoring to force confessors to reveal the confessions of their penitents.[3] One gratifying result of this activity was the financial ease afforded by the resultant large confiscations. A letter of Ferdinand's to Obregon, June 27, 1513, calls his attention to them and to those anticipated from the number of prisoners on trial, requiring greater care than had hitherto been devoted to the management; the officials were now receiving their salaries and doing their duty. In spite of this warning we find, a year later, that Obregon had abruptly quitted Palermo, leaving the affairs of the office in confusion, rendering necessary the appointment, June 15, 1514, of a successor, Garcí Cid, who was instructed to reduce it to order and to invest in ground-rents twelve hundred ounces which Obregon had deposited in a bank.[4] That the profits of persecution continued is evidenced by a gift made, March 30, 1515, by Ferdinand, to his wife, Queen Germaine, of all the con-

---

[1] Archivo de Simancas, Inquisicion, Lib. 3, fol. 202 (see Appendix).
[2] La Mantia, pp. 30–32.
[3] Amabile, Il Santo Officio in Napoli, I, 109 (Città di Castello, 1892).
[4] Archivo de Simancas, Inquisicion, Lib. 3, fol. 239, 294, 296, 314.

fiscations of that year, in the city of Syracuse and district of the Camera reginale, up to the sum of ten thousand florins—a gift which Garcí Cid was ordered to keep secret until after he should have rendered a statement of all that was on hand and was expected.[1]

It is perhaps not surprising that this increased effectiveness of the tribunal stimulated popular discontent, which found expression in a petition from the Sicilian Parliament asking Ferdinand that the Inquisition be required to observe the ancient canons and methods of procedure, for many of those burnt in the autos asserted their innocence, declaring that their confessions had been extorted by torture and dying with every sign of being good Christians. It was further asked that some limit be put to the issue of licences to bear arms and as to the kind of persons licensed; that the judge of confiscations should have a fixed salary and should not exact fees and that there should be an appeal from him to the viceroy; also that those who in good faith entered into contracts with persons reputed to be good Christians should be able to collect their debts, in place of having them included in the confiscation, the contrary practice being destructive to trade and commerce.[2] There was also a special embassy from Palermo, complaining that the inquisitors required the city authorities to renew every year the oath of obedience and that they issued licences to bear arms to men of evil life who caused much disorder and scandal.[3] Ferdinand promised relief of these grievances and, in due course, a fresh series of instructions was issued, in 1515, by Bishop Martin de Aspeitia and the Aragonese Supreme Council, or Suprema. It limited the number of familiars to thirty for Palermo, to twenty for Messina and Catania, to fifteen for Syracuse and Trapani and to not over ten in other places; they were to be men of approved character and were to carry certificates identifying them, in the absence of which they could be disarmed by the

---

[1] Archivo de Simancas, Inquisicion, fol. 331.
[2] La Mantia, pp. 38, 39.
[3] Archivo de Simancas, Inquisicion, Lib. 3, fol. 311.

secular authorities. If officials were accused of serious crime, the evidence was to be sent to the inquisitor-general when, if the proof was sufficient, the offender would be dismissed and the inquisitor who had tolerated it would be punished. Officials were deprived of the *voz activa* or right as plaintiffs to the jurisdiction of the tribunal, although Dr. Martin Real assures us that experience had already shown that they could not exist without it, so universally were they detested. Their buying up of claims and matters in litigation, in which they had the benefit of the tribunal as a court, was prohibited. The dowries of wives were protected from confiscation when husbands were convicted and dealings with those in good repute as Christians were held good, in case of confiscation, so that the claims of creditors were allowed and, if the fisc desired to seize alienated real estate, it was required to refund the purchase-money to the buyer.[1] There were various other reforms embodied in the instructions, all indicating a desire to avoid injustice to innocent third parties, but the whole is interesting rather as an exposure of customary abuses than as effecting their removal, although when, towards the close of 1514 a new inquisitor, Miguel Cervera by name, was sent to Sicily, he was ordered to obey to the letter the instructions of Torquemada and his successors and not to increase the number of officials without permission.[2]

However praiseworthy may have been the intentions at headquarters, it was impossible to control the tribunal or to allay popular hostility, which found opportunity for expression after the death of Ferdinand, February 23, 1516. Hugo de Moncada had held the office of viceroy for six years and had earned universal hatred by his cruelty, greed and lust. Among other devices, he had monopolized the corn-trade and, by his exportations, had reduced the island almost to starvation, though its fertility rendered it the granary of the Mediterranean, while the

---

[1] Archivo de Simancas, Inquisicion, Lib. 918, fol. 379.—Martin Real, *ubi sup.*
[2] Archivo de Simancas, Inquisicion, Lib. 3, fol. 314; Lib. 933.

poverty of the people was aggravated by an adulterated currency.[1] He concealed the news of Ferdinand's death, in hopes of reappointment by Charles V, but it became known and the people, led by some powerful nobles, claimed that his commission had expired. While the popular mind was thus excited, Fra Hieronimo da Verona, in his lenten sermons in Palermo, denounced as sacrilegious the wearing of red crosses on the green penitential sanbenitos of the reconciled heretics, who were very numerous, and he urged the people to tear off the symbol of Christ from the heretical penitents. His advice was followed and the aspect of the mob grew more and more threatening. Moncada attempted to quiet matters by proclaiming Charles and Juana, abolishing an obnoxious corn-tax and exhibiting letters from Charles confirming him in office. These were denounced as forgeries; a man who demanded to see them was arrested by the prefect and rescued by the people, while the prefect was obliged to fly for his life. That night, March 7, 1516, an immense crowd, with artillery taken from the arsenal, besieged the vice-regal palace; Moncada, disguised as a serving-man, escaped by a postern to the house of a friend, whence he took refuge on a ship in the harbor and sailed for Messina, which consented to receive him. After sacking the palace, the mob turned its attention to the Inquisition. Cervera saved his life by taking a consecrated host in a monstrance, under

---

[1] Argensola, Añales de Aragon, Lib. I, cap. 5.—Caruso, Memorie istoriche di Sicilia, T. VI, p. 119.

One of Moncada's arbitrary acts concerned the Inquisition. In 1517, when the receiver Garcí Cid was settling his accounts, he claimed credit for 700 ounces which he had deposited with a banker in Messina, where Moncada seized it. Cardinal Adrian the inquisitor-general thereupon ordered Inquisitor Cervera to summon the banker to return the money, for the viceroy had express orders from Ferdinand not to meddle with the property of the tribunal. If, however, the banker could prove that Moncada had taken it by force, then Garcí Cid could proceed to collect it from the revenues of the Priorazgo of St. John at Messina, which belonged to Moncada. If the banker could not prove this, he must pay the money and have recourse against the property and revenues of Moncada. Hereafter, Adrian concludes, no one shall dare to take the property of the Inquisition, for the Catholic king ordered that it should be used to purchase rents for the perpetuation of the tribunal.—Archivo de Simancas, Inquisicion, Lib. 933.

protection of which he gained the harbor, amid the jeers and insults of the people, who cried that he was an inquisitor and hunter of money, not of heretics. He took ship for Spain, while the mob released the prisoners, destroyed the records and pillaged the property of the Inquisition. The Palermitans followed this with an embassy to Charles, complaining of the evil doings of Moncada and the disorders caused by the Inquisition which had well-nigh destroyed their city. The sole object of its officials they said was to accumulate money and they would lay down their lives rather than see it restored, except under the ancient form as carried on by the bishops and Dominicans. Cervera betook himself to Flanders to solicit his restoration, but the island held out and, for three years, there was no Inquisition in Sicily, except in Messina and its territory.[1]

Enlightened by the insurrection and the Palermitan complaints, the Suprema or supreme council of Aragon, on August 29, 1516, sent to Centelles, Bishop of Syracuse, a commission to investigate the tribunal, with a list of interrogatories from which it appears that Cervera had filled the office with his kindred and servants, while every kind of pillage and oppression is suggested, even to the rifling of the treasure-chest by the officials on the day of the tumult. Bishop Centelles, however, had died on August 22d; of course no investigation was made and the Suprema contented itself with expressing, on October 27th, to Charles its gratification at his determination to restore with the greatest honor the tribunal which had been expelled with such disgrace.[2] This, however, was not so readily accomplished. Some seven months later, on June 15, 1517, Charles wrote to the Sicilian viceroy ordering Cervera to be received back and obeyed under penalty of the royal wrath and three thousand crowns but, for a time, this was a dead letter. Cervera returned to Spain when Charles went there, in

---

[1] Argensola, *op. cit.*, Lib. I, cap. 5, 34.—Fazelli de Rebus Siculis, Decad. II, Lib. 10.—La Mantia, pp. 40–42.—Dormer, Añales de Aragon, cap. 2.—P. Mart. Angler. Epistt., 593, 594.—Carta de D. Hugo de Moncada, 22 de Marzo, 1516 (Coleccion de Documentos inéditos, XXIV, 136).

[2] Archivo de Simancas, Inquisicion, Lib. 74, fol. 16; Lib. 921, fol. 38.

1517, and it was not until 1519 that Sicily was sufficiently pacified to render it expedient to send him back. A royal cédula of May 29, 1519, announces this and orders Garcí Cid, the receiver, to pay him 343 ducats for his accrued salary without deduction for absence, and, when the cédula of June 15, 1517, was published at last on July 6, 1519, it was not in Palermo but in Messina, where the Marquis of Monteleone, the new viceroy, was still residing. Meanwhile a certain Giovanni Martino da Aquino had been enjoying the title of inquisitor there, but he was removed, May 20, 1519, in favor of Cervera. A second inquisitor, Tristan Calvete had been appointed in 1517 and had been welcomed in Messina.[1]

Calvete's first act was to issue an edict, May 16, 1518, requiring, under pain of excommunication, all papers and property of the Inquisition to be returned within fifteen days and the anathema duly followed on June 6th.[2] Presumably this produced little result; Palermo, the seat of the tribunal and scene of insurrection, had not yet returned to obedience; the records had been destroyed and their lack long remained a source of embarrassment. The tribunal however, in 1519, was re-established and fully manned; it celebrated an auto de fe, June 11, 1519 and, for five or six years, there seems to have been one nearly every year, but the number of executions was not large.[3] Popular antagonism was

---

[1] Archivo de Simancas, Inquisicion, Lib. 9, fol. 39.—Franchina, *op. cit.*, pp. 122, 127.

In 1630 Messina appealed to its fidelity on this occasion, when resisting a proposition to divide the island into two viceroyalties.—Razones apologéticas de la noble Ciudad de Mecina, fol. 48 (Madrid, 1630).

[2] La Mantia, p. 42.

[3] Ibidem, pp. 45-6. The autos were:

       1519, June 11, 4 men burnt and 1 woman.
       1520, July 8, 3 " " 2 "
       1521, June 9, 1 " "
       1524, Aug. 6, 4 " " 1 "
       1525, Sept. 29, 1 " " 4 "
       1526, Aug. 1, 3 " " 1 "
             Sept. 16, 1 " "

A letter of August 19, 1519, from the Suprema to Calvete expresses the highest satisfaction with him and offers him, on his return to Spain, one of the principal

by no means disarmed, for we find Calvete issuing, September 29, 1525, two edicts, one commanding everyone to aid and favor the Inquisition and not to defend heretics, and the other summoning all cognizant of the numerous *penitenciados* and their descendants, who disregarded the disabilities imposed on them, to denounce them.[1]

There was ample cause for disaffection, arising, not from sympathy with heresy, but from the arbitrary proceedings of those who regarded persecution primarily as a source of enrichment. Instructions given, July 31, 1517, by Cardinal Adrian to Calvete, commence with the remark that all inquisitors thus far sent to Sicily had disregarded the rules of the Holy Office, both as to civil and criminal procedure, as to confiscations and as to familiars. It was therefore ordered that all officials, under pain of excommunication, should inviolably observe the instructions, including those given to Melchor Cervera; the whole body of these rules was ordered to be read in presence of all the officials assembled for the purpose, a notarial act being taken to attest the fact. Moreover, in addition to excommunication for violations of the rules, the special penalties provided were to be irrevocably enforced. Following this were particular instructions for the correction of abuses which indicate how completely the interests of the fisc and the rights of the people were subordinated to official cupidity. One of the practices prohibited shows how repulsive

---

tribunals of Castile. In 1529 we find him Inquisitor of Sarogossa.—Archivo de Simancas, Inquisicion, Lib. 74, fol. 165; Lib. 76, fol. 183.

Calvete's earlier years of office were much harassed by a suit brought against him in Rome by Juan de Leon, a canon of Córdova. Prior to 1516, Calvete as provisor of Córdova had prosecuted Leon and some others for rescuing a culprit from an alguazil. Leon nursed his wrath and when in Rome, in 1519, commenced an action against Calvete in the papal courts which caused him so much vexation that he threatened to abandon his post in Sicily and return to Spain. Charles V intervened, writing repeatedly to his ambassadors, to cardinals and to Leon himself, threatening him with the seizure of his temporalities, but the vindictive canon held good and, in 1520, obtained a judgement of 1000 ducats and costs, as Calvete could not go to Rome to defend himself.—Archivo de Simancas, Inq., Lib. 6, fol. 74, 75, 78; Lib. 9, fol. 52–54.

[1] La Mantia, p. 43.

the religion of Christ, in such hands, was rendered to converts. The inquisitors, it appears, were in the habit of making reconciled penitents and baptized neophytes labor on the fortifications of the castle; when they did not appear at the appointed hour they were fined and these fines, which were collected by Zamporron, the messenger of the tribunal, amounted to a considerable sum, of which no account was rendered.[1] In this, as in all similar denunciations of malversations and abuses, a noteworthy feature is that punishment is always threatened for the future and none is inflicted for the past; no one is dismissed and the thieving and corrupt officials are allowed unmolested to continue their career of plunder and oppression.

Apparently Cardinal Adrian was advised that his instructions were not obeyed and he sent Master Benito Mercader as "visitor" or inspector to report on the condition of the tribunal. Before this report was received, Adrian had passed through the papacy to the tomb, and it was acted upon by his successor, Manrique, Archbishop of Seville, who issued, January 31, 1525, a fresh set of instructions, based on its revelations. From this it would appear that there was little in which the inquisitors and their officials did not violate the rules, both in the conduct of trials and management of the finances. There seems, in fact, to have been a Saturnalia of peculation. Collections were made by both authorized and unauthorized persons, of which no accounts were kept. The fines and pecuniary penances, which formed so lucrative a source of income, were kept from the knowledge of the notary of sequestrations so that he could make no charge of them to the receiver. Officials claimed and received twenty or twenty-five per cent. for discovering hidden confiscated property, their knowledge of which was acquired officially. The Christian slaves of condemned heretics were sold in place of being set free,

---

[1] Archivo de Simancas, Inquisicion, Lib. 933. These instructions were probably the result of the report of a *visitador* or inspector, Juan de Ariola, sent, towards the close of 1513, to investigate the tribunals of Majorca, Sardinia and Sicily.—Ibidem, Lib. 3, fol. 251–4.

according to law. Inquisitors and their subordinates received "presents," or rather bribes, from penitents and litigants, which perhaps explains the complaint that sentences to the galleys and other penalties were not executed and that the disabilities and sanbenitos of those reconciled were not enforced. There is significance in the instructions for the collection of the two hundred gold ducats, which the late inquisitor, Melchor Cervera, had bequeathed to the Inquisition for the discharge of his conscience—probably but a small portion of the irregular gains for which he had had ample opportunity. As a whole, this inside picture of the Holy Office shows us how completely it was converted into an engine for oppression and peculation and how little there was of genuine fanaticism to serve as an excuse for its existence, but, as usual, there are no dismissals or punishments inflicted and the only remedy proposed is the formal semi-annual reading of the instructions to the officials. That they should continue to be the objects of popular detestation was inevitable, and the complaint is made that their maltreatment and the resistance offered to them remain unpunished.[1]

This was the only point on which reformation was attempted. Charles V, in a letter to his viceroy, October 22, 1525, says that he understands that the royal courts take cognizance of the cases of the officials of the tribunal, which displeases him greatly; it is his will that the Holy Office shall be cherished and favored and that in all cases, civil and criminal, its officials are to enjoy the immunities and privileges to which they are entitled; they are to exercise their functions with all freedom, under the royal protection, guarded by the penalties expressed in the royal concessions. This was supplemented by another cédula of August 25, 1526, taking the inquisitors and their officials under the royal safeguard and ordering that they should have all aid and support and protection from the secular authorities.[2]

---

[1] Archivo de Simancas, Inquisicion, Lib. 933 (see Appendix).
[2] Salelles de Materiis Tribunalis S. Inquis., I, 30 (Romæ, 1651).—Franchina, pp. 131–7.

As for the wrongs committed by the inquisitors, their continuance is shown by repeated petitions from the Sicilian Parliament, which indicate how completely the instructions of 1515 and 1517 were ignored, while Charles's replies—probably drawn up for him by the Suprema—prove how little hope there was of redress through an appeal to the throne. The Parliament represented that the Conversos who remained were few and poor, the rest having fled or been condemned, wherefore the inquisitors despoiled the native Christians of their property, to remedy which it asked as before that in future the Inquisition should be conducted by the bishops and Dominicans as of old. To this the answer was that he would consult the pope. It was also asked that Christians who had, in good faith, made contracts with reputed Catholics and thus were their creditors, should have their claims recognized and satisfied out of the confiscated property of a condemned debtor. This shows that the instructions of 1515 to this effect had been disregarded and there was little hope of improvement in Charles's assent with the nullifying proviso that there must be a prescription of thirty years' possession, concerning which he would write to the pope. A further request was that the dowries of orthodox wives should not be subject to confiscation and that children's portions should be exempted, to which the reply was "agreed as to dowries received before the commission of heresy; for the rest, the pope will be consulted." Another point was that, in case of denial of justice or evident scandal, the viceroy could appoint some prelate who, with the Gran Corte or the doctors, could decide the matter. This was rejected with the declaration that all appeals must be to the inquisitor-general. It was further asked that each inquisitor when he came should file his commission in the ordinary public registers, so that every one could learn what was his authority, for the inquisitors often exceeded their lawful powers. Complaint was also made that the officials abused their immunities and privileges by engaging in trade and it was asked that in suits thence arising they should be subjected to the vice-regal or episcopal courts, to which Charles replied that he had given orders to the inquisitor-general to see to this.¹

Thus supported, the Inquisition pursued its course and held one or more autos de fe every year, until 1534, though the number of burnings was not excessive, the summary for the nine years showing only thirty-nine victims relaxed to the secular arm, the most of whom suffered for relapse after previous conviction and reconciliation.² While thus performing its full duties to the faith, the consciousness of imperial support had not led it to mend its ways or to reform abuses, and popular opposition was undiminished, for Charles found it necessary to issue another rescript, January 18, 1535, addressed to Viceroy Monteleone, confirming at much length the privileges and exemptions of the officials from secular jurisdiction and their right to bear arms.³ When, however, in the following September, Charles visited Palermo, on his return from his crusade to Tunis, and listened to the earnest representations of the Parliament, his convictions changed—a change possibly facilitated by a subsidy granted to him of two hundred and fifty thousand ducats over and above the ordinary revenue.⁴ He suspended, for a period of five years, the jurisdiction of the Inquisition in all cases involving the death-penalty and not connected with matters of faith, and, when this term had elapsed, he prolonged the suspension for five years more.⁵ The historians of the Inqui-

---

¹ La Mantia, pp. 44–5.—Parecer de Martin Real, *ubi sup*.
² La Mantia, pp. 47–8. ³ Páramo, p. 201.
⁴ Montoiche, Voyage de Charles-Quint au Pays de Tunis (Gachard, Voyages des Souverains des Pays-bas, III, 378).
⁵ Franchina, p. 169.—"Havemos proveydo y mandado que los inquisidores del dicho Reyno no hobiesen de conocer, dentro termino de cinco años, de ninguna cosa que hoviere pena de muerte contra ningun persona natural de dicho Reyno."—A Latin version is printed by Páramo, p. 204.

The phraseology of the decree would seem to suspend the spiritual as well as the temporal jurisdiction of the tribunal and historians have generally so regarded it. This however is impossible as the former was a delegation from the pope over which the emperor had no control and any attempt to do so would have been equivalent to abolishing the Inquisition, while the auto of 1541 shows that it continued to exercise its spiritual jurisdiction. It assumed however that its capacity to suppress heresy was fatally crippled by depriving its officials of the privilege of its exclusive forum, as expressed in a document quoted by Franchina

sition tell us that this resulted in the unchecked multiplication of heretics among the noblest families, while the hatred of the people for its representatives manifested itself without fear of punishment. There can, in fact, be litte doubt that its operations were crippled on this account, for its officials were no longer shielded from popular anger as soon as offences committed against them became cognizable by the secular courts in sympathy with the offenders. Thus when the Inquisitor Bartolomé Sebastian made a visitation of the town of Jaca, with his officials and servants, and published the Edict of Faith, the inhabitants piled up wood around the house in which they were lodged and would have burnt them all had not the Baroness de la Florida assembled her kinsmen and retainers, raised the siege and enabled them to escape. Soon afterwards, when the alguazil and his assistants went to San Marcos to arrest some heretics, they were set upon by Matteo Garruba and his accomplices; he was left for dead and some of his people were slain.[1] Apparently the danger, of which these are examples, caused the inquisitors to confine their labors to the larger cities for, in January, 1543, Inquisitor-general Tavera ordered a general visitation of the island, which he says had not been performed for a long while. In June a new inquisitor, the Licentiate Gongora, was sent with special instructions to carry out this visitation and peremptory orders were issued by Prince Philip that he and his officials should be efficiently protected.[2] Another manifestation of popular repugnance was the resistance

---

(p. 69)—"Notandum est quod quando in anno 1535 fuit limitata seu suspensa jurisdictio temporalis hujus Sancti Officii in aliquibus casibus per invictissimum imperatorem Carolum V felicis memoriæ, jurisdictio spiritualis causarum fidei fuit in suspenso et quasi mortua." So a consulta of the Suprema to Philip III, October 2, 1609, refers to Charles having deprived the Sicilian Inquisition of its temporal jurisdiction, resulting in such recrudescence of heresy that he was obliged to restore it.—Archivo de Simancas, Inquisicion, Lib. 927, fol. 323.

Inquisitor Páramo, in a letter of November 8, 1600, to Philip III, states the case to be that Charles was misled by false accounts of the misdeeds of the familiars and deprived them of their immunities but, on being better informed, he restored them.—Ibidem, Lib. 41, fol. 258.

[1] Páramo, pp. 202-3.—Parecer de Martin Real, *ubi sup.*
[2] Franchina, pp. 149, 159, 163.

offered to the invariable custom in Spain of hanging in the churches the sanbenitos of the condemned, or linens with inscriptions of their names, heresies and punishment, thus perpetuating their infamy, which was one of the severest features of the penalty of heresy. Páramo explains that this was not observed in Sicily for when, in 1543, Inquisitor Cervera endeavored to introduce it, by hanging them in the church of St. Dominic, there arose so great a tumult that he was obliged to abandon the attempt and it had never since then been possible to effect it, up to his time (1598).[1] To add to the embarrassment of the tribunal, it was or professed to be impoverished. When its alguazil Marcos Calderon died, there was owing to him for arrears of salary 155 ounces, 24 tarines and 9 granos, and in February, 1543, the receiver Francisco Cid declared his inability to pay this to the heirs. To relieve him the Suprema agreed to place half the burden of this on the tribunal of Granada and, by letter of May 30, 1544, ordered Cid to pay the other half.[2]

In spite of popular disaffection and curtailment of temporal jurisdiction, the Inquisition continued its deadly work. On May 30, 1541, there was celebrated at Palermo an auto in which twenty-two culprits appeared, nineteen of them for Judaizing and three for Lutheranism—among the latter Fra Perruccio Campagna, a tertiary of San Francisco de Paola, who courted martyrdom and was burnt as an obstinate impenitent heretic.[3] By this time Lutheranism was much more dreaded than Judaism. In view of its threatening spread and of the occasional outbursts of popular detestation, there was probably little difficulty in convincing Charles that he had made a mistake in limiting the exemptions of the officials; he announced in advance his intention of not pro-

---

[1] Páramo, p. 43. I give the date of 1543 as stated by Páramo, but it is evidently an error for 1516, when the tumult occurred under Cervera.

[2] Archivo de Simancas, Inquisicion, Sala 40, Lib. 4, fol. 136. The financial mismanagement of the Sicilian tribunal was notorious. In 1560, the Contador-general Zurita states that he had finished auditing its accounts with much labor, as they had not been examined for twenty years and were in much disorder.—Ibidem, fol. 239.

[3] La Mantia, p. 50.

longing the limitation and, by letters of February 27, 1543, he ordered his Sicilian officials, after the expiration of the term, to give the Inquisition full liberty of action and not to interfere with it in any way under a penalty of two thousand ounces. When the term expired, Prince Philip, as regent of the Spanish dominions, by a decree of June 18, 1546, published the letters of 1543 and ordered their strict observance.[1]

It would seem that even before the expiration of the term the tribunal arrogantly and successfully asserted the immunity of its officials from secular law. Juan de Aragon, Duke of Terranova, was Constable and Admiral of Naples, a Spanish grandee of the first class and kinsman of Charles V, acting as President or Governor of Sicily, in the absence of the viceroy. In this capacity he had occasion to torture and condemn to the galleys Maestro Antonio Bertin, a familiar, and to imprison some other familiars. The inquisitors took up the matter and sentenced him to perform public penance, to release Bertin and to pay him a *solatium* of two hundred ducats. The case was of course carried to Spain, where both sides were heard and as usual the decision was against the crown and in favor of the Inquisition. Prince Philip conveyed this to Terranova by letter of December 16, 1543, exhorting him to submit to it willingly and not to wait to be compelled by excommunication. Terranova recalcitrated against the public humiliation and finally a letter of Philip, April 24, 1544, remitted the penance, when the duke released and compensated the criminal.[2]

---

[1] Franchina, pp. 167, 183.—Páramo, p. 204.

[2] Llorente, Historia crítica, cap. xvi, art. ii, n. 5. The date of this affair is not unimportant and has curiously been involved in doubt. As printed by Llorente, the letter of December 16, 1543, is duly signed Prince Philip and is doubtless correctly dated, as Terranova was governor in 1544 (Gervasii Siculæ Sanctiones, I, 295). It is somewhat remarkable that in the Simancas archives (Legajo 1465, fol. 60) there are two letters of Philip II on this affair, one dated from the Escorial, April 24, 1568, to the Sicilian inquisitors and the other to Terranova, dated from Madrid, April 29, 1568. The dates are evidently erroneous for in that year the Marquis of Pescara was viceroy (Gervasii, III, 121). Portocarrero also blunders in the date (*op. cit.*, n. 105), placing the affair in 1608. La Mantia moreover says (p. 52) that a MS. copy of a letter of the inquisitors,

Such an occurrence does not justify the assertion made by Prince Philip, June 15, 1546, when a new inquisitor, Bartolomé Sebastian, was sent to Palermo, that the officials of the Sicilian Holy Office were held in such contempt and were so impeded in their functions that they could scarce discharge their duties, wherefore special injunctions were laid on him to exact from all authorities the oath of obedience, while every assistance was emphatically ordered to be rendered to him.[1] In fact, almost simultaneously with these utterances, an auto de fe, held June 6, 1546, showed that there was no impediment to the discharge of the proper functions of the inquisition. In this auto there were no living bodies delivered to the stake, but the effigies of four fugitives answered the purpose of demonstrating that the authority of the tribunal was undiminished. Sebastian indicated how far that authority extended when, in 1547, he repeated the prohibition of Conversos expatriating themselves and their families under pain of confiscation, while a fine of two hundred ounces was decreed against shipmasters transporting such persons without special licence. This recrudescence of inquisitorial activity aroused the Parliament, which petitioned Charles V that the accused should have copies of the evidence against them, with the names of the witnesses, so that his faithful subjects should not perish undefended, through false testimony suborned by enmity, but the emperor turned this off with a vague promise that Sicilians should not be unduly molested. This did not soothe popular hostility, for a letter of the Regent Juana to the Viceroy Juan de Vega, September 29, 1549, thanks him for the solicitude which he has shown in protecting the rights and immunities of the Inquisition, seeing that recently some of its officials have been wounded and slain while discharging their duties. Possibly this may refer to the

---

April 10th, bears a later date. A letter of the Suprema to the inquisitors, prescribing the punishment, is dated December 15th, without indication of the year (Simancas, Lib 78, fol. 372). It speaks of two familiars tortured, orders Terranova to hear mass in a monastery as a penitent and to pay the sufferers 200 ducats, to which the officials concerned in the affair were to add 100 more.

[1] Franchina, p. 174.

case of Giacomo Achiti, who was relaxed to the secular arm, May 19, 1549, for having with others resisted and slain Giovanni de Landeras, a minister of the Inquisition. Yet whatever may have been the good will of Vega, it was impossible for a viceroy to perform his duties and remain on good terms with the Holy Office. In this same year, 1549, a certain D. Pietro di Gregorio had torture administered to a familiar, for which Alberto Albertini, Bishop of Patti and inquisitor, threw him in prison, when Vega liberated him by force and was duly reproved therefore by Charles.[1]

In the numerous autos de fe which are recorded during the following years, it is interesting to observe that Judaism sinks into the background and that the predominant heresies punished are Protestant. The Inquisition was aroused to renewed activity and its victims, whether burnt or penanced, were numbered by scores.[2] It is probable that peculation and waste continued for a letter of the inquisitors, April 2, 1560, to Philip II congratulates him on the prospect of some large confiscations impending; these, they say, will relieve the tribunal, which is deeply in debt and it is suggested to the king that if he will invest the proceeds in ground-rents, the income will go far to pay the salaries and perpetuate the institution. Apparently the suggestion was unheeded for the complaints of poverty and indebtedness continue; the convicts are mostly poor people, whose property barely meets their prison expenses, and some rich abbey is asked for, of which the revenues may be devoted to this holy cause.[3]

Whether the complaint of poverty be true or not, the inquisitors had ample opportunity of irregular gains. The privileges and immunities of its officials rendered the position of familiar eagerly sought for and, in an age of corruption, we may reasonably assume that it was liberally paid for. In addition to this, the exclusive jurisdiction over them, in both civil and criminal matters, was very lucrative, not only from the fees exacted for every transaction in suits and trials, but from the custom of

---

[1] La Mantia, pp. 52-4.—Franchina, p. 188.—Portocarrero, n. 77.
[2] Franchina, pp. 45-53
[3] La Mantia, pp. 55-6.

punishment by fines for all delinquencies. It is noteworthy that in the discussions which arose, it was assumed on all sides that the *fuero* of the tribunal was equivalent to immunity for crime, and so it was as far as corporal penalties were concerned, but pecuniary ones were a profitable substitute, which enured exclusively to the tribunal. I have not met with any trials of Sicilian officials, but this was the custom in the Peninsula and it is an unavoidable assumption that the example was followed in the island. In addition to this was the influence derivable from thus enrolling an army under the inquisitorial banner, and thus there were ample motives for disregarding the limitations placed by the instructions on the number of appointments. The viceroy, Marc' Antonio Colonna, in a letter of November 3, 1577, states that there were twenty-five thousand familiars and that the inquisitors proposed to increase them to thirty thousand; they included, he says, all the nobles, the rich men and the criminals.[1] It was practically an alliance between the tribunal on one side and the influential and the dangerous classes on the other, against the vice-regal government and the courts, rendering impossible the orderly administration of justice and the maintenance of public peace. The viceroys were involved in perpetual struggles with the Holy Office and were constantly remonstrating with the home government, but to little effect. An attempt was made to amend the situation by an agreement, known as the Concordia of Badajoz, July 4, 1580, which was, in reality, a surrender of the secular authorities to the Inquisition. In Castile, a number of the more serious crimes were excepted from the exemption of familiars, but in Sicily they were entitled to the jurisdiction of the tribunal for all offences, however atrocious. This was continued by the Concordia, which provided that, whenever a case involving an official or familiar should come before the viceroy, he should promptly hand it over to the tribunal. The inquisitors were empowered to excommunicate judges who interfered with their jurisdiction and the judge so excommunicated was required

---

[1] La Mantia, pp. 58–9.

to present himself before them, to beg for absolution and to promise obedience. Provision however was made for *competencias*, or conferences between judges and inquisitors on disputed questions when, if they could not agree, the matter was referred to the king for final decision—a process which usually prolonged it indefinitely.[1]

The secular authorities were naturally restive under this and quarrels continued. In 1589 there was an outbreak, when the Gran Corte undertook to try a familiar named Antonio Ferrante. The Inquisition claimed him; the viceroy, the Count of Alva, was less enduring than some of his predecessors; he caused the sentence of hanging to be executed and, in the ensuing recriminations, he imprisoned the consultors of the Inquisition and its judge of confiscations. Both parties appealed to Philip II who, after examining all the documents, wrote to Alba, March 29, 1590, strongly reproving him for bringing such scandal and discredit on an institution so necessary for the peace and quiet of the land. In future he must strictly observe the Concordia and the judges of the Gran Corte must present themselves individually before the inquisitors and obey their commands. Alba apparently had argued that the consultors were not formally officials, for in 1591 Philip decided that they were so and were entitled to all the privileges of that position.[2]

Philip was firmly convinced that the Inquisition was essential to keep Sicily in subjection, which accounts for his upholding it against his own representatives, but his eyes were somewhat opened by another case which was in progress at the same time. Count Mussumelli, a familiar, was charged with the murder of Giuseppe Bajola, fiscal of the Gran Corte; he was claimed by the Inquisition and took refuge in its prison. From this the Count of Alva took him forcibly, whereupon the inquisitors excommunicated the subordinates concerned in the act and, finding this ineffective, on April 6, 1590, they not only laid an interdict on

---

[1] Páramo, p. 210.—MSS. of Library of Univ. of Halle, Yc, 17.
[2] MSS. of Royal Library of Copenhagen, 214 fol.—Páramo, p. 212.

the whole city, but stretched their jurisdiction by prohibiting all vessels from leaving the port. This brought Alba to terms; Mussumelli was restored to the inquisitorial prison and the interdict was lifted.[1] The case was necessarily carried up to the king and, as usual, was referred to a *junta* consisting of two members each of the Suprema and of the Council of Italy. To the consulta which they in due course presented, Philip replied, expressing his grief at the atrocious crimes of recent occurrence in Sicily. That of the Count Mussumelli was so aggravated that its impunity would render difficult the enforcement of justice and he must therefore be remitted to the viceroy and judges of the Gran Corte. As for the Count of Rocalmuto and the Marquis of la Rochela, they were to be left to the Inquisition, in full confidence that their punishment would correspond to the enormity of their offences, for which he charged the inquisitor-general and Suprema. Moreover, to prevent such occurrences for the future, he decreed that the crime of assassination should be excepted from the immunity enjoyed by familiars and should not be made the subject of competencias. In addition to this, he proceeded to state that experience had shown the great troubles and scandals arising from nobles being officials and familiars—positions which they sought, not to discharge their duties but to commit crimes under the protection of the Inquisition, thus creating many quarrels between the jurisdictions to the discredit of both, to scandal of the people and hindrance of justice. It would therefore be well for the inquisitor-general and Suprema to order that Sicilian nobles be no longer appointed as officials and familiars and that existing appointments be called in and revoked, for he had resolved to order the viceroys and judges to hold that they are not entitled to the fuero of the Inquisition. It was unreasonable that so holy a business should serve as a cover for delinquents and evil-doers and there was ample experience that this was their sole object in seeking these positions, so that he greatly wondered that the

---

[1] Franchina, p. 78.

Inquisition should persist in a course so damaging to its reputation and so foreign to the object of its foundation.[1]

Such rebuke and such action could only have been elicited from a monarch like Philip II by a profound conviction of the unbearable abuses of inquisitorial jurisdiction. He would more wisely have followed the example of his father in suspending wholly that jurisdiction, for the tribunal continued to exercise it in a manner provocative of continual disturbance. At length, in 1595, a junta or conference was formed, consisting of two members of the Suprema, Doctors Juan de Zuñiga and Caldas, and two regents of the Gran Corte, Bruñol and Escudero, to reach, if possible, an agreement that should lead to peace. There were many discussions and tentative attempts which finally resulted in a consulta presented to Philip as a compromise acceptable to both sides. This commences by stating that the special cases in dispute had been settled or laid aside, awaiting further documents, and that for the future it had been agreed that the Concordia of 1580 should be observed with certain amendments. The Inquisition was not to protect officials or familiars guilty of treason against the viceroy or his counsellors, of assassination, of shooting from ambush, of insulting, wounding or killing any one in presence of judges of the Gran Corte or Real Patrimonio. It was the same with familiars who were notaries and committed frauds in that capacity, or were warehousemen and adulterated commodities stored with them, or dealers in provisions who used false weights, or bankers or other debtors delinquent to the Real Patrimonio, or delinquent taxpayers in general. Widows of officials were to enjoy the fuero only so long as they remained unmarried, and servants were only to be entitled to it when they were really part of the household and not merely serving for food and wages, concerning which inquisitors were strictly enjoined not to commit frauds. In Palermo and its suburbs the number of familiars was limited to one hundred; in towns of sixty hearths, to one; in other places the Suprema was to decide; they were to

---

[1] MSS. of Library of Univ. of Halle, Yc, 17.

be prohibited from carrying guns in the country and fire-arms of any kind in the cities. If a judge arrested a familiar or official, he was at once to send the papers in the case to the inquisitors that they might see whether it was excepted or whether there should be a competencia and, in the latter case, the judges were to be invited courteously to meet them and not be summoned as inferiors. The judges, when excommunicated, were to apply for absolution and not refuse as heretofore to do so, thus discrediting inquisitorial censures, but the viceroy was not to be excommunicated without the assent of the inquisitor-general. The Regent Bruñol argued earnestly in favor of including rape among the excepted crimes, pointing out how provocative it was of assassination, when the husband of a woman thus injured saw the culprit walking the streets unpunished, and he seems to have succeeded in getting it added to the scanty list of those which the Inquisition would permit to be dealt with in the secular courts.[1]

Thus far the conferees agreed, but they differed on the exclusion of nobles from official position. The members of the Suprema represented to the king that, since he had ordered their removal, the Inquisition had fallen greatly in public estimation and found much difficulty in making arrests; therefore they asked that there might be thirty, who would always be selected from the most quiet and peaceable; otherwise the tribunal would be confined to men of low extraction, who could not make arrests. To this the regents replied that the maintenance of the royal order was the only means of keeping the nobles and barons obedient to the viceroy; in Sicily more than elsewhere this was necessary and without it matters would be worse than before, when the tribunal excommunicated the viceroy in the affair of Count Mussumelli; heresy was unknown, the nobles and barons had never made an arrest and they obtained the positions solely to gain the privileges.[2] These arguments were unanswerable and the prohibition was maintained. With the accession of Philip III an attempt was again made to have it repealed; Inquisitor Páramo, in a letter of

---

[1] MSS. of Library of Univ. of Halle, Yc, 17. [2] Ibidem, *ubi sup.*

March 8, 1600, to the new king described the condition of the tribunal as most deplorable in consequence of it, but the appeal was unsuccessful. Philip contented himself with secret instructions to the viceroy to enforce the cédula of January 18, 1535, and the Concordia and to endeavor to come to some understanding with the inquisitors.[1]

So far, indeed, was the Inquisition from being oppressed, that it was seeking to assert exclusive claim to the obedience of its "subjects," as though they were released in all things from the control of the civil authorities. Thus, in 1591, the tribunal issued an edict condemning all its "subjects" who had not revealed the amount of corn possessed by them or had sold it at unlawful prices—evidently referring to certain measures taken by the government, as was frequently done in times of scarcity. The Viceroy Alba was quick to recognize this attempt to supplant the civil power and he stopped the publication of the edict. He was soon afterwards succeeded by Count Olivares, whose temper Inquisitor Páramo, with characteristic pertinacity, proceeded to test with a proclamation of April 23, 1592, published throughout the island to sound of trumpet, reciting the disturbance of public order by bands of robbers, against whom and all harboring or favoring them the viceroy had issued edicts, wherefore he summoned all those subject to the jurisdiction of the Inquisition to abstain from sheltering the said bandits, under the penalties provided by the laws and of a thousand ounces applicable to the Holy Office. Olivares was no more disposed than his predecessor to admit that his actions required inquisitorial confirmation and, on May 30th, he issued an edict prohibiting, under heavy penalties, the publication of the proclamation; if, in any place, it had been entered on the records of the magistrates, the entry was to be erased and no similar orders of the Inquisition were to be received in future. He moreover told the inquisitors that it was none of

---

[1] Archivo de Simancas, Inquisicion, Lib. 41, fol. 258, 263. In his letter Páramo mentions that not long before two Calvinist missionaries had been sent from Geneva to Sicily; the Inquisition arrested them and their converts and one of the missionaries had been burnt alive, showing the steadfastness of his faith.

their business to issue decrees on this or any other matter of general policy, but simply to obey the laws; that it had been done merely to enlarge their jurisdiction illegally and that the government could not be divided into two heads with one body.[1]

Between conflicting pretensions such as these, harmony was impossible and the conclusions of the junta of 1595 did not restore it. Collisions were frequent and the extremes to which they were sometimes carried are seen in one occurring in 1602, when the Gran Corte prosecuted Mariano Agliata, a familiar, for the murder of Don Diego de Zúñiga and Don Diego Sandoval, a captain and a sergeant of the royal troops. The inquisitors arrested him and claimed jurisdiction and, when the Gran Corte refused to abandon the prosecution, they excommunicated the judges. Excommunication by an inquisitor could be removed only by the power which fulminated it or by the pope, but the viceroy, the Duke of Feria, persuaded the archbishop, Diego de Haëdo, to absolve the judges, whereupon the inquisitors interdicted him from performing any functions until he should admit that his absolutions were invalid. At this the viceroy lost his temper and despatched, August 7th, two companies of soldiers to the Inquisition, with a gallows and the executioner. They remained in front of the building until two o'clock in the morning and returned on the 8th in greater force, erected six gallows, each with its hangman, and stood with lighted matchlocks pointed at the windows. The inquisitors were not daunted by this impotent display of force; they barred the doors, hoisted the standard of the Inquisition, with a papal flag and a crucifix, and flung out of the windows among the troops notices of excommunication. Undeterred by this, the Spaniards broke their way in and, after some parley, the inquisitors promised to absolve them. Feria had gone as far as he dared without result and the victory remained with the inquisitors, for the case of Agliata was surrendered to them, on their removing the interdict on the archbishop and the excommuni-

---

[1] Gervasii Siculæ Sanctiones, II, 329 (Panormi, 1751)

cation of the judges.[1] To emphasize Feria's defeat, Philip III, in 1603, issued a general letter to all of his viceroys, lauding the services of the Inquisition and ordering them to give it all the favor and assistance it might ask for, and to maintain intact the privileges, exemptions and liberties, assured to its ministers and familiars, by law, by the concordias, by the royal cédulas, by use and custom and by any other source.[2]

As though these sempiternal conflicts with the civil authorities were not sufficiently disturbing to the public peace, the Inquisition was involved in a similar series with the bishops, in which it did not fare so well, entrenched as they were behind the canon law, which the monarchs could not set aside. A portion of the officials of the Holy Office were clerics, of whose immunity from the secular courts there could be no question, but the bishops claimed, under divine and canon law, an imprescriptible right of cognizance of their offences, when these did not concern the faith or their official functions. The inquisitors held that they possessed exclusive jurisdiction over their subordinates and the conflict was waged with abundant lack of Christian charity, causing great popular scandal until, as we are told, the people were in the habit of asking where was the God of the clergy. The contest raged chiefly over the commissioners appointed everywhere throughout the island, whose duty it was to investigate cases of heresy in their districts and report or, if necessary, make arrests and send the culprits to Palermo for trial. In 1625 the Suprema

---

[1] La Mantia, pp. 69–70. There is a very vivid account of this affair in a letter to the Suprema from Páramo and his colleagues, written on the evening of August 9th, when they were expecting further ill treatment by the viceroy, whom they characterize in the most unflattering terms.—Bibl. Nacional de Madrid, MSS., Cc, 58, p. 35.

Páramo, in a document of March 8, 1600, had already described him as a declared enemy of the Inquisition.—Archivo de Simancas, Inquisicion, Lib. 41, fol. 249.

[2] Portocarrero, op. cit., n. 1.—Solorzani de Indiarum Gubernatione, Lib. III, cap. xxiv, n. 16.—A virtual duplicate of this letter was sent, September 10, 1670, by the Queen-regent Maria Anna of Austria, to the Prince de Ligne, then Viceroy of Sicily.—Mongitore, L'Atto pubblico di Fede de 1724, p. v (Palermo, 1724).

endeavored to effect a compromise, by designating what offences were cognizable by the bishops exclusively, what by the inquisitors and what cumulatively by either jurisdiction, for that of the bishops could not be denied and the Inquisition had no papal letters to show in support of its claims. This seems only to have emboldened the bishops and the quarrels continued. In 1630 Philip IV and the inquisitor-general wrote to the viceroy and the inquisitors, enquiring what was the established custom in such cases, but apparently the two ecclesiastical camps could not agree on terms of peace and nothing was done. In 1642 the inquisitor, Gonsalvo Bravo Grosero submitted to the Suprema a long and learned paper in which he describes the condition of the Sicilian Inquisition as most deplorable, in consequence of the implacable hostility of the bishops. It could not possibly do without commissioners, for the inquisitors could not travel around to visit the provinces; the roads were too bad and their salaries too meagre to bear the expense, as they could not venture into the country without a guard of at least forty men, in view of the robbers and bandits. There was not money to pay the commissioners a salary and their only inducement to accept the office was to gain immunity from episcopal jurisdiction. As this was virtually denied to them, it became impossible to find fitting clerics to undertake the duties, so there were many vacancies that could not be filled.

Grosero evidently did not pause to consider the reflection cast on the character of the clerics thus anxious to find refuge in the Inquisition from the courts of their bishops, but the cases which he mentions, if not exaggerated, testify amply to the virulence of episcopal vindictiveness. Recently, he says, the tribunal became involved in a quarrel with the Bishop of Syracuse over the case of a familiar. Indignant at its methods, the bishop indulged in reprisals on the unlucky commissioner of Lentini, on a charge of incontinence; he was seized by a band of armed clerics, stripped and carried on a mule to prison as a malefactor and cast into a dungeon where he lay, deprived of all communication with his friends, until the Bishop of Cefalù, then governor of the island, procured his release, but his persecution continued for two years. So the Bishop of Girgenti seized the commissioner of Caltanexeda because he had, under orders from the tribunal, stopped the prosecution of a familiar. He was confined in a damp, underground cell for forty days, until the viceroy procured his release, and his unwholesome confinement nearly cost him his life. The impelling cause of Grosero's memorial was a pending case, which scarcely evokes sympathy with his complaints. Alessandro Turano, commissioner of Burgio, had given refuge in his house to a kinsman, a monk guilty of murder, and had refused admission to the officers who came to arrest the criminal. For this the Bishop of Girgenti was prosecuting him, and Grosero appeals to the Suprema to intervene and put an end to such violations of the immunity necessary to enable the Inquisition to perform its pious work.[1] It is not likely that the Suprema succeeded in establishing concord between the irreconcilable pretensions of the two ecclesiastical bodies, but the struggle is worth passing attention as affording a glimpse into the social conditions of the period under such institutions.

Meanwhile the incessant bickering with the civil authorities continued as active and as bitter as ever. No attention was paid to the limitations prescribed in the Concordias, or to the protests of the viceroys until, in 1635, an attempt was made, in a new Concordia, to remedy some of the more crying evils by empowering the viceroy, in cases of exceptional gravity, to banish criminal officials, after notice to the senior inquisitor, so that he might appeal to Madrid, and in these cases the inquisitors were forbidden to excommunicate the officers of justice.[2] Slender as was this concession, the inquisitors, in a letter of April 26, 1652, to the Suprema, did not hesitate to assert that the exemptions of the officials were reduced to those of the vilest plebeians and that

---

[1] Biblioteca nacional de Madrid, MSS., D, 118, fol. 134, n. 47.
[2] Archivo de Simancas, Inquisicion, Legajo 1465, fol. 35.

their revenue suffered heavily through the limitation of their jurisdiction and the great reduction in the number of those who applied for appointments.[1] On the other hand, if we may believe the *Consulta Magna*, drawn up, in 1696, by a special junta composed of representatives of all the royal councils except the Suprema, the Sicilian tribunal paid no respect whatever to the Concordias, held itself as wholly independent of all rules and enforced its arbitrary acts by the constant abuse of excommunication, which rendered the condition of the island most deplorable. The inquisitors refused to meet the judges in competencias on disputed cases and though, by the Concordia of 1635, such refusal incurred a fine of five hundred ducats for a first offence and dismissal for a second, yet as the enforcement of this required the issue by the Suprema of a commission to the Council of Italy, it was easily eluded. As a matter of course the suggestion of the junta was ineffective that those oppressed by the abuse of spiritual censures should have the right of appeal to the royal judges.[2]

These quarrels and the exercise of its widely extended temporal jurisdiction by no means distracted wholly the tribunal from its legitimate functions of preserving the purity of the faith. In 1640 it held a notable auto de fe in which one case is worth alluding to as an illustration of inquisitorial dealings with the insane. Carlo Tabaloro of Calabria was an Augustinian lay-brother, who had conceived the idea that he was the Son of God and the Messiah, Christ having been merely the Redeemer. He had written a gospel about himself and framed a series of novel religious observances. Arrested by the Palermo tribunal, in 1635, he had imagined it to be for the purpose of enabling him to convert the inquisitors and through them the people. For five years the theologians labored to disabuse him, but to no purpose; he was condemned as an obstinate and pertinacious heretic and was led forth in the auto of 1640 to be burnt alive. On his way to the stake

---

[1] Archivo de Simancas, Inquisicion, Libro 38, fol. 298.
[2] Consulta Magna de 1696 (Bibl. nacional de Madrid, MSS., Q, 4).

he still expected that torrents of rain would extinguish the fires, but finding himself disappointed and shrinking from the awful death, at the last moment he professed conversion and was mercifully strangled before the pile was lighted.[1] At another auto, June 2, 1647, there were thirty-four penitents and six months later another, January 12, 1648, with thirty-seven, followed, December 13th of the same year, by one with forty-three. January 22, 1651, there was another with thirty-nine, honored moreover with the presence of Don John of Austria, fresh from the triumph of suppressing the Neapolitan revolt of Masaniello. In fact, in a letter of April 26, 1652, the inquisitors boasted that they had punished two hundred and seven culprits in public autos, besides nearly as many who had been despatched privately in the audience chamber. This would show an average of about eighty cases a year, greatly more than at this time was customary in Spain. The offences were mostly blasphemy, bigamy and sorcery, with an occasional Protestant or Alumbrado, the Judaizers by this time having almost disappeared.[2] The position of inquisitor was not wholly without danger, for Juan López de Cisneros died of a wound in the forehead inflicted by Fray Diego la Mattina, a prisoner whom he was visiting in his cell and who was burnt alive in the auto of March 17, 1658.[3] The activity of the tribunal must at times have brought in considerable profits for, in 1640, we happen to learn that it was contributing yearly twenty-four thousand reales in silver to the Suprema and not long afterwards it was called upon to send five hundred ducats, *plata doble*, to that of Majorca, which had been impoverished by a pestilence. Still these gains were fluctuating and the demands on the tribunal seem to have brought it into financial straits, from which the Suprema sought to relieve it by an appeal, August 6, 1652, to Philip IV, to grant it benefices to the amount of twenty-five hundred ducats a year.[4]

---

[1] Alberghini, Manuale Qualificatorum, p. 171 (Cæsaraugustæ, 1671).
[2] La Mantia, pp. 79–86.   [3] Franchina, pp, 100, 101.
[4] Archivo de Simancas, Inquisicion, Lib. 21, fol. 252; Lib. 23, fol. 62, 119; Lib. 38, fol. 245, 298.

The treaty of Utrecht, in 1713, gave Sicily to Savoy, but the Inquisition remained Spanish and nominally subject to the Suprema. There was, however, an immediate change of personnel, for we find the inquisitor, José de la Rosa Cozio, early in 1714, taking refuge in Spain and billeted upon the tribunal of Valencia.[1] When, in 1718, Savoy exchanged Sicily with Austria for Sardinia, the Emperor Charles VI would not endure this dependence of the tribunal upon a foreign power and procured, in 1720, from Clement XI a brief transferring the supremacy to Vienna. In accordance, however, with the persistent Hapsburg claims on the crown of Spain, the Inquisition remained Spanish. A supreme council for it was created in Vienna, with Juan Navarro, Bishop of Albarracin as chief who, although resident there gratified himself with the title of *Inquisidor-general de España*, but in 1723 he was succeeded by Cardinal Emeric, Archbishop of Kolocz. Apparently it was deemed necessary to justify this elaborate machinery with a demonstration and, on April 6, 1724, an auto de fe was celebrated at Palermo with great splendor, the expenses being defrayed by the emperor. Twenty-six delinquents were penanced, consisting as usual mostly of cases of blasphemy, bigamy and sorcery, but the spectacle would have been incomplete without concremation and two unfortunates, who had languished in prison since 1699, were brought out for that purpose. They were Geltruda, a beguine, and Fra Romualdo, a friar, accused of Quietism and Molinism, with the accompanying heresies of illuminism and impeccability. Their long imprisonment, with torture and ill-usage, seems to have turned their brains, and they had been condemned to relaxation as impenitent in 1705 and 1709, but the sentences had never been carried out and they were now brought from their dungeons and burnt alive.[2] Less notable

---

[1] Archivo hist. nacional, Inquisicion de Valencia, Legajo 13, n. 2, fol. 157. Cozio's salary in Valencia commenced with May 1st, as he had received in Palermo the advanced *tercio* of January 1st.

[2] La Mantia, p. 92.—Franchina, p. 38.—Mongitore, L'Atto pubblico di Fede celebrato à 6 Aprile, 1724 (Palermo, 1724). This work of Mongitore was reprinted in 1868, when the editor F. Guidicini mentions in the Preface that on March 9th

was an auto de fe of March 22, 1732, in which Antonio Canzoneri was burnt alive as a contumacious and relapsed heretic.[1]

Although the zeal of Charles VI led to increased activity of the tribunal in matters of faith, he was little disposed to tolerate its abuse of its temporal jurisdiction, which had led to so many fruitless remonstrances under Spanish domination. In letters of January 26, 1729, to his viceroy the Count of Sástago, he recites the complaints made to him, by the English factory, that foreign merchants were exposed to constant frauds by bankruptcies of debtors who claimed the forum of the Inquisition or of the Santa Cruzada, where creditors could get no justice or even ascertain whether the bankruptcies were fictitious or not. The emperor therefore orders that in future the Concordias shall be strictly construed and rigidly adhered to; that if the inquisitors proceed by excommunication they shall experience the effect of "los remedios economicos" (presumably the suspension of their emoluments) and that in future all mercantile cases, whether civil or criminal, shall not be entitled to the forum of the Inquisition—all of which was duly proclaimed by the viceroy in an edict of March 17th. At the same time the legal functionaries were required to investigate the whole subject and report what further measures might be essential to prevent interference with the course of justice. The result of their labors is embodied in a

---

of that year a petition was presented to the Italian Chamber of Deputies, from a Palermitan family, begging the remission of a yearly payment to the royal domain, imposed on them by the Inquisition to defray the expenses of the trial of their kinswoman, the Sister Geltruda, burnt in 1724.

It was probably the celebration of this auto that inspired an anonymous writer to denounce the inquisitorial procedure in a little work entitled "Le prove praticate nelli tempi presenti dagl' Inquisitori di Fede sono manchevole." This was answered by Doctor Don Miguel Monge, a professor in the University of Huesca in "La verdadera Practica Apostolica de el S. Tribunal de la Inquisicion" (Palermo, 1725). He seems in this to consider all criticism sufficiently answered by demonstrating that the practices complained of are in accordance with the papal instructions. The work illustrates the anomalous position of the Sicilian Inquisition at the period. It is written by a Spaniard, printed in both Spanish and Italian, dated in Vienna and dedicated to Don Ramon de Villana Perlas, a Catalan member of the Imperial Council of State.

[1] Franchina, pp. 44, 55.

Pragmatic Sanction of May 12, 1732, consisting of eleven articles, whereby it was ordered that the inquisitorial forum should not include exemption from military service and taxes; that widows of stipendiary officials should enjoy the forum only during widowhood; that the privilege of bearing arms should be exercised only when in actual service of the Inquisition; that commissions as messengers should not be given to shipmasters; nobles holding fiefs were not to be enrolled as familiars; the forum was not to exempt from serving in onerous public office and the use of excommunication in cases of impeding jurisdiction was allowed under certain limitations. This latter is explained by a decision of March 6, 1734, on cases in which the inquisitors had excommunicated D. Antonio Crimibela, a judge of the Gran Corte and D. Felipe Venuto, *capitan de justicia* of Paternò, when it was ordered that excommunications could only be employed in matters of faith and in cases where the secular tribunals had refused the conference preliminary to forming a competencia to decide as to the jurisdiction.[1]

The conquest of the Two Sicilies by Charles III, in 1734, led the inquisitors to imagine that, under a Spanish dynasty, they could reassert their superiority over the law, but they were promptly undeceived. D. Sisto Poidimani, when on trial, recused them for enmity as judges in his case and the Giunta of Presidents recognized his reasons as sufficient, whereupon Viceroy de Castro ordered them, October 2, 1735, to take no further action except to appoint some one to act in their place. To this they demurred and de Castro repeated the order, January 24, 1736, and again on February 19th. Finally, on April 21st he told them that they were actuated, not by reason but by disobedience, and that, if the order was not promptly obeyed, the senior inquisitor must sail, within forty-eight hours, for Naples to render to the king an account of his actions.[2]

The various changes that had occurred rendered the position of the Sicilian tribunal somewhat anomalous and to remedy this

---

[1] Gervasii Siculæ Sanctiones, II, 333–50   [2] Ibidem, I, 277–81.

the king obtained, in 1738, from Clement XIII the appointment of Pietro Galletti, Bishop of Catania, as inquisitor-general of Sicily, with power to deputize subordinates, who was followed, in 1742, by Giacomo Bonanno, Bishop of Patti, appointed by Benedict XIV.[1] Thus the severance from Spain was perpetuated and it was rendered independent. This seems to have revived its aggressiveness and it assumed that the limitations imposed by the Emperor Charles VI had become obsolete with the change of sovereigns for, in 1739, it endeavored to intervene in the bankruptcy case of Giuseppe Maria Gerardi, who was entitled to its forum, but the attempt was promptly annulled by the Viceroy Corsini. A further blow was inflicted by a decree of July 12, 1746, suppressing the system of competencias, for the settlement of conflicting cases of jurisdiction, and substituting, in all cases not of faith, the decision of the viceroy, who could, in matters of grave importance, refer them to the king.[2] Thus gradually the secular business of the Holy Office was circumscribed; in its spiritual field of activity there were no more burnings, though it occasionally held autos de fe, in which figured mostly women accused of the vulgar arts of sorcery, and in addition it interfered with scholars in its capacity of censor.

The enlightened views of Charles III were not abandoned, when he was summoned to the throne of Spain in 1759, and left that of Naples to his young son, Ferdinando IV, then a child eight years of age. Public opinion in Italy was rapidly rendering the Holy Office an anachronism and Ferdinando only expressed the general sentiment when, by a decree of March 16, 1782, he pronounced its suppression. He gave as a reason that all attempts had failed to make it alter its vicious system, which deprived the accused of legitimate means of defence; he restored to the bishops their original jurisdiction in all matters of faith, but required them to observe the same procedure as the secular courts of justice and to submit to the viceroy for approval all citations to appear,

---

[1] La Mantia, p. 103.—Franchina, pp. 201, 206.
[2] Gervasii, *op. cit.*, I, 286; II, 352.

all orders for arrest and all sentences proposed; moreover, he appropriated the property of the Inquisition to continuing for life the salaries of the officials, with a provision that, as these pensions should fall in, the money should be used for the public benefit. The revenues, in fact, amounted to ten thousand crowns a year and eventually they served to found chairs in mathematics and experimental physics and to build an observatory. When the royal officials took possession of the Inquisition, they found only three prisoners to liberate—women accused of witchcraft. A few more had previously been discharged, in anticipation of the suppression, by the inquisitor-general, Salvatore Ventimiglia, Archbishop of Nicodemia.[1]

In its career, since 1487, Franchina, writing in 1744, boasts that the Holy Office had handed over to the secular arm for burning two hundred and one living heretics and apostates and two hundred and seventy-nine effigies of the dead or fugitives.[2] It illustrates forcibly the changed spirit of the age that Viceroy Caraccioli, in writing to D'Alembert an account of the abolition, says that he shed tears of joy in proceeding to the Inquisition with the great dignitaries of State and Church, when he caused the royal rescript to be read to the inquisitor and the arms of the Holy Office to be erased from the portal amid the rejoicing of the assembled people.[3]

MALTA.

Malta, if we may believe Salelles, enjoyed the honor of having St. Paul as the founder of its Inquisition, when he was cast ashore there on his voyage to Rome.[4] In the sixteenth century, however,

---

[1] La Mantia, pp. 108 sqq. [2] Franchina, p. 43.
[3] Acta Historico-Ecclesiastica nostri temporis, T. IX, p. 74 (Weimar, 1783).
[4] Salelles de Materiis Tribunalium Inquisit., I, 43.

as a dependency of Sicily, it was under the Sicilian tribunal, which maintained an organization there, under a commissioner.[1] When, in 1530, Charles V gave the island to the Knights of St. John, the Sicilian jurisdiction lapsed but, even without the Holy Office, the Church had efficient machinery for the suppression of heresy. In 1546 a Frenchman named Gesuald was found to have been for ten years infecting the islanders with Calvinist opinions, and the Aragonese Domingo Cubelles, the Bishop of Malta, was at no loss in exercising his episcopal jurisdiction. Gesuald was obstinate in his faith and was duly burnt alive; on his way to the stake he called out "Why do priests hesitate to take wives, since it is lawful?" whereupon Cubelles ordered him to be gagged and he perished in silence. His converts lacked his stubborn convictions and were reconciled—among them two priests who had secretly married their concubines, for which they were condemned to wear the sanbenito. In 1553, the Grand Master, Juan de Omedes, constituted three of the knights and a chaplain as an Inquisition, but there is no trace of their labors and Cubelles continued to exercise his episcopal jurisdiction in several cases during the following years. In 1560, however, when a Maltese, named Doctor Pietro Combo, fell under suspicion, Cubelles seems to have felt uncertain what to do with him and sent him in chains to the Roman Inquisition, where he was acquitted. Cubelles informed the cardinals that the Lutheran heresy was spreading in the island and this probably explains why, by letters of October 21, 1561, the Roman Inquisition, while recognizing the episcopal jurisdiction of Cubelles, enlarged it to that of an inquisitor-general, empowering him to appoint deputies and to proceed against all persons, whether clerics or laymen, to try them, torture them, relax them or reconcile them with appropriate penance.[2]

In his zeal for the effective discharge of his duties, Cubelles sent to Palermo for detailed information as to the conduct of the Inquisition and was furnished with copies of the Spanish instructions and forms. This seems to have provoked the Roman

---

[1] Llorente, Hist. crít., cap. XIII, art. ii, n. 9.   [2] Salelles, I, 47–50.

Congregation of the Holy Office, between which and the Spanish there was perpetual jealousy, and it sent to Malta a Dominican to act as his assistant and to direct him. He was succeeded, both as bishop and inquisitor, by Martin Rojas de Portorubio, to whom in 1573 Gregory XIII sent a commission. Apparently it was impossible for the Inquisition to maintain harmonious relations with the temporal power and, already in 1574, he complained to Rome that his officials were beaten and that the Grand Master, Jean l'Evesque de la Cassière, threatened to throw him out of the window if he came to the palace. This created considerable scandal, but Rome, unlike Spain, was not accustomed to support inquisitors through thick and thin, and the result was that, by brief of July 3, 1574, Gregory revoked his commission and sent Dr. Pietro Duzzina as apostolic vicar to conduct the Inquisition. In thus separating it from the episcopate no provision was made for its expenses, but soon after this the confiscated property of Mathieu Faison, a rich heretic burnt in effigy, yielded a revenue of three hundred crowns and, when Bishop Rojas died, March 19, 1577, opportunity was taken to burden the see with a pension of six hundred more for its benefit.[1] It was thus rendered permanent, but a protracted struggle with successive grandmasters was necessary to secure for its officials the privileges of the forum and the immunities and exemptions which they claimed.[2]

Yet the Spanish Inquisition was not satisfied to be thus completely superseded by that of Rome, even in so remote and inconspicuous a spot as Malta. In 1575 Duzzina arrested a man as a heretic; it was known that testimony against him had been taken in Sicily and application for it was made to the inquisitors of Palermo. They applied for instructions to the Suprema, which ordered them not to give it but to claim the prisoner. The result was that the Maltese tribunal tried him on what had occurred on the island and discharged him.[3] This emphasized its absolute

---

[1] Salelles, I, 53–62. [2] Parecer de Martin Real, *ubi sup.*
[3] Llorente, Hist. crít., cap. XVII, art. ii, n. 10.

separation from the Spanish Holy Office and its history need not be further followed here, except to allude to the most celebrated case in its annals, when the two Quakeresses, Katharine Evans and Sarah Cheevers, moved by the Spirit, went to Malta on a mission of conversion and suffered an imprisonment of four years.[1]

---

[1] A Brief History of the Voyage of Katharine Evans and Sarah Cheevers to the Island of Malta and their Cruel Sufferings there for near Four Years. London, 1715.

CHAPTER II.

NAPLES.

IN Naples the Inquisition had been introduced by Charles of Anjou after the battle of Benevento had acquired for him the succession to the unfortunate Manfred. The house of Aragon, which followed that of Anjou, had permitted its existence, but under conditions of such subjection to the crown that it was for the most part inert. Yet Naples offered an abundant harvest for the zealous laborer. The Waldenses from Savoy, who had settled and multiplied in Calabria and Apulia, had obtained, in 1497, from King Frederic, a confirmation of their agreements with their immediate suzerains, the nobles, and felt secure from persecution.[1] Still more inviting were the banished Jews and fugitive New Christians from Spain, who found there a tolerably safe refuge. There was also a considerable number of indigenous Jews. In the twefth century Benjamin of Tudela describes flourishing synagogues in Capua, Naples, Salerno, Amalfi, Benevento, Melfi, Ascoli-Satriano, Tarento, Bernaldo and Otranto, and these doubtless were representatives of others existing outside of the line of his wanderings.[2] They had probably gone on increasing, although, in 1427, Joanna II called in the ruthless St. Giovanni da Capistrano to suppress their usury and, in 1447, Nicholas V appointed him conservator to enforce the disabilities and humiliations prescribed in a cruel bull which he had just issued.[3] Possibly, under this rigorous treatment, some of them may have sought baptism for, in 1449, we find Nicholas despatching to Naples Fra Matteo da Reggio as inquisitor to exterminate the apostate

---

[1] History of the Inquisition of the Middle Ages, II, 268.
[2] Itinerarium Beniamini Tudelens., pp. 21–5 (Antverpiæ, 1575).
[3] Wadding, Annal. Minorum, T. III, Regesta, p. 392; ann. 1447, n. 10.

Judaizers, who were said to be numerous.[1] If we may believe Zurita, when Charles VIII of France made his transitory conquest of Naples, in 1495, the Jews were all compulsorily baptized, with the usual result that their Christianity was only nominal.[2] Such unwilling converts of course called for inquisitorial solicitude but, when Ferdinand of Spain obtained possession of the land, it was the fugitives from the Spanish Inquisition that rendered him especially desirous of extending its jurisdiction over his dominions on the Italian mainland.

A single example will illustrate this and also throw light on the resistance which, as we shall see, the Neapolitans offered to the introduction of the Holy Office after the Spanish pattern. In the inquisitorial documents of the period, no name occurs more frequently than that of Manuel Esparza de Pantolosa, who was condemned *in absentia* as a heretic, in Tarragona. He had evidently sought safety in flight, abandoning his property which was confiscated and sold, June 4, 1493, for 9000 libras to his brother, Micer Luis Esparza, a jurist of Valencia, whose final payment for it is dated February 2, 1499, when the inquisitor, Juan de Monasterio, was authorized to retain a hundred ducats in reward for his labors.

Meanwhile Pantolosa had prospered in Naples as a banker and had become one of the farmers of the revenue. As a condemned heretic, however, all dealings with him were unlawful to Spaniards. It was difficult to avoid these in transactions between Spain and Naples and, in February, 1499, the inquisitors of Barcelona created much scandal by arresting a number of merchants for maintaining business relations with him, an excess of zeal for which Ferdinand scolded them, while ordering the release of the prisoners. Pantolosa seems to have held out some hopes of returning and standing trial, for a safe-conduct was issued to him, October 4, 1499, good for twelve months, during which he and his property were to be exempt from seizure, dealings with him were permitted and ship-

---

[1] Ripoll Bullar. Ord. FF. Prædic., II, 689.
[2] Zurita, Hist. del Rey Hernando, Lib. v, cap. lxx.

masters were authorized to transport him and, on the plea that he had been impeded, the safe-conduct was extended, August 22, 1500, for two years. There was manifest policy in suspending the customary disabilities for a personage of such importance, as appears from one or two instances. When, in the autumn of 1499, Ferdinand's sister, Juana, Queen of Naples, and her stepson, the Cardinal of Aragon, came to Spain, they provided themselves with bills of exchange drawn by the farmers of revenue—Pantolosa, Gaspar de Caballería and others—on Luis de Santangel, Ferdinand's *escribano de racion*, or privy purse. They could not anticipate any trouble in a transaction between officials of Spain and Naples, but Santangel, also a Converso, had reason to be cautious as to his relations with the Inquisition and he refused to honor the bills, because the drawers were fugitive condemned heretics, with whom he could have no dealings. Ferdinand was obliged to confer with the inquisitors-general, after which he authorized Santangel to supply the necessities of the royal visitors. Possibly in this case the association with Caballería neutralized Pantolosa's safe-conduct, but this disturbing element was absent from a flagrant exhibition of inquisitorial audacity when, in 1500, Ferdinand sent the Archbishop of Tarragona to Naples on business connected with his sister, the queen. Requiring money while there the archbishop sold bills of exchange to Pantolosa and, when they were presented in Tarragona, the inquisitors, apparently regarding them as a debt due to a condemned heretic, forbade their payment and sequestrated the archiepiscopal revenues to collect the amount. The bills were returned and were sent back with a fresh demand for payment, when Ferdinand intervened and, by letters of July 3d, ordered the inquisitors to remove the sequestration so that they could be paid and the archbishop's credit be preserved.[1] It

---

[1] Archivo de Simancas, Inquisicion, Libro I. An episode of this business concerned one Nofre Pelayo, a merchant of Valencia, who was arrested on the charge of concealing some of Pantolosa's property. On January 15, 1498, Ferdinand warmly praised the inquisitor for this action but he speedily changed his mind and, on March 6th, scolded him for keeping Pelayo in prison and refusing to admit him to bail. It seems that he had in his hands two hundred and fifty ducats,

is easy to understand how Ferdinand felt towards the Neapolitan asylum for condemned Spanish heretics and banished Jews and how Naples regarded the arbitrary processes of the Spanish Holy Office.

When, in 1500, Ferdinand had seized Calabria and Apulia, in fulfilment of the robber bargain between him and Louis XII, he lost little time in turning to account his new acquisition for the benefit of the Sicilian Holy Office. A letter of August 7, 1501, to his representatives recites that the inquisitors of Sicily say that they will be aided in their work by the testimony of the New Christians of Calabria, wherefore all whom they may designate are to be compelled to give the evidence required.[1] When, in 1503, Ferdinand obtained the whole kingdom by ousting his accomplice Louis, Gonsalvo de Córdova, to facilitate the surrender of Naples, made an engagement that the Spanish Inquisition should not be introduced, for its evil reputation rendered it a universal object of dread, to which the numerous Spanish refugees had doubtless largely contributed.[2] The Neapolitans also desired to destroy

---

supposed to belong to Pantolosa, but the sum was claimed by Miguel de Fluto, who luckily was a kinsman of the Neapolitan ambassador; the latter induced his master to write on the subject to Ferdinand who, on March 19, 1499, ordered the sum to be paid to the ambassador's order.—Ibidem.

These transactions are worth noting as an illustration of the destructive influence on commerce of the methods of confiscation.

[1] Archivo de Simancas, Inquisicion, Lib. I.

[2] Amabile (Il Santo Officio in Napoli, I, 93) assures us that there is no trace of such a condition expressed in the documents, but undoubtedly some compact of the kind must have been made. This is evident from the fact that when, in 1504, Ferdinand and Isabella resolved to introduce the Inquisition they formally released Gonsalvo from the obligation, giving as a reason that no Catholic was required to observe obligations in derogation of the faith—"non obstantibus in præmissis aut aliquo præmissorum quibusvis pactis, conventionibus aut capitulationibus per vos præfatum illustrem ducem aut alium quemcunque, nomine nostro vel vestro in deditione civitatis Neapolis aut alias quandocunque factis, conventis aut juratis, cum ea quæ contra fidem faciunt nullo pacto a Catholicis observanda sunt, quinimmo easdem si tales sunt quæ prædictis aliquatenus obviare censeantur cum præsentibus quoad hæc revocamus, taxamus, annullamus et irritamus, pro cassisque, irritis ac nullis nulliusque roboris seu momenti haberi volumus et habemus, cæteris autem ad hæc non tangentibus in suo robore permanentibus."—Páramo, De Origine Officii S. Inquisit., p. 192.

This is repeated more concisely in another personal letter to Gonsalvo of the same date.—Ibidem, p. 193.

the principal incentive of the existing Inquisition by a condition that confiscation should be restricted to cases of high treason, but this they were unable to secure and the final articles allowed its use in heresy and treason.¹ Ferdinand's order of August, 1501, as to obtaining evidence for Sicily, seems to have met with slack obedience, for there is a letter of November 16, 1504, from Gonsalvo to the royal officials in general, reciting that Archbishop Belorado, as Inquisitor of Sicily, had sent to Reggio, to obtain certain necessary depositions, but that the officials had prevented it, wherefore he reminds them of the royal commands and imposes a penalty of a thousand ducats for all future cases of disobedience.²

No sooner was the conquest of Naples assured than Ferdinand proceeded to clear the land of Judaism by ordering Gonsalvo to banish all the Jews. The persecution at the time of Charles VIII had left few of them *de señal*—those who openly avowed their faith by wearing the prescribed letter Tau—and Gonsalvo seems to have reported that prosecution of the secret apostates was the only method practicable. Julius II opportunely set the example by instituting a severe inquisition, under the Dominican organization at Benevento.³ Ferdinand regarded with extreme jealousy all exercise of papal jurisdiction within his dominions and to prevent the extension of this he naturally had recourse to the commission of his inquisitor-general which covered all the territories of the Spanish crown. A secret letter was drawn up, June 30, 1504, by Ferdinand and Isabella, in conjunction with the Suprema, or Supreme Council of the Inquisition, addressed to all the royal officials in Naples, reciting that as numerous heretics duly burnt

---

¹ Amabile, I, 101. When Charles of Anjou introduced the Inquisition he took the confiscations, as was customary in France, and paid the expenses, but in 1290 his son, Charles the Lame, divided the proceeds into thirds, one for the fisc, one for the Inquisition and one for the propagation of the faith, a rule which probably became permanent.—Hist. of Inquisition of Middle Ages, I, 511-12.

² Chioccarello MSS., T. VIII. This is a well-known collection of documents from the Neapolitan archives, made in the seventeenth century by Bartolommeo Chioccarello, which has never been printed. The eighth volume is devoted to the Inquisition.

³ Zurita, Hist. del Rey Hernando, Lib. v, cap. lxx. Benevento was a papal enclave in Neapolitan territory.

in effigy in Spain had found refuge there, the Inquisitor-general Deza had resolved to extend over the kingdom the jurisdiction of Archbishop Belorado, Inquisitor of Sicily, and had asked the sovereigns to support him in his labors of arresting and punishing heretics and confiscating their property. All officials were therefore ordered, under pain of ten thousand ounces, to protect him and his subordinates and to do their bidding as to arresting, transporting and punishing the guilty, all oaths and compacts to the contrary notwithstanding. At the same time a personal letter to Gonsalvo expressed the determination of the sovereigns to introduce the Inquisition, their founding of which they believed to be the cause why God had favored them with victories and benefits. Gonsalvo was warned not to allow the suspect to leave the kingdom while, to avoid arousing suspicion, Belorado would come to Naples as though on his way to Rome and Gonsalvo was to guard all ports and passes through which the heretics could escape. To prepare for the expected confiscations, the commission of Diego de Obregon, receiver of Sicily, was extended over Naples and Francisco de Rojas, then ambassador at Rome, was instructed to obtain from the pope whatever was necessary to perfect the functions of the Neapolitan Holy Office.[1]

Everything thus was prepared for the organization of the Spanish Inquisition in Naples, but even Ferdinand's resolute will was forced to abandon for the time the projected enterprise with its prospective profits. What occurred we do not know; the historian, to whom we are indebted for the documents in the matter, merely says that Ferdinand, in spite of his efforts, was prevented from carrying out his plans by difficulties which arose.[2] We can conjecture however that Gonsalvo convinced him of the impolicy of provoking a revolt in his newly acquired and as yet unstable dominions. The Neapolitans were somewhat noted for turbulence and had an organization which afforded a means of expressing and executing the popular will. From of old the citizens were divided into six associations, known as *Piazze* or *Seggi*, in which they met

---

[1] Páramo, pp. 191–4.   [2] Páramo, *loc. cit.*

to discuss public affairs. Of these five, designated as Capuana, Nido, Porta, Porta nueva and Montagna, were formed of the nobles and the sixth was the Seggio del Popolo, divided into twenty-nine districts, called Ottine. Each piazza elected a chief, known as the *Eletto*, and these six, when assembled together, formed the Tribunale di San Lorenzo, which thus represented the whole population. There were Piazze in other cities but when, under Charles V, the national Parliament was discontinued, the Piazze of Naples arrogated to themselves its powers and framed legislation for the whole kingdom. A Spanish writer, in 1691, informs us that no viceroy could govern successfully who had not dexterity to secure the favor of a majority of the Piazze, for the people were obstinate and tempestuous, easy to excite and difficult to pacify, and, if the nobles and people were united, God alone could find a remedy to quiet them.[1] In the unsettled condition of Italian affairs, to provoke revolt in such a community was evidently most unwise; there is no appearance that Belorado made his threatened visit, and when Ferdinand himself came to Naples, in 1506 and 1507, he seems to have tacitly acquiesced in the postponement of his purpose.

The popular repugnance was wholly directed to the Spanish Inquisition and there was no objection to the papal institution, which had long been a matter accepted. In 1505 a letter of Gonsalvo directs the arrest in Manfredonia of three fugitives from Benevento, who are seeking to escape to Turkey; he does this, he says, at the request of the inquisitor and of the Bishop of Bertinoro papal commissioner.[2] Evidently there must have been active persecution on foot in Benevento and, though the inquisitor is not named, he was probably the Dominican Barnaba Capograsso, whom we find, in 1506, styled "generale inquisitore de la fede" when, in conjunction with the vicar-general of the archbishop and the judges of the vicariate, he burned three women for witch-

---

[1] Ferrarelli, Tiberio Caraffa e la Congiura di Macchia, p. 8 (Napoli, 1884).—MSS. of Library of Univ. of Halle, Yc, T. XVII.
[2] Chioccarello MSS., T. VIII.

craft.[1] Yet anxious as was Ferdinand for the extirpation of heresy, he would not abate a jot of the royal supremacy and would allow no one to exercise inquisitorial functions without his licence. The correspondence of the Count of Ribagorza, who succeeded Gonsalvo as lieutenant-general and viceroy during the years 1507, 1508, and 1509, shows that Fra Barnaba held a commission directly from the king. When a certain Fra Vincenzo da Fernandina endeavored in Barletta to conduct an inquisition, Ribagorza expressed surprise at his audacity in doing so without exhibiting his commission; he was summoned to come forthwith and submit it so that due action could be taken without exposing him to ignominy. So minute was this supervision that, when Fra Barnaba reported that a colleague had received a papal brief respecting a certain Lorenzo da Scala, addressed to the two inquisitors and the Bishop of Scala, Ribagorza ordered it to be surrendered unopened to the regent of the royal chancery and that all three addressees should come to Naples when, in their presence and his, it should be opened and the necessary action be ordered. From a letter of February 24, 1508, it appears that the old Neapolitan rule was maintained and that inquisitors had no power to order arrests, but had to report to Ribagorza, who issued the necessary instructions to the officials; indeed, a commission of January 14, 1509, indicates that heretics were seized and brought to Naples before the viceroy, without the intervention of the Holy Office. At the same time, when inquisitors were duly commissioned and recognized, the authorities were required to render them all needful assistance and any impediment thrown in their way was severely reproved, with threats of condign punishment.[2]

Thus quietly and by degrees the old papal Inquisition was roused into activity and was moulded into an instrument controlled by the royal power even more directly than in Spain. Yet this did not satisfy Ferdinand, who had never abandoned his intention of introducing the Spanish Inquisition, and apparently he thought, in 1509, that the Neapolitans had become sufficiently accustomed

---

[1] Amabile, I, 97.   [2] Chioccarello MSS., T. VIII. (see Appendix).

to his rule to endure the innovation. Rumors of his purpose spread, causing popular agitation, and Julius II, who wanted his aid against the French in Northern Italy, earnestly deprecated action which might necessitate the recall of his troops to put down insurrection. To the Spanish ambassador the pope represented the danger of exciting the turbulent population; the time would come when the Spanish Inquisition might safely be imposed on Naples, but so long as the French were in possession of Genoa, the king must be cautious.[1]

Ferdinand was not to be diverted from his course by such considerations and, on August 31, 1509, a series of letters was addressed to Naples showing that the organization had been fully and elaborately prepared. Montoro, Bishop of Cefalù, whose acquaintance we have made in Sicily, and Doctor Andrés de Palacios, a layman and experienced inquisitor, were appointed to conduct the office, with a full complement of subordinates, whose liberal salaries were to be paid out of the confiscations, showing that a plentiful harvest was expected.[2] Viceroy Ribagorza and all royal officials and ecclesiastics were instructed to give them all

---

[1] Zurita, *op. cit.*, Lib. IX, cap. xxiv.
[2] A royal cédula of September 3, 1509, to Matheo de Morrano, appointed as receiver, orders him to pay the following salaries, to commence from the date of leaving home for the journey. The sums are in gold ducats:

	Salary.	Ayuda de costa.
The Bishop of Cefalù, inquisitor	300	200
Dr. Andrés de Palacios, inquisitor	300	100
Dr. Melchior, judge of confiscations	100	
Matheo de Morrano, receiver	300	150
Joan de Moros, alguazil	200	60
Dr. Diego de Bonilla, procurador fiscal	200	50
Miguel de Asiz, notary of secreto and court of confiscations	100	50
Joan de Villena, notary of secreto	100	50
Gabriel de Fet, notary of sequestrations	100	
A gaoler	54	15
Johan de Vergara, messenger	30	10
Juan Vazquez, messenger	30	10
	1814	695

Palacios was paid eight months' salary in advance by the receiver of Barcelona. —Archivo de Simancas, Inquisicion, Lib. III, fol. 1, 52.

necessary support and assistance under penalty of ten thousand ounces and punishment at the royal pleasure, notwithstanding any previous compacts or conventions, for agreements contrary to the faith were not to be observed by Catholics. On arrival they were to be established in the Incoronata or, if they preferred other quarters, the occupants were to be summarily ejected and a proper rent be paid. The Cardinal-archbishop of Naples was ordered to give them powers to act as his ordinaries and vicars; a pragmatic sanction was drawn up for publication, forbidding, under heavy penalties, the use of any papal letters of absolution until they should have received the royal assent. The local officials were also written to, ordering them to aid the inquisitors in every way and a circular to the same effect was sent to all the barons of the kingdom. As it was expected that, as soon as the letters were published, the heretics would endeavor to escape, the viceroy was ordered to take measures that none should be allowed to embark, or to send away property or merchandise, and all who should attempt it were to be delivered forthwith to the inquisitors.[1] Evidently the matter had been thoroughly worked out in detail and Ferdinand was resolved to enforce his will. Then followed, however, an unexpected delay. Ribagorza left Naples, October 8th, probably resigning or being removed owing to his conviction of the difficulty of the task imposed on him, and his successor, Ramon de Cardona, did not arrive until October 23d, showing that the change was sudden and unexpected. The Bishop of Cefalù, also, did not reach Naples until October 18th and, although officially received, he exhibited no commission as inquisitor and took no action, awaiting his colleague Palacios, whose coming was delayed until December 29th.

Meanwhile rumors of what was proposed had been spreading, popular excitement had been growing and it now became uncontrollable. It was openly declared by all classes that the Inquisition would not be tolerated and, when it was reported that, on a certain Sunday, the inquisitor would preach the customary

---

[1] Archivo de Simancas, Inquisicion, Lib. III, fol. 2–11.

sermon in the cathedral, an unanimous resolution was adopted, January 4, 1510, that such an attempt would be resisted, if necessary by force of arms. A delegation, selected as usual by all the Piazze, was sent to the viceroy and overwhelmed him with fierce denunciations of the detested institution as developed in Spain— the tortures and the burnings inflicted for the most trivial causes, the sentences against the dead and the burning of bones, the execution of pregnant women, the disinheriting of children, the scourging of naked virgins through the streets and the seizure of their dowries, the innocent impelled to flight by terror and consequently condemned in order to confiscate their property, while their servants were tortured to find out whether anything was concealed, and the stories of sacrilege invented in order to gratify rapacity. Although most of this was the ordinary inquisitorial practice, it was sufficiently embellished to show that the refugee New Christians had been busy in fanning the excitement which now burst upon the viceroy. Every delegate sought to outdo his colleagues in vociferously enumerating the horrors which justified the evil reputation of the dreaded institution, and the viceroy was told that they never would allow themselves to be subjected to the accusations of informers, whose names were concealed and whose perjuries were stimulated by a share in the spoils; the whole business was not to protect religion but to get money and they would not be dishonored and put to death and despoiled as infidels under such pretexts. If he valued the peace of the realm, he would prohibit the sermon. Cardona listened to the storm of objurgation and, when it had exhausted itself, he replied that he had the king's orders to receive the inquisitors and would obey them. This aroused a greater uproar than before and he weakened under it. He retired to consult the council and on his return he told the deputies that they might send envoys to the king to expound their views and learn his decision; meanwhile he would prevent the inquisitors from acting and they must preserve the peace.

The agitation continued; daily assemblies were held in the

Seggi and, on January 9th and 10th, a formal agreement was drawn up and executed between the nobles and the people, in which they bound themselves to sacrifice life and property sooner than to permit the introduction of the Inquisition and, at the same time, they elected Francesco Filomarino as envoy to Ferdinand. The next day a trivial occurrence nearly produced a serious outbreak, showing how dangerous was the tension of popular feeling. Luca Russo, who was one of the most active agitators, had an old quarrel, arising from a lawsuit, with Roberto Bonifacio, the justiciary of the city; he chanced to meet Colantonio Sanguigno, a retainer of Bonifacio; words passed between them and Sanguigno made a hostile demonstration, which started a rumor that Russo was slain. The shops forthwith were closed, the populace rushed to arms, shouting *ferro, ferro! serra, serra!* and the house of the justiciary was besieged by an enormous mob thirsting for his blood, but on the production of the supposed victim they quietly dispersed. During all this we hear nothing of the Bishop of Cefalù, but his colleague, Andrés Palacios, was expelled from one domicile after another; he was a dangerous inmate and finally found refuge in the palace of the Admiral of Naples, Villamari, Count of Capaccio, where he lay in retirement for some months.

Filomarino, the envoy to Ferdinand, did not start for Spain until April and the reports received from him during the summer were such that the people lost hope of a peaceful solution. Yet during the whole of this anxious time, although the kingdom everywhere was united in support of the capital, though all the troops in the land had been sent to the wars in Northern Italy and there was not a man-at-arms left, factions were hushed; Angevines and Aragonese and even Spaniards unanimously agreed that they would endure the greatest sufferings rather than consent to the Inquisition and perfect internal peace and quiet were everywhere preserved. This did not indicate that agitation had subsided, for peace was seriously imperilled on September 24th, when a rumor spread that royal letters had been received ordering the

Inquisition to be set to work. Meetings of the Seggi were held and it was proposed to close the shops and ring the bells to call the people to arms, but moderate counsels prevailed and a deputation was sent to the viceroy to assure him that they were ready to suffer all things in preference to the Inquisition. He expressed his surprise; he had no letters from the king, to whom he would write earnestly begging him to desist, and meanwhile he exhorted them to abstain from violence. Another month passed, in alternations of hope and despair; the nobles and people made a closer union, in which they pledged their lives and property for mutual defence and this was solemnized, October 28th, with a great procession of both orders, seven thousand in number, each man bearing a lighted torch.

How little Ferdinand at first thought of yielding is seen in a letter of March 18th to the inquisitors, acknowledging receipt of reports from them and the viceroy; he was awaiting the envoy and meanwhile counselled patience and moderation; they must persuade the people that matters of faith alone were concerned and when this was understood the opposition would subside. He had ordered the payment of four months' salaries and they could rely on his providing everything. Then, a few days later, he announced that the vacant place of gaoler had been filled by the appointment of the bearer, Francisco Velázquez, to whom salary was to be paid from the date of his departure. If Ferdinand had had only the Neapolitans to reckon with he would undoubtedly have imposed on them the Inquisition at the cost of a revolt, but there were larger questions involved which counselled prudence. In preparation for trouble in Naples, he began to withdraw his troops from Verona. Julius II took the alarm at this interference with his plans and urged that the Neapolitans be pacified. At the same time, with an eye to the possible revendication of the old papal claims on Naples, he sought popular favor by promises to the archbishop to revoke the commissions of the inquisitors and inhibit the Inquisition, thus creating a wholly unforeseen factor in the situation. The viceroy clearly comprehended the danger of the position, when a revolution could so readily be brought about and the people would gladly transfer their allegiance to the pope or to France, thus costing a new conquest to regain the kingdom. It is doubtful whether he acted under positive orders from Ferdinand, or whether he assumed a certain measure of responsibility, stimulated by a fresh excitement arising from a rumor that the Inquisition had commenced operations at Monopoli. However this may have been, on November 19th he sent word to the popular chiefs, inviting them to the Castello Nuovo to hear a letter from the king. Five nobles from each Seggio were deputed for the purpose, who were followed by a crowd numbering three thousand. The viceroy read to them two pragmáticas, by which all Jews and Conversos of Apulia and Calabria, including those who had fled from Spain after condemnation by the Inquisition, were ordered, under pain of forfeiture of person and property, to leave the country by the first of March, taking with them their belongings, except gold and silver, the export of which was forbidden by the laws. From this the corollary followed, that as the land would thus be purged of heresy, there would be no necessity for the Inquisition. Thus the unfortunate Hebrews and New Christians were offered up as a sacrifice to enable the government to retreat from an untenable position.

The news at first was received with general rejoicings and some quarters of the town were illuminated, but the people had not been taught to trust their rulers; doubts speedily arose that it was intended to introduce the Inquisition by stealth and, when on November 22d the heralds came forth to proclaim the new laws, they were mobbed and driven back before they could perform the duty. The next day a delegation waited on the viceroy and asked him to postpone the proclamation for two days, during which they could examine the pragmáticas. This was an assumption of supervision over the legislative function which the viceroy naturally denounced as presumptuous, but the necessity of satisfying the people was supreme and, on the next day, the Eletti by further insistence secured a preamble to the first pragmática, in which the king was made to declare formally that, in view of the ancient religion and Catholic faith of the city and kingdom, he ordered the Inquisition to be removed, for the benefit of all. In this shape the proclamation was made on November 24th, and on it was founded the claim which, for more than two centuries, Naples persistently made that exemption from the Inquisition was one of its special privileges. Andrés Palacios departed on December 3d and thus the victory was won without bloodshed, after a struggle lasting for a year.[1]

Even the pragmáticas ordering the expulsion of Jews and Conversos were not obeyed and the situation was rendered more aggravating by the facilities of escape from the Sicilian Inquisition afforded by the proximity of the Neapolitan territories. In June of 1513 Ferdinand wrote to the viceroy concerning this ever-present grievance and ordered him to hunt up all refugees and send them back with their property, while at the same time a royal letter to the alcaide of Reggio rebuked him for permitting their transit and threatened him with condign punishment for continued negligence.[2] That it continued is shown by the escape,

---

[1] Tristani Caraccioli, Epist. de Inquisitione (Muratori, S. R. I., T. XXII, p. 97).—Archivo de Simancas, Inquisicion, Lib. 3, fol. 68, 74.—Amabile, I, 101–18.—Zurita, Hist. del Rey Hernando, Lib. ix, cap. xxvi.—Spondani Annal. Eccles., ann. 1510, n. 13.

The formula withdrawing the Inquisition was "Havendo el Rey nostro Signore cogniosciuto la antiqua observancia e religione de la fidelissima Cita di napoli et de tucto questo regno verso la santa fe catholica sua Altezza ha mandato et ordinato levarese la inquisicione da dicta Cita et de tucto il regno predicto per lo bene vivere universale de tucti; et ultra questo su Altezza ha mandato publicare le infrascripte pragmatiche, dato in castello nova, napoli 22 novembre, 1510."—Amabile, p. 118.

In Ferdinand's letter books there is nothing further respecting the Neapolitan troubles until May 27, 1511, he writes to Diego de Obregon, the receiver of Sicily, that the Bishop of Cefalù returns there by his orders and, in view of his sufferings for the Inquisition his salary must be paid. Yet he died without receiving it and, on February 16, 1514, Ferdinand ordered Obregon to pay the arrears to Mariano de Acardo, in reward for certain services rendered, but this was still unpaid in January of the following year. As for Andrés Palacios, a cédula of June 6, 1511, recognized him as inquisitor of Valencia, with salary dating back to January 1st and an ayuda de costa of a hundred ducats.—Archivo de Simancas, Inquisicion, Lib. 3, fol. 145, 146, 280, 313.

[2] Ibidem, Lib. 3, fol. 238, 239.

from Sicily to Naples, in the following September, of some four
hundred of these unfortunates (see p. 12) and they doubtless
carried with them funds sufficient to close the eyes of those whose
duty it was to turn them back. There does not seem to have been
in Italy the popular abhorrence felt in Spain for the Hebrew race
or any desire for active persecution, but at the same time there
was no opposition to the existence of the Inquisition, provided
always that it was not of the dreaded Spanish type. In December
of the same year, 1513, the Dominican Barnaba, now styling himself papal Inquisitor of Naples, applied to Ferdinand, stating that
in Calabria and Apulia the New Christians lived as Jews and held
their synagogues publicly; he evidently could have had no support
from the local authorities, for he solicited the aid of the king.
Ferdinand promptly replied, December 31st, ordering him to
investigate secretly and, if he could catch the culprits in the act
he was, with the assistance of the Bishop of Isola, to arrest and
punish them and the viceroy and governor of the province were
instructed to lend whatever aid was necessary. At the same time
Ferdinand sought to make this an entering wedge for the Spanish
Inquisition, for Barnaba was told to obey the instructions of
Bishop Mercader, Inquisitor-general of Aragon, with whom he
was put into communication and to whom he reported. He
evidently did what he could, in the absence of secular support, for
a letter of June 14, 1514, to a bishop instructs him to assist Barnaba and the Bishop of Isola who are about to visit his diocese
to punish some descendants of Jews who are living under the
Mosaic Law, but his efforts were fruitless. When he applied to
the viceroy and to the Governors of Calabria and Apulia for
aid in making arrests, they replied that they would have to consult
the king. Moreover the viceroy reported that the pragmáticas
of 1511 were not enforced because they were construed as applicable only to natives and not to foreigners such as Spaniards and
Sicilians. All this stirred Ferdinand's indignation, which found
expression in a letter of June 15, 1514, to the viceroy, accusing
him and the regents and governors of sheltering the refugees,

characterizing as absurd the construction put on the pragmáticas and ordering anew that every assistance should be given to Barnaba and the Bishop of Isola. In spite of all this there was a deplorable slackness on the part of the secular authorities—the spirit of persecution seemed unable to cross the Faro. The Neapolitan officials would not arrest the Sicilian refugees without formal requisitions from the Sicilian inquisitors, brought by a duly accredited official. From what we have seen of the disorganization of the Sicilian tribunal we can readily believe their assertion that they had applied to both Alonso Bernal and Melchor Cervera, but that neither had given the matter attention. Ferdinand thereupon wrote to Cervera expressing his surprise at this neglect, especially as it was understood that the refugees had large amounts of property concealed. This seems to have produced little effect for when, six months later, Ferdinand scolded Don Francisco Dalagon, Alcaide of Reggio, about the refuge granted to the Sicilian fugitives, the alcaide replied that, if he had proper authorization he would seize them all, whereupon Ferdinand wrote, September 7th, to Cervera, ordering him to send to Dalagon a list of the fugitives, with a commission for their arrest—an order which seems to have been as resultless as its predecessors.[1]

When Ferdinand's restless energy exhausted itself ineffectually on the inertia or corruptibility of the Neapolitan authorities, there was little chance that, after his death, in February, 1516, the business of persecution would be more successfully prosecuted. There was no inherent objection to it and the old Dominican Inquisition with its limitations continued to exist but, in the absence of the secular support so essentially necessary to its success, its operations were spasmodic and it affords but an occasional manifestation of activity, of which few records have reached us. The only instances, during the next twenty years, which the industry of Signor Amabile has discovered, are those of Angelo Squazzi, in 1521 and of Pirro Loyse Carafa, in 1536.[2] It was a remarkable

[1] Archivo de Simancas, Inquisicion, Lib. 3, fol. 238, 239, 260, 261, 292, 295, 316, 317, 350.
[2] Amabile, I, 119–20.

development from the events of 1510 that the secular courts came to assume jurisdiction over heresy and claimed that the pragmática of Ferdinand deprived the bishops of cognizance of such cases. That an assumption so subversive of the recognized principles of canon law should call for protest was inevitable and, in the general Parliament of 1536, the ninth article set forth the grievance that a lay judge had gone to Manfredonia and thrown in prison several heretics. Complaint was made to the viceroy, Pedro of Toledo, of this invasion of episcopal rights, when he ordered the cases to be referred to the Bishop of Biscaglie but, in spite of this, the prisoners were not surrendered and remained for two years, some in the Castello Nuovo of Naples and some in the castle of Manfredonia and, although an appeal was made to the pope and briefs were obtained from him, these were not allowed to reach the bishop, wherefore the barons supplicated the emperor to order the cases to be remitted to the bishop and to forbid the intrusion of the secular courts.[1] The affair is significant of the contempt into which the Inquisition, both episcopal and Dominican, had fallen. Charles was in Naples in 1536, when a letter from the Suprema to Secretary Urries alludes to a previous one of February 8th, urging upon the emperor his duty to revive the institution on the Spanish model and the secretary is exhorted to lose no opportunity of advancing the matter, but policy prevailed and nothing was done.[2]

Still, there came a sudden resolve to enforce the pragmática of 1510, which seems to have been completely ignored hitherto and, in 1540, the Jews were banished, after vainly pleading with Charles V at Ratisbon. Most of them went to Turkey, and the expulsion was attended with the misfortunes inseparable from such compulsory and wholesale expatriation. Many were drowned and some were captured at sea and carried to Marseilles, where Francis I generously set them free without ransom and sent them to the Levant. Their absence speedily made itself felt through

---

[1] Giacinto de' Mari, Riflessioni .... in difesa della Città e Regno di Napoli (MS. *penes me*).

[2] Archivo de Simancas, Inquisicion, Lib. 78, fol. 39.

the deprivation of facilities for borrowing money and, to supply the vacancy, the viceroy founded the Sagro Monte della Pietà, or public pawnbroking establishment.[1] This expulsion, however, does not seem to indicate a recrudescence of intolerance and, if there were apostate Conversos and Judaizing Christians, the authorities did not trouble themselves about them. Yet the time was at hand when a more threatening heresy would arouse afresh the persecuting spirit and lead the Church to bare its sharpest weapons.

Lutheranism had not penetrated as far south as Naples, but the spirit of inquiry and unrest was in the air and a local centre of revolt developed there independently. A gifted Spanish youth, Juan de Valdés, brought up in the court of Charles V and a favorite of his sovereign, attracted the attention of the Inquisition and, to avoid unpleasant consequences, abandoned his native land in 1529. After some years of wandering he settled in Naples, in 1534, where he drew around him the choicest spirits of the time, until his death about 1540.[2] Among those whom he deeply influenced may be mentioned Pietro Martire Vermigli, Bernardino Ochino, Marcantonio Flaminio, Pietro Carnesecchi, Vittoria Colonna, Isabella Manrique, Giulia Gonzaga and Costanza d'Avalos—names which reveal to us how Naples became a centre from which radiated throughout Italy the reformatory influences of the age.[3] Valdés was not a follower of Luther or of Zwingli; rather was he a disciple of Erasmus, whose teachings he developed to their logical results with a hardihood from which the scholar of Rotterdam shrank, after the fierce passions aroused by the Lutheran movement had taught him caution. Though not driven like Luther, by disputation and persecution to deny the authority of the Holy See, there is an infinite potentiality of rebellion against the whole ecclesiasti-

---

[1] Chronicle of Rabbi Joseph ben Joshua ben Meir (Bialloblotsky's Translation, II, 318–19).—Parrino, Teatro de' Vicere, I, 175 (Napoli, 1730).
[2] Caballero, Alonso y Juan de Valdés, pp. 182 sqq. (Madrid, 1875)
[3] See Karl Benrath in *Historisches Taschenbuch*, 1885, p. 172; also his *Bernardino Ochino von Siena*, Leipzig, 1875.—Manzoni, Estratto del Processo di Pietro Carnesecchi, Torino, 1870.

cal system in Valdés's description of the false conception which men are taught to entertain of God, as a being sensitive of offence and vindictive in punishment, who is to be placated by self-inflicted austerities and by gifts of gold and silver and worldly wealth.[1] He was also largely tinged with mysticism, even to the point of *dejamiento* or Quietism, the result possibly of his intercourse with Pedro Luis de Alcaraz, in 1524, when they were together in the household of the Marquis of Villena at Escalona— Alcaraz being the leader of a knot of Alumbrados, who was severely handled by the Inquisition.[2] This is manifested in Valdés's conception of the kingdom of God, in which man renounces the use of reason and abandons himself to divine inspiration.[3] In his little catechism, moreover, there is a strong Lutheran tendency in the doctrine that man is saved by faith; there is no intercessor but Christ and the whole sacramental system, save baptism, is condemned by being significantly passed over in silence.[4] Still more significant is his classification, in the *Suma de la predicazion*

---

[1] Le Cento e dieci divine Considerationi del S. Giovăni Valdesso: nelle quali si ragiona delle cose piu utili, piu necessarie e piu perfette, della Christiana professione. In Basilea, M.D.L.

" Ingannati principalmente della superstitione e falsa religione ci fanno relatione che Dio è tanto delicato e sensitivo che per qualunque cosa si offende: che è tanto vendicativo che tutte le offese castiga: che è tanto crudele che le castiga con pena eterna: che è tanto inhumano che si gode che trattiamo male nostre persone, in fino allo sparger il nostro propio sangre, il quale egli ci ha dato: e che ci priviamo delle nostre facoltà, le quale egli ci ha dato, accio che con esse si manteniamo nella presente vita: che si gode che andiamo nudi e scalzi, continuamente patendo; che è vano e li piaccino li presenti e che gode di haver oro e belli parimenti, ed in somma che si diletta di tutte le cose delle quali un Tiranno si diletta; e si gode di haver da coloro che li sono soggetti."—Consid. XXXVII.

This edition of Basle, 1550, is the original from which the numerous translations have been made. For the bibliography, see Böhmer, *Bibliotheca Wiffeniana*, I, 124–29 (Strassburg, 1874). Also, Wiffen and Betts, "Life and Writings of Juan de Valdés," London, 1865.

Antonio Caracciolo styles Valdés "capo e maestro" of the Neapolitan heretics, who gave the Roman Inquisition early occasion to demonstrate its usefulness.

[2] Manuel Serrano y Sanz (Revista de Archivos etc., Febrero, 1903, p. 129).

[3] "Con questa risolutione condanna l'uomo il giudicio della prudentia e della ragione humana e renuncia il suo lume naturale ed entra nel regno di Dio, remettendosi al reggimento ed al governo di Dio."—Ibidem, Consid. XXV.

[4] Lac Spirituale Johannis de Valdés. Ed. Koldewey, Heilbronn, 1863.

Cristiana, of those who rely on vain ceremonial observances, with the worldly and wicked, as fit only to be ejected from the Church of Christ.[1]

All these were dangerous doctrines, even when merely discussed in the little circle of bright intelligences which Valdés drew around him. They did not, moreover, lack public exposition in a guarded way. Bernardino Ochino, the General Minister of the Capuchins, was reckoned the most eloquent preacher in Italy. In 1536 he visited Naples, where he came in contact with Valdés and preached the Lenten sermons with such success that he emptied all the other churches. On February 4th of the same year Charles V, then at Naples, issued an edict forbidding, under pain of death and confiscation, any one from holding intercourse with Lutherans and, on his departure, he impressed on Pedro de Toledo, the viceroy, the supreme importance of preventing the introduction of heresy. Envious friars accused Ochino of disseminating errors in his sermons and Toledo ordered him to cease preaching until he should express himself clearly in the pulpit as to the errors imputed to him, but he defended himself so skilfully that he was allowed to continue and, on his departure, he left numerous disciples. Three years later he returned and made a similar impression, veiling his heretical tendencies with such dexterity that they passed without reprehension. Yet the seed had been sown; it was a time when theological questions were matters of universal interest and soon the city was full of men of all ranks who were discussing the Pauline Epistles and debating over difficult texts. No good could come of such inquiries by the unlearned and the viceroy felt that some action was necessary.[2] With the year 1542 came a sort of crisis in the religious movement, not only of Naples

---

[1] Trataditos de Juan de Valdés, p. 179 (Bonn, 1880).
The germ of much of this tract may be found in the *Militiæ Christianæ Enchiridion*, Canon 5, in which Erasmus dwells on the worthlessness of external observances and stigmatizes the importance attached to them as a kind of new Judaism. Yet the *Enchiridion* was repeatedly reprinted after its first appearance, in 1502, and was approved by Adrian of Utrecht, subsequently Adrian VI.

[2] Giannone, Istoria civile del Regno di Napoli, Lib. XXII, cap. v, § 1 (Haya, 1753).

but of Italy. The Archbishops of Naples, who were customarily cardinals residing in Rome, had long neglected the moral and spiritual condition of their see but, in that year, the archbishop-cardinal, Francesco Carafa, conducted a visitation there—the first for many years—and doubtless found much cause for disquietude.[1] In that same year also, by the bull *Licet ab initio*, July 21st, Paul III reorganized the papal Inquisition, placed it under the conduct of a congregation of six cardinals, and gave it the form of which the terrible efficiency was so thoroughly demonstrated during the second half of the century.[2] In September of that year, moreover, Ochino and Vermigli threw off all disguise and openly embraced Protestantism. This naturally cast suspicion on their admirers and the viceroy commenced a persecution; preachers were set to work to controvert the heretical doctrines; an edict was issued requiring the surrender of heretical books, of which large numbers were collected and solemnly burnt, and a pragmática of October 15, 1544, established a censorship of the press. Finally, Toledo wrote to the emperor that sterner measures were necessary to check the evil and Charles ordered him to introduce the Inquisition as cautiously as possible.[3]

It seems to have been recognized as useless to endeavor to establish the Spanish Inquisition and Charles was not as firmly attached to that institution as his grandfather Ferdinand had been, but it was hoped that, by dexterous management, the way might be opened to bring in the papal Holy Office.[4] Towards the end of

---

[1] Chioccarelli Antistitum Neapol. Eccles. Catalogus, p. 321 (Neapoli, 1642).

On the death of Carafa in 1544, Paul III gave the see to his own nephew, Rainuccio Farnese, a boy of fifteen. It was then administered through vicars, the one at the time of the troubles of 1547 being Fabio Mirto, Bishop of Cajazzo.—Ibidem, p. 326.

[2] Bullar Roman. I, 762.

[3] Amabile, I, 193–6. It would seem that, at this time, the Holy See claimed inquisitorial jurisdiction over Naples, for a papal brief of June 2, 1544 orders the viceroy to arrest and send under sure guard to Rome, Vespasiano di Agnone, a wandering Franciscan friar, guilty of sacrilege and other enormous crimes.—Fontana, Documenti Vaticani, p. 131 (Roma, 1892).

[4] Antonio Caracciolo, in his MS. life of Paul IV, of which an extract is printed by Bernino (Historia di tutte l'Heresie, IV, 496) informs us that Cardinal Gio-

1546 Toledo wrote to his brother, the Cardinal of San Sisto, who was one of the six members of the Congregation, expressing his desire to introduce the Inquisition and his dread of the consequences, for the very name was an abomination to all, from the highest to the lowest, and he feared that it might lead to a successful revolution. To encompass the object, it was finally resolved to procure from the pope a commission for an inquisitor against heresy which was prevalent among the clergy, both regular and secular. The required commission was issued, in February, 1547, to the prior and the lector of the Dominican convent of Santa Caterina; Toledo did not personally grant the exequatur for it but caused this to be done by the regents of the *Consiglio Collaterale*, but this precaution and the profound secrecy observed were useless. Rumors spread among the people that orders had been received from the cardinals to proceed against regular and secular clerks; the old animosity against anything but the episcopal Inquisition at once flamed up and deputies were sent to the viceroy to beg him not to grant the exequatur. He assured them that he wondered himself at the fact; he had written to the pope that it was not Charles's will or intention that the Inquisition should be introduced and that meanwhile he had not granted the exequatur. Little faith was placed in his statements and the general belief was that Paul III was eager to create strife in Naples in order to give the emperor occupation there and check his growing ascendency. It is said that he actually sent two inquisitors but, if so, they never dared to show themselves, for there is no allusion to them in the detailed accounts of the ensuing troubles.

To carry out the plot, action was commenced in a tentative way by the archiepiscopal vicar affixing at the door of his palace an edict forbidding the discussion of religion by laymen and announcing that he would proceed by inquisition to examine into the beliefs held by the clergy. The very word inquisition was

---

vanni Piero Carafa, the head of the Roman Inquisition and afterwards Paul IV, did not want the Spanish Inquisition introduced in Naples because it was more subject to the crown than to the Holy See and the king took the confiscations.

sufficient to inflame the people; cries of *serra, serra!* were heard and the aspect of affairs was so alarming that the vicar went into hiding and the edict was removed. The Piazze of the nobles were assembled and elected deputies charged with enforcing the observance of the *capitoli*, or liberties of the city. The Piazza del Popolo was crippled, for the viceroy some months previously, in preparation for the struggle, had dismissed the Eletto and replaced him with Domenico Terracina, a creature of his own, who did not assemble his Piazza but appointed the deputies himself. Then, on Palm Sunday (April 3d), Toledo sent for Terracina and the heads of the Ottine and charged them to see that those guilty of the agitation were punished but, in place of doing this the Piazze assembled and sent to him deputies who boldly represented the universal abhorrence felt for the Inquisition which gave such facilities for false witness that it would ruin the city and kingdom, and they expressed the universal suspicion felt that the edict portended its introduction. The viceroy soothed them with the assurance that the emperor had no such intention; as for himself, if the emperor should attempt it, he would tire him out with supplications to desist and, if unsuccessful, would resign his post and leave the city. But, as there were people who talked about religion without understanding, it was necessary that they should be punished according to the canons by the ordinary jurisdiction. This answer satisfied the majority, but still there were some who regarded with anxiety the implied threat conveyed in the last phrase.

Then, on May 11th, the patience of the people was further tested by another edict affixed on the archiepiscopal doors, which hinted more clearly at the Inquisition. At once the city rose, with cries of *armi, armi! serra, serra!* The edict was torn down; Terracina was compelled against his will to convene the Piazza del Popolo, where he and his subordinates were promptly dismissed from office and replaced with men who could be relied upon. The ejected officials could scarce show themselves in the streets and three of them were only saved from popular vengeance by taking sanctuary. The viceroy came from his winter residence at Pozzuoli breathing vengeance. He garrisoned the Castello Nuovo with three thousand Spanish troops and ordered the popular leaders to be prosecuted. By a curious coincidence, one of these was Tommaso Aniello, whose homonym, a century later, led the revolt of 1647. He it was who had torn down the edict and forced Terracina to assemble the Piazza. He was summoned to appear in court, but he came accompanied with so great a crowd, under the command of Cesare Mormile, that the judges were afraid to proceed and when the people seized Terracina's children as hostages, Aniello was discharged. Then Mormile was cited and went accompanied by forty men, armed under their garments and carrying papers like pleaders; the presiding judge was informed of this and dismissed the case.

Finding legal measures useless the viceroy adopted severer methods. On May 16th the garrison made a sortie as far as the Rua Castillana, firing houses and slaying without distinction of age or sex. The bells of San Lorenzo tolled to arms; shops were closed and the people rushed to the castle, where they found the Spaniards drawn up in battle array. Blinded with rage, they flung themselves on the troops and lost some two hundred and fifty men uselessly, while the cannon from the castle bombarded the city. Angry recrimination and threats followed; the citizens determined to arm the city, not for rebellion, as they asserted, but to preserve it for the emperor. Throughout the whole of this unhappy business, they were strenuously eager to demonstrate their loyalty and, when the news came of Charles's victory over the German Protestants at Muhlberg, April 24th, the city manifested its rejoicing by an illumination for three nights. So when, on May 22d, the viceroy ordered another sortie, in which there was considerable slaughter, the citizens hoisted on San Lorenzo a banner with the imperial arms and their war-cry was "Imperio e Spagna." They raised some troops and placed them under the command of Gianfrancesco and Pasquale Caracciolo and Cesare Mormile, but it was difficult to form a standing army, owing to the question of pay, as the money had to be raised by voluntary subscription.

Bad as was the situation, it was embittered when some catchpoles of the Vicariat arrested a man for debt. On the way to prison he resisted and called for aid; three young nobles stopped to enquire the cause and, during the parley, the prisoner escaped. This enraged Toledo, who had the youths arrested at night and condemned with scarce a pretext of trial. On May 24th they were brought out on the bridge in front of the Castello Nuovo, where their throats were cut by a slave and the corpses were left in blood and mud, with a placard prohibiting their removal. This gratuitous cruelty inflamed the people almost to madness; houses and shops were closed, arms were seized and crowds rushed through the streets, threatening they scarce knew what. To manifest his contempt for the populace, Toledo rode quietly through the town, where he would infallibly have been shot had not Cesare Mormile, the Prior of Bari and others of the popular leaders earnestly dissuaded reprisals. Meetings were held in which the nobles and people formally united for the common defence, which was always regarded as a most threatening portent for the sovereign, and they resolved to send envoys to the emperor, for which office they selected the Prince of Salerno, the greatest noble of the land, and Placido di Sangro, a gentleman of high quality. Toledo summoned the envoys and told them that, if their mission concerned the Inquisition, it was superfluous, for he would pledge himself within two months to have a letter from the emperor declaring that nothing more should be done about it; if it was about the *Capitoli*, he could assure them that any infraction of the city's privileges would be duly punished; if it was to complain of him, they were welcome to go. The envoys were too well pleased with their appointment to accept his offer and wait two months for its fulfilment; the people suspected the viceroy of trickery and the envoys set out. Six days later they were followed by the Marquis della Valle, sent by the viceroy to counteract their mission;

the prince dallied in Rome with the cardinals, so that della Valle reached the court before him and gained the ear of the emperor.

Meanwhile crowds of exiles and adventurers, under chosen leaders, came flocking into the city and a guerrilla warfare was organized against the Spaniards, who had advanced from house to house up to the Cancellaria vecchia, making loop-holes in the walls and shooting everyone within range. With the aid of these reinforcements the Spaniards were gradually driven back to the Incoronata. On the other hand Antonio Doria came with his galleys, bringing a large force of Spanish troops. Of course the courts were closed and a state of virtual anarchy might be expected, yet the chronicler tells us that four things were remarkable. First, there were no homicides, assaults, or other crimes. Second, although there was no government of the city, yet food and wine were abundant and cheap and no fraud or violence was committed on those who came with provisions. Third, although there were great numbers of exiles or bandits, with their chiefs, some of them bitterly hostile towards each other, there was no quarrelling or treachery; on one occasion two mortal enemies met, each at the head of his band and a fight was expected, but one said "Camillo, this is not the time to settle our affair," to which the other replied "Certainly; let us fight the common enemy; there will be ample time afterwards for our matter." Fourth, the prison of the Vicaria was full of prisoners, some condemned to death and others held for debt, but no attempt was made to rescue them and food was sent to them as usual by women and children. Evidently the people felt that they were fighting for their liberties and would not allow their cause to be compromised by common lawlessness.

At length Toledo's preparations for a decisive stroke were completed and, on July 22d, a sortie was made in force, while the guns of the fortresses and galleys bombarded the city. There was much slaughter and some four hundred houses were burnt, whose ruins blockaded the streets. Desultory fighting continued for some days and then a truce was agreed upon until the envoys should return. On August 7th came Placido di Sangro, the bearer of a simple order, signed by Secretary Vargas, to the effect that the Prince of Salerno should remain in the court, while he should return and tell the people of Naples to lay down their arms and obey the viceroy. This cruel disappointment came near producing a violent outbreak, but the Prior of Bari succeeded in quieting the people and persuading them to obey the emperor. The next day, by order of the Eletti, a huge collection of arms was made, loaded on wagons and carried to the viceroy. Then the tribunals were opened and every one returned to his private business. On August 12th the viceroy summoned the Eletti and read to them a royal indult, which purported to be granted at his request, pardoning the people for their revolt, except those already condemned and seventeen other specified persons. Most of those deeply compromised had, however, already sought safety in flight.

This doubtful mercy did not amount to much. A bishop came, commissioned by the emperor, to try the city for its misdeeds when, as we are told, through the procurement of the viceroy, witnesses were found to swear that the cry of *Francia, Francia!* was often raised. Whether this was true or not, the letters of Diego Hurtado de Mendoza, imperial ambassador at Rome, show that active negotiations had been carried on with both France and the pope, and the sovereignty of Naples had even been offered to Cardinal Farnese, the grandson of the latter. Mendoza evidently regarded Paul III as ready to take advantage of the situation if occasion offered and, when the revolt was suppressed, he mentions that the fugitives received a warm welcome in Rome. It is not surprising therefore that the decision of the episcopal commissioner was adverse to the city, containing, among other things, a fine of a hundred thousand ducats for ringing the bells as a call to arms.

The viceroy, moreover, by no means confined himself to the persons excepted from pardon, but threw into prison all the leaders whom he could seize. He had already published a considerable list of those excluded and the seventeen also grew to fifty-six, of whom twenty-six were condemned to death, although it does not appear that any were actually executed, and the prisoners were gradually liberated, twenty-four at one time, four at another and all the rest in 1553. Among them was Placido di Sangro, whose friends could not learn the cause of his confinement and sent Luigi di Sangro to the emperor to find out. Charles said that Placido was *buon cavaliero*, but that he was a great talker and that orders had already been sent to the viceroy about him. The incident which left on the emperor the impression of Placido's loquacity is too characteristic of the former's good-nature to be omitted. Once, as he left his chamber, Placido followed him, pleading for the city; he appeared not to listen and Placido had the audacity to pluck his mantle and ask his attention. Charles turned smilingly and said "Go on Placido, I am listening." The Duke of Alva was close behind and Placido said "Signore, I cannot talk, for the Duke of Alva hears all I say," to which Charles replied, laughing, "Tell him not to hear it" and then obligingly drew Placido to one side and let him say all that he wanted. The conclusion of the whole business was that their arms were returned to the citizens and the emperor contented himself with the fine, but the hated viceroy kept his post until his death in 1553, and no assurance against the Inquisition was obtained.[1]

Yet the stubborn endurance of the Neapolitans had won a tem-

---

[1] For most of these details I am indebted to a MS. account by Antonio Castaldo, a notary who was intimate with all the leaders in these events. He was a devoted subject of Charles V and considered himself most fortunate in having been born in his time. He warmly praises the emperor's clemency towards the city. Amabile's elaborate narrative (I, 196–211) furnishes additional facts and Döllinger (Beiträge zur Polit.-, Kirch.- u. Cultur-Geschichte, I, 78–124) gives Mendoza's correspondence. See also Giannone, Ist. Civile, Lib. xxxii, cap. v, § 1.—Páramo, pp. 194–5.—Natalis Comitis Historiar., Lib. ii, pp. 35, 52 (Argentorati, 1612).—Pallavicini, Hist. Concil. Trident., Lib. x, cap. i, n. 4.—Collenucio da Pesaro, Compendio dell' Historia del Regno di Napoli, II, 184 (Napoli, 1563).—Campana, La Vita di Don Filippo Secondo, P. i, fol. 7 sqq. (Vicenza, 1608).

The narrative of Uberto Foglietta (Tumultus Neapolitani sub Petro Toleto Prorege), though he was a contemporary who tells us that he visited Naples for the purpose of ascertaining the facts, is a confused and turgid piece of rhetoric, of no historical value.

porary victory. Although they gained no formal condition of exemption from the papal Inquisition, the attempt to introduce it was, for the moment, abandoned. For awhile even the episcopal jurisdiction over heresy appears to have been inert, as it has left no traces during the next few years. This respite, however, was brief, for the tide of persecution was arising in Italy. In March, 1551, Julius III issued a savage bull, pronouncing by the authority of God eternal malediction on all who should interfere with bishop or inquisitor in their prosecution of heretics.[1] Paul III, in 1549, on the resignation of Cardinal Farnese, had appointed, as archbishop of Naples, Cardinal Carafa, who was unsparing in the extirpation of heresy and had been the leader in promoting the reorganization of the papal Inquisition in 1542, of which he was made the head. Charles V had refused to grant his exequatur to Carafa, but yielded, in July, 1551, to the urgency of Julius, and Carafa lost no time in appointing Scipione Rebiba as his vicar-general, through whom the papal Inquisition was introduced into Naples.[2] It was at first confined to his archiepiscopate, for various letters to bishops, in 1552, from the viceroy Toledo show them to be busy in the prosecution of heretics.[3] Toledo died, February 12, 1553 and was succeeded by Cardinal Pacheco, who did not reach Naples until June. The interval, under Toledo's son Luis, seems to have been thought opportune for extending the jurisdiction of the papal Inquisition for, by a decree of the Congregation, May 30, 1553, Rebiba was created its delegate and subsequently styled himself "Vicar of Naples and Commissioner of the Holy Inquisition of Rome.[4]

---

[1] Julii PP. III, Bull *Licet a diversis*, 18 Mart., 1551 (Bullar. Roman. I, 799).

[2] Chioccarello, Antistitum Eccles. Neap. Catalogus, pp. 331-2. Carafa was hostile to Spain and, on his elevation to the papacy as Paul IV, in 1555, he declared the throne of Naples vacant and fallen to the Holy See. He made an alliance with France but, in the ensuing war, he was speedily brought to terms by Alba. He retained the Neapolitan archiepiscopate for some time, doubtless in the hope of causing trouble there.

[3] Chioccarello MSS., T. VIII.

[4] Amabile, I, 214. Rebiba was promoted to the cardinalate shortly after the accession of Paul IV.

In 1555 the episcopal jurisdiction was completely subordinated to the papal, for we find several instances in which prisoners of bishops were demanded by the Roman Inquisition, when Mendoza, the lieutenant of the Viceroy Pacheco, orders them sent under good guard to Naples, in order to be transmitted to Rome and, in 1556, it would even seem that bishops were required to obtain Roman commissions, for a letter of Mendoza to the Bishop of Reggio reproves him for publishing his commission before it had received the vice-regal exequatur.[1] It was probably to reconcile the Neapolitans to this intrusion of the authority of the abhorred institution that, by a brief of April 7, 1554, Julius III abolished the penalty of confiscation, but this grace was illusory, for it required the assent of the sovereign which was withheld and the brief itself was revoked by Paul IV in 1556.[2]

It was not long after this that occasion offered to extend still more directly the authority of Rome. Early in the fourteenth century, bands of Waldenses, from the Alpine valleys, flying from persecution, had settled in the mountains of Calabria and Apulia. Their example was followed by others; they increased and multiplied in peace, under covenants from the crown and from the nobles, on whose lands they settled and made productive, until it was estimated that they numbered ten thousand souls. As a matter of self-protection they strictly prohibited marriage with the natives, they used only their own language and their faith was kept pure by biennial visits from the *barbes* or travelling pastors of their sect, but it was under a prudent reserve, for they occasionally went to mass, they allowed their children to be baptized and they were punctual in the payment of tithes, which secured for them the benevolent indifference of the local priesthood.[3] More than two centuries of this undisturbed existence

---

[1] Chioccarello MSS., T. VIII.

[2] Amabile, I, 218.—Fontana, Documenti Vaticani contro l'Eresia luterana in Italia, p. 178 (Roma, 1892).

[3] Perrin, Histoire des Vaudois, chap. vii (Genève, 1618).—Amabile, I, 236-9.— Lombard, Jean-Louis Paschale et les Martyrs de Calabre (Paris, 1881).—Filippo de' Boni, L'Inquisizone e i Calabro-Valdese (Milano, 1864).

seemed to promise perpetual immunity, but the passions aroused on both sides by the Lutheran revolt were too violent to admit of toleration earned by dissimulation. The heretical movement in Naples seems to have aroused more watchful scrutiny for, in January, 1551, the Spanish Holy Office had information, through its Sicilian tribunal, about the Waldenses, whom it styled Lutherans, and it wrote to Charles V urging him to adopt measures for their eradication.[1] Nothing came of this, however, and the peaceful sectaries might possibly have remained in obscurity had they not commenced to feel dissatisfied with their ancestral teachings and sent to Geneva for more modern instructors. Religious zeal in Geneva was at a white heat and the missionaries despatched—Giovan Liugi Pascale and Giacomo Bonelli—were not men to make compromises with Satan. They made no secret of their beliefs and they paid the penalty, the one being strangled and burnt in Rome, September 15, 1560, and the other in Palermo.[2] Pascale had been arrested, about May 1, 1559, by Salvatore Spinello, lord of La Guardia, apparently to preserve his vassals from persecution for, since the coming of the ardent missionaries, they had ceased to attend mass.[3] With his companions he was carried to Cosenza and delivered to the archiepiscopal authorities. Then the viceroy, the Duke of Alcalá, intervened in a manner to show how uncertain as yet was the inquisitorial jurisdiction, for in letters of February 9, 1560, he urged the episcopal Ordinary to try the prisoners for heresy and, to prevent errors, he was to call for advice and assistance on a lay judge, Maestro Bernardino Santacroce, to whom powers and instructions were duly sent, thus constituting a mixed tribunal under royal authority.[4] Eventually however the papal Inquisition claimed and took Pascale, who was carried to Rome and executed.

Its attention was thus called to the Calabrian heretics, but it

---

[1] Archivo de Simancas, Inquisicion, Lib. 79, fol. 135.
[2] Scipione Lentolo, Historia delle grandi e crudeli Persecutioni fatte ai tempi nostri. Edita da Teofilo Gay, pp. 227, 314 (Torre Pellice, 1906).
[3] Ibidem, pp. 251, 260   [4] Chioccarello MSS., T. VIII.

was not until November 13, 1560, that the Dominican Valerio Malvicino da Piacenza presented himself at Cosenza as inquisitor commissioned by Rome to take the affair in charge. He wandered around among the Waldensian villages of Montalto, San Sisto and La Guardia, distinguishing himself, we are told, as a glutton and drunkard, and investigating the beliefs of the people. Then at San Sisto he ordered them all to abjure their errors and wear the "habitello" or sanbenito. This they refused, nor had he more success at Montalto, though at La Guardia many abjured on his telling them that their brethren at San Sisto had done so. Castañeto, the Spanish Governor of Montalto, prepared to arrest the principal inhabitants of San Sisto, when the whole population took to the woods, and Fra Valerio returned to Cosenza to seek aid from the Marquis of Bucchianico, Governor of Calabria, who chanced to be there. He ordered the people to lay down their arms and return to San Sisto, which they obediently did, on May 8, 1561, but they took flight again on being commanded to present themselves in Cosenza with their wives and children. Castañeto then raised a force to reduce them; he allowed them to send the women and children back to San Sisto, before attacking them, but when he did so he fell with fifty of his men. This victory availed little to the victors. San Sisto was burnt; the women and children, subjected to every species of outrage, scattered through the mountains, where most of them were captured and sent to Cosenza; hunger forced the men to disband and nearly all of them fell into the hands of Bucchianico.

San Sisto being thus settled, Bucchianico proceeded to La Guardia with Fra Valerio and a commissioner named Pansa appointed by the viceroy to execute justice. Many of the inhabitants fled, but returned under promise of pardon—their flight being subsequently held as relapse into the errors which they had previously abjured. These numbered 300 men and 100 women, the latter of whom were sent to Cosenza, while the former, together with the captives of San Sisto, were carried to Montalto, where a sort of inquisitorial tribunal was formed, consisting of Fra Valerio, Pansa, and two auditors, Barone and Cove. These divided the prisoners between them and each proceeded to employ torture indiscriminately to force them to confess the foul practices ascribed to them and to profess conversion. Those who were condemned were confined in a warehouse and their sentence was read in presence of a crowd gathered from all the neighboring towns. The auto de fe which followed, June 11, 1561, is described in a letter written the same day from Montalto by a Catholic who cannot conceal his profound horror at the scene. From their place of confinement the executioner led his victims one by one, bandaging their eyes with the bloody rag which had served for their predecessors. Like sheep to the slaughter they were thus taken to the public square where he cut their throats; they were then quartered and the fragments were distributed on poles along the roads from one end of Calabria to the other—a spectacle which another pious contemporary describes as fearful to the heretic while confirming the true believer in the faith. The number thus butchered on that day amounted to eighty-eight, while in addition there were seven who had triumphed over the torture and refused to recant their heresies, and these were to be burnt alive as impenitents. Sentence of death was also pronounced against a hundred of the older women; the whole number of captives was reckoned at 1600, all of whom were condemned. The writer adds that unless the Holy See and the viceroy interfere, Bucchianico will not hold his hand until he has destroyed them all.[1]

He doubtless continued his cruel work with the rest of his prisoners, but details are lacking for our next source of information is a letter of June 27th, written from Montalto by Luigi d'Appiano (apparently an official of the Archbishop of Reggio) to the Abate Parpaglia. Rome had taken alarm at the butchery of June 11th and had commissioned the archbishop, then returning to Naples, to take charge of the affair and conduct it in more regular fashion. D'Appiano explains that the prisoners from La Guardia

---

[1] Lentolo, pp. 228–41.—Gerdes, Specimen Italiæ Reformatæ, p. 134 (Lugd. Bat., 1765).—Amabile, I, pp. 248–9.

were regarded as relapsed (and consequently to be abandoned to the secular arm), because they had abjured, while those from San Sisto, who had not, were simple heretics, whom the Church would receive back on their submission. He tells us that Bucchianico, with the commissioner and the archiepiscopal vicar of Cosenza, had concluded to impose a salutary penance on the least guilty; those more obstinate were to be sent to the galleys, and the ministers and leaders to the stake; of these five had already been sent to Cosenza to be burnt alive, after smearing them with pitch so as to prolong their sufferings and serve as a terrifying example. A reward of ten crowns a head had been offered for the capture of fugitives and they were being daily brought in. Many women prisoners, who were instruments of the devil, were to be burnt and of these five, who had confessed to the nocturnal orgies attributed to the heretics, would be executed at Cosenza the next day.[1] All children under fifteen years of age were scattered among Catholic families, at a distance of at least eight miles from the Waldensian settlements and were forbidden to intermarry.[2] How long the persecution lasted does not appear, but a letter of December 12, 1561, from the viceroy, alludes to prisoners whose trials he ordered to be expedited.[3]

That the persecution was religious and not political is seen in the fact that the people of San Sisto, who had risen in arms and had defended themselves, were treated with much less harshness than those of La Guardia whose offence was technically construed as relapse into heresy. The conditions imposed on those who were spared the galleys or the stake confirm this. The Roman Inquisition prescribed that all should wear the yellow habitello with the red cross; that all should hear mass every day, before going to labor, under heavy fines; that confession and communion should be observed on the prescribed feast-days by all of proper age;

---

[1] Amabile, I, 250, 253.—Lentolo, p. 245.
[2] Lentolo, p. 244. This rests wholly on the authority of Lentolo and probably applied only to orphans. It was a practice derived from Spain.
[3] Amabile, I, 256.

that for twenty-five years there should be no intermarriage between them; that all communication with Piedmont and Geneva should cease, together with various other prescriptions looking to the training of the children in the faith and the instruction of the elders. To these Fra Valerio added that not more than six persons should assemble together and that their native tongue, which they had sedulously preserved, should be abandoned for Italian.[1]

In the exigencies of the moment the papal Inquisition had thus obtained a recognition in Neapolitan territory for which it had hitherto been vainly struggling, but it was intermingled with the episcopal and royal jurisdictions in a manner indicating how little organization there was for action in an emergency. The royal jurisdiction, moreover, asserted itself still further when, November 13, 1561, the viceroy issued a commission to Fra Valerio as inspector of heretical books throughout the kingdom, authorizing him to go to the points of importation and empowering him to summon to his aid the secular magistrates—a commission which was renewed May 8, 1562.[2] The viceroy also enforced one of the provisions of the Spanish Inquisition, for he laid claim to the confiscations and, on September 17, 1561, he commissioned Dr. Antonio Moles to proceed to the spot and take possession of all the property of those convicted, including the debts due to them. Apparently there had been general plunder, for he was empowered to enforce the surrender of what had been taken. Dr. Moles seems to have had much trouble with clerics, who had been active in the spoiling and had committed many enormous offences; as clerics they were beyond his jurisdiction, but the vicar of Cosenza sent him an assistant to exercise the necessary spiritual jurisdiction.[3] As La Guardia and San Sisto had both been burnt and the country laid waste, there cannot have been much left to confiscate, but Dr. Moles seems to have conscientiously stripped the land bare, for when the results were sent to Naples and sold at

---

[1] Lombard, *op. cit.*, p. 105. [2] Amabile, I, 257.
[3] Chioccarello MSS., Tom. VIII.—Amabile, I, 256.

auction they produced a handsome amount of money.[1] This evidently represents only the movable property; the real-estate seems to have been granted by Philip II to the Confraternity for the redemption of captives; it was valued at 5000 ducats and was sold for 2500 by the Confraternity to Salvatore Spinello. He had been created Marquis of Fuscaldo in recompense for the zeal with which he had aided the Inquisition in destroying his vassals, and he finally sold the lands to the communities for an annual revenue of 180 ducats.[2] Strenuous as were the methods of the Inquisition, however, deeply rooted faiths have power of protracted resistance, and some correspondence of the Roman Congregation with the Duchess of Montesalto, in 1599 and 1600, would indicate that there were still remnants of these heretics in Calabria and that there was talk of establishing a school for their conversion.[3]

The Waldenses of Apulia had a milder fate. The ruin and butchery in Calabria was a warning to all parties. Their lords were powerful nobles—the Prince of Molfetta, the Duke of Airola, the Count of Biccari and others—who did not wish to see their lands laid waste and depopulated. Fra Valerio was not called in, but a papal commission was procured for Ferdinando Anna, Bishop of Bovino, in whose diocese most of the infected district lay; less inhuman measures were employed and doubtless the savage work in Calabria led the heretics to be accommodating. Only a few of the more zealous were prosecuted; the mass of the

---

[1] Collenuccio, Historia del Regno de Napoli, II, 329ᵇ (Napoli, 1563).

The process of confiscation seems to have been protracted. A vice-regal letter of January 29, 1569, states that all the proceeds had not yet been sold and orders that the matter be closed and the money be paid into the treasury.—Chioccarello MSS., T. VIII.

From a transaction in 1572 it appears that when Neapolitans were burnt in Rome, notice was sent to the viceroy in order that he might seize their confiscated estates. At the same time a statement was presented of their prison expenses, which were reimbursed to the Congregation of the Inquisition out of the proceeds.—Ibidem.

[2] Lombard, op. cit., p. 107.

[3] Decret. Sac. Congr. S. Officii, p. 221 (R. Archivio di Stato in Roma, Fondo Camerale, Congr. del S. Offizio, Vol. 3).

population submitted and seem to have been taken to the bosom of Mother Church without severe penalties.[1]

Possibly Fra Valerio may have been engaged in more congenial occupation in the province of Reggio, where at this time there were discovered some survivors of those who had embraced the doctrines taught by Juan de Valdés. The viceroy sent thither the Commissioner Panza, fresh from his labors at Montalto. He must have had inquisitorial assistance and though, in the fragmentary records, Fra Valerio's name does not appear, he was the most probable collaborator in the active work which ensued. Four citizens of Reggio and eleven of San Lorenzo were burnt, while a number abjured and escaped with imposition of the habitello.[2]

In all these proceedings there is an incongruous intermingling of jurisdictions—papal, episcopal and secular—which shows how well the people had thus far succeeded in preventing the establishment of an organized Inquisition. They looked with complacency on the sufferings of the heretics and offered no opposition to the measures adopted, satisfied with the participation of the civil and episcopal powers. They had, however, lost none of their horror of the Spanish institution and, when Philip II endeavored to force it upon Milan, their fears were aroused that it might be imposed upon Naples. In 1564 there was much popular excitement; the Piazze assembled and adopted strong declarations; Pius IV, who did not wish to see the Spanish Inquisition in Italy, seconded these efforts and peremptorily ordered the Theatin Paolo d'Arezzo—subsequently cardinal and archbishop of Naples—to accept the mission with which the city charged him to Philip, to remonstrate against the threatened introduction of the Inquisition and also to ask for the revival of the brief of Julius III abolishing confiscations. The latter request Philip refused but, in letters of March 10, 1565, he assured his subjects that he had no intention

---

[1] Amabile I, 259.   [2] Ibidem, p. 258.

of introducing the Spanish Inquisition and that trials for heresy should be conducted in the ordinary way as heretofore.[1]

The "via ordinaria" meant episcopal jurisdiction exercised in accordance with the practice of the spiritual courts in other criminal trials as distinguished from the secret procedure of the Inquisition, which denied to the accused almost every means of defence. This in the subsequent struggles was constantly cited by the Neapolitans as their protection, but it was easily evaded. The Roman Inquisition, it is true, was not allowed to organize a tribunal with an inquisitor at its head and commissioners in all the cities, as was the case in the northern provinces of Italy, and to exhibit its power with the spectacle of autos de fe, but it had its agents more or less openly and its victims were transmitted to Rome for trial and execution. Alongside of this, for a time at least, the episcopal jurisdiction over heresy was fully recognized and a number of vice-regal letters of the period show that it was vigorously exercised by some of the prelates, though whether by the *via ordinaria* or not does not appear.[2] This gratified the Neapolitans who, in 1571, sent a deputation to Archbishop Carafa to congratulate him on his holy labors against the heretics and Jews and to ask him to express to the pope their satisfaction that these people should be punished and extirpated by the episcopal Ordinaries, according to the canons and without the interposition of the secular court.[3] This is a scarcely veiled hint of the popular detestation of the Inquisition, whether Spanish or papal, and that

---

[1] Pallavicini, Hist. Concil. Trident., Lib. XXII, cap. viii, § 2.—Al nostro Santissimo Padre Innocenzio XII intorno al Procedimento nelle cause che si trattano nel Tribunale del S. Officio (MS. *penes me*).—Discorso del Dottore Angelo Gioccatano (Gaetano Agela), MS. *penes me*.—MSS. of Royal Library of Munich, Cod. Ital., 209, fol. 117-18.—Chioccarello MSS., T. VIII (see Appendix).

[2] Chioccarello MSS., T. VIII.

[3] " Delle sante dimostrazioni contro gli eretici ed Ebrei, e supplicando che voglia esser servito di far intendere à sua Beatitudine la commune sodisfazione che tiene tutta la città che questa sorte di persone siano del tutto castigate ed estirpate per mano del nostro ordinario come si conviene como sempre avemo supplicato, giusta la forma delli canoni e senza interposizione di corte secolare, ma santamente procedano nelle cose della religione tantum."—Giacinto de' Mori, Scritture e Motivi dati a' Signori Deputati di Napoli (MS. *penes me*).

this continued unabated is manifested by the Venetian envoy, Girolamo Lippomani who, in his relation of 1575, describes the Neapolitans as most religious and filled with zeal for the love of God, but nevertheless they will not endure the very name of the Inquisition and would be ready to rise against it as they have done in the past.[1]

The occasion of this address to the archbishop presumably was a lively persecution of Judaizers then on foot. There had been many abjurations, some burnings, and the archbishop was preparing to build cells attached to the walls of his palace to provide for the confinement of those sentenced to perpetual prison. There was considerable popular excitement because an inquisitorial deputy, with the title of vicar, had been sent from Rome, and there was faction among the citizens, for the number of accused was large, with kinships ramifying throughout the community. Cardinal Granvelle, then recently appointed viceroy, in a letter of July 31, 1571, to the Cardinal of Pisa, head of the Roman Inquisition, expressed his fears of a tumult; he had asked the archbishop to suspend the prosecutions and postpone building the cells; it would be better to send, as the pope desired, the accused to Rome, where they would be vigorously punished. In effect, towards the end of December, four women and three men were sent as Judaizers to Rome, where they were duly strangled and burnt on February 9, 1572.[2]

This sending of the accused to the Roman Inquisition, whether for trial or execution, gradually became the accepted custom, as a sort of compromise between the pretensions of the Holy Office and the settled repugnance of the people. It was not, however, without some complications. Of old, no arrests by the Inquisition were permitted without the royal assent in each case, but in the absence of an organized Inquisition this salutary rule seems to have been forgotten and it evidently was not observed in the Calabrian persecutions. When, however, in 1568, the authorities of Reggio were ordered by the Sicilian tribunal to

---

[1] Relazioni Venete, Serie II, T. II, p. 273. [2] Amabile, I, 312–16.

arrest and forward two individuals charged with heresy, obedience was refused and the Duke of Alcalá, still viceroy, was notified. He approved the position taken but instructed the officials to arrest the parties and hold them until the Sicilian tribunal should report whether the alleged offences were committed in Sicily or in Naples; in the former case he was to forward them; in the latter to hold them until it should be determined whether they were justiciable by the Ordinary or by the Roman Holy Office, and such was to be the rule hereafter. The Sicilian tribunal did not relish this interference with its arbitrary methods and the next month there came news that two of its emissaries had landed at Reggio, gone inland and carried off to Messina a friar from an Augustinian convent; moreover they were now endeavoring to do the same with another of the brethren. Thereupon the viceroy ordered the utmost watchfulness to be observed and, if any attempt of the kind were made, the inquisitorial agents were to be thrown in prison and held for his instructions.[1]

If this caution was necessary in dealing with a province under the same crown, much more was it applicable to the Roman Congregation of the Inquisition. No independent state could permit its citizens to be abducted, without the knowledge of the authorities, at the bidding of a foreign prince whose policy at any moment might be hostile. To submit to such a claim was an abdication of sovereignty.[2] Moreover, nearly all Catholic kingdoms had been forced, by the perpetual meddling of the papacy with their internal affairs, to adopt the rule that no papal rescript of any kind should be enforced without first submitting it to the government for its exequatur. Naples, as

---

[1] Chioccarello MSS., T. VIII.
[2] In 1597 the Venetian envoy Girolamo Ramusio alludes to the case of the Baron of Castellanetta, excommunicated by his bishop and summoned to Rome; also to that of Mastrillo, fiscal of the Vicaria, who sold a quantity of grain belonging to the Abbey of S. Leonardo which was held by Cardinal Gaetano, in consequence of which he was cited to Rome. In both cases the court intervened and prevented obedience for the reason that, if a precedent was established of allowing those cited by Rome to go, the principal royal ministers could be summoned and forced to go.—Relazioni Venete, Appendice, p. 310.

especially exposed to papal encroachments, was particularly careful as to this, and no brief, however trivial, was allowed to take effect without being submitted to the authorities for approval.¹ In 1567 we find Pius V exhaling his indignation to Philip II at the violation of the rights of the Holy See because a bishop, whom he had sent to Naples as visitor to report on the condition of the clergy, was not allowed to exercise his functions without the exequatur.²

This necessarily applied to the citations and orders of arrest with which the Roman Inquisition was endeavoring to extend its jurisdiction over Naples. In April, 1564, Hieronimo de Monte, Apostolic Commissioner in Benevento (a papal enclave in Neapolitan territory), in the case of the Marquis of Vico, was taking testimony to the effect that no one would dare to serve a summons from Rome on him without the vice-regal exequatur, as he would thus expose himself to punishment, including perhaps the galleys.³ Rome endeavored to evade this limitation on its jurisdiction and was met with consistent firmness. In 1568 Alcalá was informed that, under orders from the Inquisition, the bishop had arrested a citizen named Martino Bagnato and was holding him for transmission to Rome. The bishop was at once notified that he must surrender the prisoner to the captain of the city, to be held subject to prosecution in the *via ordinaria* by his competent judge, and the captain was ordered, in case of refusal, to take him by force. This did not avail Bagnato much, for the Roman Inquisition then wrote to the viceroy, asking to have the prisoner forwarded, which presumably was done.⁴

---

¹ Relazioni Venete, Appendice, p. 312.
² Pii Quinti Epistt., Lib. I, Ep. vi (Antverpiæ, 1640).
³ Chioccarello MSS., T. VIII.
Failing in this Cardinal Ghislieri, then at the head of the Roman Inquisition, wrote in November to Viceroy Alcalá asking that Vico be sent or be placed under bonds to present himself. To this, in April, 1565, the viceroy assented, requiring Vico to give security in 10,000 ducats to that effect; he was already in prison and condemned to banishment on complaint of his vassals; he duly went to Rome and was sentenced to compurgation and penance.—Amabile, I, 286.
⁴ Chioccarello, *ubi sup.*

There was in this merely an assertion of sovereignty and no desire to shield the heretic, for when the Inquisition accepted the inevitable and made application to the viceroy, it was granted almost as a matter of course. The formality was simple. The application was referred to the chief chaplain, who made a show of consulting with the judges of the Audiencia and reported that it was in due form, when the exequatur was granted. Occasionally, however, some question might be raised when the process called attention to some abusive extension of inquisitorial jurisdiction. Thus in 1610 a certain Fabio Orzolino asked for the exequatur on a citation which he had obtained directed to the Abate Angelo and Carlo della Rocca of Traetto (Gaeta). On this the chief chaplain reported that the parties owed to Orzolino 88 ducats, for non-payment of which they had been publicly excommunicated. Under this excommunication they had lain for a year, which, according to the canon law, rendered them suspect of heresy and thus, by a strained construction, subjected them to inquisitorial action. It is not easy to understand the decision of the chaplain that the exequatur should be granted as to the abate and not as to the layman.[1] A more wholesome case was one in 1574, shown in the application of Giovanni Tomase, Modesto Abate and Sebastiano Luca for an exequatur to the order of the Roman Inquisition to sell the property of Nicola Pegna and Giovanni Mateo of Tagio, to reimburse the applicants for expenses amounting to 338 crowns arising from false accusations of heresy brought against them by Pegna and Mateo, who had been condemned for false-witness to scourging in Rome, with the addition of the galleys for Mateo.[2]

Under this system the Roman Inquisition had a tolerably free hand in Naples and its arrests were sufficiently numerous for it to establish a regular service of vessels to carry its prisoners, transportation by sea being much more economical than by land. The latter was expensive, as we chance to learn from a letter of March 8, 1586, ordering Captain Amoroso to be forwarded by land

---

[1] Chioccarello MSS., T. VIII (see Appendix). [2] Ibidem.

because the tempestuous weather prevented vessels from putting to sea. He was to have a guard of six soldiers who were to bring back a certificate of his delivery to the Inquisition, and the expenses of the journey were to be defrayed from the property of the prisoner.[1] The sea service, however, was not without its risks. When, in 1593, Fray Gerónimo Gracian, the disciple of Santa Teresa, left Naples for Rome, it was on a *fragata de la Inquisicion*, which is described as well provided with chains and shackles for securing prisoners. It chanced to be captured by the Moors and Gracian narrowly escaped burning, as he was supposed to be an inquisitor.[2]

Still Rome was not satisfied with this and it found Viceroy Osuna (1582–86) obsequious to its exigencies. About 1585 he allowed Sixtus V to establish in Naples a regular Commissioner of the Inquisition, with jurisdiction practically superseding that of the archbishop. By this time the spirit of the Neapolitans had been effectually broken. Already, in 1580, the Venetian envoy Alvise Lando, in describing how they had been subdued by the universal misery attendant on the Spanish domination, especially under the vice-royalty of the Marquis of Mondéjar (1575–79), adds that it is the opinion of many that if the king chose to establish the Inquisition, so greatly abhorred, there would be little opposition.[3] How speedily under these circumstances the episcopal functions became atrophied is illustrated by a case occurring in 1592. In 1590 a French youth named Jacques Girard was captured by a Barbary corsair, circumcised and forced to embrace Islam. In 1592 he was sent on shore in Calabria with a boat's crew to procure water, when he escaped and, being taken for a Moor, was thrown in prison at Cosenza. He applied to the arch-

---

[1] Chioccarello MSS., T. VIII.
[2] Escritos de Santa Teresa, T. II, pp. 457, 463 (Madrid, 1869). Cf. Amabile, I, 229–30.
In 1588 we find the Congregation of the Inquisition scolding the nuncio at Naples for refusing to pay the expenses of this transportation, as his predecessors had always done.—Decret. Sac. Congr. S. Officii, p. 192 (Bibl. del R. Archivio di Stato in Roma, Fondo Camerale, Congr. del S. Offizio, Vol 3).
[3] Amabile, I, 332.—Relazioni Venete, Serie II, T. V, p. 471.

bishop for reconciliation to the Church; the prelate felt unable to act, even in so simple a matter, and wrote to the Roman Inquisition for instructions. Before these came, Jacques had been transferred to Naples; a second application was made to Rome and the necessary powers were sent to the Archbishop of Naples, with orders to report the result.[1] So, in the trial for heresy of the celebrated Fra Tommaso Campanella, in 1600, Clement VIII designated as a court his nuncio at Naples, the archiepiscopal vicar and the Bishop of Termoli, and they were to transmit to Rome a summary of the case, with their opinions, before rendering sentence.[2]

Under such a viceroy as Osuna, the inquisitorial commissioner was superfluous, for all the powers of the state were put at the disposition of the papal representatives. As early as 1582 we find the nuncio assuming jurisdiction and requesting Osuna to execute a sentence of scourging which he had passed on the Venetian Giulio Secamonte for suspicion of heresy, a request which was promptly granted. The Roman Inquisition had only to ask for the arrest of any one throughout the kingdom, when immediately orders were given to the local authorities to seize him and send him to Naples for transmission to Rome, and if necessary to take possession of and forward all his books and papers. From this the highest in the land were not secure. In 1583 Cardinal Savelli, then secretary of the Inquisition, wrote that the person of Prince Gianbattista Spinello was wanted in Rome to answer for matters of faith, when immediately Osuna issued orders to seize him wherever he might be found and bring him to the Royal

---

[1] Bibliothèque Nationale de France, fonds latin, 8994, fol. 252.

Possibly this may be partially explained by the fact that heresy was a case reserved to the Holy See, the absolution for which in the *forum internum* required a special licence (cap. 3, Extrav. Commun., Lib. v, Tit. ix). But in the *forum externum* the episcopal jurisdiction over heresy was in no way curtailed by the existence of the Inquisition (Benedicti PP. XIV de Synodo diœcesana, Lib. IX, cap. iv, n. 3). This was fully admitted by the Roman Inquisition (Decret. S. Congr. S. Officii, pp. 174-5, 177, 266-8, 272-3 ap. R. Archivio di Stato in Roma, Fondo Camerale, Congr. del S. Offizio, Vol. 3).

[2] Amabile, Fra Tommaso Campanella, II, 120-1 (Napoli, 1882).

Audiencia, where he was to give security in 25,000 ducats to present himself within a month to the Holy Office and not to leave Rome without its permission.[1]

Osuna's successor, Juan de Zuñiga, Count of Miranda, was equally subservient, but he insisted on the observance of the formalities when Rome sought to act independently without viceregal intervention. In 1587, at the order of Cardinal Savelli, the Apostolic Vicar of Lecce induced the Audiencia of the Terra d'Otranto to arrest Giantonio Stomeo. This was overslaughing the viceroy who rebuked the Audiencia, telling it that it should have referred the matter to him and awaited his instructions, meanwhile assuring itself of the person of the individual. It was purely a matter of etiquette for, in the end, after some further correspondence, Miranda ordered Stomeo to be forwarded to Naples by the first chain (of galley slaves), giving advices so that arrangements could be made for his transmission to Rome. There seems to have been some doubt as to the correctness of the stand taken by Miranda for subsequently Annibale Moles, Regent of the Vicaria, was called upon for a consulta in which he stated the rule to be that arrests for the Inquisition must always pass through the hands of the viceroy, who always ordered their execution.[2]

Rome was not satisfied with this and continued its encroachments, taking advantage of any weakness of the civil power to establish precedents and claim them as rights. In 1628 we find it represented by the Dominican Fra Giacinto Petronio, Bishop of Molfetta, who styled himself inquisitor and was especially audacious in extending his powers. He arrested Dr. Tomas Calendrino, a Sicilian, because he assisted in the escape from Benevento of a contumacious person. He was carried to the Archbishop of Naples and placed on the papal galleys for transmission to Rome, but the Neapolitan spirit was rising again and the Collaterale and Junta de Jurisdicion called on Viceroy Alba to demand his surrender under threat of not allowing the galleys

---

[1] Chioccarello MSS., T. VIII.
[2] Ibidem.

to depart and of banishing Fra Petronio within 24 hours. Alba however conferred with the nuncio and archbishop, who assured him that it was customary to arrest and send people to Rome without notice to him. In this perplexity Alba referred the matter to his master Philip IV, who warmly praised his prudence in so doing. The papal nuncio at Madrid, he said, had received orders from Rome to protest against the attempted innovation of requiring notice to the viceroy and he therefore ordered Alba, as the matter was of the highest importance, to investigate precedents of persons arrested with or without notice, and not to introduce any novelty. What was the ultimate result as respects Calendrino does not appear, but this nerveless way of treating the matter was not calculated to check the insolence of Fra Petronio who, in the course of the affair, excommunicated the judges Calefano and Osorio, summoned the auditor Figueroa to present himself to the Roman Inquisition and finally arrested him with his own armed sbirri. This was no novelty, for he had no scruple in imprisoning and maltreating royal officials for executing orders of the government.[1]

Philip was accustomed to allow his own officials to be thus abused by the Spanish Inquisition, but the Neapolitan temper was stubborn and, in 1630, the Collaterale reminded Fra Petronio that all commissions to arrest required the exequatur; it ordered him to present within three days all that he had received from Rome, and moreover forbade him to keep armed retainers. It made complaints to the king and to the Spanish ambassador at Rome, while Urban VIII issued briefs defending him, under which encouragement he continued his arbitrary methods. At length Philip, by a letter of March 18, 1631, ordered that no papal brief should be executed without the exequatur; a new viceroy, the Count of Monterey, was prompted to defend the royal jurisdiction and Fra Petronio complained to Rome that the aid of the secular arm was withheld unless he would state the names of those whom he desired to imprison. The pope appealed to Philip IV, who

---

[1] Chioccarello MSS., T. VIII.—Amabile, Inquisizione in Napoli, II, 35.

apparently had forgotten about the matter and, in a letter of November 27, 1632, asked for explanations. Then Fra Petronio commenced taking evidence against the auditor Brandolino, but when the Collaterale deliberated, January 31, 1633, on a proposition to banish him, he yielded. Monterey negotiated with Rome to have him replaced with some one less objectionable and also that the new incumbent should not hold a tribunal but should only report to the Congregation the cases occurring. Urban VIII offered to appoint any one whom they might select, and when the name was presented of Antonio Ricciullo, Bishop of Belcastro, then their ambassador at Rome, he was duly commissioned.[1]

There was nothing gained by the change. Ricciullo styled himself inquisitor-general; he held a tribunal and in his time condemned four clerics for functioning without priest's orders—three strangled and burnt in public, and one strangled privately. The pope ordered that the Dominican convent should serve as an inquisitorial prison and its prior should be a consultor, and thus after a struggle of nearly a century the papal Inquisition was fairly established in Naples.[2]

Ricciullo died, May 17, 1642, and was succeeded by Felice Tamburello, Bishop of Sora. He died in 1656 and was replaced temporarily by the nuncio Giulio Spinola, who served until 1659, when Camillo Piazza, Bishop of Dragona was appointed. That Naples should be impatient at finding itself thus gradually and imperceptibly brought under the yoke of the papal Inquisition was natural. The turbulent city had gallantly resisted, at no little cost to itself, the imposition of the Spanish Holy Office, through times in which unity of faith was seriously threatened by successive heresies. Now all such danger was past. There were no Cathari or Waldenses or Protestants to rend in Italy the seamless garment of the Church and the period was one of spiritual apathy, wholly averse to proselytism. Only the unappeasable longing of Rome to make its power manifest everywhere could explain its persistence in thus insinuating the abhorred juris-

---

[1] Amabile, II, 35–6.   [2] Ibidem, II, 37–9.

diction in a city which prided itself on its piety, on the number of churches and convents which impoverished it, on the obedience of the people to the priesthood and on the strictness of its religious observance. The only field of inquisitorial activity lay in reckless speeches which might savor of irreligion, in the blasphemy through which anger or despair found expression, in the superstitious arts of wise-women, in burning clerics who administered sacraments without having received the requisite orders and in such offences as bigamy and seduction in the confessional, all of which could only by a strained construction be deemed as savoring of heresy, and could readily be disposed of by the ordinary spiritual or secular courts. The Holy Office was a manifest superfluity and its imposition was all the more galling.

Nor was there any alleviation in the fact that the tribunal was papal and not Spanish, for there was nothing to choose between them, in spite of frequent appeals to the pledge of Philip II that the *via ordinaria* alone should be observed. There were the same confiscation and impoverishment of families. There were the same travesty of justice and denial of rightful defence to the accused. There were the same secrecy of procedure and withholding from the prisoner the names of his accuser and of the witnesses. There was the same readiness to accept the denunciations and testimony of the vilest, who could be heard in no other court, but who, in the Inquisition, could gratify malignity, secure that they would remain unknown. There was even greater freedom in the use of torture, as the habitual solvent of all doubts, whether as to fact or intention. There were the same prolonged and heartbreaking delays during which the accused was secluded from all communication with the outside world. A careless speech overheard and distorted by an enemy—or perhaps invented by him—sufficed to cast a man into the secret prison, where he might lie for four or five years, while his trial proceeded leisurely and his family might starve. It would probably end in his torture, to make him confess if he denied the utterance, or to ascertain his intention if he admitted and sought to explain it. If he succumbed in the torture he was subjected to a humiliating penance, to wearing the habitello and to infamy—probably also to confiscation. If his endurance in the torture-chamber enabled him to "purge the evidence," as the legists phrased it, he was discharged with a verdict of not proven, with nothing to make amends for his sufferings and wasted years. Such was the fate which hung over every citizen and it was felt acutely.[1] How little was required to arouse inquisitorial vigilance was shown in 1683, when Agostino Mazza, a priest employed in teaching philosophy, was thrown in prison by the Commissioner of the Inquisition and humiliated by having to abjure in public two abstract propositions which to the ordinary mind have the least possible bearing on the faith—"The definition of man is not that he is a reasoning animal" and "Brutes have a kind of imperfect reason."[2] The human intellect evidently had small chance of development under such conditions.

It is easy therefore to understand the growing uneasiness of the people when they saw the commissioner, Monsignor Piazza, appointed in 1659, gradually erect a formal inquisitorial tribunal, with a fiscal and other customary officials and a corps of armed

---

[1] These feelings are warmly but respectfully expressed in a memorial addressed to Innocent XII (1691–1700), by Giuseppe Valletta, an advocate of Naples, in support of envoys sent to negotiate with him (MS. *penes me*).

It is difficult for us to estimate the horror which, as the inquisitors boasted, the Holy Office cast over the population. They relate with pride that in Spain men cited to appear, even on matters not pertaining to the faith, but ignorant of the cause, were known to take to their beds and die of sheer terror. How much greater, then, they ask, must be the horror of those accused, suddenly arrested and cast into the strictest and most secret prison, not to mention what followed?— "Sola simplici vocatione alicujus inquisitoris in Hispania, ait Morillus citatus, per aliquem ejus ministrum, ad negotium forte particulare non pertinens ad Inquisitionem Fidei, absque eo quod vocati sciant ad quid vocentur, adeo perterrefieri homines soleant, ut aliquibus statim necessario decumbere et præ nimio dolore febri superveniente emori contigerit. At quid in casibus ubi datur præventio per accusationem aut denuntiationem et agitur de repentina captura et de carceratione rigidissima ac secretissima, ut taceam de aliis quæ hanc consequuntur, quanto magis perterrefiant capti et carcerati? quanto maiori horrore afficientur?" —Salelles, De Materiis Tribunalium S. Inquisitionis, Proleg. IV, n. 8 (Romæ, 1651).

[2] Capasso, Ragionamenti ad istanza degl' Ecc[mi] Sig[ri] della Città di Napoli (MS. *penes me*).

familiars, recruited, as we are told, from the lowest class of the population. His activity was such that he constructed eight prisons in as many convents, where even women were confined, without respect to rank or condition, under the guardianship of the *frati*. He celebrated *atti di fede* in public, where abjurations were administered, followed by scourgings through the streets, and he levied on the resources of the Regular Orders to defray the expenses of his court. Indignation gathered and, on April 2, 1661, the Piazze ordered their representative body, the Capitolo di San Lorenzo, to consider the innovations of the commissioner. The aspect of the people grew threatening and Count Peñaranda, the viceroy, ordered Monsignor Piazza to leave the kingdom, which he did on April 10th, under escort of a troop of horse to assure his safety. This did not appease the deputies who, on May 18th, presented a memorial to the viceroy, in which they further drew attention to the subject of confiscation and asked that the prohibitory bull of Julius III, in 1554, should be enforced. Consultations and negotiations were long continued during which discussion became so hot that Peñaranda threw some of the deputies in prison, but, on October 24th, he announced that Philip IV had decided that the grant of Philip II must be maintained and the *via ordinaria* alone must be followed. Nothing was said as to the abandonment of confiscation and efforts to procure it were protracted, but without success.[1]

If the Neapolitans flattered themselves that they had obtained release from the odious institution, they were mistaken. Rome continued to send commissioners and they continued to disregard the privileges of the kingdom. Another outbreak occurred in 1691 when, under orders from the Roman Congregation, its commissioner—Giovanni Giberti, Bishop of Cava—seized several persons without obtaining the exequatur of the viceroy. The

---

[1] Pietro de Fusco, Per la fidelissima Città di Napoli, negli affari della Santa Inquisizione (MS. *penes me*).—Amabile, II, 41-52.—Giannone, Lib. xxxii, cap. 5.

Pietro de Fusco tells us that confiscations were not infrequently released, as they were in 1587 to the children of Francesco di Aloes di Caserta and to the heirs of Bernardino Gargano d'Aversa, although they died as impenitent heretics.

Collaterale, or Council, notified him that there was no Inquisition in Naples and that the prisoners must be transferred to the archiepiscopal prison, under pain of legal proceedings against him. He treated with contempt the notary who bore this message and threatened him with the savage penalties provided for impeding the Inquisition, in response to which the Collaterale hustled him out of the kingdom, barely allowing him time to perform quarantine at Gaeta. Innocent XII felt this keenly, for he was a Neapolitan and had been Archbishop of Naples, and a warm correspondence ensued with the Spanish court. It was claimed by the curia that the pope was omnipotent in matters of faith; that he could abrogate local laws and enact new ones at his pleasure, while the papal nuncio at Madrid warned the king that Naples would be given over to atheism without the Inquisition and the whole vast monarchy of Spain might be destroyed. The city of Naples was equally vigorous in asserting its rights and complained of the numerous officials of the commissioner, exempted from secular jurisdiction and committing scandals with impunity. The pope threatened an interdict and the Piazze threatened to rise; the latter danger was to Carlos II the most imminent and, in 1692, he prohibited all further residence in Naples of papal delegates or commissioners. To render secure the fruits of this victory, the Piazze took the decided step of appointing a permanent deputation whose duty it was to guard the city from further dangers of the same nature.[1]

If again the good people of Naples imagined that they had at last shaken off the dreaded Holy Office they underrated the persistence of Rome. Trials for heresy continued in the archiepiscopal court, conducted in inquisitorial fashion and not by the *via ordinaria*. This caused renewed dissatisfaction and, in hopes of reaching some terms of accommodation, envoys were sent to Rome in 1693 to ask that the procedure should be open, the names of the witnesses and the testimony being communicated to the accused;

---

[1] MSS. of Library of Univ. of Halle, Yc, Tom. XVII.—Amabile, II, 54–58.—MSS. of Royal Library of Munich, Cod. Ital., 189, fol. 327; 209, fol. 111–138.

that no one should be imprisoned without competent proof against him; that the city should be allowed to supply an advocate for the poor and that two lay assistants should be appointed to see that these provisions were enforced. Prolonged discussions followed, the cardinals entrusted with the matter seeking to gain readmission for the commissioner and arguing that the bishops were mostly unfit to exercise the jurisdiction.[1] There was little prospect of reaching an agreement when Naples was startled with a wholly novel aggression. February 1, 1695, there was published in Rome by the Inquisition an Edict of Denunciation which, under its orders, was similarly published in at least one of the Neapolitan dioceses. Such edicts were issued annually in Spain, but in Naples they were unknown and the present one was evidently intended for that kingdom, for it included the episcopal ordinaries as well as inquisitors, as the parties to whom every one was required, under pain of excommunication *latæ sententiæ*, removable only by the Inquisition, and other penalties, to denounce whatever cases might come in any way to his cognizance, of a list of offences ranging from apostasy to bigamy, blasphemy and sorcery. The Deputati took the matter up in a long memorial addressed to the Collaterale, pointing out the invasion of the prerogative in publishing the edict without the necessary exequatur and the evils to be expected from converting the population into spies and creating a universal feeling of insecurity. There was also the fact that the edict assumed the jurisdiction of the Inquisition over Naples, that it made the bishops its agents, authorized as its deputies to employ the inquisitorial process, and that it comprised not only offences which the Neapolitans contended to belong to the secular courts but a general clause, vaguely embracing whatever else might be claimed as subject to the jurisdiction of the Holy Office.[2]

This shrewd device of the Roman Inquisition was successful. The bishops to a considerable extent exercised the powers dele-

---

[1] Amabile, II, 59–72; Append., 68, 71.
[2] Acampora, Ragioni a pro della Fidelissima Città di Napoli (Napoli, 1709).

gated to them and the Deputati found constant occupation in endeavoring to protect those whom they imprisoned and tried by inquisitorial methods. Then came the troublous times of the War of Succession which followed the death of Carlos II in 1700. After a fruitless struggle Philip V was obliged to abandon Naples in 1707 to his rival, Charles of Austria, and during the interval the Inquisition succeeded in re-introducing a commissioner, who made free use of his powers. The new monarch sought to secure the loyalty of his subjects and from Barcelona sent orders to his viceroy, Cardinal Grimani to support the Deputati in their efforts to uphold the privileges of the kingdom. In spite of this the Deputati were obliged to appeal to him, in a petition of July 31, 1709, representing that, after the publication of his despatch to Grimani, the ecclesiastics proceeded to the greatest imaginable oppressions and violence, so that their condition was worse than ever, wherefore they prayed for relief at his hands, so that trials should be conducted in the *via ordinaria*. To this Charles replied, September 15th, to Grimani, commanding that matters of faith should be confined strictly to the bishops, to be handled by the *via ordinaria;* any departure from this was to be severely punished and the authorities were to use the whole royal power, through whatever means were necessary, for the enforcement of his orders.[1]

This won as little obedience as the previous royal utterance and the Deputati were kept busy in attending to the cases of those who suffered from the persistent employment of inquisitorial methods—efforts which were sometimes successful but more frequently in vain. It was probably some special outrage that induced the Deputati, in 1711, to employ Nicolò Capasso to draw up a report on inquisitorial methods. The work is a storehouse of inquisitorial principles as set forth by accredited inquisitorial authorities—papal decretals and manuals of practice such as those of Eymerich, Peña, Simancas, Albertino, Rojas, the Sacro Arsenale etc., admirably calculated to excite abhorrence by laying

---

[1] Amabile, II, 74–80.—Acampora, *op. cit.*

bare the complete denial of justice in every step of procedure, the pitiless cruelty of the system and the manner in which the lives, the fortunes and the honor of every citizen were at the mercy of the malignant and of the temper of the tribunal. Yet so far from being an advocate of toleration, Capasso commences by arguing against it at much length. Religion, he says, is the foundation of social order and the principle of toleration infers toleration of irreligion. Protestants are intolerant between themselves and the Catholic system cannot endure toleration. That which is taught by the philosophers is chimerical, and a community to be stable must be united in faith, but the enforcement of this unity is a matter for the secular power. Punishment must be corporal and the Church has authority over the spirit alone, not over the body. An allusion to the *gravissime agitazioni* of the people would indicate that his labors were called forth by some action which had aroused especial resentment.[1]

It was all in vain. By the death of his brother Joseph I, Charles VI succeeded to the empire in 1711. Wars and other interests diverted his attention from Naples and, though he consistently resisted the pressure from Rome to give the Inquisition recognition, the bishops continued to exercise inquisitorial jurisdiction in inquisitorial fashion. The Deputati did what they could, but the success of their efforts depended upon the uncertain temper of the successive imperial viceroys, who, though they might sometimes manifest a spasmodic readiness to enforce the royal decrees, did not countervail the persistent ecclesiastical determination to wield the power afforded by inquisitorial methods.[2]

---

[1] Ragionamenti del Sig. D. Niccolò Capasso colli quali ad istanza degl' Ecc^{mi} Sig^{ri} della Città di Napoli prova non doversi ricevere in questo Religiosissimo Regno l'odioso Tribunale dell' Inquisizione.

I am not aware that this work has ever been printed, but it must have had a considerable circulation in MS. I have three copies, of which one is a Latin version. In one of them the prefatory address to the Deputati is dated December 3, 1711, which fixes the time of its composition. The other copies were made respectively in 1715 and 1717, indicating that it continued to be referred to.

[2] Amabile, II, 81–3.

A change was at hand when, in 1734, Carlo VII (better known as Carlos III of Spain) drove the Austrians out of Naples and assumed the throne. The kingdom, after two centuries of viceroyalties, at last had a resident monarch of its own, anxious to win the affection of his new subjects and inclined, as his subsequent career showed, to curb exorbitant ecclesiastical pretensions. His royal oath included a pledge to observe the privileges of the land, including those concerning the Inquisition granted by his predecessor. Apparently for some years there was hesitation in testing the quality of the new régime, but in 1738 and 1739, as though by concerted action under orders from Rome, Cardinal Spinelli, the Archbishop of Naples, and various bishops throughout the kingdom, undertook prosecutions in the prohibited fashion. Complaints reached the Deputati, who appealed to the king. He reproached them for negligence, ordered the proceedings stopped and the processes to be sent to Naples, and gave to Spinelli a warning that such irregularities would not be permitted. Undeterred by this, the episcopal Inquisition continued at work and in 1743 three bishops, of Nusco, Ortono and Cassano, were called to account; the papers of trials held by them were examined and pronounced irregular; in one case the Bishop of Nusco had cruelly tortured a parish priest named Gaetano de Arco, after holding him in prison for eight months.[1]

It seems incredible that under such circumstances ecclesiastical persistence should defiantly call public attention to its disregard of the laws, yet on September 26, 1746, the octave of San Gennaro —a time when the popular afflux to the churches was greatest— an *atto di fede*, conducted according to inquisitorial practice, was celebrated in the archiepiscopal church, where a Sicilian priest named Antonio Nava abjured certain errors and was condemned to perpetual irremissible prison. Popular indignation was aroused, the cry arose that Spinelli was endeavoring to introduce the Inquisition and he was insulted in his carriage by crowds as he

---

[1] Amabile, II, 84–5.—Consulta dalla Real Camera de S. Chiara alla Maestà del Re per il Santo Uffizio, Dec. 19, 1746 (MS. *penes me*).

drove through the streets. The Deputati represented to the king that they had been appealed to by three prisoners whose trials were not conducted by the *via ordinaria*, showing that the ecclesiastics were seeking to impose the abhorred Inquisition on the kingdom. Spinelli protested that the trials were open and according to the *via ordinaria* and that he was ready to obey whatever commands he might receive from the king. Carlos sent all the papers to his council, known as the Camera di Santa Chiara, with orders to investigate and report.

The Camera made a thorough examination and reported, December 19th, that Nava had lain in prison since April, 1741; another prisoner, a layman named Trascogna, had been incarcerated for three years and his trial was yet unfinished; the third, a deacon named Angelo Petriello, was accused of celebrating mass on July 24th last and was about to put in his defence. The archbishop argued that, unlike his predecessors, he did not conceal the witnesses' names and therefore the process was the ordinary one, but investigation showed that in other respects inquisitorial practice was followed and inquisitorial authorities were cited; during the trial the prisoner was kept *incomunicado* in his cell and debarred from all communication with the outside world. In the papers the expression "Tribunale della Santa Fede" was constantly used; in the marble lintel of the door leading to the rooms occupied by it the words "Sanctum Officium" were cut and the part of the prison used by it was called "del Sant' Officio." It had a full corps of special officials and in a passage-way there had been for five or six years a tablet bearing their names and positions, with the inscription "Inquisitori del Tribunale del S. Uffizio." It also had a seal different from that of the court of the Ordinary, bearing for device two hands, one of St. Peter with the key, the other of St. Paul with a naked sword and the legend "Sanctum Officium Archiep. Neap." The Camera thence concluded that it was the old Inquisition under various devices and only awaiting an opportunity to establish itself openly, as was shown by the occurrences in 1691, 1711 and 1739 and, as it was impossible to place reliance on the promises of ecclesiastics, so often made and broken, it advised that all the officials of the pretended Tribunal of Faith should be banished as disturbers of the public peace; the three processes should be sealed and filed away in the public archives, the accused should be restored to their original position and be tried again by the *via ordinaria*. Everything connected with the Tribunal should be abolished—officials, prison, seal and inscription—and notice be given that any one in future assuming such offices would incur the royal indignation. All spiritual courts should be notified that, in actions of the faith against either clerics or laymen, before arrest the informations must be laid before the king for his assent and before sentence the whole process, so as to make sure that there were no irregularities. The accused while in prison must have full liberty of writing and talking to whom he pleased and be furnished with an advocate chosen by the Deputati or the Camera. To protect the laity against prosecutions for simple sorcery or blasphemy or other matters not subject to spiritual jurisdiction, the nature of the alleged crime must be clearly expressed when applying for licence to arrest.[1]

These suggestions were promptly adopted and were embodied in a royal decree of December 29th, by which two of the officials

---

[1] Consulta dalla Real Camera de S. Chiara alla Maestà del Re per il Santo Uffizio (MS. *penes me*).

That the Neapolitan Government was not actuated by any tenderness towards heresy is manifested in a singular transaction of the period detailed in a letter of which I have copy, of July 11, 1746, from Edward Allen, the British Consul, to the Marchese Fogliani—apparently the foreign secretary. An English girl of 13, named Ellen Bowes, was forcibly abducted from her father's house, after surrounding it with about a hundred armed men. Against this outrage the consul protested as a violation of the privileges of the English nation, to which Fogliani replied, explaining the reasons which had led the king to do this and what was proposed to do with the child. Apparently she had expressed an intention to join the Catholic Church and had been taken so as to secure her conversion. Allen rejoined in a long argumentative letter and, although he pointed out that a child of such tender age could have no conception of the different religions, he felt himself obliged to disavow asking her return to her parents and limited his request to having her delivered to some one of the English nation, where she could be examined as to her motives. What was the issue of the affair does not appear from the paper in my possession, but evidently the king, after taking such a step and justifying it, could not well retreat.

were banished within eight days and similar punishment was threatened for any future attempt to exercise such functions. By January 5, 1747, the Marchese Brancone, under royal order, was able to report to the Deputati that the seal and commissions had been surrendered, the inscription over the door had been changed to "Archivium" and the name of the prison altered to prisons of S. Francesco and S. Paolo. Archbishop Spinelli was compelled to resign and, when Benedict XIV sent Cardinal Landi to Naples to seek some method of re-establishing the tribunal, he was in danger of being mobbed and was obliged to return without having secured an official audience. Thus the Inquisition ceased to have a recognized existence in Naples; the rejoicing was general and, as an expression of its gratitude, the city made a voluntary offering to Carlos of three hundred thousand ducats. Yet the Deputati did not disband; taught by past experience they kept vigilant watch to see that the detested institution or its methods were not smuggled in and that the ecclesiastical courts observed the new rules. Carlos was called to the throne of Spain in 1759, by the death of his half-brother Fernando VI, leaving Naples to his young son, Ferdinando IV. Possibly it may have been thought that during a minority there was an opportunity to revive the institution for, in 1761, the Deputati made an appeal to the king. The Regent Tanucci was not a man to relinquish the advantage gained. The decree of 1746 was again sent to all prelates with commands that it be strictly obeyed and the royal thanks were conveyed to the Deputati for their vigilance, which they were ordered not to relax.[1]

They heeded the injunction and, in 1764, they addressed to the king a memorial on the case of Padre Leopoldo di S. Pasquale, a Bare-footed Augustinian, who had been tried by his brethren on charges of financial irregularities and unchastity. Inquisitorial procedure had been employed, no opportunity for defence had been allowed and, for seven years, the unfortunate friar had been

---

[1] Lettera circolare del Marchese Fraggiani, Napoli, 1761.—Beccatini, Istoria della Inquisizione, pp. 372-77, 382 (Milano, 1797).—Amabile, *op. cit.*, II, 104-5; Appendice, 80.

subjected by his superiors to a series of inhuman cruelties.¹ What was the result I have no means of ascertaining, but this prolonged vigilance indicates the profound and enduring impression entertained of the Inquisition by the Neapolitans.

---

¹ Supplica al Re nostro Signore de' Deputati por opporsi ai pregindizj del S. Officio. *Sine nota* sed Napoli, 1764.—Le Bret, Magazin zum Gebrauch der Staaten- und Kirchengeschicte, III, 160 (Frankfurt, 1773).

CHAPTER III.

SARDINIA.

As the island of Sardinia was a possession of the crown of Aragon, it was not neglected in organizing the Inquisition. There were Conversos there and doubtless in the earliest period it served as a refuge for some of those who fled from Spain. The introduction of the Holy Office is probably to be attributed to the year 1492, when Micer Sancho Maria was appointed inquisitor.[1] He served until 1497, for a letter of December 15th of that year, from Ferdinand to Miguel Fonte, receiver of Sardinia, recites that the inquisitors-general have appointed Maestre Gabriel Cardona, rector of Peñiscola, as inquisitor in place of Sancho Marin, transferred to Sicily, and it proceeds to give instructions as to salaries, from which we learn that the organization was on a most economical scale. There was, as yet, no settled habitation for it, as a letter of March 11, 1498, to Don Pero Mata requests him to let Cardona continue in occupation of his house, as Marin had been, and one of September 24, 1500, orders that quarters be rented in Cagliari where all the officials can lodge together. There was but one inquisitor, with an assessor, no fiscal, one alguazil, a single notary to serve both in the tribunal and for the confiscations, and a receiver, with salaries too modest to offer much temptation to serve in an inhospitable land, where the principal occupation seems to be quarrelling with all the other authorities.[2] In fact the Inquisition was as unpopular in Sardinia as elsewhere, for Fer-

---

[1] Páramo, p. 219.
[2] Archivo de Simancas, Inquisicion, Lib. 1. The salaries are as follows:
Gabriel de Cardona, inquisitor, from the date of his embarcation . . . 150 ducats.
Bartolomé de Castro, assessor . . . . 50 "
An alguazil, with charge of prison, to be selected by Carmona . . . . 20 "
Bernat Ros, notario del secreto y de los secuestros . } the salaries
Yourself . . . . } heretofore paid.

dinand, in announcing to his lieutenant-general the appointment of Cardona, feels it necessary to order that he and his subordinates shall receive more favor than their predecessors, so that they may freely exercise their functions; they are not to be ill-treated by any one, nor be impeded in the performance of their duties. Ferdinand had heard how his lieutenant-general took certain wheat out of the hands of the receiver, resulting in the loss of a hundred and sixty libras, wherefore he is ordered in future to abstain from interference in such matters, as otherwise due provision will be made to prevent him.[1]

Notwithstanding these royal injunctions, Cardona was not long in becoming involved in a bitter quarrel with both the secular and ecclesiastical authorities. It appears from a series of Ferdinand's letters, September 18, 1498, that a certain Domingo de Santa Cruz—who ten years before had been the cause of similar trouble in Valencia—was imprisoned by the inquisitor and forcibly released by the lieutenant-general and the Archbishop of Cagliari, who claimed that, in furtherance of the king's interests, they had given him a safe-conduct. The archbishop, moreover, had withdrawn from Cardona a commission enabling him to exercise the episcopal jurisdiction, the coöperation of which was requisite in all judgements. Ferdinand writes in great wrath; he instructs the inquisitor to reclaim Domingo at once, to throw him in chains and hold him until the royal pleasure is known; if the lieutenant-general and archbishop resist, he is to proceed against them with excommunication; the latter are roundly scolded and ordered to surrender the prisoner and hereafter to support the inquisitor and the archbishop is told to renew the episcopal commission. Not content with this, the king orders the viguier of Cagliari, under pain of dismissal from office, to obey the commands of the inquisitor and similar instructions are sent to the town-council.[2] The inquisitor thus was made the virtual

---

[1] Archivo de Simancas, Inquisicion, Lib. 1.
[2] Páramo, pp. 220–222. For the Valencia experience of Domingo de Santa Cruz, see History of the Inquisition of Spain, Vol. I, p. 242.

autocrat of the island, but his triumph was evanescent, for on November 15, 1499, we find him in Ferdinand's court at Avila and his salary ceases on that day. He evidently left Sardinia in undignified haste and involved in trouble, for a royal cédula of November 18th commands the governor and other officials, under penalty of the royal wrath and of a thousand florins, to allow the furniture, books, bedding and personal effects of the late inquisitor Cardona to be freely shipped to him.[1] Nine months elapsed before the vacancy was filled by the commission of the Bishop of Bonavalle, August 18, 1500, to whom was granted the power of appointing and dismissing his assessor and notary—the two officials on whom, as Ferdinand tells him, the success or failure of the Inquisition chiefly depends.[2]

It is quite possible that Cardona's precipitate departure may have been motived by terror for, about that time, the receiver, Miguel Fonte, was assassinated in Cagliari, as we may assume, by some of those whom he had reduced to poverty. He was not killed on the spot; from letters of February 13, 1500, we learn that he had been carried to Barcelona, in hopes of cure, and died there. Ferdinand ordered that his widow should be treated with all consideration and that the lieutenant-general should pursue and punish the assassins. Sympathy seems rather to have been with the criminals and the royal commands were disregarded, under the frivolous pretext that it was the business of the Inquisition— a palpable falsehood, seeing that the tribunal was vacant—for which Ferdinand took his representative severely to task on August 18th. The receivership had also remained unoccupied, for it was not until August 4th that a fit person could be found, venturesome enough to tempt its dangers, in the person of Juan López, a merchant of Játiva.[3]

---

[1] Archivo de Simancas, Inquisicion, Libro 1.
[2] Ibidem. Páramo (p. 223) calls the appointee Magister Farris, subsequently created Bishop of Bonebolla—a see subsequently merged into that of Cagliari. There is no reference in Gams's *Series Episcoporum* to such a bishopric in Sardinia. Páramo interposes a Nicolas Vaguer as inquisitor, from 1498 to 1500, which is evidently a mistake.
[3] Archivo de Simancas, Inquisicion, Lib. 1.

It may well be that there was wide-spread hatred felt for the receiver of confiscations, for the correspondence of the period shows that persecution had been fairly productive, considering the poverty of the island. August 29, 1497, there is an order to pay the royal secretary Calcena, out of the property of Antoni Cones, a debt claimed by him of a hundred ducats, before any other creditors are paid. Then, on January 21, 1498, a servant of the royal household, Mosen Gaspar Gilaberte, receives a gratuity of twenty thousand sueldos ($833\frac{1}{3}$ ducats) out of the confiscation of Juan Soller of Cagliari. On March 11th we hear of a composition, made by request of the Archbishop and Syndic of Cagliari, whereby the representatives of certain deceased persons, condemned by Micer Morin, compounded for the confiscation of their property—an agreement subsequently violated by Morin, whereupon the Dean of Cagliari and other prominent persons appealed to Ferdinand. Then, October 14th, there is an *ayuda de costa* to the notary Bernat Ros to refund his expenses on a journey to the court and back. Then, October 12, 1499, there is a gratuity of two hundred and fifty ducats to Alonso Castillo, servant of Don Enrique Enríquez, royal mayordomo mayor. Soon after this Cardona, in hurrying to the court from Sardinia, brings five hundred ducats to the royal treasury. During 1500 the disorganization of the tribunal cut off receipts but, in June, 1501, we hear of six hundred and fifty ducats given to the nuns of Santa Engracia of Saragossa. In 1502 there were found some pearls among the effects of Micer Rejadel, condemned for heresy, and these Ferdinand ordered to be sent to him, covered by insurance and, in due time, on July 17th, he acknowledged their receipt, fifty-five in number, weighing one ounce and one eighth and nine grains, after which they doubtless graced the toilet of Queen Isabella. At the same time he warned Juan López, the receiver, to be careful, for there were many complaints coming in as to his methods of procedure. Some months before this, in February, Ferdinand had complimented the inquisitor on the increased activity of his tribunal and had urged him to be especially watchful as to the confiscations, so that nothing might be lost through official negligence. To assist in the enlarged business thus expected, he promised to appoint a *juez de los bienes*, or judge of confiscations.[1]

Amid this eagerness to profit by the misery which he was creating it is pleasant to find instances of Ferdinand's kindliness in special cases. Thus, January 12, 1498, in the matter of the confiscated estate of Joan Andrés of Cagliari, he releases to Beatriz de Torrellas, sister and heir of Don Francisco Torrellas, because she is noble and poor and her brother had served him, a debt of $59\tfrac{2}{3}$ ducats due by Don Francisco to Andrés, which of course Beatriz would have had to pay. A few weeks later, on February 4th, he alleges clemency and charity as his motive for foregoing the confiscation of certain houses in Cagliari, belonging to Belenguer Oluja and his wife, both penanced for heresy. October 14th of the same year he takes pity on Na Thomasa, the wife of Joan Andrés, who had been penanced when her husband was condemned; as she is reduced to beggary and has an old mother to support and two young girls of her dead sister, he orders the receiver to give her fifty ducats in charity. This same estate of Joan Andrés gave occasion to another act of liberality, February 8, 1502, in releasing to the Hospital of San Antonio a *censal* of sixty libras principal, due by it to the estate.[2] Trivial as are these cases, they are worth recording, if only for the insight which they afford on the ramifications through which confiscation spread misery throughout the land.

The season of prosperous confiscations seems to have speedily passed away and the Sardinian tribunal proved to be a source of more trouble than profit. It is true that, in 1512, Ferdinand derived a momentary satisfaction from it, when he learned that a certain Miguel Sánchez del Romero, who had been condemned and burnt in effigy in Saragossa, had escaped to the island, where the lieutenant-general had taken him into favor and made him viguier of Sassari. He promptly ordered the inquisitor to seize him

---
[1] Archivo de Simancas, Inquisicion, Lib. 1; Lib. 2, fol. 1.
[2] Ibidem. Lib. 1.

secretly at once and send him, under charge of his alguazil, to Saragossa, by the first vessel and, at the same time, he notified the lieutenant-general that any impediment offered would be punished with deprivation of office, confiscation of property and excommunication by the inquisitor.[1] This exhibition of vigor, however, did not serve to put the tribunal on an efficient basis; Ferdinand was becoming thoroughly dissatisfied and, in August, 1514, he tried the expedient of appointing as inquisitor Juan de Loaysa, Bishop of Alghero, at the other end of the island from Cagliari, without removing the existing inquisitor, Canon Aragall, but rendering him subordinate to the bishop, whose place of residence was to be the seat of the tribunal. It is significant of the decadent condition of affairs that Bernat Ros, who had become the receiver of confiscations, sent in his resignation, on the plea of ill-health, and that Ferdinand refused to accept it unless he would find some one to take his place. Presumably the trouble was that the harvest of confiscations had been gathered and spent, without making investments that would give the tribunal an assured income, and that the financial prospects were gloomy. Ferdinand realized this and his zeal for the faith was insufficient to lead him to assume the responsibility. He made out a new schedule of salaries on an absurdly low basis, amounting, for the whole tribunal, to only three hundred and thirty libras, telling the receiver that, if the receipts were insufficient, the salaries must be cut down to a sueldo in the libra for he did not propose to be in any way responsible.[2] The institution was to be self-supporting, which was perhaps the best way to stimulate its activity but, if this

---

[1] Archivo de Simancas, Inquisicion, Lib. 3, fol. 184, 185.
[2] Ibidem, fol. 306, 307, 308. The salaries ordered were:

The Bishop of Alghero, inquisitor	100 libras.
Micer Pedro de Contreras, advocate	30 "
Luis de Torres, alguazil	30 "
An escribano for both secreto and secuestros	30 "
A portero and nuncio	10 "
Bernat Ros, receiver	100 "
Mossen Alonso de Ximeno, fiscal	30 "

It is observable that no salary is provided for Canon Aragall, the other inquisitor (see Appendix).

were the object, it was scarce successful for, in January, 1515, Ferdinand writes that the baile of the island, in whose house the Inquisition was quartered, is about to return home and wants the house; as there is so little business and so few prisoners, it can get accommodation in the Dominican convent, which will serve the purpose. Loaysa's term of office was short, for he was sent to Rome as agent of the Spanish Inquisition, and the Bishop of Ales and Torrealba was appointed in his place. In announcing this to him, August 28, 1515, Ferdinand significantly warns him not to meddle in matters disconnected with the Holy Office.[1]

Notwithstanding this palpable decadence, the Sardinian Inquisition continued to exist. It was in vain that, after Ferdinand's death in January, 1516, followed by that of Bishop Mercader, the Inquisitor-general of Aragon, the people rejoiced in the expectation of its abandonment, for the representatives of Charles V, by a circular letter of August 30th to the lieutenant-general and the municipal authorities, assured them that it would be continued and ordered them to take measures for its increased activity, while the inquisitor was informed that, although Sardinia was under the crown of Aragon, it was not to enjoy the provisions of the Concordias to which Ferdinand had been obliged to assent at home.[2] Possibly the tribunal may have become more active but it was not more productive for, in 1522, the home tribunals were assessed for its support, Majorca being called upon for two hundred ducats and Barcelona and Saragossa for a hundred each.[3] About 1540, however, it seems to have discovered some well-to-do heretics, for we hear of its having three thousand ducats to invest in censos.[4] This accession of wealth, however, does not argue that its financial management was better than was customary in the Inquisition for, in 1544, a commission was sent to the Bishop of Alghero, the inquisitor, clothing him with full power to require from the receiver, Peroche de Salazar, a detailed account of his expenditures and his receipts from fines, penances, commutations

---

[1] Archivo de Simancas, Inquisicion, Lib. 3, fol. 321, 348, 349, 351.
[2] Ibidem, fol. 366; Lib. 75, fol. 40.   [3] Ibidem, Lib. 940, fol. 36.
[4] Ibidem, Lib. 78, fol. 304.

and rehabilitations, and to investigate all frauds, collusions and concealments, the terms of the commission indicating that there had long been no check on embezzlements.[1]

Such prosperity as the tribunal enjoyed was spasmodic and it soon relapsed into indigence. In 1577 we find the tribunal of Murcia ordered to pay two hundred ducats, arrearages of salary due to Martínez Villar, who had been promoted, in 1569, from the inquisitorship to the archbishopric of Sassari[2] and, in 1588, Seville and Llerena were each called upon for 119,000 maravedís to repair an injustice committed by the Sardinia tribunal on María Malla—apparently it had spent the ill-gotten money and was unable to make restitution.[3] In hopes of relieving this poverty-stricken condition, Philip II, in 1580, appealed to Gregory XIII stating that it could not sustain itself and asking for assistance, which of course meant that canonries or other benefices should be assigned to its support.[4] This appeal was unavailing for, in 1618, the Suprema represented to Philip III the deplorable condition of the tribunal, unable to defray the salaries of a single inquisitor, a fiscal, two secretaries and the minor officials; it urged him to obtain from the pope the suppression of canonries and meanwhile to meet its necessities by the grant of some licences to export wheat and horses, which the pious monarch hastened to do.[5] This did not relieve the chronic poverty and, in 1658, Gregorio Cid, transferred to Cuenca after six years and a half of service in Sardinia, represented to the inquisitor-general that the tribunal ought to have two inquisitors and a fiscal and that it was difficult to find any one to serve as a notary, for the salary was small and expenses were great; besides, the climate was so unhealthy that the tribunal often had to be closed in consequence of the sickness of the officials.[6]

---

[1] Archivo de Simancas, Inquisicion, Sala 40, Lib. 4, fol. 136.
[2] Ibidem, Lib. 940, fol. 44.   [3] Ibidem, fol. 44, 45.
[4] Biblioteca nacional de Madrid, MSS., D, 118, fol. 179, n. 55.
[5] Archivo de Simancas, Inquisicion, Lib. 19, fol. 100.
[6] Biblioteca nacional, *loc. cit.*, fol. 124, n. 44.

The tribunal was evidently a superfluity, in so far as its legitimate functions were concerned, and we may assume that it was maintained not so much to deal with existing heretics as to prevent the island from becoming an asylum for heresy. This could have been accomplished by strengthening and stimulating the episcopal jurisdiction, but the Inquisition had monopolized this and was jealous of all interference. In 1538 Paul III addressed to the bishops and inquisitor of the island a brief in which he recapitulated the provisions of the Council of Vienne requiring them to coöperate and work in harmony; he urged the bishops to be so active in repressing heresy that they should need no outside aid but, if such should be necessary, the mandates of the council were to be observed. The bishops apparently were not remiss in taking advantage of this to revendicate the jurisdiction of which they had practically been stripped and the Inquisition resented the intrusion; Charles V must speedily have made the pope sensible of his mistake for, in 1540, he addressed to the judges of the island another brief revoking the previous one and reciting that the episcopal Ordinaries were interfering with the functions of the inquisitors and must be restrained from impeding or molesting them in any way by the liberal use of censures and the invocation, if necessary, of the secular arm. This was not allowed to be a dead letter for, when in 1555 Salvator, Archbishop of Sassari, under the brief of 1538, undertook to interfere with the tribunal, Paul IV, at the request of the emperor, promptly ordered the Bishops of Alghero, Suelli and Bosa to intervene and granted them the necessary faculties to coerce him.[1]

The tribunal had little to show as the result of the jurisdiction so eagerly monopolized. In fact, its chief industry consisted in multiplying its nominal officials and familiars—positions sought for in consequence of their privileges and immunities and doubtless liberally paid for. As early as 1552, Inquisitor-general Valdés rebuked Andreas Sanna, Bishop of Ales and inquisitor, for the inordinate number of familiars and commissioners who obtained

---

[1] Fontana, Documenti Vaticani, pp. 100, 110, 169.

appointments for the purpose of enjoying the exemptions, and he ordered them reduced to the absolute needs of the Holy Office.[1] This command was unheeded, the industry flourished and the principal activity of the tribunal lay in the resultant disputes with the secular courts. So recklessly did it distribute its favors that, on one occasion, an enumeration in three villages of Gallura disclosed no less than five hundred persons entitled to the privileges of the Holy Office. The consequences of this widely distributed impunity were of course deplorable on both the peace and the morals of the island.[2]

Under such circumstances quarrels with the secular authorities were perpetual and inevitable and were conducted on both sides with a violence attributable to the remoteness of the island and the little respect felt by either party for the other. A specimen of the spirit developed in these conflicts is afforded in a brief of Paul V, March 22, 1617, to Inquisitor-general Sandoval y Rojas, complaining bitterly of a recent outbreak in which the inquisitor excommunicated two officials and the royal court ordered him to absolve them. On his refusal, the court cited him to appear and sentenced him to exile—a decree which was published in Cagliari and elsewhere to sound of drum and trumpet. Then the governor intervened in support of the court, treating the inquisitor, if we may believe the *ex parte* statement, with unprecedented harshness. He broke into the Inquisition with an armed force and ordered the inquisitor either to grant the absolutions or to go on board of a vessel about to sail for Flanders and, on his refusal, he was so maltreated as to be left almost lifeless on the floor. On a second intrusion he was found in bed with a fever; he still refused to embark and was left under guard, but he succeeded in escaping by a rope from a window and took asylum in the Dominican church, whither the governor followed him and seized him while celebrating mass, with the sacrament in his hands. This time he was kept in secure custody until he gave bonds to sail, after which, in fear

---

[1] Archivo de Simancas, Inquisicion, Sala 40, Lib. 4, fol. 208.
[2] Manno, Storia di Sardegna, II, 189–90 (Milano, 1835).

of the voyage, he submitted and absolved the excommunicates. Paul summoned the governor and his accomplices to appear in Rome and undergo the penalty of their offences, but it may be doubted whether they were obliged to obey, for Spanish jealousy of the curia was quite as acute as indignation caused by invasion of inquisitorial inviolability and appeals to Rome were absolutely forbidden to all parties.[1] It was impossible to devise any permanent basis of pacification between the conflicting jurisdictions and, up to 1630, there were enumerated no less than seven Concordias, or agreements to settle their respective pretensions, in spite of which the disturbances continued as actively as ever.[2]

During the War of the Spanish Succession, Sardinia was captured by the Allies in 1708 and, in 1718, it passed into possession of the House of Savoy. As soon as the Spanish domination ceased the Inquisition disappeared and the bishops revendicated their jurisdiction over heresy, each one organizing an Inquisition of his own, not so much, we are told, with the object of eradicating heresy as to enable them to exempt retainers from public burdens, by appointing them to useless offices.[3] Jealousy of the Inquisition had been the traditional policy of the Dukes of Savoy[4] and, as the support of the secular arm was essential to the activity of the institution, we may presume that even these episcopal substitutes faded away in silence. In 1775 a survey of the ecclesiastical and religious condition of the island makes no allusion to prosecutions for heresy although it records a tradition that, towards the end of the seventeenth century, certain Quietists and followers of Molinos had found refuge in the mountain caves.[5]

---

[1] Bulario de la Orden de Santiago, Lib. III, fol. 594 (Archivo hist. nacional).
[2] Archivo de Simancas, Inquisicion, Lib. 13, fol. 28; Lib. 20, fol. 208; Lib. 21, fol. 240; Libros 56, 57, 918.
[3] La Martinière, Le Grand Dictionnaire Geographique et Critique, IX, 237 (Venise, 1737).
[4] Sclopis, Antica Legislazione del Piemonte, p. 484 (Torino, 1833).
[5] Le Bret, Magazin zum Gebrauch der Staaten- und Kirchengeschichte, 5 Theil, p. 547 (Frankfurt, 1776).

CHAPTER IV.

MILAN.

By the treaty of Cambrai, in 1529, Francis I abandoned the Milanese to Charles V and it thenceforth formed part of the Italian possessions of Spain. In the eleventh and twelfth centuries it had been the hot-bed of heresy and it was, in the thirteenth, one of the earliest scenes of inquisitorial activity. It was there that Pietro di Verona sealed his devotion with his blood and became the patron saint of the Holy Office. With the gradual extermination of heresy, the Inquisition there as elsewhere grew inert and, even after the new and threatening development of the Reformation, when Paul III, in 1536, was alarmed by reports of the proselyting zeal and success of Fra Battista da Crema, he had no tribunal on which he could rely to suppress the heretic. In default of this he commissioned Giovanni, Bishop of Modena, who was then in Milan, together with the Dominican Provincial, to preach against the heretics and to punish according to law those whom they might find guilty, at the same time significantly forbidding the inquisitor and the episcopal Ordinary to interfere.[1]

Even when the Inquisition was reorganized by Paul III, in 1542, it was for some time inefficiently administered and lacked the secular support requisite to its usefulness. This was especially felt in the Milanese which, from its neighborhood to Switzerland and the Waldensian Valleys, was peculiarly exposed to infection. The adventure which brought the Dominican Fra Michele Ghis-

---

[1] Fontana, Documenti Vaticani contro l'Eresia Luterana, p. 87.—Raynald. Annal., ann. 1536, n. 45.

The greed of the curia in grasping at all attainable rich preferment was a fruitful source of neglect and gave opportunity for heresy to flourish. Cardinal Ippolito d'Este, who was archbishop of Milan from 1520 to 1550, during the whole of that time never entered the city.—Gams, Series Episcoporum, p. 797.

lieri into notice and opened for him the path to the papacy, shows the danger and difficulty of the situation. Heresy was creeping through the Grisons, the Valtelline and the Val di Chiavenna, forming part of the diocese of Como when, in 1550, Fra Michele was sent thither as inquisitor to arrest its progress. He found a dozen bales of heretic books consigned to a merchant in Como, to be distributed throughout Italy where, in all the cities, there were said to be agencies for the purpose. He seized the books in the custom-house, whereupon the merchant complained to the episcopal vicar, who took possession of them. Ghislieri wrote to the Roman Holy Office which cited the vicar and the canons to appear; in place of obeying, they appealed to Ferrando Gonzaga, Governor of Milan, and raised such a storm among the people that Ghislieri's life was in danger. Gonzaga summoned him to come to him the next day; he started at night on foot and it was only the accident of his taking the longer road that led him to escape an ambush where he would have shared the fate of St. Peter Martyr. Gonzaga threatened him with imprisonment, but finally allowed him to depart, when he went to Rome and so impressed the cardinals of the Holy Office that he was marked for promotion. It was not much better in 1561 when, after being created Bishop of Mondovi, he visited his diocese and returned dissatisfied, for he had been unable to secure the support of the secular arm for the suppression of heresy.[1]

---

[1] Catena, Vita del Papa Pio Quinto, pp. 6–8, 17 (Roma, 1587).

Two somewhat similar cases show that the Venetian territory was equally infected and equally indifferent (Ibidem, pp. 9, 10). One of these likewise exhibits Ghislieri's implacable persistence. Vittore Soranzo, Bishop of Brescia, was over-curious in reading heretic books. Ghislieri was sent to make a secret investigation and, on his report, Soranzo was summoned to Rome and confined in the castle of Sant' Angelo for two years. Nothing was proved against him; he was released and returned to his see, where he continued to perform his functions until 1558. In 1557 Ghislieri was promoted to the cardinalate and, in 1558, Paul IV created for him the office of supreme inquisitor—an office which he was careful not to perpetuate after he became Pius V. He had not forgotten his failure to convict Soranzo. In April, 1558, Paul IV, in public consistory, deprived of his office the unfortunate bishop, who retired to Venice and speedily died of grief.—Catena, pp. 13, 15.—Ughelli, Italia Sacra, T. IV, pp. 695–701.

In Milan, we are told, there were many heretics, not only among the laity but among the clergy, both regular and secular, some of whom seem to have been publicly known and to have enjoyed the protection of the authorities. In 1554 Archbishop Arcimboldo and Inquisitor Castiglione united in issuing an Edict of Faith, comprehensive in its character, promising for spontaneous confession and denunciation of accomplices the reward of a fourth part of the fines and confiscations that might ensue. Denunciation of heretics was also commanded, with assurance of secrecy for the informer. This Edict is moreover of especial interest as comprehending what is perhaps the earliest organization of censorship, for it required the denunciation of all prohibited books and the presentation by booksellers of inventories of their stocks, with heavy penalties for omissions or for dealing in the prohibited wares.[1] This zeal seems not to have aroused the secular authorities to a fitting sense of their duties, for a brief of Paul IV, May 20, 1556, to Cardinal Mandrusio, lieutenant of Philip II, recites how that son of iniquity, the apostate Augustinian Claudio de Pralboino, had been condemned by the inquisitor and handed over to the secular arm; how, while awaiting his fate in the public prison, a forged order, purporting to be signed by the inquisitor, had been fabricated by some lawyers, on the strength of which he escaped and, in view of all this, the cardinal is urged to see to the punishment of those concerned in the fraud, to lend all aid and assistance to the inquisitor and to be watchful against the heresies creeping in from the Grisons. It was doubtless with the hope of securing greater efficiency that, in 1558, the Inquisition was taken from the friars of San Eustorgio and confided to those of Santa Maria delle Grazie and the Dominican Gianbattista da Cremona was appointed inquisitor-general.[2]

In 1560, Cardinal Carlo Borromeo, in his twenty-second year, was, through the nepotism of his uncle Pius IV, appointed to the great archiepiscopate of Milan, which extended over all Lombardy.

---

[1] Cesare Cantù, Eretici d'Italia, III, 34–7.
[2] Fontana, Documenti Vaticani, pp. 174, 184.

Sincere as was his piety, he accepted an office which he did not fill, for he remained in Rome until the severe virtue of Pius V, in 1566, required him to reside in his see. His ceaseless labors to reform his people, both clergy and laity, his self-devotion, his charity, earned for him the honors of canonization and the admiration even of Jansenists, but the zeal displayed in the enforcement of discipline upon unwilling ecclesiastics found equal expression in the persecution of heretics. He was, in fact, the incarnation of the Counter-Reformation, in combating heresy by force as well as by depriving it, as far as possible, of its *raison d'être*. In the early years of his archiepiscopate, during his attendance on the papal court, the business of the Inquisition in Milan was carried on in most slovenly fashion. This was not for lack of any sensitiveness as to heresy for, when in July, 1561, the Franciscan Guardian of Marignano, being delayed in making a sacramental confession, exclaimed, in a fit of impatience, that confession to God sufficed, he was arrested for such heretical speech and sent for trial to Milan, under a guard of soldiers. They arrived at night and carried their prisoner to the archiepiscopal palace, where they were told to take him to the prison, but misunderstanding, as was said, their instructions, they marched him to one of the city gates and let him go, whereupon he naturally disappeared.[1] In that same month of July, Carlo's uncle, Giulio Cesare Borromeo, writes to him that the inquisitor has allowed to escape a certain chief of the Lutherans, whom he had had infinite trouble to seize; he would give a thousand ducats that the culprit had not been brought to Milan for, as a relapsed, he was already convicted. He shrewdly suspects complicity, but there is no remedy and great scandal is to be expected.[2] Matters probably did not improve when, in the Spring of 1563, the inquisitor Fra Angelo da Cremona involved himself in a bitter quarrel with Andrea Ruberto, the archbishop's vicar, over a printer named Moscheno, whom he had cast into prison and whose wife and work-people he threatened

---

[1] MSS. of Ambrosian Library, Tom. 9, F. 45, Parte Inferiore, Lettera 92.
[2] Ibidem, Tom. 51, F. 101, P. Inf., Lett. 107.

to arrest. It was a conflict of jurisdiction, the vicar claiming concurrent action and the inquisitor that his cognizance of the case was exclusive. The vicar appealed to the archbishop and represented the inquisitor in no flattering terms. The inquisitor wrote to the Roman Congregation that the vicar was a man without fear of God and was interfering to protect a heretic who was disseminating his heresies throughout the land; he had refused the vicar's request to communicate the proceedings, as he desired to preserve the privileges of the Holy Office. Carlo counselled moderation to his vicar and, as the latter was replaced the next year by Nicolò Ormanetto, he was evidently worsted in the encounter.[1]

It is not surprising that this imperfect working of the machinery of persecution should prove wholly unsatisfactory to Philip II. Twenty years had elapsed since the reconstruction of the papal Inquisition, yet in the Lombard province where, if anywhere, it should be active and unsparing and where he had ordered his representatives to give it all favor and assistance, it was proving manifestly unequal to its duties. The natural remedy lay in taking it out of hands that proved incompetent and in remodelling it after the Spanish fashion and this he resolved to do. He applied to Pius IV for the necessary briefs, but met with some delay. This was inevitable. The Roman Congregation had already ample experience of the unyielding independence of the Spanish Suprema and it could only look with disfavor on having to surrender to its rival so important a portion of its own territory, with the inevitable result of an endless series of broils in which it would probably often be worsted. At that time however Philip's request was equivalent to a command; it was difficult to frame a plausible reason for refusal and Pius gave his assent.[2] It was Philip's intention that the Milanese Inquisition should be organized on an imposing scale and he had a commission as inquisitor issued to Gaspar Cervantes, an experienced Spanish inquisitor, then

---
[1] MSS. of Ambrosian Library, Tom. 53, F. 103, P. Inf., Lett. 42, 43, 44, 45, 77, 97.
[2] Muratori, Annali d'Italia, ann. 1563.—De Thou, Hist., Lib. xxxvi.

Archbishop of Messina and recently elected to the see of Salerno, but Pius delayed the confirmation for months. Cervantes was at the council of Trent when he received the commission; he replied that, as the decree requiring episcopal residence had been adopted, he could not be absent from his see more than three months at a time, but that, if the king considered his services at Milan essential, he would resign the archbishopric. Archbishop Calini, who reports this from Trent, August 23, 1563, adds that two ambassadors from Milan had just arrived there to plead with the papal legates against the introduction of the Spanish Inquisition in their city.[1]

In fact, as soon as the rumor spread of the impending change, there arose an agitation which speedily grew to serious proportions and threatened a repetition of the experiences of Naples. The people declared that they would not submit peaceably. The municipal Council of Sixty at once arranged to send envoys to Philip, to the pope, and to the legates at Trent. The latter reached there, as we have seen, on August 22d and their instructions doubtless were the same as those prepared for the envoys to the pope, representing that the existing Inquisition was thoroughly manned and active and had the earnest support of the secular authorities, while the mere prospect of introducing the Spanish institution had so alarmed the people that many were already leaving the city, threatening its depopulation if the project were persisted in and the transfer of its commerce and industries to rival communities. The envoys to the pope were also told to invoke the good offices of Cardinal Borromeo and to point out that, as he was responsible for the Inquisition and for the defence of the faith in Milan, the necessity for a new organization would infer neglect of duty on the part of his representatives.[2]

A Milanese agent of the Cardinal-Archbishop confirmed this in a letter to him of August 25th, describing the great popular perturbation, arising not from a consciousness of the existence of

---

[1] Lettere del Archivescovo Calini (Baluz. et Mansi Miscell., IV, 329).
[2] Salomoni, Memorie Storico-Diplomatiche, p. 159 (Milano, 1806).

heresy but from the disgrace of the imputation and the dread of the facilities offered for the gratification of malignity, coupled with the destruction of the families of the accused. It were to be wished that the virtue of the people was equal to their devotion, for the ardor of their faith was seen in the frequentation of the sacraments, the great demand for indulgences and the performance of other pious works.[1] Further news was sent to him, September 1st, by his confidential agent, Tullio Albonesi, who reported that the governor, the Duke of Sessa, has not wished the city to send envoys to Philip II, for he had already taken measures to prevent the introduction of the dreaded tribunal. Still it was desirable that the cardinal, on his part, should see that this turned out to be successful, for the popular mind was so inflamed that great disorder would be inevitable and it would be well for him to let it be clearly seen that he had opposed the project so as to disabuse those who asserted the contrary.[2] The municipal authorities trusted the governor and promptly abandoned their purpose of sending envoys to the king and to the pope. These had already been chosen and had arranged for the journey, incurring expenses which had to be defrayed. Accordingly, at a meeting of the Council of Sixty, held September 24th, it was resolved that, as the governor had stopped them and taken upon himself to deal with the king and the pope, the envoys should be repaid the fifteen hundred ducats expended in preparations, on their surrendering the articles purchased for the purpose, which were then to be publicly sold at sound of trumpet in the Plaza delli Mercanti, as was customary in such cases. Besides this there had already been spent a hundred and ten ducats in twice sending letters to the pope and cardinals.[3]

The mission to Trent had proved conspicuously serviceable, for the popular resistance was efficiently seconded by the bishops assembled there. Those of Lombardy dreaded to be exposed to

---

[1] MSS. of Ambrosian Library, Tom. 23, F. 73, P. Inf. Lett. 47.
[2] Ibidem, Tom. 53, F. 103, P. Inf. Lett. 176.
[3] Archivio civico-storico à S. Carpofaro, Armario A, Filza vii, n. 43.

the experience endured by their Spanish brethren, humiliated in their dioceses by the unrestrained autocracy of the inquisitors. Those of Naples argued that, if the Spanish Inquisition were once installed in Milan, it would surely be extended to Naples, with similar results to them. Those of the rest of Italy felt that it could not then be refused to the princes of the other states, while the papal legates recognized that in such case the authority of the Holy See would be seriously crippled, for the allegiance of the bishops would be transferred to their secular rulers who could control them through the inquisitors and, in the event of another general council, it would be the princes and not the pope that would predominate in its deliberations. Earnest representations to this effect were promptly sent to Rome and great was the relief in Trent when word came that the pope was of the same opinion and would not assent to the execution of the project.[1]

Even Philip's fixity of purpose gave way before these obstacles, but he delayed long before yielding. More than two months of anxiety followed, until at length, on November 8th, he wrote to the Duke of Sessa that his report as to the condition of Milan had been confirmed by letters furnished by the Bishop of Cuenca. His dextrous management in preventing the envoys from coming was praised and, in conformity with his judgement, the Bishop-elect of Salerno was ordered not to leave Trent and the efforts to obtain faculties for him from the pope were to be abandoned. The duke was ordered to tell the people, as plausibly as he could, that Philip had never had the intention of introducing any innovation in the procedure of the Inquisition but only to appoint an inquisitor of more authority and with larger revenue, who could do what was necessary for the service of God in that infected time and dangerous neighborhood. They could rely that there would be no change and the king was confident that so Catholic and zealous a community would do its duty as heretofore.[2] The

---

[1] Lettere del Nunzio Visconti, n. 67, 68 (Baluz. et Mansi, Miscell., III, 491-2).—Pallavicini, Hist. Concil. Trident., Lib. XXII, cap. viii, n. 2-4.

[2] Archivio civico-storico à S. Carpofaro, Armario A, Filza VII, n. 40 (see Appendix).

whole letter shows how unwillingly he withdrew from a position that had become untenable and how hard he strove to obtain a capitulation with the honors of war.

Philip's failure left the Milanese Inquisition in its unsatisfactory condition. There was one burning question especially which refused to be settled. Political considerations of the greatest moment required the maintenance of friendly relations with the Catholic Cantons of Switzerland, but the Catholic Cantons were deeply infected with heresy. Moreover the financial interests of the Milanese called for free commercial intercourse with their northern neighbors while, at the same time, the rules of the Inquisition forbade the residence of heretics and dealings with them. It was impossible to reconcile the irreconcileable—to erect a Chinese wall between Lombardy and Switzerland, as the Roman Holy Office desired, and at the same time to retain the friendship of the Swiss and maintain contentment among the Lombards. Intolerance had to yield to politics and commerce, but not without perpetual protest. Tullio Albonesi writes, April 12, 1564, to Cardinal Borromeo that he had presented to the Duke of Sessa the letter asking him to cease employing those heretic Grisons, the Capitano Hercole Salice and his sons and had remonstrated with him in accordance with the information received from the inquisitor. The duke was to depart for Spain the next day, but took time to explain that the pope was misinformed as to his wishing to bring heretics to reside in the Milanese; he had arranged to pay them in their own country for the king's service and had given them greater privileges of trade than were accorded to the Grisons in general under the capitulations and, if this did not please his Holiness, he must treat with the king about it. Albonesi adds that he reported this to the inquisitor who concluded that the only way to stop the trade of these heretics with the Milanese was for the pope to appeal to Philip.[1] The next year we find the Bishop of Brescia, in a letter to Borromeo, alluding to two persons

---

[1] MSS. of Ambrosian Library, Tom. 54, F. 104, P. Inf. Lett. 48.

in his diocese suspected of heresy because they caused scandal by dealing with the Grisons.[1]

How delicate were these international relations and how little the Inquisition was disposed to respect them are manifest in an occurrence some years later, after Cardinal Borromeo had come to reside in his see. In visiting some Swiss districts of his province he promulgated some regulations displeasing to the people, who sent an ambassador to complain to the Governor of Milan. He took lodgings with a merchant and, as soon as the inquisitor heard of his arrival, he arrested and threw him in prison. This arrogant violation of the law of nations was a peculiarly dangerous blunder and, as soon as news of it reached the governor he released the envoy from prison and made him a fitting apology, but word had already been carried to the Swiss, who made prompt arrangements to seize the cardinal. Borromeo escaped by a few hours, and his obnoxious regulations were never obeyed.[2] How completely, in his eyes, all material interests were to be disregarded, in comparison with the danger of infection from heresy, is to be seen in a pastoral letter addressed, in 1580, to all parish priests—a letter which is moreover instructive as to the extent to which the ecclesiastical jurisdiction trespassed on the secular. He recites the danger to the faith arising from those who, under pretext of business or other pretence, visit heretical lands, where they may be perverted, and on their return spread the infection, wherefore he orders that no one shall make such journeys or visits without first obtaining a licence from him or from his vicar-general or from the inquisitor. All who disobey this are to be prosecuted by the Inquisition as suspect of heresy and are to be penanced at discretion. This letter is to be read from the altar on three feast-days and subsequently several times a year, while the priests are further ordered to investigate and report within a month all who are absent, the cause of their going and the length of their

---

[1] MSS. of Ambrosian Library, Tom. 56, F. 106, P. Inf. Lett. 211.
[2] Beccatini, Istoria dell' Inquisizione, p. 178.

stay.¹ The question was one which refused to be settled and was the subject of repeated decrees by the Roman Congregation, which serve to explain why the nations subjected to the Inquisition fell behind their more liberal rivals in the race for prosperity.²

With the failure to introduce the Spanish Inquisition, Cardinal Borromeo seems to have felt increased responsibility for the suppression of heresy, prompting him to efforts to render the Milanese tribunal more efficient. In his correspondence of 1564 and 1565, we find him paying the salary of the inquisitor, enlarging the archiepiscopal prison with the proceeds of confiscations and discussing the transfer of the Inquisition from the monastery of le Grazie to the archiepiscopal palace, where it would be more conveniently and honorably established. He is also recognized as its head, for Fra Felice da Colorno, the inquisitor of Como, asks his instructions about a box of books addressed to the impious Vergerio, which he has found among those hidden by the Rev. Don Hippolito Chizzuola.³ In fact, the Inquisition of the period seems to be a curious combination of the inquisitorial and episcopal jurisdictions. As early as 1549 we find the Roman Congregation giving to Antonio Bishop of Trieste a commission as its commissioner as though the ordinary jurisdiction were insufficient.⁴ In 1564 Gasparo Bishop of Asti boasts to Cardinal Borromeo of his earnest labors in keeping his diocese free of heresy, although the neighboring ones were infected; in 1565 Costaciario Bishop of Acqui excuses himself for delay in obeying the summons to the first provincial council (October 15th) because he was engaged on an important trial of a heretic whom he had imprisoned; in November of the same year Bollani Bishop of Brescia writes in considerable dread of the Signory of Venice because he had forced the podestà to abjure for some impudent and reckless speeches; he throws the responsibility on the cardinal and begs that his letter may be

---

¹ Acta Eccles. Mediolanens., I, 471 (Mediolani, 1843).
² MSS. of Ambrosian Library, H. S. VI, 29.—See Appendix.
³ Ibidem, Tom. 54, Vol. 68, F, 104, P. Inf. Lett. 63, 147, 163; Tom. 55, F, 105, Lett. 250.
⁴ Ibidem, C. 185, P. Inf. Carta 14.

burnt. A few days later he seems much relieved, for the podestà has apologized and he describes a curious assembly "la solita nostra congrega della Santa Inquisizione," which he was accustomed to hold weekly in his palace, consisting of the inquisitor, the podestà, the rettori (or Venetian governors) and some others, when the inquisitor rejoiced them by reporting that there were but two heretics in the city, one of whom was *mentecaptus*.[1]

Evidently Cardinal Borromeo was stimulating his suffragans to increased zeal and activity and when, in 1566, he came to reside in Milan, his ardor for the extermination of heresy grew apace, whether through his own convictions or through the impetuous urgency of the new Inquisitor-Pope, St. Pius V, whose aim was to subject the whole Christian world to the Holy Office.[2] There is a curious memorandum drawn up by Borromeo, detailing the

---

[1] MSS. of Ambrosian Library, Tom. 44, F, 94, P. Inf. Lett. 72; Tom. 56, F, 106, Lett. 51, 206, 211.

Brescia formed part of the Venitian territory, in which these weekly conferences of the secular and inquisitorial powers were prescribed. When the Inquisition was founded in the thirteenth century, Venice refused it admission, but in 1249 it organized a kind of secular tribunal against heresy, known as the *tre Savi dell' eresia* or *Assistenti*. At length, in 1289 it admitted an inquisitor, but adjoined to him the Assistenti, who were not to partake in the judgements but to see that he did not overstep his proper functions and to lend when necessary the aid of the secular arm. As the mainland territory of the Republic increased and the reorganized papal Inquisition appointed its delegates in the cities, the Signoria in 1548 provided that the *rettori* or other magistrates in each place should coöperate with the inquisitor and bishop as *assistenti*. Rome took umbrage at this and a prolonged negotiation ensued, which ended with the *assistenti* being accepted, with the understanding that they were to have a consultative but not a decisive vote. This gave the Signoria power to curb excesses and to save the people from being harassed with inquisitorial prosecutions for trifling cases of sorcery, bigamy, etc., which were so bitterly complained of elsewhere. If we may believe Páramo, when Philip failed to inflict the Spanish Inquisition on Milan, Pius V sought to introduce one of the same kind in Venice, but the proposition produced so alarming a popular excitement that the Signoria prevailed upon him to abandon the attempt, promising at the same time to exercise the greatest vigilance in the suppression of heresy.—Vettor Sandi, Principj di Storia Civile della Repubblica di Venezia, Lib. x, cap. iii, art. 3 (Venizia, 1756).—Albizzi, Riposta all' Historia della Sacra Inquisitione del R. P. Paolo Servita, pp. 40–58 (Ed. II, *s. l. e. d.*).— Páramo de Orig. Off. S. Inquis., p. 266.—Natalis Comitis Historiar., Lib. XIV, ann. 1564.

[2] See Appendix for a decree of Pius V, issued within a few months of his accession.

matters to be enquired into in episcopal visitations, which shows that the persecution of heresy, the efficiency of the Inquisition, the avoidance of communication with heretics and the observances of the faith were regarded by him as the points of first importance.[1] In 1568 he was suddenly summoned to Mantua as the most fitting person to put the Inquisition there into working order. The duke, Guillelmo Gonzaga, was liberally inclined and had long given trouble to the Holy Office. Pius V, soon after his accession, in 1566, had been moved to pious wrath by his refusal to send to Rome two heretics for trial. A threat to bring him to terms by open war failed and Pius would have proceeded to extremities, had he not been dissuaded by the other Italian princes.[2] He contented himself with sending orders to the inquisitor there, Fra Ambrogio Aldegato, to clear the city of heretics, who were numerous, but the frate was old; he shrank from the struggle and, pleading age and infirmity, he asked to be relieved. Pius gave him the bishopric of Casale and extended over Mantua the jurisdiction of Fra Camillo Campeggio, styled Inquisitor-general of Ferrara, who had doubtless been selected as a man of vigor for that post, in view of the encouragement to the reform given not long before by Renée de France, the Duchess of Ferrara. The new inquisitor was not favorably regarded by Gonzaga, who interfered with the public penances and abjurations imposed by him, who was slack in obeying his commands to make arrests and who even allowed suspected heretics to escape. Campeggio was more earnest than respectful in his remonstrances and mutual ill-will increased until, on Christmas night of 1567, some sons of Belial slew two Dominicans who had doubtless been overzealous in aiding the inquisitor.

---

[1] See Appendix.
[2] Bzovii Annales, ann. 1566, n. 88. This may very probably have been the occasion of the decree just referred to.

Yet the duke, in 1567, offered no opposition when Pius V ordered him to send to Rome for trial the canon Ceruti, who, in 1569, was condemned to the galleys for life. He could not have been a Protestant for his chief heresy was the denial of immortality. The intercession of the duke however, in 1572, procured his liberation and permission to keep his house in Mantua as a prison.—Bertolotti, Martiri del Libero Pensiero, pp. 43-5 (Roma, 1891).

No active efforts were made to detect the assassins; some higher authority was evidently needed and Pius V, by a brief of February 12, 1568, ordered Cardinal Borromeo to go there with all speed, to bring the duke to obedience and to sit with the inquisitor in the trial of cases. Borromeo lost no time in obeying the mandate and, on his arrival he gave the duke to understand that the pope's determination was unalterable; he would rather see all Dominicans cut to pieces, and all Dominican convents burnt, than that heresy should go unpunished in Mantua. It required resolute action for there were heretics high-placed in both Church and State; a company of sbirri had to be borrowed from Bologna, but Borromeo succeeded in breaking down all opposition. Already, by May 16th, he was able to report that his mission was accomplished and that his presence was no longer needed. On May 21st he writes that the duke has come humbly to the inquisitor to beg for release from prison and sanbenito of two penitents, which was granted, seeing that they had already been compelled to abjure publicly. As the pope had rewarded Campeggio with the bishopric of Sutri and Nepi, the duke had at once begged that the place might be filled by Fra Angelo, the vicar of the Inquisition, to all of which the cardinal points triumphantly as showing how the ducal temper had changed. Possibly some explanation of this may be sought in a request from the duke that the confiscations should be made over to him, which Borromeo was willing to meet in so far as to suggest that he be allowed one half. Another reason may perhaps be discerned in his apprehension of an attack by the Duke of Savoy, for, on June 4th, Borromeo writes that he had asked for the support of the papacy in such contingency. Be this as it may, Borromeo was able in June to return to Milan, leaving the Inquisition firmly established in Mantua.[1]

---

[1] MSS. of Ambrosian Library, Tom. 5, F, 41, and F, 177, P. Inf.

Catena relates (Vita di Pio V, p. 157) that an heretical preacher of Morbegno in the Valtelline, named Francesco Cellaria was accustomed to visit Mantua secretly as a missionary, where he had relations with some of the nobles. To put an end to this, Pius sent in disguise the Dominican Piero Angelo Casannova to the Valtelline with instructions for his capture. With a band of eight men

It is an indication of his predominating zeal for the extirpation of heresy that when, on May 16th, he begged permission to return to Milan, the reason he assigned was that he was wanted there for the long-protracted trial of Nicholas Cid. This was a case which had for years been occupying the Milanese Inquisition. The accused was treasurer-general of the Spanish forces, in whose favor Cesare Gonzaga wrote, November 2, 1565, to the cardinal, repeating what he had frequently stated before, that it was a persecution arising from malignity.[1] This ardor for the purity of the faith did not diminish with time. In his second provincial council, held in 1569, the first decree requires the bishops to promulgate an edict to be read in all the parish churches, on the first Sundays in Lent and Advent, calling upon all persons, under pain of excommunication, to denounce within ten days, to the bishop or inquisitor, any case of heresy or of reading forbidden books that may come to their knowledge. His own formula for this, in 1572, is very stringent, insisting on the denunciation of every heretic act or suspicious word.[2]

It is evident that thus far the episcopal jurisdiction over heresy was not superseded by the inquisitorial, but that both worked in harmony and, between the two, it may be questioned whether the Milanese gained much in escaping the Spanish Inquisition. As the Roman organization perfected itself throughout Northern Italy, Milan naturally was a centre of activity, as a sort of bulwark against the influence of Switzerland. The troubles arising from the inevitable commercial intercourse with the heretics, and the capitulations which provided for the residence of traders on each

---

Casannova kidnapped him at Bocca d'Adda, as he was returning from Coire to Morbegno, hurried him to Piacenza whence Duke Ottavio Farnese transmitted him to Rome. There he was condemned to be burnt alive but at the last moment he weakened and recanted, so that he was strangled before burning. He had been forced to name his accomplices in Mantua and other cities, and immediate steps were taken for securing them. The Grisons complained loudly of this invasion of their territory, but the Duke of Alburquerque, then Governor of Milan (1564–71), replied that the papal jurisdiction over heresy was supreme in all lands.

[1] MSS. of Ambrosian Library, Tom. 56, F, 106, P. Inf. Lett. 140.
[2] Acta Eccles. Mediolanens. I, 67, 469.

side, continued to be a source of perpetual anxiety and vigilance. Then the transit of merchandise had to be watched; everything destined for Milan had to be opened and searched for heretic literature, but packages in transmission were allowed to pass through, relying upon examination at the points of destination. Correspondence by mail was also the subject of much solicitude. In 1588 the Congregation of the Inquisition was excited by the news that the heretic Cantons proposed to establish in the Valtelline a school for instruction in their doctrines, whereupon it wrote urgent letters and threatened to cut off all intercourse if the project was not abandoned. In the same year it wrote to the Milanese inquisitor favoring warmly the plan of rewarding those who would capture and deliver to the tribunal heretic preachers and promising to pay for "this holy and pious work" according to the importance of the victims kidnapped, but it uttered a warning that this had better not be attempted in the Grisons, for fear of reprisals that would ruin the Catholic churches and monasteries there. In 1593 the tribunal was reminded that, while the capitulations permitted the residence of heretic merchants from the Grisons and Switzerland, the privilege was confined to them and all others must be prosecuted and punished. As for Milanese who desire to go to Switzerland, returning home several times a year, they are to be watched, and licences are not to be given to reside in places where they cannot have access to Catholic priests. Then, in 1597, there was fresh excitement over an edict of the Three Leagues, prohibiting the residence in the Valtelline of foreign priests and friars. In 1599 the zeal of the Milanese tribunal seems to have provoked reclamations on the part of the Swiss, for the inquisitor was ordered not to molest the heretic merchants but to observe the capitulations strictly. This was doubtless part of an outburst of persecution for, in 1600, orders were given to seize and retain the children of the heretics who had fled to Switzerland.[1]

---

[1] Decreta Sac. Congr. Sti. Officii, pp. 217–20 (R. Archivio di Stato in Roma, Fondo Camerale, Congr. del S. Offizio, Vol. 3).

Under Venetian rule when, in 1579, the inquisitor at Treviso was about to publish an edict prohibiting departure for heretic lands without his licence, the

It is evident that the Milanese tribunal had ample work in protecting the faith from hostile invasion. Its activity continued under the Spanish Hapsburgs until, in 1707, the genius of Prince Eugene won Lombardy for Austria, as an incident in the War of the Spanish Succession. It still existed on sufferance until the eighteenth century was well advanced. In 1771 Maria Theresa foreshadowed the end by ordering that no future vacancies should be filled and by suppressing the affiliated Order of the Crocesignati, whose property was assigned to the support of orphanages. This was followed by a decree of March 9, 1775, declaring that the existence of such an independent jurisdiction was incompatible with the supremacy and good order of the State, wherefore it was abolished and, as the inquisitors and their vicars should die, their salaries should be applied to the orphanages.[1] Thus passed away the oldest surviving Inquisition, which may be said to date from 1232, when we find Fra Alberico commissioned as Inquisitor of Lombardy.

podestà and captain of the city prevented it, for which they were praised by the Signoria and similarly the rettore of Bergamo was rebuked for permitting it.—Cecchetti, La Republica di Venezia e la Corte di Roma, I, 23 (Venezia, 1874).

Fra Paolo tells us that in 1595 Clement VII issued a decree forbidding any Italian to visit a place where there was not a Catholic church and pastor, without a licence from the inquisitors. The result of this was that traders returning from heretic lands were watched, reports were sent to Rome and they were publicly cited to appear there. The transalpine countries took offence at this and then the public citations were made at the residence of the parties. Venice sought to diminish the evil effect of this on commerce by forbidding public citations in such cases.—Sarpi, Historia dell' Inquisizione, p. 77 (Serravalle, 1638).

Simply trading with heretics, sending to or receiving from them merchandise, money or letters constituted fautorship of heresy and subjected the trader to the jurisdiction of the Inquisition.—Masini, Sacro Arsenale overo Prattica dell' Officio della S. Inquisizione, Roma, 1639, p. 16.

[1] MSS. of Ambrosian Library, H. S. VI, 29.—Le Bret, Magazin zum Gebrauch der Staaten- und Kirchengeschichte, Sechste Theil, 101 (Frankfurt, 1777).

During the 18th century the powers of the Inquisition were greatly limited by the civil authorities. In Tuscany we learn, in 1746, that in Florence and Siena no arrest or imprisonment could be made by it without the assent of the Government.—Consulta fatta dalla Real Camera di S. Chiara, in Napoli (MS. *penes me*).

CHAPTER V.

THE CANARIES.[1]

IN 1402 Jean de Bethencourt, an adventurer from Normandy, discovered or rediscovered the Canaries and made himself master of the islands of Lanzarote, Fuerteventura, Gomera and Hierro. After various changes of ownership, they fell to the crown of Castile, and Isabella undertook the conquest of the remainder of the group, the Grand Canary, Tenerife and la Palma. The sturdy resistance of the native Guanches rendered the enterprise an arduous one, consuming eighteen years, and it was not until 1496 that it was finally accomplished. That Columbus, on his first voyage, took his departure from Gomera indicates the importance assumed by the Canaries in the development of trade with the New World and this, conjoined with their productiveness, as they became settled and cultivated, rendered them a centre of commerce frequented by the ships of all maritime nations, as well as an object of buccaneering raids, in an age when trade and piracy were sometimes indistinguishable. Their proximity to Morocco and the Guinea coast moreover exposed them to attacks from the Moors and gave them an opportunity of accumulating Moorish and negro slaves, whom the piety of the age sought to

---

[1] The tribunal of the Canaries was reckoned among those of Castile and most of the new material in my possession concerning it has been embodied in the "History of the Inquisition of Spain." Its insular position, however, and the consequent attraction of foreign merchants and sea-faring men, rendered its career somewhat peculiar, and it has seemed worth while to devote a chapter to it, based on two works—

Historia de la Inquisicion en las Islas Canarias, por Agustin Millares, 4 vols., Las Palmas de Gran-Canaria, 1874.

Catalogue of a Collection of Original Manuscripts formerly belonging to the Holy Office of the Inquisition in the Canary Islands and now in the possession of the Marquis of Bute. By W. De Gray Birch, LL.D., 2 vols., Edinburgh and London, 1903.

convert into Christians by the water of baptism. In various ways, therefore, there came to be abundant material for inquisitorial activity, although the Judaizing New Christians, who furnished the Spanish tribunals with their principal business, appear to have been singularly few.

There was no haste in extending the Spanish Inquisition to the Canaries. As early as 1406 a bishopric had been founded in Lanzarote, subsequently transferred to Las Palmas in the Grand Canary, which was regarded as the capital of the group. If the successive bishops, who, with more or less regularity, filled the see, exercised their episcopal jurisdiction over heresy, their labors have left no trace. It is not until the time of Diego de Muros, who was consecrated in 1496, that we have any evidence of such action. That stirring prelate, who held a diocesan synod in 1497, announced, April 25, 1499, that, as inquisitor by his ordinary authority, he would have inquest made in some of the islands into heresy and Judaism and other crimes against the faith. What was the result, we have no means of knowing except a confession made, on May 22d, by Isabel Ramírez, of having taught a superstitious prayer which was regarded as sorcery. It is probable that Bishop Muros was warned that he was invading the jurisdiction of the Holy Office, for he sent the papers in the case to the tribunal of Seville.[1] It is noteworthy that, after the establishment of the Canary tribunal, the bishops and their provisors long continued to use the title of "ordinary" inquisitor, to which no exception seems to have been taken, although elsewhere it was contested and forbidden. The latest occasion of its employment with which I have met occurs in 1672.[2]

It was not until 1505 that the Suprema bethought itself of establishing a tribunal in the Canaries, when Inquisitor-general Deza appointed as inquisitor Bartolomé López Tribaldos. The first entry in his register is dated Tuesday, October 28, 1505, and the earliest record that we have of his activity is in 1507, when there were two reconciliations, one of Juan de Ler, a Portuguese,

---

[1] Birch, I, 5, 7–8.   [2] Millares, I, 95–6.—Birch, I, 160–7, 173.

for Judaism, and the other of Ana Rodríguez, a native, for sorceries, whose sanbenitos were duly hung in the cathedral.[1] What were the exact powers conferred on Tribaldos we have no means of knowing, but they must have been exceedingly limited, and for a long time the tribunal continued to be in close dependence on that of Seville. When, about 1520, Martin Ximenes, fiscal of the Seville tribunal, came to Las Palmas in the combined capacity of precentor of the Cathedral, provisor and inquisitor, he left as his deputy fiscal in Seville Doctor Fernando de Zamora, thus not abandoning that office. Even as late as 1548 we chance to have the record of a *consulta de fe* held by the Seville tribunal, January 13th, to decide on certain informations and cases sent to it by the Canary inquisitor Padilla. In the affair of Juan Alonso, a Morisco, it was ordered that he should be arrested and tried, when the result was to be reported for action. In that of Juan Fernández, he was to be summoned and examined as to his blasphemy and then be penanced at the discretion of Padilla and the Ordinary. Leonor de Lera was to be arrested and tried and the result be submitted. The case of Diego Martínez had apparently been concluded under Padilla, for the Seville consulta sentenced him to twelve years of galley service.[2] Thus every act, from the preliminary arrest to the final decision, was regulated from Seville. To render the position still more anomalous we hear of an *inquisidor ordinario*, Alonso Vivas, Prior of the cathedral, commissioned, in October, 1523, to try cases of faith throughout the Grand Canary as he had already done in Telde and Agüimes.[3]

Irregular and imperfect as may have been the organization of the tribunal, it yet managed to accomplish some convictions. In 1510 there was held an auto de fe in which there were three reconciliations for Judaism and one, of a Moorish slave, for reincidence in Mahometan error, while a fifth culprit was penanced for Judaism.[4] Then in 1513 occurred the first relaxation, that of Alonso Fátima, a native Morisco, who had fled to Barbary. This was

---

[1] Birch, I, 6.—Millares, I, 71. [2] Birch, I, 1, 67.
[3] Millares, I, 79. [4] Millares, I, 75.

always deemed sufficient evidence of relapse to former errors, and he was duly burned in effigy. It was probably also to 1516 that may be attributed the first relaxation in person—that of Juan de Xeres of Seville, for Judaism. It shows that the tribunal was indifferently equipped that, when he was sentenced to torture, the physician whose presence was obligatory on such occasions, Doctor Juan Meneses de Gallegas, was required personally to administer it. It was exceedingly severe, extending to eleven jars of water; the accused was unable to endure it; he confessed his faith, was sentenced to relaxation as a relapsed and for fictitious confession, and was executed on Wednesday, June 4th.[1]

Martin Ximenes seems to have performed his duties with commendable energy. He commenced by making an alphabetical register of all the parties denounced under his predecessor, comprising 139 individuals, besides various groups, such as "the Confesos and Moriscos of Lanzarote," "other Confesos, their kindred," "certain persons of Hierro" etc., which indicate how slovenly had been the procedure.[2] He made a visitation of Tenerife and la Palma, from which he returned with ample store of fresh denunciations.[3] May 29, 1524, all the dignitaries, civil and ecclesiastical, and all the people were assembled in the church of Santa Ana, where an edict was read commanding them to render aid and favor to the Inquisition, and an oath to that effect was administered. There was also an Edict of Grace, promising relief from confiscation to all who would come forward and confess as to themselves and others; also an Edict of Faith requiring denunciation of errors and specifying the various kinds of blasphemies and sorceries and the distinctive Jewish and Moorish rites; and finally an edict reciting that the Conversos were emigrating and forbidding their leaving the islands and all ship-masters from carrying away suspected persons without licence from him, under the penalties of fautorship and of forfeiting their vessels.[4]

---

[1] Birch, I, 91, 92–4. In the record concerning Juan de Xeres, the year is omitted, but as Wednesday fell on June 4 in 1511, 1516, 1533 and 1539, the probable date is 1516
[2] Birch, I, 1–5.   [3] Millares, I, 82.   [4] Birch, I, 15–33.

The terror inspired by the activity of Ximenes may be estimated from a single instance. On May 21st, Ynes de Tarifa came before him to confess that when, a couple of months before, she had heard of the burning in Seville of her son-in-law Alonso Hernández and of his brother Francisco, she recalled that after meals Alonso used to read to Francisco out of a book in an unknown tongue and, if she had erred in not denouncing this to the Seville tribunal, she begged to be treated mercifully.[1] The publication of the edicts throughout the islands brought in an abundant store of denunciations, the record for eight months, from September 13, 1524, to May 15, 1526, amounting to 167. They were nearly all of petty sorceries by women, in sickness or love affairs, but with an occasional blasphemy or suspicion of Judaism, and persons of station were not exempted, for the list comprises the Adelantado Don Pedro de Lugo and his wife Elvira Díaz, the Dean Juan de Alarcon, the Prior Alonso Bivas and others of position. The adelantado, in fact, was dead, but the accusation against his memory is sufficiently significant of the prevailing temper to be worth relating. The Bachiller Diego de Funes came forward, by command of his confessor, to state that when Diego de San Martin was holding for ransom a *Judío de señal* (one obliged to wear a distinctive mark) who had been caught on his way to Portugal, the captive was starving to death because he could not eat meat slaughtered by Christians: de Lugo charitably gave him a sheep to kill according to his rites and even himself ate some of the mutton. These petty cases kept Ximenes busy and he despatched them with promptness; the punishments as a rule were not severe—in one or two cases scourging or vergüenza, but mostly small fines, exile and occasionally spiritual penances.[2]

There were, however, cases in which the faith demanded more exemplary vindication. The island of Grand Canary, from 1523 to 1532, was ravaged with pestilence creating great misery. Among other causes of divine wrath the people included the secret apostasy of the Portuguese New Christians and of the Moorish

[1] Birch, I, 33.   [2] Ibidem, 34-64.

slaves, and demanded severe measures for its repression. It may have been with an idea of placating God that Ximenes, on February 24, 1526, celebrated the first *auto publico general de fe* with great solemnity, in which all the nobles of the island assisted as familiars. The occasion was impressive, for there were seven Judaizers relaxed in person and burnt, there were ten reconciliations, of which five were of Moorish baptized slaves, four were for Judaism and one of a Genoese heretic, in addition to which there were two blasphemers penanced.[1]

This is the last that we hear of Ximenes, whose place, in 1527, was filled by Luis de Padilla, treasurer of the cathedral. For awhile he imitated his predecessor's activity and, on June 4, 1530, another oblation was offered to God, in an auto celebrated with the same ostentation as the previous one. This time there were no relaxations in person, but there were six effigies burnt of as many Moorish slaves, who had escaped and were drowned in their infidelity while on their way to Africa and liberty. There were also the effigy and bones of Juan de Tarifa, the husband of the Ynes de Tarifa who had denounced herself in 1524; he was of Converso descent and had committed suicide in prison, which was equivalent to self-condemnation. There were three reconciliations, of which two were for Judaism and one for Islam and five penitents for minor offences.[2] The next auto was held on May 23, 1534, in which there were two relaxations of effigies for Judaism and twenty-five reconciliations—twenty-four of Moriscos and one of a Judaizer. One of the relaxations carries with it a warning, for it was of Costanza Garza, who had died in 1533 during her trial. When too late her innocence was discovered and the Suprema humanely rehabilitated her memory and her children, and ordered the restoration of her confiscated estate.[3]

Whether this aggressive vindication of the faith put an end to heresy or whether Padilla had exhausted his energies, it would be impossible now to say, but after this auto the tribunal sank

---

[1] Millares, I, 87–92.   [2] Ibidem, 96–100.   [3] Ibidem, 103–7.—Birch, I, 90.

into lethargy so complete that on February 8, 1538, the chapter notified Padilla and the secretary, Canon Alonso de San Juan, that the revenues of their prebends were stopped, for they did not assist in the choir and it was notorious that the Holy Office had nothing to do.[1] Possibly this may have stimulated action, but we have seen that in 1548 the tribunal was merely collecting evidence and obeying the instructions of the Seville Inquisition. Under this there was an accumulation of culprits for an auto held in 1557, where there were seventeen effigies burnt of fugitives— all Moriscos, except a Fleming, Julian Cornelis Vandyk. There were also four Moriscos reconciled, one of them, curiously enough, for so-called Calvinism.[2] This seems to have exhausted whatever remains of energy Padilla possessed for we hear of no further action by him, except a quarrel with the royal Audiencia in 1562, but nevertheless the tribunal shared in the suppression of prebends, and a papal brief assigning one to it was presented to the chapter, August 27, 1563, thus adding another efficient cause of dissension between them.[3] Soon after this the tribunal virtually ceased to exist. In 1565 there was a curious case, of which more hereafter, of John Sanders, an English sailor. It was carried on wholly by the episcopal provisor, during the absence of the bishop Diego Deza. There were arrest, sequestration and the collection of voluminous testimony, which was carefully sealed and despatched to Bishop Deza, to be handed to the Seville tribunal. Throughout it all, there is no trace of participation by the local Inquisition, which, in the consuming jealousy of episcopal encroachments, could not possibly have been the case had there been a tribunal in the Canaries.[4]

The policy followed thus far had evidently proved a failure, and Inquisitor-general Espinosa resolved to reorganize the tribunal and render it independent of Seville. The fiscal of Toledo, Diego Ortiz de Fúnez, was selected and was sent out as a full inquisitor, with the unusual powers of selecting and removing his

---

[1] Millares, I, 109-10.   [2] Ibidem, I, 115-18
[3] Ibidem, I, 125.   [4] Birch, II, 1018-26.

subordinates, while subjected only to the requirement of reporting his acts to the Suprema. The royal letters commanding obedience to him are dated October 10, 1567, and he left Madrid in the Spring of 1568, landing at Las Isletas on April 17th. Four days later he started for Las Palmas, accompanied in procession by all the dignitaries, secular and ecclesiastical, of the island. On May 1st all the population was summoned, under pain of fine and excommunication, to assemble the next day in the cathedral, at the reading of the Edict of Faith and to take the oath to obey and favor the Holy Office, all of which was performed with due solemnity.[1]

Fúnez carried instructions to appoint twenty familiars and no more in Las Palmas, and such as were found necessary in the other cities and islands. This was his first care, and he soon had a formidable body, recruited from the old nobility, to support his authority. Thus far the Inquisition had had no special habitation, not even a prison, and those under trial on the most serious charges were confined in their own houses or in the public gaol, where there was no provision for their segregation. Fúnez demanded a competent building, with the necessary conveniences, a demand not easily complied with in so small a place, and he finally was installed in the episcopal palace, then vacant through the absence of the bishop.[2] This of course could be but temporary and some other provision must have been made, for we are told that, when the Dutch under Pieter Vandervoez, in 1599, took possession of Las Palmas, they burnt both the episcopal palace and the building of the Inquisition. The former was not rebuilt until thirty years later by Bishop Murga and the latter, as we shall see, was reconstructed in due time on a large scale by the tribunal.[3]

A matter not easily understood is the bestowal, May 25, 1568, on Fúnez, by the dean and chapter, *sede vacante*, of cognizance of

---

[1] Millares, II, 7–20.   [2] Ibidem, pp. 15, 21–22.
[3] Murga, Constituciones sinodales del Obispado de la Gran Canaria, fol. 333 (Madrid, 1634).

superstitions and sorcery, because these crimes should not remain unpunished and his powers as inquisitor were deficient in this respect.[1] These offences in Spain were recognized as subject to inquisitorial jurisdiction when savoring, as they always were assumed to do, of heresy and pact with the demon; they formed by far the larger part of the cases coming before the Canary tribunal and the previous inquisitors had not hesitated to deal with them. They formed however a kind of debatable ground, claimed by both the secular and spiritual as well as the inquisitorial jurisdiction and Fúnez may have taken advantage of the impression produced by his reception to obtain from the chapter, in the absence of a bishop, a transfer of its powers.

Fúnez was zealous and energetic in restoring the tribunal to usefulness and, in about eighteen months, he had accumulated material for an auto de fe, celebrated November 5, 1569. For this he sent out his proclamation through all the islands so that, as he boasted to the Suprema, although the Grand Canary had only fifteen hundred inhabitants, there were fully three thousand spectators assembled. The new bishop, Juan de Azólares, took so warm an interest in the affairs of the Inquisition that he voted personally in all the cases, he walked in the procession and he preached the sermon. There were twenty-seven penitents for minor offences, involving fines, scourging, galleys and other penalties, and there were three effigies of Moriscos relaxed. One of these represented Juan Felipe, a rich merchant of Lanzarote who, on learning that a warrant had been issued for his arrest, chartered a vessel under pretext of going to Tenerife, on which he embarked with his wife and children and some thirty of his compatriots, finding a safe refuge in Morocco and furnishing material for heightening the interest of several more autos.[2]

The activity of Fúnez was not confined to the Gran Canaria for he made repeated visitations to the several islands, gathering in denunciations from all quarters, so that, between May 2, 1568, and January 4, 1571, the list of accused amounts to 544 besides

---
[1] Birch, I, 159-60.   [2] Millares, II, 23-30.

a number of collective entries, such as "*bruxas*," "the Frenchmen who took the caravel of the Espinosas," "renegades," "Moriscos of Lanzarote," "fugitive negroes" etc. The names of Englishmen and of an occasional Fleming also begin to appear. Yet the denunciations consist largely of the veriest trifles of careless speech, indicating how acute was the watchfulness excited to observe and report whatever might seem to savor of heresy. There was no safety in lapse of time, for matters were treasured up to be brought out long afterwards, when there was no possibility of disproving them. In Gomera, October 23, 1570, María Machin denounced Catalina Rodríguez for telling her of a love-charm some thirty years before; in Garachico, December 21, 1570, Marina Ferrera informs on Vicente Martin, a cleric who had gone to the Indies, who told her more than twenty-seven years before of an unnamed woman who had tried on him a conjuration to stop nose-bleeding. More serious was the accusation brought in Laguna, January 14, 1571, by Barbolagusta, wife of the Regidor Francisco de Coronado, against the physician Reynaldos, because, twelve or thirteen years before, when the husband of a patient told her to seek the intercession of the saints, he said that God alone was to be prayed to and there was no need of saints.[1]

Complaints of Fúnez must have reached the Suprema for, after a short interval, probably in 1570, Doctor Bravo de Zayas was sent out as visitador or inspector. He seems to have associated himself companionably with Fúnez as a colleague and, in August, 1571, he made a visitation of the islands, bringing back an abundant store of denunciations. The two held together an auto on December 12, 1574, in which there was but one relaxation—the effigy of a fugitive Morisco. Four slaves were reconciled, including a case which is suggestive—that of a negro of whom it is recorded that he was tortured for an hour, when the infliction was stopped because he was so ignorant and stupid. Pious zeal for the salvation of these poor savages led to their baptism after capture; they could not be intelligent converts or throw off their

---

[1] Birch, I, 133–53.

native superstitions, and no one seemed able to realize the grim absurdity of adding the terrors of the Inquisition to the horrors of their enslaved existence. When a negro slave-girl was bemoaning her condition, she was kindly consoled with the assurance that baptism preserved her and her children from hell, to which she innocently replied that doing evil and not lack of baptism led to hell. This was heresy, for which she was duly prosecuted.[1]

Under the inquisitorial code the attempt to escape from slavery thus was apostasy, punishable as such if unsuccessful, and expiated if successful by concremation in effigy. This is illustrated in an auto, held by Zayas and Fúnez, June 24, 1576, in which among sixteen effigies of absentees were those of eight slaves, seven negroes and one Moor. They had undergone baptism, had been bought by Doña Catalina de la Cuevas and were worked on her sugar plantation. They seized a boat at Orotava and escaped to Morocco, for which they were duly prosecuted as apostates and their effigies were delivered to the flames—a ghastly mockery which does not seem to have produced the desired impression in preventing other misguided beings from flying from their salvation.[2]

While Zayas thus coöperated with Fúnez, he did not neglect the special mission entrusted to him. Charges piled up against Fúnez, which he condensed into a series of thirty articles, embracing all manner of misdeeds—favoritism, injustice, improper financial transactions, illicit trading with the Moors of Barbary, ill-treatment of prisoners, lack of discipline in the tribunal, etc. Zayas and Fúnez seem to have returned to Spain towards the close of 1576, for the latter's defence against the charges is dated at Madrid, February 12, 1577. In this he answered all the points in full detail, with citation of documents; the people of the islands, he asserts, are given to perjury and, when offended, bring false accusations to revenge themselves—a habit which, it may be hoped, he bore in mind when sitting as a judge. Doubtless he had given them provocation enough to induce them to exercise their

---

[1] Millares, II, 43–44, 47, 51.   [2] Ibidem, pp. 57–61.

talents in this line against him and the numerous charges indicate a wide-spread feeling of hostility towards the tribunal. His defence was skilfully drawn and, on its face, seems to be sufficient.[1]

The Canary tribunal was thus placed upon the same footing as those of Spain, though perhaps it was subjected to a somewhat closer supervision by the Suprema than was as yet exercised at home, for we happen to have a letter of October 11, 1572, ordering that Antonio Lorenzo be released from the secret prison and be given his house as a prison. Perhaps it felt that assertion of its authority was necessary, in view of the delay and uncertainty of communication, for commercial intercourse was not frequent; as Fúnez says, about this time, it was notorious that there were no vessels sailing for two or three or even more months.[2] Be this as it may, there was another visitor sent to the Canaries in 1582, and a third about 1590. The latter was Claudio de la Cueva, whose visitation lasted until 1597 and was useful in exposing the iniquities of Joseph de Armas, who had served as fiscal for more than twenty years. A quarrel between him and the secretary, Francisco Ibañez, led to mutual accusations and the unveiling of secrets which show how the terror inspired by the Inquisition and the immunity of its officials enabled them to abuse their positions. There was a rich and respected Fleming named Jan Aventrot, married to a native widow, who was accused by a stepdaughter of eating meat on Fridays and saying that meat left no stain on the soul; also of eating meat in Lent and speaking Flemish. Aventrot was secretly a Protestant, which could readily have been developed by the ordinary inquisitorial methods, but he escaped with a reprimand and a fine of 200 ducats.[3] How this happened finds its explanation in the fact that, while he was in prison, Armas obtained from him, without payment, a bill of

---

[1] Archivo de Simancas, Canarias, Expedientes de Visitas, Leg. 250, Lib. III, Cuad. 3.
[2] Ibidem, fol. 10, 13.
[3] Millares, II, 105-6. The subsequent case of Aventrot and his nephew Jan Cote is alluded to in my History of the Inquisition of Spain, I, 300; II, 348; III, 102.

exchange on Seville.¹ He also defrauded the revenue by receiving goods imported by an Englishman named John Gache (Gatchell?) and selling them through his brother Baltasar. Hernan Peraza, alguazil of the tribunal, complained that Armas would not pay his debts and so did Daniel Vandama, a Flemish merchant. A harder case was that of a chaplaincy in the Inquisition founded by Andrés de Moron for the benefit of Juan de Cervantes, son of Gaspar Fullana, auditor of accounts in the cathedral. Armas induced Inquisitor Francisco Madaleno to take the chaplaincy from Cervantes and give it to him. When Claudio de la Cueva came, Fullana complained to him and he ordered the chaplaincy restored and the income accrued during four years, amounting to 190 doblas, to be refunded. Armas delayed payment for some months and then insisted on compromising it for 120 doblas, which Fullana agreed to, fearing that Armas, who was a canon, would induce the chapter to deprive him of his auditorship, but in place of getting money he received orders on parties at a distance. In stating this under examination by la Cueva, May 4, 1596, Fullana begged him not to insist on the restitution of the remaining 70 doblas, for Armas was a dangerous man.²

He proved so to the convent of la Concepcion, founded by Doña Isabel de Garfias, a Cistercian nun, whom Cardinal Rodrigo de Castro, Archbishop of Seville, had sent to Las Palmas for the purpose. Armas persuaded the bishop, Fernando de Figueroa, to appoint him as visitor of the convent and used his authority to cultivate a suspicious intimacy with some of the younger inmates, to the destruction of discipline and rules of the Order. When the abbess endeavored to enforce them, he deposed her and replaced her with Francisca Ramírez, a Dominican, who had accompanied her from Spain, and who was of near kin to Doña Laura Ramírez, his mistress, by whom he was said to have a child. The abbess appealed to the archbishop, who addressed, December 19, 1595, a forcible letter to the bishop, recapitulating the misdeeds

¹ Archivo de Simancas, Canarias, Exp. de Visitas, Leg. 250, Lib. I, fol. 844, 849, 872.
² Ibidem, fol. 406, 407, 411, 417–22.

of Armas and ordering him to investigate and apply the appropriate remedies, but to no purpose, and the abbess turned to la Cueva, February 28, 1596, with an earnest memorial, imploring his interposition. Armas, she said, desired her death, for when she was sick he would not allow the physician to visit her, so that she nearly died.[1] A more prominent ecclesiastic who experienced the risk of provoking him was the prior of the cathedral, Doctor Luis Rúiz de Salazar, who was also a consultor of the tribunal. They had a quarrel in the chapter; Salazar called him the son of a clockmaker and, when Armas gave him the lie, Salazar seized his cap and beat him with it. Inquisitor Madaleno promptly threw Salazar into prison and prosecuted him, but, as the affair concerned a church dignitary, he was obliged to submit the papers to the Suprema for the sentence. With unexpected moderation the latter replied, April 2, 1591 that, as the affair took place in the chapter and in the capacity of canons, the tribunal must abandon the case and allow it to be decided by whatever judges had jurisdiction—but it did not prescribe any satisfaction to Salazar for the infamy inflicted by his imprisonment.[2]

Meanwhile the tribunal had been actively performing such duties as came in its way, strengthened by the addition of another inquisitor, for, in 1581, we find Fúnez replaced with Diego Osorio de Seijas and Juan Lorenzo, who celebrated a public auto on March 12th of that year. It will be remembered that, in the auto of 1569, there appeared the effigy of Juan Felipe, who had escaped from Lanzarote, carrying with him some thirty other fugitives. The tribunal had not forgotten them and now, after duly trying them it burnt their effigies, to the number of thirty-one, including Felipe's wife and sister and three children, fifteen slaves, mostly negroes and a miscellaneous group of others. In addition there were fifteen reconciled penitents, with the usual penalties.[3]

Six years elapsed before there was another auto, celebrated

---

[1] Archivo de Simancas, Canarias, Exp. de Visitas, Leg. 250, Lib. I, fol. 568, 1115-19.
[2] Birch, I, 297-300.   [3] Millares, II, 72-4.

July 22, 1587, in which there were burnt three effigies of a remnant of the Lanzarote fugitives. There was also the more impressive relaxation of a living man—the first since that of the Judaizers in 1526. This was an Englishman named George Gaspar who, in the royal prison of Tenerife, had been seen praying with his back to a crucifix and, on being questioned, had said that prayer was to be addressed to God and not to images. He was transferred to the tribunal, where he freely confessed to having been brought up as a Protestant. Torture did not shake his faith and he was condemned, a confessor as usual being sent to his cell the night before the auto to effect his conversion. He asked to be alone for awhile and the confessor, on his return, found him lying on the floor, having thrust into his stomach a knife which he had picked up in the prison and concealed for the purpose. The official account piously tells us that it pleased God that the wound was not immediately mortal and that he survived until evening, so that the sentence could be executed; the dying man was carted to the *quemadero* and ended his misery in the flames. Another Englishman was Edward Francis, who had been found wounded and abandoned on the shore of Tenerife. He saved his life, while under torture, by professing himself a fervent Catholic, who had been obliged to dissemble his religion, a fault which he expiated with two hundred lashes and six years of galley service. Still another Englishman was John Reman (Raymond?) a sailor of the ship Falcon; he had asked for penance and, as there was nothing on which to support him in the prison, he was transferred to the public gaol. The governor released him and, in wandering around he fell into conversation with some women, in which he expressed Protestant opinions. A second trial ensued in which, under torture, he professed contrition and begged for mercy, which he obtained in the disguise of two hundred lashes and ten years of galleys. In addition there were the crew of the bark Prima Rosa, twelve in number, all English but one Fleming. One of them, John Smith, had died in prison, and was reconciled in effigy; the rest, with or without torture, had professed conversion and were sent to the galleys, some of them with a hundred lashes in addition. Besides these, this notable auto presented twenty-two penitents, penanced or reconciled, for the ordinary offences and with the usual penalties.[1]

Another auto was celebrated December 21, 1597, with a large number of penitents, but no relaxations either in person or in effigy. It was the last of these solemnities held in public, for the next one, December 20, 1608, was an *auto particular*, in the cathedral, when three effigies were relaxed.[2] In fact, while the Inquisition in Spain was consolidating its power and threatening to dominate the monarchy, in the Canaries there seems to have been an unconscious combination of opposing forces which crippled its energies and gradually rendered it inert. Yet during the early years of the seventeenth century it had vigor enough to burn two unfortunates alive. Gaspar Nicholas Claysen (Claessens?) a Hollander, had been condemned to a year of prison, in the auto of 1597, when he must have professed conversion. He seems to have imagined that he would escape recognition and, in 1611, he tempted his fate again and sought the Canaries as the captain of a merchant vessel. He was arrested April 19th and tried again. In spite of torture he maintained his faith to the last and, on January 27, 1612, he was sentenced to relaxation, as an impenitent, by the inquisitors Juan Francisco de Monroy and Pedro Espino de Brito. Then a delay of two years occurred, possibly occupied with efforts for his salvation, and it was not until February 22, 1614, that the governor, Francisco de la Rua, was summoned to hear his sentence and receive him for execution. There was a Dutch ship in the harbor and many of his compatriots in the town, so that his rescue seems to have been feared, for such is the reason given for loading him with chains and guarding him with four soldiers carrying arquebuses with lighted matches. At the appointed hour he was paraded through the streets, under a guard of soldiers, to the plaza de Santo Domingo, where he was

---

[1] Millares, II, 80–94.   [2] Ibidem, III, 9–10.

duly burnt alive. The next year, on June 2, 1615, Tobias Lorenzo, a Hollander settled in Garachico (Tenerife), who had been arrested in 1611, was burnt as a relapsed Protestant.[1]

This was the last relaxation in person, making, according to Millares, a total of only eleven since the foundation of the tribunal, but, as he omits the earliest one, Juan de Xeres, the count amounts to twelve.[2] After this a long interval occurs before there was even an effigy burnt. Duarte Henríquez Alvarez was a Portuguese New Christian, who was a collector of the royal revenues and a rich merchant in Tenerife. In his frequent voyages to Europe he fell in love with the daughter of an Amsterdam correspondent and resolved to marry her and return to the faith of his ancestors. He remitted to Holland as much money as he could without exciting suspicion, he abandoned to the Inquisition the rest of his considerable property and departed, never to return. He was duly prosecuted *in absentia* and condemned to relaxation in effigy. Permission to execute the sentence in an auto particular was asked of the Suprema and its assent was received, May 29, 1659. No time was lost; on June 1st the auto was held in the cathedral; the effigy was delivered to the corregidor and was solemnly burnt in the quemadero, being the last execution in the Canaries.[3] From this time to the end of the century the work of the tribunal was almost nothing, the records of the prison showing that there were rarely more than one or two prisoners.[4]

Before following the history of the tribunal to its decadence and extinction, we may pause to consider its condition and the various directions in which its activity was developed.

---

[1] Millares, III, 12-24.

[2] Ibidem, 163-4. The figures of Millares are drawn from the official list of *Quemados*. In 1526 there are 8; in 1587, 1; in 1614, 1; in 1615, 1.

[3] Millares, III, 26-31. The total relaxations in effigy amount to 107, as follows (Ibidem, III, 164-8):

1 in 1513	17 in 1557	16 in 1576	23 in 1591
7 " 1530	3 " 1569	30 " 1581	3 " 1608
2 " 1534	1 " 1574	3 " 1587	1 " 1659.

[4] Birch, II, 695.

Its financial resources presumably were limited. During the earlier term of its career, when it had no buildings of its own and no prison to maintain, when its officials for the most part were drawn from the chapter and other beneficed incumbents, an occasional confiscation and levying of fines probably met the moderate necessary expenses. In 1563 it had the benefit of a suppressed prebend and when, in 1568, Fúnez was sent to organize it, the energy of his administration doubtless supplied the funds necessary for the establishment which he founded. Imposing fines, however, probably was easier than collecting them, for when, in 1570, he was about to depart on a visitation of the islands he impressed upon the fiscal, Juan de Cervantes, that there were many persons who owed the fines to which they had been condemned and he was especially empowered to use all the rigor of law in compelling payment.[1] This seems to have been the only source thus far of funds, for when one of the charges against Fúnez, in the visitation, was that he kept no book for recording confiscations, his reply, in 1577, was that there had been none since that of the Felipes (in 1569) and this was so involved that he waited till he could visit Lanzarote and straighten it out.[2]

A more promising field, however, as we shall see, was now developing in the prosecution of heretic merchants and shipmasters who were seeking the trade of the Canaries, when a latitudinarian construction of the law permitted the seizure of vessels and cargoes, on which the grip of the Inquisition was not easily relaxed. Either from this or some other source the tribunal was emerging from its poverty, for a stray document shows us that, in 1602, it was investing 5000 ducats in a ground-rent, from which it was still receiving the income in 1755.[3] We also catch a glimpse of its affairs in 1654, when the Seville Contratacion sent its fiscal to the Canaries to put a stop to the exportation of wine to the Indies, the commerce of which was confined to Seville. On June 15th the tribunal addressed to Philip IV a memorial, arguing that

---
[1] Birch, I, 383–4.
[2] Archivo de Simancas, Canarias, Visitas, Leg. 250, Lib. III, Cuad. 3, fol. 20.
[3] Birch, II, 1007

to cut off this trade would be the total destruction of the islands, which now pay the king 60,000 ducats a year over the expenses of the garrison and judiciary, for the English took only the malmsey of Tenerife and the rest of the vintage, amounting to 16,000 pipes per annum, went to the Indies. The bishopric, now worth 30,000, would not be worth 10,000; as for the Inquisition, it held ground-rents on the vineyards paying 22,232 reales and 28 maravedís, which it would lose, and, as its only other source, the prebend, was worth only 300 ducats a year, its support would fall on the king.[1] The only relief obtained from the king was permission to ship 1000 tuns a year to various American ports. Whether the tribunal suffered or not we have no means of knowing, but in 1660 we find it gathering in the estate of Duarte Henríquez, burnt in effigy in 1658, and applying 1942 reales from it to the renewal of 212 sanbenitos, hung in the churches, which had become worm-eaten and indistinct with age.[2]

This does not look as if the tribunal were oppressed with poverty; in fact it must have enjoyed abundant means for about this time it completed what is described as an imposing palace for its habitation. This had a spacious patio, covered with an awning in hot weather, which led into a handsome garden, opening upon a street in the rear. To these the public was freely admitted and they formed a thoroughfare from one street to another, the object of which was to enable witnesses and informers to come without attracting attention. In the building were lodged the senior inquisitor, the gaoler and the subordinate officials, the prison and the torture-chamber being in the rear.[3] Later financial data are

---

[1] Millares, III, 153–7; IV, 19–20.

The exportation of wine from the Canaries to the Indies was an old subject of complaint in the home country. In 1573 the Córtes represented that its profits had caused the abandonment of sugar culture, which had formerly supplied the Spanish sugar market, greatly enhancing its price and deteriorating its quality, while at the same time the flourishing wine-trade was being ruined. In reply to this Philip II only promised to look into the matter and evidently nothing was done at the time.—Córtes de Madrid del año de setenta y tres, Peticion 76 (Alcala, 1575).

[2] Millares, III, 85. [3] Ibidem, 93–5.

missing, but the tribunal probably managed to meet its expenses to the end, with no greater difficulty than those of the Peninsula. From first to last it was not burdened with a punitive prison or *casa de la misericordia*, and its sentences to confinement are always to convents or to the houses of the culprits or to hold the city as a prison. The detentive or secret prison was economically administered, the ration, as we learn in 1577, being only 24 maravedís a day. The visitor, Bravo y Zayas, was assailed with many complaints by the inmates of insufficient food, which they ascribed to the knavery of the officials, but Fúnez explained it by saying that, while in the Canaries there were usually one or two months of scarcity in a year, there had been a famine lasting through 1571, 1572 and 1573, when the price of bread went up to a cuarto of six maravedís for two or three ounces and the people were reduced to eating chestnuts; meat was correspondingly scarce and the supply of fish was very uncertain. Rich and poor suffered alike and, as the prisoners' allowance was in money, their food was unavoidably diminished.[1]

Judaizing New Christians, who furnished, in the Peninsula, so abundant a source of exploitation, formed a comparatively insignificant feature in the activity of the Canary tribunal. At first there was better promise, as we have seen in the statistics of the earlier autos, but these energetic proceedings seem either to have driven them away or to have thoroughly converted them and, in the subsequent period, the cases of Judaism are singularly few, in so far as we can learn from existing documents. In 1635 there is a denunciation of a Dutchman named Rojel, who had been in Tenerife and who subsequently was seen in Holland, dressed and living as a Jew. In 1636, a man named Mardocheo, aged 80, resident of La Laguna in Tenerife, was accused of talking Judaism by a man who had been a fellow-prisoner with him in the public gaol. In 1638 the Licenciado Diego de Arteaga was suspected

---

[1] Archivo de Simancas, Canarias, Visitas, Leg. 250, Lib. III, Cuad. 3, fol. 2, 8, 10.

of being *de casta de Judío,* in consequence of irregular conduct in a procession. In 1653, Francisco Vicente, a West Indian, who had accompanied his master Diego Rodrigo Arias from Havana to London and thence to Tenerife, denounced him for taking a crucifix every night from his chest and flogging it for half an hour. In 1659 we have seen the relaxation in effigy of Duarte Henríquez Alvarez. In 1660 Fray Matias Pinto accused Antonio Fernández Carvajal of saying that he was a Jew since Protector Cromwell had broken peace with Spain. In 1662 Gaspar Pereyra, alias de Vitoria, was convicted of Judaism and sent to Seville to serve out his term of imprisonment. His grandmother had been burnt and his business as a merchant had carried him to Brazil, Angola, Lisbon, Madrid, Antwerp, Amsterdam, Middelburg and many other places, so that he had a comprehensive acquaintance with the communities of Jewish refugees everywhere, and the care with which the minute evidence that he gave concerning them was collected and ratified, although they were all out of reach, shows that the paucity of cases in the records is not the result of any lack of desire to persecute. It was natural however that the inquisitors should enquire about Gerónimo Gómez Pesoa, a rich Lisbon merchant who disappeared just in time to avoid arrest and, as an English vessel sailed that night without a licence, he was supposed to have escaped in it—a supposition fortified by learning that he had joined the colony of Conversos in Rouen and had thence gone to Amsterdam.[1] Doubtless there were more cases than these, but the records available do not furnish them.

During the sixteenth century baptized Moorish and negro slaves furnished a certain amount of business, especially when they escaped and added to the impressiveness of the autos with their effigies, but subsequently we hear little of them. When prosecuted in person it would seem that the owner was obliged to pay for their maintenance, for a warrant of arrest, in 1575, of Pedro Morisco manco, slave of Pedro d'Escalona, requires eight

---

[1] Birch, II, 534–6, 547, 548, 580, 626, 634, 646–61.

ducats to be brought with him, to be furnished by his master.[1] There is one case of a free Morisco which is not easy to understand. About 1590, Sancho de Herrera Leon, with his wife and children, was carried off in a Moorish raid. After a short time he returned and, although he asserted that he had come back to preserve his faith, he was made to abjure *de levi*, was fined in forty doblas and was exiled perpetually from Lanzarote and Fuerteventura, under pain of scourging and galleys.[2] In the seventeenth century we hear little of such cases, but in 1619 there occurs one which throws some light on the fate of the Moriscos expelled from Spain in 1610. Juan de Soto, born in Valladolid and brought up as a Christian, was seven years old at the time of the expulsion. The family passed into France; at Toulouse his parents and brothers died, but a kinsman took charge of him and carried him to Barbary, where he was circumcised and made to utter certain words in Arabic. For seven years he served various masters, who carried him twice to Constantinople, Alexandria and other places. In 1618 a fleet sailed from Algiers to the Canaries, in which he served a Turkish captain named Hamet. Sent ashore on Lanzarote with a foraging party and attacked by the natives, three were killed and he was wounded and captured. The Inquisition claimed him, which was probably fortunate for him, for, as a renegade he escaped with reconciliation and four years of sanbenito and reclusion in a convent.[3]

Renegades, in fact, were quite numerous, and the facility is noteworthy with which Christians when captured abandoned their faith. The tribunal kept a close watch on them and all who escaped from Barbary were closely questioned as to fellow-prisoners who had renegaded, when these could be prosecuted *in absentia*, or record be kept to confront them in case of their return.[4]

The vast number of denunciations which kept pouring in upon

---

[1] Birch, I, 207.   [2] Millares, II, 102.
[3] Birch, I, 416–20.
[4] Ibidem, II, 726–8, 735, 750–72, 813, 832.

the tribunal shows how sedulously the population was trained as spies and informers upon their neighbors. Many of the alleged offences were of the most trivial character, yet they have their interest as an index of the hypersensitiveness of orthodoxy with which the Spanish mind was imbued. Among the cases which Doctor Bravo y Zayas brought home with him for trial, from his visitation of the islands in 1571, was that of a man who, while dressing himself, was annoyed by the glare of the sun and pettishly exclaimed "Devil take the sun," which was gravely qualified as blasphemy. Another who, in a procession, had aided in carrying the frame on which was seated an image of the Virgin, remarked that it was a load for a camel, which was decided to be ill-sounding and offensive to pious ears. Even absence of intention did not excuse. In 1591, Gaspar López of Tenerife, when on guard one night, went through the exercise of arms with his partizan, in the course of which he happened to strike a wooden cross that was behind him, and for this he was sentenced to the indelible disgrace of appearing in an auto, followed by vergüenza—parading on an ass through the streets, naked from the waist up, while the town-crier proclaimed his misdeed.[1] This hyperæsthesia did not diminish with time. In 1665 the tribunal entertained and investigated an accusation that a certain person when praying allowed his rosary to hang down his back, which was regarded as irreverence.[2]

How readily such a system could be abused to gratify malevolence is indicated in the case of the Dominican Fray Alonso de las Roelas. In March, 1568, he made an utterance about purgatory which excited remark, and some of his brother frailes discussed it with him, when Fray Blas Merino, a prominent member of the Order, said that Roelas was simple and did not know what he said and that it was not for them to denounce him. Some years later, however, Blas Merino, in the hope of being made Provincial, was engaged in a sort of plot to get the Canaries separated from the Province of Andalusia and erected into a province of the Order. The Dominican authorities heard of this and Roelas was com-

---

[1] Millares, II, 47–54, 112. [2] Birch, II, 682.

missioned to seize all the papers connected with it and to notify
Merino to abandon the project. To revenge himself Merino
hunted up all the witnesses to Roela's utterance and persuaded
them to denounce him in 1572. Bishop Azólares, whose zeal
for the Inquisition we have seen, said that the matter was not
worth prosecuting, because Roelas did not deny purgatory, which
was a matter of faith, while its place and the character of its
torment were matters of debate with theologians. Nevertheless
Roelas was arrested and tried, and, as usual during trial, he was
recluded in the convent of his Order in Las Palmas. One midnight he came knocking at the door of the Inquisition; Fúnez
was awakened and sent him word that it was no time for him to
call and that he could come the next day. He did so and stated
that his brethren so maltreated him, because he had once served
as inspector of the house, that he asked to be placed in the secret
prisons, a request which was granted, and he stayed there until
sentenced. The sentence punished him with reclusion and he
was delivered to the prior of the convent, when they at once
commenced snarling and growling at each other like quarrelsome
dogs. Fúnez rebuked the prior, telling him to avoid such public
scandals and that he would send Roelas to the convent in Tenerife
until the Provincial should decide as to his place of reclusion.
Fúnez probably spoke from experience when he said that among
frailes there was no restraint nor truth, but only envy.[1]

The Canaries enjoyed an ample supply of *beatas revelanderas*,
but, as a rule, the tribunal did not follow the example of the
Peninsula in molesting them. One of the most renowned of these
was Catalina de San Mateo, a nun of the house of Santa Clara
in Las Palmas, who had ecstasies and revelations and was reverenced as a saint. God spoke with her familiarly through the
medium of a painted Ecce Homo, which hung in her cell, giving
her counsels and spiritual comfort and prophecies. On her death,
May 26, 1695, the body lay for three days emitting the odor of

---

[1] Archivo de Simancas, Canarias, Visitas, Leg. 250, Lib. III, Cuad. 3, fol. 6, 16.

sanctity and was viewed by a vast concourse, eager to touch it with rosaries and other objects, and all her clothes and effects were treasured as relics. All this is described in a letter of July 5th, to the Suprema, by the inquisitors Lugo and Romero, who express no doubts as to her holiness. Commencement was made to collect testimony for her canonization, but enthusiasm evaporated and the effort was abandoned. She was succeeded in popular veneration by Sor Petronila de San Esteban, of the convent of San Bernardo in Las Palmas, which she had entered in 1680, at the age of four. She was a bride of God; the child Jesus came to nestle in her arms; the man Christ came to soothe her with sweet words; legions of angels, headed by David, came to rejoice her with the music of heaven. She had terrible conflicts with demons, whom she overcame, and a little wooden image of St. John, with which she held discourse, was the medium through which she enjoyed revelations and prophecies. The Inquisition took no action to interfere with her and almost the only case in which it instituted proceedings, in such matters, was one, in 1695, against Don Miguel de Araus, confessor of two beatas in La Laguna, Francisca Machado de San José and Margarita de Santa Teresa, the former of whom boasted of the stigmata.[1]

In the later period a very considerable share of the labors of the tribunal was devoted to cases of "solicitation"—the seduction of women by their confessors. It was not until 1561 that this crime was subjected to inquisitorial jurisdiction, under the pretext that it implied erroneous belief as to the sacrament of penitence, and some time was required to settle the question of including it in the Edict of Faith calling for denunciations. The earliest case I have met occurs in 1574, when María Ramos accused her confessor, Fray Pedro Gallego.[2] After this they occur with increasing frequency and offenders appear to be treated with even more sympathetic leniency than in Spain. There was moderate rigor in the sentence of Fray Pedro de Hinojosa, denounced in 1579 by

---

[1] Millares, III, 117-23, 125-37.   [2] Birch, I, 198.

numerous maids, wives and widows, for he was deprived of the faculty of hearing confessions, he received a circular discipline in his convent and he was recluded for three years in a convent with the customary disabilities.[1] Much less severity was shown, in 1584, to Manuel Gómez Pacheco, priest of Garachico, accused by a number of women, for he was only sentenced to abjuration *de levi*, deprivation of administering the sacrament of penitence, two months reclusion in a convent and some spiritual exercises.[2] The penalties varied with the discretion of the tribunal. About 1590 Fray Antonio Pacheco Sampayo, against whom there were many accusers, was deprived of confessing, had three years of reclusion and fifty lashes in his convent, while Andrés de Ortega, parish priest of Telde, likewise accused by several women, was deprived merely of confessing women, fined in twenty ducats and severely reprimanded.[3]

Cases grow more frequent with time and, with their increasing frequency, the penalties seem to grow less. In 1694 Fray Domingo Mireles was accused by four women, with details of foul obscenity. He was sentenced to deprivation of confession and reclusion for four years, but was allowed to choose his place of retreat. He served out the term, went to Spain, and returned with a rehabilitation charitably granted by the inquisitor-general. In 1698 Fray Cipriano de Armas was prosecuted on the evidence of two women; the case was carried to the end and remitted for decision to the Suprema, which ordered its suspension. In two cases in 1742 the sentence was merely deprivation of confessing, six months' reclusion and five years' exile from certain places. In 1747 Fray Bartolomé Bello had not only seduced Maria Cabral González, but had strangled in his cell a child born to them, after piously baptizing it, but when the case reached the Suprema it was suspended. In 1750 Francisco Rodriguez del Castillo was prosecuted on very serious charges but was only suspended for two years from confessing and given some spiritual exercises. In

---

[1] Millares, II, 37–9.   [2] Birch, I, 214–17.   [3] Millares, II, 98, 102.

1755 there were nine complainants against Fray Francisco García Encinoso, who was deprived of confessing and sentenced to six months' reclusion, when he was sent to the convent of N. Señora de Miraflor, with instructions to the superior to keep the matter profoundly secret and to treat him well. In 1769 Fray Domingo Matos was sentenced only to six months' reclusion and the denial of certain privileges, which was subsequently remitted. The sympathy of the tribunal apparently was exhaustless and frequently resulted in practical immunity. In 1785, Fray Joseph Estrada, Franciscan difinidor, was accused by several women with full details, but the tribunal, on December 7, 1793, suspended the case. Then, in 1804, he was again accused by a nun in the convent of la Purisima Concepcion of Garachico. Finally, after twelve years' delay, on February 28, 1805, the tribunal ordered its commissioner to give him *audiencias de cargos*, or private examinations, on report of which the case would be voted on, bearing in mind the advanced age of the accused and the difficulty of communicating with the Suprema, in consequence of the war. This was the last of the matter for, on April 9, 1806, the commissioner at Ycod reported the death of the culprit.[1] When so serious an offence was visited so lightly, we can scarce be surprised that its subjection to inquisitorial jurisdiction failed to check it. There naturally was much difficulty in inducing women to come forward as accusers, yet the number of denunciations was large and steady. Thus, from July 26, 1706, to February 15, 1708, the total denunciations of all kinds to the tribunal was 75; of these only 22 were of men, out of which 7, or practically one-third, were for solicitation.[2]

The bulk of the business of the tribunal consisted in trials for sorcery, under which term were included all the superstitions, more or less innocent, employed to cure or to inflict disease, to provoke love or hatred, to discover theft and to pry into the

---

[1] Birch, II, 512-17, 870, 931-5, 939, 973.   [2] Ibidem, 890-2.

future, for theological ingenuity inferred pact, express or implicit, with the demon in everything which could be construed as transcending the powers of nature, except the ministrations of the priest or exorcist. Such a community as that of the Canaries, in which the primitive magic arts of the natives were added to those of their conquerors, and on these were superimposed the beliefs of Moorish and negro slaves, could not fail to accumulate an incongruous mass of superstitions affecting all the acts of daily life, and the summaries of cases printed by Mr. Birch afford to the student of folk-lore an inexhaustible treasury of curious de-details. No matter what might be the industry of the tribunal in prosecuting and punishing the practitioners of these arts, it could effect nothing in repressing them, or in disabusing popular credulity, for its very jurisdiction was based on the assumption that the powers attributed to the sorcerer were real, and he was punished not as an impostor but as an ally or instrument of the demon.

It would carry us too far to attempt even a summary of the multitudinous superstitions embalmed in the records, but a couple of cases may be mentioned which illustrate the popular tendency to ascribe to sorcery whatever excited wonder, and also the good sense which sometimes intervened to protect the innocent. In 1624, Diego de Santa Marta of Garachico was denounced as a sorcerer to the tribunal in consequence of his performance of some tricks with cards. The accusation was entertained and Fray Juan de Saavedra was ordered to investigate and report. He invited Diego to exhibit his skill and the performance took place in the cell of the Provincial, Fray Bernardo de Herrera, who was a consultor of the Inquisition, with whom were associated Padre Luzena, regent of the schools, several theological professors and Don Francisco Sarmiento, alguazil of the tribunal. Diego was not aware that he was practically on trial before this imposing assemblage, and he performed some surprising card tricks as well as sundry other juggleries. Fortunately for him the spectators were clear-sighted and Fray Saavedra reported that it was all a matter of sleight of hand, which could be detected by careful observation.[1] More serious was the denunciation, in 1803, of any one of four women named (apparently the individual was not identified) who had, twelve years before, administered to María Salome some snuff which caused her to bark like a dog. Luckily Doctor Elchantor, the inquisitor-fiscal, had a touch of the rationalism of the age. He reported that the vomiting and extraordinary movements alleged might have been produced by natural causes; that among timid and ignorant women there was a habit of attributing all disease to sorcery; that it could not be said that the snuff had been prepared with diabolic arts and that there were no other suspicions against the parties accused. He therefore advised that the papers be simply filed away, and in this Inquisitor Borbujo concurred.[2]

Although the term *bruja*, or witch, occasionally appears in the records, there would not appear to be any cases of specific witchcraft. The nearest allusions to the Sabbat occur in 1674, when Doña Isabel Ybarra testified that, a year before, Doña Ana de Ascanio told her that Don Juan de Vargas, now dead, told her that once, in returning home about midnight, he encountered a dance of women with timbrels and lighted candles. In the same year Fray Pablo Guillen deposed that at midnight he saw Guillerma Peré naked; she anointed herself and flew through the air with another woman. Connected with this was the statement that a son of Juan Hernandez, at midnight, found in the street Doña Ana María, widow of Captain Juan de Molina, entirely naked. He took her to her house, when she gave him a garment and begged him to keep silence.[3]

For a comparatively brief period the most important work of the tribunal concerned the foreign heretics—mostly Englishmen and Flemings, or rather Hollanders—who frequented the islands, whether for peaceful commerce or for piracy. As the port of call

---

[1] Birch, I, 482–4.   [2] Ibidem, II, 992–3.   [3] Ibidem, 819, 826.

in the trade with America, the islands were the favorite resort of the sea-rovers of all the nations at enmity with Spain, that is of nearly all Europe, in hopes of capturing some rich galleon or of ravaging some unprotected spot. In 1570, a Norman Huguenot, cruising off Gomera, seized a vessel starting for Brazil with forty Jesuit missionaries; he put them all to death and landed his other prisoners at San Sebastian, a port of Gomera, which next year was sacked by another French corsair.[1] To some extent, doubtless, the Inquisition was regarded as a safeguard against such marauders. In 1589, an Englishman, captured at Garachico from the ship of Vincent Pieter the Fleming, was said to have been a pirate who had pillaged in company with other Englishmen, and was brought before the tribunal, although nothing else was alleged against him. About the same time certain French "pirates," taken on the islet of Graciosa, off Lanzarote, were delivered to the tribunal, when they proved themselves to be good Catholics by their familiarity with the prayers and other observances.[2]

Much more serious was the interference of the Inquisition with those who came to trade, and it is difficult to understand how Spain could carry on any commerce with foreign nations under the impediments which it interposed. The earliest case in the records is one to which allusion has already been made, that of John Sanders who, in 1565, came as a sailor in a vessel from Plymouth, of which the master was James Anthony, the cargo consisting of 28 casks of sardines, 20 dozen of calf-skins and a lot of woollen goods, the property of the master and his brother Thomas. On arrival at Las Isletas, as Sanders could speak and write Spanish, Anthony got him to enter the goods as his own and installed him in a shop to sell them. After two or three months, one day the public scrivener, Melchor de Solis, came and demanded three reales, which Sanders refused. While they were talking he placed his hand on the wall, where there was hanging a paper print of Christ, which he had not recognized, as its face was turned to the wall and it was partly torn. Passing his hand over it, a

---

[1] Millares, II, 152–62.   [2] Birch, I, 347, 350–2.

piece fell off, when Solis charged him with tearing an image of Christ; he picked it up, reverently kissed it and replaced it. The story spread and caused scandal; in the abeyance of the tribunal, the provisor took up the matter, arresting Sanders March 29th and sequestrating the property, which consisted of 2492 reales in money, $3\frac{1}{2}$ casks of sardines and $2\frac{1}{2}$ dozen of calf-skins, all of which was duly placed in the hands of the secrestador, and, in addition, Leónez Alvarez testified that he had bought and paid for goods to the amount of 340 ducats. Under examination Sanders professed himself a Catholic; he could recite the Pater Noster and Credo and the Ave Maria without the final clause imploring the prayers of the Virgin, which he said he had never been taught; he could cross himself but did not know the peculiar Spanish form; he reverenced images of saints although the Queen of England had banished from the churches all but those of Christ and the Virgin, and he had attended mass since he came. Then James Anthony came forward and claimed the property, confirming the story of Sanders, and it was delivered to him, but not until he had furnished satisfactory security to abide the result. What was the outcome we have no means of knowing, as the papers were sent to the tribunal of Seville for its action, but the least that could happen to Sanders and Anthony was interminable delay.[1]

Trading with the Canaries evidently was a hazardous business and the danger increased as time went on, for it sufficed that the crew were heretics to justify their trial and punishment, with the accompaniment of sequestration and confiscation. Thus on April 24, 1593, a single vote ordered the arrest with sequestration of the pilot and other officers, the sailors and boys and passengers of the ship named El Leon Colorado and of all who came in the ship named San Lorenzo, both now at anchor in the port of Las Isletas.[2] The case of the Leon Colorado is suggestive. She was an English ship which, until 1587, had been employed in the Lisbon trade under a licence from the Marquis of Santa Cruz, but after

---

[1] Birch, II, 1018–26. [2] Ibidem, I, 303–4, 377.

his death she seems to have been transferred to Flanders. On this voyage she had sailed from Antwerp, a Spanish port, under a licence from Alexander of Parma, the nephew of Philip II and the governor of the Low Countries. The *escrivano* or purser of the ship, Franz Vandenbosch, while on trial, procured a certificate from the municipal authorities of Antwerp setting forth that his parents were good Catholics and so were their children, and that Franz had sailed for the Canaries with the licence and passport of the Duke of Parma. The only effect of this was a vote to torture him, on learning which he confessed that in Mecklenburg he had embraced Calvinism, and his sentence was reconciliation and confiscation, prison and sanbenito for three years and perpetual prohibition to visit heretic lands or to approach within ten leagues of the sea, for which reason he was to be sent to Spain. Another member of the crew Georg Van Hoflaquen asserted his Catholicism and adhered to it through four successive inflictions, each of three turns of the *cordeles*. Then he was ordered to be placed on the *burro* or rack, when he declared that he could no longer endure the agony and that he was a heretic. He was sentenced to reconciliation and confiscation, and three years of prison and sanbenito, with the corresponding disabilities.[1]

In these cases the adverse evidence is almost wholly derived from other members of the crews, who had no hesitation in testifying to their comrades' Protestantism. There was usually no concealment attempted but, when orthodoxy was asserted, torture was unsparingly employed. Conversion did not obtain much alleviation of punishment. Another of the crew of the Leon Colorado was Jacob Banqueresme, a Hollander, who freely admitted his Calvinism. He knew nothing of Catholicism but was ready to embrace it if it seemed to him good. Theologians were set to work and, in due time, he announced his conversion and was formally admitted to the Church, but he was sentenced to be sent to Spain and confined in a convent for two years, in order to be

---

[1] Birch, I, 374-9; II, 1048-9.

thoroughly instructed, and he was prohibited to go to heretic lands or to approach the sea within ten leagues.[1]

The result of these labors was seen in the auto of 1597, in which there were seventeen Englishmen and Flemings reconciled, with imprisonment ranging from two to eight years, and twenty-six penanced, with from one to four years of prison, the ships to which they belonged being La Rosa, San Pedro, La Posta, San Lorenzo, Leon Colorado, Margarita and María Fortuna.[2] There were no obstinate heretics and no martyrs. When this active proselytism was carried on for twenty years or more with its consequent confiscation of ships and cargoes, it is easy to understand the financial ease of the tribunal and to conjecture its influence on the commerce and prosperity of the islands.

This flourishing industry was interfered with by the treaty with England ratified by James I on August 29/19, 1604, and by Philip III on June 16, 1605. It provided that English subjects visiting or resident in the Spanish dominions were not to be molested on account of their religion, so long as they gave no occasion for scandal, and this was extended to the United Provinces in the twelve years' truce, concluded in 1609.[3] The caution induced by the treaty, even before its ratification by Spain, is exemplified in the case of Edward Monox, an English captain and merchant, charged September 10, 1604, with offences in the matter of images and with following the doctrines of Luther and Calvin. The consulta de fe, September 11th, unanimously voted his arrest with sequestration but that, before action, the papers be sent to the Suprema for its decision, in view of the considerations of state arising from the peace with England, and from the fact that he was a rich merchant who, since the death of Queen Elizabeth, had twice come with highly commendatory passports from the Spanish ambassador in London.[4]

While thus some wholesome restraint was imposed on the

---

[1] Millares, II, 148–50. [2] Ibidem, 141–7.
[3] Coleccion de Tratados de Paz; Phelipe III, pp. 161–2, 198, 465.
[4] Birch, II, 1054.

Inquisition and the vexations inflicted on merchants and seamen became much less frequent, they did not wholly cease, for the Suprema construed the treaties arbitrarily in such wise as to limit the privileges of foreign heretics as far as possible. How it still continued to throw obstacles in the way of trade may be seen in the petition of Jacob and Conrad de Brier and Pieter Nansen, merchants of Tenerife, presented May 3, 1611. The ship Los Tres Reyes arrived at Las Isletas with some goods for them; for some reason, not stated, it had been seized by the tribunal and its cargo had been sequestrated and they sought release of their property. Their prayer was granted and, on May 25th, an order was given to deliver to their agent the packages specified and their letters, subject however to the payment of the cost of disembarking the goods, the carriage to Las Palmas, the fees of the secrestador for keeping them, 24 reales to the interpreter of the tribunal for his trouble, 18 ducats 4 reales for the freight and 10 reales average to the ship, at the rate of one real per package.[1]

When war broke out with England, lasting from 1624 to 1630, of course the treaty of 1604–5 became dormant, but it was not until April 22, 1626, that a royal proclamation of non-intercourse with England appeared, confiscating all English goods imported in contravention of it, and this was followed, May 29th, by a *carta acordada* of the Suprema ordering the prosecution, in the regular way, of all Englishmen who had been delinquent as regards the faith.[2] This led to a discussion between the three inquisitors. Francisco de Santalis presented a long opinion to the effect that in Tenerife there were very many of them who, in spite of the war, remained, in place of departing as enemies. The orders of the Suprema were therefore applicable to them; Catholics incurred the risk of excommunication in supplying them with food and were exposed to the danger of infection; they were delinquents in not hearing mass or confessing and communing, and in eating meat on fast days. This was not only a great scandal, but it afforded opportunity of flight and of concealing their property,

---

[1] Birch, I, 414–16.   [2] Ibidem, II, 1069–70.

which was large. He therefore voted that secret information be taken as to their delinquencies and, when this was sufficient, that they should all be arrested and their property be sequestrated, after which the orders of the Suprema could be awaited as to their prosecution. The other two inquisitors, Alonso Rincon and Gabriel Martínez, referred to a consultation had on September 2d with the Ordinary, the consultors, and the calificadores, when it was resolved that the matter be referred to the Suprema and no action be taken till its orders were received; the royal proclamation had said nothing about residents; to seize them and their property would be a great hardship; the commissioners at La Laguna, Orotava and Garachico had been instructed to be vigilant and no denunciations had been received. It is creditable to the tribunal that it resisted the temptation of seizing the large amount of property involved, and the English appear not to have been molested.[1]

Yet the position of the foreign merchants was exceedingly precarious, as is shown by the case of John Tanner, prior to these deliberations. He was arrested and brought to the prison, November 12, 1624. On examination he stated his age as 22; he was a baptized Christian, who kept feast-days and Sundays, but did not hear mass or confess, for in his country there was no mass or confession; he knew nothing of the Catholic faith and had never been instructed in it. When asked as usual if he knew the cause of his arrest he said that he did not, unless it was because Juan Jánez, the commissioner at Garachico, had asked him for some linens and a pair of wool stockings which he refused, when Jánez called him a heretic dog and they came to blows, and then he was thrown into the public gaol. On being told, as usual, to search his memory, he added that once he went with some other Englishmen to La Laguna to see Don Rodrigo de Bohórquez, then governor of Tenerife; he asked Bohórquez to pay him 400 pesos owing to him and 2800 reales due to Robert Spencer for goods taken, when Bohórquez grew angry and said that Henry Ysan

---

[1] Birch, II, 1065-70.

was the cause of all the English making demands upon him; if he had hanged him while in his power there would be none of this and he was a heretic dog, for no one could be a Christian who was not a Roman. Tanner replied that one could be a Christian without being a Roman, when Bohórquez called for witnesses and swore that he should suffer for it. Tanner was then asked what he meant by saying that one could be a Christian without being a Roman, when he fell on his knees and begged mercy if he had erred. He was a poor youth and had a ship lying at Garachico, on which he had to pay demurrage of 120 reales a day, while the embargo on his property prevented his despatching her. At a second audience on November 19th he again begged mercy on his knees; his credit was being ruined by the demurrage on his ship, and the loss fell on his principal. Then, on the 23d, he asked for an audience in which he represented that the ships were loading and preparing to sail, while his was idle; his whole career was being wrecked; he begged them for the love of God to have mercy on him and tell him what he had done; he had lived in the religion of his fathers and must continue to do so, or he could not return to England; he had engaged to serve his master for seven years and his parents were under bonds for him. The pleadings of the poor wretch were fruitless; the case dragged on through the customary formalities and, on February 11, 1625, the consulta de fe voted that he be absolved *ad cautelam* and be recluded for two years in a convent for instruction, at the expiration of which he must bring a certificate of improvement. In accordance with this, on February 18th, he was placed in the Franciscan convent, his maintenance being paid for as a pauper.[1] Proselytism after this fashion can scarce have conduced to the salvation of souls, however much it may have replenished the treasury of the Holy Office.

With the peace of 1630 the provisions of 1604 were revived but hardly a year passed in which some Englishman was not thrown in prison and prosecuted on one pretext or another, as

---

[1] Birch, II, 1055–63.

Roderick Jones, in 1640, for saying that God alone is to be prayed to, and Edward Bland, in 1642, for having a Bible in his house.¹ In spite of this the flourishing wine-trade of the islands brought many English and Hollanders as residents, and there was even an English company established at Tenerife, where, in 1654, the tribunal reported that there were more than fifteen hundred Protestants domiciled, who were prevented from infecting the people by its incessant vigilance. The captains-general usually sought to protect them, and the influence of their ambassadors in Madrid was invoked on occasion, but, when one fell sick, the Inquisition sought to isolate him from his family and friends and put him in charge of theologians to convert him, giving rise to unseemly contests in which it was not always successful. To remedy this the tribunal, September 18, 1654, asked of the Suprema power to insist that when one of the rich Protestant residents fell sick, his compatriots should be excluded and entrance should alone be permitted to learned Catholics who might wean him from his errors.² We should probably do no injustice to the motives of the tribunal in assuming that this was dictated rather by the expectation of pious bequests than by zeal for death-bed conversions.

Foreigners sometimes sought to avert trouble by pretending Catholicism and thus placed themselves in the power of the tribunal, which was constantly on the watch for them. In 1654, for instance, Fray Luis de Betancor was summoned and interrogated as to his knowledge of such cases, to which he replied that, some twelve years before, Evan Pugh, an English surgeon, had come to Adeje to cure Doña Isabel de Ponte, and sometimes went out to hunt with her brother Juan Bautista de Ponte. He remembered that one day, when he had finished celebrating mass, he was told that Pugh had stood at the church-door with his hat in his hand, and it was currently said that he confessed to Fray Juan de Medina. Similarly, in 1674, we find the Hollander Pieter Groney testifying that when he sailed from the Texel in 1671 Juan

---

¹ Birch, II, 542, 555, 557. ² Millares, III, 83-4, 157.

de Rada was a fellow-passenger, who told him he was a Protestant and as such joined in the services during the voyage, but, when the ship was visited on arrival he swore that he was a Catholic and had since then acted exteriorly as a Catholic, though, when they lived together for a couple of months, he ate meat freely on fast days and he regarded him as a Protestant rather than as a Catholic.[1] What was the outcome in these cases cannot be told, but the investigations illustrate the careful watchfulness of the tribunal and the dangers incurred by residence within its jurisdiction. Even his official position did not protect from prosecution Edmund Smith, the British consul at Tenerife, when he was accused, in 1699, of maltreating converts to Catholicism and of persuading and threatening those inclined to it, even, it was said, shipping them away when other measures failed.[2]

In the 18th century, while foreign vessels were closely watched and a vigilant eye was kept on resident Protestants, they were no longer molested with investigations and denunciations. If, in 1728, Philip V ordered the expulsion of all foreigners, it was not on religious grounds, but to put an end to frauds on the revenue. None, however, were expelled, although some professed conversion to save themselves from annoyance.[3] A similar impulse seems to have impelled Dr. James Brown, a physician of Tenerife, who wrote, in March, 1770, to the tribunal, from the Augustinian convent of La Laguna, in which he had sought asylum from the captain-general, who was seeking to seize him and send him to England. To secure its protection he asserted his desire to abjure his errors and to be received into the Catholic Church, but in this he failed for, on July 14, he was ordered to leave the islands within forty days.[4]

The intellectual activity of the Canaries was not such as to call for much vigilance of censorship, at least during the earlier period. The *visitas de navíos*, or examination of ships arriving, for heretics

---

[1] Birch, II, 592, 825–6.
[2] Ibidem, 1070.
[3] Millares, IV, 19–20.
[4] Birch, II, 948.

and heretic books, was performed after a fashion, but the tribunal was inadequately equipped for the duty. One of the charges against Inquisitor Fúnez, in 1577, was his sending the gaoler to perform it, to which he replied that he had done so but once and that on occasions he had sent the fiscal or the secretary; it was not his business and he had no one to whom to depute it.[1]

Towards the middle of the seventeenth century there was some little activity with regard to the foreign Protestants, who were assumed to be subject to the rules of the Index. The prosecution of Edward Bland, in 1642, for possessing a Bible, seems to have attracted attention to this and, on July 5, 1645, the tribunal ordered its commissioner at Orotava to take the alguazil, notary and two familiars and visit the houses of the English heretics, secretly, without disturbance and with much discretion, asking them to exhibit all the books they possessed, examining all their chests and packages, making an inventory of all books and their authors, and making them swear before the notary as to their having licences to hold them; also whether they had been examined by the Inquisition and, if so, at what time and by what officials. If there were works by prohibited authors, or such as had not been seen by the Inquisition, they were to be deposited with a suitable person, sending a report to the tribunal, with lists of the books, and awaiting its action. If portraits or busts of heresiarchs were found they were to be seized and deposited with the books.

Under these elaborate instructions the search was duly made and the reports, if truthful, would indicate that literature and art were not extensively cultivated by the English traders. Nothing dangerous was found, though of course, as regards English books, the investigators had to accept the word of the owners. In one house they describe, as hanging on the walls of a room, very ugly half-length portraits of a strange collection of worthies—Homer, Apelles, Philo Judæus, Aristotle, Seneca, Pliny, two of Gustavus Adolphus and one without a name. It is perhaps significant that nowhere was there a Bible, a prayer-book or a work of devo-

---

[1] Archivo de Simancas, Canarias, Visitas, Leg. 250, Lib. III, Cuad. 3, fol. 20.

tion. The houses of two Portuguese traders were similarly inspected, where were found pictures of saints and of damsels with exuberant charms; also of Barbarossa and of some other pirates.[1] Possibly supervision of this kind may have continued for, on June 7, 1663, Richard Guild was summoned to the tribunal to describe six English books and four pamphlets, found in possession of Edward Baker, when among them there proved to be several controversial works as to Presbyterianism and the Independents. So, in 1670, Captain Joseph Pinero, a Portuguese, who was building a ship, was denounced for the more dangerous offence of having some Jewish books, but diligent search failed to discover them.[2]

Books, however, were not the only objects of censorial animadversion. In 1671 some plates and jars with figures of Christ, the Virgin and the saints, sold by Juan Martin Salazar of Ycod, were apparently deemed irreverent, as subordinating the divine to the commonplace of daily life, and Fray Lucas Estebes was ordered to go to his shop, with alguazil and notary, and break the stock on hand, at the same time ascertaining the name of the seller and of all purchasers. Soon after this, in 1677, an edict was issued ordering the surrender of some snuff-boxes, brought by an English vessel, which were adorned with two heads—one with a tiara and the legend *Ecclesia perversa tenet faciem diaboli*, and the other of a philosopher and the motto *Stulti sapientes aliquando*.[3]

In the latter half of the eighteenth century there seems to be more intellectual activity and desire to seek forbidden sources of knowledge, for we begin to hear of licences to read prohibited books. A register of them, commencing in 1766, shows that when obtained from the inquisitor-general they had to be submitted to the tribunal for its endorsement, but it could exercise the discretion of suspending and protesting, as in the case of one granted, in 1786, by Pius VI and endorsed by Inquisitor-general Rubin de

---

[1] Birch, II, 563–66.   [2] Ibidem, 640–2, 705.   [3] Ibidem, p. 716, 847–8

Cevallos, to Fray Antonio Ramond, on which the tribunal reports that he ought not to have it, as he is of a turbulent spirit and disorderly life. Licences generally made exception of certain specified books and authors, but sometimes they were granted without limitation. When the holder of a licence died, it was, as a rule, to be returned to the tribunal.[1]

At this period the main activity of the tribunal was in its function of censorship. It did not content itself with awaiting orders but assumed to investigate for itself; nothing escaped its vigilance, and we are told that the monthly lists which it forwarded to the Suprema of the books denounced or suppressed are surprising as coming from a province so small and so uncultured. In fact, in 1781 it expressed its grief that great and small, men and women, were abandoning themselves to reading, especially French books.[2] To do it justice it labored strenuously to discourage culture and to perpetuate obscurantism.

Yet the *visitas de navíos*, as described in a letter of August 23, 1787, were less obstructive to commerce than the practice in Spain. When a vessel cast anchor, after the visit of the health officer, the captain landed and, in company with the consul of his nation, went to the military governor, and then to the Inquisition where, under oath, he declared his nationality, his port of departure and what passengers and cargo he brought. When the vessel was discharging, the secretary of the tribunal superintended the process and noted whatever he deemed objectionable, whence it often happened that matters adverse to religion were seized.[3]

Notwithstanding all vigilance, however, the dangerous stuff found entrance. The works of Voltaire and Rousseau were widely read among the educated class and the hands of the tribunal were practically tied. It would laboriously gather testimony and compile a *sumaria* against one who read prohibited books, only to be told, when submitting it to the Suprema, to suspend action for the present. In a letter of May 24, 1788, it complained bit-

---

[1] Birch II, 940-7. [2] Millares, IV, 33-6. [3] Ibidem, pp. 36-7.

terly of this and of the consequent diminution of respect for the Inquisition. Chief among the offenders were the Commandant-general and the Regent of the Audiencia, whose cases had been sent on April 26th. Their openly expressed contempt for the tribunal perverted the whole people, who laughed at censures and read prohibited books. An object of especial aversion was the distinguished historian of the Canaries, José de Viera y Clavijo, Archdeacon of Fuerteventura. His sermons had caused him to be reprimanded repeatedly and, when his history appeared with its explanation of the apparition of the Virgen de Candelaria and other miracles of the Conquest, and its account of the controversies between the chapter and the tribunal, the indignation of the latter was unbounded. A virulent report was made to the Suprema, September 18, 1784, which remained unanswered. Another was sent, February 7, 1792, complaining of the evil effect of allowing the circulation of such writings, but this failed to elicit action, for the work was never placed on the Index.[1]

Whatever may have been its deficiencies in other respects, the tribunal seems never to have lost sight of its functions in fomenting discord with the authorities, secular and ecclesiastical. In 1521 we hear of Inquisitor Ximenes excommunicating some of the canons, in consequence of which the chapter withdrew the revenue of his prebend and sent a special envoy to the court, but he appealed to Rome and a royal cédula of July 8, 1523, ordered the chapter to make the payments.[2] Even during the inertness of Padilla's later inquisitorship, he had sufficient energy to carry on a desperate quarrel with the Audiencia. He ordered the deputy governor, Juan Arias de la Mota, to arrest Alonso de Lemos, who had been denounced to the tribunal and, on his obeying, the Audiencia arrested and prosecuted him, which led to an envenomed controversy in which excommunications and interdict were freely employed, until Philip II, February 16, 1562, ordered the liberation of Arias, adding an emphatic command in future to give to

---

[1] Millares, IV, 39, 42–44.   [2] Ibidem, I, 79–80.

the inquisitor and his officials all the favor and aid that they might require in the discharge of their duties and to honor them as was done everywhere throughout his dominions. It was doubtless in the hope of putting an end to these unseemly disturbances that Philip, by a cédula of October 10, 1567, prescribed rules for settling competencias, or conflicts over jurisdiction. The inquisitor and the Regent of the Audiencia were required to confer, when, if they could not come to an agreement, the bishop was to be called in, when the majority should decide.[1]

No regulations were of avail to prevent the dissensions for which all parties were eager and which were rendered especially bitter by the domineering assumption of superiority by the Inquisition. It was not long after Fúnez had reorganized the tribunal that he became involved in an angry controversy with Bishop Cristóbal Vera. Alonso de Valdés, a canon, incurred the episcopal displeasure by removing his name from an order addressed to the chapter for the reason that he was not present. Vera thereupon imprisoned him *incomunicado* so strictly that his food was handed in to him through a window. It chanced that Valdés was also notary of the tribunal and Fúnez claimed jurisdiction, but the bishop refused to surrender him, in spite of the fact that the absence of its notary impeded the Inquisition. The tribunal complained to the Suprema which came to its aid in a fashion showing how complete was the ascendancy claimed over the episcopal order, and how little chance a bishop had in a contest with such an antagonist. Inquisitor-general Quiroga wrote to Vera that, if the fault of Valdés was such that he should punish it, this should have been done in such wise as not to impede the operation of the tribunal. He hoped that already the case would have been handed over to the tribunal to which it belonged and that in future Vera would not give occasion for such troubles. This was enclosed in a letter of instructions from the Suprema prescribing the utmost courtesy and the most vigorous action. Fúnez is to call, with a witness, on the bishop and demand the person of

---

[1] Millares, I, 130; II, 166.

Valdés and the papers in the case, as being his rightful judge, at the same time promising his punishment to the bishop's satisfaction. If Vera refuses, Quiróga's letter is to be handed to him, and if he still refuses he is to be told that he obliges the tribunal to proceed according to law.

This so-called law is that the fiscal shall commence prosecution against the bishop and his officials for impeding the Inquisition. Then the inquisitor is to issue his formal mandate against the provisor, officials, gaolers, etc., ordering them, under pain of major excommunication and 200 ducats without further·notice, to surrender Valdés within three days to the tribunal for punishment, so that he can resume his office of notary. If this does not suffice, a similar mandate is to be issued against the bishop, under pain of privation of entering his church. If the provisor and officials persist in disobedience through three *rebeldías* (contumacies of ten days each), the inquisitor shall proclaim them excommunicated. If the bishop is stubborn he is to be prohibited from entering his church and to be admonished that if he does not comply he will be suspended from his orders and fined. If he perseveres through three *rebeldías*, letters shall be issued declaring him to have incurred these penalties and admonishing him to obey within three days under pain of major excommunication. If still contumacious, letters shall be issued declaring him publicly excommunicated and subject to the fine, which shall be collected by levy and execution. In all this he is not to be inhibited from cognizance of the case, but only that he must not impede the Inquisition by detaining its notary, and, as it is very possible that he may seek the aid of the Audiencia, if it intervenes it is to be notified of the royal cédula (of 1553) prohibiting all interference in cases concerning the Inquisition.[1]

This portentous document was received in the tribunal, April 11, 1577. It was impossible to contend with adversaries armed with such weapons and Bishop Vera was obliged to submit. Not

---

[1] Archivo de Simancas, Canarias, Visitas, Leg. 250, Lib. III, Cuad. 3, fol. 1.—Millares, II, 167-76.

content with its triumph the tribunal undertook to humiliate him still further. Doña Ana de Sobranis was a mystic who believed herself illuminated and gifted with miraculous powers. In 1572 she had denounced herself because a Franciscan, Fray Antonio del Jesús, had given her, as he said by command of God, nine consecrated hosts, which she carried always with her and worshipped. The tribunal took the hosts and dismissed the case but, as the bishop was her warm admirer and extolled her virtues, to mortify him, in 1580, the fiscal presented a furious accusation against her, as a receiver and fautor of heretics and heresies. She was arrested and imprisoned, but the tribunal had overreached itself. She had friends who appealed to the Suprema and, in May, 1581, there came from it a decision ordering a public demonstration that she was innocent and that there had been no cause for her arrest.[1]

Undeterred by the fate of Bishop Vera, his successor Fernando de Figueroa, about 1590, had a lively struggle with the tribunal. He excommunicated Doctor Alonso Pacheco, regidor of the Grand Canary and deputy governor of Tenerife, because he would not abandon illicit relations with a married woman. The tribunal intervened and evoked the case, giving rise to a prolonged competencia, which remained undecided in consequence of the death of the culprit.[2] Causes of such strife were never lacking and the first half of the seventeenth century was largely occupied by them and by an endless struggle to compel the chapter to allow to the inquisitors cushioned chairs in the cathedral.[3] On one occasion, in 1619, the chapter offended the tribunal by obeying a royal cédula and disregarding a threat which enjoined disobedience. The canons were thereupon excommunicated and appealed to the king, who found himself obliged to withdraw the cédula.[4] The overbearing conduct of the tribunal produced a chronic feeling of exasperation and the veriest trifle was sufficient to cause an outbreak. One custom provocative of much bad blood was

---

[1] Millares, II, 32–36.
[2] Ibidem, II, 104.
[3] Ibidem, III, 25, 42–3.
[4] Ibidem, I, 125–6.

that of selecting in Lent a fishing-boat and ordering it to bring its catch to the Inquisition, when, after supplying the officials and prisoners, if there was anything left it might be sold to the people. In 1629 the municipality fruitlessly complained of this to the visitor Juan de Escobar, and in 1631 there was an explosion. The Audiencia rudely intervened by throwing in prison Bartolomé Alonso, the luckless master of a boat selected, and threatening to scourge him through the streets. He managed to convey word to the tribunal, which at once sent its secretary Aguilera to the Audiencia, with a message asking the release of Alonso, but the Audiencia refused to receive anything but a written communication and Aguilera came back with a mandate requiring obedience under pain of two hundred ducats, but he was received with insults and Alonso was publicly sentenced to a hundred lashes. Then the tribunal declared the judges excommunicate, displayed their names as such in the churches and had the bells rung. The Audiencia disregarded the censures and arrested Aguilera, while the Alcaide Salazar, who had accompanied him, hid himself, but the Audiencia ordered a female slave of his to be seized and his house to be torn down, in response to which the tribunal published heavier censures and fines, demanding the release of the prisoners. Then Bishop Murga intervened and asked the tribunal to accept an honorable compromise, but it refused; he returned to the charge, urging the affliction of the people, who dreaded an interdict at a time when there was so much need of rain and when Holy Week was approaching; if reference were made to the Suprema there would be a delay of six months and meanwhile the prisoners under trial by the Audiencia would languish in gaol, for the judges would be incapacitated by the excommunication. The inquisitors, in their report to the Suprema, explained that, seeing that the people were ready for a disastrous outbreak, and as the bishop promised that the prisoners should be released at once (as they were, after a confinement of five hours) they ordered the excommunicates to be absolved and abstained from proceeding against the guilty. Then, when peace seemed restored, the quarrel broke out fiercely again, for the inquisitors demanded the surrender of the warrant of arrest, which Bartolomé Ponce, the official charged with it, refused to give up. He was arrested and as, after two days, he appealed to the Audiencia, they manacled him and ordered the arrest of the advocate and procurator who had drawn up the appeal. This secured the surrender of the document and the inquisitors felicitated themselves to the Suprema on the vigor with which they had impressed on every one the power of the Inquisition. Whether the innocent cause of the disturbance, the fisherman Bartolomé Alonso, received his lashes, seems to have been an incident too unimportant to be recorded.[1]

Rodrigo Gutiérrez de la Rosa, who was bishop from 1652 to 1658, was a man of violent temper, not as easily subdued as Bishop Vera, and his episcopate was a prolonged quarrel with his chapter and with the tribunal. In 1654, Doctor Guirola, the commissioner at Santa Cruz de Tenerife, was denounced, for his oppression, to the bishop, who ordered an investigation and his arrest if cause were found. This proved to be the case and the arrest was made, against which the tribunal protested in terms so irritating that Gutiérrez excommunicated all its officials, ringing the bells and placing their names on the *tablillas*, besides imposing a fine of 2000 ducats on each of the inquisitors. They met this by calling on the civil and military authorities for forcible aid and summoned all the bishop's dependents to assist them. Miguel de Collado, the secretary, went to the cathedral to serve these notices, on hearing which Gutiérrez hastened thither with his followers and, not finding Collado, proceeded to the house of Inquisitor José Badaran, which he searched from bottom to top for pledges to secure the payment of the fine. Word was carried to the tribunal, when the inquisitors, with a guard of soldiers, went to Badaran's house, which they found barred against them, broke open the door and a stormy interview ensued. The bishop in the cathedral, published Badaran and the fiscal as excommunicates; the inquisitors ordered the notices of excommunication removed and

---
[1] Millares, III, 51–7.

fined the bishop in 4000 ducats. To collect this, they embargoed his revenues in Tenerife and he in turn embargoed the fruits of their prebends. They obtained guards of soldiers posted in their houses and in that of the fiscal, fearing attack from the satellites of the bishop, such as he had made in 1552 in the cathedral and in 1554 at the house of the dean. In reporting all this to the Suprema, they promise to send the fiscal with all the documents by the next vessel, for the authority and power of the Inquisition depend upon the result.[1]

While this was pending a quarrel arose between the tribunal and the chapter, because the latter refused to pay to the fiscal the fruits of his prebend. Inquisitor-general Arce y Reynoso ordered the chapter to make the payment, which led the canon Matheo de Cassares and the racionero Cristóbal Vandama to commit certain acts of disrespect. To punish this the inquisitors, on November 16, 1655, arrested them, in conformity with the rules prescribed by the Suprema, in its letter of September 6, 1644, respecting the arrest of prebendaries, but, at the prayer of the chapter, they were released on the third day. They were friends of Bishop Gutiérrez, who nursed his wrath until December 26th, when there was a solemn celebration in the cathedral, at which Inquisitor Frias celebrated mass. When Inquisitor Badaran entered and took his seat in the choir, Gutiérrez in a loud voice commanded him to leave the church, as he was under excommunication for arresting clerics without jurisdiction. To avoid creating a tumult he did so; Frias celebrated mass and then joined him in the tribunal, where they drew up the necessary papers. The affair of course created an immense scandal and led to prolonged correspondence with the Suprema, which ordered it suspended April 12, 1657.[2] They were not much more successful in the outcome of the previous quarrel, although they succeeded, at the end of 1656, in procuring a royal order summoning Gutiérrez to the court. In communicating this to the bishop, December 13, 1656, the Licenciate Blas Canales advises him, if he has any money

---

[1] Millares, III, 58-68.   [2] Birch, II, 597-601.

to spare, to invest it in a jewel for presentation to the king, through the hands of the minister Louis de Haro. He probably followed the judicious counsel, for the matter ended with a decree relieving him from the fine imposed on him by the inquisitors.[1]

The next encounter was with the Audiencia, in 1661. For eight years there had been no physician in the island, when the tribunal, needing one for the torture-chamber, induced, in 1659, Dr. Domingo Rodríguez Ramos to come. He became a frequent visitor at the house of Doña Beatriz de Herrera, the *amiga* of the judge Alvaro Gil de la Sierpe, to whom she had borne several children. Sierpe became jealous and, on some pretext, Dr. Ramos was arrested, January 28, 1661, and imprisoned in chains. The tribunal asserted its jurisdiction by inhibiting the Audiencia from prosecuting the case and, on this being disregarded, the judges were excommunicated with all the solemnities. They impassively continued their functions; the tribunal then excommunicated the officials of the court, who were more easily frightened; for several months there was much popular excitement but, in October, the competencia was decided in favor of the Audiencia—doubtless because the physician was not an official of the tribunal—and a royal letter sharply rebuked the inquisitors.[2]

The tribunal was evidently losing its prestige and matters did not improve with the advent of the Bourbon dynasty. The enmity between it and the chapter continued undiminished and when, on the death of the Marquis of Celada, in 1707, his son, the Inquisitor Bartolomé Benítez de Lugo, asked that his exequies should be performed in the cathedral, the request was refused. This led to a violent rupture, in the course of which the tribunal voted the arrest of the canons, with sequestration. The chapter appealed to Philip V, who condemned the tribunal in a cédula of November 7, 1707. This did not arrive until the following year, when the chapter kept it secret until Easter; in the crowded solemnity of the feast-day, when Inquisitor Benítez was present, a secretary mounted the pulpit and read the royal decree, to his

---

[1] Millares, III, 69-70.   [2] Ibidem, 73-5.

great mortification.¹ Even worse befell the tribunal in 1714, when its inexcusable violence, in another quarrel with the chapter, led Philip V to demand the recall of the inquisitors and to enforce his commands in spite of the repeated tergiversations of the Suprema.²

As the eighteenth century advanced, the hostility of ecclesiastics and laymen towards the tribunal continued unabated, while respect for it rapidly decreased and its functions dwindled, except in the matter of censorship. A curious manifestation of the feeling entertained for it is to be found in the attitude of the parish priests with regard to the sanbenitos of the heretics hung in their churches. A report on the subject called for by the Suprema, in 1788, elicited the statement that for many years there had been no culprits of the class requiring sanbenitos. In 1756, when the walls of the parish church of Los Remedios de La Laguna were whitened, the incumbents resisted the replacement of the sanbenitos, or at least wished to hang them where they should not be seen, but the tribunal ordered them to be renovated and hung conspicuously. In the Dominican church of Las Palmas, there used to be sanbenitos, but they had disappeared and the inquisitors could not explain the cause of their removal. Eight years ago the parish church of Telde was whitened and the incumbents would not replace them; Inquisitor Padilla was informed of this, but he took no action. The only ones then to be seen in Las Palmas were in the cathedral; the building was undergoing alterations and the walls would be whitened, which the inquisitors expected would be alleged as a reason for removing them.³ Equally suggestive of the feeling of the laity is the fact that, when the position of alguazil mayor fell vacant, it was offered in vain to representatives of the principal families, who all declined under various pretexts.⁴

The sentiment of the population was duly represented by the

¹ Millares, IV, 18–19.
² For details see History of the Inquisition of Spain, I, 348.
³ Millares, IV, 23–29. ⁴ Ibidem, p. 70.

eloquent priest Ruiz de Padron in the debates of the Córtes of Cádiz, in 1813, and the suppression of the Inquisition was greeted by the ecclesiastics of the Canaries in a temper very different from that manifested in the Peninsula. The bishop, Manuel Verdugo, a native of Las Palmas, was an enlightened man, who had had frequent differences with the tribunal. The decree of suppression was received by him March 31st; it was his duty to take charge of the archives and to close the building, and he lost no time in communicating it to the inquisitors, José Francisco Borbujo y Riba and Antonio Fernando de Echanove. The chapter was overjoyed and, at a session on April 3d, it addressed the Córtes, characterizing the decree as manifestly the work of God and as removing from the Church of Christ a blemish which rendered religion odious. The same afternoon the sanbenitos in the cathedral were solemnly burnt in the patio. The bishop also reported to the Córtes that their manifesto, which had excited the canons of Cádiz to such extremity of opposition, had been duly read that morning, and that he had been greatly pleased to see that the acts of the Córtes had been received throughout his diocese with universal satisfaction. He lost no time in taking possession of the archives, but the inquisitors had already taken the precaution to remove, from the volume of their correspondence with the Suprema, two leaves in which they had spoken ill of him. The financial officials at the same time assumed charge of the landed property and censos, or ground-rents, of the tribunal, which we are told were large and numerous. Inquisitor Borbujo remained at his post, awaiting the reaction. The poets of the island were prompt in expressing the exuberance of their joy in verses, for which action was subsequently taken against the priest, Mariano Romero, Don Rafael Bento and Don Francisco Guerra y Bethencourt.[1]

When the Restoration swiftly followed, Inquisitor Borbujo received, on August 17, 1814, the decree re-establishing the Inquisition and called on the bishop to surrender the building, but the latter declared that he must await orders from competent author-

---
[1] Millares, IV, 87, 97–100.

ity. On September 29th there came an order for the re-installation of the tribunal and Borbujo made another effort to gain possession of the building and property, but it was not until a royal mandate of November 28th was received that he succeeded in doing so. The tribunal was thus fairly put on its feet again, but such was the abhorrence in which it was held that its edicts were torn down, its jurisdiction was everywhere contested, and its offices of alguazil and familiars could not be filled.[1]

Thus resuscitated, it diligently collected the pamphlets and periodicals and verses of the revolutionary period, and molested their authors as far as it could. In fact, under the Restoration, except the occasional prosecution of a wise-woman, its functions, as in Spain, were mainly political, liberalism being equivalent to heresy and, except when it had some political end in view, its efforts were ridiculed by both the civil and military authorities, which regarded it with no respect and encroached upon it from all sides. When the Revolution of 1820 broke out, news of Fernando VII's oath to the Constitution and decree of March 9th suppressing the Holy Office reached Santa Cruz de Tenerife April 29th and Las Palmas some days later. Amid popular rejoicings, the Inquisition closed its doors, delivered up its archives and the inquisitors sailed for Spain. No care was taken of the archives, which were pillaged by curiosity hunters and those whose interests led them to acquire documents concerning limpieza or old law-suits. What remained were stored in a damp, unventilated place; when removed, they were carried off by cartloads, without keeping them in any order and, in 1874, Millares describes them as forming a pile of chaotic, mutilated and illegible papers in a room of the City Hall.[2]

The reader may reasonably ask what, in its labor of three centuries, the tribunal of the Canaries accomplished to justify its existence.

---

[1] Millares, IV, 105–6. [2] Ibidem, pp. 106–9, 114–17.

CHAPTER VI.

MEXICO.

THE ostensible object of the Spanish conquests in the New World was the propagation of the faith. This was the sole motive alleged by Alexander VI, in the celebrated bull of 1493, conferring on the Spanish sovereigns domination over the territories discovered by Columbus; it was asserted in the codicil to Queen Isabella's will, urging her husband and children to keep it ever in view, and it was put forward in all the commissions and instructions issued to the adventurers who converted the shores of the Caribbean into scenes of oppression and carnage.[1] If Philip II was solicitous to preserve the purity of the faith in his own dominions, he was no less anxious to spread it beyond the seas; he prescribed this as one of the chief duties of his officers, describing it as the principal object of Spanish rule, to which all questions of profit and advantage were to be regarded as subordinate.[2]

It must be admitted, however, that the effort to spread the gospel lagged behind those directed to the acquisition of the precious metals. It is true that, on the second voyage of Columbus, in 1493, the sovereigns sent Fray Buil, with a dozen clerics and full papal faculties, but he busied himself more in quarrelling with the admiral than in converting the heathen.[3] The first regular missionaries of whom we have knowledge were two Franciscans who, in 1500, accompanied Bobadilla to the West Indies and, in a letter of October 12th of that year, reported to the Observantine Vicar-general, Olivier Maillard, that they found the natives

---

[1] Alex. PP. VI Bull *Inter cætera*, 4 Maii, 1493 (Bullar. Rom. I, 454).—Mariana, Hist. de España, T. IX, Append., p. xxvi (Ed. 1796).—Recopilacion de las Leyes de las Indias, Lib. I, Tit. i, ley 2.
[2] Recop., Lib. I, Tit. i, ley 5; Lib. II, Tit. ii, ley 8.
[3] Torquemada, De la Monarquía Indiana, Lib. XVIII, cap. 8.

eager for conversion and that they had baptized three thousand in the first port which they reached in Hispañola.¹ They were followed, in 1502, by a few more Franciscans under Fray Alonso del Espinal, a worthy man, according to Las Casas, but who could think of nothing but the *Summa Angelica* of his brother Franciscan, Angelo da Chivasso.² The first earnest effort to instruct the natives was made by Fray Pedro de Córdova, who came in 1510 with two Dominicans and was soon followed by ten or twelve more; during the succeeding years he and the Franciscans founded some missionary stations on the coast of Tierra Firme, but they were broken up by the Indians in 1523.³ As, however, we are told that none of the missionaries took the trouble to learn the Indian languages, their evangelizing success may be doubted.⁴

The efforts to organize a church establishment proceeded but slowly at first. Hispañola was divided into two bishoprics, San Domingo and la Vega. For the former, at a date not definitely stated, the Franciscan, García de Padilla, was appointed, but he died before setting out to take possession. For the latter, Pero Suárez Deza, nephew of Inquisitor-general Deza, was chosen and we are told that he governed his see for some years⁵ but, as he figures in the Lucero troubles of Córdova, in 1506, as the "archbishop-elect of the Indies" the period of his episcopate is not easily definable. However this may be, the first bishop who appears in the episcopal lists of Hispañola is Alessandro Geraldino, with the date of 1520.⁶ Cortés, who had asked to have bishoprics organized in his new conquests, speedily changed his mind and requested Charles V to send out only friars. The priests of the Indians, he said, were so rigidly held to modesty and chastity that, if the people were to witness the pomp and disorderly lives of the Spanish clergy, they would regard Chris-

---

¹ Cron. Glassberger, ann. 1500 (Analecta Franciscana, Tom. II).
² Las Casas, Historia de las Indias, Lib. III, cap. 5, 14 (Coleccion de Documentos, LXIV, 372, 422).
³ Las Casas, *op. cit.*, Lib. II, cap. 54 (Col. de Doc., LXV, 275; LXVI, 165, 180).
⁴ Torquemada, *ubi sup.*   ⁵ Ibidem.
⁶ Gams, Series Episcoporum, p. 148.

tianity as a farce and their conversion would be impracticable. Charles heeded the warning and, during the rest of his reign, he appointed as bishops only members of the religious Orders, while the secular clergy were but sparingly allowed to emigrate and those who succeeded in going earned as a body a most unenviable reputation.[1] The Church thus started grew rapidly and, towards the close of the century, Padre Mendieta informs us that New Spain (comprising Mexico and Central America) had ten bishoprics, besides the metropolitan see of the capital, four hundred convents and as many clerical districts, and that each of these eight hundred had numerous churches in its charge.[2]

It seems strange that the Spanish monarchs, combining earnest desire for the propagation of the faith with intense zeal for its purity, should have so long postponed the extension of the Holy Office over their new dominions, while thus active in building up the Church. The Indian neophytes, it is true, were not in need of its ministrations, but the colonists might well be a subject of concern. Manasseh ben Israel (*circa* 1644) tells us that, after the expulsion in 1492, many Jews and Judaizing New Christians sought an asylum in the New World and that Antonio Montesinos, a Spanish Jew who had long lived there, reported that he found the Jewish rites carefully preserved, especially in certain valleys of South America.[3] It is true that there were repeated efforts to prohibit New Christians and those who had been penanced by the Inquisition, with their descendants, from emigrating to the Indies, but this was a provision difficult to enforce, and relief from it was a financial expedient tempting to the chronically empty treasury of Spain. In the great composition of Seville, in 1509, there was a provision that, for twenty thousand ducats,

---

[1] Torquemada, *op. cit.*, Lib. xv, cap. 1, 10.—Col. de Doc., Tom. XXVI, p. 286.
See also a letter of the Franciscan Custodian Fray Angel de Valencia, to Charles V, May 8, 1552. If the description of his brother frailes by Fray Pedro Duran, in a letter to Philip II, Feb. 2, 1583, be not exaggerated, there was not much gained in restricting episcopal appointments to the regular Orders.—J. T. Medina, Historia de la Inquisicion en Mexico, pp. 11, 12 (Santiago de Chile, 1905).

[2] Mendieta, Hist. eccles. Indiana, p. 549 (Mexico, 1870).

[3] Amador de los Rios, Hist. de los Judíos, III, 378.

the disability should be in so far removed that such persons could go to the colonies and trade there for two years, on each voyage. After Ferdinand's death, this was confirmed by Charles V, but he soon afterwards, September 24, 1518, ordered the Casa de Contratacion of Seville not to permit them to embark. They complained loudly of this violation of faith and, on January 23, 1519, he ordered the Inquisition of Seville to examine the agreement and, if it was found to contain such a clause, the prohibition should be withdrawn. Six months later, on July 16th, it was renewed, exciting fresh remonstrances that they were compelled to pay the money while the privilege was denied. The matter was then referred to the Suprema, which decided that the complaints were justified, whereupon Charles, on December 13th, ordered the inquisitors of Seville to permit them to go, provided the whole amount of the composition, eighty thousand ducats, had been fully paid.[1] Thus, in one way or another, the enterprising New Christians sought successfully to share in the lucrative exploitation of the colonies, and it illustrates the ineffectiveness of Spanish administration that, in 1537, it felt obliged to call in papal assistance to supplement its deficiencies. Accordingly Paul III, in his bull *Altitudo divini consilii*, forbade all apostates from going to the Indies and commanded the colonial bishops to expel any who might come.[2] Prince Philip followed this by a decree of August 14, 1543, ordering all viceroys, governors and courts to investigate what Moorish slaves or freemen, recently converted, or sons of Jews resided in the Indies and to banish all whom they might discover, sending them to Spain in the first ships, for in no case were they to be allowed to remain.[3]

It is evident that the persevering New Christians evaded these

---

[1] Archivo de Simancas, Inquisicion, Lib. 9, fol. 71.

See also a letter from Alonzo de Zuazo to Chièvres, written from Hispañola, January 29, 1519, urging that immigrants be invited from all nations, except Moors and Jews and the reconciled New Christians with their children and grandchildren, who were prohibited by the royal ordinance.—Col. de Documentos, T. II, p. 371.

[2] Lorenzana, Concilios Provinciales de Mejico, p. 32 (Mexico, 1769).

[3] Recop. de las Indias, Lib. VII, Tit. v, ley 29.

regulations and that their success in this was a subject of solicitude, yet there was long delay in providing effectual means to preserve the faith from their contamination. It is true that, when bishoprics were erected, the jurisdiction over heresy, inherent in the episcopal office, might have been exercised on them, had not the Inquisition arrogated to itself the exclusive cognizance over all matters of faith and regarded with extreme jealousy all episcopal invasions of its province. This is illustrated by a case in 1515 which shows how indisposed it was even to delegate its power. Pedro de Leon, with his wife and daughter, had sought refuge in Hispañola, where the episcopal provisor arrested them and obtained confessions inculpating them and others. In place of authorizing him to complete the trial and punish them, the Suprema notified him that the inquisitor-general was sending a special messenger to bring them back to Seville, together with any other fugitives whom the provisor may have arrested, and he is commanded to deliver them without delay or prevarication, under penalty of forfeiture of temporalities and citizenship; moreover, the Admiral Diego Colon is commanded to render aid and favor and the Contratacion of Seville is required to furnish the messenger with a good ship to take him to the Indies and to see that on his return he has a vessel with a captain beyond suspicion and a place where the prisoners can be confined and kept secluded from all communication.[1]

This was evidently a very cumbrous and costly method of dealing with heretics, but it does not appear that the Holy Office consented to delegate its powers until 1519, when Charles V, by a cédula of May 20th, confirmed the appointment by Cardinal Adrian the inquisitor-general, of Alfonso Manso, Bishop of Puertorico and the Dominican Pedro de Córdova, as inquisitors of the Indies, and ordered all officials to render them obedience and assistance.[2] On the death of Pedro, the appointing power

[1] Archivo de Simancas, Inquisicion, Libro 3, fol. 106, 107.
[2] Ibidem, Lib. 9, fol. 37.—Llorente (Añales, II, 91) states that Ximenes, May 7, 1516, appointed Juan Quevedo, Bishop of Cuba, as delegate inquisitor-general of the Indies, with power to appoint judges and other officials, but I can find no trace of such action and, if the appointment was made, it was ineffective. The

is said to have vested in the Audiencia of San Domingo which, in 1524, appointed Martin de Valencia as commissioner. He was a Franciscan of high repute for holiness who in that year reached Mexico at the head of a dozen of his brethren and was received by the Conquistadores on their knees. We are told that he burnt a heretic and reconciled two others, which if true would show that he was clothed with the full powers of an inquisitor. He soon afterwards returned to Spain and we hear of Fray Tomás Ortiz, Fray Domingo de Betanzos and Fray Vicente de Santa María as succeeding him in 1526 and 1528, but the references to these shadowy personalities are conflicting and there are no records of their activity.[1]

With the appointment of bishops in New Spain, in 1527, and the gradual systematic organization of the hierarchy, it would seem that special inquisitorial powers were delegated to them, of the results of which we have traces in the *sanbenitos* or *tablillas* of those burnt or reconciled which were hung in the cathedrals. Early in the nineteenth century Padre José Pichardo made a list of those remaining in the cathedral of Mexico, which has recently been printed and from this we learn that an auto de fe was celebrated in 1536, at which Andreas Morvan was reconciled for Lutheranism, and another in 1539, when Francisco Millan was reconciled for Judaism and a cacique of Tezcoco was burnt for offering human sacrifices.[2] This latter stretch of authority by

first see erected in Cuba was that of Santiago, in 1522 (Gams, p. 146), and there could have been none as early as 1516, as the first expedition to the island under Diego Velázquez did not occur until 1511. Hefele (Der Cardinal Ximenes, p. 497) makes Ximenes appoint Alessandro Geraldino, Bishop of San Domingo and his colleague of la Vega inquisitors-general but, as we have seen, Geraldino was not appointed as bishop until 1522, four years after the death of Ximenes.

[1] Remesal, Historia de la Provincia de S. Vicente de Chyapa y Guatemala, Lib II, cap. iii.—Obregon, Mexico viejo, 1ª Serie, pp. 179–80; 2ª Serie, p. 390 (Mexico, 1891–5).

[2] Obregon, México viejo, 2ª Serie, p. 333.

It would seem that the sanbenitos were not hung in the cathedral until 1667, after pressure from the Suprema to compel the inquisitors to perform the work, which must have been considerable if they had to be compiled from the records. The number then hung amounted to 404.—Medina, Historia de la Inquisicion de México, p. 317.

Archbishop Zumárraga was contrary to the policy of the government and, in 1543, Inquisitor-general Tavera superseded him by sending Francisco Tello de Sandoval, inquisitor of Toledo, to Mexico to perform the same office. His commission, dated July 18th of that year, empowers him to take up and prosecute to the end all cases commenced by previous inquisitors, and a letter of Prince Philip, July 24th, to the royal officials of New Spain, commands them to give him all requisite assistance.[1] It does not appear, however, that he was furnished with officials to organize a tribunal and, as his principal charge was that of a *visitador* or inspector of the ecclesiastical establishment, it is not probable that he accomplished much as inquisitor. The list of sanbenitos shows no more autos de fe until 1555, by which time the work had fallen back into the hands of Archbishop Montúfar, for the home Government was evidently unwilling to assume the heavy cost of a fully organized tribunal, and the bishops were ready to perform its duties. When, in 1545, Las Casas, as Bishop of Chiapa, asked the royal Audiencia of Gracia á Dios to sustain him in his episcopal jurisdiction against his recalcitrant flock, he makes special reference to cases of the Inquisition as included in it and, soon after this, in Peru, Juan Matienzo says that the bishops exercised inquisitorial jurisdiction and that, when any attempt was made to appeal from them, they would elude it by claiming that they were acting as inquisitors.[2] That this was recognized at home is manifested by Prince Philip, in 1553, extending to the Indies the Concordia of Castile regulating the *fuero* of familiars, as though there was a regularly organized Inquisition throughout the colonies.[3]

In the auto of 1555, Gerónimo Venzon, an Italian, was reconciled for Lutheranism and it was followed by one in 1558, when María de Ocampo was reconciled for pact with the demon.[4] There

---

[1] Puja, Provisiones, Cédulas, Instrumentos de su Magestad etc., fol. 97 (Mexico, 1563).

[2] Coleccion de Documentos, LXX, 535.—Solorzani de Indiar. Gubern. Lib. III, cap. xxiv, n. 9.

[3] Recop. de las Indias, Lib. I, Tit. xix, ley 4. [4] Obregon, *loc. cit.*

was also an Englishman named Robert Thompson, condemned for Lutheranism to wear the sanbenito for three years, and a Genoese, Agostino Boacio, for the same crime, to perpetual prison and sanbenito. These two latter were shipped to Seville to perform their penance, but Boacio managed to escape at the Azores. In 1560 there were seven Lutherans reconciled, concerning whom we have no details; in 1561 a French Calvinist and a Greek schismatist and in 1562 two French Calvinists.[1] This shows that the episcopal Inquisition was by no means inert, and a sentence rendered by the Ordinary of Mexico, in 1568, indicates that its severity might cause the installation of the regular Holy Office to be regarded rather as a relief. A Flemish painter, Simon Pereyns, who had drifted to Mexico, in a talk with a brother artist, Francisco Morales, chanced to utter the common remark that simple fornication was not a sin and persisted in it after remonstrance. That the episcopal Inquisition was thoroughly established is indicated by his considering it prudent to denounce himself to the Officiality, which he did on September 10, 1568. In Spain this particular heresy, especially in *espontaneados*, was not severely treated, but the provisor, Esteban de Portillo, took it seriously and threw him in prison. During the trial Morales testified that Pereyns had said that he preferred to paint portraits rather than images, which he explained was because they paid better. This did not satisfy the provisor who proceeded to torture him when he endured, without further confession, three turns of the *cordeles* and three jars of water trickled down his throat on a linen cloth. This ought to have earned his dismissal but, on December 4th, he was condemned to pay the costs of his trial and to give security that he would not leave the city until he should have painted a picture of Our Lady of Merced, as an altar-piece for the church. He complied and it was duly hung in the cathedral.[2] A still more forcible

---

[1] Obregon, *loc. cit.*—Schäfer, Beiträge zur Geschichte der Spanischen Protestantismus, II, 373.

[2] Obregon, *op. cit.*, 2ª Serie, p. 61

example of the abuse of episcopal inquisitorial authority was the case of Don Pedro Juárez de Toledo, alcalde mayor of Trinidad in Guatemala, arrested with sequestration of property by his bishop, Bernardino de Villalpando, on a charge of heresy. He died in September, 1569, with his trial unfinished; it was transferred to the Inquisition on its establishment and, in the auto de fe of February 28, 1574, a sentence was rendered clearing his memory of all infamy, which we are told gave much satisfaction for he was a man much honored and the vindictiveness of the prosecution was notorious.[1]

These inquisitorial powers, however, were only enjoyed temporarily by the bishops and when, in 1570, a tribunal was finally established in Mexico, a circular was addressed to them formally warning them against allowing their provisors or officials to exercise jurisdiction in matters of faith and ordering them to transmit to the inquisitors any evidence which they might have or might obtain in cases of heresy. The bishops apparently were unwilling to surrender the jurisdiction to which they had grown accustomed, for the command had to be repeated, May 26, 1585.[2]

It is worthy of remark that there seems to have been no pressure from Rome to extend the Inquisition over the New World. St. Pius V, notwithstanding his fierce inquisitorial activity in Italy, could give Philip II the sanest and most temperate advice about the colonies. On learning that the king proposed to send thither officials selected with the utmost care, he wrote, August 18, 1568, to Inquisitor-general Espinosa to encourage him in the good work. The surest way, he says, to propagate the faith is to remove all unnecessary burdens and to so treat the people that they may rejoice more and more to throw off the bonds of idolatry and submit themselves to the sweet yoke of Christ; the Christians who go thither should be such as to edify the people by their lives and morals, so as to confirm the converts and to allure the heathen

---

[1] Medina, *op. cit.*, pp. 35–6.
[2] Solorzani *op. cit.*, Lib. III, cap. xxiv, n. 38.

to conversion.¹ To do Philip justice, he earnestly strove to follow in the path thus wisely indicated, but Spanish maladministration was too firmly rooted for him to succeed. If he could not thus render the faith attractive he could at least preserve its purity; the colonists were becoming too numerous for their aberrations to be left to episcopal provisors, overburdened with a multiplicity of other duties, and the only safety lay in extending to the colonies the Inquisition whose tribunals would have no other function.

The incentive to this, however, was not so much the danger anticipated from Judaizing New Christians as from the propaganda of the Reformers, who were regarded as zealously engaged in sending to the New World their heretical books and versions of Scripture and even as venturing there personally in hopes of combining missionary work with the profits of trade. This is the motive alleged by Philip II, in his cédulas of January 25, 1569, and August 16, 1570, confirming the action of Inquisitor-general Espinosa in founding the Mexican tribunal.² Leonardo Donato, the Venetian envoy, in his report of 1573, assents to this as the cause, not only of the establishment of the Mexican Inquisition but also of the prohibition of intercourse with the colonies to Germans and Flemings, although the latter were Spanish subjects.³ The Protestant missionary spirit in fact was, at this time, by no means as ardent as the Inquisition sought to make the faithful believe, yet it could reasonably point in justification to the number of Protestants who furnished the material for the earlier inquisitorial activity.

Although the decision to establish colonial tribunals was reached and made known in the cédula of January, 1569, Philip proceeded with his usual dilatory caution. It was not until January 3, 1570, that Espinosa notified Doctor Moya de Contreras, then Inquisitor of Murcia, that he had been selected as senior

---

[1] Bulario de la Orden de Santiago, Lib. III, fol. 79, 123.

[2] Recop. de las Indias, Lib. I, Tit. xix, ley 1.—Cf. Simancæ de Catholicis Institutionibus, Tit. xxxviii, n. 12.

[3] Relazioni Venete, Serie I, Tom. VI, p. 462.

inquisitor of the projected tribunal; he was to enjoy a salary of three thousand pesos and the fruits of a prebend in the cathedral; he was to have a colleague, a fiscal and a notary or secretary, while such other officials as might be necessary would be appointed on the spot, in accordance with instructions to be given to him.[1] Contreras declined the appointment on the ground of his health, which would not endure the voyage, and his poverty, for he was endeavoring to place his sister in a convent. Espinosa insisted, pointing out that the position would be but temporary and would lead to promotion, which was verified for, in 1573, Contreras became Archbishop of Mexico, served for a time as viceroy, and, on his return to Spain, was made president of the Council of Indies.[2] The junior inquisitor was the Licenciado Pascual de Cervantes, canon of Canaries, who was instructed to learn the duties of his office from his experienced senior. Their commissions bore date August 18, 1570, and empowered them to evoke

---

[1] This and the following details of the installation of the Mexican Inquisition I owe to a series of documents, copies of which were kindly furnished to me by the late General Don Vicente Riva Palacio.

Doctor Moya de Contreras was an old and experienced hand. In 1541 he was appointed inquisitor of Saragossa.—Archivo de Simancas, Inquisicion, Sala 40, Lib. 4, fol. 117.

[2] Torquemada, Lib. xix, cap. 29. For almost all the early inquisitors of Mexico the tribunal was the stepping-stone to the episcopate. Bonilla, who went, in 1571, as fiscal, became inquisitor in 1573 and Archbishop of Mexico in 1592. Alonso Granero, who went as inquisitor in 1574, became Bishop of Charcas the same year. Santos García was inquisitor in 1576 and Bishop of Jalisco in 1597. Alonso de Peralta, who was inquisitor in 1594, was made Archbishop of La Plata in 1609, and Lobo Guerrero, who was inquisitor in 1593, became Archbishop of Santafé in 1598.

It illustrates the character of the men occupying these positions that when Granero left Mexico for his bishopric he went by land and in Nicaragua he assumed still to be inquisitor, condemning people and fining them to defray his travelling expenses. An unlucky notary named Rodrigo de Evora wrote some satiric couplets about him, whereupon he was thrown in prison with chains on hands and feet, tortured till he was crippled with dislocated joints and then exposed in a public auto and condemned to 300 lashes and six years of galleys. The scourging was administered with excessive severity and Evora had to beg his way to Mexico to appeal to the tribunal there. He evidently was stripped of his property and among other things of four cases of Chinese ware, which Granero appropriated to his own use.—Medina, *op. cit.*, 76–78.

and continue all cases that might be in the hands of inquisitors or episcopal officials. It was not until November 13th that they set sail from San Lucar for the Canaries, where they hoped to take passage on the fleet. In this they were disappointed, as it did not call at the islands, and they were detained in Tenerife until June 2, 1571. Cervantes died on the voyage July 26th and Contreras was wrecked on the coast of Cuba, August 11th, but he found refuge on another vessel and reached San Juan de Ulua August 18th. He entered the city of Mexico September 12th, but the ceremonies of reception and installation were delayed until November 4th.[1] These were of the most impressive character. A proclamation, two days before, to sound of drum and trumpet, had summoned to be present in the cathedral, under pain of major excommunication, the whole population over twelve years of age. From the building assigned to the tribunal, the viceroy and senior judge of the royal court, followed by all the officials, conducted the inquisitor to the church, where, after the sermon and before the elevation of the host, the secretary of the Inquisition read the royal letters addressed to the viceroy and all other officials, reciting at great length the dangers of the heretic propaganda and commanding every one to render all aid and service to the inquisitors and their officials, arresting all whom they should designate and punishing with the legal penalties those whom they should relax as heretics or relapsed. Moreover the king took under his protection all those connected with the Holy Office and warned his subjects that any injury inflicted on them would be visited with the punishment due to violation of the royal safeguard. Then an edict was read, embodying the oath of obedience and pledging every one, under fearful maledictions, spiritual and temporal, to aid the Inquisition in every way and to denounce and persecute heretics as wolves and mad dogs. On this the viceroy arose and, placing his hand on the gospels which lay on a table, took the oath and all the officials present advanced in procession and followed his example.

---

[1] Medina, *op. cit.*, p. 22.

The Inquisition thus was fairly established in the city of Mexico; it issued its Edict of Faith and, on November 10th, it published letters addressed to all the inhabitants of its enormous district, stretching from the Atlantic to the Pacific and from Darien to the unknown regions to the North, commanding them and their officials to take the same portentous oath of obedience. In an age of faith, it is easy to see how profound was the impression made when the population of every parish and mission was assembled in its church and listened to such utterances in the name of Christ and the pope, with their reduplication of threats and promises, and each one was required to raise his right hand and solemnly swear on the cross and the gospels to accept it all and obey it to the letter.[1]

As communication between the tribunal and the Supreme Council in Madrid was slow and irregular, there was necessity that it should have greater independent authority than that allowed to the provincial Inquisitions in Spain, which at this period were constantly becoming more and more subject to the central head. Accordingly it was furnished not only with the general Instructions current everywhere but with special elaborate ones, providing among other matters that in the *consulta de fe*, or meeting to decide upon a sentence, if there should be *discordia* or lack of unanimity among the inquisitors and the episcopal Ordinary (who always took part in such matters) the case was not referred to the Suprema, as in Spain, unless the question was as to relaxation to the secular arm; if this was involved, the accused was to be sent to the Suprema, which decided his fate. If the sentence was to torture or reconciliation, or a milder penance, then the opinion prevailed of the two inquisitors, or of the Ordinary and one of the inquisitors, while if all three were discordant, then the consultors decided as to which of the three opinions should be adopted. Appeals to the Suprema against sentences of torture, or of extraordinary punishments, were similarly replaced by giving the prisoner another hearing, allowing the fiscal to argue

---

[1] See Appendix.

against him and reconsidering the sentence in the consulta de fe.[1] These instructions also prescribed the enforcement of the Index of prohibited books, both as to the suppression of those existing in the colony and the watchful supervision of imports, all of which Doctor Contreras hastened to execute by requiring every owner of books to present a sworn list of those in his possession. It would not be easy, however, to define whence he derived his authority for his next step, which was to forbid the departure from the land of any one without a special licence from the Inquisition—a stretch of power which we are told met with the hearty concurrence of the viceroy, Martin Enríquez, who had not otherwise manifested much prepossession in favor of the new jurisdiction thus established in his territories.[2]

The inquisitor evidently magnified his office and the result soon showed how much more efficient was a tribunal of which the energies were concentrated on a single object, than the desultory action of the episcopal provisors. He had, on his arrival, lost no time in filling up his staff by appointing an alguazil mayor, an alcaide of the secret prisons, a *portero* or apparitor and a messenger, as well as a receiver of confiscations, to whom he assigned the handsome salary of six hundred ducats, not anticipating how slender, for some time, were to be the receipts from that source. His efforts were seconded at home for, by a *carta orden* of the Suprema, January 5, 1573, the Spanish tribunals were instructed to give precedence over all other business to requests from colonial Inquisitions for evidence to be taken and furnished, experience having already shown the great benefit arising from their establishment there.[3] The publication of the Edict of Faith had brought in many denunciations; arrests were frequent and the number of prisoners soon exceeded the capacity of the improvised

---

[1] Mr. Elkan N. Adler has printed a translation of these special instructions furnished to Peru. Unquestionably the same provisions must have been established in Mexico.—Publications of the American Jewish Historical Society, No. 12.

The inquisitors were empowered to call in the judges of the Royal Audiencia as consultors in the *consulta de fe.*—Ibidem.

[2] Medina, *op. cit.*, p. 30.   [3] Llorente, Hist. crít., cap. xix, art. ii. n. 18.

prison—among them some thirty-six Englishmen, the remnant of the hundred of Sir John Hawkins's men who had taken their chances on shore after the disaster at San Juan de Ulua, in 1568.[1] The fruits of this energy were seen when the first great auto de fe was celebrated February 28, 1574, with a solemnity declared by eyewitnesses to be equal in everything, save the presence of royalty, to that of Valladolid, May 21, 1559, when the Spanish Lutherans suffered. A fortnight in advance it was announced throughout the city with drums and trumpets, the Inquisition commenced to erect its staging and the city authorities did the like for themselves and their wives, and invited the judges and their wives to seats on it. A week later, on learning that prominent officials from all parts of the country were coming, the invitation was extended to them. The population poured in from all quarters, crowding the streets and occupying every spot from which the spectacle could be witnessed. The night before was occupied in drilling, in the courtyard of the Inquisition, the unfortunates who were to appear and at daylight they were breakfasted on wine and slices of bread fried in honey.

The accounts of the auto as given by Señor Medina are somewhat confused, but from them we gather that there were seventy-four sufferers in all. Of these, three were for asserting that simple fornication between the unmarried was no sin; twenty-seven were for bigamy; two for blasphemy; one for wearing prohibited articles although his grandfather had been burnt; two for "propositions;" one because he had made his wife confess to him and thirty-six for Lutheranism, of whom two, George Ripley and Marin Cornu were burnt. These Lutherans were all foreigners of various nationalities, but mostly English, consisting of Hawkins's men. One of these, named Miles Phillips has left an account of the affair, in which he says that his compatriots George Ripley, Peter Momfrie and Cornelius the Irishman were burnt, sixty or sixty-one were scourged and sent to the galleys and seven, of whom he was

---
[1] Medina, *op. cit.*, p. 31.

one, were condemned to serve in convents; the wholesale scourging was performed the next day, through the accustomed streets, the culprits being preceded by a crier calling out "See these English Lutheran dogs, enemies of God!" while inquisitors and familiars shouted to the executioners "Harder, harder, on these English Lutherans!" Páramo, who doubtless had access to official records, tells us that there were about eighty penitents in all, of whom an Englishman and a Frenchman were burnt, some Judaizers were reconciled, together with several bigamists and practitioners of sorcery. One of these latter, he says, was a woman who had made her husband come in two days to Mexico from Guatemala, two hundred leagues away and, when asked by the inquisitor why she had done this, she replied that it was in order to enjoy the sight of his beauty, the fact being that he was the foulest of men. Bigamy, he adds, was a very frequent crime, for men thought that, at so great a distance from Spain, there was little chance of detection.[1]

Miles Phillips says that at the conclusion of the auto the victims relaxed were burnt on the plaza, near the staging. This shows that no proper preparation had been made for these solemnities and in fact, it was not until 1596 that the municipality, at a cost of four hundred pesos, constructed a *quemadero* or burning place, where concremation could be performed decently and in order. It was a ghastly adjunct to a pleasure-ground, for it was situated at the east end of the Alameda. There it remained until the stake was growing obsolete and was removed in 1771 to enlarge the promenade.[2]

This was the last inquisitorial act of Doctor Contreras, whose

---

[1] Medina, *op. cit.*, pp. 36–43.—Obregon, *op. cit.*, 2ª Serie, 84–90, 335–7.—Páramo de Orig. Officii S. Inquisit., p. 241. The "Cornelius the Irishman" of Miles Phillips's narrative was not burnt until the auto of March 6, 1575. He was one of Hawkins's men, who had married in Guatemala.—Medina, p. 51.

[2] Obregon, p. 391. In the great auto of December 8, 1596, the sentence to relaxation of Manuel Díaz states that he is to be taken on horseback to the market-place of San Ipolito where, in the place provided for it, he is to be garroted and burnt.—Proceso contra Manuel Díaz, fol. 154 (I owe to the kindness of General Riva Palacio several of the original trials connected with this auto).

promotion to the archbishopric had already taken place. He had been provided with a colleague by the promotion of the fiscal Bonilla in 1572, and the vacancy caused by his retirement was filled by the appointment of Alonso Granero de Avalos. These held an auto March 6, 1575, in which there were thirty-one culprits, twenty-five of them for bigamy and but one Protestant, the Irishman William Cornelius, who was burnt. Less important was an auto celebrated February 19, 1576, with thirteen culprits, all for minor offences, except an Englishman named Thomas Farrar, a shoemaker long resident in Mexico, who was reconciled for Protestantism. Another auto followed December 15, 1577, in which, besides the customary minor offenders, three Englishmen, Paul Hawkins, John Stone and Robert Cook, were reconciled for Protestantism and the first Judaizer, Alvarez Pliego, abjured de vehementi and was fined in 500 pesos.[1] The Judaism which thus commenced to show itself speedily furnished further victims for, in 1578, two Spaniards were burnt for it and, in 1579, another, García González Bermejero, while a Frenchman, Guillaume Potier, who escaped, was burnt in effigy for Calvinism. After this, until 1590, the tribunal seems to have become indolent; but few autos were celebrated and the culprits consisted of the miscellaneous bigamists, blasphemers, sorcerers and soliciting confessors, whose cases present no especial interest. With 1590 the yearly autos were resumed. In that year nine Judaizers at least were reconciled, one was burnt in person and one in effigy. With the advent of Alonso de Peralta as inquisitor, in 1594, the tribunal seems to have been aroused to increased activity and the auto of December 8, 1596, was a memorable one in which there were sixty-six penitents, including twenty-two Judaizers reconciled, nine burnt in person and ten in effigy. Even this was exceeded by the great auto of March 26, 1601, also celebrated by Peralta, in which there were one hundred and twenty four penitents, of whom four were burnt in person and sixteen in effigy. There would seem to have been a recrudescence of

---

[1] Medina, *op. cit.*, pp. 49-55

Protestantism, for among these were twenty-three Lutherans and Calvinists.[1]

The Inquisition thus vindicated the necessity of its existence if the land was to be purified of heresy and apostasy, for some of the Judaizers had been practising their unhallowed rites for an incredible length of time. García González Bermejero, who was burnt in 1579, had been thus outraging the faith in Mexico for twenty years; Juan Castellanos, who repented and was reconciled in 1590, had done so for forty-eight years. Although their Judaism was almost public, for they ate the paschal lamb and smeared their houses with blood, they were only discovered through the confession of an accomplice tried in Spain, who denounced González. Of a family of Portuguese Jews who suffered in 1592, and the following years, we are told that the father, Francisco Rodríguez Mattos, was a rabbi and a dogmatizer, or teacher. Fortunately for him he was dead and was only burnt in effigy, as was likewise his son, who escaped by flight. His four daughters repented and were reconciled. They were in high social position and a cultured race, for it is said that the youngest, a girl of seventeen, could recite all the psalms of David and could repeat the prayer of Esther and other Hebrew songs backwards. A brother of these girls, Luis de Carvajal, was governor of the province of New Leon and a man who had rendered essential service to the crown; for the crime of not denouncing them, he was prosecuted, publicly penanced as a fautor of heresy and deprived of his office; he relapsed, was tried and tortured in 1595 and was burnt in the auto of December 8, 1596, together with his mother and three sisters.[2] The men who founded the

---

[1] Torquemada, Lib. xix, cap. 30.—Obregon, pp. 338–52.—Medina, *op. cit.*, pp. 91–115, 123–36.

[2] Páramo, pp. 241–2.—Proceso contra Manuel Díaz, fol. 71 (MS. *penes me*).—Obregon, p. 344. The fourth sister of Carvajal was burnt for relapse in the auto of 1601 and a fifth was reconciled (Medina, pp. 131–133).

An incident of Carvajal's trial illustrates the dread excited by the pitiless Peralta, who richly earned his archbishopric. After prolonged torture and confession, Carvajal endeavored to commit suicide and then asked for Lobo Guerrero to be sent for, to whom he explained that he had begged that Peralta should

Mexican Inquisition knew their duty and were resolute in its performance. They were kept busy for, between 1574 and 1600, they despatched no less than 879 cases, or an average of about thirty-four per annum.[1] Considering the complex character of inquisitorial procedure, with its inevitable delays and consumption of time, this represents a creditable degree of industry, equal to that of the great tribunal of Toledo which, at the same period, was averaging thirty-five cases per annum.

It will be observed that no Indians figure among the victims on these occasions, since the zeal of Bishop Zumárraga, in 1536, burned the cacique of Tezcoco. In fact, the native population was exempt from the jurisdiction of the Inquisition. This exemption was originally attributable to the theory held by the Conquistadores that the Indians were too low in the scale of humanity to be capable of the faith—a theory largely relied upon to excuse the cruelties inflicted upon them. In 1517, when Las Casas was laboring in their behalf at the Spanish court, this proposition was advanced by a member of the royal council to Fray Reginaldo Montesino, who was assisting Las Casas and who promptly declared it to be heretical. To settle the question, he asked one of the foremost theologians of the time, Fray Juan Hurtado, to assemble the doctors of the University of Salamanca to decide the matter; thirteen of them debated it and drew up a series of conclusions which they all signed, the final one being that whoever defended with pertinacity such a proposition must be put to death by fire as a heretic.[2] Notwithstanding this decision, the theory was so generally asserted in the New World

---

not be present "because the mere sight of him made his flesh creep, such was the terror with which his rigor inspired him."—Adler, Trial of Jorje de Almeida (Publications of Am. Jewish Hist. Soc., IV, 42).

The complaints against Peralta accumulated until the Suprema was compelled to formulate a process against him in which the *sumaria* contained thirty-two charges, not only of arbitrary cruelty but of prostitution of his office for illicit gain (Medina, p. 216); but this, as we have seen, did not prevent his promotion to the archiepiscopate of La Plata.

[1] Obregon, p. 391.

[2] Las Casas, Hist. de las Indias, Lib. III, cap. 99 (Col. de Docum., T. LXV, p. 365).

that Fray Julian Garcés, the first Bishop of Tlaxcala, wrote to Paul III on the subject and elicited a brief of June 2, 1537, condemning those who, to gratify their greed, asserted that the Indians were like brutes to be reduced to servitude, and declaring them competent to receive the faith and enjoy the sacraments.[1] Bishop Zumárraga had already acted on this presumption when he burnt the cacique and this suggested an obstacle, almost as damaging as the popular theory, to the conversion which was the ostensible object of the conquest, for it was evident that the *doctrineros*, or missionaries, would find their labors nugatory if the Indians realized that, in embracing the new faith, they would be liable to death by fire for aberrations from it. To remove this impediment, Charles V, by a decree of October 15, 1538, ordered that they should not be subject to the inquisitorial process but that, in all matters of faith, they should be relegated to the ordinary jurisdiction of their bishops. As the papal delegation of power to the inquisitors gave them exclusive faculties in all cases of faith, this imperial rescript would have been invalid without papal sanction, but this had already been procured in the brief *Altitudo divini consilii* of Paul III, June 1, 1537.[2]

It was probably through an oversight that the commissions issued to Francisco Tello de Sandoval in 1543 and to Dr. Contreras in 1570 granted them jurisdiction without exception over every one, of whatever condition, quality or state; possibly the latter may have commenced to exercise it on the Indians, but the error was rectified by Philip II, in a decree of December 30, 1571, ordering the inquisitors to observe their instructions and the previous law, and the injunction had to be repeated in 1575. Moreover, to silence any objections as to the episcopal power, he procured from Gregory XIII a brief granting full faculties to the bishops to absolve the Indians for heresy and all other reserved

---

[1] Lorenzana, Concilios provin. de Mexico, pp. 18, 33.
[2] Ibidem, p. 82.

cases.¹ The Indians thus remained exempt from prosecution by the Inquisition—an exemption popularly attributed to their not being *gente de razon*, or not rational enough to be responsible—which libel on their intellect Las Casas considers as perhaps the worst of the many offences committed upon them.² They could, however, endure this philosophically so long as it exempted them from the Holy Office and confided them to the more temperate zeal of the bishops.³

---

¹ Recop. de las Indias, Lib. I, Tit. xix, ley 17; Lib. VI, Tit. i, ley 35.—Solorzani de Indiar. Gubern., Lib. III, cap. xxiv, n. 27, 30.

This fresh papal grant was evidently called for by the action of the Council of Trent, in 1563 (Sess. XXIV, De Reform., cap. 6) which admitted that bishops had only power to absolve for secret heresy, while even this was denied them by the bulls *In Cœna Domini* of Pius V and his successors.

² Bancroft, History of Mexico, III, 747, 750.—Las Casas, Hist. de las Indias, Lib. II, cap. 1; Lib. III, cap. 8 (Col. de Doc., Tom. LXIV, 7, 386).

³ The Dominican Thomas Gage when, about the year 1630, he was serving as a missionary priest at Mixco in Guatemala, discovered, after considerable trouble, an idol in a cave, secretly worshipped by the leading Indians of the vicinage. After relating his adventures in the search, he proceeds "I writ to the President of Guatemala informing him of what I had don and to the Bishop (as an Inquisitor to whom such cases of Idolatry did belong) to be informed of him what course I should take with the Indians, who were but in part as yet discovered unto me and those only by the relation of one Indian. From both I received great thanks for my pains in searching the mountains and finding the Idol and for my zeal in burning of it. And as touching the Indian Idolators their counsel unto me was that I should further enquire after the rest and discover as many as I could and endeavor to convert them to the knowledge of the true God by fair and sweet means, showing pity unto them for their great blindness and promising them upon their repentance pardon from the Inquisition, which considering them to be but new plants useth not such rigor with them, which it useth with Spaniards if they fall into such horrible sins."—Gage's New Survey of the West Indies, pp. 397–8 (London, 1677).

For a considerable time the Indians seem to have escaped persecution, but at length the bishops—or at least some of them—formed Inquisitions for them and conducted these in inquisitorial fashion. In 1690 the Bishop of Oaxaca, having discovered organized idolatry in eleven pueblos of the Sierra de Xuquil, held an auto in which the culprits were reconciled and penanced, twenty-six of the principal ones being condemned to perpetual prison, for which he constructed an appropriate building. Possibly the fact that persecution was unprofitable may explain the infrequency of these proceedings. The first Indian auto in the city of Mexico seems to have been held December 23, 1731, which was followed occasionally by others—bigamy, superstitions and idolatry being the common offences. In 1769 the Archbishop of Mexico published an Edict of Faith requiring denun-

While the Inquisition, as we have seen, maintained its awful dignity before the people, by the solemnity of its public functions and its severity towards the evil-minded, all was not entirely serene within its walls. In fact, its financial history illustrates so vividly some of the aspects of Spanish colonial administration that it is worth recounting in some detail. We have seen that Inquisitor Contreras was promised a salary of three thousand pesos and a prebend in the cathedral, but he was confronted with a decree of January 25, 1569, prescribing that the income of all benefices enjoyed by inquisitors and fiscals in the Indies was to be deducted from their salaries, and the retention of this provision in the Recopilacion shows that it was not of mere temporary validity.[1] It was doubtless however waived in favor of the Inquisition, as was likewise another question which speedily arose.

The tribunal was expected to become self-supporting, from confiscations, fines and pecuniary penances, but this required time and meanwhile Philip granted it a subvention from the royal treasury, to continue during his pleasure, of 10,000 pesos per annum, being 3000 each for two inquisitors and a fiscal and 1000 for a notary. Although the tribunal started with but one inquisitor, the thrifty receiver, or treasurer, collected the salaries of two and, when called to account, claimed that he spent the money on the maintenance of poor prisoners. The treasury officials had no authority to allow this and refused further disbursements till the amount was made good but, when Philip was appealed to, he ordered, by a cédula of December 23, 1574, the receiver's claim to be allowed.[2] Thus early began the long-continued bickering between the Holy Office and the treasury, which Philip had already, in 1572, endeavored to quiet by instructing the inquisitors to obtain their salaries direct from the viceroy and

---

ciations of Indian practices to his *Tribunal de Fe*. This excited the indignation of the Inquisitors who vainly demanded its suppression and then appealed to the Suprema, probably with no better success.—Medina, pp. 371-8

[1] Recop. de las Indias, Lib. I, Tit. xix, ley 26.
[2] Archivo de Simancas, Inquisicion, Libro 40, fol. 24; Libro 926, fol. 169.

not from subordinates, whom he forbade them to prosecute or excommunicate for the purpose of enforcing their demands.[1]

While Philip had provided liberally for the superior officials, he had taken no thought of the minor positions and, in spite of the solemnity of the autos de fe and the successful persecution of heresy, the internal working of the tribunal was pursued under difficulties, in the absence of resources from confiscations. A curious insight into these troubles is afforded by some correspondence of 1583 with Inquisitor-general Quiroga by the two inquisitors, Santos García and Bonilla. It seems that their *portero* or apparitor, Pedro de Fonseca, had exhibited to them a commission, which he had secretly obtained from Quiroga, promoting him to the post of notary of sequestrations. They met this piece of jobbery with the favorite inquisitorial formula—*obedecer y no cumplir*, obeying without executing—for they say they obeyed it without admitting him to the office until they could consult the cardinal. This notariate, they say, is the least necessary of offices, as there are no sequestrations or confiscations, and they have no other portero and no money wherewith to pay a substitute: besides, Pedro is destitute of all qualifications for the position. If a good salary could be assured, proper persons would apply for the position but, in the absence of salaries, the offices have not a good reputation and people say they are bestowed on any one who will accept them. In view of the poverty of the tribunal and small prospect of improvement they repeat what they had previously said that, if the king will not provide for it, it had better be abolished rather than maintained precariously, with the officers relying on the hope of confiscations that never come, so that one resigns today and another tomorrow, leaving only the alcaide and portero, who are so poor that they would also have gone if they saw other means of escaping their creditors. It is therefore suggested that, in addition to the two inquisitors, the fiscal and the notary, salaries be furnished of 600 ducats for an alguazil, 500 for an alcaide or

---

[1] Solorzani de Indiar. Gubern., Lib. III, cap. xxiv, n. 13.

gaoler and 400 for a messenger—or otherwise that, as in Spain, a canonry be suppressed for the benefit of the Inquisition, in each of the eleven bishoprics of the district, though this would have its disadvantages in view of the poverty of the churches and paucity of ministers. Then, in another letter the inquisitors announce that they have filled the vacant post of alguazil by appointing Don Pedro de Villegas, for whom they ask Quiroga to send a commission; it is true, they say, that he is too young, but then both he and his wife are *limpio*—free from any taint of heretic blood—and he has the indispensable qualification of possessing means to live on without a salary and that, in the present condition of the Inquisition, is the main thing to be considered.[1]

It is an emphatic testimony to the exhaustion of the royal treasury that so pious a monarch as Philip II should have shown indifference to this deplorable condition of a tribunal which had already given evidence so conspicious of its services to the faith, but he remained deaf to all appeals and it was left to struggle on as best it could. As the number of its reconciled penitents increased it felt the need of a *carcel perpetua* or penitential prison, for their confinement and, having no funds wherewith to purchase a building, it besieged the Marquis of Monterey, the viceroy, for an appropriation. In 1596 he yielded in so far as to authorize the treasurer to lend the tribunal 2000 pesos, on its giving security to return the money in case the royal approbation should not be had within two years. The term elapsed without it, but Philip III, September 13, 1599, graciously approved the expenditure, at the same time warning the viceroy not to repeat such liberality without previous permission.[2] Even though the monarchs were thus niggardly, there were advantages in serving the Inquisition which in many cases answered in lieu of salary, for official position conferred the *fuero* or right to the jurisdiction of the Inquisition as well as substantial exemptions. As early as 1572, Philip II decreed that, during the royal pleasure, the inquisitors,

---

[1] Archivo de Simancas, Inquisicion, Leg. 1157, fol. 66.
[2] Ibidem, Libro 40, fol. 31.

the fiscal, the judge of confiscations, one secretary, one receiver, one messenger and the alcaide of the secret prison should be exempt from taxation and the royal officials were ordered, under penalty of a thousand ducats and punishment at the king's pleasure, to observe this and protect them in all the honors and exemptions which such officials enjoyed in Spain.[1]

A further, although illegal, relief was found by sharing in the *repartimientos* under which the Indians were allotted to Spaniards who lived upon their enforced labor. It is to this cruel system that Las Casas, Mendieta and Torquemada attribute the rapid wasting away of the natives and the hatred which they bore to the Spaniards. Among other attempts to diminish the evils arising from the system, repeated laws of 1530, 1532, 1542, 1551 and 1563 prohibited the allotment of Indians to any officials or to prelates, clerics, religious houses, hospitals, fraternities, etc. In spite of this, as soon as the Inquisition was established, it claimed and was allowed its quota in the allotments. It watched vigilantly, moreover, to see that it was not defrauded in any way, for one of its earliest recorded acts, in 1572, was the prosecution of Diego de Molina, the *repartidor de los Indios* of San Juan, because, in allotting the Indians of that place, the twelve assigned to the Inquisition proved to be boys and incapables, while the useful ones, who could be hired out advantageously, such as carpenters and masons, he gave for bribes to others. He was mercifully let off with five days' imprisonment and a forcible warning and doubtless served as a wholesome example to other partitioners.[2] Like most of the salutary legislation of Spain, it seems to have been impossible to enforce the prohibition, and that the Inquisition continued to enjoy the unpaid service of Indian

---

[1] Recop., Lib. I, Tit. xix, ley 14. In 1626, however, Philip IV ordered them to be compelled to pay the *alcavala* or commutation of the tax of ten per cent. on all transactions like other subjects and, in the Concordia of 1633, the exemption from royal taxes and imposts was wholly withdrawn.—Ibidem, Lib. I, Tit. xix, leyes 15; 30, § 5.

[2] MSS. of Royal Library of Munich, Cod. Hispan 79, Leg. 1, fol. 1.

serfs is manifested by its being specifically included in subsequent repetitions of the law in 1609, 1627 and 1635.[1]

When, as we have seen, the Judaizers commenced to appear among the penitents in the autos de fe, the longed-for relief derivable from confiscations, fines and penances was at hand. Spanish finance was already suffering the distress which was to become so acute and the treasury naturally looked to find its burden lightened by the income from these sources. It looked in vain, for whatever the tribunal acquired from its victims it retained and it persisted, with incredible audacity, in refusing even to render an account, although the confiscations belonged to the crown which never renounced its claim to them. In 1618 a royal cédula required the receiver to render itemized statements of all receipts and expenditures; in 1621 Philip IV sought to enforce this by ordering his viceroys in the Indies not to pay salaries until proof should be furnished that the confiscations were insufficient to meet them in whole or in part, and this was to be observed inviolably, no matter what urgency there might be, but repetitions of the decree, in 1624 and 1629, show how completely it was ignored.[2] Not the slightest attention was paid to these repeated royal commands and, to the last, the Inquisition never permitted either the king or the Council of Indies to know what it acquired in this manner, although the sums were large and the tribunal became wealthy through investments of the surplus, besides making, with more or less regularity, very considerable remittances to the Suprema.

Finding himself thus baffled by the immovable resistance of the Holy Office, Philip, in 1627, sought to relieve his treasury by despoiling the Church. He reported to Urban VIII that he expended 32,000 ducats a year on the tribunals of Mexico, Lima and Cartagena, wherefore he prayed that the bull of Paul IV, January 7, 1559, suppressing a prebend in every cathedral and

---

[1] Recop., Lib. vi, Tit. xii, ley 42.
[2] Recop., Lib. i, Tit. xix, leyes 10, 11, 12.—Solorzani de Ind. Gubern., Lib. iii, cap. xxiv, n. 11

collegial church in Spain, for the benefit of the Inquisition, might be extended to the Indies. Urban complied in a brief of March 10, 1627, whereupon Philip ordered the archbishop and bishops to remit to the senior inquisitors of their respective tribunals the fruits of the prebends as they should fall in, furnishing, at the same time, to the royal officials a statement of the sums thus paid, so that the amount should be deducted from the salaries.[1] Receipts from this source commenced at once and went on increasing as vacancies occurred, amounting, according to the estimate of the Council of Indies, to 30,000 pesos per annum for the three tribunals, while the Suprema admitted that those of Mexico and Lima produced about 11,000 pesos each, but those of Cartagena, it said, yielded only about 5000.[2]

During this time there had been frequent collisions between the inquisitors and the treasury officials, arising from the refusal of the former to reveal the amount of the confiscations and penances and the obedience, more or less persistent, of the latter to the royal commands to require such statements as a condition precedent to paying the royal subvention. In these collisions the inquisitors enforced their demands as usual by prosecution and excommunication, giving rise to unseemly controversies

---

[1] Recop., Lib. I, Tit. xix, leyes 24, 25. In the earlier period of the colonial Inquisition, the inquisitors sometimes, as we have seen, held prebends in addition to their salaries, but this privilege was subsequently withdrawn, at the instance of the Council of Indies, on account of the poverty of the churches.—Solorzani, *op. cit.*, Lib. III, cap. xxiv, n. 78.

[2] Archivo de Simancas, Inquisicion, Lib. 40, fol. 54, 128, 139.

The canonries fell in gradually. October 24, 1636, the Suprema reports that up to that time, only those of Mexico, Puebla, Oaxaca and Guatemala, had become available, the aggregate revenues of which did not amount to the royal subvention. The tribunal had reported, January 23d, that a vacancy had occurred in the cathedral of Guadalajara and the king is urged to lose no time in ordering its suppression.—Ibidem, Lib. 21, fol. 67.

About the middle of the century the tribunal enjoyed canonries in Mexico, Puebla, Oaxaca, Chiapa, Yucatan, Guatemala, Mechoacan, Guadalajara and Manila. In Mexico the sees of Guadiana, Honduras and Nicaragua, and in the Philippines those of Cebu, Cagayan and Nueva Segovia were too poor, some of them not even having prebendaries, and the bishops were supported by the treasury.—Medina, p. 209.

and, when the Suprema forbade their use of such measures, they were reduced to impotence. In a letter of February 13, 1634, they complained bitterly of this; during 1633, they said, in spite of all their efforts, they received no money until October, after all the royal officials had been paid and, as they had no other means of support, they were exposed to the deepest humiliations.[1] The suppressed canonries, however, introduced an element of pacification and, in the Concordia of 1633, between the Suprema and the Council of Indies, a plan to harmonize differences was agreed upon which was a practical surrender to the Inquisition. It provided that every year, before the first *tercios* (four months' instalments in advance) were paid, the receivers should render a sworn itemized statement of all receipts and expenditures, including confiscations, fines and penances, in accordance with the royal cédulas and, when this was delivered to the viceroy, the tercios should be paid in advance without delay. If the treasury officials should take exception to any portion of the statement, they were to forward it with their comments to the Council of Indies, but this was not to interfere with the prompt payment of the salaries and the inquisitors were to furnish the Suprema with their explanations. If the statement should show a surplus applicable to the salaries, this was, if agreed to by both parties, to be deducted from the second tercio; but if the inquisitors presented any reasons why this tercio should be paid in full, the treasury should pay it and the question be referred for settlement to the two Councils. The inquisitors were not to proceed against the treasury officials with censures or fines or other penalties, but were to apply to the viceroy, to whom positive instructions were sent to pay them punctually, both the arrearages then unpaid and the current salaries, while any fines or penalties that had been imposed were to be withdrawn or, if collected, to be refunded.[2]

This elaborate arrangement is only of importance as showing

---

[1] MSS. of David Fergusson Esqr.
[2] Archivo de Simancas, Inquisicion, Lib. 40, fol. 44.—Recop., Lib. i, Tit. xix, ley 30, § 1.

that, in spite of the suppressed canonries, the treasury was still required to support the tribunal and that the latter could be bound by no agreements however solemnly entered into. Except at Cartagena it was never carried into effect. No statement of receipts was ever rendered. In 1651, Count Alva de Aliste, the viceroy, reported to Philip IV that he had no means of learning what the confiscations amounted to but, on cautiously sounding the inquisitors, they told him that they reported them to the Suprema and would obey its instructions. They might well keep the facts secret. In the exterminating persecution of the wealthy New Christians, during the decade 1640–50, of which more hereafter, the confiscations were very large, placing the tribunal at its ease for all future time, besides what was embezzled by the inquisitors. The auto of 1646 yielded 38,732 pesos; that of 1647, 148,562. What was gathered in two autos held in 1648 does not appear, but between November 20, 1646, and April 24, 1648, the inquisitors remitted 234,000 pesos in bills of exchange while the crowning auto of 1649 furnished three millions more.[1] In spite of this enormous influx of wealth, the Inquisition still maintained its grip on the royal subvention of 10,000 pesos per annum, though for how long it is impossible to determine with positiveness. In the prolonged controversy which raged between the Suprema and the Council of Indies over the relations of the colonial tribunals, the former, in 1667, positively declared that, after 1633, there had been no subvention paid in Mexico or Lima and this assertion was repeated in 1676, but the statements of the Suprema are so full of duplicity that no reliance can be reposed in them.[2] On the other hand, in 1668, we find the Council of Indies earnestly advising the king to withdraw the subvention on the ground that the tribunals were rich and could support

---

[1] Medina, p. 209.
[2] Archivo de Simancas, Inquisicion, Lib. 40, fol. 85, 139. In these papers the Suprema had the hardihood to assert that the prebends were suppressed in order to enable the tribunals to meet expenses over and above the royal subvention for salaries, although all the documents show that the object was to relieve the treasury.

themselves, as they do in Castile; in 1675 it speaks of the payments as still continuing and urges their discontinuance without consulting the Suprema, as it is a matter wholly within the control of the treasury and, in 1676, Carlos II answered the Suprema by demanding a prompt decision as to a proposition made by the Council of Indies to discontinue the subventions enjoyed by the three tribunals for the salaries of their officials.[1] When they were definitely discontinued it would be impossible to assert, but it is probable that those of Mexico and Lima were stopped in 1677, while that of Cartagena was prolonged even later. In 1683 Inquisitor Valera of that tribunal complained that, owing to the exhaustion of the public treasury through wars and piratical attacks, an arrearage had accumulated of thirty-three *tercios*. He claimed that the king was indebted to the tribunal in the sum of 58,000 pesos and he urged its transfer to Santa Fe, where the royal treasury was in better condition to meet the obligation. The transfer was not made, payments of the subvention became more and more irregular and we shall see that in 1706 the tribunal was still unavailingly endeavoring to enforce them.[2]

In a letter to the king, July 31, 1651, the viceroy, Alva de Aliste, took the ground that the subvention had been merely a loan, to be repaid when confiscations should come in, and as, within the last few years, these had been large enough to settle the debt, he had had the accounts examined and had found that, since the beginning, there had been advanced for salaries 559,189 pesos, 6 tomines and 5 granos and, for other purposes, 6837 pesos, 5 granos, wherefore he suggested that the king should compel restitution of this amount.[3] To a treasury so desperately embarrassed as that of Spain the prospect of such relief was most welcome. Philip referred the viceroy's letter to the Council of Indies, which delayed its reply till December 12, 1652, when it advised the king that examination showed that the salaries were

[1] Archivo de Simancas, Inquisicion, Lib. 40, fol. 91, 103.
[2] J. T. Medina, La Inquisicion en Cartagena de Indias, p. 310 (Santiago de Chile, 1899).
[3] Archivo de Simancas, Inquisicion, Legajo 1465, fol. 78.

to be defrayed by the confiscations, which were to be reported to the treasury. The only light that could be thrown upon the subject was to be sought in the registration, by the Contratacion of Seville, of the amounts of silver passing through it from Mexico and Peru and from these registers it appeared that the colonial tribunals had remitted to the Suprema the aggregate of 76,965 *pesos de ensayados* and 85,454 *pesos de á ocho*, thus showing that those tribunals had revenues largely in advance of their needs. In view of the magnitude of the sums furnished by the treasury, the extensive confiscations, the income of the suppressed canonries and the dire necessities of the royal finances, it therefore advised the king to call upon the Suprema for restitution and to furnish statements of the amount of the confiscations from the beginning. To this the king replied, in the ordinary formula of approval "It is well and so have I ordered."[1] When the Suprema was concerned, however, obedience by no means followed royal orders and so it proved in this case.

Philip's weakness was shown in his next despatch to the viceroy, February 1, 1653, in which he said that he had determined that the Suprema should arrange to make restitution and that, to facilitate a proper adjustment of the matter, it should furnish a statement of all confiscations from the beginning, "for neither my Council of Indies nor my viceroys have been able to obtain this, but only the records of the shipments of silver from the Indies."[2] There is no evidence that the Suprema made any attempt to obey the royal commands or that it paid any attention to a reiterated demand made on August 12, 1655. Then the effort seems to have been abandoned and the matter was allowed to slumber until attention was called to it again in 1666. Philip had written, August 12, 1665, to the Marquis of Mansera, then

---

[1] Archivo de Simancas, Libro 40, fol. 57.

[2] Ibidem, fol. 74.

The Contratacion could furnish only the records of silver passing through it, which were always liable to seizure by the king. The great remittances of 1646 and 1648 were cautiously made in bills of exchange, and this was probably the rule.

Mexican viceroy, urging him to extinguish the debt of 1,333,264 pesos, by which amount the Mexican treasury was in arrears with its payments. The viceroy replied, September 5, 1666, pointing out the difficulty of accomplishing this and, at the same time, keeping up the remittances by the fleet, which were imperatively required by the absolute needs of the monarchy. He added that one of the chief causes of the indebtedness was the large sums withdrawn from it by the salaries and expenses of the Inquisition since its foundation in 1570; this had been intended as a loan, until it could be repaid from the confiscations, fines and penances but, although these had been large, restitution had never been made. The cédula of 1653 had inferred that the matter would be settled between the two councils and therefore the viceroys were powerless, but he suggested that the tribunal was rich and held large amounts of property; it had the disposition, which it might not have in future, to commence making this just and long overdue payment. This despatch the Council of Indies reported to the queen-regent, together with copies of the royal cédulas of 1653 and 1655, in order that she might compel the Suprema to make restitution, not only of the sums reported by Count Alva de Aliste, but of what had since been paid to the tribunal, seeing that it had the means to do so and was remitting such large amounts to the Suprema.[1]

It is scarce worth while to follow in detail the discussion which ensued, lasting, with true Spanish procrastination, until 1677, when the effort to make the Inquisition refund seems to have been abandoned out of sheer weariness. Of course the feeble queen-regent and the feebler boy-king, Carlos II, failed in the attempt and the only importance to us of the debate lies in the falsehoods and prevarications of the Suprema's defence. It was notorious that there had been heavy confiscations, for persecution, as we have seen, had become active and exceedingly profitable as the half-century had drawn to a close. The tribunal had grown rich and had made large investments, besides the

---

[1] Archivo de Simancas, Inquisicion, Lib. 40, fol. 77.

enormous remittances to the Suprema, and these had been derived almost exclusively from the confiscations and penances. Yet the Suprema endeavored to make it appear that financially confiscation had been a failure. There had been some confiscations, it admitted, in Mexico and Lima; there was the one of Diego López de Fonseca, amounting to 79,965 pesos, but Jorje de Paz of Madrid and Simon Rodríguez Bueno of Seville had come forward with claims amounting to more. They had asked to have the money sent to the receiver of Seville for adjudication and, on its arrival, the king had seized it and, by a cédula of July 14, 1652, had bound himself to satisfy the claimants, which he did by assigning to them certain matters. It was true that, in 1642, a number of Judaizing Portuguese had been discovered in Mexico, of whom some had moderate fortunes and one was reputed to be rich, but on the outbreak of the Portuguese rebellion, for fear that the viceroy would embargo their property, they had concealed it, and although the Inquisition had published censures, only a little had been discovered, while there came forward creditors with evidences of claims amounting to 400,000 pesos, so that it was difficult to make the confiscations meet them, to say nothing of the heavy expenses of feeding the prisoners, hiring houses to serve as prisons and the increased number of officials required. Besides this, there was protracted and costly litigation in investigating the claims and detecting suspected frauds. For this, Archbishop Mañozca was appointed visitador; on his death Medina Rico was sent out for the same purpose and, when he died, the matter had not been settled, nor has it yet.[1] If the

---

[1] Archivo de Simancas, Inquisicion, Lib. 40, fol. 85, 139.

The letter-book of the tribunal from 1642 to 1649 is largely filled with minute instructions as to the sequestrations which accompanied arrests and the management of the property seized. Though called sequestration this was really confiscation for, without awaiting the conviction of the accused, the assets were converted into money as rapidly as possible, by auctions in which of course much was sacrificed. The proceedings were most arbitrary. In a letter of October 21, 1645, the commissioner at Vera Cruz is instructed as to some cocoa belonging to prisoners, either on hand or expected to arrive. Trains of pack-mules were to be seized, no matter under what engagements they might be, to hurry the goods

Suprema was to be believed, confiscation cost more than it came to.

In the same way it sought by garbled statements to conceal the fact that it was secretly deriving a considerable revenue from the colonial tribunals, thus proving that they were possessed of superabundant means. In its private accounts for the year 1657, there is an item of 10,000 ducats from those of Mexico and Lima, with the remark that this is always in arrears and is now two years overdue[1]—for the tribunals were as anxious as the Suprema to conceal their gains. Yet it could not hide the fact that it was in receipt of large remittances through the Contratacion of Seville and the Government, in its extremity, had an awkward habit of seizing what took its fancy and possibly paying for silver in vellon, for we chance to hear of such an occurrence in 1639 and again in 1644.[2] The Council of Indies, as we have seen, did not fail to call attention to the large amounts which it was thus receiving, but it airily replied, in its consulta of November 16, 1667, that the three tribunals had, at various times, remitted the aggregate of 130,803 pesos, 3 reales, as the proceeds of sales of *varas* or offices of alguazil, and that this and much more, from the home tribunals, amounting in all to over 700,000 pesos, had been contributed to the necessities of the State. It repeated this, May 11, 1676, with the addition that the colonial tribunals had sent about 8000 pesos to the fund for

---

to Mexico and no other cocoa was to be allowed to come, so that this might bring a better price. A few weeks earlier, on September 25th, orders were sent for the arrest of Captain Fernando Moreno of Miaguatlan (Oaxaca), who was claimed to be a debtor to the fisc. He was to be seized suddenly and hurried off, heavily ironed, to Mexico, while his property was taken possession of. He was engaged in large transactions of making advances to Indians for cotton yarn and cochineal and minute instructions were given as to gathering in the product of these advances, which would be an affair of time. All this work had to be gratuitous. When on one occasion a familiar and a notary charged for their labor, they were compelled to refund and were told that the honor of serving the Inquisition was sufficient payment.—MSS. of David Fergusson Esqr.

[1] Bibl. nacional, MSS., D, 150, p. 224.
[2] Archivo de Simancas, Lib. 40, fol. 218, 328.

the attempted canonization of Pedro Arbués and that there were also remittances for the *media añata* of the officials and for the deposits of aspirants to office to defray the expenses of the investigations into *limpieza*—the whole manifesting extreme desire to divert attention from the confiscations.¹ In spite of these subterfuges there can be no question that the tribunals of Mexico and Lima accumulated vast amounts of property. The magnificence of the palace of the Mexican tribunal, rebuilt from 1732 to 1736, shows that it could gratify its vanity with the most profuse expenditure.² That it was fully able to do this without impairing its revenues may be assumed from the assertion, in 1767, of the royal fiscal, when arguing a case of competencia before the Audiencia, that if its accumulations were not checked, the king would have but a small portion of territory in which to exercise his jurisdiction.³ Certain it is that the tribunal continued to be able to render large pecuniary support to the home institution. In 1693 we hear of a remittance of 93,705 pesos and in 1702 of 19,898 in spite of heavy defalcations by the receivers. This was followed by remittances of 40,000 pesos in 1706, of 16,500 in 1720, and of 31,500 in 1727. In 1771 the tribunal lent to the viceroy, for the emergencies of the war with England, 60,000 pesos, which were repaid, and, in 1795, a further loan was made of 40,000 to aid in the war then raging.⁴ As

---

¹ Archivo de Simancas, fol. 85, 139. In 1631 the *vara*, or wand of office of alguazil, was sold in Castile and, in 1634, the Suprema sought to extend this to the Colonies, under pretext of applying it to the repairs of the Castle of Triana, the home of the tribunal of Seville. The Council of Indies stoutly resisted it and a consulta of November 16, 1638, shows that the struggle was still going on (Ibidem, Libro 21, fol. 162). The Suprema finally won, but of course it absorbed the proceeds and the castle was repaired by means of the levy known as the *Fabrica de Sevilla*, which continued to be collected in the nineteenth century.

It is probable that the amount attributed to the sale of *varas* is largely exaggerated. In 1652 there came a remittance from Mexico of 2298 pesos, of which 1711 were the proceeds of sales and 587 for the *media añata*—a tax of half of the first year's salary of those appointed to office (Ibidem, Lib. 40, fol. 295).

² Obregon, *op. cit.*, 1ª Serie, p. 188.
³ Archivo de Simancas, Inquisicion, Lib. 28, fol. 276.
⁴ Medina, pp. 213, 348, 379, 405.

late as 1809 the Government seized a remittance from it to the Suprema of 60,131½ pesos and gave a receipt for the proceeds, being 915,886 reales, for which, after the Restoration, we find the Suprema claiming restitution.[1] In spite of these reiterated drains we shall see hereafter what wealth the tribunal possessed when suppressed.

If we are to trust the list of sanbenitos hung in the cathedral of Mexico, after the great auto of 1601, there ensued a period of comparative inaction for nearly half a century, in which Protestants almost disappeared and were replaced by comparatively few Judaizers.[2] The sanbenitos however represent only the serious cases and the tribunal continued to gather its customary harvest of bigamists, blasphemers, sorcerers, solicitors and other minor offenders, some of whom yielded a liberal amount of fines.[3] In fact, a report of the cases pending in 1625 amounts to the very considerable number of sixty-three, showing that there was ample business on hand, receiving attention with more or less

---

[1] Archivo de Simancas, Libro, 435, 2°.

[2] Obregon, *op. cit.*, 2ª Serie, pp. 352–55. From 1601 to 1646 the only sanbenitos were—

1603. A Fleming relaxed for Calvinism, one Judaizer reconciled and one relaxed in effigy and two mulattos reconciled for heresy.

1605. An Irishman reconciled for Lutheranism and a Portuguese for Judaism. There were however 36 penitents in this auto of whom 21 were negroes and mulattos for blasphemy. When in 1605 the general pardon for Judaizers descended from Portuguese reached Mexico, there was only one to be liberated.—Medina, pp. 143, 146.

1606. A mulatto relaxed for administering sacraments without ordination. There was however another person guilty of the same offence, a married priest and a blasphemer.—Medina, p. 145.

1621. A German reconciled for Lutheranism

1625. Three Judaizers reconciled.

1626 One Judaizer relaxed in effigy.

1630. Three Judaizers reconciled.

1635. Four Judaizers reconciled, one relaxed in person and four in effigy. This is evidently incomplete. Medina, p. 165, reports that in this auto there were twelve Judaizers reconciled and five effigies of the dead relaxed.

1636. One Judaizer relaxed in effigy.

[3] Medina, pp. 146–50.

diligence.¹ After this however the activity of the tribunal diminished so greatly that, on July 12, 1638, it reported that it had not a single case pending, and a year later that it had but one, which was against a priest charged with solicitation in the confessional.² This is a singular tribute to the efficacy of the Edict of Faith—a proclamation requiring, under pain of excommunication, the denunciation of all offences enumerated under it, of which any one might be cognizant or have heard of in any way. According to rule, this should be solemnly published every year in all parish and conventual churches; it kept the faithful on the watch for all aberrations and rendered every one a spy and an informer. It had, however, at this time, fallen into desuetude. In a letter of February 13, 1634, the inquisitors say that for ten years the publications had been suspended in consequence of the indecency which attended it after the viceroys refused to be present, owing to quarrels as to ceremonial, and they ask that a royal order should be issued through the Council of Indies requiring the attendance of the civil magistracy in the procession and publication.³

Nearly ten years more, however, were to elapse, before the questions of etiquette and precedence were settled, and at last, on March 1, 1643, the Edict was read with all solemnity in the cathedral of Mexico and was followed by an abundant harvest of denunciations.⁴ How numerous these habitually were may be gathered from partial statistics of those received after a publication of the Edict in 1650. These were recorded in eight books, of which four, representing presumably one-half, have been preserved, containing altogether two hundred and fifty-four cases of

---

¹ MSS. of David Fergusson Esqr. The cases reported consisted of

Judaism	22	Personating priesthood	4
Solicitation	12	Illuminism	2
Sorcery	8	Miscellaneous	11
Bigamy	4		

² Medina, p. 168.
³ MSS. of David Fergusson Esqr.
⁴ Medina, p. 169.

the most varied character, as may be seen by the summarized classification below.[1]

The most significant feature in this mass of so-called testimony is the manner in which the most trivial acts inferring suspicion were watched and denounced, so that every man lived under a universal spy-system stimulated by the readiness of the Inquisition to listen to and make record of the veriest gossip passing from mouth to mouth. Thus one informer relates how in 1642, eight years before, he saw Simon de Paredes quietly put to one side on his plate a piece of pork that came to him from among the miscellaneous contents of the olla. Another gravely deposes how a man had casually told him that he had heard how a miner named Blas Garcés, of the mines of Los Papagayos, now dead, had once taken some of the herb Peyote to find some mines of which he had chanced to see specimens, and the marvels which thence ensued.[2] From the book of *Membretes* kept by the tribunal

---

[1]
Solicitation in the confessional	14
Sorcery and divination	112
Consulting diviners	13
Judaism (besides 11 in Pernambuco)	41
Disregard of disabilities of descendants	8
Bigamy	4
Abuse of Inquisition by culprits	2
Remaining under excommunication for a year	4
Revealing confessions	1
Heretical blasphemy	6
Incest	1
Neglect of observances	5
Mental Prayer better than Oral	1
A little girl for breaking an arm of an image of Christ	1
A boy of 6, for making crosses on the ground, stamping on them and saying that he was a heretic	1
Priest saying mass without confessing	1
Personating official of Inquisition	1
Celebrating mass without ordination	2
Impeding the Inquisition	7
Insults to images	6
Concubinage better than marriage	3
Irregular fasting	1
Propositions	12
Various suspicious acts	1
Marriage better than Religious Life	1
Criticizing the Inquisition	1
Denying a debt due to the confiscated estate of a culprit	1
Marriage in Orders	1
Priest saying 4 masses in one day	1
For being the grandson of a man relaxed in Portugal	1

(MSS. of David Fergusson Esqr.).

Nearly all the accusations of sorcery are of Indians, negroes or mulattos. A note states that the testifications against Indians are not indexed because the Inquisition has not jurisdiction over them.

[2] The plant named Peyote had intoxicating and narcotic properties causing pipe-dreams and visions. It was largely used by diviners and was strictly prohibited by the Inquisition.

it would appear that when this kind of evidence did not lead to a prosecution it was carefully preserved and indexed for reference in case of subsequent testimony against an individual. Such was the training of the population and such was the shadow of terror under which every man lived.

Meanwhile, during the quiescent period of the tribunal, the class of New Christians, who secretly adhered to the ancient faith, increased and prospered, accumulating wealth through the opportunities of the colonial trade which they virtually monopolized. Their fancied security, however, was approaching its end. The vigorous measures taken in Spain, between 1625 and 1640, to exterminate the Portuguese Judaizers, revealed the names of many accomplices who had found refuge in the New World; these were carefully noted and sent to the colonial tribunals.[1] Moreover, from 1634 to 1639, the Lima Inquisition was busy in detecting and punishing a large number of its most prominent merchants guilty of the same apostasy, who had relations with their Mexican brethren, revealed during the trials. The tribunal seems to have been somewhat slow in realizing the opportunities thus afforded, but in 1642 there opened an era of active and relentless persecution which was equally effective in enriching its treasury and in purifying the faith. To prevent the escape of its victims, on July 9th it sent orders to Vera Cruz prohibiting the embarkation of any Portuguese who could not show a special licence from it. A wealthy merchant named Manuel Alvarez de Arrellano had already sailed for Spain, but his ship was wrecked on Santo Domingo and he was compelled to return to Havana. The tribunal was on his track and, on December 1st, it sent orders to its commissioner at Havana to arrest him, seize all his property, sell it at auction and send him in chains with the proceeds to Vera Cruz. This was successfully accomplished and, in acknowledging his arrival, the tribunal gave further instructions as to some cases of cochineal, which it understood to have been saved from the wreck.[2]

---

[1] Archivo de Simancas, Inquisicion, Lib. 812; Cuenca, fol. 2.
[2] MSS. of David Fergusson Esqr.

There was small chance of escape for any culprit. The New
Christians were closely connected by family, religious and business
ties, and each new prisoner was forced to implicate his friends
and kindred. Gabriel de Granada, a child of 13, arrested in
July, 1642, was made to give evidence against 108 persons, including his entire family.[1] There were then three inquisitors, Francisco
de Estrada y Escobedo, Bernabé de la Higuera y Amarilla and
Juan Saenz de Mañozca, whose names became a terror to the
innocent as well as to the guilty. Their cruel zeal is manifested in
a letter to the Suprema virtually asking authority to relax ten
persons, although they had confessed and professed repentance
in time to entitle them, by the rules of the Inquisition, to reconciliation.[2] It was a wild revel of prosecutions and condemnations.
Medina Rico, the *visitador* or inspector who came in 1654, reported
that, in reviewing the proceedings, he found that no attention
had been paid to the defences presented by the accused, although
in many cases they were just. A single case will indicate the
heartlessness of the tribunal. September 24, 1646, Doña Catalina
de Campos sought an audience to say that she was very sick and
near unto death and that she would die in the Catholic faith in
which she had lived. She was sent back to her cell, no attention
was paid to her and some days later she was found dead and
gnawed by rats.[3]

The result of this method of administering justice was a succession of *autos particulares*, in 1646, 1647 and 1648, followed by an
auto general in 1649.

In 1646 there were thirty-eight Judaizers reconciled and, as
reconciliation, in addition to prison and sanbenito, inferred confiscation, the harvest as we have seen was large. In 1647 the

---

[1] MSS. of David Fergusson Esqr.

[2] Carta de 27 Nov. 1643 (MSS. of David Fergusson Esqr.). These prisoners were all reconciled in the subsequent autos except three who died in prison and were relaxed in effigy.

For the individual offences of these inquisitors and their subordinates in cruelty, rapacity, embezzlement and licentiousness, as reported by the *visitador* Medina Rico, see Medina, pp. 261–2.

[3] Medina, pp. 239.

number was twenty-one.[1] In 1648 there were two autos—a public one on March 29th and an *auto particular* in the Jesuit church on March 30th. In the former there were eleven penitents for various offences, eight Judaizers penanced and eight reconciled, two reconciliations for Mahometanism, twenty-one effigies of Judaizers burnt and one burning in person. In the latter there was one penitent brought from the Philippines for suspicion of Mahometanism, who escaped with abjuration *de levi* and servitude for life in a convent for instruction; there were two for personating priesthood and administering sacraments without orders, who received 300 and 200 lashes respectively and were sent to the galleys; one for marrying in orders, who abjured *de vehementi* and was sent to serve in a hospital for five years; a bigamist who had 200 lashes and the galleys; a *curandera*, who employed charms to cure disease and was visited with 200 lashes and perpetual exile from Puebla, and finally there were twenty-one Judaizers. Of these, two escaped with fines of 2000 and 3000 ducats respectively and perpetual exile from Mexico, one was only exiled and eighteen were reconciled with confiscation and various terms of imprisonment, in addition to which five of them were scourged and, of these latter, two were also sent to the galleys.[2]

The great *auto general* of April 11, 1649, marks the apogee of the Mexican Inquisition and of this we have a very florid account, written by an official.[3] A month in advance the solemn proclamation announcing it was made in Mexico, March 11th, with a gorgeous procession, to the sound of trumpet and drum, and this had previously been sent to every town in New Spain, so that it was published everywhere at the same hour. Consequently, for a fortnight in advance of the appointed day, crowds began to pour in, some of them from a distance of a hundred or two hun-

---

[1] Medina, pp. 181, 182.
[2] Medina, p. 183.—El Museo Mexicano, Mexico, 1843, pp. 537 sqq. Reprinted also, with some abbreviation as an appendix to a translation of Féréal's *Mystères de la Inquisition*, Mexico, 1850.
[3] My copy of this scarce tract unfortunately lacks the title page, which I am thus unable to give. It was printed in Mexico in 1649.

dred leagues, till, as we are told, it looked as though the country had been depopulated. The reporter exhausts his eloquence in describing the magnificence of the procession of the Green Cross, on the afternoon preceding the auto, when all the nobles and gentlemen of the city, in splendid holiday attire, took part, and the standard of the Inquisition was borne by the Count of Santiago, whose grandfather had done the same in the great auto of 1574 and his father in that of 1601. A double line of coaches extended through the streets, from the Inquisition to the plazuela del Volador, where the ceremonies were to be performed, and so anxious were their occupants not to lose their positions that they remained in them all night and until the show was over. It might seem that all Mexico, from the highest to the lowest, was assembled to demonstrate the ardor of its faith and to gain the indulgence which the Vicar of Christ bestowed on those who were present at these crowning exhibitions of the triumph of the Church Militant. Inside of the Inquisition the night was spent in notifying of their approaching fate those who were about to die and in preparing them for death.

Of the one hundred and nine convicts there was but one Protestant, a Frenchman named François Razin, condemned to abjure for vehement suspicion of heresy and to two years' service in a convent for instructions; as he was penniless, we are told that he was not fined. There were nine Judaizers who abjured for vehement suspicion and were banished to Spain; three of them, being impoverished, were not fined but on the other six were imposed mulcts, ranging from 1000 to 6000 ducats, amounting in all to 15,000 ducats and one in addition had 200 lashes. There were nineteen reconciled, whose estates of course were confiscated, as also were those of the relaxed, seventy-eight in number. Of these, fifty-seven were effigies of the dead, of whom ten had died in prison, two of the latter being suicides, in addition to which were eight effigies of fugitives. Thirteen were relaxed in person, but of these twelve were garroted before burning, having professed repentance and conversion in time. Only one was burnt alive—

the hero of the occasion, Tomás Treviño of Sobremonte. His mother had been burnt at Valladolid, and nearly all of his kindred, as well as those of his wife, had been inmates of the Inquisition. He had been reconciled in the auto of 1625 and there could be no mercy for a relapsed apostate, though he could have escaped the fiery death by professing conversion again. He had lain in prison for five years during his trial, always denying his guilt, but when notified of his conviction, the night before the auto, he proclaimed himself a Jew, declaring that he would die as such, nor could the combined efforts of all the assembled confessors shake his resolution. To silence what were styled his blasphemies, he was taken to the auto gagged, in spite of which he made audible assertion of his faith and of his contempt for Christianity. It is related that, after his sentence, when he was mounted to be taken to the quemadero, the patient mule assigned to him refused to carry so great a sinner; six others were tried with the same result and he was obliged to walk until a broken-down horse was brought, which had not spirit enough to dislodge its unholy burden. An Indian was mounted behind him, who sought to convert him and, enraged at his failure, beat him about the mouth to check his blasphemies. Undaunted to the last, he drew the blazing brands towards him with his feet and his last audible words were—"Pile on the wood; how much my money costs me!"[1]

The inquisitor-general, Arce y Reynoso, on October 15, 1649, congratulated Philip IV on this triumph of the faith, which had been the source of joy and consolation and universal applause, whereat the pious monarch expressed his gratification and desired

---

[1] In addition to those who appeared in the auto there were two women condemned to relaxation, Isabel Núñez and Leonor Vaz who, the night before in the prison, sought audience with the inquisitors, professed conversion, and were withdrawn. They were reconciled in church, April 21, with irremissible perpetual prison and sanbenito.

Besides the summary in the text, the list of sanbenitos for this year includes the names of Francisco López de Aponte, relaxed in person for atheism and Sebastian Alvares for obstinacy in various errors (Obregon, p. 372), but they are not in the official relation and, as they occur again in 1659 (p. 381), there is obviously an erroneous duplication.

the inquisitors to be thanked in his name. As summarized by Arce y Reynoso the results of the four autos were two hundred and seven penitents of whom a hundred and ninety were Jews, nearly all Portuguese. There was one drawback to his satisfaction. The penitents sentenced to banishment were directed to be sent to Spain, and repeated royal orders required that they should be transported free of charge, but the captains of all vessels, both naval and commercial, refused to carry them without pay and, as they had been stripped of all their possessions, they could not defray the passage-money themselves, while the Inquisition made no offer to supply the funds. Consequently they remained in Vera Cruz or wandered through the land, throwing off their sanbenitos and infecting the population with their errors. Arce y Reynoso suggested to the king that he should give them rations while on board ship so as to help to bring them over. It never seemed to occur to him that the Inquisition, which was enriching itself with their confiscations, could spare the trifle requisite for the execution of its sentences on these homeless and penniless wretches.[1]

After this supreme manifestation of its authority, the Inquisition became again somewhat inert, for its attention was largely absorbed in settling the details of the confiscations which involved the greater portion of Mexican commerce.[2] The tribunal had its routine business of bigamists, soliciting confessors and women guilty of so-called sorcery—cases usually despatched in the audience-chamber—though there was an *auto particular* celebrated October 29, 1656. In 1659, however, there was a public auto on November 19th which, though not large, merits attention by its severity and the peculiarity of some of the delinquents. Of these there were thirty-two in all—twelve blasphemers, two bigamists, one forger, one false witness, one for violating the secrecy of the prison, one who had been reconciled for Judaism

---

[1] Archivo de Simancas, Inquisicion, Libro 38, fol. 96, 101.

[2] When, in 1654, Medina Rico came as visitador, he found 1200 cases pending in suits against the fisc of the tribunal.—Medina, p. 212.

in 1649 and had thrown off the sanbenito, a woman for suspicion of Judaism, an alumbrado, or mystic, with visions and revelations. Then there were two sisters Romero, prosecuted for fraudulent visions and revelations, of whom one was acquitted and the other had 200 lashes and ten years' service in a hospital—a third sister having been penanced in the auto particular of 1656. There was also Manuel Méndez, a Portuguese, suspected of Judaism, who had died in prison and was now acquitted. Another Portuguese, Diego Díaz, was not so fortunate; he had been condemned in 1649 to abjuration *de vehementi* and perpetual banishment, but he did not leave Mexico; arrested February 26, 1652, he had lain in prison awaiting an auto and was now sentenced to be burnt alive as pertinaciously impenitent; by mistake the executioner commenced to garrote him, but was stopped by the alguazil mayor, who ordered the fire lighted, so that he had both punishments. Similar was the case of Francisco Botello, arrested in 1642, sentenced in 1649 to 200 lashes and banishment, remaining in Mexico, arrested again in 1650 and now garroted and burnt. These two cases indicate the treatment accorded to those alluded to above, who, after being stripped of their property, were ordered to leave the country, but were not furnished with means to do so.

Another convict, Francisco López de Aponte, was accused of pact with the demon and of heresies. He gave signs of insanity, but on examination by physicians was pronounced sane. Under severe torture he remained perfectly quiescent and insensible to pain, which could only be explained by diabolical aid, so he was shaved all over and inspected carefully for charms or for the devil's mark, but in vain. A second torture was endured with the same indifference and he was condemned to relaxation as an apostate heretic. On the night before the auto he said to the confessor who endeavored to convert him "There is no God, nor hell, nor glory; it is all a lie; there is birth and death and that is all." During the auto he manifested no emotion and was burnt alive as an impenitent.

Juan Gomez had been arrested, May 28, 1658, as an Illuminist and *herége sacramentario*, for teaching many opinions contrary to the Catholic faith. Condemned to relaxation, he maintained his heresies until, during the auto, he weakened and professed repentance, notwithstanding which he was burnt alive.

Pedro García de Arias was a wandering hermit who, although uneducated, had written three mystic books containing erroneous doctrine. When on trial he claimed that he had never committed sin, and he abused the Inquisition, for which he was scourged through the streets with 200 lashes. When notified of his condemnation to relaxation he protested that he would not beg for mercy, but on the staging he asked for an audience, in which he insisted that there were no errors in what he had written. Nevertheless he was garroted before burning, when his books, hung around his neck, were consumed with him.

Sebastian Alvárez was an old man who claimed to be Jesus Christ, but was pronounced to be sane by the experts who examined him. He persisted in his delusion and was sentenced to relaxation. On the staging he asked for an audience and was remanded to the Inquisition, where two days later he had an audience and, as he still asserted himself to be Christ, he was sentenced to burning alive if he did not retract. On the way to the quemadero he retracted and was garroted before burning.

In this curious assemblage of eccentric humanity, the most remarkable of all was an Irishman named variously William Lamport or Guillen Lombardo de Guzman. He had lain in prison since his arrest as far back as October 25, 1642, on a denunciation that he was plotting to sever Mexico from Spain and make himself an independent sovereign, for he claimed to be the son of Philip III by an Irish woman, and thus half-brother to Philip IV. This was his real offence, but the Inquisition claimed jurisdiction because he had consulted an Indian sorcerer and certain astrologers to assure the success of his enterprise. The details of his scheme show that it was suggested by the success with which, in June, 1642, Bishop Palafox, acting under secret orders from Philip, had ousted from the viceroyalty the Marquis of Escalona, who was suspected of treasonable leanings towards João of Braganza and the revolted Portuguese. With the aid of an Indian singularly skilled in forgery, Lamport had drawn up all the necessary royal decrees which would enable him to seize control, on the arrival of the expected new viceroy, the Count of Salvatierra. Yet he was no common adventurer, but a man of wide and various learning, thoroughly familiar with English, French, Spanish, Italian, Latin and Greek, with the classical poets and philosophers, with the Scriptures and the fathers and with theology and mathematics. This was proved by the memorials which he drew up in prison, without the aid of books, yet full of citations and extracts in all languages and of scripture texts. These were scrutinized by the calificador who verified the citations and found them all correct and who moreover certified that there were no errors of faith.

In the account of his life, which all prisoners of the Inquisition were required to give, he stated that he had been born in England, from which he had fled in his twelfth year because of a pamphlet entitled *Defensio Fidei* which he had written against the king. After marvellous adventures in many regions, in which he had rendered services to Spain, Philip IV had summoned him to Madrid, where Olivares patronized him. He was then sent to Flanders to aid the Cardinal Infante, to whose success he largely contributed, especially at the battle of Nördlingen (1634). After much other service, Philip gave him the title of Marquis of Cropani and the viceroyalty of Mexico, from which he was to eject the occupant—and for this he held forged royal cédulas. That there was some residuum of truth at the bottom of his story would appear from his familiarity with details of persons and events, and there is no doubt that he was an object of interest in Madrid, for a royal cédula of May 13, 1643, ordered the case to be expedited and that after his punishment all his papers should be given to the judge, Andrés Gomez de Mora. Why the case should then have been protracted for seventeen years is inexplicable, unless it was designed to keep him imprisoned for life, but, however that may be, he continued to be a source of solicitude, not unkindly, for the Suprema, under royal orders, wrote June 21, 1550, that he should be given a cell-companion to alleviate his confinement if he so desired and that every care should be taken of his life. Again, on July 7, 1660, when the Suprema received the account of his relaxation, it wrote to ask why this had been done against its express orders. Altogether the case is a mystery to which the clue is lost.

Diego Pinto, the companion given to share his confinement, was soon won over to join him in a plan of escape, which was executed December 26, 1650, with remarkable skill and perseverance. In place of flying to some safe retreat Lamport spent the night in affixing in various prominent places certain writings which he had prepared, and in persuading a sentinel at the palace to convey one to the viceroy urging him to arrest the inquisitors as traitors. Towards dawn he induced a householder to take him in and awaited the result of his papers, besides writing others, when the host became apprehensive and made him remove to another house. No time was lost by the tribunal in issuing a proclamation, describing his person and ordering his capture under severe penalties; his host promptly reported him and he was carried back to the Inquisition, when he was lodged in an exceptionally strong cell, his feet in stocks and his hands in fetters. In January, 1654, he asked for writing materials, with which he composed a tremendous attack on the Inquisition, and during the winter he utilized the sheets of his bed to write a book, which when transcribed proved to be a treatise in Latin verse which filled 270 closely written pages. He had now lain twelve years in prison without trial; his overwrought brain was giving way and his insanity became more and more manifest. At last the time for the auto approached and, on October 8, 1659, without further audience, the accusation was presented; the trial proceeded swiftly and on November 6th sentence was pronounced, condemning him to relaxation for divination and superstitious cures showing express or implicit pact with the demon, besides which he had plotted rebellion and was a heretic sectary of Calvin, Pelagius, Huss, Luther and other heresiarchs and an inventor and dogmatizer of new heresies. As a special punishment for his defamatory libels and forgery of royal decrees, he was to listen to his sentence on the scaffold with a gag and hanging by his right arm fastened to an iron ring. During the night before the auto he assailed with opprobrious epithets the holy men who sought to save his soul; he exclaimed that a hundred legions of devils had entered his cell with them and finally he covered his head with the bed-clothes and refused to speak. At the auto on the staging he was like a statue and at the stake he escaped burning alive by throwing himself against the iron ring encircling his throat with such force that it killed him.[1]

The last act of the tragedy was the burning of the effigy of Joseph Bruñon de Vertiz, a priest whose offence was that he had been the dupe of the imposture of the Romero sisters and had reduced to writing their visions and revelations. Arrested September 9, 1649, he speedily admitted that he had been deceived and cast himself on the mercy of the inquisitors, vainly endeavoring to ascertain what was the nature of the charge against him so that he could confess and retract whatever errors were imputed to him. It was not, however, the *estilo* of the Inquisition to do more than to tell the accused to search his memory and clear his conscience and after eighteen months of this suspense Bruñon's mind commenced to give way. He was left in his cell apparently forgotten, except when he would seek an audience to ask for writing materials with which, in 1652 and 1654, he drew up and presented attacks upon the tribunal of a character to show that he was becoming insane through despair. No notice was taken of these ebullitions and on April 30, 1656, he died without the sacraments, after six years and a half of incarceration, during which he had never been informed of the charges against him. His body was thrust into unconsecrated ground and the trial was continued against his fame and memory as an

---

[1] Medina, pp. 271–311.

alumbrado heretic, in an accusation presented May 11, 1657. There was no defence possible by his kindred; he was duly condemned and in this auto of November 19, 1659, his effigy was brought forward, clad in priestly garments, the impressive ceremony of degradation was performed and it was cast into the flames with his bones exhumed for the purpose.[1]

Cruel as all this performance may seem to us, it was in strict conformity with the convictions of the age and, when Philip IV received the report of the auto, he warmly congratulated the inquisitor-general on the vigilance which preserved the purity of the faith by inflicting merited chastisement.[2]

With this auto the murderous activity of the tribunal may be said virtually to end. Until the end of the century its business consisted almost exclusively in the commonplace routine of bigamists, blasphemers, petty sorcerers, soliciting confessors, clerics administering the sacraments without priest's orders and the like. Thus in an auto celebrated January 15, 1696, out of twenty-six penitents, there was but one heretic with a sanbenito; there was a Greek schismatic reconciled and the rest were sixteen bigamists, one Franciscan tertiary for Illuminism, a woman for imposture and four men and two women for the superstitious practices conveniently classed as sorcery with explicit or implicit pact with the demon.[3] Yet during this half-century there were a couple of cases showing that a nearly bloodless career was not due to any surcease of fanatic zeal. In November, 1673, was arrested a wandering hermit named Juan Bautista de Cardenas, charged with being *iluso y alumbrado*, with grave suspicion of sacramentarian heresy. After giving the customary account of his life he took refuge in absolute silence, which suggested that he was possessed by a demon, but exorcism proved unavailing. Sharp torture was then tried, but it elicited only the usual

---

[1] Proceso contra Joseph Bruñon de Vertiz (MSS. of David Fergusson Esqr.). I have considered this curious case at greater length in "Chapters from the Religious History of Spain," pp. 362–73.
[2] Archivo de Simancas, Inquisicion, Lib. 60, fol. 189.
[3] Obregon, *op. cit.*, 2ª Serie, pp. 380–4.

shrieks of pain. The conclusion drawn from this was that he was a contumacious heretic and in July, 1675, he was condemned to relaxation, when, on being notified of it, he only said that if he was carried to the quemadero he would die for God. The tribunal however did not dare to execute its own sentence and sent the papers to the Suprema which, June 22, 1676, altered it to abjuration *de levi*, deprivation of the habit he wore and exile from the cities of Mexico and Puebla, adding that the torture had been abusive seeing that he had not been formally testified against for heresy. The other case was that of Fray Francisco Manuel de Cuadros, who had left his Order and practised as a *curandero*, or curer of disease by charms. He was thrown in prison, November 14, 1663, and during his trial, which was protracted for nearly fifteen years, he confessed to being an agnostic, except as to the existence of God, but he admitted that he was ignorant and half-crazy. At the auto of March 20, 1679, he was condemned to relaxation after degradation, but at the quemadero he showed signs of repentance, in virtue of which he was admitted to the sacraments and was strangled before burning.[1]

In the public autos there is no trace of one of the principal duties of the Inquisition in the repression of the prevalent crime of the seduction of women by their confessors, euphemistically known as solicitation in the confessional. Even as bigamy had been brought under inquisitorial jurisdiction by the somewhat forced assumption that it implied erroneous belief in the sacrament of matrimony, so solicitation was held to infer in the confessor error as to the sacrament of penitence. At least this was the reason alleged when, recognizing that the spiritual courts were useless to check the practice, Paul IV, in 1561 entrusted its suppression in the Spanish dominions to the Inquisition, and Gregory XV, in 1622, extended this to other lands in which the Holy Office existed. Priests, however, for the avoidance of scandal, were never paraded in public autos, unless they were

---

[1] Medina, pp. 328, 330.

16

to be deprived of their orders; their sentences were read in the audience-chamber with closed doors and in the presence only of a selected number of their brethren, to whom the fate of the culprit should serve as a wholesome warning.[1] While, therefore, the knowledge of this offence was sedulously kept from the public, it gave the tribunal considerable occupation. The morals of the Colonial clergy, for the most part, were notoriously loose and, in the solitary missions and parishes among the natives, evil passions had free rein.[2] This was enhanced by the almost assured prospect of immunity, for the women seduced were the only possible accusers and it has always proved exceedingly difficult to induce them to denounce their seducers. Naturally therefore the Inquisition, on its establishment, was speedily called upon to prosecute such culprits and, up to 1577, it already had five cases.[3] It seems however not to have enforced its exclusive jurisdiction over the offence if we may judge from the proceedings in the case of Fray Juan de Saldaña, in 1583, for when it assumed the prosecution he was undergoing six months' imprisonment by his superiors because at Tequitatlan he had violated an Indian girl and, when she refused to continue the connection, he had her arrested and flogged, after which she submitted. Though only 34 years of age he was a person of consideration in his Franciscan Order, he had occupied various positions of importance and at this time was guardian of the convent of Suchipila, where he seduced three sisters, his penitents, the daughters of Diego Flores, the *encomendero* of Suchipila and a person of distinction. There seems to have been little or no concealment about it; he boasted openly of the women he had seduced, Spanish as well as Indian, not only in Suchipila

---

[1] In the auto of 1601 the priest Juan Plata appeared as a penitent and was suspended from orders for connivance in pretended revelations of a nun of the Puebla convent of St. Catherine of Siena. He was also a *solicitante*, having seduced her in the confessional, but this was studiously omitted from the sentence read.—Medina, *op. cit.*, p. 125.

[2] Oviedo y Valdés, Las Quinquagenas de la Nobleza de España, I, 383 (Madrid, 1880).—Concil. Mexican. I, ann. 1555, cap. lvii.—Mendieta, Hist. eccles. Indiana, Lib. IV, cap. xlv.

[3] Medina, p. 54.

but in his visitations, and he evidently had no idea that he was incurring risk of the Inquisition, for when remonstrated with he asked what his prelates could do to him—it was only a dozen strokes of the discipline and a year's suspension from his guardianship. When brought to trial he was frank in his admissions; two years before he had been deprived of confessing Spanish women, but as guardian he had licence to do so; he mentioned seven Indian women whom he had seduced in confession besides a mestizo and several Spaniards. In these cases, the accusation of the fiscal and the exordium of the sentence are eloquently rhetorical as to the heinous guilt in one, clothed with the awful power of the priesthood, using that power to lead astray the souls seeking salvation through him, but when it came to defining the penalty there is a tenderness which suggests that in reality the offence was regarded as much less important than aberration on some minute point of faith. When his sentence was read, May 5, 1584, he was subjected to the discipline for the space of a *miserere;* he was deprived of the faculty of confessing, was suspended from orders for six years, was recluded for two years in a convent with the customary disabilities and was banished for six years from the see of Guadalajara.[1]

Such treatment was not adapted to strengthen the carnal-minded against temptation so severe and the vice flourished accordingly. As the inquisitors stated in a letter to the Suprema of May 22, 1619, it was a very frequent offence in those parts and many confessors regarded it as trivial,[2] and the list of cases of solicitation for the years 1622–4 contains fifty-six names, of which seven were from Manila, for the Philippines were a dependency of the Mexican tribunal. That leniency increased with time may be assumed from the case, in 1721, of Fray Francisco Diego de Zarate, President of the Mission of Santa María de los Angeles of Rio Blanca, a Franciscan entrusted with many important positions. The summary in his trial states that the evidence

---

[1] MSS. of David Fergusson Esqr.
[2] "Que es delito muy reiterado en estas partes y muchos confesores hacen poquisimo caso dél."—Medina, p. 162.

collected proved a hundred and twenty-six acts of solicitation with fifty-six women and that it was his habit to solicit every one who came to him to confess. It is impossible to conceive anything more brutal than some of the details of the evidence; the offence in many cases was almost public and might have continued indefinitely had he not banished from Rio Blanco a woman and her family because she resisted him, whereupon she talked and created a scandal that rendered action necessary. Of the women, twenty-one were Indians, eight were Spaniards (one of them his near relative), eight Mulattos, four Mestizos and fifteen whose race is not specified. When the accusation, detailing all the cases, was read to him, he admitted its correctness and indeed he had previously made a written confession which contained a large number that had escaped the investigations of the prosecution. Aggravated as was this case Fray Francisco escaped with a second reading of his sentence in the Franciscan convent, where a circular discipline was administered, perpetual deprivation of confessing and of active and passive voice in his Order, six months' suspension from celebrating mass and two years' reclusion in a convent, of which the first was to be passed in a cell with fasting on bread and water on Fridays and Saturdays, and the last place in choir and refectory.[1] Yet inadequate as was the habitual treatment of the offence by the Inquisition, it was regarded as unduly harsh by the clerical authorities. The inquisitors, in a letter of 1666 to the Suprema, by way of illustrating the prevalent laxity of the Religious Orders, mention that after they had penanced four frailes for solicitation, they were applied to to remove the restrictions which prevented the culprits from being promoted to prelacies.[2] Self-denunciation,

---

[1] MSS. of David Fergusson Esqr.
[2] Medina, p. 320.

In 1664 the tribunal asked to have its jurisdiction extended over unnatural crime and bestiality, which it described as exceedingly prevalent, especially in the Religious Orders, but the Suprema refused.—Ibidem, p. 321.

It was beyond the power of the Suprema to accede to this without a special papal delegation. In Spain this had been granted to the tribunals of the Kingdoms of Aragon, but not to those of Castile.

as in Spain, was tolerably certain to win virtual immunity. In 1712, Luis Marin, vicar of Nativitas, accused himself by letter, to which the tribunal promptly responded by summoning him to appear within thirty days, but that only a reprimand was intended is evident from the summons being accompanied with a faculty to absolve him from the excommunication incurred, sent to Padre Fernández de Córdova, S. J., who was instructed to counsel him to abstain for the present from confessing women.[1]

The very miscellaneous functions assumed by the Inquisition in extending its jurisdiction over a variety of matters foreign to its original purpose is illustrated by a fortuitous collection of 397 cases between its commencement in 1572 and the year 1800. In these the offences alleged are[2]—

Bigamy	76	Heresy	20
Judaism	71	Propositions	13
Offences against the Inquisition	49	Illuminism	12
Solicitation	44	False witness	10
Blasphemy	39	Personating priesthood	7
Sorcery and superstitions	29	Miscellaneous	27

The considerable proportion of offences against the Inquisition arose from the perpetual troubles caused by what was known as its temporal jurisdiction, apart from its spiritual sphere of action. Every one connected with it in an official capacity, however insignificant, with his family, servants and slaves, was entitled, in a greater or less degree, to the *fuero*, or jurisdiction of the Holy Office, and to exemption from pleading or prosecution in the secular court if a layman, or the episcopal court if an ecclesiastic. As favoritism rendered this privilege virtually an immunity for crime it was eagerly sought and, as it was the source of influence and of profitable business, the tribunal endeavored to extend its jurisdiction in every way, with little regard to the limits imposed by law. This led to constant conflicts between the rival jurisdictions, in which the tribunal used without scruple its faculties of excommunication and of treating any opposition as an attempt

---

[1] MSS. of David Fergusson Esqr.   [2] Ibidem.

to impede its freedom of action, a crime to be prosecuted and severely punished. In Spain these irreconcilable pretensions were the cause of constant troubles, the settlement of which was through the process known as *competencia*, carrying them up to the Supreme Council of the Inquisition on the one hand and to the Council of Castile or of Aragon on the other, with the monarch as the final arbiter. In the Colonies, however, as we shall see, this system was practically eluded, and the tribunals became even more arbitrarily lawless than those of the home country, sometimes abusing their power after a fashion that involved the whole land in confusion, for in matters of faith they had no superior, short of the inquisitor-general, and it rested with themselves to define what was, directly or indirectly, a matter of faith.

There were two classes of officials whose claims to the *fuero* were different. Those known as *titulados y asalariados* were directly employed in the tribunal, holding commissions from the inquisitor-general, enjoying salaries and understood to devote themselves exclusively to its service. For them and their families and dependants the fuero was complete, in both civil and criminal matters, and both active and passive—that is, whether as plaintiff or defendant. They were comparatively few in number, their position was unchallenged and, whatever may have been the injustice and oppression thence arising, there was little occasion for dispute. Beyond these were the unsalaried officials— commissioners and their notaries and alguazils, stationed at all important centres, consultors, *calificadores* or censors and, above all, familiars numerously scattered throughout the land. All these pursued their regular avocations and only acted when called on for special service; they received no salary, but the positions were eagerly sought, chiefly on account of the privileges and immunities which they conferred. Of these the familiars were by far the most numerous and troublesome. In Spain the definition of their privileges had been the subject of numerous settlements known as Concordias and, when Philip II established the colonial tribunals, he endeavored to forestall trouble by extending to them the Castilian Concordia of 1553, which was much less favorable to the familiars than those of the kingdoms of Aragon and, at the same time, he sought to limit the number of appointees.

Among the documents issued in 1570 is a cédula addressed to the colonial authorities, in which Philip conveys to them the regulations adopted by the inquisitor-general. In the city of Mexico there are allowed twelve familiars, in the cathedral towns four, in other towns one. Lists of these and of all changes are to be furnished to the local magistracy, so that they may see that the number is not exceeded and, in case of improper appointments, they are to report to the tribunal or, if necessary, to the inquisitor-general. In civil suits the familiars are not entitled to the fuero, whether as plaintiffs or defendants. In criminal matters not as plaintiffs while, as defendants, they are to enjoy it except in cases of treason, unnatural crime, raising popular commotions, forging letters of safe-conduct, resistance to royal commands, abduction or violation of women, highway robbery, house or church breaking, arson of houses or harvests and "other crimes greater than these" and also in resistance or disrespect to the royal judges. Excepted also is official malfeasance in those holding public office. Arrest by secular judges is permitted, in cases entitled to the fuero, provided the culprit is handed over to the Inquisition, together with the evidence, which is to be at his expense. If the offence is committed outside of the city of Mexico, the offender cannot return to his place of residence without exhibiting a copy of the inquisitorial sentence, with evidence of its fulfilment. By a cédula of May 13, 1572, moreover, offences committed against Indians were added to the excepted cases.[1]

This all appears definite enough, but it was easily evaded. At first there seems to have been a disposition to conform to its

---

[1] Biblioteca nacional de Madrid, Seccion de MSS., X, 157, fol. 240 (see Appendix).—Royal Library of Munich, Cod. Hispan. 79.

intent. In 1575 a familiar named Rodrigo de Yepes, who had given the lie to, and repeatedly struck in the face, the alcalde of Valladola, was arrested by the civil magistrate and claimed by the tribunal but, after a competencia, or discussion of the case by the civil and inquisitorial authorities, the latter admitted that it was excepted and surrendered him. On the other hand, in 1615, Diego de Carmona Jamariz, a familiar of Puebla, was arrested for the murder of his enemy, Joan de Olivárez, and was surrendered to the Inquisition without a competencia, although murder would seem to be a greater crime than highway robbery or burglary. The widow prosecuted him before the tribunal, but it was useless and the case was dropped. In Spain, the Inquisition had devised the ingenious argument that, until a crime was proved, it could not be classed as excepted and therefore the affair was under its jurisdiction until conviction, which enabled it to protect its familiars, and this plea was used, in 1616, in the case of Gonzalo Antúnez Yáñez, a familiar, prosecuted by order of the viceroy.[1]

It was not only the familiars who gave trouble, but the numerous other unsalaried officials. The commissioners with their notaries and alguazils formed little groups in the provincial towns, of which the members supported each other and set the magistrates and courts at defiance. In the original instructions issued to the inquisitors they were admonished to be careful in the selection of commissioners, who were not to interfere with the constituted authorities or to provoke quarrels, but were merely to execute the mandates of the tribunal and to report on such matters as should present themselves.[2] Distance and the difficulty of communication, however, rendered them prone to abuse their position, and in this they were emboldened by the unwavering support of the tribunal. Throughout all the

---

[1] These cases are derived from the Munich MS., last cited, entitled "Extractos de Causas [de] Familiares y Ministros que no son Oficiales que ay en la Camara del Secreto de la Inquisicion de Mexico en este presente año de 1716."

[2] E. N. Adler, The Inquisition in Peru (Publications of the American Jewish Historical Society, No. 12).

Spanish Colonies the commissioner was an object of dread and the subject of perpetual complaint on the part of the secular and ecclesiastical powers. The general sentiment is expressed, as late as 1777, by Santiago Joseph, Bishop of Cuba, in a letter to Inquisitor-general Bertran. All the commissioners whom he had known, he said, had been ignorant persons, with the exception of one whose term of service was brief. There was no salary to attract competent men and the place was taken only to serve as an excuse for neglecting all clerical functions and duties. The commerce of Havana brought numerous heretics who scattered their poison and he dared not interpose for fear of the consequences of invading inquisitorial jurisdiction. The existing incumbent paid no attention to this and, when not absent, was wholly occupied in stirring up quarrels with the civil authorities.[1]

The commissioners of Mexico fully justified this characterization by the good bishop. In the great majority of cases the hopelessness of resistance to their arbitrary acts caused submission, but occasionally one emerges to light which illustrates the spirit animating the Inquisition and its officials. In 1699, Father Pistoya, S. J., the ecclesiastical judge of Sinaloa, prosecuted Martin de Verastegui for incestuous adultery with María García. Thereupon his intimate friend, Pérez de Ribera, the commissioner, to protect him, promptly appointed him notary, an act for which he had no authority. Pistoya sent the evidence in the case to the royal court of Guadalajara (Jalisco), which ordered the Governor of Sinaloa, Don Jacinto de Fuensaldaña, to arrest the guilty pair, embargo their property and send them to the royal prison of Guadalajara. Ribera claimed him as an official of the Inquisition and, on refusal, excommunicated the governor and the military officers who had executed his orders and posted them as such on the tablillas of the church. The

---

[1] J. T. Medina, Hist. de la Inquisicion de Cartagena p 437. See, also, p. 278. Cf. Archivo de Simancas, Inquisicion, Libro 61, fol. 251.—MSS. of Library of University of Halle, Yc 17.

tribunal sustained its commissioner; the governor was obliged to appear before it and beg for absolution; the commissioner was empowered to take testimony in the case and report it to the tribunal, which naturally found the parties innocent and Verastegui was rewarded with a genuine notary's commission in lieu of the fictitious one which had protected him from justice. It is no wonder that, in replying to their report of another outrageous case in 1695, the Suprema had sharply rebuked the inquisitors, ordering them to act with justice and moderation and prevent the complaints of their proceedings, which came daily to the king from the Council of Indies, but the case of Verastegui shows how little respect they paid to the admonition.[1]

Yet, with all this, there were comparatively few of the bitter struggles, so frequent in Spain during this period, between the royal and inquisitorial jurisdictions. It was not that the inquisitors were less arbitrary and audacious than at home, for their distance from the court rendered them even more independent, but that the secular magistracy felt its weakness and offered less resolute resistance. Spain was far off and the viceroy, though representing the royal autocracy, was under strict orders to show every favor to the Inquisition. There was kept in the royal chancellery the formula of a letter to all viceroys, emphasizing the great services of the Inquisition to religion and to the king and ordering it to be favored and guarded in all its privileges, exemptions and liberties, including those of its officials and familiars. Adherence to this would be regarded as most acceptable service and the contrary would not be permitted.[2] This portentous document was sent to the Viceroys of Mexico and Peru in 1603 and was doubtless repeated to them whenever necessary, as it was to other royal representatives at subsequent periods. As a rule however the viceroys and the tribunal were at odds and their quarrels were not conducive to popular tranquillity or edification. More than once we find viceroys like

---

[1] MSS. of Royal Library of Munich, Cod. Hispan. 79.
[2] Solorzani de Indiar. Gubern., Lib. III, cap. xxiv, n. 16.

Mancera, Cerralbo and Gelvez threatening the inquisitors with banishment.[1]

As a matter of course, under such auspices, colonial inquisitors could never be restrained within the limit of their rightful prerogatives, great as these were. A royal cédula of January 20, 1587, scolds those of Lima for illegal protection of their familiars and for vexing the local magistrates by summoning them from long distances before the tribunal. Another of March 8, 1589, rebukes them for creating too many familiars and other officials. Another of August 23, 1595, reprimands those of Mexico for supporting a familiar in refusing to render an account to the royal chancery of his functions as custom-house officer at Vera Cruz.[2] These complaints were of almost daily occurrence until at length Philip III sought to cut them off at the root by forming a junta of two members from each of the Councils of the Inquisition and of Indies to advise him. After mature deliberation they did so and the result is what is known as the Concordia of 1610. The prohibitions embodied in this are eloquent of the audacity of the inquisitors in exceeding their functions, abusing their authority in matters wholly outside of their jurisdiction and exercising an insufferably vexatious petty tyranny, the exasperating effect of which was intensified by the immunity enjoyed by the servants and slaves of the officials. These were justiciable only by the tribunal, which invariably protected them, so that the community was exposed without redress to the insolence of a class peculiarly apt to abuse its privileges.

Under pain of forfeiture of office the inquisitors were forbidden, directly or indirectly, by themselves or their kindred, to farm the public revenues or to prevent their being farmed to the highest bidder. Neither they nor the salaried officials were to engage in any kind of trade, under the same penalty. They were not to claim the right of seizing articles at an appraised price, except under urgent necessity for the support of the prisoners or buildings

---

[1] Medina, p. 315.   [2] Solorzano, *loc. cit.*, n. 61.

of the Inquisition. Their negroes were not to carry arms except when accompanying their masters. They were not to defend commissioners or familiars in frauds on the revenue nor in refusing to render an account of deposits made with them by order of court. They were not to detain the couriers and messengers who served as a rudimentary post-office and were to remove the prohibition against vessels leaving port or passengers departing without their licence. They were not to arrest the royal alguazils except for grave and notorious excess against the Inquisition. They were to be allowed one alguazil in Vera Cruz and were to dismiss all those appointed elsewhere.[1] They were not to protect familiars, who held public office, when prosecuted for official malfeasance, nor commissioners who held benefices for offences committed in their character of incumbents. They were not to order universities to grant degrees in contravention of their statutes, nor were they to interfere in matters of government apart from their functions. They were not to excommunicate a viceroy in cases of competencia, nor was the viceroy to evoke to himself a case that might lead to a competencia. A provision was also made for the settlement of competencias without the tedious resort to the councils in Spain. If the senior judge and senior inquisitor could not agree in their conference, the inquisitors were to name three ecclesiastical dignitaries to the viceroy, who was to select one; he was to be adjoined to the judge and inquisitor and the majority was to decide or, if there were three discordant opinions, the viceroy was to choose between them.[2]

This project for the settlement of competencias was ineffective. A cédula of February 7, 1569, had extended to the colonies the system in force at home, and under it there had been in Mexico,

---

[1] This prohibition was removed in the Concordia of 1633.
[2] Recop. de las Indias, Lib. I, Tit. xix, ley 29.

The vexatious petty tyranny in which the tribunal indulged is illustrated by the case of a law-student, Diego de Porras Villerías, about 1600, who was fined in 100 pesos and banished for a year because he refused to honor a requisition for two cartloads of lime for the prison which it was constructing.—Medina, p. 137.

during the remainder of the century, seven cases; there was one in 1601 and another in 1602, after which they ceased.[1] Solorzano tells us that they were not revived by the new regulations, which omitted to specify the place where the conferences were to be held, and the judges and inquisitors each summoned the others to come to them. The judges had old custom and royal cédulas on their side, but the inquisitors refused compliance because the orders had not been transmitted to them through the Suprema which they claimed was requisite to their validity, and thus important cases, both civil and criminal, remained undecided, to the great injury of individuals and the public. Moved by the complaints thus occasioned, Philip III, in a cédula of November 19, 1618, ordered that the conferences be held in the vice-regal palace, where the senior judge was to have precedence over the inquisitor, and this was repeated in a cédula to the court of Lima, May 28, 1621, but again the inquisitors of both Mexico and Peru refused obedience on the same pretext as before. Thus cases continued undecided until the urgency of the Council of Indies led Philip IV to consult both councils and, in 1636, he ordered that the judge and inquisitor should meet before the viceroy, the one who was senior in office taking the right hand.[2] This compromise did not suit the pretensions of the Holy Office for precedence and it gained the victory in a cédula of May 30, 1640, which recites that, after many conferences, it was determined that the senior judge must go to the Inquisition, where the senior inquisitor was to have precedence, when the competencia was to be settled under the provisions of the Concordia of 1610.[3] Apparently this assumption of their inferiority was insufferable to the judges, for no formal competencia occurred between 1602 and 1711. Matters in dispute were occasionally referred to the councils in Spain, but this was of little benefit

---

[1] Solorzani *op. cit.*, Lib. III, cap. xxiv, n. 60.—MSS. of Royal Library of Munich, Cod. Hispan. 79.—Archivo de Simancas, Inquisicion, Lib. 60, fol. 1, 60, 66 *sqq*.
[2] Solorzano, *loc. cit.*, n. 63–73.
[3] Archivo de Simancas, Inquisicion, Libro 17, fol. 1.

for it was usually the last heard of the case.[1] To appreciate fully the cruelty of all this, we must reflect that perhaps some accused person or unlucky alguazil, arrested for executing the orders of his superiors, might be languishing in gaol for a life-time, awaiting the settlement of a conflict of jurisdiction which could never be settled.

Whether or not the other prescriptions of the Concordia of 1610 were better observed than those concerning competencias it would be difficult to determine, but the presumption is adverse. At all events, inquisitorial ingenuity was constantly devising new methods of aggression and further complaints led Philip IV to assemble a junta of two members of each council, whose conferences resulted in the enactment of another Concordia, published April 11, 1633. Many of its clauses relate to the ever-present question of precedence, which need not detain us here, except the suggestive one that, at bull-fights in the plaza, the first courses are to be performed before the secular authorities, unless the latter, of their own accord, desire that honor to be paid to the inquisitors. Equally suggestive in another way are the prescriptions that commissioners shall treat the public courteously and that inquisitors shall treat the judges with respect and shall cease molesting the officers of the royal courts with censures and summoning and detaining them. They are again forbidden to engage in trade and are told not to interfere with the elections of secular officials nor, in times of scarcity, are they to persecute with excommunications the guards in charge of boats bringing grain, but are to apply to the viceroy, who will promptly supply their wants. The prohibition of detaining ships is repeated, but they are allowed to grant licences for sailing and for individuals to depart, which practically amounted to the same thing. The inquisitors seem to have gained their point as to the right of seizing goods and materials at a "just price," for this is allowed, subject to some limitations. The inviolability of the domicile of inquisitors is admitted in the provision that it is not to be abused

---

[1] Munich, MSS., Cod. Hispan. 79.

by secreting goods to the prejudice of third parties; and, in the case of salaried officials, it is limited by a clause that when it is necessary for officers of justice to enter the house of such official, or of the widow of one during her widowhood, notice shall first be given to the tribunal, which shall appoint one of its ministers to be present, with an appointee of the viceroy or court and, if such an appointment is not made within two or three hours, the entry can be made without longer waiting. One of the petty privileges which gave rise to constant exacerbation is indicated in the provision that, of the cattle slaughtered in the public shambles, there shall be given weekly the chine and chitterlings of ten oxen—two to each of the inquisitors, one to the alguazil and secretaries, one to the receiver and notary of sequestrations, and the rest to the poor prisoners; this is said to be all that the tribunal is entitled to and anything more must be paid for, nor shall its servants take the chitterlings and sell them.[1]

Concordias were only attempts to restrain existing abuses and they could not provide for the perpetual new aggressions suggested by the facile weapon of excommunication through which the Inquisition could overcome the resistance of the secular authorities. The distribution of quicksilver, for instance, to the miners was a matter jealously reserved to the viceroy and the junta of the treasury but, when the Inquisition wanted it for some mines belonging to it in Zacatecas, it forced, by threats of excommunication, the royal officials to supply its demands. Viceroy Mancera, in a letter of December 8, 1666, complains of this and of a case in which the royal treasurer of Guadalajara owed a personal debt to the tribunal of 980 pesos and the commissioner there, by order of the acting inquisitor and visitador, Medina Rico, forced the auditor of the treasury to pay it out of the royal funds, by threats of excommunication and of a fine of 500 pesos. Mancera endeavored by courteous remonstrance to obtain restitution but, after the inquisitors had insulted him, he only succeeded in getting 600 pesos returned. In reporting

---

[1] Recop., Lib. I, Tit. xix, ley 30.

these matters to the king, the Council of Indies pointed out forcibly how incompatible with subordination and good government were these arbitrary extensions of inquisitorial jurisdiction over matters wholly foreign to the objects of its institution.[1]

Indeed, the existence of so uncontrollable and disturbing an element goes far to explain the ill-success of Spanish colonial administration. In 1615, Fray Isidro Ordoñez, commissioner in San Francisco del Nuevo Mexico, under pretext of a fictitious order from the tribunal, gathered a band of soldiers and citizens, to whom inquisitorial orders were supreme, and seized Don Pedro de Peralta, Governor of New Mexico, and held him in irons for nine months. Peralta managed to complain to the tribunal, which summoned Ordoñez to the capital and assigned to him his convent for a prison, but Peralta obtained no satisfaction beyond a declaration that there had been no cause for his arrest, while Ordoñez, in place of the severe punishment which he merited, was permitted to attend the general chapter of his Order in Rome, as procurator of the province of Mexico.[2] Another Governor of New Mexico, Diego de Peñalosa, fared even worse when, for indiscreet words about priests and inquisitors and expressions verging on blasphemy, he was exposed to the humiliation of appearing as a penitent in the auto de fe of February 3, 1668— thus virtually incapacitating him for further service.[3] It was not without grounds that the Council of Indies, in 1696, addressed a formal remonstrance to Carlos II, recapitulating a long array of abuses and violences, showing the impossibility of enforcing observance of the Concordias or obedience to the royal commands. Prelates and governors were alike sufferers from the irrepressible audacity which admitted no responsibility to any one, so long as it was upheld and justified by the Suprema at home, and the council supplicated the king, if not for the total extinction of

---

[1] Archivo de Simancas, Inquisicion, Lib. 60, fol. 199.
[2] Munich MSS., Cod. Hispan. 79.
[3] Medina, p. 323. Possibly this may explain his treasonable project of transferring the northern provinces of Mexico to France.

the tribunal, at least for the dismissal of the officials. Without some thorough change the retention of the colonies could scarce be hoped for, as all the population was inspired with a common hatred arising from its violence.[1]

As the council says, prelates were as liable as royal officials to be subjected to the lawless action of the tribunal. There never were lacking pretexts for quarrel. In 1617 Archbishop Pedro de Villareal fared badly in a rupture caused by his inserting in an edict some matters which the tribunal claimed to belong to its jurisdiction. In 1623 Bishop Bohorques of Oaxaca had the same experience because he styled himself Inquisidor Ordinario. The episcopate of Archbishop Matheo Sagade Bugueiro, from 1655 to 1662, was a succession of bitter dissensions, during which Bernardino de Amezaga, chief notary of the court of testaments, was arrested by the tribunal, deprived of his office and banished, while Francisco de Bermeo, contador of the Santa Cruzada, was kept long in prison, fined 200 pesos and a negro slave of his was sold to defray it. In 1658 the archbishop made a demand that all edicts read in his cathedral must first be shown to him in order to satisfy him that they contained nothing that invaded his jurisdiction, and his action in enforcing this claim led the tribunal to publish a manifesto declaring that, under the bull *Si de protegendis*, he had incurred degradation and relaxation to the secular arm.[2]

There was one case, however, in which the tribunal and the Archbishop of Mexico combined for the persecution of a bishop, for Juan de Mañozca, the archbishop from 1643 to 1653, was cousin of the inquisitor of the same name. The saintly Bishop Juan de Palafox of Puebla, in his capacity of visitador and protector of the Indians, incurred the enmity of the archbishop and of the Viceroy Salvatierra, and an occasion of gratifying it occurred

---

[1] Archivo de Simancas, Inquisicion, Lib. 60, fol. 362.

[2] Archivo de Simancas, Inquisicion, Lib. 946, fol. 282, 360, 400.—Por el Tribunal del S. Officio de Mexico sobre el Impedimiento que a puesto D. D. Matheo Sagade Bugueiro, Arzobispo de la dicha Ciudad (communicated by D. Fergusson Esqr.).

17

when he undertook to guard his episcopal jurisdiction against the encroachments of the Jesuits. They appointed *jueces conservadores* to protect their interests and the tribunal rushed eagerly into the fray, with which it had absolutely no right to intervene.[1] It ordered the suppression of the writings and edicts of Palafox and forbade any interference with those of the conservators; it sent a commissioner to Puebla who terrorized the community by arresting prominent priests and citizens of the bishop's party, parading them through the streets in chains and sending them to Mexico, where they were thrown into the secret prison, thus inflicting indelible disgrace on them and their posterity. In spite of the exemption of Indians from inquisitorial jurisdiction, he flogged nearly to death, with four hundred lashes, an unfortunate Indian who, at the command of a citizen, had taken down one of the conservators' edicts. Palafox was advised that he too would be arrested and fled to the mountains, where he lay concealed for several months.[2] When, in 1647, he appealed to the Suprema, powers were sent to the Bishop of Oaxaca to investigate and report, but Archbishop Mañozca threw every impediment in his way and, in his capacity of visitador of the

---

[1] The visitador Medina Rico characterizes without reserve this unjustifiable action of the tribunal "sin causa, motivo, ni razon alguna, se introdujeron à inmensos procedimientos en la materia, y esto no con igualdad y justicia, sino con manifiesta pasion contra el dicho señor Obispo, su provisor, criados, allegados y afectos." They represented to Viceroy Salvatierra "que era sospechoso en la fe y tizon ardiente del infierno y otras cosas gravisimas semejantes à las referidas."—Medina, pp. 241, 242.

[2] Obras de Juan de Palafox y Mendoza, Tom. I, Prolegom.; T. XI, pp. 241, 289, 328, 466–7 (Madrid, 1762). The fullest account, however, of the arbitrary proceedings of the Inquisition is contained in a letter, omitted for cause from his collected works, written from Chiapa, August 10, 1647, to the Inquisitor-general Arce y Reynoso. It was printed by Puigblanch, Cadiz, 1813, and by Medina, pp. 242–60.

It is worthy of note that at this time the Jesuits were laying the foundation of their curious autocratic empire of Paraguay, by a quarrel with Bernardino de Cardenas, Bishop of Asuncion, known as *el Padre de los Indios*. To prevent his visiting their missions they drove him by force of arms from his episcopal see. The struggle lasted from 1644 to 1660, when the Holy See decided in favor of the bishop.—Coleccion de Documentos tocantes á la Persecucion contra D. Fr Bernardino de Cardenas, Madrid, 1768.

Inquisition, assumed to annul his commission. He appealed to the Bishop of Yucatan, then Governor of New Spain, and to the Audiencia for support, but the archbishop threatened to excommunicate them all and they prudently declined the conflict. Palafox represents to the Suprema that his life was in danger and he begs to be allowed to return to Spain.[1] The combination of the archbishopric and Inquisition, under the two Mañozcas, evidently held the whole land in its grasp, and no one was hardy enough to oppose it. Palafox was obliged to abandon Mexico, but he eventually secured a decision in his favor on an appeal to Rome.

An episode of this case is worth recounting in some detail, not only as illustrating inquisitorial methods but as a rare instance of a victim obtaining a measure of satisfaction. Doctor Juan de la Camara, a canon of the cathedral, was a man of noble birth, proud of his unblemished *limpieza*, and his appointment as visitador of the see of Guadalajara indicates the estimation in which he was held by his superiors. Unfortunately he was a friend and correspondent of Palafox. When, in 1646, a bitter libel was circulated against the latter, one of the judges of the Audiencia, Alonso González de Villalba, was included in it. Palafox endured the attack in silence and endeavored to make Villalba follow his example, but the latter was so incensed that he wrote a reply in which he handled roughly the inquisitor Mañozca. He showed it to his neighbor Camara, who returned it without comment and said nothing about it except to Don Antonio Urrutía de Vergara, to whom he mentioned it in order that he might tell the archbishop, and to a Doña Catalina de Diosdado, to whom he merely said that he had seen two scandalous papers and that, if the author confessed to him, he would not absolve him.

There was a chance that among his papers something might be

---

[1] Archivo de Simancas, Inquisicion, Lib. 38, fol. 64.
We shall meet Archbishop Juan de Mañozca hereafter in his earlier capacity of Inquisitor of Cartagena, where he earned an infamous notoriety.

found to compromise Palafox, so an order of arrest with sequestration of property was made out, February 7, 1647. At eight o'clock in the morning Camara was roused from his bed and taken in his own carriage to the secret prison, where he was confined in a cell of which the window had been blocked up, so that the single candle to which he was restricted was his only light by day and night. Here he was kept *incomunicado* for twenty days. After the tenth day, however, on which he was examined, the obstructions were removed from the window and, after the twentieth, his brother, Fray Diego, and some other friends were permitted to see him on obtaining a special licence for each visit. Meanwhile his papers had been carried off to the tribunal, without being inventoried as required by the Instructions; on the day after his arrest his household effects were inventoried and placed in the hands of the receiver, Juan González de Castro, as depository, but they were not removed from the house and no care was taken to ensure their safety.

At nightfall of March 15th he was taken back to his house and told that it was henceforth to be his prison, under pain of excommunication and a thousand ducats. On April 1st his prison was enlarged to the city, under the same penalties, and he was enabled to resume his duties at the cathedral. Of course the immurement in the secret prison, with sequestration of property, of so prominent an ecclesiastic, caused a general sensation; it was at the height of the prosecution of the Judaizers and the inevitable conclusion was that they had implicated him, so that a stain was cast upon his honor which no subsequent exculpation could wholly efface. His papers were withheld from him; his house had been richly furnished, with abundance of silver plate and linen, much of which had disappeared, and he seems to have deplored especially the loss of eighteen ounces of amber. His trial remained unconcluded and his repeated applications for a decision and for the restoration of missing property were filed away without action. His only hope of escape from prolonged and intolerable suspense lay in appealing to the

Suprema. The inquisitors had already sought to prejudice it against him for, in a letter of May 20th, they spoke of the incredible efforts and diabolical means employed to intimidate them from the performance of their duty in the matter of Palafox; Camara was an accomplice of Villalba in publishing the libel; he had perjured himself in his confessions and might be assumed to be the author of the worst passages in it. In spite of this the Suprema, by a decree of September 28, 1647, ordered his release, on the security of his oath, and the sequestration of his property to be removed.

Camara succeeded in secretly obtaining from the king an order, November 16, 1647, permitting him to go to Spain, but he was impoverished and sent his brother, Fray Diego, to act for him. The mission occupied Diego for several years, but he finally procured from the Suprema a commission to the Inquisitor Higuera to try the case promptly for, during all this time, it had been held suspended over Camara's head. This was presented, February 15, 1650, and, on the following July 12th, Higuera, who was at odds with Mañozca, rendered a sentence acquitting him and restoring him to his previous good fame, so that his arrest should work no prejudice to him or to his kindred and their descendants; also that the chapter should pay him all the accrued fruits of his prebend and that his papers and property should be returned to him. From this Camara appealed to the Suprema, which confirmed it, July 7, 1651; then the fiscal of the Suprema appealed and it was again confirmed, July 31st. The whole prosecution was thus stamped as being malicious and groundless, but nevertheless Camara in vain endeavored to regain possession of his papers and of his missing effects.

Archbishop Mañozca died in 1653; the affair of Palafox had created no little scandal in Spain and, in 1654, a new visitador, Pedro de Medina Rico, was sent out with instructions especially to investigate it. Camara promptly set forth his grievances, in September, in a complaint against Estrada and Higuera—for apparently Mañozca, as the subject of the libel, had not sat in the trial. On December 1st he made his formal charges in a criminal action against them, laying his damages at 12,000 pesos, which he claimed to be the amount which the affair had cost him in losses and expenses. It was a bold undertaking and probably unexampled, and he found it impossible to secure the necessary legal assistance for, on January 20, 1655, he represented that none of the procurators of the Audiencia would serve him, wherefore he prayed for an order on Juan de Escobar to appear for him. It was granted and enforced with a penalty of fifty pesos, under pressure of which Escobar took charge of the case. In the same way his witnesses refused to appear until he procured orders on them, with censures for disobedience. The action went slowly on through its various stages; the inquisitors made no effort to justify what they had done and confined their defence to alleging that the affair was a *cosa juzgada*, which could not be reopened, and to interjecting appeals to the Suprema at every adverse interlocutory decree. It was not until May 31, 1656, that Medina Rico pronounced sentence to the effect that Camara had proved his case completely and that Estrada and Higuera had alleged nothing to palliate their grave offence, the punishment of which he reserved for future decision. As to what affected the interest of the plaintiff, he condemned them jointly and severally to pay him two thousand pesos. The receiver, or depository, was ordered to restore to him everything shown in the inventory and, if it appeared that articles were not deposited with him, the inquisitors must make them good under penalty of a thousand pesos. From this the inquisitors appealed and, after protracted argument, Rico suspended the order to pay the two thousand pesos until the Suprema should decide the appeal, but that the rest of the sentence should be executed without awaiting its action. Then followed a long and confused litigation with the executor of the receiver de Castro, who had been dead for many years and his estate distributed. The documents preserved end with November 14, 1657, at which time they were made up for transmission to the Suprema and what was its final decision cannot be told.¹ It is evident that Camara obtained little compensation for his sufferings, but at least he had the satisfaction of seeing his persecutors punished, although inadequately, for official offenders were always treated tenderly by the Inquisition. Medina Rico, as the result of his visitation, formulated hundreds of charges against them, collectively and individually, and rendered sentence, May 17, 1662, in the audience-chamber, where all the officials were assembled. Estrada was condemned to severe reprimand, to a fine of 1500 pesos and to four years' suspension, though, as he had died October 26, 1661, the penalty fell only on his heirs. Higuera was sentenced to a fine of a hundred pesos and two years' suspension, which he endured until May 16, 1664. Mañozca was visited more heavily with a fine of 1300 pesos and nine years of suspension.² This he could afford to disregard for, in the autumn of 1661, he had been provided with the bishopric of Santiago de Cuba whence, in 1666, he was transferred to that of Guatemala and finally, in 1675, he obtained the wealthy see of Puebla, from which he had driven Palafox. Retributive justice, however, at last overtook him, for he died before he could take possession.³ Such were the men who largely filled the tribunals and episcopates of the Colonies.

Among the privileges claimed by the Inquisition was exemption from military service. This was strictly limited by the Concordia of 1633. Officials holding commissions from the inquisitor-general were exempted from appearing in the general musters, but familiars were not, unless actually on duty for the tribunal and, if the enemy was in sight, all were liable to service, save those necessary to guard the papers and records of the tribunal, to whom certificates were to be given. As might be expected, however, little respect was paid to these provisions. In 1685, the alcalde of Puebla called a muster of the citizens to march

---

[1] MSS. of David Fergusson Esqr. The sentence in this case is so unusual that I give the essential portion of it in the Appendix.
[2] Medina, p. 266.   [3] Gams, Series Episcoporum, s. vv.

to the succor of Campeachy. Hipolito del Castillo, alguazil and familiar, claimed exemption, to which he was clearly not entitled. The alcalde threatened to send him on a mule to Campeachy and in effect threw him into prison, placed his head in the pillory and made him pay a fine of 120 pesos. The commissioner at Puebla defended Castillo and, on appeal to the Inquisition, it ordered the money to be returned. Again, in 1718, when eight companies of merchants were formed in Puebla, by order of the viceroy, to make the rounds of the city and drive out malefactors, Martínez de Castro, a familiar and trader, was enrolled; he protested and appealed to the Inquisition, which ordered his discharge, in which the authorities immediately acquiesced.[1]

The inquisitorial function of censorship was by no means neglected. Even before the establishment of the tribunal, it was felt necessary to guard the faithful from the infection of heretical books and, in 1561, Inquisitor-general Valdés sent to Archbishop Montufar a commission empowering him to examine the book-shops for that purpose.[2] This conveyed no censorial power, but Páramo proudly asserts that, almost at the inception of the Holy Office, calificadores were appointed who exercised a most vigilant supervision over all books introduced into the colony, even over those which had passed the examination of the Suprema itself, and who occasionally had the satisfaction of showing that books widely circulated in Spain required expurgation. In fact, a letter of the Suprema respecting the Index then in preparation shows that, as early as 1573, censures of books were received from Mexico. The position of calificador, like that of inquisitor, seems to have been a stepping-stone to the bishop's chair, for the first one was Domingo de Salazar, promoted, in 1581, to the archiepiscopate of the Philippines; the second was Bartolomé de Ledesma, who in 1581 became Bishop of Oaxaca, and the third was Pedro de Ribera, who in

---

[1] Munich MSS., Cod. Hispan, 79.
[2] Archivo de Simancas, Inquisicion, Lib. 940, fol. 2.

1594 was elected Bishop of Panama, but died on the road to take possession.¹ Apparently the office was one not always easy to fill. In a letter of September 1, 1655, the tribunal informed the Suprema that it was in need of correctors of books and calificadores and it sent the genealogy of Padre Juan Hortiz, Rector of the Jesuit College, as a fit person, though he had not studied theology; the tribunal of Logroño thereupon reported favorably as to his *limpieza* and, on November 11, 1659, after four years of delay, the commission for him was sent.² It will be seen from all this that the Mexican Inquisition exercised an independent function of censorship; the earliest printing-press in the New World was established in the city of Mexico and its products were supervised by the tribunal, which condemned them, when necessary, without awaiting a reference to distant Spain. Prohibitory edicts, moreover, emanating from the home censorship, were duly published from every parish pulpit between the Caribbean and the Pacific.³

As was the case in Spain, censorship was not confined to literature but extended to works of art which might offend sensitiveness either of modesty or of veneration. The degree to which this might interfere with affairs of daily life depended upon the discretion of the tribunal, as was instanced by an edict of March 2, 1600. This prohibited all crosses, heads of Christ, the Virgin and the saints and scenes from sacred history carved or engraved or painted or embroidered on furniture, bed-clothing, napery, utensils of all kinds, or other places where these sacred symbols might be exposed to disrespect, and everything of the kind was to be surrendered for the erasure of the images. As Spanish

---

¹ Páramo, p. 243.—Archivo de Simancas, Lib. 940, fol. 6.
² MSS. of David Fergusson Esqr.
³ See the Author's "Chapters from the Religious History of Spain," p. 73.

There was no little scandal, in 1768, when it was discovered that the receiver of the tribunal, Vicente de las Heras Serrano, had sold for 850 pesos to the Licentiate Juan José Azpeitia a number of the prohibited books which had been seized. No great damage to the faith could have ensued if they were all like Milton's Paradise Lost, for the possession of which a French surgeon, Carlos Loret, was forced to abjure and was banished to Spain.—Medina, p. 434.

piety had luxuriated in the use of such emblems wherever possible, this raised a cloud of questions, which Fray Diego Múñoz, commissioner at Mechoacan, endeavored to settle in instructions issued to his delegate at Querétaro. Thus branding-irons for cattle and horses, that had a cross on them, were to be surrendered; as for beasts already so branded, the marks were to be erased where possible. Men tattooed with crosses or the name of Jesus were to efface them within fifteen days. Thimbles so adorned, if of gold or silver, were to be returned after filing off the symbols. Moulds for pastry with sacred heads were allowable, because the pastry was eaten and not treated with indecency, and it was the same with tapestries and wall-hangings. That the opportunities afforded by this decree were not neglected is indicated in a complaint to the tribunal from Juan Rodríguez of Querétaro, who relates that Fray Francisco de Parra, Guardian of the Franciscan convent, under orders from Múñoz, had seized and carried off to the convent a bedstead of gilt wood, costing 500 pesos, because it had some carved heads, which were not of Christ or angels; also counterpanes, pillows, curtains, towels, etc., because they had crosses or the word Jesus embroidered on them, and finger-rings with five stones set as a cross. Others had suffered in the same way, and Rodríguez prayed for the restoration of the articles.[1]

Incident to the censorship was the *visita de navíos*, or search of all vessels on their arrival, regarded as an indispensable duty to prevent the importation of forbidden books and the immigration of suspected heretics and Judaizers, as well as to ascertain whether, during the voyage, any one on board had committed acts subjecting him to inquisitorial jurisdiction. As in Spain, this performance inevitably led to friction with the secular authorities of the sea-ports. As early as 1584 there is a prosecution of Hernando de Moxica, alcalde mayor, and of Diego de Yepes, regidor of Vera Cruz, for impeding the commissioner in

---

[1] MSS. of David Fergusson Esqr.

A similar prohibition of the irreverent use of crosses and images is embodied in the Peruvian Edict of Faith of 1641.—Adler, The Inquisition in Peru (American Jewish Historical Society, No. 12)

this work and speaking disrespectfully of it, resulting in a fine of five hundred pieces each, with excommunication until they should withdraw their opposition.[1] Of course it was difficult to control the officials of the tribunal in the matter of fees and to keep the peace between them and the royal representatives as to questions of precedence, points which the Concordia of 1633 endeavored to regulate by fixing the fee at four pesos, of which two accrued to the commissioner and one each to the alguazil and notary, an amount never to be exceeded, no matter how many assistants might be employed, while existing orders were to be strictly observed as to their concurrence with the royal officials.[2] Of course it was not easy for the Inquisition to maintain supervision over so extended a coast. In a consulta of February 15, 1620, the Suprema informed Philip III that there had recently been printed in Holland large numbers of Spanish Bibles to be sent to the colonies and, as the Inquisition was unable to prevent their introduction unaided, the king was asked to instruct the royal officials to exercise greater vigilance. To this he assented and the request was renewed, June 28, 1629. It was probably to meet this that, in 1633, an agreement between the Suprema and the Council of Indies permitted the appointment of an alguazil in Yucatan to aid in searching the ships arriving at the ports.[3]

With the advent of the Bourbon dynasty, there occurs, in Mexico as in Spain, a disposition on the part of the secular authorities to restrain the overbearing petulance and audacity of the Holy Office. It is true that the tribunal obtained a victory in 1712, in a quarrel with the Royal Audiencia which had prosecuted its notary, and it was so overjoyed that it hastened to communicate the fact to the tribunal of Lima so that it might serve as a precedent. It related how the royal cédula of 1640, repeated in

---

[1] Munich MSS., Cod. Hispan. 79. See "Chapters from Spain," p. 86, for instructions to the commissioners in the performance of this duty.
[2] Recop., Lib. I, Tit. xix, ley 30.
[3] Archivo de Simancas, Inquisicion, Lib. 20, fol. 10; Lib. 40, fol. 44.

1667 and 1701, had been strictly observed, when the senior judge came to the competencia and occupied the lowest seat and the decision was that the notary was entitled to the *fuero* of the Holy Office.[1] Though competencias thus commenced to reappear they did not always end so satisfactorily. In 1722, Joseph Freire de Somorostro, commissioner in Zacatapan, was fined 500 pesos and suspended for six years from his functions as an advocate by the royal court, for an offence against its authority. He appealed to the tribunal which, in its customary threatening methods, demanded that the papers in the case be delivered to it within fifteen days, but they were withheld. It succeeded better in the case of Alonso Diaz de la Vega, alguazil of Goamantla who, in 1723, was concerned with his son in a quarrel, in which a man was killed. They were arrested and prosecuted, but the tribunal interfered vigorously, obtained possession of both father and son, gave notice that prosecutors must present themselves within eight days and, as none appeared, discharged the accused—thus affording convincing proof of the advantage of the fuero to criminals. It showed, however, a juster sense of the limitations of its jurisdiction in another case of the same year which illustrates the tendency of its officials to obstruct the secular authorities. The Castellan of Vera Cruz complained to the viceroy of the commissioner, Gregorio de Salinas, who had assisted the mutineers of the fleet in demanding their pay and had defended the asylum of the convent of San Francisco, in which they had taken refuge. The viceroy forwarded the statement to the tribunal, which forthwith ordered the commissioner to desist; the Inquisition had nothing to do with the matter; if he had assembled the officials of the Inquisition with their badges and had taken them to the convent to defend its right of asylum, he had done very wrong and must instruct each of them, before a notary, to keep aloof and he must, in the same way, withdraw the delegated power given to the superior of the convent. It does not appear however that the peccant commissioner was punished in any way

---

[1] MSS. of David Fergusson Esqr.

for this inexcusable prostitution of the authority of the Holy Office. Another case, in the same year, illustrates the multifarious ways in which these petty local officials abused the mysterious attributes with which they were invested. Valdés la Vandera, commissioner of Valle de Santa Barbara, claimed fees for all interments to which he was invited, even when he did not wear surplice and cap as ordered by the Constitucion Sinodal and, not content with this, charged double fees; he also demanded that, in the assemblies of Corpus, San Pedro and other feasts of obligation, he should have the highest place, in virtue of being commissioner. The clergy complained to the tribunal, which condemned his pretensions and ordered him to desist.[1]

The enlightened despotism of Carlos III brought increased tendency to curtail the privileges of the Inquisition and to curb its audacity. A cédula of February 29, 1760, declares that the titular and salaried officials shall enjoy the fuero only as defendants, in both civil and criminal matters, and wholly withdraws that of the familiars. Also that in clear and notorious cases there shall be no competencia, but that the viceroy, as the personal representative of the sovereign, shall decide what is fitting to prevent invasion of the royal jurisdiction.[2] The transitory liberalism of the period greatly diminished the traditional awe inspired by the Inquisition. About the year 1767, it had a serious conflict with the Audiencia, over the case of a Doctor Bechi, in which the royal fiscal, during his argument, treated it with scant respect, reciting how Charles V had been obliged to limit its jurisdiction in Sicily, how the reigning monarch had exiled from court the Inquisitor-general Quintano Bonifaz, and hinting not obscurely that, if it was abolished, substitutes for it could be found—all of which was made the subject of bitter, and apparently fruitless, remonstrance to the king by the Suprema, in a consulta of February 29, 1768. This unprecedented freedom

---

[1] Munich MSS., Cod. Hispan. 79.
[2] Note to Recop., Lib. I, Tit. xix, ley 29. For further details as to this see below, under Peru.

of speech reveals the existence of a belief in some impending change, and this was stimulated by the startling expulsion of the Jesuits, skilfully managed by the viceroy, the Marquis de Croix, June 25, 1767. The foundations of the ecclesiastical structure seemed to be crumbling and there arose a universally accredited rumor that the Inquisition would be the next to suffer. So definite did this become that the day was fixed for September 3d and the precaution taken by the viceroy, in anticipation of disturbance, by keeping troops under arms all that night, especially in the quarter where the Inquisition was situated, only strengthened the delusion. So firmly rooted was this that, when the night passed away without the expected event, the archbishop called upon the viceroy to learn for himself the truth of the belief that the suppression had only been postponed until certain pending trials shoud be completed.[1]

During this period of decadence the functions of the tribunal, in its proper sphere of action, amounted to little more than punishing a few bigamists, so-called sorcerers and soliciting confessors. In 1702 it reported only four cases pending—three for

---

[1] Archivo de Simancas, Inquisicion, Lib. 28, fol. 272, 276.

Obregon (*op. cit.*, p. 227) relates an anecdote of this period which would seem incompatible with the existing discredited position of the Inquisition. One Ash Wednesday, when the canons of the cathedral called upon the Marquis de Croix, as customary, to present him with ashes, he kept them waiting in his antechamber, to the intense indignation of those dignified personages. They complained to the inquisitors, who summoned the viceroy to appear before them. He obeyed, but he went attended by a guard and some pieces of artillery. He was haughtily received until he took out his watch and casually remarked that he hoped the audience would be brief for, if he was not back in the street in ten minutes, the cannon would open on the building and reduce it to ruins. The dignity of the inquisitors disappeared; they promptly dismissed him and were in agony as he leisurely sauntered forth.

If such an occurrence took place it is attributable with more verisimilitude to the period of the Marquis de Croix in Mexico than to the earlier time of the Marquis de Castelfuerte in Peru, of whom a precisely similar story is told, except that he gave the tribunal an hour for consideration. In his case the summons to appear is ascribed to his rough treatment of the Franciscans, July 5, 1731, when two of them were killed in a disturbance at the execution of Dr. Joseph de Antequera.—Palma, Añales de la Inquisicion de Lima, p. 184 (Madrid, 1898).

bigamy and a Jesuit, Padre Francisco de Figueroa, for what was known as flagellation, or stripping female penitents and using the discipline on them, an offence akin to solicitation.[1] Yet in an auto of 1704 it exhibited eight bigamists and two sorcerers and, in one of 1708, it had thirteen penitents of whom five were bigamists. There was an exception in 1712 when it had the fortune to present a Judaizer who had denounced himself and begged for mercy, notwithstanding which he was condemned to appear in an auto with a gag and to irremissible prison and sanbenito for life. In 1712-13 there were eleven convictions for solicitation and in 1722 an auto with twelve penitents, of whom nine were bigamists, followed soon afterwards with five cases of solicitation. So it went on, gradually diminishing and affording less and less justification for the existence of the tribunal with its large revenues, though when it had an opportunity it demonstrated that it retained its capacity for evil, as in the case of a naval lieutenant, Manuel Germa de Bahamonde, arrested February 24, 1735, for heretical propositions and, after nine years of incarceration, pronounced insane in 1744, when he was sent to the castle of San Juan de Ulua pending transmission to Spain.[2]

After 1750 there was some increase in business, arising from the prevalence of blasphemy and irreligion in the army, especially in the regiments of foreigners, and cases became more numerous among foreign residents accused of heresy and free-thinking. It was doubtless owing to this that Fernando VI, in a decree of December 31, 1756, imposed the death penalty on recruits who pretended Catholicism in order to enlistment—a severity modified in 1765 by Carlos III to expulsion from the kingdom.[3] In spite of these measures, the tribunal, in a letter of April 28, 1766, complained of the number of foreigners sent to Mexico among the troops—their disseminating the heresies of Luther and Calvin and of total irreligion, and their justification of England, thus diminishing the horror and detestation felt by the natives for

---

[1] Medina, p. 338.   [2] Ibidem, pp. 339–45.
[3] Archivo de Simancas, Inquisicion, Legajo 1465, fol. 81.

the English, which it was so desirable to maintain. The Suprema represented this to Carlos, who thereupon ordered that no soldiers should be sent to the Indies who were not assuredly Catholics.[1]

The increasing discredit into which the tribunal had fallen and the widely spread rumors, as we have seen, of its approaching suppression, seem to have stimulated it to a recrudescence of activity in an effort to assert its continued existence. It celebrated an auto, September 6, 1767, with four culprits—one of them, María Josefa Pineda Morales, for bigamy, who had been arrested as long before as in 1760. Then on March 13, 1768, it held another with seventeen penitents. Cases of solicitation also became more frequent as the century drew to its close.[2] A new field of activity, moreover, was opened to it by the outbreak of the French Revolution, when the propaganda of the rights of man increased the importance of the Inquisition as an agency of repression. Already, in 1770, an edict ordered the denunciation within six days of confessors who should use the confessional to encourage ideas contrary to the submission due to the sovereign. The accession of the reactionary Carlos IV and the dread of revolutionary principles began to afford a harvest of cases in which politics had more to do than religion. There were many Frenchmen in Mexico following their trades; they were naturally partizans of the new order of things; their influence was dreaded for they spread their opinions among the people and the organization and methods of the Inquisition rendered it the most efficient instrument for the detection and punishment of liberalism.[3]

A typical example was that of two Frenchmen, the Capitan Jean Marie Murgier and Doctor Joseph François Morel, accused of a conspiracy to cause a revolution and arrested in 1794. Murgier feigned sickness and, when visited by Dr. José Francisco Rada, he asked the gaoler for a glass of water and during his absence blocked the door with his trunk. Then he seized Rada's

---

[1] Medina, pp. 358–63.—Archivo de Simancas, Inquisicion, Legajo 1465, fol. 81.
[2] Medina, pp. 365, 388. [3] Ibidem, pp. 396, 432.

sword and declared that he would kill both him and himself unless the tribunal would liberate him with a full acquittal and furnish him with a pair of loaded pistols. The confusion of the tribunal was great; parleying went on from 10.15 A.M. to 4.30 P.M., when it was decided to break down the door. Guards with hatchets attacked it and Murgier ran himself through with the sword. His comrade Morel cut his throat with a pair of snuffers February 11, 1795. They were prosecuted after death and furnished occasion for the last public auto, August 9th of that year, where their effigies and bones were burnt as those of heretics, deists and materialists. At the same auto there figured the first Judaizer for many years—Rafael Gil Rodríguez, a cleric in the lower orders, who had been arrested October 9, 1788. He proved exceedingly obstinate and was sentenced to relaxation on February 9, 1792, after which he was held awaiting an auto. His resolution failed on the morning of the fatal day, he professed repentance, was reconciled, and thus saved the Inquisition the shame of burning a fellow-creature alive at the close of the eighteenth century. The other penitents were Jean Langouran of Bordeaux, who was reconciled for Lutheranism and atheism, and Jean Lausel of Montpellier who abjured de levi for suspicion of Free-Masonry.[1]

It was not however Frenchmen alone who suffered for their political opinions. José Antonio Rojas was denounced by two ladies, in correspondence with whom he had expressed his liberalism too freely. In September, 1804, he was condemned, as a formal heretic and materialist, to reclusion in the College of the Propaganda Fide at Pachuca, but he escaped to the United States where he relieved his feelings in a tremendous pamphlet against the Holy Office, which was duly prohibited in an edict of March 6, 1807. The distinguished publicists, Juan Wenceslao Bosquera and José Joaquin Fernández de Lizardi, known as *El Pensador Mexicano*, were also prosecuted for writings that evinced too ardent a spirit of patriotism. It was also doubtless

---

[1] Medina, pp. 387, 397–405.

for offences of the same nature that Fray Juan Antonio de Olabarrieta was reconciled for atheism in 1803, and his sanbenito was suspended in the cathedral, for the charge of atheism or any kindred form of speculation was, as we have seen, a convenient one to bring political liberalism under inquisitorial jurisdiction.[1]

Under the pressure of the time the censorship was sharpened with special rigor and severity. A curious instance of the strictness with which the laws against prohibited books were enforced is afforded by an episode, in 1806, of the Louisiana Purchase. As this rendered necessary a delimitation of the boundary between Mexico and the United States, Carlos IV ordered an investigation and report from the viceroy, who employed Fray Melchor de Talamantes to make it. He found it necessary to consult the works of Robertson and Raynal, but these were in the Index and he applied to the Inquisition, through the viceroy, for the requisite licence, saying that, although the books were detestable, the information they contained, and especially their maps, were important for the public service. The request was refused and, as a compromise, a formal commission was given to two *calificadores*, Fray José Paredo and Fray José Pichardo, to examine the dangerous books and report to Talamantes such information on the subject as they might find.[2] When Spanish diplomacy was thus hampered by such scruples it is no cause of surprise that the eminent historian of Mexico, Lucas Alaman, was prosecuted for reading prohibited books and even the episcopal dignity

---

[1] Obregon, *op. cit.*, 2ª Serie, pp. 389, 392–3.

Lizardi's troubles did not end with the extinction of the Inquisition. In 1822 he issued a defence of Free-Masonry which excited clerical wrath. In Puebla, a priest, after arousing the people with his sermons, headed a mob which broke into a printer's shop, carried off the obnoxious books and made an auto de fe of them, leading to a tumult in which three men were killed and a number were wounded. About the same time Lizardi was obliged to appeal to the Córtes for protection against his public excommunication by the archiepiscopal provisor.— El. Sol, pp. 122, 146, 152 (Mexico, 1822).

[2] I owe to the late General Don Vicente Riva Palacio the documents in this matter.

of Manuel Abad y Queipo, Bishop-elect of Valladolid (Mechoacan) did not save him from trouble for the same offence.[1]

Yet this reactionary tendency was accompanied with an increasing disposition to enforce the subordination of the Inquisition and to render it an instrument of the Government. A royal cédula of December 12, 1807, takes additional precautions to prevent illegal increase in the number of familiars and officials and to give the secular authority a closer supervision over them. When secular assistance, moreover, was called for, it could no longer be commanded as a right, except in matters of faith; if the temporal jurisdiction was concerned, the Inquisition was put on a level with other ecclesiastical courts, and the magistrate was instructed to examine the merits of the case and to give or withhold his aid accordingly.[2] As agitation in Mexico increased with the news of the abdication of Carlos IV and the Napoleonic usurpation, foreshadowing the Revolution, the political importance of the Inquisition, as an agency of repression, became greater and its so-called sacred functions were more and more subordinated. Successive edicts of August 27, 1808, and April 28, June 16 and September 28, 1809, were directed against all proclamations and emissaries seeking to pervert the loyalty of the colonists in favor of the ambitious schemes of the French, and the doctrine of popular sovereignty was denounced as manifest heresy[3]—a doctrinal definition which was effectively used during the debate on the suppression of the Holy Office, in the Córtes of Cádiz, which had affirmed that sovereignty. Even in a matter so foreign to politics as solicitation in the confessional, it is suggestive to observe that, in the trial for that offence of Dr. Pedro Mendizabal, cura of the parish of Santa Ana (1809–1819) his correct political conduct is urged upon the inquisitors as a matter for their favorable consideration—which may possibly have conduced to his escape in the face of convincing evidence.[4]

---

[1] Obregon, *op. cit.*, 2ª Serie, p. 393.
[2] Note to Recop., Lib. I, Tit. xix, ley 1. Cf. Lib. III, Tit. i, ley 2.
[3] See in Appendix the Edict of January 26, 1811. Also Obregon, 2ª Serie, p. 393.
[4] Proceso contra Dr. Pedro Mendizabal, fol. 13 (MS. *penes me*).

The political functions assumed by the Inquisition become especially manifest in its trials of the two chief martyrs of the war of independence—Hidalgo and Morelos. The former of these, Miguel Hidalgo y Castilla, the parish priest of los Dolores, who first raised the standard of revolt, in conjunction with Allende, Aldama and Abasolo, and who was elected generalissimo of the insurgent army, was a singularly interesting character.[1] Born in 1753, he received his education at the royal university of San Nicolás at Mechoacan, where he became rector and theological professor. In the formal accusation during his trial it is asserted that he was known while there as *el zorro*, or the fox, on account of his cunning, and that he was finally expelled because of a scandalous adventure, in the course of which he was obliged to escape at night through a window of the chapel. Taking orders, he finally settled as *cura* at los Dolores where, in spite of a large revenue, he encumbered himself with debts. He loved music and dancing and gaming and his relations with women were of a character common enough with the clergy of the period. His abounding energy led him to establish potteries and to introduce silk-culture, which may doubtless account for his indebtedness. He was regarded as a prodigy of learning and kept up his intellectual pursuits, translating tragedies of Racine and comedies of Molière, the latter of which he caused to be acted in his house, his favorite being Tartufe. The priest, García de Carrasqueda, who enjoyed his intimacy for twelve or thirteen years, when on trial by the Inquisition, deposed that they used to read together Cicero, Serri, Fleury's Ecclesiastical History, Rollin's Ancient History and an Italian work on commerce by Genovesi and that he praised highly the orations of Æschines and Demosthenes, Bossuet, Buffon's Natural History, Pitaval's Causes Célèbres and various historical works. He was fond of debating questionable points in theology, emitting opinions not wholly orthodox on

---

[1] I owe the following details to a transcript of his trial, made from the original in 1865 by Don José María Lafragua and kindly communicated to me by David Fergusson Esqr.

such subjects as the stigmata of St. Francis, the House of Loreto, the Veronica, whether St. Didymas or Gestas was the penitent thief, the inheritance of original sin, the identity of the three kings and the like, while his high reputation for learning caused him to be regarded as an authority. Altogether he presents himself to us as a man of unusual physical and intellectual energy, not over nice as to the employment of those energies, of wide culture, of vigorous and enquiring mind and of small reverence for formulas or for authority.

Such a character was not likely to escape the attention of the Holy Office. On July 16, 1800, Fray Joaquin Huesca, a teacher of philosophy in the Order of Merced, denounced him to the commissioner of Mechoacan for various unorthodox utterances, at which Fray Manuel Estrada, of the same Order, had been present, and Estrada, on being summoned, confirmed and amplified the accusation. In transmitting these depositions to the tribunal, July 19th, the commissioner reported that Hidalgo was a most learned man, who had ruined himself with gambling and women, that he read prohibited books and, while professor of theology, had taught from Jansenist works. The tribunal necessarily started an investigation, which lasted for more than a year and included the testimony of some thirteen witnesses, resulting in proof of a wide variety of most heretical utterances, any one of which, if pertinaciously maintained, would have sufficed to consign him to the stake. Moreover, he was described as revolutionary in his tendencies, speaking of monarchs as tyrants and cherishing aspirations for liberty; he was well-read in current French literature and had little respect for the censorship—in short he was what was subsequently termed an *afrancesado*. The commissioner of San Miguel el Grande reported, March 11, 1801, much about Hidalgo's disorderly life and that he carried about with him an Alcoran but, in a second report of April 13th, he stated that in the recent Easter, Hidalgo had reformed, a matter which was widely discussed and seems to have aroused general attention. In due time, on October 2,

1801, the fiscal reported on this accumulated testimony that, if Hidalgo had uttered the propositions ascribed to him, he should be arrested with sequestration of property, but the witnesses were contradictory and Estrada had the reputation of an habitual liar. He therefore recommended that the case be suspended and the papers be filed for future reference, to which the tribunal assented.

The case rested until July 22, 1807, when a priest named José María Castilblane came forward to say that, in 1801, Estrada had told him scandalous and heretical things about Hidalgo. More serious was a denunciation made, May 4, 1808, by María Manuela Herrera, described as a woman of good character who frequented the sacraments. By command of her confessor she deposed that she had once lived with Hidalgo as his concubine, when he told her that Christ had not died on the cross, but that it was another man; also that there was no hell—this latter she supposed being to quiet her conscience, as they had an agreement that she was to provide him with women and he was to provide her with men. This was again laid before the fiscal who reported, June 8th, in favor of awaiting further proof. Then, on March 15, 1809, Fray Diego Manuel Bringas deposed that he had found Hidalgo in possession of prohibited books, such as Serry's History of the Congregations *De Auxiliis*, under his own name and that of Augustin Leblanc, also his Dissertations on Christ and the Virgin, in which he speaks without measure of María de Agreda; that Hidalgo praised this work and called María a deluded old woman.[1] Still, with singular moderation, no action was taken to restrain Hidalgo's audacity and, had he been content to let politics alone, it is safe to say that the Inquisition would not

---

[1] The learned Dominican Jacques Augustin Serry's *Historia Congregationum de Auxiliis*, issued also under the pseudonym of Augustin Leblanc, appeared in 1700 and was promptly condemned in Spain in 1701 (Index of 1707, I, 776), but is not on the Roman Index. His *Exercitationes de Christo ejusque V. Matre* are in both Indexes. For a Jesuit opinion of the former work see Father Colonia's *Bibliothèque Janseniste*, p. 186 (Ed. 1735).

María de Agreda was a Spanish mystic of the seventeenth century whom Spain has repeatedly, up to modern times, endeavored to get canonized.

have troubled him, so inert had it become in the exercise of its ostensible functions.

When, however, he started the revolution, September 16, 1810, this lethargy gave place to the utmost activity. The official Gazette of September 28th asserted that he was disseminating among the people the doctrine that there is neither hell, purgatory nor glory; an extract from this was sent to the commissioner at Querétaro, with instructions to obtain its verification, which he had no trouble in doing, although the evidence was hearsay. Without awaiting this, however, the testimony which had been so long slumbering in the *secreto* was laid before *calificadores*, October 9th, with orders to report at once. This they did the next day, to the effect that, as he was a sectary of French liberty, they pronounced him a libertine, seditious, schismatic, a formal heretic, a Judaizer, a Lutheran, a Calvinist, and strongly suspect of atheism and materialism. The same day the tribunal resolved that, as he was surrounded by his army of insurgents and could not be arrested, he should be summoned by edict to appear within thirty days. On the 13th the edict was printed, on the 14th it was posted in the churches and was circulated as rapidly as possible throughout the land.

The edict is a singular medley of politics and religion, illustrating the dual character of the Inquisition of the period and the enormous advantage to the Government of possessing control over the ecclesiastical establishment, whereby an attack on the civil power could be made to assume the appearance of an assault on the faith. All the heretical utterances, discredited nine years before by the action of the tribunal, are put forward as absolute facts. It is impiety that has led him to raise the standard of revolt and to seduce numbers of unhappy dupes to follow him. In the inability to reach him personally, he is summoned, under pain of excommunication, to appear for trial within thirty days, in default of which he will be prosecuted *in rebeldía* to definitive sentence and burning in effigy if necessary. All who support him or have converse with him and all those who do not denounce those who favor his revolutionary projects are declared guilty of the crime of fautorship of heresy and subject to the penalties decreed for it by the canons. When to this are added the proclamations of excommunication issued against the insurgents by the Archbishop of Mexico and the bishops of the disturbed districts, it will be seen how powerful was the restraining influence exercised by the Church over a population trained to submission, and how intense were the passions that braved its anathema.[1]

In fact, the hatred of the creoles and the Indians for the *Gachupines*, or Spaniards, was so bitter that four-fifths of the native clergy espoused the cause of the insurgents, in spite of the censures of the Church, and questions of faith became inextricably involved in the contest between the factions. To the loyalists, Hidalgo became a heretic or indeed a heresiarch, and the confessional was so largely used by them that the insurgents became guilty of a new heresy, by asserting that confession to a Gachupin priest was invalid. They found great comfort, moreover, through their belief in the protection of Our Lady of Guadalupe, who was universally revered, and especially by the Indians, as the sovereign patroness of Mexico. On the fateful 16th of September, when Hidalgo was marching on San Miguel el Grande at the head of his little band of insurgents, in passing through Atolonila, he chanced to take an image on linen of the Guadalupe Virgin and give it to one of his men to carry as a banner. It was adopted by the other bands as they rose and it became the standard of the insurrection, usually accompanied with an image of Fernando VII and of the eagle of Mexico, and the inscription "*Viva nuestra Señora de Guadalupe! Viva Fernando VII! Viva la America y muere el mal gobierno!*" Second in rank as a tutelary power of the insurrection was Our Lady of Puebla and against these the

---

[1] These comprehensive excommunications led to a result not particularly creditable to the Church. A writer in 1822 calls attention to the fact that, while the leading insurgents who were captured were formally reconciled before they were shot, the mass of the people, who had never paid any attention to the censures, were freely received to the sacraments without having been absolved.—El Sol, México, Feb. 27, 1822, p. 107.

loyalists pitted a new-comer, Our Lady of los Remedios, who was denounced as a Gachupina by the natives. There is a subject of study for the student of mythology in this modernization of the triform Hecate and in the revival of Homeric divinities presiding over the two sides of the battlefield.

The Inquisition labored earnestly to get evidence of sacrilegious acts on the part of the insurgents and, as they were beaten back, it had its emissaries in the territory from which they had been driven, collecting testimony as to individuals who had sympathized with them or had opposed the posting of its edict. The most active of these was Fray Simon de la Mora, who accompanied the royal army in its advance. He reported that it was useless to attempt to enumerate the common people, but he sent the names of fifty-nine persons of standing, many of them ecclesiastics, with the evidence against them, and the notes on the margin of the MS. show that they were forthwith entered for prosecution.

The edict was duly posted in the towns occupied by the army but, in the course of a night or two, it was generally torn down or defaced with paint, in spite of the heavy penalties incurred for thus impeding the Inquisition. Hidalgo felt it necessary to issue a manifesto in defence, protesting that he had never departed from the faith and pointing out the contradictory character of the heresies imputed to him. To this the Inquisition replied with another edict, January 26, 1811, reiterating its charges, stigmatizing him as a cruel atheist and prohibiting certain proclamations issued by the insurgents.[1]

---

[1] See Appendix. One of the insurgent proclamations shows the savage character of the warfare. It sets forth the terms and conditions of the struggle of which the following may serve as a specimen—

4. The European who resists with arms will be put to the sword.

5. When threatened with siege or battle, before commencing we will put to the sword the numerous Europeans in our hands and will then abide the fortunes of war.

6. The American who defends a European with arms will be put to the sword.

Thus was justified the execution of Hidalgo and his chiefs. Whatever sympathy we may feel for the cause, we must admit that the cruelty marking the strife was equally shared and that the fate of Maximilian was foreshadowed.

Meanwhile his trial, *in absentia*, was proceeding through its several stages as deliberately as though he were an ordinary heretic in time of peace. On November 24, 1810, the tribunal declared that, having evidence that, on October 27th, he had knowledge of the edict, the thirty days' term should run from October 28th. On November 28th, therefore, the fiscal demanded that he should be treated as *rebelde*, or contumacious, and that ten days, as usual, should be allowed him to appear in person. The prescribed three terms of ten days each, with two days additional, were scrupulously observed. Then further delay followed and it was not until February 7, 1811, that the formal trial began with the presentation by the fiscal of the accusation. This was in the ordinary form, reciting that Hidalgo was a Christian, baptized and confirmed, and as such enjoying the privileges and exemptions accorded to good Catholics, "yet had he left the bosom of holy Church for the filthy, impure and abominable faith of the heretic Gnostics, Sergius, Berengar, Cerinthus, Carpocrates, Nestorius, Marcion, Socinus, the Ebionites, Lutherans, Calvinists and other pestilential writers, Deists, Materialists and Atheists, whose works he has read and endeavored to revive and to persuade his sect to adopt their errors and heresies, believing wrongly, like them, as to various articles and dogmas of our holy religion and revolutionizing the whole bishoprics of Mechoacan and Guadalajara and great part of the arch-diocese of Mexico, being moreover the chief cause of the great abominations and sins, which have been and still are committed. All this and more, which I shall set forth, constitute him a formal heretic, apostate from our holy religion, an atheist, materialist and deist, a libertine, seditious, schismatic, Judaizer, Lutheran and Calvinist, guilty of divine and human high treason, a blasphemer, an implacable enemy of Christianity and the State, a wicked seducer, lascivious, hypocrite, a cunning traitor to king and country, pertinacious, contumacious and rebellious to the Holy Office, of all of which I accuse him in general and in particular." The fiscal then proceeds to recite the evidence taken since 1800, followed by a long statement of Hidalgo's share in the insurrection and winding up with the customary petition that, without requiring further proof, the accused shall be condemned to confiscation and relaxation, in person if he can be had and, if not, in effigy; or, if the evidence be deemed insufficient, he shall be tortured if attainable.

The inquisitors received the accusation and gravely ordered, according to form, that a copy be given to Hidalgo and, in view of his contumacious absence, that due notification be made in the halls, which was accordingly done and record made. Then, on February 19th, the fiscal accused the contumacy of the absent and fugitive Hidalgo in not answering and asked that the case be concluded and received to proof. The inquisitors assented and the proof was presented. May 20th, the fiscal demanded the publication of evidence, which was duly ordered to be made, with the ordinary suppression of their names. A large portion of this consisted of evidence taken during the insurrection, showing acts of sacrilege, contempt for the Inquisition and its edicts and the like, on the part of Hidalgo and his followers. A copy of this was ordered to be given to him and that he answer it in the next audience, of which announcement was made in the halls and duly recorded. It was not until June 14th that the next step was taken, in ordering a copy of both accusation and testimony to be given to him and that by the third day he put in his answer, with the assent of his advocate, an advocate being provided for him in the person of the Licenciado José María Rosas. Then another witness was found in the priest García de Carrasquedo, a prisoner on trial, to whom allusion has been made above. His evidence was taken June 21st and, on the 27th, was submitted to calificadores who, on August 12th, presented a long and learnedly argumentative report, in which they characterized the several propositions with the customary choice selection of objurgatory epithets, as *falsa, impia, temeraria, blasfema, malsonante, sapiens hæresim, llena de escandalo, erronea, sapiens errorem Lutheranorum, Judaica y formalmente hæretica, injuriosa al espiritú de la S. M. Iglesia*, and they concluded that, if he who uttered them did so with full knowledge of their import, he was a formal heretic. This was practically the last act of the long drawn-out comedy, although some additional testimony concerning Hidalgo was taken and recorded, February 10 and 20, 1812, in the trial of the habitual liar, Fray Manuel Estrada. Events had moved faster than the Inquisition. After the disastrous day of the Bridge of Calderon, Hidalgo in his flight had been captured, March 21, 1811, at Bajan, and carried two hundred leagues farther north to Chihuahua, where he was executed, July 31st, before the calificadores had finished their formulation of his heresies. No notice of this was given to the Inquisition, which was treated with a singular discourtesy, savoring of contempt. The explanation of this probably is that, if it had been apprised of the capture, it could rightly have claimed the prisoner as a heretic, primarily subject to its supreme and exclusive jurisdiction; there might have been danger in escorting him back through the recently disturbed provinces; the processes of the Inquisition were notoriously slow and, after it had tried the culprit and he had abjured and been penanced in an auto de fe, he would still have to be condemned in a military court. It was in every way wiser to try him and despatch him in far-off Chihuahua, and the local military and ecclesiastical authorities coöperated to this result, leaving the Inquisition to find out what it could, and not even forwarding a supplication which Hidalgo addressed to it, on June 10th.

The tribunal waited patiently for eleven months after the catastrophe and then, on June 25, 1812, it wrote, with much solemnity, to its two commissioners in Chihuahua, reminding them that the edict of October 13, 1810, rendered it their duty to keep it advised of the capture of Hidalgo and of all subsequent occurrences. They should have gone to him in prison and exhorted him to make a declaration on all points contained in the edict and whatever else weighed upon his conscience. All signs of repentance should have been observed and reported, and at least his confession to his judges, in so far as the Inquisition was concerned, should have been sent to it. The alcaide, the ecclesiastics and the military officers must now be examined as to his state of mind during his imprisonment, so that the tribunal may be informed as to his repentance or impenitence and thus be enabled to render justice. The two commissioners are to work in harmony, with power of subdelegation, and they are made responsible, before God and the king, for the due discharge of their duties.

The Holy Office evidently took itself seriously and considered that judgement as to Hidalgo's heresies still lay in its hands. There must have been a flush of indignation and wounded pride when, on January 2, 1813, the inquisitors received from Sánchez Alvarez, one of the commissioners, an answer dated October 27, 1812, reporting that he had applied to Nemesio Salcedo, the commandant-general, who had ordered him to suspend all action and that he, Salcedo, would explain the absolute necessity for this. The tribunal had to wait until February 27th before it received Salcedo's explanation, dated October 22d, showing how its supreme jurisdiction had been overslaughed with as little ceremony as that of a pie-powder court. With profuse expressions of respect, Salcedo stated that the peace and prosperity of the provinces required that the matter should not be agitated. Hidalgo was not a heretic and would not have been permitted to receive the sacraments and ecclesiastical burial, had he not been duly absolved and reconciled to the Church. A royal order, he said, of May 12, 1810, had conveyed papal inquisitorial faculties to the bishops, and the Bishop of Durango had subdelegated Doctor Francisco Fernández Valetin, the doctoral canon of his church, thus constituting him a papal inquisitor.[1] To him, as such, were communicated the answers of Hidalgo on his trial, who ratified them in his presence; he also verified the manifesto of Hidalgo, which was published, and he absolved him. In addition he saw

---

[1] In estimating the veracity of this curious tale, we must bear in mind that both Fernando VII and Pius VII were at the time prisoners of Napoleon. There was, it is true, a Spanish Regency and the Córtes of Cádiz which used the royal name, but it is inconceivable that, even if it had access to the pope, it would have taken such a precaution at a time when there was no anticipation of rebellion in the colonies.

the supplication of Hidalgo to the Inquisition, which would have been forwarded sooner but for the danger of its being intercepted and which was now enclosed, together with the other necessary papers. These were extracts from Hidalgo's examination, his manifesto to the insurgents and the supplication in question.

It was somewhat brutal to have kept the tribunal so long in the dark on a matter touching its highest privilege and to have detained for sixteen months, on a frivolous pretext, a supplication addressed directly to it, but its position was becoming precarious and it dared not complain. Napoleon's suppression of the Inquisition of Spain, in 1808, did not count for much, but the Córtes of Cádiz had enacted a liberal Constitution in 1812 and simultaneously the preliminary skirmishing for the abrogation of the Inquisition preoccupied all minds. It was enacted February 22, 1813, and, though the news had not as yet reached Mexico, the result could scarce have been doubted when the tribunal took action on March 13th. It evidently placed no faith in the story of a papal inquisitor, suddenly created in the wilds of Chihuahua, for it wholly ignored his action. The fiscal reported to the tribunal that, in spite of Hidalgo's supplication for pardon and endeavors to satisfy the charges against him, there were not merits enough to absolve his memory and fame nor, at the same time, to condemn him, as it appeared that he had made a general confession and had been reconciled, whereupon the tribunal ordered the case to be suspended and the papers to be filed in their proper place—an expression of dissatisfaction and an admission of powerlessness. On March 29th it acknowledged Salcedo's letter and drily thanked him.

Hidalgo's supplication to the Inquisition, written in his prison on June 10, 1811, is a long and dignified declaration of submission, calmly and clearly reasoned and manifesting full command of his theological learning. But for his confinement, he said, he would hasten to throw himself at the feet of the tribunal, not only to seek pardon for his insubordination, but to vindicate himself from the charge of heresy and apostasy, which was insufferable to him. He answered the various accusations of the edict, denying that he had led an immoral life and exculpating himself with much dexterity from the heresies imputed to him, but if, he added, the Inquisition deemed his utterances heretical, although he had not hitherto so considered them, he now retracted, abjured and detested them. He concluded by begging to be relieved from the disgrace of heresy and apostasy; the tribunal could repose entire faith in his statements for, if he had committed those crimes, the circumstances in which he now found himself would impel him to confess them freely, in order to gain the pardon and absolution that would open to him the gates of heaven and would close them, if withheld, in consequence of his denial.

The frame of mind revealed in this document, which is unquestionably genuine, serves to refute the imputation of forgery so generally ascribed to Hidalgo's manifesto of May 18th, addressed "A Todo el Mundo" and published in order to quiet the population. Its effusiveness and extravagance of repentance, and the earnestness of its exhortations to his followers to submit, have not unnaturally created suspicion, from their violent contrast to the deep convictions and reckless energy with which he precipitated and sustained the insurrection, but it can be accepted as authentic without impugning his good faith. He was impulsive and enthusiastic and was liable to the revulsions incident to his temperament. His cause had been disowned by God; he had been captured as a fugitive within a few months after he had been at the head of eighty thousand men. The grave was yawning for him, as the portal to the hereafter, in which there was, in his belief, no escape from eternal torment for one who died as a rebel to the Church. He was a fervent Catholic, whose excommunication cut him off from the sacraments essential to salvation, unless he could prove himself worthy of them by earnest repentance and by the amendment which could only be manifested through zeal in undoing that which had brought upon him the anathema. That under such pressure he should seek to avert the endless doom by heart-felt contrition was natural, however strange it may seem to those brought up in a different faith, who can sympathize with his aspirations for liberty but cannot realize the emotions enkindled by his religious convictions.

The decree of the Córtes of Cádiz, February 22, 1813, suppressing the Inquisition was published in Mexico June 8th. Under it the property of the tribunal was applicable to the treasury for the reduction of the public debt and was forthwith sequestrated; there were no prisoners, the few political ones having been transferred to various convents some days in advance. We have an authentic account of the transaction, made December 20, 1814, after the Restoration, by the alcaide of the secret prison. He says that the decree had been eagerly expected; the tribunal and its ministers were regarded with contempt and its privileges were set at defiance. Immediately after the publication, Viceroy Calleja announced to the senior inquisitor the cessation of its functions; the next day the official commissioned for the purpose came to take possession and commenced an inventory. The building was thrown open to gaping crowds, who gave free vent to their detestation of the institution. On the 11th, the money in the chest was removed; the records concerning the faith were delivered to the Archbishop Bergosa y Jordan, while the papers connected with property were taken by the Intendente of the Government, who confided them to the writer and allotted to him offices in which to keep them. In the Inquisition building was established the lottery, and the adjacent houses of the inquisitors served to lodge its officials, while the main building was used as a barracks and the prisons were turned into shops for tailors, shoemakers and other workers for the army. The total amount sequestrated was 1,775,656 pesos, 5½ reales, consisting of—

Money in the coffers	66,566	pesos, 2½ reales.
Capital invested	1,394,628	" 1½ "
Due on income of censos	181,482	" 1.7 gr.
Fifteen rented houses	125,000	"
Furniture, etc., sold at auction, July 19	8,000	"
	1,775,676	" 5½ reales.

The alcaide proceeds to give us details as to the organization and finances of the tribunal. Besides the inquisitors and fiscal there were seven secretaries, a messenger, a treasurer, a contador, a purveyor of the prison, an alcaide and his assistant, a notary of the sequestrations, two officials of the *secreto*, an advocate of the fisc and an advocate of prisoners—a largely superfluous force for the trivial work to be performed. The pay-rolls amounted to 33,000 pesos per annum, the subvention to the Suprema was 10,000, and the expenditure for maintaining prisoners, repairs, church functions, etc., brought the annual outlay to 55,000 or 60,000, while the income was 85,000, to which was added 32,000 from the canonries, amounting in all to 117,000—about double the expenses, showing how profitable had proved the purification of the faith.[1]

On August 31st the archbishop reported to the Government that the decree of suppression had been read in the cathedral on the three Sundays following its receipt. The sanbenitos were at once removed from the places where they were hung; the Prior of the Hospital of San José asked for them to clothe the insane, but the viceroy took them for the troops. The Archbishop requested to have the prohibited books, which were stored in four rooms of his palace, and they were given to him. He was an old inquisitor and lost no time in assuming the jurisdiction over heresy restored to the episcopate by the decree of suppression. As early as June 10th, he issued a pastoral ordering denunciation to him of all persons suspect of heresy and, on September 27th, he published another calling for the surrender of all prohibited books by those who did not hold licences.[2]

The decree of suppression provided for the continued salaries of the officials and after this the two senior inquisitors disappear—Bernardo de Prado y Obejero and Isidoro Sainz de Alfaro y Beaumont—probably returning to Spain, where refugees from the American tribunals were taken care of. The junior, Manuel de Flores, remained and was ready to resume his functions

---

[1] Medina, pp. 456–61.   [2] Ibidem, pp. 461, 463.

whenever the "suspension," as he called it, was removed. His foresight was speedily rewarded, for one of the first acts of Fernando VII on his restoration was the decree of May 4, 1814, abrogating the Constitution of Cádiz, declaring invalid all laws enacted under it and even menacing with the death-penalty all who should keep copies of them. This of itself virtually revived the Inquisition, but legislation was required to reorganize it and this was effected by a decree of July 21.[1] Inquisitor Flores had not waited for this, as we find that he had already for some time been gathering evidence against Manuel Abad y Queipo, Bishop-elect of Mechoacan, which he transmitted, August 31st, to the Suprema for its action.[2]

It was not until December 23d that Viceroy Calleja notified him to re-establish the tribunal, in execution of the royal decree of July 21st; this he followed on January 4, 1815, with a proclamation embodying the decree and announcing that the tribunal had been restored to its jurisdiction and that its property had been returned to it. The archbishop also issued a pastoral requiring all denunciations to be made to it and Flores, on January 21st, published an Edict of Faith ordering the denunciation, within six days, of all heresies, prohibited books and all words of disrespect towards the Holy Office that might subsequently be uttered.[3] The tribunal however, was in a sadly dilapidated condition. The alcaide in a letter of December 30, 1814, reports that the restoration of property consisted in the written securities and the real estate, but only 773 pesos of the money had been returned. Notice had been given that the fruits of the canonries and interest on the censos were to be paid as formerly to the tribunal. The purchaser of the furniture, which had been sold at auction in July, was nominally a merchant but in reality the Count of la Cortina, from whom they were endeavoring to get it back at the price which it had brought, but much had been resold; the

---

[1] Coleccion de Cédulas etc. de Fernando VII, pp. 8, 85 (Valencia, 1814).
[2] Archivo de Simancas, Inquisicion, Libros 877, 890.
[3] Medina, pp. 467-9.

building had to be refitted for their use and altogether they were in great distress.¹ To add to their troubles, the tribunal was so thoroughly discredited that its jurisdiction was invaded on all sides in a manner indicating the contempt in which it was held. Viceroy Calleja issued a proclamation condemning to the flames the Constitution adopted by the insurgents October 22, 1814, at Apatzingan, together with various of their sermons, addresses, etc. and ordering them to be denounced to him under pain of death. Then, on May 24, 1815, he sent a copy of this to the tribunal, inviting it to take action and use all rigor for their suppression. This provoked the liveliest resentment of Flores who complained bitterly to the Suprema, June 29th, of the intrusion on his jurisdiction and of the discourtesy manifested in not previously submitting to him the offending papers. He also enlarged on the harshness with which the decree of suppression had been enforced in 1813 and of the imperfect restitution of property which Calleja had publicly asserted to have been made. He had also endeavored to compel the officials to render military service, but this had been successfully resisted. In spite of all this indignation, however, the insurgent documents were duly censured by the calificadores and, on July 9th, Flores issued an edict condemning them and specifying their errors. The chapter of the cathedral (*sede vacante*) had also on May 26th published an edict requiring the surrender of these documents to it under pain of excommunication and threatening all priests and beneficiaries who should not exert themselves against the rebels. This was a palpable intrusion on inquisitorial jurisdiction which was deeply resented, and there was also a quarrel with the royal Audiencia which the tribunal accused of invading its jurisdiction and disregarding its *fueros* in the matter of a pasquinade of which the Audiencia had taken cognizance.²

Under these circumstances it is easy to understand how eagerly Flores seized the opportunity of asserting himself afforded by the capture, November 15, 1815, of the insurgent chief José

---

¹ Medina, pp. 469–70.   ² Ibidem, pp. 479–92.

María Morelos, who shares with Hidalgo the foremost place in the Mexican Valhalla.[1]

Born in 1764 of humble parents, he was an agricultural laborer up to the age of 25, when he returned to his native Mechoacan and applied himself to the study of grammar, philosophy and morals. Entering the Church, he took full orders and, after serving temporarily the cure of Choromuco, he obtained that of Caraguaro, which was under the rectorship of Hidalgo. It must have been a slender benefice for, in his examination, he explained his not having taken the indulgence of the Santa Cruzada by the plea that before the insurrection he was too poor to pay for it and afterwards the insurgents regarded it as invalid and as merely a device to raise money for the war against them. His morals were those of his class; he admitted to having three children, born of different mothers during his priesthood, but he added that his habits, though not edifying, had not been scandalous, and the tribunal seemed to think so, for little attention was paid to this during his trial and, in the *calificacion* which preceded his sentence, it is not even alluded to. He joined Hidalgo, October 28, 1810, and must have quickly distinguished himself, for that chief gave him a commission to raise the Pacific coast provinces and, after the rout of the Bridge of Calderon, the burden of maintaining the unequal war fell mainly on Morelos, who was raised successively to the grades of lieutenant-general and captain-general, with the title of Most Serene Highness.

Unlike Hidalgo, who was hurried off to Chihuahua, Morelos when captured was brought to the city of Mexico for trial and execution, arriving there on November 21st. He was carried to the Inquisition, not as its prisoner, but for safe-keeping "on deposit" and Flores, to preserve the secrecy of the Holy Office, made it a condition that the guard accompanying him should not go up stairs or penetrate beyond the first court-yard. It

---

[1] The following details of the trial of Morelos are derived from a report, accompanied by the documents, made by Flores to the Suprema, November 27 and December 29, 1815. It is in the archives of Simancas, Inquisicion, Sala 49, Legajo 1473.—See also Medina, pp. 513–45.

was not until 1.30 A.M. of the 22d that he was lodged in the secret prison, in a cell so dark that he could not read the breviary, which was given to him on his request. The 22d was occupied with an effort to get permission to try him—a competencia carried on in a spirit very different from the masterful audacity of old. Viceroy Calleja desired that Morelos should be degraded from the priesthood, within three days, by the episcopal jurisdiction, in order that his execution should be prompt, and testimony for that purpose was already being taken by the secular and spiritual courts acting in unison. Flores therefore had no time to lose in putting forward the claim of the tribunal, and the fiscal drew up an elaborate paper showing that there were points in the case which came within its jurisdiction. On the 23d a *consulta de fe* was assembled, consisting of the episcopal Ordinary of Mechoacan, and the consultores of the Inquisition, which represented to the viceroy that, although Morelos was subject to both the secular and spiritual courts, it was persuaded that for other crimes he was justiciable by the Inquisition and that his trial by that tribunal would redound to the honor and glory of God as well as to the service of the State and the king and be efficacious in undeceiving the rebels. Moreover, it promised that the trial should be concluded within four days. Somewhat unwillingly, Calleja granted the request and no time was lost in commencing the most expeditious trial in the annals of the Holy Office—a grim enough comedy to gratify the vanity of the actors, for it could have no influence on the fate of the prisoner, save perhaps in removing the excommunication under which he inferentially lay. Flores, in boasting of this activity, adds that they were much embarrassed by Morelos being frequently taken from them for examination in the other courts, which indicates that the authorities regarded the Inquisition as merely a side-show.

Hurried as were the proceedings, there was due observance of all the formalities required by the cumbrous methods of the Holy Office. That same day, November 23d, the fiscal presented his *clamosa*, basing it on Morelos having signed the constitutional decree of November 22, 1814, as well as various proclamations condemned as heretical by the Inquisition;[1] also on his celebrating mass while under excommunication, and his reply to the Bishop of Puebla, when reproached for so doing, that it would be easier to get a dispensation after the war than to survive the guillotine; also on an edict of Bishop Abad y Queipo of Mechoacan, July 22, 1814, declaring him to be an excommunicated heretic. There was still time for a morning audience and the prisoner was brought before the tribunal, where he was subjected to the customary examination as to his genealogy and whole career, and the first monition was given to save his soul by confessing the truth. In the afternoon he had his second audience and monition. On the morning of the 24th came the third audience and monition, during which he admitted that, at Teypan, he had captured a package of the edicts against Hidalgo and had utilized them to make cartridges. The pompous formulas, urging him to discharge his conscience so that the Inquisition might show him its customary mercy, must have seemed a ghastly jest to a man who knew that his captors would shortly have him shot, and they contrast grotesquely with the feverish anxiety of the tribunal to have a share in the performance.

That same afternoon the fiscal presented the accusation and, considering the haste in which it was prepared, its long accumulation of rhetoric is creditable to the industry of the draughtsman. He describes Morelos as abandoning the Church for the filthy and abominable heresies of Hobbes, Helvetius, Voltaire, Luther and other pestilent writers, rendering him a formal heretic, an apostate from the holy faith, an atheist, materialist, deist, libertine, seditious, guilty of divine and human high treason, an implacable enemy of Christianity and the state, a vile seducer, hypocrite, traitor to king and country, cunning, lascivious, pertinacious and rebellious to the Holy Office. He shows how

---

[1] The Constitution of Nov. 22, 1814, which based all government on the will of the people clearly came under the edict of August, 1808, which denounced the doctrine of popular sovereignty as manifest heresy. For the same reason the Constitution of Cádiz was heretical.

rebellion is heresy and all rebellious acts are directly or indirectly heretical. To Morelos, in the bottom of his heart, Christ and Belial are equal; he is even suspect of toleration and, as usual, the accusation concludes by asking for confiscation and relaxation. The remainder of the afternoon and the morning audience of the 25th were occupied with the defendant's answers to the twenty-four articles of the accusation. From what he said it appears that insurgents claimed to be opposing the French domination in Spain, and that Ferdinand's restoration in 1814 was largely disbelieved or was assumed to be only another phase of Napoleon's supremacy, showing that Ferdinand could not be a sincere Catholic.

That same morning the publication of evidence was made, consisting wholly of documents, such as the Constitution of October 22, 1814, sundry proclamations signed by Morelos and his printed letter to the Bishop of Puebla, together with the letter of the Bishop of Mechoacan declaring him to be an excommunicated heretic. He was ordered to answer with the advice of his counsel and the three advocates of prisoners were named to him, of whom he selected Don José María Gutiérrez de Rosas. He was sent to his cell to be brought back directly for an interview with his counsel, who was sworn in as customary. There was no time to make copies of the papers, so the unusual course was adopted of entrusting the originals to Rosas, with instructions to return them and present the defence within three hours. In the afternoon he did so and the result showed him to be a ready writer, but he was more occupied in justifying himself for undertaking the defence than in making a plea for Morelos. He savagely denounced the insurrection and the Córtes of Cádiz, whose principles it represented, and he concluded abruptly with a few lines, alleging the repentance of the defendant, from which he hoped for absolution. The inquisitor thereupon ordered the fiscal to be notified and the case to be concluded.

The next morning, November 26th, Flores assembled his calificadores and exhibited to them the proceedings and the condemnations of the insurgent Constitution and proclamations. Fray Domingo Barreda opined that the accused savored of heresy, but the rest were unanimous that he was a formal heretic, who denied his guilt and was not only suspect of atheism but an atheist outright. In the afternoon was held the *consulta de fe* to decide upon the sentence. Without a dissentient voice it agreed that a public auto should be held at 8 o'clock the next morning in the audience chamber, in the presence of a hundred prominent persons to be designated by Flores. That Morelos should there be declared guilty of malicious and pertinacious imperfect confession, a formal heretic who denied his guilt, a disturber and persecutor of the hierarchy and a profaner of the sacraments; that he was guilty of high treason, divine and human, pontifical and royal, and that he should be present at the mass in the guise of a penitent, in short cassock without collar or girdle and holding a green candle, which, as a heretic and fautor of heretics, he should offer to the priest. As a cruel persecutor of the Holy Office, his property should be confiscated to the king. Although deserving of degradation and relaxation, for the crimes subject to the Inquisition, yet, as he was ready to abjure he was, in the unlikely case of the viceroy sparing his life, condemned to perpetual banishment from America and from all royal residences and to imprisonment for life in the African presidios, with deprivation of all preferment and perpetual irregularity. His three children were declared subject to infamy and the legal disabilities of descendants of heretics. He was to abjure formally, and be absolved from the excommunications reserved to the Holy Office; he was to make a general confession and through life to recite the seven penitential psalms on Fridays and a part of the rosary on Saturdays. Moreover a tablet was to be hung in the cathedral, inscribed with his name and offences.[1]

The next morning, November 27th, as Flores reports, the auto was duly celebrated in the most imposing scene ever witnessed in the audience chamber, which was crowded with five hundred

---

[1] See Appendix.

of the most important personages of the capital. The mass was followed by the impressive ceremony of degradation from the priesthood, performed by the Bishop of Oaxaca. Morelos was delivered to the royal judge and returned to the secret prison whence, at 1.30 of the following night, he was transferred to the citadel. Flores might proudly claim to have vindicated the jurisdiction of the Holy Office, at some sacrifice of its dignity, in the shortest trial of a formal heretic to be found in its records. The object of the indecent haste required by Calleja is scarce apparent, for Morelos was not executed until December 22d.

The tribunal continued to perform its functions. In 1817, the prosecution of Don José Xavier de Tribarren, for reading prohibited books, revealed that Don Cayetano Romero of Guetaria in Guipúzcoa was equally guilty, and the Suprema in Madrid forthwith ordered the tribunal of Logroño to take action against him.[1] The latest notable victim was Fray Servando Teresa de Mier Noriega y Guerra. After holding him for some time in prison, the tribunal, in anticipation of its extinction, sent him to the viceroy as an important offender against the State, with a paper describing him as hating, from the bottom of his heart, the king, the Córtes and all legitimate government, and even as lacking respect for the Holy See and the councils of the Church, his dominant passion being revolutionary independence, which he had vigorously promoted in both North and South America, by his writings full of passion and venom.[2]

This useless prolongation of existence was soon to end. One of the first measures of the revolution of 1820, which restored the Constitution of 1812, was the royal decree of March 9th, suppressing the Inquisition. Before this reached Mexico offi-

---

[1] Archivo de Simancas, Inquisicion, Lib. 559.

[2] Obregon, 2ª Serie, p. 395. Mier's crowning offence was a book with the suggestive title "Informe y Pedimento Fiscal presentado por los Locos ante el Supremo Tribunal de la Razon humana."—Archivo histórico nacional de Madrid, Inquisicion de Valencia, Legajo 100.

He escaped to the United States and returned to Mexico in 1822, when he was imprisoned by Dávila, Governor of the castle of San Juan de Ulua, but was speedily released.—El Sol, p. 117 (Mexico, 1822).

cially, the Viceroy Count of Venadita had seen it in the *Gaceta de Madrid* and had arranged for the extinction of the tribunal. The officials ceased their functions on May 31st; as before, they had transferred their political prisoners to the public prison and those for matters of faith to various convents, the archives were delivered to the custody of the archbishop and the officials hastened to find other homes. Then, on June 14th, the viceroy sent orders for compliance with the decree and, on the 16th, the Inquisitor Antonio de Pereda reported that the tribunal had ceased in all its functions and remained in a condition of absolute extinction. The papers of pending trials were distributed among the appropriate diocesans and the Intendente took possession of the property.[1] The officials straggled back to Spain, where they were provided for in common with those of the Peninsula. In the accounts of 1833 there still appear as in receipt of salaries the senior inquisitor, Antonio de Pereda, the secretaries Venancio de Pereda y Cassolla and José María Briergo, and the *nuncio y portero*, Tomás del Perojo.[2]

Thus forlorn and discredited passed away the tribunal which had in its prime cast terror over all the provinces between the two oceans, but the impression which it had produced did not disappear with it. In 1821 Don Celestino de la Torre reprinted a savage attack issued in Spain, under the title of "Memorial de la Santa Inquisicion," which he says, in a prefatory note, is for the disillusionment of the *serviles* who sigh for the restoration of the Holy Office. It is still more significant that, in the agitation caused, in 1833, by the effort of the Government to reduce the Church to acquiescence in the new order of things, there appeared a little anonymous tract entitled "Mientras no haya Inquisicion se acaba la Religion"—"Without the Inquisition, Religion is destroyed"—arguing that heresy can never be suppressed without the use of force; excommunication, censures and argument are of no avail and the faith of Christ can only be preserved by

---
[1] Medina, p. 505.
[2] Archivo hist. nacional de Madrid, Inquisicion, Legajo 6462, Cuaderno 1, fol. 68; Cuaderno 2, fol. 2.

arming the bishops with all the powers and methods of the Inquisition and enforcing their penal sentences by the State. The bishops, in fact, were quite ready to assume its functions as far as they could for, as late as 1850, on the appearance of a translation of Féréal's *Mystères de l'Inquisition*, with notes by Don Manuel de Cuendias, a diocesan *junta de censura* was held which, without hearing the accused, passed a sentence of excommunication on the editor and on all who should read the book, all of which was publicly proclaimed by edict. This was based on a consulta presented to the junta by Doctor Sollano, who lamented the abolition of the Inquisition and proved satisfactorily that heresy merits the death-penalty.[1]

THE PHILIPPINES.

When Spain, in 1566, undertook the conquest of the Philippines, they were not erected into a separate government but were placed under the vice-royalty of New Spain or Mexico, with a governor or captain-general in command. When, in 1581, the bishopric of Manila was founded, it was suffragan to the archbishopric of Mexico and was not erected into a metropolitan see until 1595. The islands therefore were included in the district of the Mexican Inquisition, but they were too sparsely occupied by Europeans for the tribunal to think it necessary to establish an organization there. When, however, the first bishop, the Dominican Domingo de Salazar, reached his see in 1572, his zeal led him at once to establish an episcopal Inquisition with a fiscal and other officials, and the regular inquisitorial procedure; he soon found culprits and held a formal auto de fe, exercising his assumed authority with excessive severity. Don Francisco de Zuñiga, a youth of 20, in a discussion, had thoughtlessly declared forni-

[1] *Defensa del Editor de la Obra titulada los Misterios de la Inquisicion*, México, 1850.

cation to be no sin; then on reflection he denounced himself, but notwithstanding this he was obliged to appear in an auto with a gag, and was banished for ten years, with a threat of two hundred lashes if he returned. Canon Francisco de Pareja, suspected of being one of the Alumbrados of Llerena, when arrested for solicitation, hanged himself in prison. Some of Salazar's penitents on reaching Mexico complained to the tribunal and thus aroused its attention to this invasion of its jurisdiction, when it lost no time in vindicating its rights. March 1, 1583, it sent a commission as commissioner to the Augustinian Fray Francisco Manrique, a man of prominence in his Order, which was the most influential in the islands, and at the same time it notified Salazar that it had done so in consequence of his having assumed to act as inquisitor.[1]

Bishop Salazar, who was on the point of celebrating an auto de fe, was by no means disposed to abandon the authority which he had assumed. He refused to recognize the commission of Manrique and threatened with excommunication all who should do so. The Licenciado Juan Convergel Maldonado, who supported Manrique, was thrown into prison so harsh that he became insane, when Salazar sent him to Mexico, and Benito de Mendiola, who had served as Maldonado's messenger, was likewise imprisoned. The traditional rivalry between the seculars and regulars and between the different Orders brought to the bishop ample support from the clergy, the Franciscans and the Jesuits—a high authority among the latter, Padre Alonso Sánchez, even declared that those who recognized the commissioner committed mortal sin. For six months Fray Manrique kept up the struggle and then abandoned it, writing to the tribunal, April 1, 1584, that, to avoid scandal he would do nothing more until it should have provided a competent remedy. The tribunal took prompt and effective steps. It wrote to Manila revoking all the acts of the bishop and to the Suprema, January 17, 1585, reciting the cir-

---

[1] J. T. Medina, El Tribunal del Santo Oficio de la Inquisicion en las Islas Filipinas, pp 16, 28-9 (Santiago de Chile, 1899).

cumstances and pointing out the grave consequences that would follow when Salazar's success should lead other bishops to follow his example. Through the Suprema it also addressed a letter to Philip II, who responded, May 26th, with a cédula to the bishop, telling him that he had invaded the jurisdiction of the Inquisition and ordering him to abstain from interfering in any way in affairs pertaining to it or with the duties of its commissioners. This was decisive but it was uncalled for. Salazar had already seen his error, had recognized Manrique and had handed over to him the papers in all the cases—seven in number—then pending before him. Thus the jurisdiction of the Mexican tribunal was permanently established over the islands, although subsequently there were one or two attempts made to organize an independent Inquisition there.[1]

In this the tribunal regarded rather its own ambition to extend its jurisdiction than the interests of the faith, for the whole career of the Philippine commissionership manifests the impossibility of conducting such a business at the distance of a hundred and forty degrees of longitude, when perhaps a year or two might pass without a vessel reaching Acapulco from Manila. The duties and powers of a commissioner were strictly limited and defined. As a rule he could do nothing except in execution of orders from the inquisitors; without such orders he could not make arrests, unless there was immediate danger of the escape of the accused; he could only gather information, report it and await instructions, and it was the same with regard to sequestration; if involved in a competencia he could issue inhibitions on the rival judges, but he could not put into execution the censures and penalties threatened in the formulas unless authorized by the tribunal.[2] In the detailed instructions sent to Manrique along with his commission there is little concession made to the difficulties of distance and communication by enlarging his powers. Although he is not allowed to sequestrate property, he is to inventory it and see that

---

[1] Medina, *op. cit.*, pp. 17-28, 30-1, 36-8, 141-51.
[2] Instruccion que han de guardar los Comisarios, n. 16, 17, 18, 30.

it is left in charge of a proper person, but this must be an arrangement between the accused and the depository in which the Inquisition assumes no responsibility. He is expressly told that he can make no arrests without orders, but an exception is made in the case of bigamy, on account of its frequency, when, if he obtains positive evidence against a culprit, he can arrest him and send him to Mexico, confining him in the royal gaol at the public expense, while awaiting a vessel. On the other hand, he is not to interfere with the secular or spiritual courts when they prosecute for bigamy and, if they offer to surrender an offender, he is to tell them to send him to Mexico, but not at the expense of the Inquisition.[1] Subsequently, in 1611, another exception was made, in the crime of solicitation in the confessional. The tribunal wrote to the Suprema that, in consequence of the number of denunciations, and in view of the need of the culprits' presence in the Philippines, whither they had been sent at the royal expense, it had ordered that only two who seemed most guilty should be shipped to Mexico for trial and sentence. It further suggested that in future the commissioner should have power, in conjunction with a judge or other qualified person, to try the cases and send merely the papers to Mexico where the sentence should be rendered. To this the Suprema assented, adding that, in view of the distance and delay, the prisoner should meanwhile be discharged on bail—which indicates that in these cases the commissioner could arrest.[2] This does not seem to have been strictly carried out for, in 1613, we chance to hear of three culprits of this kind, sent from Manila to Mexico, with the papers, for sentence. One of these, Francisco Sánchez de Santa María, was accused by twenty-three native women, and another, Don Luis de Salinas, had been shipwrecked on the coast of Japan and the papers had been lost; he succeeded in getting back to Manila, where the commissioner tried him again and despatched him to Mexico.[3]

---

[1] Medina, *op. cit.*, pp. 178-9, 181-2.   [2] Ibidem, pp. 38-9.
[3] Medina, *op. cit.*, pp. 42-3.
We have seen above (p. 243) that, in the list of cases of solicitation pending before the Mexican tribunal in the years 1622-3-4, there were seven from Manila.

Another exception to the prohibition of arrest was made in the case of soldiers who deserted to the Dutch or to Moros and embraced their faith. What to do with these cases presented a problem concerning which the Mexican tribunal consulted the Suprema, as burning them in effigy might prevent their coming back. The Suprema thereupon submitted the matter to Philip III, representing that the soldiers were exposed to such privations that they were forced to fly and find refuge wherever they could, and meanwhile it advised the tribunal to await the action of the royal councils. To this the tribunal replied at much length, May 20, 1620, stating that no action had as yet been taken in such cases, but that the commissioner was ordered to proceed against the culprits and, on convicting them, to send them to Mexico for sentence. The whole discussion, however, was purely academical; there is no trace of such culprits being forwarded to the tribunal and this, possibly, for the very good reason that the military authorities punished the offence with death, when they could lay hands on the delinquents.[1] There was another class of cases in which the commissioners seem to have exercised the power of arrest. In 1666 we find the tribunal complaining to

---

Of these, as we chance to learn from other documents, three, Fray Domingo Fernández, Fray Melchor de Manzano and Fray Martin de la Anunciacion, were all denounced, by different women, on March 31, 1622, to Fray Miguel de San Jacinto, commissioner for the province of New Segovia. As that day was the Thursday after Easter, this was probably the result of confessing to a rigid confessor who refused absolution until denunciation should be made. Another one was Padre Pedro Ramírez, S. J., denounced to the Manila commissioner, Fray Domingo González, Aug. 16, 1622.

The comparative infrequency of Jesuit culprits may perhaps be partially explained by a remarkable precaution adopted by the Society. A deposition under oath, Jan. 20, 1625, made in the Philippines by Padre Baltasar de Silva, states that experienced and trustworthy women, whom they called syndics, were employed to confess to Jesuits and tempt them to a certain point. The result was reported to the rector and if one was found to respond to the advances, he was transferred to some other place before he reached the point of himself soliciting. The Order looked with aversion on the requirement of denunciation to the Inquisition and took this method of averting it. In Manila, about 1605, one of these syndics was Doña Mariana Garvi, who was succeeded by Doña María Marmolejo.—MSS. of David Fergusson Esqr.

[1] Medina, *op. cit.*, pp. 48–50.

the Suprema that soldiers, to escape the rigor of military law, sought prosecution by the Inquisition in order to be arrested and sent to Mexico and to this end would blaspheme or utter heretical propositions. Many of them died on the passage and the expense of this bore heavily on the tribunal. For this the Suprema had no remedy to suggest except the plan adopted with soliciting confessors.[1] With these exceptions and the *visitas de navios*, or searching vessels for prohibited books, the duties of the commissioner were restricted to receiving denunciations, taking testimony, reporting to Mexico and executing such orders as he might receive from there. Still, they were personages of importance; although frailes living in their convent cells, they organized an imperfect kind of court; they had their assessors, notaries, treasurers, consultors and calificadores, their alguazil mayor and familiars and deputized their powers to sub-commissioners in the various parts of the islands.

Of real inquisitorial work for the purity of the faith we hear little. During the sixteenth century the only evidences of activity are three cases of Judaizers—Jorje and Domingo Rodríguez of Manila, reconciled in the Mexican auto of March 28, 1593, and Diego Hernández, regidor of Vitoria, accused by his cook of ordering her to cut chickens' throats instead of strangling them; his property was sequestrated and evidence against him was sought in Oporto from whence he came, but he died during these prolonged preliminaries.[2] The seventeenth century is similarly barren, affording few instances except the occasional bigamists and soliciting confessors, military culprits and sometimes a few Dutch prisoners of war. In the Mexican auto of 1648 there appeared Alejo de Castro, an octogenarian sent from Manila on suspicion of Mahometanism, sentenced to perpetual exile from the Philippines and to servitude for life in a convent for instruction in the faith.[3] A more noteworthy culprit was Padre Francisco Manuel Fernández, S. J., a devotee of Luisa de los Reyes,

---

[1] Medina, *op. cit.*, pp. 53–4.   [2] Ibidem, pp. 33–4.
[3] El Museo Mexicano, 1843, p 361.

a Tagal beata who had ecstasies. He declared that she had died many times and that God had resuscitated her so that she should suffer for the souls in purgatory; he compared her for sanctity to St. Teresa, St. Catherine and St. Inez and insisted that when he kissed her, embraced her and handled her indecently, he had no sensual feeling. It was a clear case of Illuminism against which the Inquisition waged unsparing war, nor was Fernández the only culprit, for another Jesuit, Padre Javier Riquelme was also compromised. Luisa was prosecuted in 1665 and testimony was taken against the Jesuits, but the Mexican tribunal reported, July 17, 1770, to the Suprema that the case had been suspended owing to the activity of the Jesuits in the islands, who always made the cause of their members their own. It complained bitterly of the way in which they impeded the Inquisition and frustrated its labors, when any Jesuit was concerned, whether for solicitation or other offence. They were not to be believed, for there was the case of the French Father Pierre Peleprat, whose detention was ordered, when they asserted that he was dead, but subsequently it was reported that this was not so but that he had been sent to France.[1]

The eighteenth century offers a similarly eventless record. So great was the inertness that the Edict of Faith, which was the chief source of denunciations and which should be published yearly in all parish churches, became virtually obsolete. From the time of Commissioner Paternina, who published it in 1669, forty-nine years elapsed before it was again published, in 1718, by Commissioner Juan de Arechederra; and Fray Juan de la Concepcion, writing in 1790, tells us that it had never been published since then.[2] It was a somewhat remarkable and uncalled-for burst of energy on the part of Commissioner Bernardo de Ustáriz, in 1752, when a score of Moro sailors of an English ship performed some pagan rites with songs and incense and he applied to the archbishop and then to the governor for aid to punish the scandal.

---

[1] Medina, *op. cit.*, pp. 59–66.
[2] Fray Juan de la Concepcion, Historia general de Philipinas, T. IX, pp. 202–4.

Both declined, when he got General Antonio Romero, who was a familiar, to undertake an investigation. Then force was needed to arrest the culprits and a prison to confine them, and Romero sought the Marquis of Ovando, the governor for this, but Ovando replied that the matter was under his exclusive jurisdiction, an assertion which he repeated to Ustáriz, adding that he intended to punish the guilty. Ustáriz complained of this to the tribunal, which declared, February 19, 1754, that the governor had failed in his duty; that his assertion of cognizance of such cases should be expunged from any instrument in which it appeared, and that the commissioner and notary should notify him of this in person. The Suprema, however, took a cooler view of the matter, pointing out that, by the Treaty of Utrecht in 1713, English subjects could not be prosecuted for practising their religion in Spanish territory, but at the same time it approved of the action of the tribunal and promised to ask the king to make due provision for the future.[1] Seeing that baptism was necessary to give jurisdiction to the Inquisition and that natives, even when converted, were not subject to it, this sudden access of zeal on the part of Ustáriz would appear somewhat supererogatory.

Ustáriz also showed his energy, in 1750, by arresting Pierre Fallet, a Swiss of Neuchâtel and a convert from Calvinism. In 1742 Commissioner Arechederra had taken from him two indecent prints; in 1748 Commissioner Juan Alvárez had deprived him of another and denounced him to the Mexican tribunal as suspect of heresy. The tribunal, on March 14, 1748, ordered his arrest with sequestration, at the same time dismissing Alvárez for his indiscretions and replacing him with Ustáriz. The sequestration showed that Fallet's property consisted of some uncollectable credits and many debts but, among his books on history, voyages and mathematics, in English, French, Flemish, Spanish, Latin and Greek, were found two prohibited ones—Rapin's History of England and a "Historia publica y secreta de la corte de Madrid." He was duly sent to Mexico, where he entered the secret prison,

---

[1] Medina, *op. cit.*, pp. 151–4.

January 17, 1752, with broken health. An accusation of seventy-six articles was accumulated against him, but his sentence on August 8th consisted merely of abjuration for light suspicion, three months' reclusion in the Jesuit College for instruction and some spiritual penances. This laborious trifling, so ruinous to the unfortunate subject, was crowned by the Suprema, which pondered over the case until March 7, 1772, when it ordered its suspension. Fallet, meanwhile, had been allowed to return to the Philippines, where his conduct was reported as exemplary.[1]

Censorship of a similarly futile kind was exercised in the denunciation of objectionable books or passages, which had to be forwarded to Mexico for action. Of this a single example will suffice. At the end of the sixteenth century, the Dominican Fray Francisco de San José was one of the most zealous and successful missionaries. He left a number of works in Tagal, some of which were printed, while others reposed in MS. Among the latter was a volume of sermons that had considerable repute, and in this the Augustinian Fray Juan Eusebio Polo, in 1772, discovered a passage conveying the Dominican view entertained at the period, as to the Immaculate Conception of the Virgin. Not daring to denounce it to the Dominican commissioner, he did so directly to the Mexican tribunal, adding that he could not send the MS., because it was borrowed, but he furnished certificates of two of his Augustinian brethren as to the accuracy of his translation. This was forwarded to the Suprema which, on January 27, 1774, ordered a copy of the book to be searched for in Mexico and Manila, the translation to be examined by experts, the matter to be voted on and then referred back to Madrid. Apparently this ended the case.[2]

If the natives were exempt from inquisitorial jurisdiction, they were subject to that of the missionary fathers and it may be questioned whether in this they were to be envied. About 1756 an obstinate revolt in the Island of Bonol throws some light on the relations between the converts and their spiritual guides. A

---
[1] Medina, *op. cit.*, pp. 141–51. [2] Ibidem, pp. 161–3.

district belonging to the Jesuits was placed under the control of Padre Morales who, observing that one of his subjects did not attend mass or frequent the sacraments, ordered him to be arrested. The man was known to be a desperate character and it was not until Morales laid explicit commands on the alguazil mayor of the village that the attempt was made, which resulted in the killing of the alguazil and the flight of the culprit. Francisco Dagohoy, brother of the slain, brought the corpse to Morales for Christian burial, which the padre refused, unless the regular fees were paid, intimating moreover that the alguazil had died under excommunication as a duellist. Naturally exasperated, Dagohoy, who was a leader among his people, assembled them, set forth their wrongs eloquently and had little difficulty in persuading them to follow him to the mountains, to the number of some three thousand. Entrenching themselves, they kept up a predatory warfare, in which Morales was killed and also an Augustinian Fray Lamberti. The rigor with which the taxes were exacted by the Spaniards drove many to join them and the rebellion was still flourishing in 1792, in spite of repeated overtures and offers of pardon—indeed, it may be doubted whether it was ever completely pacified under Spanish domination.[1]

While this Philippine branch of the Inquisition accomplished so little for the faith, it was eminently successful in the function of contributing to the disorder and confusion which so disastrously affected Spanish colonial administration. As everywhere else, the immunity of the officials was a fruitful source of trouble. In 1601, Benito de Mendiola, a familiar, was prosecuted in the secular court for the murder of Roque Espina de Cáceres, secretary of the governor, but the commissioner interposed and a long competencia followed, at the end of which, after a delay of ten years, the papers in the case were ordered to be surrendered to him by a decree of the Suprema of November 28, 1611. In

---

[1] Juan de la Concepcion, XIV, 81–107.—Buzeta, Diccionario de las Islas Filipinas, I, 395 (Madrid, 1850).

consideration of the distance and delay, Mendiola was liberated on bail; the widow of his victim desisted from the prosecution and finally, after further postponement caused by the difficulties of communication, the Mexican tribunal sentenced him to four months' banishment, two months' suspension from his office as notary and a fine of fifty pesos—a punishment sufficient to show his guilt and his escape from justice.[1]

The same question came up, in 1635, under Governor Sebastian Hurtado de Corcuera, whose stormy term of office was a continuous succession of broils with the several ecclesiastical jurisdictions. The Archbishop Hernando Guerrero was engaged in a mortal struggle, first with the governor and then with the Jesuits, in which his experience singularly resembled that of Bishop Palafox of Puebla. He was twice excommunicated, his temporalities were seized and he was relegated for a time to Corregidor Island. Compelled to a humiliating submission, he took the precaution of making a preliminary protest before the notary Diego de Rueda, whereupon the governor seized Rueda and threw him into the castle of Santiago. It chanced that he was a familiar; the commissioner, Fray Francisco de Herrera, claimed him and excommunicated the *juez conservador* of the Jesuits, who had excommunicated the archbishop. The juez yielded to the superior jurisdiction of the Inquisition and ordered Rueda released, but the Governor stood firm and when Herrera sent two frailes of his order with a demand for the prisoner, Corcuera seized them and sent them to Cavite with orders to confine them in their convent.[2]

---

[1] MSS. of Royal Library of Munich, Cod. Hisp. 79.

[2] Juan de la Concepcion, V, 276, 278. Puigblanch (La Inquisicion sin Mascara, Cádiz, 1811, p. 402) is in error in attributing the persecution of Archbishop Guerrero to the Inquisition and has misapprehended Palafox's allusion to it. In both cases it was the Jesuits acting through *jueces conservadores*, who, by a monstrous abuse, assumed to exercise full papal powers, but in Mexico the Inquisition was with them and in Manila it was against them.

The ecclesiastics had full revenge on Governor Corcuera when, in 1644, he was succeeded by Diego Fajardo. In fortifying Manila against an expected attack by the Dutch, his lines ran through an Augustinian convent. He offered the frailes another house, but they refused to move and he tore down the building

This was probably but a small part of Herrera's contests with the civil power for, in 1636, Corcuera applied to the Mexican tribunal asking that frailes be no longer appointed as commissioners, on account of the disturbances which they excited; if clerics of prudence were selected, peace would be preserved and the scandals caused by the Dominicans would be averted. In 1638 the Council of Indies renewed the request to Philip IV, asking that prebendaries of the churches should be chosen; Philip sent corresponding instructions to the Suprema but, on its remonstrating, he referred the matter back to the Council and nothing was done.[1]

Corcuera's successor, Diego Fajardo, had an opportunity of learning the extent to which the audacity of a commissioner could reach, and the utter disregard of all considerations of public policy. About 1650, an order came to the commissioner to seize, with the utmost secrecy, the governor of one of the provinces, who was also commandant of a fortified post. The commissioner quietly summoned his alguazil mayor and a sufficient number of familiars, sailed for the province, surprised the governor in his bed, carried him off and imprisoned him in a convent until there should be a vessel sailing for Acapulco. Fajardo was an irritable and passionate soldier, whose governorship was a continuous broil with the warring jurisdictions of the colony, and who could appreciate the risk of depriving a fortified place of its commander, at a time of perpetual warfare with the Dutch and the natives. His wrath was expected to be extreme at the contempt thus shown for his office and for the safety of the colony, but his reverential fear of the Inquisition overcame all other considerations and, when informed of the matter, he gently rebuked the commissioner for not having afforded him the opportunity of earning the graces and indulgences granted for participation in so pious a work, as

---

about their ears. When out of office they prosecuted him and obtained a verdict of 25,000 pesos. He must have been a rarely honest governor, for he was unable to pay it and they kept him in harsh gaol for five years. On his liberation, Philip IV appointed him Governor of the Canaries.—Concepcion, VI, 185-93.

[1] Medina, *op. cit.*, p. 46.—Archivo de Simancas, Inquisicion, Lib. 21, fol. 154.

he would have eagerly served as an alguazil in making the arrest.[1]

Yet perhaps the most troublesome of the commissioners with whom the Inquisition afflicted the islands was the Augustinian Fray José de Paternina Samaniego. He was grossly ignorant and had led a disorderly life in both Spain and Mexico. His fellow Augustinian, Fray Cristóbal de Leon, told him that he was unworthy to occupy so high an office, for he was an apostate whom the General of the Order had condemned to the galleys when visiting the convents of Old Castile, whereupon he accused Cristóbal to the provincial as a Jew and a usurer, causing his imprisonment with such harshness that it cost him his life. Yet this was the man whom the inquisitor-general sent to the Philippines, in 1663, as commissioner. His unfitness soon manifested itself, and his prelates wrote to the Mexican tribunal recommending his replacement; other remonstrances were sent to the Suprema, which ordered the collection of material against him, and nothing further was done.[2]

On board the ship which carried Paternina to Manila there was another passenger, Don Diego Salcedo, a Fleming who, as *maese de campo*, had rendered distinguished service in the Flemish wars, and who was coming to the Philippines as governor. The two men conceived a mutual dislike which was heightened when Salcedo dismissed from command of the fleet Don Andrés de Medina, who was a close friend of the commissioner, and refused employment to his nephew, González Samaniego. Still bitterer grew his hatred when Salcedo succeeded him in the favors of a married woman, whose paramour he had been, and he openly declared that he would be revenged.

Salcedo was arbitrary and covetous; he must have made full use of the opportunities afforded by his position, for at his death his fortune was reckoned at 700,000 pesos—much of which he had the prudence to remit to Mexico. He was not popular; he was speedily involved in the dissensions which seemed inevi-

---

[1] Juan de la Concepcion, VI, 316.   [2] Medina, *op. cit.*, pp. 84–6.

table, with Archbishop Poblete, and a faction was formed against him at the head of which stood the commissioner. A conspiracy for his ruin was organized and in February, 1666, there came to the Mexican tribunal letters from Paternina, from the archiepiscopal notary and from the Castellan of Manila accusing him of indifference to the service of God and the king and of his communication with Dutch heretics. Then the archbishop, in a letter of June 20, 1666, to the inquisitor-general, represented that Salcedo surrounded himself with Flemings and Dutchmen, one of whom was a Calvinist; that he never attended mass on feast-days or heard sermons; it was not known that he confessed or took communion except at Easter; that he created scandal by his relations with a married woman and that his cupidity was insatiable. This brought from the queen-regent a letter of November 11, 1666, to Salcedo, reprimanding him for his disregard of church observances, but nothing more. Paternina sent fresh accusations to the tribunal, and the archbishop and the Bishop of Cebu wrote to the Viceroy of Mexico; then the tribunal ordered its commissioner at Acapulco to examine secretly the passengers and crews of vessels arriving from the Philippines and all the accumulation was sent to the Suprema which, on November 22, 1667, ordered the case to be suspended; Paternina must act with caution and, if he obtained further information, he was to forward it.

The failure of his plans thus far showed Paternina that he must assume the responsibility. Archbishop Poblete died December 8, 1667, and it was not until September, 1668, that the commissioner was ready to take vigorous action, assured of the support of two judges of the Audiencia who hoped to succeed to power, of high officials with whom Salcedo had quarrelled, and of individuals to whom promises were made of offices, *encomiendas* and other advantages, while there was the enticing prospect of plunder in the sequestration of the governor's fortune. It was not difficult to obtain from his enemies evidence such as it was—evidence which the Mexican tribunal subsequently pronounced not only to be factitious on its face, but to amount at most only to a presumption *plusquam leve.* This was submitted, September 28th, to nine frailes as calificadores, some of whom pronounced the accused to be vehemently suspect of the errors of Luther and Calvin. Then three consultors were called together—the Dean José Millan de Poblete, nephew of the archbishop, the archiepiscopal provisor, Francisco Pizarro de Orellano, and the Licenciado Manuel Suárez de Olivera, from whom Salcedo had taken 12,000 pesos and who was soon afterwards prosecuted for Judaism. These worthies on October 6th decided that the commissioner could proceed to arrest, seeing that the three prescribed conditions were more than fulfilled. Of these conditions the most important, in the present case, was the danger of immediate escape of the accused, for which, as an afterthought, there was subsequently collected testimony so transparently futile that the Mexican tribunal described the danger of flight as a mere baseless pretext.

The forms having thus been observed, Paternina, on October 8th, issued the warrant of arrest addressed to the Admiral Vizcarra y Leiva as alguazil mayor—Vizcarra having been one of the principal witnesses. It ordered him to seize Salcedo wherever he could be found, to sequestrate his property and deliver it to Fray Mateo Ballon, guardian of the Franciscan convent. Salcedo was aware of the machinations against him, but imagined himself in full security and took no precautions. The warrant was delivered to the admiral at 9 P.M. on October 9th and between 12 and 1 A.M. he entered the palace with a band of Franciscan frailes armed with pikes, swords and bucklers. They seized Salcedo in bed, fettered him and, without allowing him to dress, carried him as he was in a hammock to the Franciscan convent and threw him into a narrow cell. After a few days he was removed to the house of the Capitan Diego de Palencia, his declared enemy, and then to the Augustinian convent of San Pablo, where Paternina kept him *incomunicado* and chained to the wall. The day of the arrest the judges ordered the bells of the cathedral to be rung as a sign of rejoicing that they had assumed the government. In fact, one of the judges, Juan Manuel de la Peña Bonifaz, an accomplice in the conspiracy, assumed the nominal government and there ensued a period of terror for all who were not of their faction. Paternina became the virtual ruler and he inspired general fear by banishing ten or twelve of the principal citizens, by forbidding any one to speak of the affair under heavy penalties and excommunication, and by bringing charges against a number of persons of being hostile to the Inquisition. The rich sequestration became an object of plunder. A nephew of Bonifaz profited largely from it, nor was Paternina neglectful of the chance, for we happen to hear of his entrusting 20,000 pesos to the Capitan Pedro Quintero, to be used for his benefit, and also of his extorting bribes from shipmasters for delivering to them goods embargoed with those of the governor. In short, as the Mexican tribunal reported to the Suprema, they committed a thousand iniquities.

How long Salcedo lay in his chains does not appear, but it must have been more than eighteen months, for he was probably shipped to Mexico during the summer of 1670. He died at sea November 24 of that year, making a most Christian end, for he confessed three times. A further proof of his orthodoxy may be found in the fact that he appointed as his executor the Mexican Inquisitor Ortega Montañes—a position which the Suprema forbade him to accept—and the estate was handed over, when the sequestration was lifted, October 31, 1671, to Don Gerónimo Pardo, Auditor of the Audiencia, who held powers from Salcedo's sister and three brothers.

The vessel by which Salcedo was shipped did not reach Acapulco until January 7, 1671, being the first that had come for two years. It brought the earliest direct intelligence of the events at Manila and the report of Paternina, but the news had already arrived there by way of Batavia, Holland and Madrid. In Madrid it had naturally aroused the Council of Indies which presented to the queen-regent a consulta embracing three propositions: I. If the commissioner made the arrest without orders from the tribunal, he should be severely punished for exposing the colony to risks so great. II. If the arrest was by order of the tribunal, it should have notified the Viceroy of Mexico in order that he might make provision for simultaneously filling the vacancy. III. That precise instructions for the future should be given for the arrest of persons of that rank, in conformity with the royal cédulas and concordias providing for such cases. To this the Suprema, still completely in the dark as to the circumstances of the case, replied somewhat superciliously that, if the commissioner had exceeded his duty, he would be punished appropriately; that the arrest was not ordered by the tribunal but, if it had been, no notice was due to the viceroy in matters of faith; the cédula of April 2, 1664, provided for the government of the Philippines in cases of vacancy, which is all that human foresight can anticipate. No new instructions were necessary, as such cases were already provided for in the existing regulations; sentences on persons of the rank of Don Diego Salcedo were not executed without consulting the Suprema, except when irremediable injury might be anticipated from delay, and it was an accepted rule that, in important cases of faith, all such personages were subjected to the Inquisition. To this the Council of Indies rejoined by insisting that it should not be left to the discretion of a commissioner to determine whether the danger of delay justified arresting a governor and imperilling the safety of the colony; the tribunal should give notice to the viceroy, without violating the secrecy of the Inquisition, and it concluded by asking that definite instructions be given to the inquisitor-general and Suprema that in matters of such importance such action should be taken as would avoid the danger of a recurrence of similar proceedings. Even the Council of Indies did not venture to hint that the governor of an important colony, if suspected of heresy, could not be suddenly arrested, and it only objected to this being done without preliminary precautions.

In June, 1670, the news of Salcedo's arrest filtered through Madrid to Mexico but it was not until January 7, 1671, that the official report from Paternina reached Acapulco. The tribunal, in forwarding, January 18th, an abstract of this to the Suprema, made haste to exculpate itself from all responsibility, pronouncing the whole affair to be the greatest abuse ever committed by an official, especially by one of the Inquisition, a trampling on justice, with grievous discredit to the prudence and equitable procedure of the Holy Office, arising from hatred of Salcedo and carried out by a conspiracy between Paternina and the judges who desired to seize the government. This rendered necessary exemplary punishment, so that all might understand that the tribunal did not undertake to punish crimes that did not pertain to it, nor serve as an instrument for the gratification of passion, and this demonstration should be made in Manila, in order that the honor and fame of Salcedo might be restored, although he had lost life and fortune. The tribunal therefore, while awaiting instructions, proposed to suspend Paternina and give his office to another, with orders to shut him up in a convent and also to raise the sequestration. This it did and appointed as his successor Fray Felipe Pardo, though when the Suprema, June 4, 1671, confirmed the suspension, with incredible blindness, it replaced him with the Dean José Millan de Poblete, who had been his active accomplice. Pardo however probably retained the office, as the dean had been promoted to the bishopric of Canaries, and one of the results of the affair was to transfer the commissionership from the Augustinians to the Dominicans.

Paternina escaped the punishment which he merited for he died, January 18, 1674, like his victim, on the voyage to Acapulco. The Suprema had ordered his imprisonment and trial, but the sentence was not to be executed without its confirmation. Despite its assurance to the Council of Indies that nothing more was necessary to regulate arrests of governors, it issued, under pressure from the queen-regent, June 30, 1671, a carta acordada prescribing special rules for such occasions. Meanwhile in Manila there had been a natural revulsion. The new governor, Manuel de Leon y Saravia, took full advantage of the opportunity to emancipate the secular power from the predominance of the ecclesiastical.

He withdrew the sequestrated property out of the hands of the treasurer of the Inquisition; he released Juan de Berestain who had been imprisoned as an accomplice of Salcedo; he prosecuted and banished the Franciscan provincial and the guardian of the Franciscan convent, and the good frailes complained that they were persecuted as by an enemy; and we are assured that he reduced the power of the Holy Office until its officials were so despised that if they had to arrest the vilest individual no one would help them.[1]

There is nothing more connected with the Philippine commissionership that is worth relating, except to explain the disappearance of its records. When the British captured Manila, October 5, 1762, these were not removed from the city. No attention was paid to them at first but, on March 12, 1763, an English Catholic and Don César Fallet, who had been penanced by the Inquisition, informed the commissioner, Fray Pedro Luis de Serra, that he was about to be arrested and the archives to be seized, whereupon he burnt them all and when the English came they found nothing. He was taken before the authorities where he told what he had done; the tribunal approved of his action and sent him renewed instructions.[2]

Although not directly connected with our subject, there is interest in observing the zeal with which the purity of the faith was conserved in the Far East. The commissioner, Juan de Arechederra, in a letter of July 6, 1724, from Manila to Francisco de Garzeron, inquisitor and inspector of Mexico, encloses a sentence rendered in Canton by Fra Giovanni Bonaventura de Roma, as delegate judge and commissioner of Giovanni de Cazal, Bishop of Macao, on Antoine Guigue, a French missionary convicted of

---

[1] Medina, *op. cit.*, pp. 87–130.—MSS. of Royal Library of Munich, Cod. Hispan. 79.—Archivo de Simancas, Inquisicion, Lib. 60, fol. 209, 249. It is perhaps worth remarking that Juan de la Concepcion makes no allusion to this episode, so prominent in the history of the Colony and so little creditable to his Augustinian Order.

[2] Medina, *op. cit.*, pp. 156–7.

Jansenism. Guigue, it appears, had obeyed orders in publishing the appeal of his archbishop, Cardinal Noailles, to a future council against the bull *Unigenitus*, he had maintained that councils are superior to popes, that popes sometimes erred and other Jansenist heresies, besides receiving and circulating Jansenist books. Moreover it was asserted that he had been guilty of solicitation when on missions in the interior. He had not obeyed the citations and had allowed the trial to go by default, wherefore his sentence was publicly read, March 1, 1724, in the church Siaò Nân Muen of Canton. He was suspended from all priestly functions, he was ordered to leave the province and betake himself to a convent in which he was to remain, performing certain spiritual exercises, until he had satisfied the pope, and all this under penalty of perpetual imprisonment for disobedience.[1] The Emperor of China at the time was ordering all Christian missionaries to leave his dominions, but the common danger was insufficient to allay the strife arising from Pasquier Quesnel's speculations on sufficing attrition.

---

[1] MS., *penes me*.

CHAPTER VII.

PERU.

WHEN, on January 9, 1570, Servan de Cerezuela arrived at Lima to open a tribunal of the Inquisition, the condition of Spanish South America was such as to call for energetic action if the colony was to respond to the hopes of those who had so earnestly urged the Christianization of the New World. The establishment there of the Holy Office had been asked for by many who viewed with dismay the prevailing demoralization, and we shall see whether its influence proved to be for good or for evil. Peru had been conquered by adventurers inflamed with the thirst of gold, who in the eager search for wealth had thrown off the restraints of civilized life. The Church exercised little or no moral power for, as the existing Viceroy, Francisco de Toledo, reported, he found on his arrival that the clerics and frailes, bishops and prelates, were lords of the spiritual and acknowledged no superior in the temporal. The king was exposed to constant outlay in granting free passage by every fleet to great numbers of clerics and frailes who came under the pretext of converting and teaching the Indians, but, in reality, many devoted themselves to accumulating wealth, plucking the Indians in the endeavor to return to Spain with fortunes. These priests kept prisons, alguaziles and chains, seizing and punishing all who offended them and there was no one to call them to account. The bishops pretended to have royal licences to return to Spain, laden with the silver which they had not already gathered and despatched in advance, and it was the same with the frailes.[1]

---

[1] Medina, Inquisicion en las Provincias del Plata, pp. 43–7.

Thanks to the researches of native scholars there is ample material for the history of the South American Inquisition. The most prominent of these gentle-

This deplorable statement is confirmed and strengthened by Toledo's successor in the vice-royalty, the Count del Villar, in 1588. The secular clergy, he says, from the bishops to the lower grades, have come to Peru, not to save the souls of the Indians but to gain money in any manner and return to Spain, while those who are ordained in the country are mostly soldiers discharged for ill-conduct or men of bad character. The regular Orders are no better, except to some extent, the Franciscans and more especially the Jesuits. The royal officials use their positions to make money and oppress the people. Few immigrants seem to come with the intention of honest labor, but are mostly vagrants living on the hospitality of those who will receive them. The descendants of the *conquistadores* claim positions in virtue of the services of their ancestors and, as they increase in number with each generation, it is impossible to satisfy them or the impostors who pretend to be descendants. With all this the Christianiza-

---

men is Don José Toribio Medina who has gathered a wealth of documents in the Spanish archives on which are based the works to which I am principally indebted. These are

"Historia del Tribunal del Santo Oficio de la Inquisicion de Lima (1569–1820)." 2 vols., 8vo, Santiago de Chile, 1887.

"Historia del Tribunal del Santo Oficio de la Inquisicion en Chile." 2 vols., 8vo, Santiago de Chile, 1890.

"El Tribunal del Santo Oficio de la Inquisicion en las Provincias del Plata." 1 vol., 8vo, Santiago de Chile, 1900.

"Historia del Santo Oficio de la Inquisicion de Cartagena de las Indias." 1 vol., 12mo, Santiago de Chile, 1899.

Don Ricardo Palma of Lima has contributed a useful compendium—"Añales de la Inquisicion de Lima," Lima, 1863. Third edition, Madrid, 1897.

Don Vicuña Mackenna has given some exceedingly curious details of the procedure of the tribunal in his "Francisco Moyen ó lo que fué la Inquisicion en América," Valparaiso, 1868, of which an English translation by Dr. James W. Duffy appeared in London in 1869.

Various relations of autos de fe have been reprinted in the "Documentos Literarios del Perú," Tomo VII, Lima, 1876.

Unfortunately, the main source of information, the records of the tribunal itself, are no longer available. They were preserved almost intact, at the suppression in 1820, and were lodged in the Archivo nacional, in the convent of San Agustin, but were dispersed in 1881 when Lima was occupied by the Chilian army. Before this event, through the kindness of Doctor Paz-Soldan, I procured copies of some interesting documents, referred to in the following pages under the old numbers. The Spanish archives have also furnished me some material.

tion of the Indians makes little or no progress. Altogether he assumes that the immigration, both lay and clerical, is thoroughly vicious, while the creoles, or native whites, are no better.[1] It is a community living in idle self-indulgence on the Indians and the Government.

As regards matters of faith, in the absence of the Inquisition, the jurisdiction over heresy, inherent in the episcopal office, had reasserted itself and was exercised by the bishops. As early as May 15, 1539, the Dominican Provincial, Gaspar de Carvajal, is found acting as inquisitor for the Bishop Fray Vicente de Valverde and, on October 23 of the same year, the secular magistrates honored a demand from the bishop for the process against Captain Mercadillo, in order that, as inquisitor, he should take cognizance of certain ebullitious of blasphemy. This inquisitorial power was exercised to its highest expression, for, in 1548, the first Archbishop, Gerónimo de Loaisa, held an auto de fe in Lima, wherein Jan Millar, a Fleming, was burnt for Protestantism. In 1560 the episcopal Provisor of Cuzco held an auto in which were relaxed the Morisco Alvaro González and the mulatto Luis Solano as dogmatizing Mahometans; in 1564 he celebrated another in which Vasco Suárez, Antonio Hernández and Alonso de Cieza were penanced, while Lope de la Peña was reconciled for Islam. In 1565 the Dean of la Plata reconciled Juan Bautista for Protestantism and condemned him to confiscation and perpetual prison and sanbenito.[2] Evidently the episcopal Inquisition was active; in 1567 the synod of Lima adopted regulations to govern its functions and when, in 1583, the provincial council, under St. Toribio, confirmed the acts of that synod, it was obliged, doubtless on representation by the tribunal, to except those regulations as matters which had passed beyond its control.[3] The bishops, however, did not surrender their jurisdiction without impulsion,

---

[1] Medina, Inquisicion de Lima, II, 469-73.
[2] Ibidem, I, 26; La Plata, I, 16-18.
[3] Concil. Limens. Provin. I, Act. II, cap. 1; Act. v, cap. 1 (Haroldus, Lima Limata, pp. 5, 42).

for, as we have seen (Mexico, p. 199), the Suprema was obliged to order them, in 1570, to transfer all cases to the tribunal and it was found necessary to repeat this in 1586.

When the transfer was made there were four cases pending in Lima and ninety-seven in Cuzco, concerning which the fiscal reported that the Ordinaries had prosecuted many that were not matters of faith and were habitually settled for a trivial payment in oil. Inquisitor Cerezuela set a good example by suspending three and ordering the rest to be filed for reference in case of relapse.[1] One of the cases thus inherited by the tribunal may be briefly sketched as affording a vivid picture of the methods in vogue and the use made of the Inquisition, whether episcopal or Spanish.

Francisco de Aguirre was one of the prominent conquistadores. He had come well equipped to Peru in 1533, he had borne an active share in the conquest of Chile and then in that of the extensive interior province known as Tucuman, of which he became governor. Of this he was deprived, but about 1566 he was reappointed on the occasion of an Indian revolt, in which the Spaniards were murdered and only a handful of soldiers held out in the town of Santiago del Estero. With his customary energy Aguirre collected a force, defeated the Indians in a battle, in which he lost one of his sons, and re-established the Spanish dominion. Then he headed an expedition in search of a port on the Atlantic to afford easier access to the territory, but when near his destination his troops mutinied and carried him back as a prisoner to Santiago del Estero. To justify this the mutineers claimed to have acted under orders of the Inquisition of the Bishop of la Plata, with whom Aguirre had quarrelled on the subject of tithes. There were witnesses in plenty to hasty and irreverent speeches by the veteran soldier; for two or three years he was kept in prison, at a cost to him, as he declared, of thirty thousand pesos, and on October 15, 1568, by judges acting under commission of Bishop Navarrete "inquisidor ordinario y general" he was sentenced.

---
[1] Medina, La Plata, 19.

His imprisonment was accepted as a punishment; he was fined in fifteen hundred pesos and costs and was required to appear as a penitent in the church of Santiago del Estero and make formal abjuration of his objectionable speeches. This he performed, but on the pretext of informality he was obliged to undergo the humiliation a second time, April 1, 1569, in la Plata. Of this a notarial act was sent to the Council of Indies to show that he was unfitted to be Governor of Tucuman, but it was too late, for in August of that year he received the royal confirmation of his appointment with orders to proceed at once to his seat of government. On the march a cleric with an order from the bishop sought to stop him, but he disobeyed and paralyzed the unfortunate messenger by sternly asking him "If I should kill a cleric, what would be the penalty?"

So far he had had to deal with the episcopal Inquisition in the hands of an opposing faction; even severer experiences were in store for him from the Holy Office, used as an instrument by the Viceroy Toledo who desired to get rid of him. One of the earliest acts of the Lima tribunal was to entertain a denunciation of him, in which his intemperate utterances were again brought forward, together with the further accusation that he had banished from Tucuman all who had been concerned in his prosecution and that he had said that he had been forced to confess to what he had not done. March 14, 1570, Cerezuela ordered his arrest with sequestration of property; Toledo undertook to execute the mandate and in reporting to the king stated that Aguirre's government was such that most of the inhabitants were leaving the province. To arrest such a man was not an easy matter, but it was effected and he was brought three hundred leagues to Lima. Delays were unavoidable in obtaining and ratifying testimony at such a distance, through a hostile Indian country which, as the tribunal stated, was entered only once a year. Aguirre offered to waive the formality of ratifying the testimony in order to expedite the process, but the fiscal insisted on regularity and the trial dragged wearily on, as new evidence came in, mostly as to his arbitrary government and other matters with which the tribunal properly had no concern. Aguirre fell dangerously ill and was transferred, July 19, 1572, to the house of a familiar, where he was kept strictly *incomunicado* and from which he was brought back, April 24, 1574, to listen to the publication of evidence. It was not until late in 1575 or early in 1576 that sentence was rendered condemning him to hear mass as a penitent on a feast-day when no services were allowed in any other church; he abjured *de vehementi*, was cast in all costs, was recluded for four months in a convent and was banished perpetually from Tucuman. The trivial character of the charges is seen in the special stress laid on his having used charms to cure wounds and toothache, which he was forbidden to do in future—innocent charms, as he explained, employed only because no physician was at hand and surely pardonable in the wild warfare in which he had worn out his life. He retired to the city of Serena which he had founded, old, sick and penniless. He had spent thirty-six years and some three hundred thousand pesos in the king's service; three of his sons, his brother and three nephews had died in the same service, and he was too poor and oppressed with debts to make his way to court and ask reward for his labors. To complete the destruction of his influence his two remaining sons were prosecuted on frivolous charges, but the cases seem to have been suspended after the desired result had been attained. His son-in-law, Francisco de Matienzo, who had endeavored to prevent his arrest, was prosecuted and fined in three hundred pesos. There were also seven other prosecutions against his followers, resulting in the imposition of fines.[1] Had all viceroys, like Francisco de Toledo, known how to control the Inquisition it might have been made a useful political instrument but, as we shall see, succeeding inquisitors

---

[1] Medina, La Plata, pp. 21–41, 85–111.

Another distinguished conquistador, Felipe de Cáceres, was prosecuted by Pedro Fernández de la Torre, Bishop of la Plata, who carried him to Spain, about 1580, but died on the passage and Cáceres was delivered to the tribunal of Seville.—Ibidem, p. 116.

preferred to follow their own ends and it became a perpetually disturbing influence.

The bishops did not willingly acquiesce in the surrender of a jurisdiction which could be so profitably employed. That Archbishop Loaiza showed a recalcitrating temper is manifested by a letter of the Suprema directing that he should not style himself "inquisidor ordinario" in his pastorals and edicts. Another letter permits him to inspect the commissions of the inquisitors and their instructions if he desires, but it must be in the audience-chamber as they are not to be removed from there, except the printed instructions, of which a copy may be given to him on condition of his allowing no one to see it. There was evident friction despite the injunctions of the Suprema that a good understanding should be maintained.[1] This was increased when, in 1574, a royal cédula addressed to the bishops ordered them to exercise special vigilance and make secret inquiry about disguised Lutheran preachers who were said to be on their way to Peru. The prelates assumed this to be a grant of renewed inquisitorial power and undertook to exercise it, giving rise to no little trouble. Sebastian de Lartaun, Bishop of Cuzco, not only published edicts trespassing on inquisitorial jurisdiction but boasted that, if the inquisitors came into his diocese, he could punish them, and he arrested and imprisoned in chains their commissioner Pedro de Quiroga, a canon of his cathedral, publicly and under circumstances creating great scandal. The tribunal retaliated by summoning to Lima the bishop's provisor Albornoz and throwing him in the secret prison; furthermore it imprisoned the priest Luis de Arma, who had assisted in chaining Quiroga, as well as the episcopal fiscal Alonso Duran and a cleric named Bejerano for the same offence, to which the bishop responded by seizing Quiroga's temporalities and forbidding him to enter the church. The tribunal, in 1581, reported the situation to the Suprema, which replied that nothing was to be conceded to the Ordinaries save what was allowed by the laws and the royal

---

[1] Archivo nacional de Lima, Protocolo 223, Exped[te] 5270.

cédulas; from the Bishop of Cuzco's edict the matter pertaining to the Inquisition was to be struck out and he was to be duly warned. A second notice was to be given to the Bishop of Panamá of the cédulas forbidding his interference in matters of faith and, if he continued to disobey, the Suprema was to be advised. The same was to be done with other bishops similarly offending, and special attention was directed to the acts of the Bishops of Popayan and Tucuman. If we may believe the reports made by the tribunal to the Suprema the episcopate was filled with most unworthy wearers of the mitre and the Archbishop of New Granada was the only one who had fully obeyed the orders to hand over all inquisitorial cases. The officials of the Inquisition, it said, were hated equally by the bishops and by the royal judges, who lost no opportunity of oppressing and humiliating them.[1]

Thus early commenced the antagonism between the Inquisition and the episcopate which continued during its whole career to be a disturbing element in the Spanish possessions. In 1584 we find Inquisitor Ulloa complaining to the Suprema of the action of the recent provincial council of Lima in secretly writing to the king about the evil character of the commissioners selected. This, he asserts, arose from his refusal of the request of the Bishops of Cuzco, la Plata and Tucuman to make them commissioners in their respective dioceses. The bishops, he adds, were opposed to the introduction of the Inquisition, because it limited their jurisdiction, and they and the royal courts were constantly causing trouble in spite of the extreme modesty and deference shown by his officials.[2]

Such was the soil in which the Inquisition was to be planted when Philip II resolved to confer upon the New World the blessing of the institution. Its inception bore a marked resemblance to that of Mexico. January 28, 1569, Inquisitor-general Espinosa

---

[1] Medina, Lima, I, 173–177, 179–80.—Archivo nacional de Lima, *ubi sup.*
[2] Medina, Lima, II, 424.

wrote to the Licentiate Servan de Cerezuela, in Oropesa, that the king proposed to establish a tribunal in Peru and that he was selected as an inquisitor, with a salary of three thousand pesos, each of four hundred maravedís, a part of which would be drawn from the fruits of a prebend in Lima. He was ordered to start without delay for Seville, whence he would sail with a colleague, a fiscal and a notary, in the fleet carrying the Viceroy Francisco de Toledo, who would deliver to him his commission and instructions. Similar orders were sent to the other inquisitor, Dr. Andrés de Bustamente, and five hundred ducats were given to each to defray their expenses. Commands were issued to the bishops to surrender all cases pertaining to the tribunal; to the courts not to interfere with the confiscations; to the viceroy to render it all favor and support and to provide a proper building for its occupancy and prisons; to all officials to take the oath of obedience and to lend whatever aid might be required.[1]

The fleet sailed March 19, 1569; Domínica was reached April 28th, Cartagena May 8th and Nombre de Dios, June 1st. There their funds ran out and no one would lend them a real without interest until Judge Barros of Panamá furnished them two thousand pesos out of moneys deposited in his court. While thus delayed they heard several cases and rendered sentences. Bustamente with the notary Arrieta left Nombre de Dios on June 23d, but he was so affected by the escape of two of his slaves, as we are told, that he fell sick and died on June 30th. Cerezuela and the fiscal Alcedo remained to attend to a case which developed itself on the day fixed for their departure. Six witnesses testified that a Portuguese named Salvador Méndez Hernández had been burnt in effigy in Seville; they arrested him and wrote to Seville for the process, but as they had no arrangements for detaining him, he was released under oath, which he naturally forfeited. Cerezuela reached Panamá on July 18th, when he summoned the viceroy and the judges of the Audiencia to take the oath of obedience to the Inquisition. On the 22d there was a solemn cere-

---
[1] Medina, Lima, I, 2–4.

mony, with a procession to the church of San Francisco, where his commission was read, he issued a mandate and the viceroy and officials and the people all took the oath. Sail was made from Panamá, August 15th, and Lima was reached November 28th. A house was selected and the viceroy was called upon to give it to them; another adjoining was rented for the officials and, on January 29, 1570, there was a solemn function in the cathedral, such as we have seen in Mexico, when the tribunal was officially acknowledged, its authority asserted and the Edict of Faith was published, calling upon every one to denounce all offenders of whom he was cognizant, directly or indirectly.[1]

Although Cerezuela was accused to the Suprema, by his notary Arrieta, as wholly ignorant of inquisitorial practice, of allowing himself to be easily influenced, and of neglecting to appoint familiars, he speedily manifested an energy inspiring all classes with fear of a tribunal which was superior to all distinctions of station, and whose jurisdiction was limited only by its own definitions. Scarce had the edict been published when arrests began of bigamists, blasphemers and persons whose utterances were not cautiously restrained—Alcedo, the fiscal, reports three in one day. Two canons of the cathedral and their advocate were prosecuted for some false swearing before the ecclesiastical court, which the theologians managed to find heretical, and, in spite of the intervention of the archbishop, Cerezuela tried them and amerced them in eight hundred pesos for the benefit of the tribunal. Then he prosecuted two royal officials, for raising difficulties in supplying his demands for the maintenance of poor prisoners, and fined them in eighty ducats.[2] Presumably he desired to produce a profound impression upon the public and for this the solemnity of a public auto de fe was essential. This rendered inadvisable the customary prolonged delays of inquisitorial action and already, on November 15, 1573, it was held in

---

[1] Medina, Lima, I, 6–18.—See also Elkan N. Adler, The Inquisicion in Peru (Publications of the American Jewish Historical Society, No. 12), who prints a translation of the special instructions of the Suprema.

[2] Medina, Lima, I, 29–31.

the principal plaza, with the usual oaths administered to all present and the preaching of a sermon. The different bodies of dignitaries of course quarreled as to the places assigned to them, but Cerezuela settled their conflicting pretensions and the awful ceremony was performed effectively. The penitents were not numerous. The Corsican, Joan Bautista, had been penanced for Protestantism by the archbishop and again had been sentenced to perpetual prison by the Bishop of los Charcas; now as an impenitent, he was condemned to two hundred lashes through the streets and to lifelong galley-service. The Frenchman, Jean de Lion, for the same heresy abjured *de vehementi*, was confined for ten years to the city of Lima, and contributed a thousand pesos towards the cost of erecting the staging at the auto. Ynes de los Angeles received a hundred lashes for bigamy, and Andrés de Campos the same for violating the secrecy of the Inquisition. The crowning attraction of the spectacle, however, was another Frenchman, Mathieu Salado, who was generally reputed to be insane. He had been denounced for "Lutheranism" in May, 1570, but after arrest and examination had been discharged as irresponsible. New evidence was received however and, in November, 1571, he was again put on trial. He held that Erasmus and Luther were saints enlightened by God; he denounced the popes, the clergy and the whole establishment; he denied purgatory and indulgences, images and the mass. He was decided to be of sound mind and, as he was pertinacious, he was sentenced to relaxation after a preliminary torture *in caput alienum*, all of which was duly executed, but whether he was burnt alive or after strangulation we are not informed.[1]

The tribunal which had thus asserted its power was necessarily organized on the Castilian pattern, with normally two inquisitors, a fiscal (or, as he was termed in later times, an inquisitor-fiscal), a notary or secretary, a receiver of confiscations or treasurer, an ornamental alguazil mayor and another for work, an alcaide

---

[1] Medina, Lima, I, 49-55.

or gaoler with assistants, a nuncio, a portero or apparitor, an advocate of prisoners, a barber, a physician and a surgeon. These were the salaried officials and in addition there were commissioners at distant points, familiars, consultores and calificadores. There seems to have been an effort from the first to restrict the lists of unsalaried officials, whose overgrown numbers in Spain were the source of constant trouble, owing to their exemption from the secular courts and being justiciable only by the tribunal. Thus the consultores were limited to six and the familiars to twelve in the city of Lima, four in each cathedral city and one in each town inhabited by Spaniards, and their *fuero* was defined, as in Mexico, to be that of the Castilian concordia of 1553, which limited, to a considerable extent, their exemption in criminal cases.[1]

Distance and delay in communication necessarily rendered the tribunal more independent in action than was permitted in Spain at this time, but the Suprema endeavored to maintain supervision and subordination as far as it could. It was unavoidable that the tribunal should be allowed to appoint to the minor and unsalaried positions, but its appointments were reported to the Suprema, which thereupon issued the commissions and sometimes, at least, made appointments itself. In the original instructions of 1570 power was granted to create commissioners and familiars; in 1576 this was extended to notaries and other officials, while in 1589 it appears to be restricted to cases of necessity in the city of Lima.[2] Yet when the Suprema chose to exercise the appointing power it had no hesitation, as when, in 1615, it ordered Don Gil de Amoraga to be received as commissioner of Panamá and Don Fernando Francisco de Ribadeneira as commissioner of Tucuman, if the place was vacant, and if not, as soon as it should become so. As time went on, cases of this kind became more frequent. As regards commissions, a letter

---

[1] Archivo nacional de Lima, Protocolo 223, Exped.^{te} 5270.—Palma, Añales, 8–11.—Medina, Lima, I, 6.

[2] Archivo de Simancas, Inquisicion, Legajo 1465, fol. 23.

of May 26, 1620, orders that the physician, the barber and the surgeon are to furnish their proofs of *limpieza,* or purity of blood, when their names can be forwarded and the inquisitor-general will issue their commissions. When, in 1584, the tribunal granted to a familiar of Panamá the title of alguazil, with a *vara alta de justicia,* or the privilege of carrying a tall wand as the symbol of his office, the audiencia of Panamá complained to the king and the Suprema called upon the tribunal for an explanation, pending which the *vara* was not to be carried.[1]

The provisions for cases which in Spain were referred to or appealed to the Suprema and inquisitor-general have already been detailed in the chapter on Mexico and need not be repeated here. It will be recalled that they conferred on the colonial tribunals almost complete independence, so that they escaped the encroachments which at home eventually rendered the provincial Inquisitions scarce more than bureaus for the collection of evidence and for the execution of the decrees of the Council. The Suprema, it is true, occasionally made its power felt by sending out a *visitador* or inspector, with faculties more or less extensive and by removing or transferring an inquisitor against whom complaints were too vigorous to be disregarded, but the only regular supervision that could be exercised lay in the requirement of full semi-annual reports of the business of the tribunal and the condition of pending cases. It may be questioned, however, whether this could have been performed with regularity during the earlier periods for, as late as 1680, the tribunal was notified that an arrangement had been made with the king by the consulado of Seville whereby despatches could be sent twice a year.[2]

The Edict of Faith was ordered to be published regularly in all parish and conventual churches, a command which was doubtless obeyed with reasonable regularity, but there was a curious ignorance displayed of the vastness of South America and its lack of

---

[1] Archivo de Simancas, *loc. cit.*
[2] Medina, Lima, I, 5.—Archivo nacional de Lima, Protocolo 228, Exp^{te} 5289.

means of intercommunication, when the inquisitors were required to perform an annual visitation of their district. Of course this instruction received no attention; indeed the only attempt recorded is that of Inquisitor Ulloa, who found it convenient, in 1594, to be absent from Lima and employed his time, until his death in 1597, in wandering over the land and harassing the people.[1]

As in Mexico, Indians were excepted from inquisitorial jurisdiction and, in matters of faith, were subject to the bishops. This was not relished. Fray Juan de Vivero wrote to Philip that the Inquisition should punish them, though not as severely as Spaniards. The notary Arrieta advised Cerezuela to disregard the instructions and to prosecute them, just as he had seen in Seville unbaptized slaves punished for perverting their Christian comrades. Cerezuela reported that baptized Indians publicly persuaded their fellows that what the missionaries told them was false, but the Suprema was firm and ordered him not to interfere even with dogmatizers who told their people not to believe the missionaries.[2]

Cerezuela's zeal was also rebuked when he represented that foreigners who came to Peru usually sought at once to penetrate into the interior, wherefore he proposed that the commissioners at Cartagena and Panamá should turn them back and not permit them to enter, but the Suprema replied that their entrance was not to be impeded nor were they to be prosecuted unless they committed offences coming within the jurisdiction of the Holy Office, or were detected in bringing prohibited books. At the same time it ordered a careful inquest as to all strangers scattered through the land and, when this should be verified with due secrecy, the commissioners were to be instructed to admit to reconciliation those found transgressing and, if they refused conversion, they were to be prosecuted with the full severity of the canons.[3] If

---

[1] Archivo de Lima, Protocolo 223, Exp.to 5270.—Medina, Lima, I, 301–18.
[2] Medina, La Plata, p. 57.—Archivo de Lima, *ubi sup.*
[3] Medina, Chile, I, 363, 365.—Archivo nacional de Lima, *ubi sup.*

the tribunal thus was prevented from regulating ingress, it assumed full control over egress, for in June, 1584, it issued a proclamation that no one should leave the kingdom without its licence, under pain of excommunication and fines, and shipmasters were ordered to take no passengers without it—an assumption of power which won the approbation of the Suprema, with the suggestive warning that the licences must be issued without charge. This arbitrary exercise of authority was even extended to prohibiting any vessel from leaving port without a licence, and the abuse became so intolerable that, as we have seen (Mexico, p. 252), its removal formed part of the Concordia of 1610. The tribunal chafed under this and, when it was busy in arresting nearly all the Portuguese merchants in 1636, it complained to the Suprema that its hands had been tied; to prevent the escape of those who might be guilty it had applied to the Viceroy Chinchon who, as a governmental act, ordered that for a year no one should be given passage without a licence from the Inquisition; he would willingly have done more, but he had to pay some regard to the Concordia. The Suprema was impressively asked to see that this matter should be corrected, as otherwise the faith and the fisc would suffer. It was probably on this occasion that occurred a detention of the fleet when ready to sail, to which I have met with an allusion, because licences had not been procured for the passengers.[1]

The chief obstacle to the thorough organization of the Inquisition was the immense extent of the territory subjected to a single tribunal. Until the kingdom of New Granada was cut off, in 1610, by the establishment of a tribunal at Cartagena, this comprised the West India Islands and the whole of South America, save the undefined limits of Portuguese Brazil.[2] The three centres of Lima, Santiago de Chile and Buenos Ayres were far apart in

---

[1] Medina, Lima, I, 172; II, 58.—Archivo nacional de Lima, Protocolo 228, Expte 5287; Protocolo 223, Expte 5270.

[2] The prosecution, about 1580, of Fray Andres Vélez, Provincial of San Domingo, shows that the islands were subject to the Lima tribunal.—Archivo de Lima, Protocolo 223, Expte 5270.

distance and still farther in the character of the intervening territory, much of as yet scarce explored, the Indians but partially subdued and the Spanish settlements few and far between. Chile, indeed, could be reached by sea, in a voyage usually of two or three weeks, but the difficulties of communication with the interior provinces and those of the River Plate were embarrassing. When the tribunal consulted the Suprema about them it could only reply that cases arising in Paraguay and la Plata must be dealt with as best they could; the accused at a distance should be ordered to present themselves to the tribunal and not be arrested unless there were manifest heresy or evidence justifying sequestration[1]—a suggestion dictated rather by thrift than mercy.

The device which was effective in Spain, of commissioners in all centres of population and familiars scattered everywhere, was only a partial remedy for the difficulty. The power of the commissioner, as we have seen, was jealously limited; he could execute orders, take testimony and report, but he was forbidden to arrest unless there was imminent danger that a culprit might fly; in no case could he conduct a trial; his functions were purely executive and in no sense judicial. A vast proportion of the cases tried by the Inquisition were for offences comparatively trivial—blasphemy, careless or irreverent remarks, or the more or less harmful superstitions classed as sorcery—and the transmission of denunciations for such matters, over hundreds of leagues of forest and mountain, and awaiting a reply with instructions, was manifestly too cumbrous a process to be practical; the half-breed crone, the vagrant soldier or the wandering pedlar, who were the usual culprits in such cases, would be dead or vanished before an order of arrest could be received.

Peru was no more exempt than Mexico from the troubles caused by these outlying officials who felt themselves virtually independent and became intolerable pests in their districts. The object of acquiring the position was to obtain exemption from justice. They were answerable only to the tribunal, hundreds of leagues

---

[1] Archivo nacional de Lima, Protocolo 223, Expte 5270.

away; if laymen, the secular courts, and if ecclesiastics, the spiritual judges, could not touch them. They were above all local law; they could indulge with impunity all evil passions, they could tyrannize at will over their neighbors, and even in civil matters they could set justice at defiance. It was idle for the Suprema to urge great care in their selection and strict investigation into their conduct when visitations were made, with rigorous punishment for their excesses. The material to select from was not abundant and was mostly evil; visitations never took place as planned, and punishment was rare. The repeated orders not to appoint frailes except in case of necessity and, when it was obligatory, to prefer Dominicans, is not to be regarded as a reflection on the regular Orders, but as arising from the desire to maintain discipline in the Orders, because, when a fraile obtained a position in the Inquisition, he threw off subjection to his prelate, and the injunction not to support them in disobedience was rarely observed.[1]

A memorial presented, in 1592, to the inquisitor-general, in the name of the clergy of Peru, complains of the appointment as commissioners of vicious, dishonest and turbulent persons, and confirms it by statements in detail concerning those of Cuzco, Potosí, Popayan, Camana, Arequipa, Guaymanga and Payta, while the familiars were no better. Successive inquisitors, from Cerezuela to Juan de Mañozca, admitted the fact but justified themselves by the argument that they had to take what they could get; the material to select from was too scarce to admit of selection, with the result that the officials abused their power in innumerable ways.[2] The only serious effort made to repress these evils was when Juan Ruiz de Prado was sent, in 1587, to Lima as *visitador*, clothed with full power to correct the abuses which had excited general complaint. He reported that much of his time was occupied in prosecuting commissioners and their notaries, who had

---

[1] Archivo nacional de Lima, *ubi sup.*—Archivo de Simancas, Inquisicion, Legajo 1465, fol. 23.
[2] Medina, Lima, I, 204–223; La Plata, 62–3, 113.

committed the gravest excesses; the tribunal, while cognizant of their evil ways, had only taken action in so far as to deprive two of them of their commissions, giving as an excuse that if it punished them it could find no others to take their places. Among those whom Prado disciplined was the priest Martin Barco de Centinera, commissioner of Cochachamba, well known as the author of *La Argentina*. The charges against him were grave but Prado did not wish to bring him three hundred leagues to answer them, so they were sent to him with orders to return them with his defence. It was proved that he treated the people of his district like Jews and Moors, that he revenged himself on all who offended him, and that he usurped the royal jurisdiction. At public banquets he drank to intoxication, he talked openly of his successful amours, he kept a married woman as a mistress and was generally scandalous in conversation and mode of life. Prado fined him in two hundred and fifty pesos and incapacitated him from holding office in the Inquisition.[1]

A single spasmodic effort such as that of Prado could effect no permanent result and, if it was difficult for the people, oppressed by these petty local despots, to make their wrongs known, it was equally difficult for the Lima tribunal to exercise its authority over such vast distances. The cruelty and injustice to which this exposed the accused were also extreme. On a simple denunciation, possibly for a trivial offence, and without proper preliminary investigation, he might be sent, perhaps in chains, from Buenos Ayres to Lima, exhausting in expenses whatever fortune he possessed. A practical illustration is furnished by the case of Francisco de Benavente, denounced in 1582, to the Commissioner of Tucuman because, when some one remarked that the Church was permanent, he had replied that it was not well said. The commissioner commenced to take testimony which so alarmed Benavente that he travelled six hundred leagues to present himself to the tribunal in Lima, which suspended the case and he

---

[1] Medina, Lima, I, 261; La Plata, 113–15.

travelled home again.[1] To a great extent this explains the inordinate procrastination in many of the trials, while the victim languished in his cell, for the evidence might have to be sent back for ratification, or fresh testimony might be sought and when, after years had been consumed in these preliminaries, he put in his defence, the interrogatories for his witnesses would be despatched over the same distance and their return would be awaited. These causes of delay were aggravated by the habitual negligence and indifference of all the officials concerned, so that a large portion of a man's life was often consumed in prison for an offence which ultimately might only merit a reprimand, or for which he might be acquitted.

Some relief was afforded when, in 1611, the tribunal of Cartagena was founded for the northern coastal territory and the islands. This was probably intended as the commencement of a systematic subdivision of the vast district for, a few years later, in anticipation of the erection of the bishopric of Buenos Ayres in 1620, the Suprema presented to Philip III an elaborate consulta strongly urging the establishment there of a tribunal. It pointed out that the arrests made in Lima showed the country to be full of Portuguese Judaizers, who had every facility of entrance and departure at Buenos Ayres. From there to Lima there were seven hundred leagues; the roads were good, the country populous and the Portuguese drove a thriving trade, enriching themselves and perverting the Indian converts. A commissioner would not answer, for he had to send seven hundred leagues to Lima, with as many in return, before he could act, while a tribunal could take note of every passenger landing or departing, and not only defend the faith but avert the political dangers threatened by the correspondence of these foreigners with the enemy. Besides, it was a great hardship when a man, for a slight offence such as blasphemy, had to be taken under guard for seven hundred leagues, at great cost, to be sentenced perhaps to abjure *de levi* and to hear a mass. If the projected cathedral were founded a prebend could be taken

---

[1] Medina, La Plata, p. 116.

to diminish the expense and a single inquisitor would suffice, as in Majorca.[1]

Given the necessity for the Inquisition, the arguments were unanswerable, but they elicited no response for the crown was impoverished and shrank from having to support another tribunal. About 1620 another effort was made by the procurator of the Atlantic provinces, in a memorial repeating the same arguments and suggesting that a district be formed of Rio de la Plata, Paraguay and Tucuman up to the boundaries of los Charcas, thus extending some three hundred leagues and leaving four hundred for the Lima tribunal.[2] This was referred to the Suprema which presented a consulta urging favorable action February 1, 1621, but the illness and speedy death of Philip III intervened and on March 31, 1623, it applied again to Philip IV, supporting its arguments with letters from the tribunal of Lima and the commissioner at Buenos Ayres, but to no effect. The next move came from the king, who, on April 12, 1630, communicated to the Suprema a paper describing how the Dutch lost no opportunity of introducing heretical books and perverting the natives of those regions. He thought it would be well to found an Inquisition in Buenos Ayres and, if the expenses were too great, there might be an inquisitor and a fiscal, while the other offices could be filled by wealthy men who would gladly serve gratuitously. Or, if this were too costly, a Dominican fraile could fill the post of inquisitor as in Naples and other parts of Italy, and he ordered the Suprema to arrange the matter accordingly. We shall see that in Peru, as in Mexico, the tribunal and Suprema evaded all efforts to relieve the royal treasury of the burden and can scarce wonder that Philip, with all his fanaticism, was economically disposed, but this did not suit the ideas of the Suprema. It replied in a consulta of April 17th, insisting that an inquisitor, fiscal, notary, alcaide and portero, with salaries and expenses aggregating at least six thousand ducats a year, were indispensable.

---

[1] Archivo de Simancas, Inquisicion, Libro 45, fol. 210.
[2] Medina, La Plata, pp. 200-7.

The other officials, whose time would not be exclusively occupied, might be selected from among opulent persons, and that by aiding to suppress the contraband trade of the Dutch the royal revenues could be correspondingly increased. The prospect of this outlay refrigerated Philip's zeal, and he returned the consulta with the endorsement that the disadvantages prevented the execution of the project; the Lima tribunal must appoint a commissioner of special ability and the governor would be ordered to assist him.[1]

This rebuff silenced the Suprema for the time but, on September 19, 1630, it returned to the charge. The Lima tribunal, in a letter of June 28, 1629, had related how a soldier in the port of Buenos Ayres, on the look-out for a vessel, had picked up on the shore a sealed package addressed "A las justicias del Perú" and on opening found it full of attacks on the papal and monarchical authority. This showed, it said, the audacity with which the heretics were disseminating their doctrines in those regions. They were also circulating tracts which had been seized, one of which was enclosed to prove to the king the necessity of ordering efficacious support to the Inquisition by the royal officials, and how desirable it would be to establish a tribunal at Buenos Ayres.[2] This appeal likewise fell on deaf ears and, on November 26, 1636, the Suprema forwarded to Lima the king's reply with corresponding instructions.[3]

The suggestion was renewed, March 1, 1636, by the fiscal of the Audiencia of la Plata, but this time the proposed seat of the tribunal was in Tucuman. This led the king, November 2, 1638, to ask for information from the audiencia, the viceroy and other authorities. To this the President of Charcas replied, warmly approving of the project, but for a wholly different reason, saying that during his years of service he had observed the great oppression of the people by the commissioners, maltreating them on

---

[1] Archivo de Simancas, Inquisicion, Libro 20, fol. 46.
[2] Ibidem, fol. 66.
[3] Medina, La Plata, pp. 207-8. I give the date as printed but think it probable that a typographical error has converted 1630 to 1636.

trivial pretexts, ordering them to appear at Lima with excessive cost and irreparable disgrace and molesting them in many ways, for which they dared not seek redress, for it lay at such a distance and the remedy was to them so horrible. The audiencia answered, March 10, 1640, recommending Córdoba de Tucuman as the most desirable seat. Two inquisitors and a fiscal, with salaries of two thousand pesos and a secretary with one thousand would suffice and would be largely defrayed by the fines and confiscations. Viceroy Chinchon delayed responding until September 29, 1641, when he said that it would be advantageous but costly; the salaries would have to be large, for living was dear, and the confiscations would be insufficient; in the last auto, although the culprits were many and of much reputed wealth, the property had almost wholly disappeared. Chinchon's successor, the Marquis of Mancera, had already written, June 8, 1641, that Chinchon had handed the matter over to him; he had referred it to the President of Chuquisaca, whose report he enclosed, and he dwelt upon the evil of the Portuguese who entered Paraguay by San Pablo and spread over the land.[1]

By this time the Portuguese and Catalan revolts gave Philip ample occupation, and the absolute exhaustion of the treasury forbade all thoughts of incurring avoidable expenses. When these pressing necessities diminished, the suggestion was renewed in 1662; the erection of an audiencia in the growing city of Buenos Ayres led the Lima tribunal to urge the establishment of an Inquisition there or in Córdoba de Tucuman. Communication with Spain was easy from there and two inquisitors would suffice, or one and a fiscal. The Suprema warmly advocated the measure, but favored Córdoba, which was only eight days' journey, or even only five, from Buenos Ayres. The failure of this effort seems to have discouraged further official attempts and we hear nothing more of the matter for nearly a century. In 1754 the Jesuit Pedro de Arroyo wrote to the procurador of his province in Spain, calling attention to the necessities of an additional

---
[1] Medina, La Plata, pp. 209–14; Lima, I, 331.

tribunal. That of Lima was so far off—a thousand leagues, he said—that it was of no use to them. In the twenty years spent in those provinces, he had never heard of an arrest by the Inquisition except one in Buenos Ayres, and then the prisoner escaped before reaching Lima; there was, however, a case of a cleric of Paraguay who spontaneously obeyed a summons to Lima. A commissioner had told him that, in ten or eleven years, he had had ten or eleven cases, which he had investigated and reported to Lima, but had never had a reply, except in the first case and this was not until two years had elapsed, by which time the culprit had disappeared. A second tribunal was now more necessary than ever, as the Portuguese were inundating the land. In the jurisdiction of Buenos Ayres they were said to number six thousand, and there was the same proportion in other districts; in that of Córdoba, the audiencia banished them some years ago, but they merely moved their residence and their places were taken by other Portuguese. About the same time Pedro de Logu, a calificador in Buenos Ayres, called attention to the mischief to religion arising from the scum collected there and subjected to no supervision; the powers of the commissioner were limited, he had no profit from his work and the introduction of prohibited books was frequent. These unofficial representations seem to have elicited no attention, but more authoritative was the memorial, in 1765, of Pedro Miguel, Archbishop of la Plata, whose residence there for twenty years had shown to him the necessity of a tribunal in Buenos Ayres. To this the fiscal of the Council of Indies replied, December 13, 1766, with an indifference which forms the measure of inquisitorial decadence. The rarity, he says, of cases of faith, attributable to the care exercised in preventing the immigration of descendants of infected persons, rendered it unnecessary to burden the fisc with the expenses of another tribunal; besides, the difficulty of reaching Lima restored to the bishops their inherent jurisdiction in such matters and they could sufficiently protect the faith.[1] It may

---

[1] Medina, La Plata, pp. 215-24; Lima, I, 332.

be hoped, for the good archbishop's peace of mind, that he did not avail himself of this unofficial authorization to set up an episcopal Inquisition.

It may be gathered from these ineffectual efforts to multiply tribunals that the financial question was as important in South America as we have seen it in Mexico. The experiences of the two Inquisitions were similar. When Cerezuela and his colleague went to Lima, they bore instructions to the royal officials to disburse to the receiver of confiscations ten thousand pesos a year for the salaries of the two inquisitors, the fiscal and the notary.[1] This made no provision for other inevitable expenses. The theory on which the Holy Office was based was that it should be self-sustaining—supported by the fines and confiscations which it inflicted—and that when these were in excess the surplus should enure to the royal fisc. In Lima, more clearly than in Mexico, Philip defined repeatedly that this royal subvention should continue only as long as there was deficiency from other sources of income. In the quarrels which speedily arose between the tribunal and the viceroy, Toledo kept it in some sort of subjection by making the inquisitors apply to him personally for their salaries. This was highly distasteful, and they seem to have endeavored to escape from it by excommunicating the royal officials who declined to honor their demands, for cédulas of July 17 and 27, 1572, addressed to the viceroy and inquisitors, prohibited them from drawing on the royal treasury and enforcing payment with censures; they were to hand in their accounts which were to be promptly paid, until the fines and penances and confiscations should suffice. If this meant that they should render accounts of these other sources of income, it received no attention. In Lima as in Mexico no effort on the part of the government could

---

[1] Medina, Lima, I, 2. Vicuña Mackenna asserts (Francisco Moyen, p. 112) that Philip granted the tribunal a dotation which produced an annual revenue of 32,817 pesos, 3½ reales, but this is a self-evident error, probably based on the king's assertion to Urban VIII that he spent 32,000 ducats a year on the three tribunals of Mexico, Lima and Cartagena.

obtain an insight into the finances of the tribunal and the royal subvention was indefinitely prolonged.¹

Still this did not provide for the salaries of the minor officials and the other unavoidable expenses. For awhile doubtless the tribunal felt the pinch of poverty. We find the Suprema suggesting that, if the prisons are insufficient, they can be made good out of the fines and penances; the alguacil is to be dismissed and, if another is appointed, he must serve without salary; possibly the viceroy may be induced to grant pensions on some of the vacant *repartimientos* of Indians. The tribunal astutely raised the question of the *ayuda de costa*, or supplementary payment to meet the expenses of the visitations, which it had no intention of making, and it was told to consult the viceroy and report, after which the Suprema would consult the king. In this it doubtless failed, but we chance to hear of an ayuda de costa paid as a reward for the auto de fe of 1578. Philip was by no means disposed to be liberal. In 1593 a question arose as to the salary of a fiscal *ad interim* and he rather grudgingly, by a cédula of February 7, 1594, ordered that one-half might be paid, until the confiscations should suffice.²

Meanwhile the activity of the tribunal was rapidly enabling it to emerge from its penury. Its correspondence with the Suprema between 1570 and 1594 shows that confiscations were continually decreed and were apparently profitable. Frequent references occur to the estate of a Dr. Quiñones, who owned a mine which was to be rented until sentence was pronounced and then was to be sold; he also had a library which seems to have been of value and was to be disposed of either in bulk or at retail. Up to 1583 the total receipts from confiscations amounted to thirty-eight thousand pesos, or an average of nearly three thousand per annum.³ Fines were also lucrative. Between 1571 and 1573

---

¹ Archivo de Simancas, Inquisicion, Libro 40, fol. 20, 21, 54, 91.—Medina, Lima, I, 187.—Archivo nacional de Lima, *ubi sup*.
² Archivo nacional de Lima, *ubi sup*.—Archivo de Simancas, Inquisicion, Libro 40, fol. 30.
³ Archivo nacional de Lima, *ubi sup*.—Medina, Lima, I, 202.

there were twenty-seven cases sentenced in the audience-chamber, yielding in all twenty-six hundred pesos of which a thousand were levied on Rodrigo de Arcas, parish priest of Ribera, for solicitation in the confessional. Between 1581 and 1585 fifty-seven cases, similarly sentenced in private, furnished eighty-three hundred pesos. In 1583 there came a piece of good fortune in a legacy of Pedro de la Peña, Bishop of Quito, who left to the tribunal twenty thousand pesos to build a chapel for his interment. The house and prison thus far occupied were unfitted for the growing activity of the tribunal; with the legacy and the proceeds of sale of the existing building, a much finer structure was erected, including a prison with twelve cells. With increasing business came increasing income and, while the pretext of poverty continued to be put forward to the king, the tribunal soon began to accumulate capital and place it at interest. In 1596, Inquisitor Ordoñez, while blaming the receiver Juan de Saracho, admitted that he had succeeded in amassing twenty thousand pesos, part of which sum was invested in censos or ground-rents. To this Ordoñez, by a happy stroke, added seven thousand more from the estate of Pedro González de Montalban, whose property had been sequestrated. He was very sick and obtained his liberation by making a will in favor of the tribunal.[1] The Portuguese Judaizers now began to occupy a constantly increasing share of the tribunal's attention, opening up a most prosperous field of operations. The time had come when the temporary subvention should be withdrawn, but the tribunal continued quietly to demand and receive it.

It was impossible to keep wholly secret the absorption of large estates and the investments of accumulating capital. The attention of Philip III was called to the matter and, in a letter of June 4, 1614, to the viceroy, he recited the conditions on which the grant had been made; he had learned that the salaries continued to be paid by the treasury, in spite of the receipt from these sources of amounts sufficient to defray them in whole or in part,

---

[1] Medina, Lima, I, 47-9, 188-95, 200, 304.

and he therefore ordered that, when the salaries were paid, the viceroy should inform himself of the receipts from other sources and deduct them from the charge on the treasury, making full reports to the king. This was evaded by the receiver giving a certificate such as he saw fit, of what moneys he had on hand, which naturally was found to be a worthless safe-guard, and the viceroy was ordered to require from the receiver a statement of all receipts every year. It was found impossible to procure this and Philip, in a letter to the Viceroy Squillace, April 26, 1618, after recalling all the previous attempts, ordered him to appoint from the treasury two experienced accountants to audit the receiver's accounts and report the result to the king. The accountants were duly appointed, but the receiver refused absolutely to exhibit his accounts—he had sent them to the inquisitor-general as he was required to do by his instructions. This exhausted the royal patience and one of the first acts of Philip IV was a letter to the viceroy, June 11, 1621, ordering the suspension of payments until the inquisitors should furnish authentic evidence that the confiscations had not sufficed to meet them. This went on for two years, the inquisitors preferring to forego the subvention rather than to expose the flourishing condition of their finances. They brought incessant pressure to bear, however, and finally induced Viceroy Guadalsacar, under a resolution of the treasury officials, to resume payments on the presentation of certain certificates of the contador, the scrivener of sequestrations and the receiver. On learning this the Council of Indies made a thorough investigation of the whole matter and reported that, in view of the exhaustion of the royal treasury, and that since the foundation of the tribunal, up to 1625, it had consumed six hundred and sixty-two thousand ducats without having returned anything from the fines and confiscations, it was wholly wrong that the money should have been used by the officials in buying lands and censos which they were now enjoying. To put an end to this the king, April 20, 1629, issued a cédula ordering that the conditions expressed in 1621 should be inviolably observed, no matter what might be the exigency, under pain not only of the royal displeasure but that all such disbursements should be charged to the viceroy and be deducted from his salary. To insure observance this cédula was to be entered on the books of the treasury and all auditors were to be governed by it.¹

These were brave words but it is probable that the Inquisition found means to render them nugatory, while an apparent compromise was sought at the expense of a third party—the Church. We have seen (Mexico, p. 216) how a prebend in each cathedral was suppressed at the first vacancy and the fruits were paid to the tribunal. The process was necessarily slow, commencing with the brief of Urban VIII, March 10, 1627, and delayed by waiting for the successive vacancies and also by resistance, in some cases, of the cathedral chapters.² It was

---

¹ Archivo de Simancas, Inquisicion, Libro 40, fol. 34, 35, 36, 54.—Recop. Lib. I, Tit. xix, ll. 10, 11, 12.—Solorzani de Indiar. Gubernat., Lib. III, cap. xxiv, n. 11.

² In the chapter of Santiago de Chile, one of the canons, Francisco Navarro, soon after the arrival of the royal order suppressing a prebend, withdrew to the convent of San Francisco. It was claimed that his retirement vacated the benefice; the matter was referred to the king who decided, by a decree of August 31, 1635, that this was the case. The canons adopted the favorite device of obeying without executing and were supported by the Audiencia, much to the disgust of the Dean, Tomas de Santiago, who was commissioner of the Inquisition. Meanwhile another of the canons, Gerónimo Salvatierra, died and the question was finally settled by a royal order of April 6, 1638, pronouncing the vacated prebend to be that of Salvatierra.

Commissioner Santiago had become violently inimical to some of the canons in the course of this dispute and undertook to gratify his revenge, when Manuel Bautista Pérez of Lima was burnt and his property was confiscated. One of his debtors to the amount of 2000 pesos was a prominent merchant of Santiago, Pedro Martínez Gago, whose property was seized by Santiago; some of the canons were indebted to him for trifling amounts and Santiago persecuted them. The quarrel assumed portentous dimensions through the violence of his proceedings and liberal use of excommunication, when a new bishop Fray Gaspar de Villaroel, made his appearance, and undertook to reduce Santiago to submission. In this he disregarded all the immunities of the Inquisition and, being supported by the civil power and the judiciary, he vindicated his episcopal supremacy by arresting the contumacious commissioner and imprisoning him in chains. Santiago boldly strove to make head against the united secular and ecclesiastical power of the province, but was finally forced to submit. Villaroel does not seem

virtually completed in 1635, when Philip wrote to the treasury officials, September 26th, that the senior Inquisitor, Juan de Mañozca, had advised him that the suppression of the prebends for the payment of salaries had been effected. The orders with regard to this are to be executed and, as he supposes that the arrearages of salaries have been paid, he writes to Mañozca that in future the prebends are to be applied to the salaries as the treasury is in urgent need of relief—which shows that up to that time the king had continued to pay them and even to make good the arrearages, in spite of the decisive provisions of 1629.[1] The prebends thus obtained were eight in number, in the cathedrals of Lima, Quito, Trugillo, Arequipa, Cuzco, Paz, Chuquisaca and Santiago de Chile. They produced, as we have seen, eleven thousand pesos a year, thus more than replacing the subvention. Further documents fail us here but, from the experience of Mexico and Cartagena, it is fairly to be assumed that, in spite of the prebends and of the large confiscations now coming in, the tribunal managed to continue drawing the subvention and, in 1677, there was still discussion of the subject.[2]

The time, in fact, had come when the finances of the tribunal were to be placed on an enduring foundation. We shall see hereafter the details of the *complicidad grande*, when nearly all the leading merchants in Lima, of Portuguese extraction, were arrested on charges of Judaism and their property was sequestrated. Arrests had commenced in 1634 and the tragedy culminated in the great auto of January 23, 1639. What was the amount acquired by the tribunal can never be known, but popular report estimated it as a million of pesos, and we have seen that Viceroy Chinchon reported that it virtually disappeared without any one knowing where it went. Philip IV, whose necessities

---

to have suffered for his audacity. In 1651 he was transferred to the see of Arequipa and in 1658 he became Archbishop of la Plata. When he died there, in 1665, his whole fortune was found to consist of six reales.—Mackenna, La Revista de Buenos Aires, Mayo, 1870, p. 102.

[1] Archivo de Simancas, Inquisicion, Libro 40, fol. 46.
[2] Ibidem, fol. 54.

were daily becoming greater, was led by the report of the enormous sequestrations to seek an explanation of the Suprema, which replied to him, December 19, 1636, that the sequestrations had been large but they shrank to almost nothing from the claims of creditors, some of which came from Spain.[1] Disappointed in this he wrote, March 30, 1637, congratulating the inquisitors on their zeal and suggesting that it appeared to him just that out of them the fisc should be reimbursed for its outlays on their salaries, and that enough should be set aside to provide for the future in case the prebends did not suffice. The inquisitors replied, with outward demonstrations of respect, that they would report to the Suprema to which the funds belonged; that as yet there had only been sequestrations, while innumerable claims on the property had been presented, and that many prisoners had been found innocent and their estates had been restored to them—to five of these, Pedro de Soria, Andrés Muñoz, Francisco Sotelo, Antonio de los Santos and Jorje Danila there had thus been returned a hundred and seventy-four thousand pesos. Philip made an attempt to investigate the matter by appointing, in 1643, with the assent of the Suprema, Dr. Martin Real as visitador to examine into the finances of the tribunals of Lima and Cartagena, but, as we shall see, he was baffled in Cartagena and, after stormy experiences, returned to Spain without reaching Lima.[2] Repulsed thus at every point, Philip resorted to somewhat arbitrary measures. In 1644 we find the Suprema complaining of the seizure at Seville of two or three large sequestrations sent there from Lima for settlement with creditors, and again of twenty thousand ducats' worth of wool taken by him, of which Alfonso Cardosso & Co. were demanding the surrender as owners.[3]

What share of the spoils the Suprema obtained it would be impossible to say. We happen to hear, in 1640, of twelve thousand pesos brought to it from Lima by Juan de Arostegui, which is doubtless only a portion of the amount doled out to it by the

---

[1] Archivo de Simancas Inq., Libro 21, fol. 72.   [2] Medina, Lima, II, 165–66.
[3] Archivo de Simancas, Inquisicion, Libro 36, fol. 74.

tribunal.¹ The latter, in fact, in its reports habitually belittled the results obtained or anticipated; it treated the Suprema as the Suprema treated the king. In reporting the arrests, in 1636, it was careful to point out that, although the prisoners were reputed to be wealthy and lived with ostentation, it was a deception, for in reality they were trading on borrowed money and had little of their own. This was a repetition of what it had said in 1631, when persecution of the Portuguese had already been going on for some years—the sequestrations made much show but with slender results; the real estate of the accused was held in order to gain the reputation of wealth, while in reality it was so encumbered as to be valueless, and the personal property was so concealed as to be undiscoverable.²

There were other productive sources of income besides the confiscations. One of these which was especially profitable was the "quebrantamientos de escrituras de juego." Gambling was almost universal and disgusted gamesters would frequently swear off under a penalty, attested by a notarial act; the pledge would inevitably be broken and the forfeit was usually contributed to the pious uses of the Inquisition. A statement of the deposits in the *arca de tres llaves*, or money-chest of the tribunal, from May 4, 1630, to August 31, 1634, shows 1449 pesos from fines, 4909 from donations and 35,829 from the *quebrantamientos*, or in all 42,187, representing an annual income of nearly nine thousand pesos from these sources alone.³ When to this we add the confiscations, the prebends and the constantly increasing returns from accumulating investments, it will be seen that the tribunal was rapidly growing in wealth and how factitious were the pleas on which it maintained its grip on the royal subvention.

When, in 1631, the office of alguazil was made saleable considerable sums were collected from this source. In 1641 the position of alguazil mayor of Santiago de Chile—a purely ornamental office, unsalaried but with contingent privileges—was bid up to

¹ Archivo de Simancas Inquisicion, Libro 21, fol. 261.
² Medina, Lima, II, 48, 167.   ³ Ibidem, 166.

6500 pesos.[1] As these commissions, however, were issued by the inquisitor-general it is probable that they were duly accounted for. Indeed, we have seen (p. 224) that the Suprema endeavored in this way to explain the remittances which it could not conceal.

Increasing wealth naturally led to multiplication of offices and generally careless expenditure. In 1674 the receiver or treasurer lamented that he had striven in vain to reduce the affairs of the tribunal to order. The revenues had fallen to 35,951 pesos and the expenses exceeded them. Still, he held that, in spite of the considerable remittances to the Suprema and the overgrown payroll, the income could be made to suffice if it were not for the expenditures of the inquisitors on their houses and their frequent elevation to bishoprics, after which they persisted in drawing their salaries.[2]

---

[1] Medina, Lima, II, 167.
[2] Ibidem, 251.

A statement of expenses for 1681 shows:

Salaries of fourteen officials	pesos 23,528.0
Yearly remittance to the Suprema	9,926.3
" " to its Secretary	496.2
" " to two other secretaries and two clerks at 275	1,100.0
	11,522.5
Maintenance of poor prisoners	850.0
Extraordinary expenses	2,800.0
Expenses of the cámara del secreto	250.0
	38,950.5
Spent in seven years on the houses of inquisitors	7,000.0

In giving this Medina (pp. 252–3) calls attention to the fact that in this enumeration are not included the salaries of a number of other officials mentioned by the receiver, as follows:

A third secretary	1000
Notario del juzgado	1400
Contador	200
Juez de los bienes confiscados	1000
Advocate of prisoners	200
Steward	300
Solicitador	100
Barber	100
	4300

There is significance in the annual payments to the secretaries of the Suprema whose good will might at any moment be useful.

The investments of the tribunal were principally in censos—rent-charges on real estate. When these fell into arrears the property was put up and sold at auction, apparently still subject to the rent, the arrearages being collected from the purchase-money, and the numerous references to these transactions show that they were by no means infrequent. Still, the Inquisition assumed that it was an indulgent creditor. When, about 1705, several successive bad harvests had rendered the farmers unable to pay their rents, they petitioned the viceroy for a reduction of the principal. In transmitting this request to the king, the viceroy asked the opinion of the various tribunals, to which the Inquisition replied that the principal should remain intact as the deficient harvests were temporary and the land retained its value: that it was different in Chile, where the censos on urban property were reduced in principal after the earthquake which ruined the buildings. The tribunal therefore recommended a postponement of arrears and reduction of interest until the bad season should pass; this was what it had done with its debtors; it had not thrown them in prison or put up the farms at auction, even though the arrears were large, proceeding with benignity and equity and treating each case on its merits.[1]

Under a succession of venal and unprincipled inquisitors, the finances of the tribunal became involved in confusion and the magnitude of the amounts at stake shows how successful it had been in accumulation. In 1733 the two inquisitors were Gaspar Ibañez de Peralta and Christóbal Sánchez Calderon. The former was old and failing and the latter was engaged, under the name of his chaplain, in mercantile operations with the funds of the tribunal with such success that, in 1739, he remitted eighty thousand pesos to Spain and had purchased a valuable property near Lima. He also spent five thousand in decorating his house, and when the security of the temporary receiver Juan Estéban Peña expired he opposed its renewal, resulting in heavy loss when Peña became bankrupt. The new receiver, Manuel de Ilarduy

---

[1] MSS. of White Library, Cornell University, n. 616, fol. 65.

speedily fell into default for more than two hundred and thirty thousand pesos and there were other deficiencies. In 1735 Diego de Unda was sent from Spain as fiscal with special orders to investigate the finances. In 1736 he reported that he found everything right except that when Calderon insisted that Ilarduy should render his accounts and deposit all funds in the chest and on the receiver's refusal, had embargoed his property, Ibañez verbally suspended the embargo, so that when, on the next day, the embargo was renewed, it was found that large amounts of silver and merchandise had been removed and there only remained a little silver dish and some vessels in his oratory. Still Ilarduy was forced to pay fifty thousand pesos and furnish securities amounting to a hundred and ten thousand more.

It seemed impossible to secure honest officials. Unda had brought with him as secretary of the tribunal Ignacio de Irazábal, who was made auditor. He was detected in passing false accounts for Ilarduy and was dismissed, as likewise was another secretary, Gerónimo de la Torre. The struggle between Calderon and Ilarduy became mortal, and the amounts at stake must have been large for the latter sent emissaries to Spain with a hundred thousand pesos with which to bribe the Suprema to dismiss the inquisitor. He succeeded in having a visitador sent with full powers to investigate and punish, with results that we shall see hereafter. It is only necessary here to say that Calderon's and Unda's property was sequestrated, to be released in 1747 by orders of the Suprema. A new factor had appeared on the scene when, in 1737, Mateo de Amusquíbar came as fiscal, to be not long afterwards promoted to the inquisitorship. He formed an alliance with Ilarduy; they were both Biscayans and the Biscayan faction became supreme. Unda died, May 27, 1748, and Calderon was living in retirement on his plantation. The vacancy was filled, in 1751 by Diego Rodríguez Delgado who came with special orders to investigate the finances. He promptly reported that it was impossible to examine the accounts of the receiver, which were in a state too confused to admit of verification. He had learned that the cost of maintaining the prisoners did not amount to more than a thousand pesos per annum, while it was charged at four thousand. There were seventy thousand due on the rents of farms and fruits of prebends and, by the reduction of exorbitant salaries this amount when collected could readily be increased to a hundred thousand, more than enough to rebuild the inquisition and its chapel, which had lain in ruins since the earthquake of 1746. Under the preceding receiver, the confiscation of Pedro Uban, condemned in 1736, had amounted to more than sixty thousand pesos, but no trace could be found of the existence or the expenditure of this sum. No reform however was possible in view of the alliance between Amusquíbar and Ilarduy. No reform, in fact, followed, although after all the actors had passed away, Calderon's property was seized to make good the deficit of Antonio Morante, an administrador whom he had appointed and kept in office without requiring security and, in 1773, a suit was in progress with the executor of his estate for over thirty thousand pesos, the outcome of which the records fail to inform us. Altogether, through these quarrels we obtain an inside view of venality and corruption which probably were not confined to this period. In 1751 we learn that Amusquíbar, on entering office in 1744, had remitted nineteen thousand pesos to the Suprema, since when nothing had been sent. The income had fallen to thirty thousand and there was little more than forty thousand in the chest.[1]

The inevitable results of dishonesty and disorder were heightened by external causes and, in 1777, we find the resources of the tribunal materially reduced. After the earthquake of 1746 the rate of interest on the censos had been lowered from five per cent. to three. There were few profitable confiscations to make

---

[1] Medina, Chile, II, 396; Lima, II, 315–19, 326, 331, 352–3.—Archivo nacional de Lima, Protocolo 225, Exp^{te} 5278.—Memorias de los Vireyes, IV, 490.

A salutary regulation required each viceroy, at the expiration of his term, to draw up an account of his experience and of the condition of affairs for the benefit of his successor. These, so far as recovered, were printed at Lima in 1859, under the title of *Memorias de los Vireyes*.

good the deficit, the fruits of the prebends were falling off and their collection was becoming difficult. In 1777 that of Quito owed about ten thousand pesos, that of Trujillo eleven thousand, that of Arequipa, owing to the decline in prices was greatly diminished in value. Salaries were in arrears to the extent of twenty thousand pesos and the efforts of the receiver to make collections were fruitless. The houses of the inquisitors were unfinished and Inquisitor Lopez Grillo was obliged to rent one, at the distance of a block from the tribunal. In 1784 the earthquake in Cuzco caused a further decline in the canonries of la Paz, Arequipa and Cuzco; an urgent request was made for the suppression of the office of the third inquisitor, and authority was asked to sell property in order to pay salaries.[1] All this betokens real distress and yet, although the administration of affairs can scarce be thought to have improved in the following years, when, in 1813, the decree of suppression was received in Lima and the property of the tribunal was inventoried for the benefit of the royal treasury, there were found in its chests ready money to the amount of 68,834 pesos, $3\frac{1}{4}$ reales, besides 2400 pesos of jewels confiscated on Inquisitor Unda and 2500, the valuation of the furniture of the chapel. From the statement of the auditor it appeared that the capital of the censos and value of the plantations belonging to the tribunal amounted to 1,508,518 pesos. A portion of this, however, was not its property but was held in trust for special purposes. Of the money on hand, 47,433 pesos were funds of the tribunal, while 13,325 pesos, 2 reales appertained to the Colegio de Santa Cruz, founded by Mateo Pastor de Velasco and Bernardino Olave for female foundlings, and placed under the charge of the Inquisition, also 8076 pesos, $1\frac{1}{4}$ reales was the balance on hand of a foundation known as of Zelayeta and Nuñez de Santiago. The capital of the Colegio de Santa Cruz amounted to 394,502 pesos, $6\frac{1}{2}$ reales; that of the other foundation is not stated but, assuming them together to be

---

[1] Medina, Lima, II, 382–3.

500,000 pesos, it would leave about a million for the accumulations of the tribunal.[1]

The men who were at the head of the tribunal, whatever may have been their reputation at home, were not, as a rule, able to resist the demoralizing influences around them, intensified by the irresponsible autocratic power conferred by their position. The only effective control possible to the Suprema lay in the appointment of a visitador or inspector, clothed with superior authority, and this was an expedient rarely resorted to, especially as the inspector was exposed to the same temptations and was apt to yield to them. The Suprema was not kept in ignorance of the derelictions of its appointees, for the inquisitors rarely worked in harmony. Deadly quarrels arose between them and they abused each other without stint in their communications to headquarters, while their subordinates were equally free in exposing the malfeasance of their superiors. The publication of much of this secret correspondence and of complaints of aggrieved parties by Señor Medina thus gives us an exceptional opportunity to gain an insight into the interior life of a tribunal and into its use of the enormous power which it enjoyed.

We have seen that the second inquisitor, Bustamente, died at Panamá, and that Cerezuela was alone in opening the tribunal. The fiscal, Alcedo, and the notary, Arrieta, were quarrelling mortally with each other, and both were writing to the Suprema, criticizing Cerezuela's inexperience and lack of self-assertion, and asking that the new inquisitor to be sent should be a man of greater force. Their wishes were gratified when Antonio Gutiérrez de Ulloa arrived, March 31, 1571. It was not long before his arbitrary and scandalous conduct aroused indignation, but those who dared to complain were made to suffer. Secret information, however, was conveyed to the Suprema and the viceroy, the Count del Villar, was unreserved in his communications to the king, representing that Ulloa kept spies in the viceregal palace, who carried off papers and documents and that he had

---

[1] Mackenna, p. 116.—Medina, Lima, II, 392.—Memorias de los Vireyes, VI, 51.

indirectly farmed the quicksilver mines of Guancavelica, making large sums to the detriment of the royal interests. A cleric named Gaspar Zapata de Mendoza, as representative of the clergy of Peru, after several vain attempts, managed to escape to Brazil; he was captured by the French and carried to Dieppe, whence he made his way to Spain, but it was not until 1592 that he was able to present in Toledo a memorial to Inquisitor-general Quiroga in which the conduct of Ulloa was set forth in detail. His promiscuous amours with maids and married women were notorious; he publicly kept as a concubine Catalina Morejon, a married woman, who used her influence to dictate appointments and modify sentences until, after repeated efforts, Villar succeeded in banishing her. On one occasion a husband found him in bed with his wife; Ulloa threatened him as inquisitor and he slunk away; another husband was less timid, he killed the wife and chased the adulterer through the streets. He was in the habit of walking the streets at night dressed as a cavalier, brawling and fighting, and on one Holy Thursday he supped with a number of strumpets. He and the Dominican Provincial, Fray Francisco de Valderrama, each had as mistress a relative of the other; when the three years of the provincialate ended, Valderrama aspired to be prior of the Lima convent, but the new Provincial, Agustin Montes, refused to appoint him because he was a bastard, whereupon Ulloa went to the convent, thrust a dagger to the provincial's breast and swore he would kill him, when Montes yielded. He was involved in perpetual contests with the judges and royal officials, whom he treated without ceremony or justice, interfering with their functions, of which a number of cases were given which, if not exaggerated, show that the land was at the mercy of the inquisitorial officials, who murdered, robbed and took women at their pleasure, and any who complained were fined or kept chained in prison. The limitations of the fuero enjoyed by the ministers of the Holy Office were disregarded and no one could obtain justice against them.[1]

---

[1] Medina, Lima, I, 44, 47, 204, 223.

Before this black catalogue of crime reached the Suprema, the complaints had shown that some interference was necessary, and it had sent as visitador Juan Ruiz de Prado, who reached Lima February 11, 1587. He had full authority to prosecute any members of the tribunal and to send them with the evidence to Spain for judgement, but those who anticipated relief were disappointed. As Villar writes, he took up his residence with Ulloa, and his officials were lodged with those of the tribunal, who made much of them. He made no secret that he came to take care of Ulloa's honor, so that all complainants were frightened off. Villar had his special grievances which show how impossible was efficient government, when a power existed within the state superior to the state itself. News was received that two ships had sailed from England for the Pacific; two Englishmen, John Drake, cousin of the famous Sir Francis, and Richard Farrel, who had been wrecked in the River Plate, had been sent to the Inquisition, as was the fashion with heretic prisoners; the viceroy desired to examine them to learn, if possible, something about the threatened corsairs and he asked the inquisitors to send the men to him or, if that was not possible, to allow one of his officers to examine them, or again, if that was impossible, to examine them themselves and communicate to him what they could learn; Ulloa was willing but Prado refused, saying that he would communicate with the Suprema who could inform the king, thus postponing for a year the information wanted at the moment. Then there came an alarm about some English ships on the coast, and Villar ordered all who were liable to military service to be in readiness to defend Callao. Ulloa and Prado assumed that their officials and familiars would fulfil their duty by guarding the buildings of the Inquisition, and gave instructions not to obey the viceroy's orders, who vainly pointed out to them that, in defending the city, their men would be defending the Inquisition. At the auto of 1587 they virtually took possession of the city, treated the viceroy as a private person subject to their orders, and grossly humiliated him, to all of which he submitted for the sake of peace. They meddled in everything, and with their unlimited power of excommunication and fines, no one dared to resist them. They summoned his secretaries before them and forced them to reveal everything, even of the most confidential character, and to produce official papers, of which they retained copies. They appointed royal officials as familiars, thus releasing them from all responsibility to the viceroy, to the courts and to their superiors. Villar declared himself helpless to remedy all this unless the king would interfere.[1]

The memorial of Mendoza tells the same story of the alliance between the visitador and the inquisitor, and mentions a case of a priest named Hernan Gutiérrez de Ulloa, who had lent a considerable sum to Inquisitor Ulloa and being unable to obtain repayment had procured a papal brief against him. Prado took the brief from him, fined him heavily, suspended him for a year from his benefice and sentenced him to four years' reclusion, the result being that he died under the persecution.[2]

The evil friendship between these men did not last long and, in January, 1588, Prado commenced the real duties of his office. He overhauled all the proceedings of the tribunal since its foundation, examining 1265 documents, his notes on which covered 1650 pages and fully substantiated his conclusions as to its irregular methods, its cruel delays, and its inflicting public penances for matters not of faith and beyond its jurisdiction. He reported that he had drawn up 216 charges against Ulloa, many of them applicable also to Cerezuela. There were six about his relations with women, involving much publicity and scandal, and there would have been more had he cared to investigate further in this direction. He said that Ulloa had accumulated considerable sums which he sent to Spain; he was virtually the farmer of the

---

[1] Medina, Lima, I, 223–47, 251. After Villar's term was ended, in 1590, the inquisitors prosecuted his secretary, Juan Bello, because, when some one insisted on having certain papers, Bello exclaimed impatiently that he could not have them even if God wished it, and also because he had said that he would rather have to do with demons than with the frailes.—Ibidem, p. 258.

[2] Ibidem, p. 217

quicksilver mines of Guancavelica, for when bids were invited he frightened off all bidders except his brother and an accomplice, who obtained the contract for twenty or thirty thousand pesos less than others were ready to offer. He kept around him a band of disreputable creatures, who ministered to his vices and were above the law. No one could collect debts of them, for when suit was brought he would order it discontinued and he was obeyed. When he was sole inquisitor he used to go hunting for a fortnight at a time, leaving the accused in prison and delaying their cases. Sometimes he took with him a certain mestizo who had a quarrel with another mestizo and was prosecuted in the royal court. Ulloa demanded the case, claiming that the defendant was his servant; the court demurred as the man was not *de familia* but only an occasional employee, whereupon he excommunicated the judge and all the alcaldes; they surrendered the case which was settled before him for eight pesos.[1]

When Prado presented the 216 charges, Ulloa quietly allowed a year to elapse before undertaking to answer them. Prado seems to have been in no hurry. Four years had been spent in the visit and the Suprema had repeatedly ordered his return, which he answered by alleging Ulloa's repeated absences, sometimes for months together, during which he could not leave the tribunal; then he gave sickness as an excuse, or that he had not a real with which to pay for the voyage. Finally he sent the papers by the secretary, Martínez de Marcolaeta, who started from Callao May 6, 1592, and reached Spain the same year. After this Ulloa no longer kept terms with him and ordered him to leave the tribunal, which he refused to do. Ulloa then denounced him to the Suprema, pointing out that he could have sailed at any departure of the fleets but that he desired to remain because he was in partnership with an Augustinian fraile, Francisco de Figueroa, whom he appointed commissioner at Trujillo and then at Potosí, where they made twenty-five thousand pesos. Ulloa publicly spoke of him in terms too opprobrious for any lackey

---

[1] Medina, Lima, I, 262, 264, 274, 277–80, 282.

to endure, and the fiscal, Arpide, joined in accusing him of unlawful gains, in granting licences to leave the country, and of protecting unworthy persons by appointing them as familiars. The Suprema attributed the quarrel to the close friendship which Prado had formed for a Dr. Salinas, a man of notoriously bad character, whom he had made advocate of prisoners and then of the fisc, in which capacity he had his suits brought before the tribunal, to the wronging of third parties.[1]

Finally the orders of the Suprema became so pressing that Prado was obliged to leave Lima, April 14, 1594, Ulloa managing so that he received no salary for his return. From Havana he sent a report of his visit, which was approved, not without some rebuke. Of the 216 charges against Ulloa, 118 were accepted and, by sentence of December 15, 1594, he was suspended for five years, fined and ordered to present himself before the inquisitor-general for reprimand—a sentence suggestive of the customary indulgence shown to official malfeasance. Prado also proposed thirty-one articles of reform, the most important of which was the deprivation of the fuero, in criminal cases, of familiars and servants of commissioners; subordinates of the tribunal were to have regular salaries so as to remove the temptation of accepting bribes, and there were many other suggestions for improving the operation of the tribunal, diminishing injustice and relieving the people from abusive extortions. The Suprema approved of all this and directed Prado to return to Lima and put the reform into execution, but, when these orders reached Havana, Prado had sailed for Spain; he did not get back to Lima until 1596, by which time Ulloa had escaped his sentence by dying and there is little trace of any reform by Prado, who died January 18, 1599.[2]

Meanwhile the vacant inquisitorship had been filled by the arrival, February 4, 1594, of the Licentiate Antonio Ordóñez y Flóres. Ulloa at once announced his intention of visiting the district, which he carried out in spite of his colleague's protest to delay until he should have familiarized himself with the busi-

---

[1] Medina, Lima, I, 283-6.   [2] Ibidem, pp. 327-8.

ness of the tribunal. Ulloa traversed the land spreading terror wherever he went by the indulgence of his passions. A memorial to the inquisitor-general, from a gentleman named Diego Vanegas, son of a judge of the Contratacion of Seville, affords an illustration of the reckless abuses possible under such institutions. When Ulloa, on his way to Charcas, stopped at Cuzco and lodged in the house of Francisco de Loaysa, a servant of the latter came where Vanegas and some friends were talking in the public square, and began boasting of the powers of the inquisitor which were the greatest on earth; there was, he said, the Licentiate Parra who had some words with a servant of Ulloa, in consequence of which he was arrested; Ulloa called him a dog of a Jew, an *ensambenitado*, with other insults and threw him in prison. Vanegas remarked that they did not wish to hear anything more about it, and for this he was seized and carried before Ulloa who called him a scoundrel, an Indian, a dog and other opprobrious epithets. Then summoning his servants, about twenty persons rushed in whom he told to kill the rascal. One of them gave him a severe cut on the head while the rest pummelled him. Doña Mariana, wife of the host, entered and interceded for him; Ulloa declared that he was going to give him five hundred lashes, but on her entreaty he diminished it to three hundred, then to two hundred and finally consented to send him to the corregidor with orders to banish him. Ulloa left Cuzco the next day but, hearing on the road that Vanegas had said that he would go to Spain to complain, he sent back orders to seize him. Vanegas was taken from his bed where he was recovering from his wounds, was thrown in prison in chains and the next day was carried to Siguana where Ulloa swore him on the cross, made him sign a paper without reading it and carried him to Potosí, where he lay chained in prison for four months. Thence he was sent two hundred leagues to Santa Cruz de la Sierra, as a soldier condemned to serve for three years on the frontier or in the galleys. Then he was returned in chains through Potosí to Misque, being wounded in an attempt to escape. Carried fifty leagues farther, still in chains, he effected his escape and, after many perils in four hundred leagues of travel, he reached Lima, where he reported to the viceroy and with his permission and that of Ordóñez he was allowed to sail for Spain to present his complaint.[1]

Ulloa continued his so-called visitation in this fashion until orders came in October, 1596, to Cepeda, President of the Audiencia of la Plata, to notify him that his commission would terminate in four months. He appealed to the viceroy who told him that he must obey it, and Cepeda ordered him to leave Potosí. He refused, alleging his health, but the corregidor, Alonso Osorio, communicated to him a further order of the Audiencia, requiring him to do so in ten days. He still pleaded sickness, but Osorio arrested him and all his servants and, after three days, ejected him from the city. He reached Lima, July 7, 1597, and died six days later at the age of 63. He attributed his disgrace to the report of a visitador of the Audiencia of Lima that he and his brother, whom he had made alguazil of the tribunal, had embezzled some three hundred thousand pesos.[2] If there were even partial truth in the statement the plea of the poverty of the tribunal can be understood.

Meanwhile Ordóñez had commenced his official career by letting it be known that all who had claims to collect within the district of the Inquisition could assign them to him, and they would divide the proceeds. This was an open invitation to the commission of fraud, resulting, as the secretary reported, in converting the Holy Office into a business office. He also took money from the chest—at one time as much as ten thousand pesos—which he confided to a merchant to trade for him in Mexico. Before the year was out, the receiver and the secretary were making bitter complaints of him to the Suprema—he was young, inexperienced, violent tempered and abusive. Those who came voluntarily to the tribunal to discharge their consciences were so ill-treated that they declared they would rather go to hell. He would order the secretary to alter the evidence and, if a witness

---

[1] Medina, Lima, I, 301, 313-17.   [2] Ibidem, pp. 317-18.

remonstrated, he would be abused and threatened. On his part he wrote equally unfavorable accounts of his subordinates; he knew that they assailed him but he ascribed this to the friends of Ulloa and Prado.[1]

Whether the Suprema believed these accusations or not, Ordóñez was not disturbed and continued to be sole inquisitor, with the exception of the brief second term of Prado from 1596 to 1599, until the arrival of Francisco Verdugo, a new inquisitor, towards the close of 1601. He was a man of different type, who had been advocate in the tribunal of Seville and fiscal in that of Murcia. While a strenuous persecutor of heresy, he was not inclined to abuse his office and he shortly reported to the Suprema that they had suspended a hundred *informaciones*—cases in preparation— which were without sufficient proof or were matters that did not concern the Holy Office. Ordóñez continued in office until 1612, when he became Archbishop of the Nuevo Reino de Granada, a promotion that was not to his taste, as he complained that the revenues of the see were insufficient for his decent support. Doubtless it afforded fewer opportunities than the inquisitorship.[2]

His successor, Andrés Juan Gaitan reached Lima, October 12, 1611; he had been fiscal of the tribunals of Cuenca and Seville and was therefore experienced in the work. About the same time Panamá, New Granada and the Antilles were detached from the tribunal of Lima on the founding of that of Cartagena.[3] In October, 1623, Verdugo left Lima to occupy the see of Guamanga, to which he had been promoted. For several years he and Gaitan had been on such bad terms that they would not speak to each other, and Gaitan had moreover quarrelled with the Viceroy Guadalcázar, who had resumed a certain repartimiento of Indians that he had granted to the inquisitor. His enforcement, moreover, of the royal orders about the payment of salaries was bitterly resented by the officials and intensified the embroilment. The vacancy left by Verdugo was soon filled by Juan de Mañozca who, after founding the tribunal of Cartagena, was sent as visitador

---

[1] Medina, Lima, I, 301-3.   [2] Ibidem, I, 329, 348.   [3] Ibidem, II, 5.

of the Audiencia of Quito and, in place of going there directly, came to Lima and occupied the position of inquisitor *ad interim* much to Gaitan's disgust. He reported to the Suprema that the condition of the tribunal was deplorable; unless some action was taken there would be no Inquisition, but only a gang of men obeying a will the most obdurate and most terrible that he had ever met, under which the tribunal was diverted from its proper functions to serve Gaitan's interest or caprices, for good or for ill. There was nothing with which he did not interfere, and that with such violence that he offended all good men, and even his own faction followed him rather through force than willingly. The fiscal was a coward; it was a pity to pay their salaries for they did nothing but impair the authority of the Holy Office.[1]

In October, 1625, Juan Gutiérrez Flóres arrived to take Verdugo's place. In consequence of Mañozca's representations he was ordered to make a secret report, which was equally unfavorable. Gaitan, he said, controlled the tribunal absolutely and supported all the claims of the officials without regard to justice. This was thoroughly understood by the people, and we can readily imagine the oppression and terrorism which afflicted the community. Flóres died, September 22, 1631; and the tribunal was reinforced by the appointment of Juan de Mañozca and Antonio de Castro y del Castillo. Gaitan continued to serve for some years, though infirm with age and sickness, accused to the last of abusing his position for gain.[2] There soon followed the Portuguese *complicidad grande*, of which more hereafter, and this, with the complications of the resultant confiscations, for years afforded the tribunal abundant occupation more or less legitimate. With its consequent enrichment there came torpidity and for many years it did little work and its annals are bare. In June, 1688, there came as inquisitor Francisco de Valera, transferred from the tribunal of Cartagena, in order to restore peace to that city, disturbed, as we shall see hereafter, by a prolonged conflict between him and the bishop, Benavides y Piedrola. This transfer

---

[1] Medina, Lima, II, 14–15.   [2] Ibidem, p. 16, 76–8.

had been arranged for 1685, but he had delayed obedience, awaiting the arrival of a successor and, on reaching Lima, he was met with a command from the Suprema to return to Spain, which he evaded on the ground that this would leave but a single inquisitor. He paid no attention to a royal cédula of April 1, 1691, ordering Viceroy Monclova to send him at once to Spain without listening to excuses, but this was to be expected, for royal commands were not obeyed by inquisitors unless they were transmitted by the Suprema. Finally the latter ordered his jubilation or retirement on half-pay—the usual punishment of inquisitors whose offences were too flagrant to be overlooked. This reached Lima in 1703, when the tribunal submissively answered that it would obey the command with due exactitude, but that Valera had died on the previous second day of August.[1]

Valera had imparted some vigor to the tribunal and had held public autos in 1693 and 1694, but there was not another until 1733. His death had seriously crippled the tribunal, for his colleague Burrelo had died in 1701, the third inquisitor Suárez was old and disabled by asthma, and the fiscal, Ponte y Andrade, was so prostrated with gout that, for twenty-two months prior to November, 1704, he could not venture out of doors. By this time the civil business of the tribunal was greater than that of the royal Audiencia and it necessarily fell into confusion, while matters of faith were neglected. Suárez asked the Suprema for help and it was rendered after the customary fashion, for the fiscal Ponte was appointed inquisitor and an old professor of law, who had sought the priesthood, Gaspar Ibañez, was made fiscal. Quarrels arose immediately, for Ibañez received his commission by private hand and was sworn in immediately, while that of Ponte came by the galleons. Suárez, who was a friend of Ibañez, endeavored to enforce the latter's seniority, which carried with it considerable emoluments, and this was resisted by Ponte. By this time there was no distinction of grade between inquisitor and fiscal; the latter had the title of inquisitor-fiscal, and the

---

[1] Medina, Lima, II, 253; Cartagena, pp. 343–44.

functions were interchangeable, although no one could perform both—that is of prosecutor and judge—in any given case. Ponte, in 1707, exhaled his griefs to the Suprema; his colleagues, he said, acted irregularly; Ibañez assumed to be both fiscal and inquisitor in the same case; the situation was desperate and the civil business was at a standstill.[1]

For more than a quarter of a century there was no improvement. Slender as was the business of the tribunal in matters of faith, it was greatly in arrears. Ibañez, who had become senior inquisitor, was sometimes unable to sit for three months at a time. Holidays, beyond those on the register, were taken until they amounted to half the days in the year. Gutiérrez de Cevallos, one of the inquisitors, on being made Bishop of Tucuman, in 1730, reported to the Suprema that he had been unable to expedite matters; there were prisoners who had been confined for thirteen years, of which eleven had passed since he had, as fiscal, presented the formal accusations—and we shall see that six more were to elapse before these dreary trials came to an end in the *quemadero*.[2]

Ibañez finally fell into dotage. Sánchez Calderon had become his colleague and Diego de Unda came as fiscal in 1735, to be rated as inquisitor when Mateo de Amusquíbar, in 1737, assumed the former position, to be in turn made inquisitor, in 1744, when he had attained the age of thirty, which was the minimum for that office. Allusion has been made above to the quarrels over the mismanagement of the finances by the receiver Ilarduy, with whom Amusquíbar formed an alliance. Amusquíbar wrote to the Suprema most damaging reports as to his colleagues; the irregularities committed in serious trials for heresy and the monstrous contradictions in civil cases. Unda, he said, acceded to all that Calderon did, and Calderon followed his own whims in opposition to the precise orders of the Suprema, while the same disregard of instructions was shown in appointments and in dismissals from office. There had, indeed, been gross irregularities in the trial culminating in the great auto of December 23, 1736,

---

[1] Medina, Lima, II, 212-14.   [2] Ibidem, pp. 283, 285.

in which a woman and two effigies had been relaxed. One of the effigies was that of a Jesuit Padre, Juan Francisco de Ulloa, who had died in 1710 with a reputation of sanctity; the Jesuits had made great efforts to avert it and were deeply incensed at the disgrace inflicted on the Society. This may perhaps aid to explain why, when Calderon and Unda sent their official relation of the cases, the Suprema had replied that it felt the greatest sorrow and scandal in seeing how the affairs of religion were treated, in offence both of religion and justice, and of the honor of the Holy Office, with the threat that, if in future the laws were not observed, the inquisitors would be dismissed. Calderon and Unda, moreover, were greatly discredited by their amours. They kept as concubines two sisters, Magdalena and Bartola Romo, the daughters of the alcaide of the prison. Magdalena had three daughters whom Calderon educated in the monastery of las Catalinas, where they were known as *las inquisidoras*. Romo was an accomplice of Ilarduy, but when Calderon and Unda dismissed others who were compromised, they retained him on account of their relations with his daughters.[1]

These scandals and Calderon's commercial enterprises were weapons used by Ilarduy who, as we have seen, sent to Spain emissaries with a hundred thousand pesos to accomplish Calderon's downfall. One of these, Felipe de Altolaguirre, Ilarduy's son-in-law, before his departure, openly boasted that he would not return without securing Calderon's dismissal, and after he came back he publicly spoke of having bribed the inquisitor-general and Suprema, while Ilarduy said that it had cost him forty thousand pesos.[2] What was attained was the appointment of a visitador, armed with supreme powers. The person selected was Pedro Antonio de Arenaza, inquisitor of Valencia, who was promised a salary of fourteen thousand pesos and perquisites. If Calderon is to be believed, Altolaguirre, the envoy of Ilarduy, told him that there

---

[1] Medina, Lima, II, 311–14, 317.—Joseph Bermudez de la Torre y Solier, Triunfos del S. Oficio Peruano, Lima, 1737.—Palma, p. 107.

[2] Medina, Lima, II, 318–19.

were rich pickings to be had from the fines to be imposed on the inquisitors; that he could make large profits from merchandise which he could carry with him; that he would have the appointment of corregidores in Piura and el Cercado, yielding him thirty-six thousand pesos; that his travelling expenses would be paid and that, on his return to Spain, he could not get a seat in the Suprema unless he took with him a hundred thousand pesos.[1] His experience in Madrid had evidently familiarized him with the depth of corruption existing there.

The impression conveyed by this is confirmed by the commercial aspect of the visitador's voyage, strangely at variance with its object of reforming abuses. To escape the risk of English cruisers, Altolaguirre and Arenaza sailed from Lisbon to Rio, the visitador taking with him a large assortment of goods and some negro slaves for sale. Rio was reached in the middle of 1744 and Buenos Ayres in November, whence they passed to Santiago and arrived in Lima early in March, 1745. On March 15th Arenaza presented his credentials and at once examined the funds in the chest. Two weeks later, when Unda went to the chapel as usual to hear mass, Arenaza's notary told him to go to Amusquíbar's house. As he was about to enter, the notary made him get into a carriage standing at the door, when, accompanied by a secretary, he was carried to the Franciscan convent in the neighboring village of la Magdalena, with orders to speak to no one. His property was at once embargoed, his house locked up and placed under guard.

Calderon was arrested in even more unceremonious fashion. He had been sick in bed for three days when Yrazabal, the alguazil mayor, who had been reinstated, penetrated to his apartments. His physician and chaplain, who were with him, were dismissed and an order was read suspending him from office, embargoing his property and ordering his departure for Limatamba. Yrazabal collected all the keys, and at once commenced an inventory which consumed two days. Calderon remained in bed under

---

[1] Medina, Lima, II, 319.

guard, with orders to speak to no one and no one was allowed to leave the premises. The next day he was sent, in Amusquíbar's coach, to Limatamba, where two Dominicans were ready to guard him and, on May 3, he was carried to Guaura. For a month there was busy search for the sequestrated property. Calderon declared that it consisted mostly of deposits confided to him, and he says that he was offered reinstatement and the withdrawal of the visitation, if he would give security for fifty thousand pesos and Unda for twenty thousand.[1]

Meanwhile Arenaza was openly retailing his negroes and his goods, through his secretary Gabiria, in rooms obligingly placed at his disposal by the Jesuits in their college. Ilarduy collected for him the proceeds and the traffic was so successful that Arenaza was speedily able to remit to Spain forty thousand four hundred pesos. The friendly assistance of the Jesuits was due not only to their rancor against Calderon, but also to their desire to shield one of their members, whose arrest had been ordered and evaded by hurrying him away and procuring the arrest of another party in his place. They were Arenaza's advisers and Calderon's transfer to the secret prison had been determined when an unlooked-for event changed the aspect of affairs. The Inquisitor-general, Manrique de Lara, died January 10, 1746, and was succeeded, July 26th, by Pardo y Cuesta. Calderon received the news by way of Potosí and claimed that Arenaza's commission expired with the grantor. He hastened to Lima where he recused Arenaza as his judge, threatened to shoot him and asked the Count of Superunda, then viceroy, to give him no support. Superunda was strongly in favor of Arenaza and ordered Calderon to leave the city within ten hours, nor does it need Calderon's accusation that he was bribed to this by the Jesuits. Arenaza, in a letter to his brother, asserts that Calderon attempted to buy him off and, when this failed, threatened him, but he would gain nothing by this "for I am resolved rather to be fried in a frying-pan in the public plaza."[2]

---

[1] Medina, Lima, II, 320–22.   [2] Ibidem, pp. 322–26.

Calderon's faction in the city had been active in discrediting Arenaza with pamphlets, lampoons and caricatures. The viceroy stood by him, holding that his commission emanated from the Suprema and had not lapsed, but still he sought to effect a settlement. At one time it was agreed that the inquisitors should resume their offices and the sequestrations be lifted, on their giving security in fifty thousand pesos to answer judicially to the charges but, from some cause, the arrangement fell through. Then came the great earthquake of October 28, 1746, followed by pestilence, which, for a time, suspended all action. Calderon had his agents at work with the Suprema, which resolved, in April, 1747, that the inquisitors should be restored and the sequestration be lifted; that Arenaza's functions should be limited to the subordinate officials, and that the viceroy should select some one to replace him as respected the inquisitors. It was nearly a year before these orders reached Peru, but, on March 4, 1748, Calderon and Unda entered the city triumphantly, in coaches escorted by a crowd of negroes and mulattos, with bands of music and scattering of flowers, while the bells of the convents of which they were patrons sounded a joyous peal, the demonstration continuing for two days.

Arenaza was humiliated and, when Superunda received a commission in blank for a new visitador, the warning was quite sufficient to deter any competent person from accepting the perilous position. All to whom it was offered declined, pointing out the fate of Arenaza and the danger of arousing enmities that would blast their honor and reputation. Superunda therefore brought Arenaza and the inquisitors together and, after a long conference, it was agreed that the sequestration should be lifted and that they would sit with Arenaza in the tribunal, but they failed to comply with their promise and the business was carried on by Arenaza and Amusquíbar. Unda died, May 27, 1748, of apoplexy following a visit paid to a house where he had illicit relations with the daughters. His funeral was dismal, even Calderon refusing to be present, saying that he had died as he had lived.

Superunda reported to the inquisitor-general that affairs were beyond remedy by a continuance of the visitation, and Arenaza was ordered to return to Spain. This order reached Lima at the close of 1750 and he sailed from Callao August 11, 1751, complaining bitterly that his salary of fourteen thousand pesos had been cut down to fifty-nine hundred. Amusquíbar, however, states that he was paid in addition eighteen thousand five hundred for his outward expenses and living and eight thousand for those of his return, which conflicts with the statement of Viceroy Superunda that he embarked wholly destitute of money. He died on the passage at Cartagena, but his secretary went on to Spain with the papers of the visitation.

The decision of the Suprema had suspended Calderon until he should answer judicially the charges made against him, and he consequently lived in retirement, while the tribunal was carried on by Amusquíbar and Rodríguez Delgado, who had been sent out to replace Unda. As usual they quarrelled and, in 1754, Amusquíbar formally demanded that his colleague should be removed by promotion to the episcopate, for he was inquisitor only in name, being utterly inefficient and incapable. Rodríguez, on his side, described Amusquíbar as arbitrary and impenetrably obstinate; a case had been ready for final sentence for a year, yet he could not be brought to agree as to its settlement. The sudden death of Rodríguez, however, October 31, 1756, restored peace and José de Salazar y Cevallos, who was appointed in his place, died in November, 1757, before he could assume possession, so that Amusquíbar remained sole inquisitor. He paid so little attention to his duties that in five months he was only three times in the audience-chamber and, on the plea of illness, he absented himself from Lima and appointed as his representative the fiscal, Bartolomé Lopez Grillo, an act which excited much adverse comment.

Meanwhile nothing was heard as to the dealings of the Suprema with the papers of the visitation. They seem to have been gone over with even more than customary deliberation and we chance to learn that, in 1762, Calderon was charged with improper conduct of the cases of Bartolomé Cortez de Umansoro and Andrés de Muguruza. In 1763 the Suprema adopted the expedient of sending to the Viceroy Armat y Yuniant blank commissions by which to appoint two competent ecclesiastics who with Amusquíbar should form the court to try the charges. The instructions reached Lima in 1764, by which time both Calderon and Amusquíbar had passed away and thus, some twenty years after its inception, the visitation died a natural death, every one concerned in it having passed to a higher jurisdiction.[1]

A paralysis had fallen on the tribunal and from this time its functions almost ceased, although its organization was kept complete and its pay-roll suffered no diminution. One of its last autos was held in 1773, in which only eight penitents appeared. Possibly this torpidity only rendered its official positions more attractive, for they came to be a matter of almost open bargain and sale. In 1789, Cristóbal de Cos, chief clerk in the secretariat of the Suprema, commenced to traffic in them through his agent, Fernando Piélago, one of the secretaries of the Lima tribunal. To save the expense of transportation, the Suprema had for some time adopted the practice of appointing natives or residents of Peru, which may have given rise to the sale of offices or may, perhaps, only have rendered it notorious, for Cos could not have transacted the business without the connivance and participation of his superiors. Piélago himself had paid three thousand pesos for his position, and Manuel de Vado Calderon the same, for the office of secretary of sequestrations. Narciso de Aragon gave six hundred for a minor position and three cases are mentioned in which sums were paid for jubilation, or retirement on half-pay, with the privilege of appointing a successor. The culmination was reached in the career of Pedro Zalduegui,

---

[1] Medina, Lima, II, 326–8, 331, 353–6.—Memorias de los Vireyes, IV, 69–72, 490–91.—Archivo nacional de Lima, Protocolo 225, Exp^{tes} 5276, 5278.

It is to the credit of Arenaza that, in the earthquake of 1746, which ruined the buildings of the Inquisition, the prisoners were rescued by his efforts, he himself sustaining injury and one of his servants being killed.—Medina, II, 331.

who commenced as sweeper and sacristan of the chapel of the tribunal. He was wholly illiterate, but he was a shrewd trader and he paid the capellan mayor of the tribunal a thousand pesos to surrender his place to him. Finally, through Piélago and Cos, he bought the position of inquisitor for the sum of fourteen thousand ducats; there was little concealment in the transaction and the scandal was great. The Suprema was obliged to order an investigation which it confided to the Inquisitors Abarca and Matienzo. In a letter of November 8, 1794, they confirmed the reports as to the sale of offices and the incompetence of those who bought them. Against this Zalduegui, in 1796, defended himself, by asserting that the trouble arose from his refusal to join with his colleagues in their mismanagement of the affairs of the tribunal for their private interests. At length he manifested his gross ignorance in a controversy with Bartolomé Guerrero on the intricate question of sanctifying grace; they obliged him to define his position and, on the strength of the doctrinal error involved, they prosecuted him and suspended him from office. That the Suprema restored him is fairly suggestive of another payment and he retained his office till the last.[1]

Inquisitors of the character thus indicated, owning no superior save the distant inquisitor-general and Suprema, armed with the terrible power of excommunication which none but themselves could remove, judging all and judged by none, could not fail to be a disturbing element in the colonial administration. They were at the head of a body of officials and familiars, scattered over the land, who enjoyed exemption from all other jurisdiction,

---

[1] Medina, Lima, II, 384–6, 398.

W. B. Stevenson, Secretary to Lord Cochrane, who was brought before the tribunal in 1813, shortly before the decree of suppression was received, gives a vivid description of Zalduegui—"I knew the inquisitors—but how changed from what at other times I had seen them! The pursy swarthy Abarca, in the centre, scarcely half filling his chair of state—the fat monster Zalduegui on his left, his corpulent paunch being oppressed by the arms of his chair, and blowing through his nostrils like an over-fed porpoise—the fiscal, Sobrino, on his right, knitting his black eye-brows and striving to produce in his unmeaning face the semblance of wisdom."—Twenty Years' Residence in South America, I, 264 (London, 1825).

secular and ecclesiastical, and who were sure, whatever crimes they might commit, to find protection and mercy in the tribunal. Even their servants and slaves had the benefit of this *fuero* and formed a peculiarly obnoxious class in the community. The maintenance and extension of these privileges involved the tribunal in constant strife with the authorities, lay and spiritual, quarrels which were carried on with a violence frequently destructive to the public peace. The governmental officials, however high-placed, who sought to curb inquisitorial arrogance, could have slender hope of support from their royal master. As we have seen in the chapter on Mexico, there was preserved in the Madrid archives the formula of a letter addressed to viceroys, insisting on their subservience to the Inquisition. This in 1603 was duly sent to the Marquis of Monterey, Viceroy of Peru.[1] How often this was repeated it would be impossible to say, but in 1655, at least, it was sent to the Count of Alba by Philip IV, as a warning in consequence of some squabbles in which he came to be involved with the tribunal.[2] When the colonial Inquisitions were founded, Philip II, by a cédula of August 16, 1570, took the inquisitors and all the officials under the royal protection and decreed that any one, no matter of what rank, who disturbed or injured them should incur the penalty of violating the safeguard, and this was repeated by Philip III in 1610.[3]

Francisco de Toledo, the first viceroy who had to deal with the Inquisition, was a man of decided character who, by holding the purse-strings, managed to keep within bounds Cerezuela, who was of a yielding disposition. There was dissension however, for which Alonso de Arceo, canon of la Plata, decried him as a heretic and a forger, whom the tribunal dared not accuse, but when Toledo asked it to prosecute him, it evaded the request.[4] The next viceroy, the Count del Villar, was weaker, while Ulloa, as we have seen, enforced the prerogatives of the Holy Office

---

[1] Hoyo, Relacion del auto de fe de 20 Dic. de 1694 (Lima, 1695).
[2] Medina, Lima, II, 183-5.
[3] Recop. de las Indias, Lib. I, Tit. xix, ley 2.   [4] Medina, Lima, I, 181.

with a masterful hand. The quarrels which arose were long and intricate and were conducted in a way to abase thoroughly the vice-regal authority. We have seen that Villar banished Catalina Morejon to put an end to the scandal of her relations with Inquisitor Ulloa; this may have been either the cause or a result of the ill-feeling between them, but motives for dissension could not be lacking, when the domineering spirit of the tribunal refused obedience to all constituted authority, and could always frame some excuse for asserting its superior jurisdiction.

May 30, 1587, the English made a descent on Payta, where they burnt some churches and convents and desecrated some images. They had been piloted into the port by Gerónimo de Rivas, an inhabitant of Payta, whom they had captured at sea and who remained after their departure. The deputy corregidor naturally arrested him and Villar ordered him to be sent by land to Lima for examination. In some way the inquisitorial commissioner, the Mercenarian Fray Pedro Martínez, was interested in him and to save him claimed and obtained him from the corregidor as a fautor of heretics, justiciable by the Inquisition. He was forwarded by sea to Lima and was withheld from the viceroy. In August Fray Martínez came to Lima to attend a chapter of his Order, which made him comendador of his ruined convent so that he could rebuild it. Villar, who felt much aggrieved, forbade the Provincial, Fray Thomas de Valdez, to issue the commission, but'the tribunal interposed and by threats of excommunication compelled its delivery. Soon after this, at the auto of November 30, 1587, there arose a quarrel, probably about the distribution of seats, which resulted in the excommunication of the viceroy, who was compelled to seek absolution.

Villar sustained an even more humiliating defeat in another encounter which exhibits the elasticity of inquisitorial jurisdiction. A young man named Antonio de Arpide y Ulloa (possibly of kin to Inquisitor Ulloa) came to Lima, with orders to admit him to a "lance" in the lancers of the guard, which was accordingly done. Ulloa appointed him fiscal of the tribunal, although, according to the Visitador Prado, he was naturally ill-conditioned, a youth in all things, careless in his office, and it was a scandal to see a fiscal wearing the garments of a layman. Villar thereupon discharged him from the guard, replacing him with Don Luis de Nevares, for the sufficient reason that the two positions were incompatible and that no one could enjoy two salaries. Arpide petitioned the tribunal for relief; as its official he was entitled to its fuero and the viceroy had no authority over him. The tribunal confirmed this view; the viceroy had no right to dismiss him, and it ordered, under a penalty of a thousand pesos, the officers of the guard to strike from the rolls the name of Nevares and replace that of Arpide, to whom the salary must be paid. The officers represented that they were under the viceroy's orders, when they were told that they had thus incurred excommunication and the penalty. The affair was put into the shape of a suit between Arpide and Nevares, in which the tribunal of course gave a decision in favor of the former and, when the latter appealed the Suprema, it refused to allow the appeal.

There was another source of trouble in the case of Dr. Salinas, a man of evil reputation, who was appointed advocate of prisoners. Previous to this appointment he had uttered disparaging remarks about the viceroy, and had a quarrel with his secretary Juan Bello. Villar procured the assent of Ruiz de Prado and arrested Salinas, prosecuted him and subjected him to severe torture in the course of the trial. Then the tribunal interfered and Villar surrendered him and all the papers. This did not satisfy Ulloa and Prado, who forgot their mutual strife and united to give the viceroy a final blow, as his five years' term of service was drawing to an end. Formal proceedings were commenced against him. September 26, 1589, Arpide as fiscal presented his *clamosa* or indictment, representing that Villar had always been disaffected to the Inquisition, had talked against it, had impeded it and had diminished its authority as far as he could. In the case of his secretary, Juan Bello, he had sent a threatening message; at the auto of November 30, 1587, he had invented means to deprive it of the services of its officials; as soon as Dr. Salinas received an appointment, he had prosecuted him for trifling words uttered long before; in the case of Gabriel Martínez de Esquivel, familiar in Huanuco, he had ordered him to report forthwith in Spain to the Council of Indies and, when asked by the tribunal for his reasons, he had made an offensive reply; he had even made investigations against the persons and reputations of the inquisitors themselves. From all this, which was notorious, it followed that he had incurred the pains and censures provided by the bull *Si de protegendis* of Pius V (April 1, 1569), against all who offend or despise the officials of the Inquisition, wherefore the tribunal was asked to declare him to have incurred these censures, notwithstanding any absolution *ad cautelam* which he might have obtained, so that he might serve as an example to all Christian people of their obligation to respect and reverence everything connected with the Holy Office.

Without going through the prescribed formalities of submitting the matter to calificadores and assembling consultores and, without hearing the accused, the tribunal that same morning decreed that Villar had incurred the censures of the bull of Pius V, while for the other penalties prescribed in it he was remitted to the Suprema. To this the viceroy replied, October 3d, that he had only sought to perform the duties of his office, but seeing that they had declared him to be under the excommunication of the bull, as an obedient son of the Church he begged for absolution and asked that it be speedy, as he was under orders to sail for Spain. For an answer to this he waited until the 16th, when he sent a judge and alcalde de corte, both consultors of the Inquisition, to the tribunal to enquire about his petition. There was read to them a reply, dated on the 14th, to the effect that the inquisitors had repeatedly intimated to him that he had incurred these censures and, in fact, it was so self-evident that every one could have known it, for every one knows that all incur them who impede the Inquisition directly or indirectly, or who ill-treat, in word or deed, the inquisitors or officials to the injury of their reputation and authority, and that good intentions are powerless to avert it. The viceroy's acts had been so notorious that it was needless to recite them and, before absolution could be granted, condign satisfaction must be rendered for them, especially to Dr. Diego de Salinas, while, as regarded the injuries to the Holy Office, he was referred to the Suprema. As it had long been evident that he was under these censures, without seeking their removal, and as he was about to undertake a long and perilous voyage, the inquisitors had been moved by loving charity to bring him to a recognition of the condition of his soul. They were ready to absolve him as soon as he should do what was requisite and, in consideration of his station, he should be spared the solemnities required by law.

After some parleying this portentous document was delivered to Villar on the 19th and on the 27th he replied at much length. He had never been told that he was under excommunication, or he would at once have applied for absolution. He had always favored and enriched the Inquisition; he had not proceeded against Dr. Salinas till assured by Prado that he could do so, and he had surrendered him and the papers, January 11, 1589, as soon as he was summoned. Then Prado, after consulting Ulloa, had given to Fray Pedro de Molina a commission to absolve him *ad cautelam*, in case he had incurred excommunication for that or anything else, and he had received the absolution with great satisfaction, but the certificate had been withdrawn more than a month ago, and since then he had abstained from hearing mass or taking the sacraments, except on the feast of San Francisco (October 4th) when he had special licence from the inquisitors. He did not know how he was to give satisfaction to Dr. Salinas, as the matter had been remitted to the Suprema which, with the king, would do as they might see fit. Meanwhile, as a gentleman and an humble and obedient son of the Church, he again prayed for absolution.

The victory of the tribunal and the humiliation of the viceroy were complete. When the inquisitors read his petition, October

27th, they issued to Antonio de Balcázar, provisor of the archdiocese, a commission to absolve him, at the same time admonishing him to present himself to the Suprema as early as possible. They also gave him the papers of the suit brought against him by Dr. Salinas, in order to enable him to make his defence before the Suprema. Villar received the absolution with much humility and satisfaction, as a great favor from the inquisitors, and on the 28th the provisor was summoned, who solemnly absolved him in the chapel of the palace.[1]

Yet Villar was so little reassured that, on his voyage home, he wrote from Havana to implore the protection of the king from the enmity of Salinas. He rehearsed the services of his ancestors to the monarchy, while of his children five sons had been killed and one crippled in the king's wars with heretics and infidels, two more were then serving and two were in training for service, while two had died in the priesthood. His fears were probably groundless for the Suprema, in a letter to Prado, blamed him for the dissensions in the tribunal which it attributed to his favor for Salinas, a man of such evil life and tortuous methods that he alone would throw any republic into discord. Apparently it did not as yet know that the secret of the influence of Salinas was the relations of his sister-in-law with Prado, a scandal which continued until Prado's recall.[2]

It has seemed worth while to give somewhat in detail the particulars of this obscure quarrel to illustrate the position adopted by the tribunal towards the highest authorities, its arrogant assumption of superiority, and the readiness with which its jurisdiction could be extended in any desired direction. It can easily be perceived how difficult was the task of the viceroys to maintain an efficient government, and to keep the peace with so independent and so unruly a factor in the land. But few of them escaped collisions, although it does not appear that in any subsequent case the quarrel went so far as the institution of a formal

---

[1] Archivo nacional de Lima, Protocolo 228, Exp.te 5287 (see Appendix).
[2] Medina, Lima, I, 263, 285-6, 290-2.

prosecution against the personal representative of the king. It is not surprising therefore that, however pious were the viceroys, they were almost unanimous in deprecating the acts and the influence of the Holy Office. The Count del Villar naturally exhaled his woes in long and lugubrious epistles to the king. His successor, the Count of Cañete, as early in his term as 1589, complained bitterly of the exemptions through which all connected with the Holy Office admitted responsibility to no one. This gave rise to endless trouble, for every one who was summoned to have his accounts examined, or who refused to pay his dues to the royal treasury, procured a familiarship or some office and with it secured exemption. Even Alvaro Ruiz de Navamuel, the government secretary, had himself made a familiar and auditor, and assumed that he was not subject to investigation. The royal officials were familiars—one of them at Arequipa, when called upon for his accounts, refused because he was a familiar.[1] Government conducted after this fashion seems like *opéra bouffe*.

In like manner the Viceroy Luis de Velasco, in 1604, represented strongly to Philip III the intrusion of the tribunal on other jurisdictions and its overbearing methods, so that the superior royal officials, on whom rested the peace and quiet of the land, had to abandon their rights to avoid scandals. As for himself, sometimes he temporized, sometimes he yielded, and sometimes he pretended not to see, in order to avoid dissension, for, when the tribunal was opposed, it made public demonstrations, which degraded the authority of the vice-regal office and of the Royal Audiencia. So, in 1609, the Viceroy Marquis of Montesclaros, in representing some scandalous ill-treatment of the alcaldes of the city, declared that the inquisitors were arbitrary and assumed that there was no power superior to them to restrain or even to resist them.[2] It was probably representations such as these which led to the concordias of 1610 and 1633. In these some of the more flagrant usurpations of authority were forbidden, but the

---

[1] Medina, Lima, II, 444. [2] Ibidem, 444, 449.

underlying principles were unchanged and we have seen how, in Mexico, the attempted reform was frustrated.

The Viceroy Count of Alba de Aliste was involved in many encounters with the tribunal, for which, as noted above, in 1655, Philip IV sent him a copy of the circular letter of 1603 commanding respect and obedience. This did not prevent him, in 1657, from writing that the reiteration and multiplication of its excesses of jurisdiction might render it necessary for him to break with it altogether, as the only way of maintaining the authority of the Government.[1] With the advent of the Bourbon dynasty, the consequent infusion of Gallicanism in Spain, and the resolute assertion of the regalías, the authority of the viceroys was more fully recognized, and we hear less, in the eighteenth century, of their struggles to maintain it against the tribunal. Yet the latter did not cease to assert the superiority of its jurisdiction and to extend it as far as possible, giving rise to a perpetual succession of embittered contests with the other judicial organizations, to the detriment of the public peace and the weakening of the functions of government. Even after its decadence had fairly set in, as late as 1773, the Viceroy Manuel Amat y Yunient writes that the Inquisition, so necessary for the purity of the faith, would be more useful and respected if it would confine itself to its proper functions, for its cognizance of civil cases has always led to collisions with the royal courts, which are particularly prejudicial at this distance from the king and, though there have been concordias and royal cédulas to prevent them, there are never lacking occasions to revive the contention to the great disquiet of the people.[2]

The eighteenth century, in fact, presents an almost continuous series of quarrels with all the different jurisdictions, the existence of which so greatly weakened the organization of the Spanish colonial system, and these quarrels were fought out with a persistent bitterness, sometimes degenerating into violence, which taxed to the utmost the efforts of the viceroys as peacemakers.

[1] Medina, Lima, II, 454.   [2] Memorias de los Vireyes, IV, 487.

Into the trivial details of these dreary conflicts it is not worth while to enter at length, but a single case may be briefly described, to illustrate the ferocity displayed by all parties and the confusion arising from the complexity of the multiplied judicial systems which influenced Spanish development so unfortunately.

On November 11, 1723, two brothers, the Licentiates Juan and Martin Lobaton, presented themselves before the tribunal to claim its protection. Juan was cura or parish priest of Soras and commissioner of the Inquisition in Guancabelica; Martin was cura of Viñao and "persona honesta" or cleric called in to be present when witnesses ratified their evidence. Both parishes were in the see of Guamanga, then *sede vacante* and governed by the chapter, which had required Juan to account for the property of an Indian woman, a parishioner who had died some two years previous, and it had ordered him not to leave Guamanga, under penalty of excommunication, whereupon he had promptly fled to Lima. In his case, the fiscal reported that the matter did not concern the Inquisition and the papers were returned to the episcopal Ordinary. Martin had assisted his brother's flight and for this he was confined to his house by the episcopal authorities and a coadjutor appointed, to the great scandal and destruction, we are told, of the parish. In this case the tribunal assumed jurisdiction; it ordered him, June 2, 1724, to be restored and his property released, on his giving security, and the chapter was ordered to prosecute before the Inquisition whatever charges it had to bring against him.

Martin meanwhile had the town of Guamanga as a prison. On the afternoon of April 30th, as he was standing in the street, the dean of the chapter, who was also commissioner of the Inquisition, passed in his carriage, then got out and scolded him roundly for not taking off his hat. Martin withdrew, but the dean, still unsatisfied, went to his house with the alcalde, broke open the door and embargoed all his goods—even to his clothes and breviary—then summoned the chapter and by 5 o'clock had him excommunicated and fined twenty pesos, as the papers stated, for not removing his hat to the dean an hour before, and notices of the excommunication were duly affixed to the doors of the churches.

When the inquisitorial sentence of June 2d was served upon the chapter it said that it had nothing against Martin, but when his embargoed property came to be restored much of it was found to have been stolen by the depositaries to whom it had been confided. The tribunal held the chapter responsible and ordered the loss to be made good, under threat of excommunication. The chapter replied, September 29th, that the case belonged to the bishop and chapter and its previous surrender of the papers had been without prejudice. Then Fray Luis de Cabrera, prior of the Augustinian convent, to whom the sentence had been sent as executor, excommunicated the chapter. The archdeacon as Commissioner of the Cruzada, declared the excommunication void, ordered the notices to be removed, and replaced them with others excommunicating Cabrera as a disturber of the Bull of the Cruzada. Cabrera responded by excommunicating the alguazil and notary of the Cruzada and, on October 2d, the archdeacon pronounced these excommunications to be null.

When the tribunal heard of this, by orders of October 18th and 27th it declared the excommunications on both sides to be null; it put the matter of the chapter in the hands of Luis de Mendoza, rector of the Jesuit college, and it ordered Cabrera to push the restitution of Martin's property, but not to employ censures without instructions. This was the situation when the new bishop, Alfonso Roldan, arrived at Lima and, on its being stated to him, he expressed himself as satisfied. Then Martin came before the tribunal asserting that one of the depositaries, Juan Joseph Lasco, who had stolen most of the goods, had pawned some silverware of his with a merchant named Joseph de Villanueva, and asking their restoration on his proving property. Consequently on March 14, 1725, orders were sent to Cabrera that, if the silver were proved to be Martin's, it should be deposited in safe hands. This was done on April 5th, when Villanueva deposed that Lasco had pawned with him ninety-three marks of silver plate. He was ordered to deposit it and promised to do so but, on the 7th, he testified that the day before the bishop had ordered him not to surrender the silver but to tell Cabrera to throw up the commission of the Inquisition and any other that he might hold. This was followed by the archdeacon notifying Martin to go to his parish in sixteen hours and, on his representing the impossibility of this, as he had been a prisoner for a year and was deprived of his property, he was posted as an excommunicate. After considerable delay he was absolved and was told to stay in the city, but on falling sick and unable to assist in the church, he was excommunicated again and recluded in his house.

All this is a one-sided relation, furnished by the tribunal to the Suprema. It evidently omits much that would show the tribunal in a less favorable light, as the outcome indicates, for in it there is nothing to justify the intervention of the viceroy and Audiencia. Yet we learn from another source that Cabrera had arbitrarily excommunicated and fined the alcalde of Guamanga who complained to the Audiencia, and on October 30, 1724, the viceroy notified the tribunal that the Audiencia, after considering the evidence, had resolved that the Inquisition should restrain its officials. A correspondence ensued, continued until the summer of 1725, in which the tribunal complained that the viceroy and Audiencia were assuming to be the superiors of the Inquisition, in violation of the laws and the royal cédulas. The affair finally took the shape of a competencia referred for settlement to the Suprema and the Council of Indies. The Suprema took high ground; it alone could review the acts of the tribunal or entertain appeals, and no other authority had power to intervene. This might have answered under Philip IV, but times had changed. A decree of Philip V, February 1, 1729, ordered it to correct the excesses of the tribunal by such means as it deemed requisite, and to this it replied, April 16th, that it had revoked the acts of the tribunal in the affair of Martin Lobaton, ordering the surrender of all papers to the Ordinary and judge of Cruzada before whom he must plead; that it had entirely disapproved the proceedings of the tribunal and that it had instructed the inquisitors hereafter to observe the provisions of the law.[1]

The Cruzada jurisdiction which emerges in this case was another of the subdivisions of judicial authority, which so fatally complicated the administration of justice in the Spanish dominions and furnished an abundant source of quarrels. The indulgence known as the Santa Cruzada supplied a large revenue to the crown and the organization for its sale was elaborate. At its head was a chief commissioner who held exclusive jurisdiction, civil and criminal, over his subordinates and, although this was by law confined to their official acts, yet it was, as we have just seen, extended to protect them in every way.[2] While the case just mentioned was in progress, another prolonged quarrel arose, similarly involving all three jurisdictions. Don Antonio de Marcategui, the priest of Quiquixana, was also a commissioner of the Inquisition. As such he was already engaged in a contest with the episcopal provisor of Cuzco, in which the Suprema decided against him and ordered all his acts to be revoked. While this was pending he celebrated mass in the chapter's chapel of the Virgin, on a feast-day, without first settling with the Cruzada for the indulgences gained there by the worshippers under some old concessions. For this Don Juan de Ugarte, commissioner of the Cruzada in Cuzco, on January 8, 1724, notified him that he was fined in three hundred pesos, and also excommunicated him without trial. Marcategui went to Cuzco and laid the matter before Bishop Arregui, who sided with Ugarte. After some further trouble the corregidor was sent to arrest him and sequestrate his property; he gathered together some Indians and Spaniards for resistance but thought better of it and escaped to Lima when, on appealing to the Inquisition, it declared all the pro-

---

[1] Bibl. nacional de Madrid, Seccion de MSS., R, 102, fol. 169.—Archivo de Simancas, Inquisicion, Libro 27, fol. 90, 106.—Memorias de los Vireyes, III, 85.
[2] Nueva Recopilacion, Lib. I, Tit. x, ley 10, n. 5.

ceedings to be invalid and ordered the surrender to it of all the papers. The bishop however sent his papers to the viceroy and Ugarte his to the Cruzada tribunal of Lima. The inquisitors demanded the former from the viceroy and asked him to compel the Cruzada to surrender the latter, but the viceroy refused, alleging that what he held concerned the royal *patronato* and that he had no control over the Cruzada, whose jurisdiction was ecclesiastical, exempt and privileged. To a second demand, he expressed the wise determination not to get entangled in ecclesiastical matters and jurisdictions, and he further claimed cognizance of the case of the corregidor, whom the Inquisition was prosecuting for sequestrating Marcategui's property and attempting his arrest. He stubbornly rejected repeated requests and he finally ordered the tribunal to suspend its summons to Ugarte to appear before it. The case was carried to Spain to vex the souls of the Suprema, the Council of Indies and the Commissioner of the Cruzada. In 1729 the king decided against the Inquisition and ordered the case to be surrendered to the Cruzada and the episcopal court, but it still dragged on and, in 1733, a royal decree ordered the Inquisition to obey the Concordias and the laws, but even this was not the end; how it was finally settled matters little; its only interest lies in illustrating the hopelessly impracticable character of Spanish colonial organization and administration.[1]

These defeats of the Inquisition were followed soon afterwards by a still greater invasion of the privileges of the inquisitorial employees. A citizen of Lima pursued a slave into the house of a salaried official, whereupon the tribunal forthwith ordered his arrest. The royal Audiencia intervened, representing to the viceroy, the Marquis of Castel-Fuerte, that the officials enjoyed only the passive and not the active fuero; that the pretensions of the Inquisition, if admitted, would destroy the royal jurisdiction, and that an order should be issued requiring the aggrieved party

---

[1] Bibl. nacional de Madrid, MSS., R, 102.—MSS. of Archivo nacional de Lima, Legajo 225, Expediente 5278.—Memorias de los Vireyes del Perú, III, 86–93.

to plead in the Audiencia. This opinion the viceroy sent to the tribunal with a request that it should abstain. It replied that the official had withdrawn his complaint on account of the apologies made to him, but that the tribunal could not assent to the position of the Audiencia without committing the grave fault of crippling its powers. A considerable correspondence ensued in which the Audiencia asserted decisively that, in matters not connected with faith, the officials of the Inquisition did not enjoy the fuero and much less the active fuero; that there were no laws or customs to contravene the settled principle that the plaintiff or prosecutor must seek the court of the defendant. To this the tribunal replied that the Audiencia had no authority to frame general rules in contravention of laws and customs, and that the matter must be settled by the Suprema. Castel-Fuerte rejoined that the competence of the royal court was not to be impugned, that the Suprema had cognizance only of matters of faith and that to admit the contrary was to place the whole administration of justice at the mercy of the tribunal.[1]

These were brave words which a century earlier would have consigned the utterer to disgrace. They were the denial of the privileges and exemptions which the Inquisition had enjoyed for nearly two centuries and a half, and their significance lies in their expression of the tendencies of the period. In time those tendencies brought about their inevitable development. In 1744 there was a contest over the will of D. Felix Antonio de Vargas, in the consulado or commercial court. A secretary of the tribunal claimed to have an interest in the estate, and it consequently asserted jurisdiction over the whole affair. This was resisted by the consulado, and Viceroy Villagarcia ordered a *sala de competencia* to decide between the conflicting claims, according to established rule. The tribunal refused, on the ground that its rights were too clear to be called in question. While this was pending, Superunda succeeded to Villagarcia and, after no little trouble, he induced the visitador Arenaza to agree to a *sala*

---

[1] Memorias de los Vireyes, III, 94–100.

reflexa, to determine whether a *sala de competencia* should be held. Then there came fresh trouble on the side of the senior judge of the Consulado, but finally the decision was reached that the officials of the Inquisition were entitled to the active fuero. When Superunda reported the matter to Fernando VI there resulted the royal cédula of June 20, 1751, declaring that the officials should enjoy only the passive fuero, and this in both civil cases and those criminal ones not excepted by the concordias, while their servants and the familiars were wholly deprived of it. In the case in question, the papers were to be surrendered to the Consulado; in future no sala reflexa was to be held and, when the matter was so clear as in this one, the viceroy should decide it, as the effort was manifestly an assault on the regalías.

By this time Arenaza had departed and the inquisitors were Amusquíbar and Rodríguez. The latter was disposed to accept the royal cédula without dispute, but Amusquíbar refused to obey it on the ground that it had not come with the confirmation of the Suprema. A long wrangle ensued, but at length another cédula of February 29, 1760, was received, ordering the observance of the previous one, and this time it was accompanied by a corresponding decree of the Suprema. These were communicated to the tribunal, March 24, 1761, which, seeing that further resistance was useless, promptly promised obedience. This was followed by a demand for the papers of the estate of Vargas, which, after an interval of seventeen years, was at length placed in train for adjudication.[1]

This settled the question as to the civil jurisdiction of the tribunal and simultaneously another case put an end to conflicts over criminal matters. A negro slave of the alguazil mayor had been arrested for some offence; the tribunal demanded the prisoner with its customary threats of fines and excommunications. The affair was pending when the cédula of 1760 was received; the Audiencia thereupon served on the tribunal an inhibition to issue letters of excommunication and fine against the alcaldes del

---

[1] Memorias de los Vireyes, IV, 73–6, 300.

crimen and proceeded to try the slave. The cédula was sent to all the judicial officers of the vice-royalty and they were ordered to defend the royal jurisdiction in all cases covered by it. To the arrogant temper of Amusquíbar this limitation of the traditional jurisdiction of the Inquisition must have been gall and wormwood, but it was worth much to the peace of the land. In 1796, the Viceroy, Frey Francisco Gil de Taboado y Lemos, tells us that it had put an end to the former conflicts between the jurisdictions.[1]

We have seen how neglectful was Amusquíbar of the real duties of his office, but he found time and energy to keep Barroeta y Angel, the Archbishop of Lima, in a condition of exasperation for years, and in this he seems to have had the support not only of the Suprema but of Fernando VI. What was the origin of the dissension between them does not appear, but Barroeta lost no opportunity of exercising his authority for Amusquíbar's annoyance and always to his own discomfiture. The rupture must already have been pronounced when, October 4, 1752, Barroeta wrote calling his attention to the fact that his licence as confessor had not been renewed, while in spite of this he continued his visits to the nunneries of the Recollects, which was unfitting his position and was prohibited; his ceasing these visits would relieve the Archbishop from further proceedings. This sharp provocation was disarmed by cool insolence. Amusquíbar delayed a reply until November 14th, when he simply said that he had postponed acknowledging the note in order to be temperate, and he now omitted answering it in order not to fail in the respect due to his own office and the dignity of the archbishop. Barroeta transmitted the correspondence to the Suprema for redress and obtained none. Amusquíbar, however, ceased his visits but kept up a correspondence. So it was, in 1756, when Barroeta called upon Amusquíbar and Rodríguez for a statement of settlements with creditors and sales of farms belonging to chaplaincies, in order that he might see that the

---

[1] Memorias de los Vireyes, IV, 300–2; V, 50.

souls of the founders were reaping the benefits designed in the foundations. The inquisitors replied that it was impossible and, on his asking why, replied that it was on account of the mode of his demand; the archbishop could send his fiscal and any special question about any special foundation would be answered. Again he forwarded the letters to the Suprema but its only action was to file them away. He had equal ill-luck in all the questions that he raised. In 1751 the Suprema sent to Amusquíbar its approval and that of the king, as to his conduct in an encounter with Barroeta over jubilee faculties for absolving for heresy. Then Barroeta claimed that the inquisitors should submit to him their licences to celebrate and hear confessions, but the king decided against him. Barroeta transferred the delegation of his inquisitorial jurisdiction from his Ordinary to another person; the tribunal disputed it and the king decided in its favor. He undertook to deprive the inquisitors of their faculties as confessors, and only provoked fresh rebukes from Spain. He issued an edict on fasting which the tribunal prohibited; then he printed it at the end of his Synodal Constitutions only to have the prohibition confirmed and the decision approved by the Suprema. There was a question about the notary of the episcopal court going to the tribunal to report certain acts, in which the Suprema sustained its action, and the visits of ceremony between them was a fruitful source of controversy.[1] Barroeta died, December 10, 1757, his whole episcopate marred with these little squabbles. It is all very petty, but it illustrates how the relations of the Inquisition with the spiritual authorities were as unfriendly as with the temporal.

Thus far we have considered the activity of the tribunal in matters foreign to its original purpose, which, indeed, were the most important portion of its record. As regards its proper function, that of maintaining the purity of the faith, its chief

---

[1] Archivo de Simancas, Inquisicion, Sala 39, Legajo 52.—Archivo nacional de Lima, Protocolo 225, Expedte 5278.

business in Peru, as in Spain, was with a class of cases which could only by forced construction be considered as heretical. Bigamists furnished a large proportion of penitents—the adventurer who left a wife in Andalusian Córdoba was apt to take a new one in Córdova de Tucuman and chance might at any time bring detection, while, even in Peru itself, distances were so great and intercommunication so difficult, that the seeker after fortune was easily tempted in his wanderings to duplicate the sacrament of matrimony. Blasphemy was another prolific source of prosecution, for the gambling habit was universal and lost none of its provocative character in crossing the ocean. Sorcery moreover, including the innumerable superstitions for creating love or hatred, curing or causing disease, bringing fortune or averting misfortune, and foretelling the future, which were technically held to include implicit or explicit pact with the demon, brought an ample store of culprits before the tribunal. To the mass of superstitious beliefs carried from home by the Spaniards were speedily superadded those of the native wise-women and a sprinkling taught by Guinea negro slaves. We find but few whites among these offenders, but every other caste is represented— negro, mulatto, quadroon, mestizo and sambo and sometimes Indian, for in this crime the jurisdiction of the Inquisition over the Indians seems to have been admitted. One feature of Indian sorcery which constantly meets us is the use of the drug coca, owing to the marvellous properties attributed to it, akin to the *peyote* which, in Mexico, was employed to produce fatidical dreams and revelations. Both of these were strictly prohibited by the respective Inquisitions.[1]

No specific cases of witchcraft occur in the autos de fe, but, in 1629, a special Edict of Faith directed against the occult arts and sorcery was published, enumerating all the forbidden practices in minute detail and forming a curious body of superstitions

---

[1] For the large part played in South American sorcery by coca see Granada, *Reseña de antiguas y modernas Supersticiones del Río de la Plata*, pp. 26, 30, 201, 208–9, 498, 501, 578 (Montevideo, 1896).

and folk-lore, much more extensive than anything of the kind issued in Spain. It brought in, we are told, numerous denunciations, but the practices were ineradicable and continued to flourish until the end. The virtual paralysis of the tribunal in the later years of Amusquíbar caused many complaints, among which was one from Córdova de Tucuman to the Suprema, representing that, in the interior provinces, sorcery was universal; there was no case of sickness that was not attributed to it, but denunciations and testimony sent to the tribunal received no attention and, as the civil magistrates were precluded from acting, it flourished unrepressed.[1]

Propositions, which furnished so large a portion of the work of the Spanish tribunals, afforded a much smaller percentage in Peru. This is probably attributable to lack of intellectual activity, for some of the cases tried indicate that the susceptibility of the Inquisition was as delicate as in Spain, and that there was the same readiness to denounce any careless speech or ill-sounding remark uttered in vexation or anger. Thus, in 1592, Felipe de Lujan was tried because, when looking at a picture of the Last Judgement, he said it was not well painted, for Christ was not with the Apostles. Juan de Arianza had the indelible disgrace of appearing in the auto of February 27, 1631, because, when reading the Scriptures, he exclaimed "Ea! there is nothing but living and dying," which sounded ill to those who heard it. A case, which came near to ending in tragedy, was that of Antonio de Campos who, for uttering certain heretical propositions and adhering to them pertinaciously, was condemned to relaxation. Fortunately for him the expense of a public auto was too great to be incurred for him and the Suprema was consulted, in 1672. During the delay thus caused it was found that his real name was Fray Teodoro de Ribera and that his brain had been turned by a potion given to him by a woman. This afforded a solution and he was handed over as insane to his Provincial. A case in 1721 is noteworthy as illustrating the dangers

---

[1] Medina, Lima, II. 35-41, 357

which environed all speculations connected with the Church. A Frenchman, known as Juan de Ullos, was denounced for saying that neither the pope nor a general council was the head of the Church. In due course this proposition was submitted to two calificadores, Padre Luis de Andrade, S. J., and the Mercenarian Fray Francisco Galiano. It was probably through some vague reference to Gallicanism that they reported that the qualification was difficult because the accused was a Frenchman, and for this they were imprisoned, with sequestration of their property.[1]

As we have already seen in Mexico (p. 241), one of the most frequent offences, not strictly heretical, with which the Inquisition had to deal, was that of so-called solicitation—the seduction of women by priests in the confessional, but as these offenders never appear in the relations of the autos, they are only to be gathered from more or less imperfect records. Prior to 1578 there had been various cases, about one of which, that of Antonio Hernández de Villaroel, the tribunal reported that it could not diminish the penalty of perpetual deprivation of confessing women, because this had been ordered by the Suprema in the case of Rodrigo de Arcos, and this was construed as a general law. If so, it was not long in force for, about 1580, we find Juan de Alarcon deprived for only three years. In a collection of cases between 1578 and 1581 there are seven of solicitation and between 1581 and 1585 there are eight. Thus they are constantly appearing and, in 1595, we are told that there were twenty-four priests in prison awaiting sentence, one of whom, Juan de Figueroa, was testified against by forty-three women. In 1597 seven priests were prosecuted from the province of Tucuman alone, where, among the Indian converts, few confessors seem to have had scruples.[2]

In view of the heinousness of the offence the treatment of culprits in Spain was remarkably lenient, but this was surpassed by the tenderness shown to them in Peru. Another fraile from

---

[1] Medina, La Plata, pp. 129–37; Lima, I, 311; II, 45, 225, 273.
[2] Medina, Lima, I, 139, 147, 188–95; La Plata, 122.—Palma, Añales, p. 51.

Tucuman, the Dominican Francisco Vázquez, was sentenced, in 1599, for this and for twenty-four scandalous propositions, but for this cumulation of offences he escaped with deprivation of confessing women and reclusion for a year in a convent. At the same time the Franciscan Bartolomé de la Cruz, Guardian of the convent at Santiago de Estero, against whom fifteen women testified, was deprived of confessing and had some spiritual penances. Fray Andrés Corral, Guardian of the convent at las Juntas, testified against by twenty-eight women, had aggravated the offence by committing rape in the church and for this he was banished from Tucuman and subjected to a discipline. On the other hand Rodrigo Ortiz Melgarejo, the only priest in Asuncion, denounced himself to the commissioner in 1594, to the delegate in Asuncion and to the tribunal in 1596, for guilt with seven women. He was obliged to go to Lima, where he presented himself in 1600. He was regarded as excessively scrupulous, he had performed a journey of over a thousand miles and this seems to have been thought an ample punishment. The fact that there was no evidence against him shows that the commissioner and his delegate regarded the matter as too trivial to gather testimony about it.[1]

In some of these cases the customary reading of the sentences before colleagues of the culprits was omitted because, as the tribunal explained, there were so many of them of various Orders that the omission seemed best to spare the honor of the religious bodies; the character of the Indian female witnesses was doubtful, but experience showed that they spoke truth, for most of the accused confessed and this was confirmed by the evil lives and example of all the frailes summoned from Tucuman. This had led the tribunal to deprive them perpetually of confessing women, even when the witnesses were Indians and few in number, especially as all those priests and frailes were very ignorant and profligate.[2]

Inquisitor Ordoñez, as we have seen, was not especially sensitive

---

[1] Medina, La Plata, pp. 122-5.   [2] Ibidem, pp. 125-6.

or straight-laced, but he felt compelled, in a letter of April 20, 1599, to call the attention of the Suprema to the frequency of solicitation, especially in Tucuman, where, as he said, it appeared that there was scarce a priest not guilty of it, and the worst feature was that some of them told the Indian women that the sin was no sin when committed with them, and it was consummated in the churches. He therefore asked authority to increase the punishment indicated in the Instructions and the Suprema accordingly gave permission to add service in the galleys—a permission, however, of which the tribunal seems never to have availed itself. So far from there being an improvement, the tribunal was led to issue, in 1630, a special edict to the effect that, notwithstanding the clauses in the annual Edict of Faith, the crime continued to prevail; that confessors ignored that it was strictly reserved to the Inquisition, and absolved the guilty as well as the penitents, without requiring the latter to denounce their seducers as prescribed by the papal decrees; further, that learned persons when consulted furnished opinions that these cases did not come within inquisitorial jurisdiction; wherefore all persons were required, within six days after notice, to denounce these offenders under pain of excommunication *latæ sententiæ*.[1]

It was all in vain and solicitation continued until the end to furnish a notable portion of the dwindling business of the tribunal. As late as 1806 the fiscal Sobrino reported to the Suprema that the worst criminals were to be found in the vice-royalty of Buenos Ayres, which was hastening to its ruin, especially through irreligious propositions and solicitation. Possibly wholesome severity might have placed some check on the persistency of the crime, but the same inexplicable tenderness continued to be shown to culprits. In 1737, Pedro de Zubieta, canon of Lima, denounced himself for soliciting Doña Lorenza de Fuentes, a nun in the convent of la Concepcion—a confession which she confirmed to some extent. Then Sor Eugenia Evangelista, of the convent del Prado, denounced him with details of the filthiest and most cor-

---
[1] Medina, Lima, I, 313; II, 474–8.

rupting talk. As, however, he was a person of consideration, the tribunal, before taking action, consulted the Suprema, with the result that, in 1743, he was merely reprimanded and advised to give up hearing confessions. Almost equal leniency was shown, in 1793, to the priest Fermin de Aguirre, whose sentence was read in the presence of twelve priests, when he abjured *de levi* and had some spiritual penances.[1]

More nearly akin to the real business of the Inquisition was its dealing with the class known as *beatas revelanderas*—women professing a holy life, specially favored by heaven with trances, revelations and visions, and gifted with spiritual attributes and powers. Popular superstition rendered this a profitable trade in Spain, where the Holy Office was perpetually engaged in exposing and punishing their impostures; Peru was equally afflicted; indeed, the boldness and grossness of their demands upon the credulity of the people exceeded even that displayed in the mother country.

Almost the first occupation of the new tribunal was a case of this kind. About 1568, in Lima, a young *endemoniada*, named María Pizarro, had visitations from the angel Gabriel, in which many things were revealed to her, including the Immaculate Conception. She was exorcised by numerous frailes, who accepted these revelations and carried them out to their ultimate conclusions. Conspicuous among these were the Padres Luis López and Gerónimo Ruiz Portillo, two of the three Jesuits selected by S. Francisco de Borja as the first missionaries of the Society sent to Peru, where they were received as angels of light. There were also several Dominicans—Fray Francisco de la Cruz, professor of theology and a man of such high repute that the Archbishop of Lima had proposed him as coadjutor—Fray Pedro de Toro, Fray Alonso Gasco, prior of the convent of Quito, and others of minor importance. Early in 1571 Gasco denounced himself to the Bishop of Quito and surrendered sundry objects which had been

---

[1] Medina, La Plata, p. 266; Lima, II, 307, 381.

blessed by the demon, among them a copy-book of blank paper, two pens and a cloth. The paper had the faculty that whatever was written on it was true, even in doubtful matters, and the cloth was a cure for disease. The bishop sent Gasco to the tribunal, where he was imprisoned, May 8, 1572; the others and María Pizarro were arrested at different times.

None of them seem to have denied their belief in the revelations. María fell sick, after making a full confession, in which she accused herself of having served as a succubus to the demon, and Padre Luis López of having corrupted her, of which she gave full details. She was several times thought to be dying, when her confessions were read over to her, which she altered several times, finally disculpating López and asserting herself to be a virgin—all of which was disproved. She died, December 11, 1573, and was secretly interred in the convent of la Merced.

The most conspicuous figure in the affair was Francisco de la Cruz; he stoutly maintained his belief that the revelations came from the angel, and he persistently asserted the doctrines deduced from them. The calificadores pronounced them to be heretical in the highest degree and him to be a heretic more dangerous than Luther, for under his teachings priests would be permitted to marry, laymen to practise polygamy, confession would be abolished and excommunication be disregarded, duels be allowed and soldiers permitted to enslave the Indians. Such a man teaching such principles could cause a revolution and overthrow the Spanish sovereignty. Moreover, by Doña Leonor de Valenzuela, a married woman, he had a child named Gravelico who was to be another Job and John the Baptist; he was now beginning to talk and to say that God was his father and the Virgin his mother. He was too dangerous an imp to be at large; the tribunal prudently seized him, secretly shipped him to Panamá and had him forwarded to Trujillo and placed with Don Juan de Sandoval. The fraile himself on trial was stubbornly pertinacious; his advocate and a *patron theológico* abandoned his defence, whereat he expressed his satisfaction; his sanity was called in question, but he defended his opinions with such dexterity that this excuse was abandoned; four theologians were let loose upon him to strive for his conversion, but his convictions were unalterable. There was no alternative but to condemn him to relaxation as a pertinacious and impenitent heretic, which was duly agreed to, July 14, 1576, after his trial had lasted for nearly five years. Then, on May 18, 1577, he was tortured without success to discover his intention in his heresies, and he waited for nearly a year more until the final act of the tragedy in the auto of April 1, 1578. As he was said to have repented at the last, he was probably strangled before burning.

The trial of Fray Pedro de Toro was approaching its conclusion, after more than three years of incarceration, when, in September, 1575, he was reported to be dangerously ill. A sentence of reconciliation was adopted and he was allowed to be sacramentally absolved. Early in January, 1576, he was nearing his end and on the 13th he was transferred to the house of a familiar, where he died on the 16th. He was secretly buried in the church of San Domingo and was reconciled in effigy in the auto of 1578.

Fray Alonso Gasco, although self-denounced, was moderately tortured on intention. He was sentenced to appear in the auto, to abjure *de vehementi*, to six years' reclusion in a monastery, he was deprived of celebrating for one year and perpetually of active and passive voice, teaching, preaching and confessing, and was to be sent to Spain to perform his penance. After the auto he was duly shipped by the fleet, April 20th, but on the voyage he talked about his case, which was forbidden by the Inquisition, and the tribunal asked the Suprema to prosecute him again. His place of reclusion was the convent of Jerez de la Frontera.

The Mercenarian, Fray Gaspar de la Huerta, was the *profeta oculto* of the revelations, and was mixed up in the affair; besides, he had administered sacraments without being in full orders and had managed communications in prison between the accomplices. He appeared in the auto, was degraded from his orders, received two hundred lashes and was sent to the galleys for life.

Then there was a poor man named Diego Vaca, who could neither read nor write, but who had some dreams which Cruz and Toro regarded as revelations. He was put on trial, but acknowledged his errors and the case was dropped. The Dominican Provincial, Fray Andres Velez, was brought into the affair because the prisoners had written to him and he had replied that efforts were making in Spain, with influence and money, to obtain relief from the tyranny of the inquisitors. Proceedings were commenced against him but he got wind of them and escaped to Spain early in 1575. The tribunal asked the Suprema to have him returned but he succeeded in averting this.

In all this affair some mysterious influence protected the Jesuits, who escaped prosecution with their accomplices. After the auto, however, Padre López was imprudent enough to say that Cruz had been insane, in spite of which the inquisitors had made a heretic of him and that he would not wish to have Cerezuela's conscience. The tribunal thereupon referred to its records which proved him to have been the principal exorciser of María Pizarro and to have corrupted her. It further gathered testimony showing him to be an habitual solicitor in confession and among his papers was found a tract impugning the rightful possession of Peru by Philip II—a document so treasonable that the viceroy sent a copy of it to the king, for such action as he might deem fit, seeing that López was one of the most prominent and influential of the Jesuits. On his trial, López admitted the evidence as to solicitation and confessed to other cases, although he argued that they were not technically *in actu confessionis*. He was spared appearance in an auto. His sentence was privately read in presence of eight Jesuit confessors and then again in the Jesuit college in presence of all the Jesuits, where a discipline was administered lasting the space of two *Misereres*. It bore that he was to be sent to Spain by the first fleet, being strictly, during the interval, confined in the college, *incomunicado*. In Spain he was to be recluded for two years in the Jesuit house of Triguera, after which for four years he was to be confined in some designated place and ten leagues around it; he was deprived perpetually of confessing women and for two years of confessing men. He was duly forwarded in the next fleet.¹

Doña Luisa Melgarejo was a bolder practitioner than María Pizarro. She had been the mistress of Dr. Juan de Soto, who had been compelled to marry her. For twelve years she carried on a profitable trade in ecstasies, revelations and other manifestations, and was largely consulted about marriages, undertaking voyages, obtaining positions and other similar matters, which brought in corresponding fees. Unbelievers compared her to the image of a saint and Dr. Soto to the basin under it for receiving offerings. When she was arrested, November 14, 1623, her writings, consisting of fifty-seven *cuadernos*, were seized in the hands of two Jesuits, Padres Contreras and Torres, and were found to be full of alterations and erasures by them to eliminate numerous heresies. Apparently the collusion of Jesuits indicated caution, and Inquisitor Gaitan, May 1, 1624, reported the matter to the Suprema and asked for instructions, with what result the records fail to inform us.² She did not appear in the auto of December 21, 1625, in which there figured four similar *embusteras*, who had traded on ecstasies and revelations. Three of these, María de Santo Domingo of Trujillo, Isabel de Ormaza and Isabel de Jesus of Lima, had given proof of exuberant imaginations in speculating upon the inexhaustible appetite for marvels.³

In the auto of March 16, 1693, there appeared Angela de Olivitos y Esquivel as an *embustera hipocrita*. She was a sempstress by trade and had not lived a moral life, as she had borne a child to one of her devotees. She was sentenced to reclusion for five years in a designated place and not to talk or write about revelations.⁴ She was probably an humble imitator of the queen of impostors, Angela Carranza. This remarkable woman was born in Tucuman about 1638. In 1665 she came to Lima and com-

---

¹ Medina, Lima, I, 57–117. ² Ibidem, II, 34–5.
³ Ibidem, pp. 27, 28, 30.
⁴ Hoyo, Relacion del Auto de Fe de 20 Diz. 1694, fol. 54 (Lima, 1695).

menced to have trances which she took care to be in public and mostly in the churches. In 1673 she began to write out her revelations, and learned men became her amanuenses till the product amounted to fifteen volumes of a thousand pages each, in a small and close handwriting. Her only qualifications were an exhaustless imagination and amazing audacity. In her youth her unchastity had been notorious and she confessed it in her trial; she was self-indulgent in eating and sleeping, foul and indecent in her talk and had no shame in exposing her person. Such was the impostor who for fifteen years, by mere dint of self-assertion, made herself feared and revered not only in Lima but throughout Peru. As Inquisitor Valera says, in his report of the case, "She, who was the common sewer of errors, was regarded as a paradise of perfections. In the mistaken apprehensions of men she was the saint of the age, the wonder of the world, the mistress of mysticism, the advocate of the people; so frequent were the accepted miracles, ecstasies, trances, intelligences and revelations that heaven was regarded as condensed in her.... Rosaries and beads were taken to her house not one by one but in whole chests and they passed to Spain and even to Rome with her renown .... In the common belief of the kingdom, naught was lacking to her but canonization and the altar. Fragments of what she had touched were cherished with the belief that they would soon become relics....She deceived the human race in this kingdom—viceroys, archbishops, bishops and prelates." She threatened and prophesied death to those who displeased her, and few there were who could resist the superstitious terror that came over them when she uttered her evil forecasts. Those who did not believe in her she maligned, and we are told that it greatly injured their prospects on account of her repute, not only among the vulgar but among the learned and wise, who regarded her words as oracles from heaven. The profound faith which she inspired is illustrated by the incident that when, after the earthquake of 1687, there was an inundation, and at night the report was spread that the sea was engulfing the land, there was a panic in which all who could fled to the mountains. A man in charge of the chest in which her writings were kept said to his assistant that there was no danger of the sea rising to the writings of the angel, even if it covered the whole earth, so the two mounted the chest and stood there until the terror passed.[1]

It argues a surprisingly low level of intelligence that men of the highest station in State and Church, of presumable culture in the learned professions, and of common-sense in the business walks of life, should have accepted without question the vulgar absurdities, poured forth in a constant stream, which reduced the awful mysteries of the spiritual world to the basest condition of common life, and represented the vituperative, coarse, grasping, self-indulgent woman, whom they saw leading an animal existence, as the one human being selected by God to be the repository of his powers over heaven, purgatory and hell, so that the Holy Ghost had told her that she was the daughter of the Father, the mother of the Son, the spouse of the Holy Ghost and the *sagrario* of the Trinity, and once, in presence of the Trinity, the Son made her take his seat for he wished her to form the Trinity with the Father and Holy Ghost. She threatened that she would wake up the pope and cardinals and knock them on the head to make them define the mystery of the Immaculate Conception. Once on entering the church of the Incarnation she met the Virgin, who offered her the breast; on sucking she complained that the milk was salt, and the Virgin replied that it had become so in waiting for her. Christ, with the Virgin, angels and saints, once entered her chamber; he asked for a chair and wanted to know whether he had to sit on the bench with the rest, after which the bench was greatly prized by her devotees as a relic. It would be endless to repeat all these absurdities which met with such devout credence and a single one of her stories will suffice. In a field of straw she saw Christ walking hand in hand with a young girl dressed as a beata. Filled with jealousy she set fire to the straw

---

[1] Hoyo, Relacion, fol. 2, 3, 34, 36, 38, 39, 43, 44, 45, 48.—Medina, Lima, II, 258.

and left Christ burning, and when the angels remonstrated she said she was going to purgatory to release souls and then to hell to do the same. She went to purgatory and released many souls, but some would not go, among them her father, who said that his time would not come until she was dead, when she replied that he would have to wait, for she was still a young girl.[1]

She did a thriving business in many ways. She carried to heaven beads, rosaries, candles, bells, swords and rosemary, which were blessed on various saints' days and possessed special virtues accordingly. They were brought to her for the purpose by the basketful and, on one occasion, Christ was vexed and said "This is a huckster business." When she was condemned and they were brought in they filled a room in the Inquisition. Once she lent her shoes to the Virgin, whereupon Christ gave to her shoes the same virtue as that of the rosaries, which made a great demand for her old shoes. This kept her in foot-gear, for new shoes were constantly brought to exchange for her old ones. Her intervention was continually invoked in cases of sickness and difficulty, and her prophetic power was sought in marriages, voyages and enterprises of all kinds. These she sold at a round price and she had a cashier who kept an itemized account of her receipts—so much for a case of mumps, so much for fever, so much for the miracle of the ingots—and some of the entries were of one and two thousand pesos.[2]

After fifteen years of success, there would seem no reason why this career might not have continued until her death, to be followed with a demand for her canonization supported by ample store of miracles. Possibly there may be truth in the story that, on a rainy day in the calle del Rastro, she disputed the sidewalk with a Franciscan fraile, who rudely elbowed her into the mud. This caused such indignation that the offender expiated his clownishness with two months in the convent prison, when, to satisfy his rancor, he kept close watch on her and obtained proof that she was a sinner, whereupon he denounced her to the Inqui-

---

[1] Hoyo, fol. 16, 27, 28, 40, 42.   [2] Ibidem, fol. 17, 18, 39.

sition.¹ If so, the denunciation came to one ready to act upon it in spite of the shock given to public opinion. Inquisitor Valera, whose resolute aggressiveness had rendered his career in Cartagena one of perpetual turbulence, had just been transferred to Lima, and doubtless eagerly seized the occasion to make an impression in his new post. Angela de Dios, as she called herself, was arrested December 21, 1688. The trial lasted for six years, owing doubtless to the immense mass of her writings to be examined, and her numerous heresies to be characterized and condemned, for she had ventured upon dangerous theological ground and had constructed a grotesque theogony to prove the Immaculate Conception. In her prolonged incarceration she professed to be still comforted by visits from Christ and the Virgin; she bore her confinement cheerfully, was eager for her three meals a day, and was generally found snoring when her cell was entered.²

Her system of defence was shrewd. She denied having given assent or belief to what was expressed in her writings; she had merely recited what she had seen and heard in her trances and submitted it to the learned men who were her confessors. Finally on June 2, 1694, she asked for an audience in which she said that, enlightened by God through this holy tribunal, she had been illuminated to detest the doctrines and propositions in her writings, which she now saw were heretical and blasphemous and defamatory. There had been, she said, no deception on her part as to her visions, and she had referred them to those whose virtue and religion enabled them to counsel her. Under their command she had reduced them to writing; she had wanted to burn the writings, but had been forbidden to do so and had never seen them after they left her hands. Now that the tribunal had condemned them she asked pardon of God and of his judges and ministers, for she saw that she had been deceived. Nothing more could be required and her sentence soon followed, which bore that she was to appear in a public auto, to abjure *de vehementi*, to be confined in a monastery for four years, to be deprived

---

¹ Palma, p. 67.   ² Hoyo, fol. 8, 9, 11, 49–50.

of pen and ink, and never to treat of revelations, together with sundry spiritual exercises and ten years' exile from Lima and Tucuman, while a public edict ordered the surrender of all beads, rosaries, nail-parings and other objects treasured as relics.[1]

A public auto was arranged for December 20, 1694, but, so great was the popular revulsion of feeling against her, that it was not deemed safe to let her appear in the procession from the Inquisition to the church of San Domingo. She was secretly conveyed thither in a closed carriage two hours before day-break, and after the ceremonies she was not returned to the tribunal with the other penitents. She was kept until late in the afternoon and then, by a back door, was placed in the carriage with two persons of rank. In spite of these precautions some boys divined the truth and commenced stoning the carriage. Crowds gathered and a guard of soldiers was brought, but to little purpose, for the stones flew thicker and thicker; one of the occupants was seriously injured and it was as though by miracle that the carriage reached the Inquisition without being wrecked. Similar caution was observed in keeping her there for a month and conveying her to her place of reclusion. Meanwhile all over Lima boys were celebrating mock autos, carrying her effigies in procession and scourging and burning them.[2] It was probably the number and high station of her devotees that prevented a general prosecution, for only her three confessors, Ignacio Ixar, priest of San Marcelo, and the Augustinians, Fray José de Prado and Fray Agustin Roman, were arrested and tried.[3]

Among her revelations were some concerning an Indian tailor, Nicolás de Aillon known as Nicolás de Dios, who died November 7, 1677, with the reputation of a servant of God, and was represented as having been carried immediately to heaven by Christ, taking with him a crowd of souls from purgatory. His widow sought to establish his sanctity and the Jesuit, Bernardo Sartolo, wrote a book, published in Madrid in 1684, in which he accepted Angela's story as true and praised without stint the tailor's

---

[1] Hoyo, fol. 50–1.   [2] Ibidem, fol. 51–3.   [3] Medina, Lima, II, 262.

confessor, Fray Pedro de Avila Tamayo, who had been punished by the Inquisition as a scandalous corrupter of women in the confessional. When the book reached Lima it excited a lively discussion and was prohibited by the tribunal. The efforts to canonize Aillon, however, were not relinquished, for, in 1711, papal letters were received by the archbishop, ordering him to collect information as to the life and virtues of the candidate. What was done is not recorded, but we may assume that the response caused the affair to be dropped.[1]

The popular detestation excited by Angela Carranza seems to have served as a deterrent on impostures of the kind, for no other cases are on record until about 1720, when a quadroon named María Josepha de la Encarnacion was prosecuted for visions and revelations. She was not treated as leniently as Angela for, although she was perfectly harmless and had attempted no speculations on her devotees, and although, during her trial, she was so ill that she had to be transferred to a hospital, she was visited with the cruel punishment of two hundred lashes through the streets of Lima.[2] If subsequent cases occurred, their records have failed to reach us.

Mystic Illuminism and Quietism, which called for such energetic repression by the Spanish tribunals, seem to have had little currency in the more stagnant spiritual life of Peru. There is only one group of cases in the records, but these cast so much light on inquisitorial methods that they deserve treatment in some detail.

In November, 1709, there died at Santiago de Chile the Jesuit Padre Francisco de Ulloa, a man of little education but of high spiritual gifts, nourished on the mysticism of Tauler. He had devoted himself to the direction of consciences and had a circle of about thirty devotees, many of them nuns, who reverenced

---

[1] Medina Lima, II, 262, 264.—Index Prohib. et Expurg., 1747, I, 124. The title of Sartolo's book was "Vida admirable y muerte prodigioso de Nicolás de Ayllon y con nombre mas que curioso Nicolás de Dios, natural de Clayo en las Indias del Perú." Madrid, 1684.

[2] Medina, Lima, II, 241.

him as a saint. On his death-bed he committed his flock to another Jesuit, Padre Manuel de Ovalle, who found on assuming charge that, although they confessed freely, he could not penetrate into the spiritual recesses of their souls. Suspecting that there lay concealed the doctrines forbidden in Molinos, Madame Guyon and Fénelon, he pretended to be himself in search of the higher spiritual experiences; he drew up a series of propositions, among which were some of those condemned, and submitted it to a few of the leading spirits who accepted it, thus committing themselves to the dangerous doctrines of the absolute abandonment of the soul to God, the non-resistance to temptation, the idleness of exterior observances, and the impeccability of the confirmed adept. After six months spent in this pious treachery, and having secured written evidence of these heresies as entertained by José Solis and Pedro Ubau, he denounced them, June 14, 1710, to the tribunal of Lima, with all others whose names he had ascertained. He admitted that Solis and Ubau, Doña Petronilla Covarrúbias, José González, Doña Josefa Maturano and others, who were leaders among them, were persons of pure life, and that some whose careers had been evil, after practising the exercises prescribed by Ulloa, became virtuous and deeply religious, but this had no bearing on their heresy. At Concepcion there was another proselyte, Fray Felipe Chavarri, whose errors were shown by a letter which he enclosed. Still another leading spirit was Juan Francisco Velazco, an expelled Jesuit, who resisted Ovalle's advances. Some extravagances on his part attracted public attention and finally became so marked that he was confined in the public prison.

Anything akin to Molinism was regarded as dangerous in the highest degree, but the Lima tribunal was so inert that it was not until December 10, 1712, that the Commissioner Manuel de Barona summoned Ovalle to confirm his denunciation. On this same December 10th, another Jesuit, Antonio María Fanelli, wrote to the tribunal enclosing some writings of Solis and reciting the obstructions placed in the way of his attempts to have the affair investigated at Santiago, where all were connected by intermarriages and friendships. The writings of Solis were submitted to a calificador, Maestro Dionisio Granado, who reported, December 22d, that they contained the heresies of Molinos, Luther and Calvin. After this there was a pause until February, 1714, when Commissioner Barona received further denunciations of Solis from the Jesuit Claudio Cruzat and the Mercenarian Nicolás Nolasco. These were soon followed by a deposition of Mariana González showing that Solis's teachings were pure Illuminism of the Quietist school. She had been under Ulloa's direction for two years before his death, and he taught the same doctrines. Altogether her testimony was of the most damaging character, and she added the names of eighteen of Ulloa's disciples. Stirred by this Barona procured evidence from others of the group and sent the whole to the tribunal. On the strength of it the fiscal, August 27th, presented a *clamosa* against Solis as a follower of Molinos and demanded his arrest with sequestration. Ibañez, who was sole inquisitor at the time, on September 1st signed a decree for the prosecution of all the disciples of Ulloa, but on November 9th, in view of the importance of the case, he ordered a fresh *calificacion* and inquiries to be made as to the standing of Ovalle. Fray Antonio Urraca was sent as a special commissioner *ad hoc* to Santiago to verify the evidence and gather fresh testimony.

Urraca lost no time in proceeding to Santiago where he remained until 1718 employed on the work, and it was not until February 10, 1719, that he presented himself to the tribunal to report. Solis, Ubau and Velazco had already been received as prisoners in November, 1718. In sending them, Commissioner Barona stated that Solis, through poverty, had gone to the mines, where he had been arrested. Velazco had been crazy for two years and was found on a ranch with no property but a poor bed. Ubau had four thousand pesos in his possession; his arrest had caused great excitement, for he was accountant for nuns and frailes, for the cabildo of the city and for merchants, universally respected for uprightness and punctual in his religious duties.

Thus far, although dilatory in action, the proceedings of the tribunal had been unexceptionable. Molinism was an aberration that had excited too much abhorrence for any substantial accusation of it to be neglected. All reasonable effort had been made to obtain and to verify evidence; there seems to have been no desire to persecute the bulk of the disciples of Ulloa and attention was concentrated on three who were regarded as leaders and dogmatizers. After this, however, there is much to criticize in the prosecutions. Ubau, who was perfectly sane when incarcerated, began to manifest symptoms of mental alienation which developed into complete insanity. In February, 1733, he was transferred to the convent of the Recollects and finally to the insane department of the hospital of San Andrés. Velazco pleaded that he had been insane for nine years, with lucid intervals; his health speedily broke down, consumption set in and he was transferred, March 15, 1719, to the hospital of San Andrés where he died on the 19th and his body was returned to the tribunal to be thrust into the ground. Proceedings were continued against his memory and fame, the advocate of prisoners arguing that irresponsibility precluded his condemnation for formal heresy. As for Solis, the accusation against him consisted of eighty articles and assumed that he was wholly an apostate from the faith. He protested that he had persuaded himself that God had revealed to him the spiritual way; this had been his fault, for which he begged mercy and was ready to accept any penance that might be imposed. His advocate defended him by pointing out the deceitful way in which Ovalle had beguiled him into error, by submitting to him propositions of Molinos which he had admitted under examination that he did not understand. He had never even heard the name of Miguel de Molinos, so he could not be termed his disciple and, if he had erred, it had been in following his confessor Ulloa. As for Ulloa, the prosecution of his memory and fame was carried through its regular course. The accusation represented him as a dogmatizer of the heresies of Luther, Calvin, Molinos and Ubicler (Wickliffe). There were a hundred and sixty articles and twenty witnesses to prove them. When a defender was called for, by command of the Jesuit Provincial the procurador-general of the province of Chile presented himself and the most strenuous efforts were made to protect the honor of the Society. Padre Firmin de Irisarri, who conducted the defence, says that there was no proof that Ulloa had ever taught the worst of the propositions ascribed to him, and he throws the whole blame on the artifice of Ovalle betraying three unlettered laymen into accepting doctrines which they were led to believe were entertained by him to whom the dying Ulloa had entrusted them.

As far as the living were concerned, the cases were concluded and ready for sentence in 1725. Then ensued an inexplicable delay until 1736, when Calderon and Unda were in control of the tribunal. The last *auto general* celebrated in Peru was announced for December 23d and was solemnized in the public plaza, with exceptionally imposing ceremonies, in the presence of the viceroy, the Marquis of Villagarcía, and of all the magnates. The effigies of Ulloa and Velazco were brought forward, condemned and burnt; that of Solis was reconciled in view of his submission. The unfortunate Ubau, in spite of his insanity, had been condemned, December 1st, to be relaxed as an impenitent heretic who denied his guilt, and, as his mental condition would have precluded repentance, he would have been burnt alive, but for some reason he was not brought forward and was allowed to linger in the hospital until he died in 1747. The sentence, however, confiscated his property which, as we have seen (p. 353) amounted to more than sixty thousand pesos and disappeared without leaving a trace. It would scarce be doing injustice to Calderon and Unda to suggest that the taking up of these cases, after ten years' interval, may have been to conceal the abstraction of the sequestration.[1]

When the Visitador Arenaza and the Inquisitor Amusquíbar, in 1746, arraigned their predecessors they laid special stress on

---

[1] Medina, Chile, II, 276–356, 450.—Bermudez de la Torre, Triunfos del Santo Oficio Peruano, Lima, 1737.

the irregularities and excesses which characterized the conduct of these cases. In that of Ulloa, the consulta de fe voted *in discordia;* another consulta was called, from which the two consultors who had voted in favor of the accused were excluded; another Ordinary, who had as consultor condemned Ulloa's papers, was substituted for the previous one, and two new consultors were summoned, who were only allowed a morning in which to examine the voluminous documents, and the consulta was held on a feast-day when Ibañez refused to act.

Even before this, however, the Suprema had commenced action. The Jesuits had been profoundly stirred by the condemnation of Ulloa and the suspension in the churches of the sanbenito of a member of their Order. It was doubtless owing to their influence that the Suprema, March 10, 1738, ordered all the papers in the case of the Molinists to be sent to Spain and the sanbenitos of Ulloa to be removed from the churches of Lima and Santiago. This last command was unwillingly obeyed and, in reporting its execution, January 10, 1739, the tribunal remonstrated bitterly as to the disastrous results to the authority of the Inquisition and to the faith. The papers were duly forwarded, but were detained in Panamá until 1746, when they were despatched by way of Brazil. It was not, however, until 1762 that the Suprema delivered its judgement. It called attention to the many irregularities and inexcusable delays in the case of Solis, but did not modify the judgement. In that of Velazco, it revoked the sentence as unjust, absolved his memory and fame, ordered his property to be restored to his heirs, less the expenses of maintenance, and that a certificate rehabilitating them be given and the sanbenitos be removed from the churches. The review of the trial of Ulloa was long and minute, pointing out its innumerable irregularities and denials of justice; there was no proof that he ever held the doctrines imputed to him and no effort to ascertain the truth; a false and imperfect report of the case, moreover, had been made to the Suprema.[1]

---

[1] Medina, Chile, II, 388–91, 442–8.

There were six other disciples of Ulloa who were treated in the same inexcusable fashion. Two or three of them had appeared before the Santiago commissioner, in 1710 and 1718. Nothing more was done with them until the affair was revived for the auto of 1736, when they were arrested and brought to Lima and tried. It is scarce worth while to detail the cases. It suffices to say that two of them died in consequence, and that in at least two of the cases the Suprema, in 1762, set aside the sentences as unjustifiable. The auto of 1736 had not escaped severe criticism in Lima, which the tribunal repressed by trying two of the critics and fining them in five hundred pesos each. A third was a Jesuit, Padre Gabriel de Orduña, whom Calderon and Unda apparently were afraid to handle. The evidence was sent to the Suprema, which replied that Ibañez should summon him and warn him to treat the Holy Office with due respect. This became known in Lima to the mortification of the inquisitors who suspended the case.[1]

In the chief matter for which the tribunal was founded—the protection of the colony from the presumable missionary efforts of the Protestants—it found little to do. No case of proselytism has been found among the records thus far and those of voluntary Protestant residents are few and far between. The archbishop, as we have seen, had disposed of Jan Miller in 1548, and in the first auto de fe, in 1573, there appeared Joan Bautista and Mateo Salado. In 1581 there was a courageous martyr in the person of Jan Bernal, a Flemish tailor who had been arrested and forwarded by the Commissioner of Panamá. At first he professed conversion and begged mercy, but he regained his fortitude and declared that it was better to burn in this world than the next. To this he adhered in spite of strenuous efforts to convert him. He was tortured *in caput alienum* without success and was sentenced to relaxation. He was pertinacious to the last and must therefore undoubtedly have been burnt alive. In the auto of

---

[1] Medina, Chile, II, 450–61.

November 30, 1587, there appeared Miguel del Pilar, a Fleming, whose constancy was punished by relaxation and burning.[1] Then a long interval occurs until 1625, when a man called Adrian Rodríguez of Leyden was induced to profess conversion and was reconciled with eight years of galleys and a sanbenito for life. A century elapses when, in 1730, there was an *autillo* for Robert Shaw, a Nova Scotian, who deserted from Clipperton's expedition and penetrated to Cuzco, where he was arrested as a heretic and sent to Lima. He professed readiness for conversion and was confided for instruction to Dr. Thomas Correy but soon ran away, carrying with him 160 pesos and some jewels. He took service with a butcher in Puno, was discovered and taken back to Lima, where he escaped with some spiritual penances. About ten years later, James Haden of Boston was prosecuted as a heretic and was converted.[2] The extreme sensitiveness which would not permit Spanish soil to be polluted by a Protestant foot is seen in the case of Pierre Fos, a French Protestant of Protestant descent, who was cook to Viceroy Superunda. He attended mass and passed for a Catholic, but betrayed himself and was arrested in 1758. He confessed at once and said he would become a Catholic if he could obtain his parents' consent; then, after three days of prison, he announced his conversion to save his soul. Instructors were given to him and his trial dragged on through all its cumbrous forms until his sentence was read in an auto of May 18, 1763. It condemned him to abjure *de vehementi*, to be paraded in *virgüenza* through the streets, to confiscation of half his property, reclusion for instruction during two years, after which he was to be shipped to Spain, consigned to the commissioner at Cádiz. The last papers in the case are the receipt for his person by the captain of the good ship los Placeres, Callao, April 2, 1765, and the receipt from the receiver, April 22d, for the documents concerning his property. It was doubtless his pretended Catholicism that justified this severity.[3]

---

[1] Medina, Lima, I, 150–6, 257.   [2] Ibidem, II, 29, 287, 310, 375.
[3] Archivo nacional de Lima.

It is a curious illustration of the Spanish theories concerning heresy and its cognizance by the Inquisition that even heretics, whose presence was involuntary as prisoners of war, were held to come within its jurisdiction, and the Lima tribunal had much more to do with such subjects than with those who ventured intentionally within its grasp. In 1578 it wrote to Juan Constantino, its commissioner at Panamá, that it understood that the English corsairs who appeared there were heretics and that it would proceed as such against any who were captured. They robbed the commissioner and left him in his shirt, they broke the chalice and patena and cast into the sea the altar and missal. The commissioner on his part denounced the General of the armada del Mar de Norte for keeping in his service two or three Englishmen as trumpeters and an artilleryman, whom he ought to have delivered to the Inquisition of Seville.[1] Sometimes the secular authorities maintained a cumulative jurisdiction with a result grotesquely horrible. Thus, in 1581 there were four English prisoners surrendered to the tribunal which tortured them severely for intention and sentenced John Oxenham, "captain of the robbers at Ballano," to reconciliation, confiscation and the galleys for life; Thomas Xervel (Harvey ?), master of the ship, to reconciliation, ten years of galleys and subsequent perpetual prison; John Butler, pilot of the ship, to abjure *de vehementi* and six years of galleys; the fourth, Henry Butler, a young brother of the last, was not tried. It sounds like a ghastly jest to learn that the alcaldes had already sentenced the first three to be hanged and the last one to perpetual galleys; they were all returned to the secular court and the sentences were duly executed. As they had evidently all been converted, the tribunal at least had the pious satisfaction of saving their souls.[2] About 1585 there is a brief entry of a dozen or so of Englishmen captured at Guayaquil and taken to Lima. The Viceroy Count del Villar asked them whether they were baptized and on learning that they were thus answerable to the Inquisition, he handed them over to the tri-

---

[1] Medina, Chile, I, 363.   [2] Medina, Lima, I, 157; Chile, I, 359.

bunal. What were their sentences and whether the secular court reclaimed them does not appear.[1]

The next adventurers who suffered appeared in the auto of November 30, 1587. John Drake, a cousin of Sir Francis, passed the Straits of Magellan and was lost on the Pacific coast. Thirteen of the crew saved themselves and fell among cannibal Indians with whom they lived for about a year. Drake and two others fled in a canoe down the River Plate to Buenos Ayres, one of them being lost in the Paraguay. Drake and his comrade Richard Ferrel were seized, sent across the continent to Arica and thence to Lima, where they were tried by the tribunal. They professed conversion; Drake was sentenced to reconciliation and seclusion for three years in a monastery with prohibition to leave the country. Ferrel must have been somewhat more stubborn, for he was tortured and condemned to reconciliation, four years of galleys and perpetual prison.[2]

The auto of April 5, 1592, was graced with two groups of English prisoners. Four of these had been captured on the island of Puná and had lain in prison for five years. The secular authorities seem to have abandoned jurisdiction by this time and left them wholly to the Inquisition. Walter and Edward Tillert, brothers, were relaxed as persistent heretics, but weakened at the last moment and were strangled before burning. Henry Axli (Oxley?) was pertinacious to the end and was burnt alive. The fourth, Andrew Marle (Morley ?), a youth of eighteen, professed conversion and was reconciled, with two years reclusion among the Jesuits for instruction.[3]

The other group consisted of three "pirates," from the expedition of Thomas Cavendish, who sailed from Plymouth July 21, 1586. He reached the Straits of Magellan January 3, 1587, emerged March 15th and on April 9th anchored in the roadstead of Quintero, a little north of Valparaiso. At Santiago a force had been raised in anticipation of their coming, and when the

---

[1] Archivo nacional de Lima, Protocolo 228, Exp^{te} 5287.
[2] Medina, La Plata, pp. 117–19.   [3] Medina, Lima, I, 296–8.

English, in need of wood and water, had landed a party, they surrounded twelve men, who had straggled to a ravine, and carried them to Santiago. There nine of them were summarily hanged, to the great benefit of their souls, for they professed conversion. The other three were shipped to Lima, and delivered to the Inquisition where their trials lasted for three years. Of these William Stephens said his parents were both Catholics, and his mother had died in gaol for possessing beads and images; he had observed the religion of his country but was in heart a Catholic; he was reconciled with four years prison and sanbenito. Thomas Lucas had a Protestant father and Catholic mother; he had always been a Protestant but was now a Catholic; he was reconciled, with four years of galleys, six years of prison and sanbenito, and was never to leave Lima. William Hilles was but 17 years old; he had been a Protestant but was now a Catholic; he was reconciled, with six years of galleys and perpetual prison and sanbenito.[1] Cavendish, it may be added, captured a treasure-ship, imitated Drake in circumnavigating the globe and was knighted by Queen Elizabeth.

More disastrous was the expedition under Richard Hawkins, which sailed from Plymouth in July, 1593, with three vessels, of which one was wrecked and one returned. Hawkins cast anchor at Valparaiso, April 24, 1594, where he captured four little vessels and ransomed a larger one. When he sailed, the corregidor manned one of the abandoned barks and despatched it to Callao with news of the corsairs. It made the voyage in fifteen days, enabling the Viceroy, Hurtado de Mendoza, to fit out a squadron under his nephew Beltran de Castro, who encountered Hawkins, July 2, in the Bay of Atacames, near Quito. After a desperate fight, Hawkins surrendered under promise of treatment as prisoners of war, and the extraordinary rejoicings with which the news of the victory were received in Lima are a measure of the terror excited by these dauntless sea-rovers. The terms of capitulation were scandalously violated; of the seventy-five prisoners taken,

---

[1] Medina, Chile, I, 371–80.

sixty-two were sent to the galleys at Cartagena, and thirteen were brought to Lima, where the Inquisition claimed them, on information that they were heretics, and they entered the secret prison, December 4, 1594. Possibly it may have been the irregularity attaching to the infraction of the terms of surrender that hastened the trials, for eight of the prisoners appeared in the auto of December 17, 1595, together with seven other Englishmen, captured at la Yaguana and forwarded from Santo Domingo. There were no martyrs among them. All professed conversion and were reconciled with various terms of reclusion except one, William Leigh, who was sentenced to six years of galleys and perpetual irremissible prison.[1]

Richard Hawkins, whose trial ended July 17, 1595, was too sick to appear in the auto and was transferred to the Jesuit college. His chivalrous bearing won for him general good will, and on his recovery he was placed at the disposition of the viceroy who was earnestly desirous that the terms of surrender should be observed. There was correspondence on the subject. The Suprema wrote, October 5, 1595, to suspend the sequestrations of the Englishmen, and in future not to sequestrate in such cases, for soldiers ought not to be deprived of the spoils won from their enemies. The tribunal, it said, was not to interfere in the cases of those sent to the galleys at Cartagena, but, as to Hawkins and his comrades, they were to be delivered to the viceroy, without proceeding further in their cases and, when they were fully instructed in the faith, it was to do justice, proceeding in their cases with much care and consideration. These instructions were of course too late, and in reply the tribunal asked whether their sanbenitos should be removed from the churches and whether, in case they relapsed, they should be subject to relaxation. The conclusion reached was that the sanbenitos were to be removed, the reclusion revoked, the sequestrations restored and that they were not subject to the penalties of relapse for reincidence. The succeeding viceroy, Velasco, desired to send them all to Spain, but this was

---

[1] Medina, Chile, I, 381; Lima, I, 305-7.

opposed by the tribunal because their penances had not been completed; Hawkins ought also to be kept on account of his knowledge of the navigation of those seas. The last information concerning them occurs in a letter of the Royal Audiencia, May 21, 1607, showing that they had passed out of the hands of the tribunal. It says that the Viceroys Cañete and Velasco had sent to Spain all those captured in 1594 except Richard Hawkins, Captain John Ellis, Hugh Carnix (Charnock ?) and Richard Davis, who were kept because they were experienced seamen and Davis was useful in the position assigned to him. Now permission has been given to them to sail in the outgoing fleet, consigned to the Contratacion of Seville.[1] We know that Hawkins eventually reached England and was knighted.

In time there came a recognition of the rights of prisoners of war, even though they were heretics and were claimed by the Inquisition. In the auto of December 21, 1625, there appeared Pieter Jan of Delft, who had been captured and condemned to death as a pirate, though the sentence was not executed. He refused to be converted and was sent to the galleys, but was subsequently liberated under a royal cédula as a prisoner of war. Fanaticism, however, was difficult to extinguish. When, about 1650, the Dutch endeavored to establish themselves at Valdivia, Viceroy Mancera sent a well-equipped fleet and army to drive them out. The captain of the first vessel that reached there, on learning that the Dutch commander had died and been buried, caused the corpse to be dug up and burnt. From the absence in the subsequent records of cases of prisoners of war, however, it is safe to assume that by this time the barbarity of giving them the alternative of conversion or the stake had been abandoned. There was, it is true, an intervention of the tribunal in the case of the Dutch ship St. Louis, captured at Coquimbo in 1725, but

---

[1] Medina, Chile, I, 385–90.
The question as to the ownership of confiscations made on heretic prisoners was a nice one. When some Englishmen were captured in Vallano the tribunal laid claim to the gold that was taken with them. How the dispute was settled does not appear.—Archivo nacional de Lima, Protocolo 223, Exp^{te} 5270.

it was not unreasonable. The fiscal Calderon, learning that among the prisoners there were French Huguenots and Dutch heretics and Jews, and that the Viceroy Castelfuerte thought of utilizing the sailors on his own ships, represented to the tribunal the grave dangers of such a course, when the Inquisitor Gutiérrez de Cevallos, induced the viceroy to abandon the plan and to bring to Lima about a hundred who had been left sick at Coquimbo.[1] As none of them appeared in the succeeding auto it is inferable that they were not subjected to prosecution for heresy.

The most serious business of the tribunal, in the line of its proper functions, was with the apostasy of the Jewish New Christians. From the very foundation of the colonies, as we have seen in the preceding chapter, restrictions were laid on the emigration of Conversos and a law of 1543, preserved in the Recopilacion, orders that search be made for all descendants of Jews who were to be rigorously expelled.[2] In spite, however, of the jealous care observed to preserve the colonies from all danger of Jewish infection, the commercial attractions were so powerful that the New Christians eluded all precautions. At first, however, they occupied but a small portion of the energies of the tribunal. It is true that among the earliest denunciations received, in 1570, were those of the Licenciate Juan Alvarez, a physician, and of his brother-in-law Alonso Alvarez with his wife, children and servants, for Judaism, but as their names are absent from the subsequent auto it is presumable that they were found innocent.[3] The first appearance of Jews is in the auto of October 29, 1581, when Manuel López, a Portuguese, was reconciled with confiscation and perpetual prison, and Diego de la Rosa, described as a native of Quito, was required to abjure *de levi* and was exiled—showing that the evidence against him was very dubious.[4] After this there are none until the great auto of April 5, 1592, in which there were two, Nicholas Morin, a Frenchman, and Francisco Díaz,

---

[1] Medina, Lima, II, 33; Chile I, 366, 369.   [2] Recop., Lib. vii, Tit. v, ley 29.
[3] Medina, Lima, I, 29.   [4] Ibidem, p. 157.—Palma, Añales, p. 21.

a Portuguese, the former required to abjure *de levi* and the latter reconciled.[1]

The conquest of Portugal, in 1580, had led to a large emigration to Castile, where Portuguese soon became synonymous with Judaizer, and this was beginning to make itself manifest in the colonies. The auto of December 17, 1595, gave impressive evidence of this. Five Portuguese—Juan Méndez, Antonio Núñez, Juan López, Francisco Báez and Manuel Rodríguez—were reconciled. Another, Herman Jorje, had died during trial and his memory was not prosecuted. There were also four martyrs. Jorje Núñez denied until he was tied upon the rack; he then confessed and refused to be converted, but after his sentence of relaxation was read he weakened and was strangled before burning. Francisco Rodríguez endured torture without confessing; when threatened with repetition he endeavored unsuccessfully to commit suicide; he was voted to relaxation with torture *in caput alienum*, and under it he accused several persons but revoked at ratification. He was pertinacious to the last and was burnt alive. Juan Fernández was relaxed, although insane; the Suprema expressed doubts whether he had intelligence enough to render him responsible. Pedro de Contreras had been tortured for confession and again *in caput alienum;* he denied Judaism throughout and was relaxed as a *negativo;* at the auto he manifested great devotion to a crucifix and presumably was strangled; in all probability he was really a Christian.[2]

This bloody work affords a foretaste of what was to come. At the auto of December 10, 1600, there were fourteen Portuguese Judaizers. Twelve of them had professed conversion and were reconciled; with two, convictions were too strong and they were burnt alive—Duarte Núñez de Cea and Baltasar Lucena, whose last words were that he denied Christ.[3] The auto of March 13, 1605, exhibited sixteen Judaizers reconciled in person and one in effigy. Six who had fled were burnt in effigy and three less

---

[1] Medina, Lima, I, 297.—Palma, p. 49. [2] Medina, Lima, I, 305, 307–10.
[3] Ibidem, I, 321–23.

fortunate were burnt in person. Besides these was Antonio Correa who, during his trial, was converted by the inspiration of God; he was reconciled with three years in prison, which he served in the convent of la Merced and then was sent to Spain, dying, in 1622, as a fraile in Ossuna, in the odor of sanctity, which has rendered him the subject of several biographies.[1]

The auto of June 1, 1608, afforded but one case, and that an unusual one—Domingo López, tried for Judaism and acquitted. This may be explained by the fact that the Portuguese New Christians had purchased, in 1604, a general pardon in Spain, which reached Peru in 1605 and for a time repressed inquisitorial activity in this direction. In 1610 there was a noteworthy case of Manuel Ramos, one of the fugitives who had been burnt in effigy in 1605. He had been captured and on being tried was now acquitted.[2] In an auto of June 17, 1612, there were five reconciliations for Judaism.[3] From this time for some years there were only scattering cases. Possibly the terrible energy manifested by the tribunal had served as a deterrent and checked the Portuguese influx, but if so the impression was but temporary. We have seen (p. 337) the complaints that arose about this time concerning the Portuguese immigration by way of Brazil and Buenos Ayres. This increased greatly when, in 1618, a Portuguese inquisitor came to Rio de Janeiro, published an Edict of Faith and then in a few days made many arrests and sequestrated property to the amount of more than 200,000 pesos. The frightened Judaizers sought refuge in Spanish territory and kept the commissioner at Buenos Ayres, Francisco de Trejo, in a state of continual anxiety. He reported, January 15, 1619, that since the new governor, Diego Martin, had come the *visitas de navíos* had been interrupted and he asked for such positive instruc-

---

[1] Medina, Lima, I, 337–9. It must be borne in mind in all these cases that "reconciliation" to the Church entailed confiscation and was usually accompanied with other penalties more or less severe according to the record of the culprit and the readiness with which he had confessed and recanted as indicative of the sincerity of his conversion. There might be prison and sanbenito for a term or for life, scourging or the galleys.

[2] Ibidem, p. 341, 347. [3] Palma, Añales, p. 31.

tions that the authorities should understand that no foreigners could land until he had inspected the ship. His protests were unavailing. By the middle of April there had arrived eight ships bringing Portuguese passengers, who had paid Castilians to take them as servants so that they might enter. Governor Martin was alert and threw them in prison, in order to send them back, but many managed to get through. Some of them were married in prison to Buenos Ayres women, so as to give them a standing in the community; others broke gaol and took refuge in convents, when the frailes refused to surrender them, giving security to the governor that they would prove themselves to be not of the prohibited class, whereupon they scattered to the interior and the man who had furnished the security calmly paid the forfeit. It is true that forty of them were sent back, but it was evidently impossible to exclude these proscribed and hunted beings who were so persistent and resourceful. The tribunal, in fact, was apparently not averse to obtaining fresh material for condemnation and confiscation, for it did not authorize the commissioner to arrest suspects and send them back, but only to compile information about them and forward it to Lima, keeping advised as to their destinations so that they could be seized when wanted.[1] The immigration continued and, in 1623, the tribunal called the attention of the Suprema to the increasing numbers of Portuguese, who were spreading throughout the interior provinces. This continued and, in 1635, the fiscal of the Audiencia of Charcas represented forcibly to the king the evil of the innumerable Jews who had entered and were constantly coming.[2]

The tribunal resumed its labors and, by December 21, 1625, it was ready with an auto in which ten Judaizers were reconciled. Two had committed suicide in prison and were burnt with their bones. Two more were relaxed—Juan Acuña de Noroña, who was described as impenitent and must have been burnt alive, and Diego de Andrada who gave signs of repentance at the last and was probably strangled before burning.[3]

---

[1] Medina, La Plata, 155–61.   [2] Ibidem, 164–66.   [3] Medina, Lima, II, 27–31.

In 1626 there commenced a trial which illustrates forcibly the inexorable discipline of the Church, rendering it the supreme duty of the Christian to persecute and destroy all heresy. Francisco Maldonado de Silva was a surgeon of high repute in Concepcion de Chile. He was of Portuguese descent. His father had suffered in the Inquisition, had been reconciled and brought up his children, two girls and a boy, as Christians. Francisco was a good Catholic until, at the age of 18, he chanced to read the *Scrutinium Scripturarum* of Pablo de Santa María, Bishop of Búrgos—a controversial work written for the conversion of Jews.[1] So far from confirming him in the faith it raised doubts leading him to consult his father, who told him to study the Bible and instructed him in the Law of Moses. He became an ardent convert to Judaism, but kept his secret from his mother and two sisters and from his wife, for he was married and had a child, and his wife was pregnant when he was arrested. During her absence, a year or two before, he had circumcised himself. At the age of 35, considering that his sister Isabel who was about 33, was mature enough for religious independence, he revealed his secret to her and endeavored to convert her, but in vain, and he was impervious to her entreaties to abandon his faith. They seem to have been tenderly attached to each other; he was her sole support as well as that of her mother and sister, but she could not escape the necessity of communicating the facts in confession to her confessor. The prescriptions of the Church were absolute; no family ties relieved one from the obligation of denouncing heresy, and she could not hope for sacramental absolution without discharging the duty. We can picture to ourselves the torment of that agonized soul as she nerved herself to the awful duty which would cost her a lifetime of remorse and misery

---

[1] Pablo de Santa María was originally the Rabbi Selemoh Ha-Levi, one of the most learned of Jewish doctors. Converted in 1390, he rose to be regent of Spain in the minority of Juan II, papal legate *a latere* and bishop successively of Cartagena and Búrgos. His book was regarded as convincing and was repeatedly printed. Two editions appeared in Strassburg about 1471 and my copy is of Búrgos, 1591.

when she obeyed her confessor's commands and denounced her brother to the Inquisition.

The warrant for his arrest was issued December 12, 1626, and executed at Concepcion April 29, 1627. His friend, the Dominican Fray Diego de Ureña, visited him in his place of confinement, May 2, and sought to convert him, but he was resolved to die in the faith in which his father had died. So when transferred to Santiago, the Augustinian Fray Alonso de Almeida made similar efforts with like ill-success; he knew that he should die for the faith, he had never spoken to any one but his sister and she had betrayed him. He was received in Lima July 23d and was admitted to an audience the same day. When required to swear on the cross he refused, saying that he was a Jew and would live and die as such; if he had to swear it would be by the living God, the God of Israel. His trial went on through all the customary formalities, protracted by the repeated conferences held with theologians who endeavored to convince him of his errors. Eleven of these were held without weakening his pertinacity until, on January 26, 1633, the consulta de fe unanimously condemned him to relaxation.

A long sickness followed, caused by a fast of eighty days which had reduced him almost to a skeleton covered with sores. On convalescing, he asked for another conference, to solve the doubts which he had drawn up in writing. It was held June 26, 1634, and left him as pertinacious as ever. Meanwhile the prison was filling with Judaizers, of whom a number had been discovered in Lima. He asked for maize husks in place of his ration of bread, and with them made a rope by which he escaped through a window and visited two neighboring cells, urging the prisoners to be steadfast in their law; they denounced him and he made no secret of it, confessing freely what he had done. It was a mercy of God, we are told, that his prolonged fast had rendered him deaf, or he would have learned much from them of what had been going on.

The tribunal was so preoccupied, with the numerous trials

on foot at the time, that Maldonado was left undisturbed, awaiting the general auto that was to follow. We hear nothing more until, after an interval of four years, a thirteenth conference was held at his request, November 12, 1638. It was as fruitless as its predecessors and, at its conclusion, he produced two books (each of them of more than a hundred leaves), made with marvellous ingenuity out of scraps of paper and written with ink made of charcoal and pens cut out of egg-shells with a knife fashioned from a nail, which he said he delivered up for the discharge of his conscience. Then on December 9th and 10th were held two more conferences in which his pertinacity remained unshaken. The long tragedy was now drawing to an end after an imprisonment which had lasted for nearly thirteen years. He was brought out in the great auto of January 23, 1639, where, when the sentences of relaxation were read, a sudden whirlwind tore away the awning and, looking up, he exclaimed "The God of Israel does this to look upon me face to face!" He was unshrinking to the last and was burnt alive a true martyr to his faith. His two paper books were hung around his neck to burn with him and assist in burning him.[1]

This auto of 1639, the greatest that had as yet been held in the New World, was the culmination of the "complicidad grande"— the name given by the inquisitors to a number of Judaizers whom they had discovered. As they described the situation, in a report of 1636, large numbers of Portuguese had entered the kingdom by way of Buenos Ayres, Brazil, Mexico, Granada and Puerto Bello, thus increasing the already numerous bands of their compatriots. They became masters of the commerce of the kingdom; from brocade to sack-cloth, from diamonds to cumin-seed, everything passed through their hands; the Castilian who had not a Portuguese partner could look for no success in trade. They would buy the cargoes of whole fleets with the fictitious credits

---

[1] Medina, La Plata, pp. 172–97; Lima, II, 146.—See also a paper by George Alexander Kohut in Publications of the Am. Jewish Historical Society, XI, 163 (1903).

which they exchanged, thus rendering capital unnecessary, and would distribute the merchandise throughout the land by their agents, who were likewise Portuguese, and their capacity developed until, in 1634, they negotiated for the farming of the royal customs.

In August, 1634, Joan de Salazar, a merchant, denounced to the Inquisition Antonio Cordero, clerk of a trader from Seville, because he refused to make a sale on a Saturday. On another occasion, going to his store on a Friday morning, he found Cordero breakfasting on a piece of bread and an apple and, on asking him whether he had not better take a rasher of bacon, Cordero replied "Must I eat what my father and grandfather never ate?" The evidence was weak and no immediate action was taken, but, in October, the commissioners were instructed secretly to ascertain and report the number of Portuguese in their several districts. The matter rested and, as nothing new was developed, in March, 1635, the evidence against Cordero was laid before a consulta de fe and it was resolved to arrest him secretly, without sequestration, so that the hand of the Inquisition might not be apparent. Bartolomé de Larrea, a familiar, called on him, April 2d, under pretence of settling an account, and locked him in a room; a sedan-chair was brought, and he was conveyed to the secret prison. His disappearance excited much talk and he was supposed to have fled, for the supposition of arrest by the Inquisition was scouted, seeing that there had not been sequestration.

Cordero confessed at once that he was a Jew and, under torture, implicated his employer and two others. These were arrested on May 11th and the free employment of torture obtained the names of numerous accomplices. The prisons were full and to empty them an auto in the chapel was hurriedly arranged and preparations were made for the hasty construction of additional cells. On August 11th, between 12.30 and 2 o'clock, seventeen arrests were made, so quietly and simultaneously that it was all effected before the people were conscious of it. These were among the most prominent citizens and greatest merchants of Lima, and we are told that the impression produced on the community was like the Day of Judgement. Torture and inquisitorial methods elicited further information resulting in additional arrests; the affrighted Portuguese began to scatter and, at the request of the tribunal, the Viceroy Chinchon prohibited for a year any one to leave Peru without its licence.

Up to May 16, 1636, the date of a report made to the Suprema, there had been eighty-one arrests; there was evidence against eighty more but, for lack of prison accommodation, their seizure was postponed. The old prison had sixteen cells, nineteen new ones had been constructed, then an adjoining house was bought and seventeen more were fitted up in it. This influx of wealthy prisoners put the fidelity of the gaolers to a strain which it could not stand. The old alcaide, Bartolomé de Pradeda, excited suspicion by buying property beyond his legitimate means; he was investigated and found to be selling favors to those under his charge, revealing secrets, permitting communications and the like. He deserved severe punishment but, in view of his twenty years of service, his seven children and his infirm health, he was allowed to ask permission to retire to his country place. He was replaced by Diego de Vargas, who soon had to be dismissed for the same reasons. Joseph Freile was appointed assistant, but was soon found guilty of similar offences and was sent to the galleys. His successor was Benito Rodríguez, who likewise succumbed to temptation, but he was a familiar and was only dropped. Another was Francisco Hurtado de Valcázar, who subsequently appeared in an auto for the same reasons.

One matter which vexed the souls of the inquisitors was the effort made by the threatened Portuguese to hide their property from sequestration. A proclamation was issued, ordering all who knew of such matters to reveal them within nine days under pain of excommunication and other penalties. This was successful to some extent, but the difficulties in the way were illustrated in the case of Enrique de Paz, for whom Melchor de los Reies secreted much silver, jewels and merchandise. Among other things he deposited with his friend Don Dionisio Manrique, Knight of Santiago, senior alcalde de corte and a consultor of the tribunal, a quantity of silver and some fifty or sixty pieces of rich silks. Manrique did not deny receiving them, but said that the same night Melchor ordered them taken away by a young man who was a stranger to him. The inquisitors evidently disbelieved the story; they reported that they had unsuccessfully tried friendly methods with Manrique and asked the Suprema for instructions.

The sequestration of so much property brought all trade to a stand-still and produced indescribable confusion, aggravated, in 1635, by the consequent failure of the bank. The men arrested had nearly all the trade of the colony in their hands; they were involved in an infinity of complicated transactions and suits sprang up on all sides. Creditors and suitors pressed their claims desperately, fearing that with delay witnesses might disappear, in the widening circle of arrests. There were many suits pending already in the Audiencia which were claimed by the tribunal and surrendered to it. It was puzzled by the new business thus thrown upon it; to a suit there had to be two parties, but the prisoners could not plead, so it appointed Manuel de Monte Alegre as their "defensor" to appear for them, and it went on hearing and deciding complicated civil suits while conducting the prosecutions for heresy. Mondays and Thursdays were assigned for civil business, and every afternoon, from 3 P.M. until dark, was devoted to examination of documents. The inquisitors claimed that they pushed forward strenuously in settling accounts and paying debts, for otherwise all commerce would be destroyed to the irreparable damage of the Republic, which was already exhausted in so many ways. This did not suit the Suprema, which, by letters of October 22d and November 9, 1635, forbade the surrender of any sequestrated or confiscated property, no matter what evidence was produced of ownership or claims, without first consulting it. This exacting payment of all debts and postponing payment of claims threatened general bankruptcy when the rich merchants were arrested, for their aggregate liabilities amounted to eight hundred thousand pesos, which was estimated as equal to the whole capital of Lima. To avert this, some payments were made, but only on the strength of competent security being furnished.

In the excitement of the hour and the mad rush for arresting everybody who might be an apostate, much injustice was committed which aggravated the confusion. Thus on May 8, 1636, Santiago del Castillo, was arrested, a merchant whose licence to sail for Spain was to be signed that afternoon. With him were seized fifty-five bars of silver and ten thousand pesos in coin; he was administrator of customs and it was reckoned fortunate that over thirty thousand pesos belonging to the king had been handed over so that it could be sent by the fleet. He was receiver in the bankruptcy of Joan de la Queba, and as such held about seven thousand pesos which were given to Judge Martin de Arriola to be apportioned among eight hundred creditors. Castillo's estate was large but he was involved in suits, besides holding considerable property belonging to others, and claims began at once to be presented. All this was wholly superfluous, for on October 23, 1637, he was discharged as innocent and the sequestration was lifted. Alonso Sánchez Chaparro was liberated, February 9, 1637, and more than sixty thousand pesos were returned to him. There were several other acquittals, and a number of cases were suspended involving the release of large sums which ought never to have been tied up.

Meanwhile the trials of the accused were pushed forward as rapidly as the perplexities of the situation admitted. Torture was not spared. Murcia de Luna, a woman of 27, died under it. Antonio de Acuña was subjected to it for three hours and, when he was carried out, Alcaide Pradeda described his arms as being torn to pieces. Progress was impeded, however, by the devices of the prisoners, who were in hopes that influences at work in Spain would secure a general pardon like that of 1604. With this object they revoked their confessions and their accusations of each other, giving rise to endless complications. Some of the latter revocations, however, were genuine and were adhered to, even through the torture which was freely used in these cases. Besides this, to cast doubt on the whole affair, they accused the innocent and even Old Christians, which accounts for the acquittals mentioned above. The inquisitors add that they abstained in many cases from making arrests, when the testimony was insufficient and the parties were not Portuguese.

The tribunal was manned with four inquisitors, who struggled resolutely through this complicated mass of business, and at length were ready to make public the results of their labors in the auto of January 23, 1639. This was celebrated with unexampled pomp and ostentation, for now money was abundant and the opportunity of making an impression on the popular mind was not to be lost. During the previous night, when their sentences were made known to those who were to be relaxed, two of them, Enrique de Paz and Manuel de Espinosa, professed conversion; the inquisitors came and examined them, a consulta was assembled and they were admitted to reconciliation. There was great rivalry among men of position for the honor of accompanying the penitents and Don Salvadoro Velázquez, one of the principal Indians, *sargento mayor* of the Indian militia, begged to be allowed to carry one of the effigies, which he did in resplendent uniform. Conspicuous in a place of honor in the procession were the seven who had been acquitted, richly dressed, mounted on white horses and carrying palms of victory.

Besides the Judaizers there were a bigamist and five women penanced for sorcery. There was also the alcaide's assistant Valcázar, who was deprived of his familiarship and was exiled for four years. Juan de Canelas Albarran, the occupant of a house adjoining the prison, who had permitted an opening through the walls for communications, received a hundred lashes and five years of exile, and Ana María González, who was concerned in the matter, had also a hundred lashes and four years of exile.

Of the Judaizers there were seven who escaped with abjuration *de vehementi*, various penalties and fines aggregating eight hundred pesos. There were forty-four reconciled with punishments varied according to their deserts. Those who had confessed readily as to themselves and others were let off with confiscation and deportation to Spain. Those who prevaricated or gave trouble had, in addition, lashes or galleys or both. Of these there were twenty-one, the aggregate lashes amounting to four thousand and the years of galleys to a hundred and six, besides two condemnations for life. In addition to these were the mother of the Murcia de Luna who died under torture, Doña Mayor de Luna, a woman of high social position, and her daughter Doña Isabel de Luna, a girl of 18, who, for endeavoring to communicate with each other in prison, were sentenced to a hundred lashes through the streets, naked from the waist up. There was also one reconciliation in effigy of a culprit who had died in prison.

There were eleven relaxations in person and the effigy of one who had committed suicide during trial. Of the eleven, seven are said to have died pertinacious and impenitent and therefore presumably were burnt alive, true martyrs to their belief. Of these there were two especially notable—Maldonado whose case has been mentioned above, and Manuel Bautista Pérez. The latter was the leader and chief among the Portuguese, who styled him the *capitan grande*. He was the greatest merchant in Lima and his fortune was popularly estimated at half a million pesos. It was in his house that were held the secret meetings in which he joined in the learned theological discussions, but outwardly he was a zealous Christian and had priests to educate his children; he was greatly esteemed by the clergy who dedicated to him their literary effusions in terms of the warmest adulation. He owned rich silver mines in Huarochiri and two extensive plantations; his confiscated house has since been known as the *casa de Pilatos*, and his ostentatious mode of life may be judged by the fact that when his carriage was sold by the tribunal it fetched thirty-four hundred pesos. He had endeavored to commit suicide by stabbing himself, but he never faltered at the end. He listened proudly to his sentence and died impenitent, telling the executioner to do his duty. There was one other prisoner who did not appear. Enrique Jorje Tavares, a youth of 18, was among those arrested in August, 1635. He denied under torture and after various alternations became permanently insane, for which reason his case was suspended in 1639.

The next day the mob of Lima enjoyed the further sensation of the scourging through the streets. These exhibitions always attracted a large crowd, in which there were many horsemen who thus had a better view, while boys commonly pelted the bigamists and sorceresses who were the usual patients. On this occasion the tribunal issued a proclamation forbidding horses or carriages in the streets through which the procession passed, and any pelting of the penitents under pain, for Spaniards, of banishment to Chile, and for Indians and negroes, of a hundred lashes. There were twenty-nine sufferers in all; they were marched in squads of ten, guarded by soldiers and familiars, while the executioners plied the scourges, and the brutalizing spectacle passed off without disturbance, and with the pious wish of the tribunal that it would please God to make it serve as a warning.[1]

The holocaust had been duly offered to a Savior of love and mercy; the martyrs had sealed in flame and torment their adherence to the Ancient Faith, and the mob had had its spectacle. Satisfied with the results of their pious labors for the greater glory of God, the inquisitors calmly went forward to gather in the gleanings from the ruined commerce and industry of the kingdom, to retain what they could for themselves and to account for as little as they might to their superiors. The process was long and complex and it was years before all the tangled skeins were ravelled out, and the clamorous creditors of the victims had their claims satisfied or rejected.

---

[1] Medina, Lima, II, 47–168, 176. Medina prints the Relation of the auto by Fernando Montesinos. A brief abstract of it is given by Pellicer, *Avisos históricos*, under date of Feb. 7, 1640 (Valladares, Semanario erúdito, XXXI, 129).

There were still some remnants of the the hated Portuguese to be dealt with. After the auto, seven cases, which had been pending for three years or more, were suspended, followed, in 1639 and 1640, by others of reconciliation or suspension. In 1641 there was an auto, November 17th, in which three Judaizers were reconciled and seven others sentenced to confiscation and a hundred lashes apiece. There still remained of the "complicidad grande" Manuel Henríquez, who had been arrested in December, 1635, and had confessed under torture, after which he revoked, and several extravagances led to his being thought crazy, but in 1647 he was condemned to the stake. The tribunal however waited for other victims to justify the expense of an auto and, in 1656, he was still lingering in prison; he was not burnt until 1664 in company with the effigy of Murcia de Luna, the victim of torture. The Inquisition, in fact, had passed its apogee and had become inert as its wealth increased. In 1648 it reported that its only prisoner was Manuel Henríquez, who was awaiting the execution of his sentence.[1]

This was not because the Portuguese had been exterminated. They were still numerous, although the revolt of Portugal, in 1640, had rendered them, if not as yet foreigners, at least citizens whose loyalty might well be suspect. Political as well as religious motives may therefore be ascribed to the action of the Viceroy Pedro de Toledo, Marquis of Mancera, at the instance of the Audiencia, under impulsion of the tribunal, when, in 1646, he issued an edict that all Portuguese should present themselves with their arms and should leave the country. More than six thousand are said to have come forward and by payment of a large sum to have obtained a revocation of the measure—a venal transaction which formed the basis of one of the accusations brought against Mancera in the *residencia* or customary investigation at the close of his term of office.[2]

Either the tribunal had become too indolent for active work,

---

[1] Medina, Lima, II, 169, 175, 177–8.—Palma, Añales, p. 41.
[2] Palma, Añales, pp. 38–9.

or the Portuguese population had been cowed into sincere acceptance of Catholicism, for we hear little subsequently of Judaism. It was not that sensitiveness to Jewish observances had decreased, for in 1666 Juan Leon Cisneros was accused of buying scaleless fish on Fridays and of not sending his children to school on the Sabbath, for which suspicious actions he was sentenced to abjuration.[1] From that time there is a long interval and even the ferocious recrudescence of persecution in Spain, during the first third of the eighteenth century, awoke but a feeble echo in Peru.

The next two cases that present themselves are highly significant of inquisitorial methods. About 1720 Alvaro Rodríguez was prosecuted for Judaism but died in prison and his case was never concluded. Still his sequestrated property, amounting to fourteen thousand pesos, was remitted to the Suprema, although the Inquisition had no claim on it, for he had left no relatives in Peru and Philip V had ordered the seizure of all Portuguese property as a measure of retaliation in the relations between the two countries. The other case was that of Don Teodoro Candioti, a Levantine Christian, who had married in Lima. He was arrested, probably somewhat before 1722, on suspicion of Judaism arising from his keeping the day before Christmas as a fast, according to the custom of his country. He had also said that St. Moses was a great saint and as such was venerated in his land. There was some talk of his being circumcised, but this was unfounded. He died in prison, May 19, 1726, making a most Christian end and saying that salvation was to be had by keeping the law of God, through the grace of Jesus Christ. His body was thrust into one of the graves of the tribunal but the Suprema ordered, November 24, 1728, that his bones should be secretly transferred and buried with Christian rites in the parish church and that an entry be made in the parish register of his burial as of the day of his death, without stating that he had died in prison, and further that a certificate of no disability be given to his widow and children, including capacity to hold

---

[1] Medina, Lima, II, 189-90.

offices in the Inquisition. Evidently the falsification of church records was a matter of course when the injustice of the Inquisition was to be concealed. The tribunal itself had still less scruple. It replied, August 26, 1729, that it had already, on December 23, 1727, reported the translation of the remains to the church of the Dominican college of St. Thomas; another exhumation seemed unnecessary, but it had had the required entry made in the parish register. The widow had presented the genealogies of her two sons, Don Antonio and Don Juan Candioti, asking that they be made familiars and, as the viceroy was much interested in the family, the request had been granted.[1] This case brings before us one of the deplorable results of the system of secrecy; a husband and father disappears into the prison; he dies, and his family only learn his fate after seven years of suspense.

A more flagrant case was that of Doña Ana de Castro, a married woman of good social position but of dubious character, as she was reported to have sold her favors to one of the viceroys and to many of the rich colonial nobles. Accused of Judaism, she persistently denied; when, in 1731, her case was reported to the Suprema, she had been voted to relaxation with preliminary torture, to which the Suprema replied, February 4, 1732, that if the torture and efforts of the theologians did not bring repentance, the sentence was to be executed, but, if she confessed and gave signs of repentance, she was to be reconciled. She was held until the solemn public auto of December 23, 1736, when she was relaxed to the secular arm as a Judaizing Jew, convicted, negative and pertinacious. On her way to the brasero she is said to have shed tears, but the alguazil mayor paid no attention to them and she was duly burnt—probably without preliminary strangulation. All, apparently, was in accordance with routine procedure but, when the records came to be investigated in the visitation of Arenaza, Amusquíbar reported that the day before the auto she sought two audiences; no record was made of what

---
[1] Medina, Lima, II, 276-80.

occurred, but there could be no doubt that she confessed more than enough to entitle her to reconciliation; even if she did not entirely satisfy the evidence, what more could be expected of a poor woman in such agitation of mind and ignorant of the trap laid for her by Calderon, who acted as fiscal? The printed official account of the auto rather superfluously recites how she was notified of her sentence at ten o'clock of December 21st, after which two theologians, relieved every hour until 6 A.M. of December 23d, labored vainly to induce her to confess and to return to the faith. Amusquíbar, on the contrary, states that there was no record that she was notified of the sentence; that the book of votes did not contain such a sentence and that, even if there was one, it was invalid in consequence of the absence of the Ordinary; moreover that, in spite of her confessions, no new consulta de fe was summoned to consider them. Altogether, if Amusquíbar is to be believed, it was a cold-blooded judicial murder contrived, like the burning of Ulloa in effigy, for the purpose of rendering more impressive the spectacle of the auto de fe. In the same auto there was a reconciliation in effigy of Pedro Núñez de la Haba, a Judaizer of Valdivia, who had escaped from prison after his case was finished. If recaptured he was to be confined in the castle of Chagre, until he could be sent to the penitential prison of Seville, and was to have two hundred lashes for his flight. A small *auto particular* followed, November 11, 1737, in which Juan Antonio Pereyra, a Portuguese, was sentenced to abjure *de vehementi*, two hundred lashes, ten years of presidio at Valdivia and half confiscation.[1]

These are the only cases of Judaism recorded at this period and if the number is so scanty this must be attributed to the lack of Judaizers and not to indifference of the tribunal. How ready it was to prosecute is exhibited in the next case, that of Don Juan de Loyola y Haro, a scion of the family of St. Ignatius and an elderly gentleman of high consideration. He was arrested, July

---

[1] Bermudez de la Torre, Triunfos del Santo Oficio Peruano, fol. 59–60, 154–55, 178.—Palma, Añales, pp. 105–6.—Medina, Lima, II, 312.

9, 1743, on a charge of Judaism based on the flimsiest testimony of a negro slave. Other evidence was gathered, but with it the commissioner of Ica wrote that the current belief regarded it as a conspiracy on the part of his slaves, and that this had been confessed by one of the witnesses when dying. In spite of this his trial continued, nor was he released when, in February, 1745, the four false witnesses were arrested. He fell sick; in July he was transferred to a convent, where he died, December 27th of the same year, and was secretly buried in the chapel of S. María Magdalena. Evidently his family were kept in ignorance until an auto was held October 19, 1749, when the witnesses were punished and a great parade was made of the equity of the tribunal. His effigy was carried in procession, bearing in one hand a palm-branch and in the other a gold baton symbolical of his military rank as maestre de campo. His acquittal was read, empowering his brothers to carry the effigy around the town on a white horse, to exhume the remains and bury them where he had indicated on his death-bed, and certificates were granted to them that his imprisonment inflicted no disabilities on his kindred. On the next day the procession of the white horse took place with much pomp and circumstance. The Suprema, on reviewing the report, pronounced the whole proceedings to be vicious from the start and destitute of all the safeguards provided against injustice.[1] It is perhaps worth noting that most of it occurred after Calderon and Unda had been superseded by Arenaza and Amusquíbar. With this the formal persecution of Judaism in Peru comes to an end, except that, in 1774, the tribunal wrote to the Suprema that the only cases then pending were thirteen for Judaizing, but that they had no basis.[2]

With regard to the general character of the punishments inflicted it may be remarked that they vary capriciously, in accordance doubtless with the temper of the inquisitors, whose discretion had few limits. In the earlier days there would seem

---

[1] Medina, Lima, II, 336, 341–52. [2] Ibidem, p. 378.

to be a tendency to greater rigor than that customary in Spain. In the auto of 1578 the sentences, as a rule, are exceedingly severe.[1] When Judaism came to be conspicuous, the penalties which we have seen inflicted were very similar to those imposed for the same offence by the home tribunals. As the galleys went out of fashion and were replaced by forced labor in the presidios, the principal destination to which culprits were sent was Valdivia, though occasionally they were assigned to Callao, Chagre or other ports where fortifications were under construction. Scourging, as in Spain, was a favorite resort, without distinction of sex. We have seen how ruthlessly it was employed in the great auto of 1639 and this continued as long as the tribunal was active. In the auto of 1736 there were sixteen sentences of two hundred lashes, half of them on women, for bigamy, sorcery and other similar offences. In that of 1737 there were only nine penitents, five of them being women; all of them were sentenced to two hundred lashes apiece, but this was remitted in the case of one of the men.[2] In addition to the suffering, there was the severest of humiliations for those sensitive to shame. The so-called penitents were marched in procession through the streets, naked from the waist up, with insignia or inscriptions denoting their offences, while the executioner plied the lash. The assembled mob was in the habit of manifesting its piety by stoning the poor wretches, to repress which the tribunal occasionally issued a proclamation, such as we have seen in 1639. Similarly, before the auto of October 19, 1749, it forbade the throwing of stones, apples, oranges or other missiles at the penitents, under pain of a hundred pesos for Spaniards and ten pesos with four days of prison for others.[3] Although there are frequent sentences to imprisonment for longer or shorter terms, there is no allusion anywhere to a *casa de la misericordia* or *de la penitencia*, as it was called in Spain, in which the penitents could perform their penance.

---

[1] Palma, Añales, pp. 14–19.
[2] Bermudez de la Torre, Triunfos, pp. 136–57, 172–78.
[3] Palma, Añales, p. 139.

Occasional instances in which they are ordered to be shipped to the home country renders it probable that this was the usual recourse in such cases. Exile was a frequent penalty, sometimes to a designated place, but more frequently from certain cities or districts, where the culprit had committed offences; when this happened to be his native home, where his trade or profession was established, it might be a most severe infliction, depriving him of his means of livelihood; when the culprit was a vagrant or an old sorceress it mattered little.

The inexplicable inconsistency in the adjudgement of penalties, when gauged by any rational standard, can best be understood by the contrast in a few cases. The tenderness displayed towards the abuse of the confessional has already been alluded to. The same is seen in some of the sentences for crimes of a still more serious character. Thus in the auto of July 12, 1733, Sebastiana de Figueroa, a mestiza aged 60, for sorceries including adoration of the demon and causing sickness and deaths, offences for which in a secular tribunal she would have been executed without mercy, yet escaped with abjuration *de vehementi*, half confiscation, two hundred lashes (which were remitted) and four years of exile to a designated place.[1] In the auto of 1736, María Josepha Canga, a free negress, who had made her husband insane with sorceries and herbs, so as to have freedom for adultery, merely abjured *de levi*, with four years' service in the hospital of San Bartolomé. In the same auto, Juan González de Ribera, a mestizo, had gone to the Indians, adopted their ways, professed their religion and, worst of all, had induced several Spaniards to do the same, in addition to which he had taken three wives. He was thus a dogmatizer and was condemned as a bigamist, idolater, sorcerer and diviner, and yet he merely abjured *de vehementi* and had three years hard labor on an island off Callao.[2]

With this ill-judged mercy may be contrasted the case of François Moyen, a Frenchman of varied talents and wide culture,

---

[1] Barnuevo de Peralta, Relacion del Auto de 1733, Lima, 1733.
[2] Bermudez de la Torre, Triunfos, fol. 146, 152.

skilled as an artist and musician, whose evil fortune threw him upon the tender mercies of Amusquíbar. Born in 1720, he led a somewhat adventurous life; that he was a believing Catholic is seen in a vow of pilgrimage to Compostela, made during danger in a voyage—a vow which he duly performed in 1739, during a residence in Lisbon. In 1746 he sailed from there to Rio de Janeiro, with the Count de las Torres, who had important business in Chile. At Buenos Ayres they parted, the count hastening across the Pampas, while Moyen tarried there for awhile, his vivacity and his accomplishments rendering him a general favorite. During his stay he again manifested his devoutness by performing the spiritual exercises of St. Ignatius. About the middle of 1748, at the request of the count, who had gone to Lima, he started to rejoin him by way of Potosí, in company of a band of traders. With light-hearted carelessness, he talked freely, in the confidence of the road and the bivouac; as a Frenchman of the Gallican school and accustomed to the freedom of speech in Paris, he said much that he had better have left unsaid, with a singular imprudence in view of his acquaintance with the methods of the Portuguese Inquisition, his criticism of which formed one of the counts in his indictment.

He became an object of suspicion to his companions, especially to a Gallego named José Antonio Soto. Potosí was reached March 27, 1749, where a considerable stay was made, during which Moyen expended four pesos in masses. Two days after arrival, Soto denounced him to the commissioner José de Ligaraza Beaumont y Navarra, who secretly summoned the other travellers and muleteers, and gathered testimony swelling the *sumaria* to some two hundred pages. It was loose and thoughtless talk capable in the hands of the inquisitorial theologians of deductions most damaging—predestination in its most absolute form, polygamy justifiable, marriage not a sacrament; masses, prayers and indulgences were useless to souls in purgatory; limbo and purgatory were doubtful; the pope was not the head of the Church and had no power to bind or to loose; councils were superior to popes;

it was wrong to condemn people for lack of knowledge of the son of a carpenter, and much more of the same kind. The ingenuity of the calificadores, in fact, injected heresy into the simplest remarks. When he reproved a muleteer for abusing a mule and said that it was a creature of God, this was held to prove that he was a Manichean. One brilliant night, looking at the stars, he observed that their multitude was superfluous, thus assuming that God had erred in creation, which was heretical blasphemy, constituting him an heretical blasphemer. A criticism of the luxury of the clergy, with a reference to the poverty of the Apostles, showed him to be a Wickliffite.

Commissioner Ligaraza assembled a consulta, which voted for the arrest of so dangerous a heretic. It was executed May 14th and he was imprisoned in chains. At first he was kept *incomunicado*, but subsequently visitors were admitted who provoked him to risky discussions and then gave evidence against him, in which, among other matters, a debate on the Eucharist told heavily against him. He became an epileptic and suffered frightfully from his chains and the cold climate. The commissioner had no funds for his maintenance; he endeavored to support himself by painting, but this was insufficient and his only solace, his violin, was taken and sold, reducing him to such despair that he attempted suicide. The commissioner was in no haste and did not report the arrest until June 9th nor transmit the evidence until December. On May 9, 11 and 12, 1750, the tribunal extracted from it forty-four heretical propositions and ordered Moyen's transfer to Lima.

This journey, which commenced July 12th, consumed two years. Moyen's health had been wrecked in his confinement and his epileptic fits recurred almost daily. Several times he nearly died; at Chuquito he received the viaticum. It was not until April, 1751, that Cuzco was reached, when he chanced to interest a lawyer named Tomas de Lecaros, who entered security for him and carried him to Arequipa, in vain search for improvement. There he met an English hatter named William—a good Catholic who attended mass daily—who counselled hypocrisy and silence about religious matters in a land where there was an Inquisition. Moyen chanced to mention this in his examinations; the Englishman was arrested and ruined.

On the return to Cuzco, a halt was made at Urcos, eight leagues distant. Amusquíbar, on September 14, 1751, called for his appearance within two months; the commissioner of Cuzco sent his notary, when Moyen drew a dagger and attempted resistance but was overpowered. Some three months later Fray Juan de San Miguel wrote to the tribunal that Moyen was hardened in his heresies and scattered them freely around Cuzco. That place was left, January 29, 1752, fortunately prior to the reception of an order from Amusquíbar to forward him in chains. March 26th he was delivered to the tribunal, broken and prematurely old with the sufferings of these three preliminary years of his trial.

Proceedings dragged on with the customary delays. The accusation, presented October 13th, represented him as a formal and pertinacious heretic and a follower of the sects of Luther, Calvin, Jansen, Quesnel, Manichee and Mahomet, besides being strongly suspect of Judaism. Discussion over these articles lasted until May 18, 1753, when he professed profound repentance for having discussed religious matters and begged for mercy. During the prolonged delays which ensued his sufferings in the prison were severe—in themselves an excessive punishment for reckless speech. Besides his continual epileptic fits, his feet were eaten up by chigoes; his chains chafed his ankles into sores, which threatened gangrene of one leg, and when, to avert this, on November 13th, the alcaide was directed to remove one of the shackles, the other was left on. In spite of this he made several attempts to escape— once by endeavoring to set fire to the door of his cell with the candle allowed to him at night, whereupon he was deprived of it. Again he succeeded in reaching the house of the Count of las Torres, only to be remanded, and on a third effort his plans were betrayed by a prisoner in an adjoining cell.

Two years were consumed in sending the evidence to Potosí

for ratification and awaiting its return, although at first it had been ratified *ad perpetuam*. It was not received until April, 1755, and then its publication was delayed until September 3d. After this followed the customary examinations on the evidence, which were prolonged until March 14, 1758—a delay largely caused by Moyen's constant epileptic attacks. His counsel did not present the defence until November 8, 1759, and then the consulta de fe was not assembled until January 15, 1761. It considered the case until February 14th, when the definitive vote was taken, under a protest that torture was not ordered in view of the weakened condition of the accused. The sentence finally was published in the auto of the following April 5th. It condemned him to abjure *de vehementi*, to ten years' forced labor in an African presidio (Oran, Ceuta or Melilla), or in the penitential prison of Seville, as the inquisitor-general might prefer, and to two hundred lashes, which were commuted to vergüenza in consideration of his infirmities. The humiliating parade of the vergüenza through the streets of Lima was duly performed the next day; on the 11th he was shipped in irons by the galleon San Juan Bautista, reaching Cádiz in November; in December he was sent to Seville to which the African presidio was commuted. No consideration seems to have been given to the sufferings of the thirteen years of imprisonment since his arrest, nor to the wreck of a joyous and promising life for a few inconsiderate utterances.

Amusquíbar sought to justify the excessive delays of the trial by the quarrels in which he was involved, by his own sickness and that of the accused, but the Suprema did not accept these excuses and replied that the ten years intervening between the receipt of the prisoner and the sentence was an excessive delay and grave omission of the tribunal.[1] There was in all this no special malignity; it was simply the habitual application of the system with callous indifference as to the results to the accused.

[1] Mackenna, Francisco Moyen, *passim*.—Palma, Añales, pp. 129-32.—Medina, Lima, II, 374.

Not the least important function of the Inquisition was the censorship of the press. Although in Spain this was reserved to the Suprema, and the tribunals could only refer to it books which they regarded as suspect, distance rendered independent action necessary in the colonies. From an early period the Lima tribunal examined books and prohibited such as it saw fit. The importation of printed matter was also, as in Spain, subject to its supervision. The original instructions, borne by Cerezuela, enjoined special watchfulness by the commissioners at the seaports, to prevent the introduction of all works that were on the Index. To insure this, at first no books were admitted except through Callao, and the commissioner at Panamá was required to keep a close watch on everything destined for that point. Nothing could be shipped from there without his licence, nor could any package be opened except in his presence. The same vigilance was exercised at Callao, and all books were sent to Fray Juan de Almaraz, Prior of San Agustin, for examination. As the settlement and commerce of Buenos Ayres developed, similar precautions were observed there. There was always a haunting dread of the efforts attributed to the Protestants to smuggle heretic books into the land. In 1605 there was a scare of this kind, based on rumors that ships from Lisbon manned by Flemings were bringing such works in casks purporting to contain wine or salt, and special orders were issued to the commissioner to be doubly watchful.[1] As in Spain, this system was a serious impediment to trade, and led not infrequently to collisions with the secular authorities. It required that all ships on arrival should be visited by the commissioner before any passenger or merchandise was landed, and that the latter, when brought on shore, should be opened in his presence and be minutely inspected.

Even so high an ecclesiastical dignitary as the Archbishop of Lima was not exempt from the censorship of the tribunal. We have seen how Amusquíbar used this power for the humiliation of Archbishop Barroeta, nor was this the only instance. Juan de

---

[1] Medina, Lima, I, 5, 172, 330; II, 368.

Almoguera, who was archbishop from 1674 to 1676, while yet Bishop of Arequipa, had been strongly impressed with the dissolute lives of the priests among the Indians and, in 1671, he published in Madrid a series of Instructions, which the inquisitors held to be not only defamatory to the priests, but to contain propositions adverse to the Holy See. The archbishop defended himself by asserting that his doctrines were approved by the most learned men of Peru, and that the facts which he cited were perfectly true, for which he appealed to the testimony of the inquisitors themselves. They admitted this, but nevertheless they caused the edict of prohibition to be published everywhere.[1]

The reformatory legislation of Carlos III, from 1762 to 1768, limiting the unrestricted control of the Inquisition over the prohibition of books, was long in reaching Peru. In 1773 Viceroy Amat y Yunient says that although he had not yet received the cédula of 1768 officially through the Council of Indies, yet he defines its provisions as a guide. It put in force the Constitution *Sollicita ac provida* of Benedict XIV, entitling authors to be heard in defence of their books; it prevented the prohibition of books *ad interim* until a final decision was reached; where expurgations were ordered they were to be made known so that owners could delete the objectionable passages, and all edicts were to be submitted to the viceroy before publication.[2] The demand for literature must have been greater than would be anticipated, for, in 1772, there was a discussion between the viceroy and the tribunal over the proceedings in opening and examining 165 cases of books.[3]

At this period the censorship was exercised largely through the civil authorities. February 28, 1787, the Viceroy Count de Croix reported to the king the execution of his orders of 1785 in the suppression and burning of certain books, the seizure of all copies that could be traced to the possession of booksellers or of individuals, and the issue of an edict prohibiting the printing of anything

---

[1] Medina, Lima, II, 249.   [2] Memorias de los Vireyes, IV, 472.
[3] Archivo nacional de Lima, Protocolo 225, Exp.te 5278.

without a licence, even the University not being permitted to publish the eulogies and addresses customary on the arrival of a viceroy, or the Latin orations with which the studies were annually opened. The Inquisition is only alluded to in connection with the examination of importations, none being delivered from the custom-house without preliminary inspection by the commissioner of the tribunal, in connection with an appointee of the government.[1] As in Spain, this censorship extended over morals as well as over religion and politics. In 1796, Antonio Ortiz, the commissioner at Buenos Ayres, was much exercised over certain wall-papers received from Barcelona. Some of them had mythological figures, such as Hercules, Venus and the like, which he considered intolerable. There was another one representing the globe adorned with flowers and presided over by Cupid with a lighted torch, as though to burn it with his impure fires, all of which he was impelled to cut up into small pieces.[2] As we have seen in Mexico, even ill-advised symbols of devotion were prohibited. When, at the suppression in 1813, the building of the Inquisition was entered, Stevenson describes seeing there among the mass of prohibited books, a quantity of cotton handkerchiefs on which was printed a figure of Religion with a chalice in one hand and a cross in the other—a device which the manufacturer had fondly believed would render them popular, without reflecting upon the desecration inseparable from their use.[3]

From this time the principal work of the tribunal was in the enforcement of the prohibition of literature regarded as dangerous to State or Church. Camilo Henríquez, priest of the Padres Crucíferos de la Buena Muerte, was a prominent object of persecution. In 1809 he was denounced for reading prohibited books; his cell was searched without success, but the accuser insisted and on a more minute investigation his mattress was found to be stuffed with the dangerous material. He was arrested and, in 1810, was banished to Quito, but instead of obeying he joined the

---

[1] Memorias de los Vireyes, V, 85.   [2] Medina, La Plata, II, 256.
[3] Stevenson, Twenty Years in South America, I, 269

insurgents of Chile and distinguished himself by supporting the revolution in *La Aurora*, the periodical which he founded. Under the Restoration, the tribunal had little real work to do except to issue edicts prohibiting European periodicals, political pamphlets and other productions in which it could discover opinions inimical to the established order in politics and religion.[1]

In the turbulent atmosphere of the early nineteenth century, the authority of the Inquisition naturally declined, especially as the character of the inquisitors was so unfitted to inspire respect. Its suppression by the decree of the Córtes of Cádiz, February 22, 1813, was evidently seen in advance to be inevitable and was fatal to its influence. Shortly before that decree was received Stevenson relates that he was summoned before the tribunal, in consequence of a discussion in a coffee-house with a Fray Bustamante, respecting the image of the Madonna of the Rosary. If we may believe his story of the audience, he treated the inquisitors with slender reverence and escaped with an admonition to avoid religious disputes, and to bear in mind that in the dominions of his Catholic Majesty all men were subject to the Inquisition.[2] When the decree of suppression was published, he had an opportunity of accompanying the first party that entered the building, so long an object of universal dread. The prison cells were all open and empty; he describes them as small but not uncomfortable. In the audience-chamber, back of the judges' dais, there hung on high a life-sized image of Christ; its head was so arranged as to be movable by a person secreted behind, on a signal from the inquisitor, producing a profound impression on the awestruck culprit, who was denying his guilt. From his description of the torture-room it would seem that the tortures employed, though cruel enough, were less severe than those formerly in use—the *cordeles* and *jarras de agua*, the *mancuerda*, the *trampazo* and the *garrucha*. There was a rack on which the arms and legs could be stretched; a kind of pillory for scourging with scourges,

---

[1] Palma, Añales, p. 176, 210.
[2] Stevenson, Twenty Years in South America, I, 261–67.

some of which were of wire chains with sharp points; "tormentors" of netted wire with points, arranged to fit the wrists or waists, the legs or arms, and thumb-screws—a grisly collection, but less likely to endanger life and limb than the older atrocities. The crowd which found admittance carried off some of these as mementos and also some of the records, but the archbishop the next day published an excommunication against all who should not return what they had taken, and most of the documents were restored.[1]

We have seen that the money found in the chest was taken by the authorities and this of course was retained, but the salaries of the officials were continued. The suspension was short-lived, ending with the decree of July 21, 1814, re-establishing the Inquisition, when the three inquisitors, Abarca, Zalduegui and Sobrino, resumed their places, but the old awful authority could not be revived. They complained bitterly of the viceroy, who showed himself, they said, hostile to the re-establishment. He delayed issuing the decree, treated them with discourtesy and refused to refund the money. They depicted the deplorable condition of the tribunal, destitute of means to pay salaries in arrears, or even to make arrests that had been resolved upon prior to the suppression, while the buildings were dirty and out of repair.[2] We can readily imagine that the progress of the War of Independence left little leisure or disposition on the part of the authorities to listen to their complaints. How completely decadent was their authority, is seen in a letter from the Suprema ordering them to summon an Englishman named John Robinson and point out to him that he had been admitted to residence on condition of not talking about religion, or dogmatizing against Catholicism, and they were moreover to seek an interview with the viceroy, to ask his aid in restraining the man and to report the result.[3] Times had changed since François Moyen was so inhumanly persecuted for his loquacity.

---

[1] Stevenson, *op. cit.*, I, 267-74.—Medina, Lima, II, 398.
[2] Medina, Lima, II, 400.   [3] Palma, Añales, p. 211.

Still, they were not without some remnants of authority. The University of Lima had sent an address to the Córtes of Cádiz, congratulating it on the decree of suppression. This was an offence not to be overlooked and, April 7, 1815, the Suprema sent an order to dismiss all the signers of the paper who held office under the tribunal. Accordingly, on October 29th, Fray Josef Recalde was summoned to surrender his vestment and badge as a calificador. To this he replied, November 3d, with a supplication not to expose him to such a dishonor; the paper had been presented to him for signature by the beadle of the University, saying that it was an act of obedience to the Córtes and he, being busy, had signed it without reading it, as he was accustomed to do with the numerous papers requiring his signature. On this Inquisitor-fiscal Sobrino reported that Recalde only intensified his offence, and he proceeded to accuse the University of misleading youth and allowing them to read prohibited books, while Recalde's statement only showed how recklessly its members joined in anything resolved upon by the leaders. Both papers were forwarded, December 13th, to the Suprema for its judgement, but whether Recalde was reinstated does not appear from the documents at hand.[1]

The officials continued to draw their salaries, but there is little trace of their activity. The latest indication I have met of their performance of duty is a letter from the Suprema, July 11, 1817, to the tribunal of Logroño, asking for information to guide the tribunal of Lima in a case of alleged bigamy on the part of Don Fernando Díaz, then a resident of Cuzco.[2] In that same year a "voluntary" subscription in aid of the government was organized, to which the contribution of Inquisitor-fiscal Sobrino was niggardly, leading to his being reprimanded from Madrid.[3] In 1819 the tribunal was reorganized. The senior inquisitor Abarca was dead and Zalduegui was dean; he and Sobrino were jubilated on one-quarter of their salaries and the tribunal consisted of Cristóval

---

[1] Archivo de Simancas, Inquisicion, Legajo 1473.
[2] Ibidem, Libro 559.
[3] Palma, Añales, p. 213.

de Ortegon as senior, Anselmo Pérez de la Canal as junior and José Mariano de Larrea as fiscal.

Their term of office was short. The final decree of suppression, March 9, 1820, was long in reaching Peru, where it was not promulgated until September 9th, with orders to communicate it to all the archbishops of the district and to take the necessary steps for assuming possession of the property. This was done decently and in order. On September 18th Viceroy Pezuela ordered the intendant of the province, in concert with the two regidores of Lima, to proceed in accordance with the decree of February 22, 1813, to occupy the property, including its patronage and pious foundations, and to make an exact inventory. This was followed, September 20th, with instructions that at 8.30 A.M. of Friday, September 22d, possession should be taken, and the ex-dean was notified to be ready in order that it should be executed with promptitude. At nine o'clock on Saturday the intendant and the regidores met in the Inquisition and made an inventory of all property found there. In pursuance of Article 10 of the decree of 1813, the commission of three, on September 28th, issued an order calling on the ex-receiver-general, Carlos Lizon, for an authentic list of all the officials with their salaries, so that the latter might be paid. This was superfluous; from time immemorial the custom had been to pay all salaries in advance, in instalments of four months. The inquisitors had providently taken care of themselves and their subordinates and, on August 29th and September 1st, had issued orders on Receiver Lizon for the *tercio adelantado*, commencing September 1st, so that he was able to exhibit the corresponding receipts, amounting to 9472 pesos and a fraction, indicating on annual pay-roll of 28,417 pesos.

That the inventory only showed a few items of volumes of records is testimony of the completeness with which everything had been appropriated. Although the work of the tribunal had shrunk almost to nothingness, all the offices had been kept filled and the roster was as complete as it had been in the period of the greatest activity.[1] It is presumable that, as in Mexico, they went to Spain and were provided for there.

The total amount of work accomplished is estimated by Medina as three thousand cases tried, but this is probably too liberal an allowance. His exhaustive researches have resulted only in an enumeration of 1474 cases.

These consist of—

Laymen	1126	Dominicans	34
Women	180	Mercenarians	36
Secular clergy	101	Augustinians	26
Franciscans	49	Jesuits	12

[1] Archivo nacional de Lima, Inventarios Originales, No. 1.

It may be of interest to put on record the personnel of the tribunal and the salaries at the moment of extinction:

	Pesos.	Reales.	Mrs.
Inquisidor mas antiguo Cristóval de Ortegon	4962	9	30
Inquisidor Anselmo Pérez de la Canal (at ¾ of salary as ordered by Suprema)	3722	3	14
Do. fiscal José Mariano de Larrea (Do.—but with 148 additional as Juez de los bienes)	3870	3	6
Jubilado Dean Pedro Zalduegui (at ¼ salary)	1240	6	16
" Inquisidor José Ruiz Sobrino (Do.)	1240	6	16
Secretario del Secreto Manuel de Arizcurrunaga	1700		
Do. Franco de Echavarria Momediano	1700		
Do. Ramon del Valle	1700		
Do. Carlos Delgado (at ½ salary)	850		
Do. Jubilado Pablo de la Torre (Do.)	850		
Secretario de Secuestros Jacinto Jimeno	1000		
Receptor-general Carlos Lizon, 1900, together with 250 for collecting rents	2150		
Contador Ildefonso Gereda	500		
Abogado del Fisco Manuel de la Fuente y Chaves	350		
Procurador del Fisco Mariano González	300		
Alcaide de Carceles J. Baut. de Barnechea	900		
Nuncio A. D. Eustaquio	830		
Portero de Camara Manuel Leon	500		
Ministro de vara Teodoro Marino	50		
	28,417	5	14

In addition Teodoro Marino is ordered to receive 33 pesos 2½ reales for four months' service as portero at the rate of 100 pesos per annum. Also there is a salary of forty reales per month as sweeper, divided between Fray Manuel Bahamonde and Fray Manuel Tinoco, who are each to receive five pesos for the months of July and August. The peso, or piece of eight reales, is the Spanish dollar.

The offences prosecuted were

Propositions	140	Blasphemy		97
Judaism	243	Sexual errors		40
Moors	5	Bigamy		297
Protestants	65	Sorcery		172
Solicitation	109	Miscellaneous and not specified		306

For the 250 years of existence, the estimate of a total of 3000 cases would make 12 per annum, or 1 per month, but in the first 20 years of the tribunal the cases amounted to 1265, which would reduce the average of the other 230 years to about 7½, and it would be safe to assume for the last century an average of not more than 3 or 4 a year.[1]

For this slender result, to say nothing of the large expenditure, the colony was kept in a constant state of disquiet, the orderly course of government was well-nigh impossible, intellectual, commercial and industrial development were impeded, universal distrust of one's neighbor was commanded by ordinary prudence, and the population lived with the sense of evil ever impending over the head of every one. That there was any real danger to the faith in Peru is absurd. Possibly the tribunal may have been of some service in repressing the prevalence of bigamy among laymen and of solicitation among the clergy, but the fact that these two offences remained to the last so prominent in its calendar would show that it accomplished little. As regards sorcery and superstitions, which pervaded all classes, in the mixed population of Europeans, Indians, negroes and half-breeds, with an accumulation of superstitious beliefs drawn from so many sources, the number of cases is surprisingly small, especially as the exemption of Indians from inquisitorial jurisdiction seems to have been disregarded in this offence. In the repression of the practices which were regarded as implying pact with the demon the Inquisition may be said to have virtually accomplished nothing. It would be difficult to find, in the annals of human misgovernment, a parallel case in which so little was accomplished at so great a cost as by the Inquisition under Spanish institutions.

---

[1] Medina, Lima, II, 466-7

CHAPTER VIII.

NEW GRANADA.

ALTHOUGH the *Nuevo Reino de Granada* originally formed part of the Viceroyalty of Peru, it was the earliest settlement on the continent of South America. When Balboa, in 1514, reported his rich discoveries in Darien, no time was lost in sending out Pedro Arias Dávila as governor, who landed at Santa Marta. He took with him as bishop Fray Juan de Quevedo, who formed one of his council with a right to vote, thus founding at the start that curious complication of jurisdictions which exercised so unhappy an influence on the development of the Spanish colonies. The see of Santa Marta, however, was not founded until 1531 and, as settlements were pushed into the interior, Santa Fe de Bogotá was established as the capital, where the Audiencia, or high court, was organized in 1547 and governed the colony until 1564, when Andrés Díaz Venero de Leiva was sent out as president.[1] It was not erected into a viceroyalty until 1719, from which it was reduced to its former state in a few years, to be restored again in 1740.[2]

In 1532 the see of Cartagena was founded and, in 1547, that of Popayan. In 1553 came the Franciscan Fray Juan Barrios with a bull of Julius III by which the see of Santa Marta was transferred to Santa Fe and erected into an archbishopric, thus sundering it from the metropolis of Lima. Santa Marta was reduced to an abbacy, to be subsequently re-erected. Cartagena

---

[1] José Manuel Groot, Historia eclesiastica y civil de Nueva Granada, I, 1, 7, 98 (Bogotá, 1869–71).
[2] J. A. García y García, Relaciones de los Vireyes del Nuevo Reyno de Granada, pp. xvi–xix (New York, 1869).

was dismembered from Santo Domingo and the archiepiscopal province included it with Popayan and Santa Marta. In the absence of the Inquisition, Archbishop Barrios exercised its functions and, in a series of Synodal Constitutions, issued in 1556, he ordered that no books should be possessed or sold without being first examined by the bishop or his deputies, under the penalty of fifty pesos.[1]

When, in 1570, the tribunal of Lima was established, its authority extended over all the Spanish possessions from Panamá to the south. The organization of so extended a territory was a work of time and the material at hand for it was of the worst description, as we have seen in the preceding chapter. It was not until 1577 that Inquisitor Cerezuela appointed a commissioner for Santa Fe, when his choice fell upon D. Lope Clavijo, dean of the metropolitan chapter. In the exercise of his new authority, Clavijo naturally became involved in bitter quarrels with the archbishop, Luis Zapata de Cardenas. His character reflected no credit on the Holy Office, if it be true as reported that his official apartments became a receptacle for women, on some of whom he committed violence, and that the nuns of Tunja were obliged to forbid his entrance into their parlor, in order to escape his licentious conversation. The Commissioner of Popayan, Gonzalo de Torres, was no better and was the source of infinite trouble to the bishop, until the visitador, Juan Ruiz de Prado, summoned him to trial in Lima, on a prosecution containing twenty charges. He seems, in 1589, to have been deprived of his office, which, as Archbishop Lobo Guerrero said to the Suprema, he used only as a means of committing offences against God. We hear also of Juan García, Commissioner of Cumaná, appointed by Inquisitor Ulloa, as a reward for committing perjury against an enemy of the latter. His adulteries and incests with maids, wives and widows, mothers, daughters and sisters, were notorious and he had caused the death of more than a hundred Indian laborers without baptism or confession. Like the others, he only

---

[1] Groot, I, 84, 504.

sought the place for the protection afforded from punishment for his crimes.¹

Under worthies such as these, it is easy to understand that little attention was paid to the purification of the faith among the colonists. The cases sent to Lima for trial were few and unimportant. There were no Protestants among them; the only accusation of Judaism was that of Juan de Herrera, in 1592, of which he was absolved in 1595, after undergoing torture; the rest were the ordinary run of inquisitorial business—sorcery, bigamy, blasphemy and propositions, more or less innocent. That the commissioners, however, did not neglect opportunities that presented themselves may be assumed from the case of Juan Fernández, a merchant who, in 1588, denounced himself to the Commissioner of Cartagena because, on hearing that a man had hanged himself he had exclaimed "May God forgive him!" This proposition was decided to be heretical; Fernández was arrested, with sequestration of property, and was sentenced to abjure *de levi*, to hear mass as a penitent, and to pay a fine of a hundred pesos.²

It was evident that, if the faith was to be properly guarded, some authoritative tribunal nearer than Lima or Mexico was necessary for the vast territory which included the whole sweep of the Antilles and the coast of Tierra Firme from Panamá to Guiana. As early as April 8, 1580, Inquisitor Cerezuela wrote that the people of New Granada were asking for one, in view of their distance from Lima; this was great—fully six hundred leagues—and there would be no inconvenience in such a step except that he has understood that there were no suitable persons there to serve as consultors and calificadores.³ Again, in 1600, Inquisitor Ordóñez y Flores represented to the Suprema the enormous extent of the territory assigned to the Lima tribunal and suggested two new ones—one at La Plata and the other at

---

¹ J. T. Medina, Historia del Tribunal del Santo Oficio de la Inquisicion de Cartagena de las Indias, pp. 19–23, 430 (Santiago de Chile, 1899).
² Ibidem, pp. 27, 29.   ³ Ibidem, p. 423.

Santa Fe. The latter should include the sees of Popayan, Cartagena, Santa Marta and Venezuela, making a district four hundred leagues in length, in which it was impossible to provide commissioners; at present there was but one, with whom communication was so difficult that sometimes two years passed without hearing from him. A year earlier, in 1599, Archbishop Lobo Guerrero had written to the king to the same effect. He described the land as the most vicious and sinful in the Spanish dominions, and the faith as on the point of destruction; the distance to Lima was so great that offenders either died or escaped on the road and there was no money to meet the cost of sending them.[1]

The same cry went up from the islands. In 1594 the Council of Indies suggested to the king that, in view of the failure of all efforts to suppress the dealings of the people of Santo Domingo with the English and French corsairs, and with pirates of all nations, the inquisitor-general should commission the Archbishop of Santo Domingo as an inquisitor. On this being submitted to the Suprema it replied that there were disadvantages in the plan and the true remedy would be to establish a tribunal on the island, which could be done on the most economical basis. Philip II ordered a junta of a member of each council to consider a grant of inquisitorial power to the archbishop for a term of three or four years.[2] Nothing was done. The king shrank from the expense of a new tribunal and the Suprema was too jealous of the episcopate to delegate its power to the archbishop. A similar fate awaited a complaint of Bishop Martin of Puerto Rico, in 1606, as to the influx of heretic traders and sailors with their books, to remedy which he urged that a tribunal be established in Santo Domingo, or that delegated power be granted to the bishops, including authority to appoint alguaziles and familiars with the recognized privileges and exemptions.[3]

---

[1] Medina, pp. 37–41.
[2] Archivo de Simancas, Inquisicion, Lib. 45, fol. 182.
[3] Medina, p. 434.

There can be no doubt that many representations of the same import poured in upon the court and finally, in 1608, the Council of Indies formally urged the erection of a tribunal in Santo Domingo. After due discussion, it was resolved to include in the district all the lands surrounding the Caribbean, except Central America, and, as its inquisitors subsequently boasted, it enjoyed the most extensive territories of any tribunal, embracing the archbishoprics of both Santa Fe and Santo Domingo and the bishoprics of Cartagena, Panamá, Santa Marta, Popayan, Venezuela, Puerto Rico and Santiago de Cuba.[1] Its seat was fixed at Cartagena, as a central point and leading port of entry, which had had time to recover from its devastation by Drake in 1585. Its position and its safe and capacious harbor, easily defensible by fortifications, rendered it the entrepôt of the trade with the Pacific, and the place where the treasures of the colonies were gathered for transhipment to Spain, while the pearl fishery of Margarita and the productions of a province rich in mineral and agricultural wealth gave it a large and lucrative commerce. As the seat of a tribunal it had the advantage that, unlike Lima and Mexico, it was not a capital where the humors of inquisitors could be in some slight degree controlled by a viceroy and a royal Audiencia. They had only to deal directly with a local governor and municipal authorities on the one side, and with a simple bishop on the other; there was little to restrain them, short of the Suprema beyond the Atlantic, and we shall see that they took full advantage of their position in the endless embroilments which formed their chief occupation. The history of the tribunal is to be found not so much in its autos de fe as in the guerrilla war which for a century it maintained with the authorities, civil and ecclesiastical, rendering decent and orderly government impossible and going far to explain the decadence and decrepitude of the colony.

Extensive as was the district of the tribunal, it sought to extend its authority still farther over Florida. As early as 1606 there

---
[1] Medina, p. 46.

is a curious letter from Fray Juan Cabezas, Bishop of Cuba, reciting that the tribunal of Mexico had appointed Fray Francisco Carranco as commissioner in Havana—under what authority does not appear. On the news of his coming the good bishop fled from Havana and took refuge in St. Augustine, whence he despatched his provisor to Spain to protest against the announced intentions of Carranco to include Florida within his jurisdiction. This had caused lively anxiety among the garrison, some three hundred in number, who with the friars were the only Spaniards there. The Indians as yet were so little rooted in the faith that recently in the missions they had slain four or five of the missionaries. There were, he adds, many women and children, for most of the soldiers were married and the effort was made to induce all to marry, for the hardships of the place were such that, without these ties, the governor would not venture to send any one away with the expectation of his return.[1] In 1621 there was some discussion as to sending a commissioner there, but nothing was done. Then, in 1630, Inquisitor Agustin Ugarte y Saravia reported from Cartagena that he had sent to the Governor of St. Augustine, Luis de Rojas y Borja, commissions in blank for a commissioner and familiar, fearing that, if appointees were sent, he would not receive them, as the settlement was wholly military, even the Franciscan missionaries being rated as soldiers.[2] It is not likely that the governor filled out the commissions, for Florida remained deprived of the blessing of the Holy Office. In 1692 another attempt was made. The Cartagena tribunal appointed Fray Pedro de Lima as commissioner with power to nominate subordinates, without requiring proofs of limpieza. Of this he availed himself to create a notary, an alguazil mayor and four familiars, thus establishing a tribunal of his own. The governor, Don Diego de Quiroga y Lanada, took the alarm and wrote earnestly to the Council of Indies. All this, he said, was simply to escape the royal jurisdiction; Fray Pedro, as a friar, was ineligible to the post of commissioner; the

---

[1] Medina, p. 433.   [2] Ibidem, pp. 155, 163.

tribunal of Cartagena had no jurisdiction over Florida, where, by the Concordias, there was to be no Inquisition and, if cases of faith arose, they were to be treated by the cura or the ecclesiastical Vicariate. The Council of Indies, December 9, 1695, reported this to the king, asking that the Suprema be told to order the Cartagena tribunal to desist; to this Carlos II assented and the attempt to establish an Inquisition in Florida seems to have ended here.[1]

[1] MSS. of Library of University of Halle, Yc, 17.—Archivo de Simancas, Inquisicion, Libro 60, fol. 352; Lib. 61, fol. 524, 534.

It does not seem that the tribunal of Cartagena had any part in a curious attempt to introduce the Inquisition into Louisiana, which was ceded to Spain by the Treaty of Paris in 1762. The disaffected colonists drove out their new masters in 1768, but were subdued the next year by O'Reilly. In 1772 the Governor, Don Luis de Unzaga, in a report to the Bishop of Havana, said "It is not the practice here to force any one to submit to the Church, and the process of excommunication is held in utter abomination." This toleration continued and, in 1789, the Governor Estevan Miró was surprised to receive from Fray Antonio de Sedella—one of a band of Spanish Capuchins who had been sent to New Orleans in 1772—a communication stating that, in a letter of December 5th, he had received from the proper authority a commission as commissioner of the Inquisition, with instructions to perform his duties with the utmost zeal and fidelity; that, having made his investigations with the greatest secrecy and precaution, he notified the governor that, in execution of his instructions, he might soon, at some late hour of the night, deem it necessary to require some guards to assist him in his operations. That same night, April 29th, he was aroused from sleep to find at his door an officer with a file of grenadiers, when he thanked them and said that he had no use for them that night. To his astonishment he was told that he was under arrest; he was hurried on board a vessel which sailed the next day for Cádiz, and the Inquisition was nipped in the bud. Miró seems to have been called upon for an explanation, for in a despatch of June 3d he declared that he shuddered when he read Sedella's note. He had been ordered to foster immigration from the United States, under pledge of no molestation on account of religion, and the mere name of the Inquisition in New Orleans would not only check immigration but would be capable of driving away those who had come, and, in spite of his action with Sedella, he dreaded the most fatal consequences from the mere suspicion of the causes of his dismissal. His justification seems to have been accepted, for the attempt was abandoned.—Gayarré, History of Louisiana. The Spanish Domination, pp. 56, 69, 269–71 (New York, 1854).—Fortier, History of Louisiana, II, 62, 140, 327.

It may be assumed that the motive of commissioning Sedella was rather political than religious. The uprising in France was calling for active measures by the Inquisition in Spain to keep out revolutionary principles; Louisiana was French and its loyalty to Spain was doubtful, so that the Inquisition would be useful both as a source of information and an instrument of repression.

On June 29, 1610, Mateo de Salcedo and Juan de Mañozca—the latter a name of evil import to the Spanish colonies—the newly appointed inquisitors for Cartagena, set sail from Cádiz, with a fiscal, alguazil, notary and messenger, and power to appoint all necessary subordinates, whose commissions would be issued by the Suprema. On August 9th they arrived at Santo Domingo, where they were received with all honor and published the Edict of Faith; they received some self-denunciations, they appointed the Dominican Provincial as temporary commissioner, and the archbishop surrendered the papers of all cases heard by him and his predecessors. Sailing on September 4th, they reached Cartagena on the 21st, where their reception by the civil and ecclesiastical authorities was conducted with great pomp. On the 26th the royal letters were read and the oaths of obedience taken; three houses were rented for their occupation until a suitable building could be rented. The king allowed them 8000 pesos for their installation, with which they bought the houses in which they were lodged, paying half in cash and, with the remainder of the money, building a prison with thirteen cells.[1] For the support of the officials, as in the case of Mexico and Lima, the king provided a subvention of 8400 ducats a year, until the fines and confiscations should suffice to defray expenses; but, profiting by experience, he endeavored to guard against the habitual deceit of the tribunals. In his cédula of March 8, 1610, to the treasury officials of Cartagena, he ordered that sum to be paid out of any funds in the treasury or, if those were not sufficient, then out of what came in from the province, but, in order to know how much of this subvention should be paid, the receiver of the tribunal was required to furnish every year a statement of the confiscations and of all moneys applicable to the salaries, which were to be duly deducted from the treasury payments.[2] We shall see, as in Mexico and Peru, how fruitless was the precaution against audacious inquisitorial mendacity.

---

[1] Medina, pp. 42–50, 76.—Archivo de Simancas, Inquisicion, Leg. 1465, fol. 23.
[2] Archivo de Simancas, Inquisicion, Lib. 40, fol. 51.

EARLY OPERATIONS

The tribunal found little to do in justification of its existence. It was not until February 2, 1614, that it held its first auto de fe, in which it presented about thirty penitents, whose offences consisted of trivial propositions, blasphemies, superstitious arts and the like. Nevertheless the ceremonies were conducted with all solemnity to impress the population, and a long and grandiloquent report was sent to the Suprema. Four readers of the sentences were employed, so that the reading could be continuous, yet such was the verbosity that the ceremonies lasted from half-past nine in the morning until after sunset and the auto had to be finished by torch-light. There were about a dozen sentences of scourging through the streets and when, on the next afternoon, the infliction was to commence, a motley crowd of negroes, mestizos, mulattos and Spaniards, estimated at four thousand, assembled, armed with oranges and other fruits wherewith to pelt the victims. The escort provided for them was afraid to venture forth until the inquisitors made proclamation threatening a hundred lashes for any such manifestation of pious zeal, when every one dropped his missile and the punishment was carried out in peace.[1]

Besides these there had been despatched in the audience-chamber sixteen cases, one of which is worth mentioning as an example of the spirit in which the inquisitors commenced their duties. For some matter of slight importance, Doña Lorenza de Acereto, a noble married woman, had been penanced by the episcopal provisor Almanso, prior to the founding of the tribunal. Probably stimulated by the Edict of Faith she was impelled to denounce herself to it and Mañozca, who had some private grudge to satisfy, imprisoned her for eight months and then sentenced her to a fine of 4000 ducats and exile for two years. When the sentence was read, she appealed to the inquisitor-general but, as she was leaving the room, she was warned that she would be immured for life in the secret prison and, in dread of this, she withdrew the appeal. It chanced that Almanso was soon after-

---

[1] Medina, pp. 82–96.

wards sent to Madrid by his bishop to complain of the tribunal; he represented this matter to the Suprema, which sent for the papers of the trial and, on examining them, suspended the case as groundless.[1]

It was in unimportant routine work of this kind that the inquisitors employed the intervals of their quarrels with the civil and ecclesiastical authorities. Cartagena numbered a population of only five hundred Spaniards; the rest were negro slaves, Indians and the half-castes so numerous in the Spanish colonies. The Indians were not subject to inquisitorial jurisdiction and among the whites there was not intellectual energy sufficient to produce serious heresy. Mañozca, in fact, in a letter of March 17, 1622, to the Suprema describes them as wholly devoted to the pursuit of gain and utterly regardless of honor and reputation, from the Governor down. There is no one, he says, who will trouble himself with useful works, and virtue and honor are contraband, for they are only prized where there are virtuous and honorable men.[2] There were left the negroes and mixed races, ignorant and superstitious. The slaves had brought from the Guinea coast the mysteries of Obeah and dark practices of sorcery. The native Indians had ample store of superstitions, to cure or to injure, to provoke love or hatred; the colonists had their own credulous beliefs, to which they added implicit faith in those of the inferior races. The land was overrun with this combination of the occult arts of three continents, all of which were regarded by the Inquisition, not as idle fancies, but as the exercise of supernatural powers, involving express or implicit pact with the demon. Had the tribunal seriously labored to eradicate them, it would have had ample work for its energies, but the offenders were slaves or paupers; there was neither honor nor profit in their prosecution, and consequently no energy. Indeed Mañozca, in the letter just quoted, endeavored to be released from the task—perhaps the only instance on record of an inquisitor desiring

---

[1] Medina, pp. 100–1.
[2] Archivo de Simancas, Inquisicion, Libro 30, fol. 180.

to abandon a portion of the jurisdiction for which the Holy Office was wont to struggle so desperately.

He gives a fearful account of the witchcraft practised by the negro slaves in the mines of Saragossa, in Antioquia, who kill, cripple and maim men and women and suffocate children and destroy the fruits of the earth. There are about four thousand of them, brought from Guinea, who, though baptized, are wholly untaught in the faith, and are more like brutes than men. The missionaries among them pay no heed to their instruction but are wholly absorbed in the search for gold. The district is remote and mountainous and only to be reached by footpaths; the smallest coin there is gold and to arrest a culprit costs more than his value as a slave. The tribunal has no funds to bring them hither for trial and their maintenance in gaol is a heavy burden on the owners. Four have been tried and condemned to reconciliation and perpetual prison, but the Inquisition has no penitential prison and, if there was one, they would starve to death, as they could not earn their support and the alms of the pious would not reach so miserable a set of beings. They have therefore been put into the Hospital General, where they can be employed and hear mass and perform their penance. As for the great mass of the culprits, it would be impossible for the tribunal to arrest and try them— the cost would be enormous and the result, according to law, would be to set them free, which would fill the land with demons, nor would the owners permit their capture, in the certainty of losing them. To meet these difficulties Mañozca therefore suggests a general pardon, after which the civil authorities shall have cognizance of their crimes and punish them otherwise than with the benignity habitual with the Inquisition. The Suprema was hardly prepared thus to surrender even so unprofitable a portion of its jurisdiction and, in forwarding this letter to the king, urged that an Edict of Grace should be proclaimed; that he should assist the tribunal with the funds necessary for the support of the officials and the expense of its functions, and that the Council of Indies should order the royal officials to inflict severe punishment, in so far as they had jurisdiction, and should assist the Inquisition in making arrests and other acts. To this Philip IV drily replied that the Council of Indies would order the governors to apply such remedies as they deemed advisable.[1] All parties thus sought to wash their hands of this troublesome and costly affair, and witchcraft and sorcery continued to flourish.

They were not confined to the slaves in the mines of Antioquia and, some ten years later, there was an outburst which offered fairer inducements to repay prosecution. A great assembly of witches was discovered among the negroes of the town of Tolú— an accessible sea-port, about sixty-five miles from Cartagena— where the witnesses testified to all the classical features of the Sabbat—flying through the air, dancing around a goat, kissing him *retro* and all the customary performances. Since the great auto de fe of witches at Logroño in 1610, the Suprema had grown skeptical and cautious as to these superstitions, and had impressed on the tribunals the necessity of acting with great reserve in all such cases. In reporting this matter therefore, September 25, 1632, the inquisitors said that they had observed these instructions and had arrested only a mulatto woman and a mestiza, who had persistently denied the charges. Still the testimony continued to pour in, spreading the epidemic to Cartagena and implicating Spaniards of consideration and property, for witnesses who confessed to having been at the Sabbat were free to designate whomsoever they chose as having been present—a fact which explains the rapid multiplication of accomplices, whenever a persecution commenced. Animated by the prospect thus opened, the inquisitors threw aside their caution; they accepted the most absurd stories and attributed to witchcraft many cases of ordinary sickness occurring in the town. They erected additional prisons to receive the culprits and sentenced to burning two of those accused as leaders—negresses named Elena de Vitoria and Paula de Eguiluz, but the sentence of the former was revoked by the Suprema and, when that of the latter was received, it

---

[1] Archivo de Simancas, Inquisicion, Libro 30, fol. 178.

sent orders that no sentence of relaxation should be executed until a copy of the process was submitted to it.

Torture was freely employed, resulting in an auto de fe held, March 26, 1634, where twenty-one witches were exhibited, whose punishment mostly consisted of scourging, although one, Ana de Avila, a mestiza widow, who had overcome seven turns of the *mancuerda* in her torture, was fined 1000 pesos. A sentence of absolution was read of Ana Beltran, who had been tortured without confession for an hour and a half and had died of its effects. This was followed, June 1, 1636, by another auto with sixteen penitents, among whom was Elena de Vitoria. Another was Guiomar de Anaya, who had overcome the torture and was sentenced to exile and a fine of 200 ducats. Paula de Eguiluz was reconciled in an auto of March 25, 1638, after six years of imprisonment, and was condemned to two hundred lashes and irremissible prison. It seems that she enjoyed a high reputation as a physician and was allowed to leave the prison in the practice of her profession, numbering among her patients even the inquisitors and the bishop, Cristóbal de Lazárraga. She was permitted to cast off the sanbenito and appeared in a mantle bordered with gold and in a sedan chair; she earned much money and was charitable in relieving the necessities of her fellow-prisoners.[1]

In the other chief source of inquisitorial business—blasphemy— the mercifulness of the Suprema brought about a curious and unexpected result. The most usual expletive, *reniego á Dios*— I renounce God—was reckoned as heretical and therefore subject to the jurisdiction of the Holy Office, but it was so frequent that the Suprema ordered it to be punished only with a reprimand. As the inquisitors complained, in a letter of June 28, 1619, the effect of this was that, when a master flogged a slave, at the first lash the latter promptly renounced God; he thus became, on the spot, subject to the exclusive jurisdiction of the tribunal; the flogging ceased and he was handed over to it, to go through the formality of a trial, at the end of which he was discharged

---

[1] Medina, pp. 211-19, 225-6.

with a scolding. This was a process which might be repeated indefinitely, to the manifest detriment of the discipline indispensable to slavery.[1]

It was not till the tribunal had been established for more than ten years that it had any serious business in vindicating the faith. In an auto de fe celebrated March 16, 1622, there were four negro witches reconciled, two negro sorceresses punished and one bigamist banished from the Indies. In addition to these there was a Protestant burnt alive—an Englishman named Adam Edon (Haydon?). He had been sent, in 1618, by an English merchant, to purchase tobacco in Cumaná, where he was arrested in 1619 and sent to Cartagena. For two years the most earnest endeavors to wean him from his errors were fruitless, and his fate was inevitable. Mañozca, in his report, described him as a most engaging person; at the *quemadero* he was not chained as usual to the stake, but he calmly sat on a faggot and remained motionless till life was extinct, a veritable martyr to his convictions.[2]

After this auspicious beginning there opened a prospect of greater usefulness. At an auto de fe of June 17, 1626, solemnized with great magnificence, there were twenty-two penitents, of whom one was a Calvinist and seven were Judaizers. Of the latter, Juan Vicente had already been reconciled in Coimbra and again in Lima. Under the canon law, a single relapse entailed relaxation; this he had been spared in Lima, and his persistent backsliding left no hope of ultimate conversion, so he was duly consigned to the flames.[3] After this there was an interval during which inquisitorial energy had to be content with witches, blasphemers and the like, until the raid made on the Portuguese merchants in Lima gave occasion for similar action in Cartagena. One of the accused, in the former city, gave evidence against a compatriot in the latter; it was duly forwarded and the arrest was made March 15, 1636. The circle spread until there were twenty-one in prison. Torture was savagely employed and one of the prisoners, Paz Pinto, a man widely esteemed, died from its effects.

---

[1] Medina, pp. 118–19.   [2] Ibidem, pp. 158–9.   [3] Ibidem, pp. 175–94.

Most of the cases were ready for an auto held March 25, 1638, at which eight were reconciled and nine were absolved. There were no relaxations, but the confiscations, as we shall see, put the tribunal in possession of ample funds.[1]

Little remains to be said as to the activity of the tribunal in its appropriate sphere, although its contributions from time to time to the Suprema show that it occasionally obtained some wealthy penitent to strip, among the inconspicuous mass of blasphemers, bigamists and sorceresses. Its energies became more and more devoted, during the remainder of the century, to internal dissensions and quarrels with the secular and ecclesiastical authorities, leaving small leisure for its proper functions. Such was its inertia in this respect that we are told that there was no publication of the annual Edict of Faith between 1656 and 1818.[2] Then it was dealt a heavy blow in the capture of Cartagena, in 1697, by the French adventurers under the Baron de Pointis and his buccaneer allies, after which it was sacked by the latter. A few days after the commencement of the bombardment April 10th, the tribunal abandoned the city, carrying some of its prisoners to Majates, about fourteen leagues distant, where an auto de fe was held, with three penitents, and those whose cases were not ready were sent further inland to Mompox. When the fort of Bocachica was taken, the French found there nine prisoners accused of bigamy; eight of these joined the enemy and the ninth, Pedro Sarmiento, voluntarily went to Mompox and surrendered himself. The town capitulated May 6th and, when the French entered, they promptly sought the Inquisition, where they took the vestments of the officials and the sanbenitos and mitres of the penitents and held in the plaza a mock auto de fe, reading sentences and parodying the solemnities. Inquisitor Lazaeta was anxious to obtain

[1] Medina, pp. 222–7.
[2] Groot, II, 473. This is not strictly correct. After an interval of many years, Inquisitor Valera published the edict in Lent, 1684, when it brought in denunciations which doubled the number of cases in hand (Medina, p. 308). Probably this was the last until the nineteenth century.

possession of certain papers and employed the good offices of Don Sancho Jimeno, the castellan of Bocachica, whose gallant defence had earned the respect of the enemy. He had been rereleased but returned to Cartagena to defend himself against certain charges, after which he requested of the leaders permission to get the papers; the mere mention of the Inquisition provoked a tempest of passion, but after it had cooled off he asked leave to get some papers of his own and, while collecting them, he succeeded in including those desired by the inquisitor. After the invaders had sailed, Lazaeta returned to Cartagena, June 22d. He found the building much damaged by the bombardment; it had been sacked and the chests broken open and left empty, but the records were untouched. With a donation which he begged and 12,000 pesos obtained from the governor, he had everything in order by the end of August, but this proved the turning-point of the tribunal which thenceforth declined rapidly.[1]

Repairs to its habitation became necessary in 1704, but these were inefficiently performed and, in 1715, the tribunal was obliged to shift its quarters to the house of the senior inquisitor and even this had been so maltreated in the bombardment that it threatened to fall. The trouble culminated in 1741 when Admiral Vernon bombarded Cartagena; a bomb dismantled the Inquisition and it had to be torn down, though the records escaped as they had prudently been transferred in advance to Tenerife, near Santa Marta. It was a quarter of a century before Carlos III, in 1766, granted for the rebuilding 12,600 pesos from the revenues of the vacant archbishopric.[2]

All this was but a symptom of the general decadence of the tribunal. In 1747 the Inquisitor, Francisco Antonio de Ilarduy, wrote that the only consultor he had was also the advocate of the fisc and of the accused; for three years there had been but one calificador, and the provincial at Seville had been vainly urged to send out frailes; there were but two familiars, who were

---

[1] Medina, pp. 346–51, 364.—Groot, I, 331–6.   [2] Medina, pp. 369–70.

engrossed in earning their living and no one cared to accept the position; for seven years the Suprema had not taken the trouble to reply to the applications for advice and instructions. Ilarduy vainly tendered his resignation, but it was not accepted until at length he obtained a transfer to Córdova and left Cartagena in 1754. Under such conditions there was little done and the Inquisition lost its terrors. The royal permission to draw articles of necessity from foreign sources brought to Cartagena Danish, Dutch and other heretic ships, in which there came Jews whom the governor, in spite of the reclamations of the tribunal, allowed to establish themselves and to walk the streets like natives. The tribunal appealed to the Archbishop-viceroy, Antonio Caballero y Góngora, who contented himself with ordering that the limitation of importations to articles of necessity should be enforced.[1]

A typical case was that of Don David de la Mota, who came in 1783, and who made no secret of being a Jew. The tribunal summoned him and swore him in the Jewish fashion, when he said that he was born in Velez-Malaga; his parents had been penanced and his grandfather had been burnt by the tribunal of Granada; he had married a Jewess in the Danish island of Santa Cruz and had been circumcised fifty years before in Santa Eustacia. It indicates the altered situation when this case, which formerly would have been treated with little ceremony, was the subject of doubt and discussion. The inquisitors forbore to arrest him, for he represented foreign interests, which would have complained to the consul and he to the ambassador. They accordingly shrank from the responsibility and let him go. In Spain the exclusion of Jews was still rigidly enforced and, when they reported their action to the Suprema, it censured their timidity and ordered them always to arrest such parties when the evidence sufficed. It was the same in other parts of the district. In Santo Domingo the governor was liberally inclined and, in 1783, the Archbishop complained to the Suprema that, during the previous year, a Jew named José Obediente had come and

---
[1] Medina, pp. 358, 371.

was allowed to go about freely, to entertain persons of distinction and even to be present in the solemnities of Holy Week. The commissioner had vainly appealed to the authorities, and the archbishop was afraid to say anything, for fear of public disturbance. This year he had come again, bringing six or seven others, who kept house and lived like any other residents.[1] It was not the Jews alone whom the tribunal, in its weakened state, was afraid to attack. In 1784, the royal auditor at Mompox, Don Francisco Antonio Antona, was denounced for having, at a banquet given by a priest, proposed for discussion some manifestly heretical propositions. In place of prosecuting him, the inquisitors consulted the Suprema alleging, as a reason for their timidity, the character of the accused, the relations of his wife with the best families, and the protection given to him by the viceroys in the conduct of his office.[2] A tribunal thus shorn of its audacity could only be an object of contempt.

There was, however, a little recrudescence of activity as the progress of free-thought and the approach of the Revolution called for the exercise of the functions of censorship. This has been well-nigh in abeyance. The edicts prohibiting books, as sent out by the Suprema, were regularly published as matters of routine, but they were regarded by no one. In fact, the intellectual torpor of the colony was so profound that there was little danger of the spread of dangerous literature. In 1777 Cartagena could not even support a small printing-office, and the inquisitors complained that they had to copy the edicts by hand; there had been a printer, but the poor man had sold his stock elsewhere and no one had ventured to replace him.[3] Seizures of prohibited books had been exceedingly rare. In 1661 some copies had been suppressed of "Horas y oraciones devotas," printed in Paris in 1664. In 1668 there was a little flurry when, on one of the affluents of the Orinoco, a Dutchman was found in possession of copies of a work in Spanish, apparently printed in Holland, entitled "Epistola á los Peruleros," consisting of a Calvinistic

---

[1] Medina, pp. 359-61.   [2] Ibidem, pp. 374-6.   [3] Ibidem, p. 378.

catechism and exhorting the colonists to withdraw their allegiance from Spain and ally themselves with the Dutch, whose colony of Guiana was dangerously near. In 1732 a little book called "Paraiso del alma" was seized in Santa Fe and, in 1757, some copies of Bishop Palafox's "Ejercicios devotos." The moral phase of censorship had manifested itself in 1736, when the commissioner at Panamá took from the French astronomers, on their way to the equator to measure an arc of the earth's surface, an engraving of a woman which he regarded as indecent, but when he sought to get possession of another, said to be even worse, they assured him that it had been burnt and threatened to complain to the king of the insult offered to them. So, in 1807, there were denounced to the tribunal some watches brought by a Danish vessel, of which the cases were enamelled with indecent pictures; the enamels were destroyed and the watches were restored to the owner.[1]

In 1774 a more difficult question was forced upon the tribunal. José Celestino Mutis, distinguished both as priest and physician and professor in the Colegio Mayor of Santa Fe, in 1773, presided over some conclusions in which the Copernican theory of the solar system was defended. In June, 1774, the Dominicans of the Universidad Tomistica resolved to celebrate other conclusions to prove the contrary by Scripture and St. Augustin and St. Thomas, and that the Copernican theory was intolerable for Catholics, indefensible and prohibited by the Inquisition. Mutis addressed a defence of Copernicus to the viceroy, who sent a copy to the commissioner; he transmitted it to the tribunal, which submitted it to two calificadores. One of these reported that the propositions were not subject to theological censure; the other held that the Copernican system was opposed to Scripture and no Catholic could defend it. The matter then passed into the hands of the inquisitor-fiscal, who argued that all authors of greatest repute detested the system as absolutely contrary to Scripture, repeatedly condemned by the Roman Inquisition and,

---

[1] Medina, pp. 379–80, 390.—Archivo de Simancas, Inquisicion, Lib. 25, fol. 52.

as some say, by Urban VIII. He was especially shocked by an assertion of Mutis that the king had ordered all Spanish universities to teach the works of Newton which were based on Copernicus. Dr. Mutis, he added, was the first and only one who, in this kingdom and perhaps in all America, had publicly declared himself in favor of this system. Thereupon the tribunal, at a loss what to do in a matter beyond its comprehension, sent all the papers to the Suprema for instructions, and the latter discreetly filed them away without answering.[1]

Of more practical importance was the manifesto of the French Constituent Assembly on the rights of man, of which a Spanish version appeared under the title of *Derechos del Hombre*. This was condemned in Cartagena by edict published December 13, 1789. Then, in 1794, there was a sudden command for its vigorous suppression. In almost identical phrase the Viceroys of New Granada and Peru wrote to their respective tribunals, describing it as a work destructive of social order and advocating toleration. Every pains, they said, must be taken to hunt up every copy and to ascertain when and how and from whom they came. The tribunals accordingly exerted their utmost diligence, but were not rewarded by finding a single copy.[2] Probably equal ill-success attended their efforts to obey the orders of the Suprema to suppress *Gli Animali parlanti* of Giambattista Casti and to spare no pains in ascertaining the possessors of the poem which, as a clever satire directed against the vices and follies of kings and courts, was especially distasteful to an autocratic monarch. The work had appeared in Paris in 1802 and these orders came from the Suprema under date of May 23, 1803, although the formal decree suppressing it was not issued until June 23, 1805, to be followed, August 6th, by a similar papal prohibition.[3]

---

[1] Medina, pp. 380-6.

[2] Ibidem, pp. 387-9. During the suppression of the Inquisition, it was reprinted and largely circulated, forming the subject of a severe edict in 1814 (Ibid., p. 390).

[3] Ibidem, p. 390.—Suplemento al Indice Expurgatorio, p. 10 (Madrid, 1805).—Index Pii PP. VII, p. 53 (Romæ, 1819).

If the results of the labors of the tribunal in defence of the faith were thus meagre, it was far more successful in its true vocation of creating scandal, by incessant quarrels with the civil and ecclesiastical authorities, and by its internal discords. Hardly had it been organized when the Easter solemnities of 1611 offered occasion for dissension, over questions of etiquette and precedence, with the secular and spiritual powers, giving rise to antagonism throughout the district, especially on the part of the bishops, who grudged the deprivation of the jurisdiction which they had been accustomed to exercise in matters of faith. They continued to disregard the exclusive functions of the inquisitors, who complained bitterly of them as ignorant prelates, with officials whose ignorance was equalled by their turbulence; they had few duties to occupy them and they desired to retain this jurisdiction because of the hold which it gave them over their subjects. It probably would be unjust to estimate them by one of their number, Fray Juan González de Mendoza, Bishop of Popayan, who, on his arrival at Cartagena in 1610, introduced the practice of divination with sticks, which he asserted to be allowed by the Inquisition and to be used by the queen and the Duke of Lerma. It spread rapidly among all classes and, as all divination was held to imply pact with the demon, the inquisitors were greatly exercised and inquired anxiously of the Suprema, January 31, 1611, what they should do about it, to which apparently they received no answer.[1]

Mañozca, arrogant, unscrupulous and ambitious, was the leading spirit of the tribunal. He speedily made it apparent that, under his guidance, it was to be the dominant power in the community, and that its awful authority was to be restrained by no considerations of law or justice. The governor, Diego Fernández de Velasco, was good-natured and made every effort to keep on good terms with the inquisitors, but his moderation only encouraged their insolence and at length, in a letter of July 4, 1613, to the king, he poured forth his grievances. The tribunal, he

---

[1] Medina, pp. 74–8, 80.

said, sought to render itself the supreme master and had become so feared that the whole province was terrorized, so that, not only for the inquisitors but for their servants and slaves, there was no law but their own will. They were accustomed to arrest butchers, fishermen, bakers and other dealers in provisions; to seize with violence the goods of merchants and to summon and scold them for objecting. In two cases Mañozca forced parties who imported cargoes of slaves to give him some of them, whom he sold. They took, without notice, prisoners from the public prisons and, on one occasion, when the gaoler asked for a voucher, as requisite for his justification, the messenger wounded him on the head with his sword and was not punished. The governor added numerous instances of outrages on all classes, winding up with himself, as having been publicly proclaimed as excommunicated in all the churches.[1]

The regular Orders had equal cause of complaint and managed, with some trouble, to send to Spain a procurator to represent that everything in the convents was regulated by Mañozca's powerful hand, whence it resulted that many estimable frailes were unjustly punished, while those were untouched who deserved to be castigated and reformed. This brought upon Mañozca, from the Suprema, a severe reprimand with orders to abstain from such interference.[2] Apparently the warning was disregarded if we may believe a memorial addressed by a fraile, May 12, 1619, to the king, representing that to leave Mañozca at his post was to keep a monster in the seat of an angel of light. This was substantiated with ample details of his scandalous mode of life, his nocturnal sallies in disguise and the general terror which he inspired, for terrorism was the means by which he had become the ruler of all. When the secular authorities sought to banish the courtezans and concubines he prevented it and, when the preachers preached against them, he issued what he called an *instruccion de predicadores* in which he called them dishonoring names and covered them with ridicule. The writer relates a

---
[1] Medina, pp. 129–31.   [2] Ibidem, p. 134.

number of cases by which it appears that Mañozca controlled the local courts and officials, dictating sentences and procuring that his supporters escaped justice and won their suits, however unrighteous. Moreover he gave occasion for an indefinite amount of smuggling; arrivals were reported to him in advance of the custom officials, and he received bribes—negro slaves and other things of value—to enable the owners to defraud the customs— a matter presumably easy of accomplishment through the supervision of all arrivals, by which the Inquisition was empowered to prevent the intrusion of heretics and the importation of heretic books.[1]

Quarrels with the bishops were incessant and only the bishop of Cuba, Alfonso Henríquez de Almendáriz, who was old and self-willed and prompt in quarrel, held his own, leading to numerous complaints of him by the tribunal.[2] Then, towards the middle of 1619, there came a new governor, García Giron, with whom there was speedily trouble. A negro slave of Inquisitor Salcedo was refused meat by a negro in the market; he complained to his master who gave him a paper requiring the dealer to supply it. Armed with this, he struck the negro several times with the flat of a *machete*, took what meat he wanted and told the man that, if he wanted pay, he could send for the money. Thereupon Giron ordered a prosecution; the inquisitors sent for the notary employed in it and ordered him to surrender the papers under the customary threat of fine and excommunication; the governor ordered him not to obey, but he was finally obliged to pay the fine and deliver the papers.[3]

Complaints against Mañozca came pouring in upon the Suprema, especially from members of the regular Orders, including whole convents, until it found itself obliged to have an investigation made into his life and morals. The result justified the accusations and it ordered him to present himself in Madrid. He had no trouble in gathering certificates—which no one dared to refuse —as to his good character and conduct, with which he sailed for

---

[1] Medina, pp. 135–45. [2] Ibidem, pp. 103, 154–55. [3] Ibidem, p. 112.

Spain, towards the end of July, 1620. There he succeeded so completely in exonerating himself that, in April, 1621, the inquisitor-general wrote that his presence in the court being no longer necessary, for the business on which he had been summoned, he had been ordered to return to his post. Thus, after a year's absence, he reoccupied his seat in the tribunal, but only for a short time. With the customary policy of the Holy Office, he was promoted to the more important tribunal of Lima, to be elevated, in 1643, as we have seen, to the archbishopric of Mexico. He remained, however, in Cartagena, until the arrival of his successor, Agustin de Ugarte y Saravia, in the middle of 1623.[1]

During his absence at the court, his colleague Salcedo had become involved in a furious quarrel with the bishop, Diego de Torris Altamirano, by forcibly taking from his prison a priest named Pedro de Quesada, condemned to degradation and death for robbery and murder. Quesada, through his confessor, informed the tribunal that he had a deposition to make; Salcedo sent a message informally to the provisor to send the culprit, who would be returned, but when the messenger went for him, he was found fast in the stocks and the key carried off. The bishop declared that he should not be delivered without a written demand, but Salcedo sent a party of familiars, who carried him off by force and then returned him within an hour—the object being simply to humiliate the bishop and demonstrate the superior authority of the Inquisition.[2] Salcedo and Altamirano both died in 1621, but the new bishop, Francisco de Sotomayor, who arrived in 1622, became immediately involved in a serious quarrel with Mañozca, which had to be referred to Spain for settlement.[3]

In 1630 the Council of Indies presented to Philip IV a formal complaint in thirty-four articles against the tribunal of Cartagena, which very probably contributed to the enactment of the Concordia of 1633.[4] Meanwhile a new governor, Francisco de Murga,

---

[1] Medina, pp. 146–9, 160.   [2] Ibidem, pp. 152–3.
[3] Archivo de Simancas, Gracia y Justicia, Inquisicion, Leg. 621, fol. 26.
[4] Archivo de Simancas, Inquisicion, Lib. 20, fol. 59.

had resolutely undertaken to abate the insolence of the inquisitors and had become involved in specially bitter quarrels with the inquisitor Vélez de Asas y Argos, who had been promoted, in 1626, from the position of fiscal. In a letter of December 12, 1632, the inquisitors describe him as the most dangerous man on earth, for he daily framed a thousand devices to trip them up and, if this could not be stopped, there would be no living in the city. He was certainly audacious for one day he took from the executioner a negro who was being scourged through the streets for heresy. For this they excommunicated him, but when they sent officials and familiars to notify him, he clapped them all into gaol and held them there under heavy guard for twenty-four hours. Then he called a junta in the house of the bishop and, by its advice, asked for absolution, which was administered in a manner so humiliating that the Council of Indies presented a formal complaint to the king. This did not tend to harmony and the quarrel went on, to the discomfiture of the tribunal, showing what a determined man could do, when supported by the universal detestation in which the Inquisition was held. In fact, as the inquisitors complained, in a letter of August 8, 1633, the mass of the people held them in mortal hatred, which they could explain only by the wiles of the devil seeking to obstruct their pious work.[1]

Meanwhile the home authorities were leisurely engaged in endeavoring to reconcile the irreconcileable. A consulta of the Suprema, March 23, 1633, suggested measures to that effect but in vain. Philip IV adopted a more practical course in ordering the Suprema to summon Vélez to Spain, but it disobeyed and, when he repeated the order, it replied, May 3, 1635, that it was ready to obey but had deferred in expectation of his replying to its consulta of May 26, 1634; besides, it had not yet received the papers containing the inquisitors' side of the matter. To this the king replied by curtly commanding immediate compliance, but it still dallied and it was not until 1636 that Vélez was com-

---

[1] Medina, pp. 201-3.—Archivo de Simancas, Inquisicion, Lib. 20, fol. 177, 299.

pelled to sail for Spain. At the same time the Suprema admitted the fault of the tribunal by ordering the inquisitors, March 15, 1636, not to plot and conspire against Murga nor, after his retirement, against his deputy and officials. The sincerity of this was soon put to the test. Murga had died before Vélez left Cartagena and, in April, 1636, the tribunal was delighted to receive orders to arrest his deputy, Francisco de Llano Valdés, who was asserted to be the cause of all the troubles. The order was joyfully obeyed, but to little effect. In prison Llano Valdés became intimate with Inquisitor Cortázar, for both were Biscayans; a false certificate of illness was procured from the physician and he was given his house as a prison; he was soon seen on the streets again and was even called in frequently to administer torture, as the tribunal had no official skilled in the art.[1]

The death of Murga did not end the debate, which was transferred to Spain, where Vélez arrived in December, 1636. It dragged on with customary procrastination. The Suprema urged his return to Cartagena, declaring that his service had been most satisfactory, and that he had been dishonored by being summoned to Spain without cause, which could only be repaired by his restoration. The Council of Indies insisted that he had exposed Cartagena to destruction and that he should be provided for with a post in Spain. Philip IV sought to compromise the matter by deciding against his return and that he should have one of the best Spanish tribunals—it being the ordinary policy of the Inquisition that when a man had proved his unfitness in one position, he should be promoted to a higher station in which to exercise his powers of evil. Finally it was settled that he should have the great tribunal of Mexico, but the commander of the fleet, Don Carlos de Ibarra, ordered him to take ship direct to Honduras and made public proclamation that no one should receive him on board or carry him to Cartagena, under pain of treason and confiscation. Then the Suprema, September 30, 1639, made a

---

[1] Archivo de Simancas, Inquisicion, Lib. 61, fol. 51; Lib. 21, fol. 8.—Medina, pp. 204, 207.

final effort to obtain his restoration to Cartagena, but this failed and he at last took his seat in the Mexican tribunal.[1]

Vélez had been on terms not much better with his colleague, Martin de Cortázar y Ascarate, who accused him of endeavoring to encompass the death of Llano Valdés in prison and of seeking to rule the tribunal with a faction of the officials, consisting of the fiscal Juan Ortiz, his son, the secretary Luis Blanco and the other secretary, Juan de Uriarte, father-in-law of Blanco. As for Cortázar himself, two of the consultors, Juan de Cuadros Peña and Rodrigo de Oviedo, wrote to the Suprema, August 10, 1635, representing his utter ignorance; he knew no Latin and his Castilian was so imperfect as to be unintelligible; he was proud and haughty and his cruelty was evinced by the savage tortures which he inflicted on the accused. Then, on November 16, 1640, Ortiz was promoted to the inquisitorship and his family had complete control.[2]

They used their power for their own enrichment, dividing among themselves the moneys in the coffer and paying no debts unless they were bribed. That they should soon be involved in strife with the municipality, was inevitable. In 1641 an excessive scarcity caused by the ravages of locusts led the cabildo, or city authorities, to prescribe maximum prices for provisions and to order an examination into the quantities of produce in the several plantations, so as to prevent exportation. Ortiz and his officials claimed exemption from these regulations; he ordered the secretary of the cabildo to furnish him with its proceedings, that he might see which of the regidores voted for them, so that he might imprison them, as was done with Don Cristóval de Bermúdez and Don Baltasar de Escovar, on complaint of the servants of the officials, for distributing provisions equally—arbitrary imprisonment without observing any formalities or opportunity for defence. Then, as the secretary did not comply with the demand, he was similarly thrown in prison. When meat was brought into

---

[1] Archivo de Simancas, Inquisicion, Lib. 21, fol. 82, 88, 196.
[2] Medina, pp. 233–7.

the city for distribution the servants of the officials claimed whole carcasses, which they cut up and retailed at excessive prices. Driven to extremities, the city complained to the king of the violence of the tribunal and the excesses of its officials, when Ortiz again demanded a copy of the proceedings of the cabildo, leading to further intolerable vexations, which caused it to send the regidor, Nicolás Heras Pantoja as procurator to ask for a visitador.[1]

This imprisonment in the secret prison, we may remark, was an inveterate abuse; it was in itself the severest punishment, as it implied heresy and inflicted indelible infamy on the individual and his posterity. It was the subject of repeated complaints and, at last, a consulta of the Council of Indies, June 14, 1646, led the king to order the Suprema to instruct the Cartagena tribunal not to molest the people; when any one was arrested for matters not of faith, he must be placed in a decent prison, outside of the Inquisition. The Suprema had already taken such action in letters of April 28, 1645, and it repeated this July 28, 1646. Yet a letter from Cartagena of June 10, 1649, represented that, in spite of these orders, the inquisitors continued to throw many people into the secret prison, for causes not of faith, till at length three citizens who had been thus dishonored supplicated the king to remedy the great injuries thus inflicted. The Council of Indies, in a consulta of February 21, 1650, represented strongly to the king the disorders arising from the disregard of his commands and urged that positive orders to obey be given to the inquisitors. This he sent with his endorsement to the Suprema, which, on April 8th, wrote to the tribunal to observe its previous instructions—but without producing permanent effect.[2]

Meanwhile the prayer of the city for a visitador had been answered after a fashion, though not in consequence of its supplication. According to a statement of the Suprema in 1646, it had, at the close of 1642, determined to send an inspector to Lima

---

[1] Archivo de Simancas, Inquisicion, Lib. 61, fol. 270.—Medina, pp. 238-9.
[2] Archivo de Simancas, Inquisicion, Lib. 38, fol. 122.

and Cartagena, as those tribunals had not been visited since their foundation. There had recently been great sequestrations and confiscations, giving rise in Lima to over two thousand lawsuits, while in Cartagena it was necessary to investigate the settlements made with the claimants and the net collections secured. There were no charges, it said, against the inquisitors and it was only the financial matters that were concerned. There was hesitation as to the selection of a visitor; he had to be an old inquisitor and no one would accept the position without the assurance of a good benefice in the Indies or of a place in the Suprema itself. To give him more authority it was resolved to make him a member of the Suprema and to swear him in before his departure. Unfortunately the choice fell upon Dr. Martin Real, then serving in the tribunal of Toledo, a man of learning and imbued with the highest conceptions of inquisitorial authority, who had acted as visitor in Sicily, where he earned the reputation of a breeder of troubles, through his ungovernable temper and headstrong character. This was known to the Suprema, but it was thought that what he had suffered in consequence of it and the warnings that would be given would render him cautious. Philip IV objected, in view of what had occurred in Sicily, and suggested other names, but yielded on condition that he should not take the oath as councillor until the day of his departure. Then the Council of Indies protested against the appointment as dangerous to the peace of the colonies, but the Suprema represented that the matter had gone too far to be reconsidered without disgracing Real; that the opposition came from those who desired to prevent the visitation and that it did not concern the inquisitors but only the confiscations. The king made no further objection and Real was duly commissioned and departed early in 1643.[1]

The result justified fully the apprehensions of Philip and the Council of Indies, but it may be doubted whether the most even-tempered visitor, honestly bent on performing his duty, could have averted an explosion. The object of the mission was the

---

[1] Archivo de Simancas, Inquisicion, Lib. 61, fol. 130.

investigation of the finances; there can be little question that, as in the other tribunals, false reports had been made as to the results of the enormous confiscations accruing from the prosecution of the Judaizing New Christians, and an inspection of the accounts was to be prevented at all hazards. The city was in a state of combustion with the chronic quarrels between the tribunal and the civil and military authorities. Real's temper would not allow him to be neutral and it was easy to create a situation which should preclude the dreaded investigation. Such, at least, is the most rational explanation of the events as they can be disentangled from the somewhat conflicting accounts that have reached us.

Towards the end of July, 1643, Real arrived in Cartagena and with him came a new inquisitor, Juan Bautista de Villadiego, a man nearly seventy years of age, and a fiscal, Pedro Triunfo de Socaya. Real's first act was to forbid Ortiz and Uriarte from entrance to the secreto, evidently with a view of examinating their accounts without interference, at the same time handing them appointments to equivalent positions in Llerena and Logroño— the favorite method used by the Suprema when officials had destroyed their usefulness where they were. Villadiego however refused to let Real have the keys of the money-chest, so the object of his visitation was frustrated and he revenged himself by exceeding the powers of his commission and assuming control of the tribunal. To obtain the keys of the coffer he led a disorderly crowd to Villadiego's house, broke it open, personally assaulted him, seized the furniture and sold it at auction to pay the fine which he had imposed on him. Real further espoused the cause of the governor and cabildo and interfered by liberating a secretary whom Villadiego had arrested in order to learn who had voted against him. Then Villadiego endeavored to establish a rival tribunal in his own house and appointed officials to run it, a schism which lasted for two months, until Real judicially sentenced him to consider his house as a prison. Villadiego thereupon, on the night of February 11, 1644, with his own hands, posted notices that Real was excommunicated and Real retorted by arresting him.

He was replaced by Juan Pereira Castro, who took possession as inquisitor, August 22, 1644, and lost no time in organizing a faction among the officials and the clergy against Real and was concerned in libels upon him which were posted on the night of September 3d. For this, on insufficient evidence, Real arrested Ortiz de la Masa, an ecclesiastic of high standing, and proposed to torture him, which created an immense scandal among both clergy and laity. Pereira in vain endeavored to release him and, on January 25, 1645, he and Real exchanged excommunications, resulting in an interdict under which the city lay for many months. A few days later, on January 28th, Pereira, the fiscal Socaya and the notary, Tomás de Vega, locked themselves up in the tribunal for fear of arrest, and there they remained for seven months, solacing their self-inflicted captivity with feasting and gambling, while Real could neither get his salary nor the papers which were necessary for the business of his visitation. Many of those whom he had treated harshly hurried to Spain and brought suits against him in the Suprema, and we hear of Socaya sending with them forty bars of silver to substantiate their complaints.

The Suprema was not a little perplexed by the turn which affairs had taken. It ordered Villadiego to be restored to his place in the tribunal, an order received February 17, 1645, but it was accompanied with a summons to present himself at court within four months. This he disobeyed and recommenced to hold a tribunal in his own house, with the object, as Pereira wrote in February, 1646, of diverting attention from the scandals of his licentious life. To this Villadiego retorted by accusing Pereira of defending the gaoler in his crimes with female prisoners and of holding indecent banquets with him and the fiscal. The only immediate solution to the troubles seemed to lie in the recall of Real; he was ordered home and left Cartagena at the end of October, 1645. As the time of his arrival in Spain approached, the Suprema grew uneasy at the prospect of receiving him as a member and, February 16, 1646, it presented a consulta to Philip IV containing a condensed narrative of his doings and representing that his seat in the Council was intended, not as a reward for past services but as an incentive to those he was to render; his visitation had cost 20,000 pesos and had brought no results, nor was it held advisable that he should be allowed to repeat his performances in Lima. Besides, it would be indecent for him to sit in judgement on the numerous suits brought against him in the Suprema so that, all things being considered, it was suggested that his membership should be suspended until those suits were settled—a suggestion to which the king cordially assented.[1]

The inquisitors were not so busy quarrelling among themselves but that they had leisure to keep up dissensions with the secular authorities. A bitter struggle with the governor was occupying the court in 1644 and 1645, leading the Junta de Guerra de Indias, on November 9th of the latter year, to urge that instructions he sent to the tribunal not to excommunicate the governor and captain-general on account of the evils that would result.[2] Then a consulta of the Council of Indies, March 7, 1647, complained of the invasions of secular jurisdiction, in violation of the Concordia of 1610, causing regrettable disturbances. It alluded especially to a competencia with the royal Audiencia of Santa Fe over a civil case of the familiar Rodrigo de Oviedo y Luron, in which 1500 pesos were deposited with Capitan Francisco Beltran de Cairedo to await the adjudication of the claims of his creditors, when the tribunal stepped in and seized the money, although it had no jurisdiction over the civil cases of familiars. The Council therefore asked that the tribunal be ordered to abstain from civil cases and that its competencias with the Audiencias of Santa Fe, Panamá and Santo Domingo be settled—an appeal to which the

---

[1] Medina, pp. 239–45, 247–8, 257.—Archivo de Simancas, Inquisicion, Lib. 61, fol. 130, 270.

[2] Archivo de Simancas, Inquisicion, Lib. 61, fol. 164, 175.

king returned no answer, as he doubtless transmitted it to the Suprema, where it probably lay buried.¹

As long as Real was on the ground, Villadiego and Pereira united in efforts to destroy him, but as soon as he departed they quarrelled and, in February 1646, Pereira commenced a prosecution against his colleague for holding a tribunal in his own house. The only hope of restoring the Inquisition to decency and usefulness seemed to lie in another visitation. This time the choice fell upon Pedro de Medina Rico, Inquisitor of Seville, whom we have already met in his subsequent discharge of similar duties in Mexico. He arrived in Cartagena, December 11, 1648, and found everything in disorder. As he wrote, May 19, 1649, the prisoners were rotting in the dungeons, some of whom had been lying there for eight years. He set vigorously at work with the cases, but it was difficult to make progress. There was no clock in the city; the hours were announced by the soldiers of the guard in the streets with a bell, but they were irregular and little attention was paid to them. The officials came late to their duties and left early; Pereira was especially brief in his attendance and, when he came, thought of nothing but getting away. Medina Rico therefore begged the Suprema to send out a fitting person to serve as secretary and also two inquisitors of learning and probity; Pereira was worthy of severe punishment and ought on no account to be allowed to remain.²

Medina Rico of course was at once involved in bitter antagonism with the officials whom he had come to reform; his powers however were limited and he was unable to use censures or arrest, which put him at a disadvantage, and there were no such exhibitions of violence as characterized the visitation of his predecessor. The Governor Pedro Zapata, moreover, took sides with the incumbents and wrote to the Council of Indies complaining that the city had been kept in a turmoil for ten years, attributable to the delay of the visitadors in completing their visitations. Real had been there for two years and returned, leaving the task incomplete and

¹ Archivo de Simancas, Inq., Lib. 61, fol. 251.   ² Medina, pp. 249–50.

now Medina Rico has been at work for a year, with no prospect of completion, on account of which the city is in great affliction, dreading a renewal of former disturbances. Philip transmitted this to the Suprema, March 13, 1649, ordering, for the sake of peace, that Medina Rico be instructed to finish as speedily as possible. To this the Suprema replied that the illness of Pereira had thrown the unfinished business of the tribunal on Medina Rico, but that orders had already been despatched to him to complete his task without loss of time. Zapata continued his complaints and the Marquis of Miranda de Auta, President of the Audiencia of Santa Fe, joined in condemning his arbitrary acts; in civil cases he had arrested the procurators of pleaders and he had issued letters to the judges of the Audiencia threatening that in three days they would be posted as excommunicates.[1]

Medina Rico's task was difficult for the abuses of the tribunal were so inveterate that the sharpest measures were necessary. Real's report, based on 231 witnesses, brought sixty-eight charges against Villadiego and a hundred and thirteen against Pereira, but his hurried departure had prevented his submitting it to the accused for their defence and it therefore could not be acted upon. Fresh evidence was naturally hard to obtain. The people knew the power of Pereira and Uriarte and that they were favored by the governor and the Bishop of Santa Marta; they had seen the failure of Real's visitation and anticipated the same result from the present one, when vengeance would follow on all who deposed against them. Medina Rico was therefore obliged to proceed cautiously. He states that he had to take precautions against attempts on his life by Uriarte and that such fears were not groundless for there was evidence in his hands that the former notary, Luis Blanco del Salcedo, was poisoned by his wife and the Inquisitor Juan Ortiz, then receiver, who subsequently married her; Inquisitor Cortázar was poisoned by Ortiz and Uriarte, who intercepted his letters accusing them to the Suprema. Rodrigo de Oviedo was killed by order of Uriarte, whose accom-

---
[1] Archivo de Simancas, Inquisicion, Lib. 38, fol. 31; Lib. 61, fol. 251.

plice he had been. There was, he said, every facility for such crimes in this land filled with evil negroes; it was held for certain that in this way perished Bishop Cristóbal de Lazárraga and all his family; to poison was attributable the death of Juan de Lorrigui, acting fiscal, and also that of the governor who was in office at the time of his arrival.[1]

In spite of these apprehensions he gathered evidence, confirmatory of Real's charges and of subsequent misdeeds and, under pressing orders to betake himself to Mexico, towards the summer of 1650 he drew up accusations against the inquisitors and the chief officials. Those against Pereira were virtually the same as Martin Real's. Villadiego he accused of friendship with Jews who had been penanced, of receiving gifts and loans from them and using them as agents to sell goods for him; he was continually exacting gifts and abused those who refused them and there was also his general licentiousness with women. The fiscal, Bernardo de Eyzaguirre, was charged with embezzling the money of the prisoners. Secretary Uriarte he accused of selling his influence to the kindred of those on trial, giving them information and advice and arranging to bribe the consultors and episcopal Ordinary; of encompassing the death of his accomplice Rodrigo de Oviedo, who threatened to denounce him; of falsifying the accounts and robbing the tribunal to the amount of 200,000 pesos; after the death of Cortázar, he had a secret door made by which he entered the secreto to commit these thefts and he embezzled the property of the accused by bribing those in charge of it, in addition to all which his life was scandalously incontinent. Against Juan Ortiz he reproduced the sixty general charges made by Real and added seventy-nine special ones of the same character—bribery, receiving presents, appropriating the property of prisoners, falsified accounts, subornation and violence—when a butcher did not give him the best meat, he summoned him to the tribunal and struck him a blow on the head that left him senseless.[2]

In July, 1650, there arrived a new fiscal, Juan de Mesa, who was

---

[1] Medina, pp. 260-1.   [2] Ibidem, pp. 250-59.

to be associated with Medina Rico, in case Uriarte recused him, as in fact he did. Pereira had become so apprehensive as to the results of the visitation that Mesa, on August 4th, in handing him the charges, told him that they would kill him. It so turned out. Pereira took them and pondered over them until midnight. In the morning he sent for a physician who at once told him that his case was hopeless and, on the 13th, he was dead. Uriarte followed him to the grave, on February 1, 1651, and Medina Rico's task was accomplished. He was under orders to start for Mexico, but was detained by prolonged illness and did not leave Cartagena until June 8, 1654.[1]

The perennial quarrels with the authorities continued, of which the Council of Indies complained in a consulta to Philip IV, May 14, 1652.[2] Matters were not improved when, about this time, there came a new inquisitor, Diego del Corro Carrascal, followed shortly by Pedro de Salas y Pedroso as fiscal, who was soon promoted to the inquisitorship. He was so completely dominated by his senior that the Suprema took him to task, after which he manifested his independence by perpetual *discordias*, which left the accused perishing in the prison, awaiting the slow decisions in Spain. Corro Carrascal moreover was rebuked by the Suprema for cruelty and for speculating on the operations of the tribunal by having the confiscations bought in for him at the auctions at low prices. His dissolute life was so notorious that Governor Zapata said that his going out at night in disguise and having amours with married women passed into a proverb.[3] The dissension between the inquisitors grew bitterer until, in 1658, they had a common object of dislike in a new fiscal, Guerra de Latrás, a man who had had a somewhat distinguished career as doctor of laws, professor and author, and who had served in various important positions. The Suprema had often reproved the tribunal for its disregard of established procedure and Guerra sought

---

[1] Medina, pp. 261–3.
[2] Archivo de Simancas, Inquisicion, Lib. 61, fol. 251.
[3] Medina, pp. 263–5.

to reduce it to order, bringing upon himself the hostility of the inquisitors, who characterized his representations as childish. Early in 1660 he had a fall from his mule and broke his arm, which incapacitated him from writing; the inquisitors refused to allow him to employ an assistant and the business of the tribunal was paralyzed. In 1665 Corro Carrascal was made President of New Granada, Salas fell sick and was absent for weeks at a time and, in this atrophy, the Inquisition ceased to inspire awe or even respect. The opportunity was propitious for the secular power to reassert itself, and the Governor, Benito de Figueroa y Barrantes, availed himself of it. August 23, 1666, meeting the executioner who was scourging two penitents through the accustomed streets, he sent three of his soldiers to release them. The tribunal prosecuted the soldiers and, on the 29th, had two of them arrested by its secretary, Gonzalo de Carvajal, who, in the process, fired a shot and had a struggle with one of the soldiers. Figueroa thereupon surrounded the Inquisition with guards to starve out the inmates; Guerra sought an interview and agreed to surrender the prisoners but, four days later, the governor arrested Carvajal, threw him fettered into the public prison, sequestrating his property and taking his confession in the torture-chamber. Guerra and Salas proceeded to prosecute the governor and proclaimed a *cessatio a divinis*. The bishop intervened and Carvajal was relieved of his chains, but remained in prison. The affair completely discredited the Inquisition; as the new fiscal, Montoyo y Angulo, reported, April 16, 1669, there was no petty official who did not think himself able to give orders to those of the tribunal.[1]

It had not, however, as yet reached the depth of its degradation. Salas had died, December 28, 1667; Guerra had been promoted some months earlier to the inquisitorship and he too died March 21, 1671, leaving the fiscal Luis de Bruna Rico alone. Then, August 19, 1673, there came a new inquisitor, Juan Gómez de Mier, followed, in 1674, by a colleague, Alvaro Bernardo de Quirós, and a new fiscal, José de Padilla, Bruna Rico having been transferred

---
[1] Medina, pp. 280-88.

to Lima. The colleagues speedily quarrelled and Padilla joined Mier to oppose Quirós. The latter, on his arrival, had observed the abuses current in the importation of merchandise and slaves and wrote on the subject to the Council of Indies. The governor, who was compromised, succeeded in winning him over, so that he spent most of his time in the governor's house card-playing and wrote to the Council, withdrawing his charges. It was too late, however, for Juan de Mier y Salinas, a judge at Santa Fe, was commissioned to investigate and came to Cartagena, where he lodged in the house of his uncle, the Inquisitor Mier. The two commenced making arrests and the inculpated took asylum in the churches. Among them was a friend of Quirós, who exerted himself in vain to protect him, and in failing to do so broke definitely with his colleague. He allied himself closely with the governor, for whom he drew up edicts, notably one in 1678 which, under pretext of a threatened attack by the French, discharged all the prisoners and put an end to the prosecutions. He is described as wandering around at all hours of the day and night, mingling with every body, even dancing in public and universally despised. Mier's association with his nephew the judge brought upon him a shower of denunciations; he held relations with the English of Jamaica, who sent him negroes; these he entered at night as prisoners of the Inquisition, guarded by the alguazil mayor, through whom, moreover, he sold positions—commissionerships and the like—to all who would pay for them. The fiscal Padilla shut himself up in his house and would see no one. The master spirit of the tribunal was the secretary, Miguel de Echarri, to whom were attributed all the evil deeds of Mier. Every one went to him for the distribution of favors; his anteroom was like that of a viceroy and presents were showered upon him; he was assiduous in the gambling-houses and, as Fray Juan Cabeza de Vaca had written, January 30, 1670, "while he is in this city there will neither be peace in the tribunal nor will the people be without a demon to disturb everybody and keep them in open war."[1]

---

[1] Medina, pp. 297–301.

This state of affairs continued for years. Mier was transferred to Mexico and Quirós to Lima in December, 1681, leaving as sole inquisitor Padilla, who died March 31, 1682, appointing as successor ad interim the Archdeacon Andrés de Torres. Matters took a new aspect with the arrival, March 27, 1683, of a new inquisitor, Francisco Valera, who had filled important offices in Lima. He dismissed Torres and made Echarri fiscal; he gave five hours a day, in the tribunal, to cases of faith and three hours in his house to affairs of property. He pushed the pending trials to conclusion and in five months, August 29th, he celebrated an auto de fe.[1] Under such a man the tribunal was speedily lifted from its degradation, but he had the defects of his qualities, and his imperious temper speedily involved him in a struggle of which the scandal was greater than that of any previous one.[2]

In 1681, two years before Valera's arrival, there had come to Cartagena a new bishop, Manuel de Benavides y Piedrola, who seems to have been impulsive and inconsiderate. Almost at once he fell into trouble by listening to the prayer of the nuns of Santa Clara, who desired to transfer their obedience from the Franciscans to the episcopal provisor, leading to a contest which was envenomed by the bishop's endeavor to restrain the disorderly intercourse between friars and nuns. Castillo de la Concha, the President of New Granada, ranged himself against the bishop, on whom a sentence of banishment was pronounced, to which he replied by casting an interdict on the city and leaving it. The populace took sides with a vehemence which led to frequent riots and almost to civil war, during which the nuns sustained a siege of six months.

Valera, on seeing the condition of affairs, endeavored to make peace and sought the bishop in his retreat, but was unsuccessful and his disappointment was aggravated by the bishop's refusal

---

[1] Medina, pp. 302–5.

[2] Of this quarrel we have two accounts. That of Sr. Medina (pp. 311–24), drawn from the records of the Inquisition, is naturally favorable to Valera. The other side is given by Groot (I, 286–306; II, 584) from a MS. relation. I have endeavored to elicit the truth from the conflicting statements.

to allow him to celebrate mass in his own house during the interdict. On his return to Cartagena he boldly celebrated mass, which greatly encouraged the anti-episcopal faction. Matters however seemed to be settling down, when, by order of President Castillo, Diego de Baños, Bishop of Santa Marta, came to Cartagena and removed the interdict. The two bishops exchanged excommunications and the quarrel became fiercer and more intricate than ever. Castillo ordered Benavides to leave the diocese, but he refused and excommunicated the governor and all the authorities; in fact, his enemies said that he had a mania for such censures and once excommunicated an object which he saw through the blinds of a balcony, without knowing whether it was a bag of cocoa or a sack of wool.

Valera was not long in being involved in the conflict. The authorities had armed the citizens and broke by force into the cathedral, seizing three ecclesiastics, whom the governor threw into the fort of Bocachica; one of them, Baltasar de la Fuente, was a commissioner of the tribunal and claimed the fuero, but Valera refused to come to his assistance. When, however, the governor ordered Benavides to withdraw the censures, the latter excommunicated Gerónimo Isabal, the advocate who signed the letter, and it chanced that he was also acting advocate of prisoners in the tribunal, though without a commission, and Valera sprang to his assistance and demanded the papers. Benavides retorted with an edict declaring that Isabal was not entitled to the fuero for defect of title, that Valera had incurred censures for not protecting la Fuente and that he, as episcopal inquisitor, would supply any deficiencies in the tribunal. One account states that as Valera kept himself housed, the bishop went there personally and affixed the edict to his door; another asserts that he led a mob of negroes and mulattos to seize the inquisitor, who barely escaped by a back door and took refuge in the tribunal.

The edict was printed and posted throughout the town, when the alguazil mayor of the Inquisition tore it down and arrested the ecclesiastics who were concerned in it. Benavides went to the tribunal to rescue them and was contumeliously refused admittance; the governor came and a scene ensued, the accounts of which are irreconcileable, but which served still further to scandalize the people and inflame the passions of both sides. The unlucky clerics, after two years of prison, were fined and exiled. Benavides meanwhile had the cathedral bells tolled for an interdict, when all the other bells in the city were rung to drown them— a brazen warfare to which the people had become accustomed. Then he ordered a *cessatio a divinis*, but the convents refused to observe it; the Bishop of Santa Marta pronounced it null and Valera posted a declaration that he raised it. The Audiencia of Santa Fe had ordered the expulsion of Benavides and now it fined him 4000 pesos for delay in executing the decree. The cathedral was surrounded with guards; the chapter fortified it, but the Bishop of Santa Marta had the doors broken open and ordered the chapter to declare the see vacant. On their refusal, the provisor, treasurer and *maestre-escuela* were arrested and the cathedral was handed over to priests of his faction. A certain Don Gómez de Atienza declared that he wished Benavides had come forward to resist this desecration, for he would have finished him. The vengeance of heaven was not long delayed, for that night a tempest of unexampled violence burst over Cartagena; the lightning sought out Atienza in the midst of his family and slew him, while another bolt struck his farm in the country, burnt his granaries and killed his mules. He was buried with much pomp by the Bishop of Santa Marta and his dead mules were hidden, to keep the people in ignorance.

A new governor, Juan Martínez Pando, on his arrival was ordered by the Audiencia to remove Benavides, but it was impossible to ship him away, for the buccaneers commanded the sea. He was confined in his house under strict guard and his temporalities were seized. The clergy and people who were faithful to him were arrested, banished and their properties confiscated. The nuns of Santa Clara refused to recognize the confessors appointed for them, when the convent was broken open and in spite of their resistance they were beaten and confined on bread and water, while some of them were put in irons. The Archbishop of Santa Fe had ordered the Bishop of Santa Marta to retire and leave Benavides in possession, but the mandate was taken from the messenger, was pronounced to be forged, and prosecutions were brought against all who professed obedience to it.

Matters took a sudden turn when there came a royal cédula of May 16, 1683, addressed to Valera ordering him to replace Benavides in his see, which he accordingly did with extraordinary pomp. That he was master of the situation was generally recognized and peace for a time was restored, although he refused the bishop's demand for the return of the clergy and domestics whom he had exiled. Then Benavides' position was further strengthened by a papal brief of November 3, 1683, based wholly on the adverse representations of the Audiencia, ordering the nuns of Santa Clara to be remitted to his care. Thus the original cause of quarrel was settled and the troubles which followed were a simple trial of strength between the episcopacy and the Inquisition.

Passions had not yet exhausted themselves and the struggle for supremacy had not been decided. A new element of discord came with the arrival in November, 1684, of another inquisitor, Juan Ortiz de Zárate, who regarded Valera as having been timid and irresolute in the quarrel and boasted of his own unyielding firmness. Causes of dissension were not lacking and open war broke out when Benavides removed, perhaps with unnecessary violence, seats which the inquisitors had placed in the church, giving as a reason the "tertulia" or talkative crowd thus attracted. Thereupon they excommunicated the bishop and ordered his name to be omitted from the mass, to enforce which they excommunicated, fined and banished the dean and the Prior of San Agustin for including it. The bishop had torn down the edicts of his excommunication, had ostentatiously celebrated mass and had ordered the arrest of the clergy who would not assist him, which led the tribunal to order him to keep his house as a prison, an order enforced by obtaining from the governor a guard which rendered him practically a prisoner. During this turmoil it is easy to imagine the condition of the community, terrorized by the Inquisition. The majority of the people, we are told, favored the bishop, but were afraid of the absolute power exercised by the tribunal, with the support of the governor. The better part of the clergy saved themselves by flight and there was general demoralization. To render their victory complete the inquisitors assembled the chapter in order to have the see declared vacant. All but two voted in the negative and left the room, when the remaining two declared the vacancy and elected provisors to govern the diocese.

Then three vessels arrived from Spain which it was hoped would bring despatches putting an end to the troubles. Nothing was given out as to their nature, but it was observed that each night the guard at the bishop's palace was reduced until it was entirely withdrawn and Benavides was released after a confinement that had lasted from April 13 to August 22, 1687. At the same time there arrived Gómez Suárez de Figueroa as inquisitor to replace Valera, who had been transferred to Lima early in 1685 but who had awaited the arrival of his successor; he sailed September 2, 1687, reaching Panamá on the 23d and Lima in June, 1688.

Suárez at first seemed inclined to deprecate the excesses of his predecessor, but the traditions and interest of the Inquisition were too strong and he soon yielded to them. The tribunal still held the bishop to be excommunicated. The news of the terrible earthquake of Lima, March 9, 1687, improved by the preachers, caused a wave of religious fervor in which many persons abandoned their scandalous lives and applied to Benavides for licences to marry but, when the banns were published, the inquisitors excommunicated the officiating priests. They also gave notice that all who communicated with the bishop must seek absolution at their hands—an absolution which they ostentatiously administered. Seeing them thus determined to carry on war to the knife, he resolved to publish a papal brief of January 15, 1687, which he had received. This treated the matter as exclusively a quarrel between him and Valera; it recognized fully the justice of his side and stated that the nuncio at Madrid had been ordered to prevail with the king that all his rights should be restored to him and that he should have public satisfaction for injuries endured. Although this brief had passed the Royal Council, when he applied to the civil authorities for aid in its publication this was refused and when he circulated copies the inquisitors stigmatized it as a forgery. They filled their prison with the bishop's supporters and they garrotted in the plaza a Franciscan named Francisco Ramírez, without observing any formalities or even degrading him from holy orders—a tragedy in which the governor, Francisco de Castro, acted the part of executioner.

A new governor, Don Martin de Ceballos y la Cerda, brought with him a royal cédula, ordering the restitution of the bishop to his full rights and jurisdiction. This was received with rejoicings, which showed how few had been really opposed to him, although terrorism had forced men to dissemble. One article of the cédula, however, commanding the restitution of all fines and confiscated property, was not obeyed, because the judge commissioned to enforce it belonged to the inquisitorial faction and had the support of Ceballos, with whom the bishop had speedily quarrelled. This encouraged the tribunal to a renewal of molestation. When the bishop ordered the prosecution of Doctor Francisco Javier de Cárdenas, for abuses committed in a visitation, the inquisitors threatened the provisor that, if he did not release Cárdenas, he should be imprisoned as the bishop had been. During the troubles the tribunal had been conducted without the necessary concurrence of an episcopal Ordinary. To remedy this, Benavides appointed Don José Pedro Medrano to act, but the inquisitors took away his commission and refused to allow him to serve. Seeing that the contest was endless, the bishop resolved to present himself at the court and embarked in an English vessel for London, but hearing in Jamaica of the expulsion of James II, he returned to Cartagena to await the arrival of the Spanish galleons. When they came, they brought a despatch calling him to Madrid and he accompanied them on their return.

At this point the narrative in both Groot and Medina fails us and we know nothing of his reception at court, except that it was not wholly to his satisfaction. We learn from a consulta of the Council of Indies, in 1696, that Innocent XI had rendered a decision invalidating the excommunications uttered by the inquisitors and affirming those proclaimed by the bishop and that all comprised under the latter must obtain absolution. To do this would be so unexampled a humiliation that the Suprema had not enforced it, and Benavides had, without asking the royal permission, gone to Rome to accomplish its execution. This placed him in antagonism with all Spanish traditions and, in 1695, the ambassador was endeavoring to obtain papal authority to carry him back to Spain, but apparently without success, for in 1696 he was still there. The indomitable old man died in Cádiz, but in what year is not known and the see remained vacant until 1713.[1]

However the Suprema may have interposed to prevent the humiliation of the inquisitors, it set its seal of disapprobation on Valera. His transfer to Lima indicates that it considered, early in the quarrel, that his usefulness in Cartagena was ended. His action during the interval between 1685 and 1688 evidently confirmed the unfavorable impression and, as we have seen, he was met, on his arrival at Lima, with orders from the Suprema to return to Spain—orders which he evaded—and in 1691 the Viceroy Moncada was instructed by the king to ship him home. As this was merely a royal command, it received no attention, and he continued to exercise his functions; apparently he had profited by experience for we hear of no controversies with either the spiritual or temporal power. With the advent of the Bourbon dynasty, however, there came a determination to curb inquisitorial exuberance and his Cartagena performances were not for-

---

[1] MSS. of Library of Univ. of Halle, Yc, 17.—Medina, p. 324.

gotten. In 1703 there came orders from both the king and inquisitor-general to jubilate him on half his salary, the other half being applied to the Church of Cartagena, in consideration of the controversy which he had with it, thus condemning him to make to it such reparation as he could. The sentence came too late, however, as he had died on August 2, 1702.[1]

Governor Ceballos had no reason to congratulate himself on siding with the tribunal against Bishop Benavides. Its excesses had convinced the court that some thorough change was necessary if peace and harmony were to be restored in the colony and a Junta of two members each, of the Suprema and of the Council of Indies, was ordered to carry it into effect, but these intentions were balked by the members of the Suprema never meeting their colleagues.[2] Nothing was done and the absence of the bishop left the tribunal in absolute command of the city. How despotically it exercised its authority is shown in a plaintive despatch of Governor Ceballos, January, 1693, reciting how the butcher of the public shambles having refused to give the preference to a negro of Inquisitor Suárez, the latter sent the gaoler of the secret prison to bring the butcher bound to the prison or, if he could not be found, then one of the regidores of the city in his place. The butcher was found and thrown into the prison, where he was still lying. The governor says that he was afraid to take the proper steps and contented himself with addressing a civil request to Suárez, which was disregarded. He found it impossible to get legal evidence as to the affair, for witnesses were in such terror that they would make no formal depositions. On January 13th, after drawing up a despatch on the subject, he went to his residence, whither came Secretary Luna of the tribunal, accompanied by a mob of followers and, with much disturbance, required him under threat of major excommunication and other censures to sign letters declaring that the case belonged to the jurisdiction

---

[1] Cuaderno de Cumplimientos, fol. 62 (MSS. of White Library, Cornell University).

[2] Archivo de Simancas, Inquisicion, Lib. 60, fol. 352.

of the Inquisition and that he abandoned it; also that all references to the matter be erased from the books of the municipality and all the papers be delivered to the tribunal. In this strait he consulted with Don Francisco Gorrechategui, President of the Royal Audiencia of Santa Fe, and Don Fernando de la Riva Aguero, Judge of the Audiencia of Panamá, but they could render him no assistance; he was helpless and, for the sake of peace, he submitted to the demands of the Inquisition.[1] When such was the condition to which the tribunal had reduced the civil and military power in Cartagena, we need no further explanation of the ease with which the French adventurers captured it in 1697.

That catastrophe, as we have seen, was the turning-point in the history of the tribunal, which thenceforth rapidly declined. In 1705, Pablo de Ozaeta took possession as fiscal and found himself alone, in consequence of the severe illness of Inquisitor Lazaeta, until the arrival of Manuel de Verdeja y Cosio as his colleague. There was a lively quarrel on foot with the governor, Juan Díaz Pimienta, to whom the tribunal had imputed the concealment of the property of a person deceased. The two secretaries, Echarri and Ventura de Urtecho, took his part and were excommunicated and arrested, Urtecho being banished for eight years and Echarri ordered to leave the city within twenty-four hours, while his son was thrown into the secret prison. On the other hand, Pimienta seized Luis de Cabrera, the notary of sequestrations, and threw him into the fort of Bocachica, where he died in the course of eight months, and, on another occasion, acting on a royal order, he took, from Lazaeta's house, Julian Antonio de Tejada, who had been sent out to report on the capture. To avenge these insults, the tribunal commenced twenty-four prosecutions against the governor, but it was in no position to assert itself. In a letter of February 27, 1706, it exhaled its griefs. Ozaeta and Verdeja were ailing—one wanted to go to Spain and the other to be transferred to Mexico. Everything was in ruin; the money coffer was empty; for ten years no galleons

[1] MSS. of the Library of the Univ. of Halle, Yc, 17.

had arrived; Pimienta slighted Lazaeta at every turn, so that for eighteen months he had been obliged to shut himself up in his house. As for Ozaeta, Verdeja, in a letter of September 13th, accused him of devoting himself wholly to trade. He had brought merchandise with him and was the agent of foreign merchants, whose goods he introduced without paying duties, and there was no business of this kind, throughout the extensive district of the tribunal, that was not under his control. He was allowed to enjoy this profitable commerce until 1716, when he returned to Spain and was rewarded with an appointment to the tribunal of Llerena.[1]

He was replaced in Cartagena by Tomás Gutiérrez Escalante who did as little honor as his predecessor to the Holy Office, though he retained his position until his death, in 1738. He was involved in bitter quarrels with the governor, Francisco Baloco, of which the details are lacking, though we may assume that he was in fault, for constant complaints of him were sent to the Suprema, and the Bishop Molleda y Clerque (1734-41) accused him of interfering in matters beyond his jurisdiction and that in his house there was nothing but banquets and gambling. One of these feasts was given in honor of the saint's day of a young mulatto girl whom he kept and whom his guests had to honor.[2] After this we cease to hear of troubles with the civil authorities, but the dissensions between the officials of the tribunal continued to the end of the century and the exhortations and commands of the Suprema were fruitless in maintaining harmony.[3]

The financial history of the tribunal, at least during the seventeenth century, is similar to that which we have already traced in Mexico and Peru. As we have seen, when Philip III established it in 1610 he was careful to specify that the royal subvention of 8400 ducats was to continue only as long as the confiscations and fines and penalties were insufficient; the receiver was ordered to furnish a yearly statement of his receipts which were to be

---

[1] Medina, pp. 365-7.   [2] Ibidem, p. 368.   [3] Ibidem, pp. 372-6.

deducted from the payments to be made by the treasury. Clearly as this program was laid out, it is perhaps needless to say that it never received the slightest attention from the tribunal. It had not been long in operation when the fruits of its industry began to pour in. A letter of July 22, 1621, conveyed the pleasing information that it had secured the handsome sum of 149,000 pesos from the confiscated estate of the Judaizer Francisco Gómez de Leon.[1] Windfalls such as this were of course exceptional, but a more or less steady stream of smaller amounts can scarce have failed to reward its activity. Still this brought no relief to the royal treasury, which was regularly called upon for the subvention and, in 1630, we chance to hear of the complaints of the treasury officials, who were summoned before the tribunal and scolded when they had not funds wherewith to meet the demands promptly.[2] In 1633 there duly came the suppression of a canonry in every cathedral of the district for the benefit of the tribunal—a measure designed for the relief of the royal treasury—but the revenues of the prebends were quietly absorbed without relaxing hold on the subvention.

Wealth flowed in with the discovery of Judaizers in 1636, whose confiscations were announced in the auto de fe of March 25, 1638. That of Juan Rodriguez Mesa amounted to 65,000 pesos; that of Blas de Paz Pinto to 50,000; of Francisco Rodríguez Pinto to 40,000, while the smaller ones brought the aggregate up to 200,000, as reported, June, 1638, by Andrés de Castro the receiver who assuredly did not exaggerate, and besides this there were confiscations in Havana amounting to 150,000.[3] In 1639 there came orders to sell at auction three *varas* of alguaziles, one each in Santa Fe, Caracas and Popayan, but competition was not eager and we do not know the amount realized.[4] The tribunal was evidently accumulating abundant capital, although it was obliged to contribute a part of its gains to the Suprema. In 1644 the latter alludes to a remittance shortly expected from Cartagena

---

[1] Medina, p. 157.   [2] Archivo de Simancas, Inquisicion, Lib. 20, fol. 59.
[3] Medina, p. 230.   [4] Ibidem, p. 231.

of about 10,000 ducats; by a letter of September 24, 1650, it appears that the tribunal admitted to having on hand 187,677 pesos; according to a certificate of June 30, 1659, there had been deposited in the money coffer 430,414 pesos and, although there had been more than 100,000 remitted to the Suprema, there was ample left. In addition there were houses and lands; there were 95,332 invested in censos, yielding about 4000 a year but the royal subvention was still regularly collected, the 8400 ducats being reckoned at 11,500 pesos.[1]

The subvention continued to be paid though, with the increasing penury of the Spanish treasury, it was apt to be in arrears. In 1670 we find the Suprema ordering the tribunal to use gentle methods; it learns that the garrison is unpaid and therefore the fault may be with the governor; the last payment collected was for the *tercio* (four months) of November, 1668, and the annual amount alluded to is 8400 ducats. The tribunal was not satisfied and, in its replies of May 6 and October 8, 1671, it asks for permission to apply pressure; the governor excuses himself by the expenditures necessary to provide for the safety of the place, but these pretexts will never be lacking, the civil salaries are regularly paid and the garrison is partially so. Yet the arrearage to the tribunal had been diminished and was reduced to only three tercios, showing that at least two years' subvention had been collected during the past twelvemonth.[2] Then the arrearage increased and on April 17, 1674, the tribunal reported it at nearly eighteen months, whereupon the Suprema, February 3, 1675, addressed a strong remonstrance to the queen-regent, threatening that if the officials were not paid regularly they would be obliged to desert their posts; it recapitulated the financial history of the tribunal; the royal grant, in 1610, of 8400 ducats per annum, until the confiscations and fines and penances should suffice, followed by the suppression of the prebends in 1633, and it had the effrontery to assert that since then the prebends and fines and

---

[1] Archivo de Simancas, Inquisicion, Lib. 36, fol. 74.—Medina, pp. 262, 265–66.
[2] Archivo de Simancas, Inquisicion, Lib. 40, fol. 112, 120.

penances had been deducted from the subvention; the royal officials asserted that there were no moneys appropriated for the purpose, and that they could not pay without special orders, wherefore the queen was asked to make the subvention a first charge on the treasury. Against this the Council of Indies protested vigorously on March 9th, going over the whole history of the matter and pointing out that whatever was paid to the Inquisition must be withdrawn from the protection of the coasts, ravaged constantly by the buccaneers, and especially of Cartagena, which was the object of their special cupidity. In fact, large expenditures were making on the defences of the city, which was the entrepôt of the shipments of the precious metals to Spain; as the Council stated, the royal treasuries of Santa Fe and Quito had already been drawn upon to the amount of 17,390,300 mrs. for that purpose.[1]

The debate went on, without either side abandoning its position. The Suprema, on May 11, 1676, insisted that the subvention was a necessity for the tribunal. Five of the canonries produced a total of only 2535 pesos and the sixth, of Puerto Rico, only about 100; the revenues from investments were 5491 pesos while the expenses were 18,770, so that even with the subvention there was a deficit. It is evident that not much faith was felt in these figures, for the Count of Peñaranda, in a consulta of December 10, 1677, pointed out that there never had been any statement furnished as to the amount of the confiscations and fines and penances, nor had any effort been made to obtain from Cartagena and Peru, as there had been from Mexico, restitution of the sums improperly obtained from the treasury, to which they were evidently large enough to afford sensible relief.[2]

In some Cartagena documents of 1684 we find the first evidence that the treasury had the benefit of other receipts of the tribunal. On June 2d the receiver presented to Inquisitor Valera a dolorous complaint as to the financial condition. In the

---

[1] Archivo de Simancas, Inquisicion, Lib. 40, fol. 122, 132.
[2] Ibidem, fol. 139, 54.

failure to collect the royal subvention it had been impossible to pay the salaries and other expenses without drawing upon the funds held for creditors of confiscated estates awaiting settlement. The buildings of the Inquisition and its houses were out of repair and threatening ruin; the last payment obtained from the treasury was up to the end of October, 1678, since when there had accrued 61,764 pesos, 5 reales, 22 mrs. from which was to be deducted, of collections from the canonries, 8221 pesos, 3 quartellos, leaving a balance due of 53,543 pesos, 4 reales, 31 mrs., which Valera was urged to collect in order that the fund held for creditors might be reimbursed and the necessary repairs made to the buildings. Thereupon Valera addressed to the governor, Don Juan Pando de Estrada, a vigorous appeal, embodying the receiver's statement of the account and asking at least for a partial payment. The governor submitted this to the treasury officials, who admitted the correctness of the statement, and from their figures it appears that in the settlements from November 1, 1675, to October 31, 1678, due allowance had been made for receipts from the canonries —but they add that in 1680 a royal cédula had ordered the archbishop and bishops to report to them all payments to the tribunal on account of the canonries, an order which had been obeyed only by the Bishop of Cartagena. They professed the utmost desire to pay the Inquisition and deplored their inability, in view of the demands of the home government for remittances and the indispensable outlays for the maintenance and safety of the city.

This the governor transmitted to the tribunal with the assurance of his deep regret and a request for a statement of its other receipts, in order that an accurate balance could be reached. Valera met this last demand by procuring from the receiver and his predecessor sworn statements that nothing had been received from confiscations, fines and penances, the truth of which may be doubted in view of the receiver's previous complaint as to the use made of the sums in litigation with creditors of confiscated penitents— but he added that, if there had been receipts from these sources, they were especially appropriated to the secret and necessary expenses of the Inquisition, which was a manifest falsehood. Moreover, as the tribunal was a creditor of the treasury, and it appeared that there were no funds applicable to the discharge of the debt, it had a right to have a detailed statement of receipts and expenditures, to lay before the king, with a request for relief. What reply the governor made to this impudent demand, we have no means of knowing, but we may assume that the tribunal fared no better in the future. It had appealed, October 1, 1683, to the Suprema, setting forth its deplorable condition; as it was forbidden to use pressure, it was at the mercy of the officials and it asked that the treasurers of Santa Fe and Quito be instructed to remit directly to its receiver. For some reason this appeal was not considered by the Suprema until April 10, 1685, and then it was simply ordered to be filed away with the other papers.[1]

We may reasonably assume that much of the distress, thus movingly represented, was fictitious, to parry the demands of the Suprema for the contributions which it was accustomed to exact. Notwithstanding the recalcitrancy of the royal officials, the tribunal by diligent siege managed to extract an occasional payment and, though it unquestionably suffered heavily at the capture of Cartagena, in 1697, what with the prebends and the occasional fortunate capture of a wealthy penitent, it would seem not to have suffered from the lack of means. At least so the Suprema thought when, in a letter of June 15, 1705, it ordered the tribunal to be prompt in remitting the contribution demanded of it. Thus spurred, on February 27, 1706, it sent 6000 pesos, which it stated it had been obliged to borrow, as it had no resources save to pledge repayment out of the first moneys it should receive, and it expected to do this out of the estate of Don Juan de Zavaleta, the settlement of which was hourly expected. It went on to give a dolorous account of its condition. The capture of the city had left it in a miserable state—all the money in its coffers was taken and all its buildings and houses were damaged. Its

---

[1] Archivo de Simancas, Inquisicion, Lib. 40, fol. 155, 151.

chief means of support, it says, is the royal subvention, but for six years it had failed to receive any important assistance from this; arrearages due amount to more than 140,000 pesos and its applications to the treasury are met with enmity and ill-will. The suppressed canonries produce less than 5000 pesos a year; as for the houses, they have declined greatly in value; for more than ten years the galleons have ceased to visit the port and commerce has so decreased that the houses are generally untenanted and repairs consume most of the rentals received.[1]

In this sombre description there is doubtless a large element of truth. The kingdom of New Granada, though less than two centuries old, was already decaying and the Inquisition necessarily suffered with the rest of the community. Its poverty became so pressing that, in 1739, the houses held by it were sold on ground-rents. To add to its misfortunes, as we have seen, in 1741, during the bombardment by Admiral Vernon, a bomb dismantled the Inquisition so that it had to be torn down and it was not rebuilt until 1766. Still the tribunal managed to exist and when, in 1811, it was expelled from Cartagena, it had 4000 pesos in its coffer.[2]

When came the Revolution the Inquisition evidently had lost all claim on the respect of the people and was one of the early objects against which popular detestation was directed, rendering its career in those turbulent times different from that of its sister tribunals. Before Hidalgo raised the banner of revolt, in September, 1810, already in July insurrection had broken out in Santa Fe and, on August 13th, a revolutionary Junta was established in Cartagena, although complete independence of the Spanish crown was not yet contemplated. Matters remained for a year in this uncertain condition, during which the tribunal sought to ingratiate itself with the rising forces of Revolution by acquitting and discharging a patriotic priest, Juan A. Estévez

---

[1] Archivo de Simancas, Inquisicion, Lib. 40, fol. 116.
[2] Medina, pp. 367, 400.

sent to it by the Santa Fe Government to be imprisoned and punished for a sermon characterized as seditious; and it furthermore dismissed its commissioner, Doctor Lasso, who had started the prosecution—a service warmly recognized by the Supreme Junta in a manifesto of September 25, 1810.[1]

As in Spain, the Liberals were careful to proclaim their adhesion to the principle of intolerance. The Constitution of Cádiz in 1812 declared that the Catholic, Apostolic, Roman faith was the religion of the State and that no other worship, public or private, would be permitted, while the Articles of Federation of the Provinces of New Granada enumerated among their duties that of maintaining the Catholic religion in its purity and integrity.[2] Yet when the Revolution culminated for the time in Cartagena, November 11, 1811, by an armed rising of the people, one of the demands made on the Junta was that the Inquisition be suppressed and the inquisitors be handed their passports. The Junta was prompt in executing the popular wishes. The same day it issued a decree that all who did not favor independence should leave the country within eight days, and it summoned the various corporations to come forward and take the oath of independence.[3] The next day, notice was sent to the tribunal that its existence was incompatible with the new order of affairs, and that the inquisitors, with such officials as desired to follow them, must sail for Spain within fifteen days, while those who remained must forthwith take the oath; all papers were to be transferred to the bishops of the dioceses to which they referred and the property was to be made over to the public treasury. To this the inquisitors replied, on the following day, that the decision had been extorted by an armed mob and, as soon as popular agitation should subside, they expected to resume the august functions confided to them by Divine Providence. Insistence, however, brought compliance and, on November 28th, they announced their readiness to go, though not to Spain; the authorities took possession of all their property and the papers connected

---

[1] Groot, II, 230. [2] Ibidem, pp. 226, 232. [3] Ibidem, pp. 230–1.

therewith, but it was not until December 17th that their passports were sent, and further delays postponed their departure until January 1, 1812, when they sailed for Santa Marta. There they erected their tribunal and remained for about a year, when the occupation of the place by the revolutionary forces caused their transfer to Puertobelo. When Santa Marta was regained by the royalists they returned there and soon afterwards they received news of the suppression of the Inquisition by the Córtes of Cádiz in February, 1813. This rendered their condition more precarious than ever. In a report of July 8, 1815, they state that on their ejection from Cartagena, they notified the various chapters to preserve the fruits of their prebends for them; those of Santiago de Cuba, Havana and Panamá came regularly, but were paid into the royal treasury; those of Puertobelo and Santo Domingo were held back through fear of pirates; that of Caracas by the revolution, so that they were in arrears of their salaries by five tercios and had been living on borrowed money.[1] If their salaries were but twenty months in arrears, in July, 1815, it indicates that the previous complaints of poverty had been exaggerated and it suggests that, in spite of the seizure of property, they had succeeded in carrying from Cartagena a fair supply of funds.

The triumph of the Spanish War of Independence and the restoration of Fernando VII in the Spring of 1814 changed the face of affairs. The whole power of the monarchy could be directed to the subjugation of the revolted colonies and, in 1815, a heavy force was sent, under Don Pablo Morillo, to effect that of New Granada. Although the Inquisition had been revived in Spain by royal decree of July 21, 1814, it was not until March 31, 1815, that the joyful news reached Santa Marta, where the inquisitors celebrated it with a solemn mass and Te Deum and the announcement that they resumed their duties, although, to keep up the semblance of a tribunal, they had appointed as fiscal the alcaide of the secret prison and as secretary the alcaide of the

---

[1] Medina, pp. 398–407.

penitential prison. Morillo reached Santa Marta on July 24th and on August 15th he advanced to reduce Cartagena, accompanied by the senior inquisitor, José Oderiz, whom he appointed as *teniente vicario general* of his army. After a siege of a hundred days, in which the inhabitants were almost destroyed by famine and pestilence, Cartagena fell on December 6th and Oderiz at once took measures to seize prohibited books and resume his authority. The other inquisitor, Prudencio de Castro, deferred the transfer of the tribunal until May, 1816, awaiting the restoration of sanitary conditions in the unhappy city, and it could not fully commence operations until January 21, 1817, the date at which the two secretaries, who had remained behind, were reinstated in office, after undergoing the process of "purification," to remove all taint of liberalism. Morillo himself had accepted the position of honorary alguazil.[1]

On April 29, 1818, there was a solemn publication of the Edict of Faith and of the Edict of Grace of the Suprema for heresies occasioned by the war. This was followed in the afternoon by a procession through the streets carrying the banner of the Inquisition; the standard-bearer was Colonel Jiminez, accompanied by the principal officers of the army, to whom the ceremonial was a farce, for we are told that they were nearly all Free-Masons.[2] It was not until near the end of the year, however, that the organization of the tribunal was completed, by the arrival of the new fiscal, José Antonio de Aguirrezabal. Although thus ready for business, it had little to do, in the disturbed condition of the land, and it was in no condition to render active service. As it reported, September 25, 1819, it was suffering acutely from poverty, without means to repair its building which threatened ruin; it was unable to imprison offenders because they could not be fed; the salaries were unpaid and the officials had no means of livelihood, for there were no charitable hands to solace their misery. In fact, its last case was that of Don Rafael Barragan of Santa Fe, for propositions.

---

[1] Medina, pp. 408–12.—Groot, II, 473.   [2] Groot, II, 472–3.

His accusation dated back to 1813; after infinite trouble he was thrown into the secret prison and, in September, 1818, his sentence was read in the audience chamber with closed doors; he abjured *de levi* and was absolved *ad cautelam*.[1]

The Revolution of 1820 in Spain revived the energies of the patriots who felt that they had little to fear from further efforts of subjugation. The suppression of the Inquisition by the royal decree of March 9, 1820, seems to have attracted little attention in New Granada and, if the tribunal continued to exist, it must have disappeared when Cartagena was captured by the revolutionists in October, 1821. Still, on September 3d of that year the Vice-president of the United States of Colombia, Doctor José María Castillo, deemed it necessary to issue a decree declaring the Inquisition abolished. No traces of it should be allowed to exist and therefore the authorities of Cundinamarca were ordered not to permit the commissioner in Santa Fe to exercise his office. In future no inquisitorial edicts should be published, no books should be suppressed except by the Government and no ecclesiastical authority should supervise their importation. As the commissioner at Santa Fe, Doctor Santiago Torres, had previously died in exile, the zeal of the vice-president was somewhat superfluous except in so far as the edict deprived the bishops of censorship.[2]

Shortly after this the Congress of the United States of Colombia adopted a law declaring the Inquisition extinguished forever and never to be re-established. All its properties were appropriated to the State. The bishops were restored to their ancient jurisdiction over matters of faith, but appeal from their decisions lay to the civil courts. This however applied exclusively to Catholics. Foreigners of other faiths were assured against molestation on account of religion, so long as they observed due respect to the national one, and finally the civil power assumed to regulate the external discipline of the Church, such as the prohibition of books and similar matters.[3] As the United States of Colombia then

---

[1] Medina, pp. 414–16.   [2] Groot, III, 124, 142–3, 151.   [3] Ibidem, pp. 143–44.

embraced the whole of the Spanish South American possessions, north of Peru, these liberal principles were effective over a wide expanse of territory and, when the victory of Ayacucho, December 10, 1824, finally destroyed the Spanish power in Peru and liberated the colonies, the last chance disappeared that the reactionary government of Spain might attempt to revive the Inquisition.

Many causes contributed to the decay of the Spanish colonies, but among them not the least was the impossibility of settled and orderly administration occasioned by the multiplicity of rival jurisdictions, inherited from the medieval conceptions of the relations of Church and State. There were the military represented by the viceroy, and the civil by the Audiencia; the spiritual, exercised by the bishops over the secular clergy; the numerous Regular Orders, exempt from the bishops and subjected each to its own provincial; the Cruzada, whose numerous officials owed obedience only to the Commissioner General or his representative, and finally the Inquisition which claimed supremacy over all, in a sphere of action the limits of which it defined practically at its pleasure. Of these the most disturbing element was the Inquisition, armed with the irresistible weapon of excommunication, by which it could paralyze its antagonists at will, and the arbitrary power of arrest, which inspired general terror. We have seen what manner of men it was that Spain habitually sent to the colonies to wield this irresponsible authority, the use which they made of it and, when their abuse of it became unbearable, how they were rewarded by transfer to better tribunals or to episcopal seats. The commissioners whom they distributed through the provinces aped their masters and carried oppression and discord to every corner of the land, while the ægis of protection was extended over every criminal who could claim any connection, however illusory or fraudulent, with the tribunals.

Complaints to the Council of Indies came pouring in by every fleet from bishops, governors, officials and individuals. These were duly laid before the king, who referred them to the Suprema; it would promise to call for a report from the tribunals and this would be the last of the matter, for however severely it might berate its subordinates in secret, it steadfastly defended them in public. In 1696 the Council submitted an elaborate consulta to Carlos II, recapitulating a number of flagrant cases, occurring from Mexico to Cumaná, and its fruitless efforts to obtain redress; it pointed out how completely the tribunals disregarded the provisions of the Concordias and the impossibility of securing their observance; it suggested various reforms, the most radical of which was depriving the Inquisition of its temporal jurisdiction; it declared the matter to be of greater importance than any other that could arise in the monarchy, and it concluded with an earnest and eloquent appeal for immediate action. The Inquisition, it said, was founding a supreme monarchy, superior to all others in the State. It was regarded with universal hatred in all the regions of the Indies and with servile fear by all, from the lowest to the greatest.[1]

Of course nothing was done and the condition of the colonies went on steadily deteriorating. To this the Inquisition contributed not only as a leading factor in internal misgovernment, but also by its hideous system under which the affluence of the tribunals depended upon the confiscations which they could levy. We have seen how large a part this played in their financial vicissitudes and how it was regarded on all hands with eager expectation, and it is doing no injustice to the kind of men sent out as inquisitors to assume that it was a motive far more potent than the desire to maintain the faith with exact justice. To say nothing of the cruel wrongs inflicted on countless victims, commerce could not flourish when the gains of the trader only served to render him a tempting prey to such men, armed with irresponsible power exercised through the inquisitorial process and shielded from criticism by the secrecy of procedure and the stern

---

[1] MSS. of Library of University of Halle, Yc, 17.

punishment administered for complaint. The Suprema was constantly calling for remittances and, to satisfy its exigencies and their own wants, there could be small hesitation in prosecuting any merchant whose success might excite cupidity, especially when trade was so largely in the hands of descendants of New Christians. The benumbing effect of this on the withering prosperity of the colonies is self-evident.

How it fared with New Granada, under all the various depressing influences of Spanish policy, is described in a report, made in 1772, by Francisco Antonio Moreno y Escandon. The condition of the colony is represented as most deplorable and the tone of the report is that of utter hopelessness, in view of the universal decay and dilapidation. The local officials everywhere were indifferent and neglectful of duty; the people steeped in poverty; trade almost extinct; capital lacking and no opportunities of its employment, for the only source of support was the cultivation of little patches of land and the mining of the precious metals. There were no manufactures and no means of retaining money in the country, for, though it was bountiful in products, it was unable to cultivate for export in consequence of the restrictions imposed by the home Government; if freedom of export could be had for its cocoa, tobacco, precious woods, etc., it would flourish. The mines were still as rich as ever, but their product was greatly decreased; the province of Chico, which had large mineral wealth, was approachable by the river Atrato but, since 1730, the navigation of that stream was forbidden under pain of death. It is true that, in 1772, Viceroy Mexia obtained permission to send two vessels a year up the river, but the permits for this were held at a prohibitory price. The commerce with Spain consisted in one or two ships, with registered cargoes, annually from Cádiz to Cartagena, whence the goods were conveyed into the interior, but so burdened with duties and expenses that there was no profit in the trade. In the consequent absence of all industry every one sought to obtain support from the Government by procuring some little office. The frontier territories were "Missions," under charge of frailes, the different Orders having charge of the various stations, while the Government defrayed the expenses and furnished guards of soldiers, which entailed heavy outlays with little result. They had all been established for at least a century but had failed to advance the propagation of the faith, for the Indians, when apparently converted and brought into *pueblos* or villages, would run away and take to the mountains. This Moreno explains by the absence of the apostolic spirit on the part of the missionaries, who undertook the career only to enjoy a life of ease and sloth.[1] The spirit of the secular clergy was even more reprehensible, if we may believe the relation drawn up by Viceroy Manuel de Guirior, in 1776, for the guidance of his successor. The deplorable condition of the Church he ascribes to its subordinating its spiritual duties to the exaction of taxes and tithes, in illustration of which he states that the parish priests omitted from their registers the records of marriages, baptisms and interments, in order to evade payment of the excessive fees levied by the bishops on their official functions.[2] To appreciate the full import of this we must bear in mind that on the completeness and accuracy of the parish registers depended the position in the community of every individual.

This degrading secularization of the Church was not confined to New Granada. When, in 1735, Don Jorje Juan and Don Antonio de Ulloa were sent to Quito, in company of the French men of science, to measure an equatorial degree of the earth's surface, they were commissioned to investigate and report as to the condition of the colony in all its various aspects. The voluminous and detailed report which they presented, some ten years later, to the Marquis of la Ensenada, under Fernando VI, gives a vivid picture of the disorders of clerical life. Public prostitutes were scarce known in the cities, for licence and con-

---

[1] Relaciones de los Vireyes del Nuevo Reino de Granada, pp. 26–8, 41–3, 67, 95, 97.
[2] Ibidem, pp. 112–14.

cubinage were so universal that there was no call for professionals. Dissolute as were the laity the clergy were worse, and of the clergy the regular Orders bore the palm for the effrontery of their scandalous mode of life—excepting, indeed, the Jesuits who are highly praised for their assiduity in their duties and the strictness with which the regulations of the Society were enforced, by the expulsion of all unworthy members. The disorders of the others are attributed to their wealth and idleness. The position of a provincial of any of the larger Orders, for the regular term of three years, was worth from 300,000 to 400,000 pesos, derived from the patronage of guardianships, priories, parish churches and plantations, which were distributed to those of his faction who would pay proportionately for them—payments for which they recouped themselves by grinding exactions on their parishioners and subjects. The convents were dens of prostitution, occupied only by those who could not afford separate establishments. The wealthier ones lived in their own houses with the concubines whom they changed at will and the children in whom they took no shame, and these houses were the scenes of gambling, dancing and drinking, causing frequent scandalous disorders which the police were unable to check, as the civil power had no jurisdiction over the clergy. Notwithstanding this extravagance, their revenues were so large that all the best lands in the colony were rapidly passing into their possession, and this was especially the case with the Jesuits, who husbanded their resources and managed their extensive properties with businesslike precision. What plantations were left to the laity were mostly burdened with heavy ground-rents and there was danger, if the process were not checked, that eventually the whole land would pass into *mainmorte*. As regards the missions, the report bears the same testimony as we have seen in New Granada. With the exceptions of the Jesuits, the Religious Orders, whose presence in the colony was based on the pretext of spreading the faith, were too worldly and indolent to devote themselves to that duty and the Jesuits were apt to find that when they sought to civilize their converts, these interesting neophytes would murder them and take to the mountains.[1]

All this frightful demoralization was beneath the attention of the Inquisition. Its business was the salvation of souls by enforcing unity of faith, and its duties as to morals were confined to destroying such works of art as it considered to be improper. Yet Ensenada, if he took the trouble to read the report so laboriously prepared, might reasonably ask himself whether a system which led to such results was fitted either for the spiritual or the material benefit of the populations subjected to the Spanish monarchy.

---

[1] Noticias secretas de America, pp. 489–536, 382–3 (Londres, 1826).

Juan and Ulloa were distinguished men of science, *Tenientes Generales* of the Navy and members of the British Royal Society and of the Royal Academies of Paris, Berlin and Stockholm. Their report was so damaging as to the defenceless condition of the ports that it was jealously kept secret until, after the independence of the colonies had rendered this unimportant, a copy was procured by Don David Barry and printed in London. From casual allusions by the authors, they seem to have been good Catholics and punctual in religious observance.

APPENDIX.

I.

KING FERDINAND TO THE SICILIAN INQUISITION, OCTOBER 25, 1512,

(Archivo de Simancas, Inquisicion, Libro III, fol. 202).
(See p. 12).

EL REY.

Inquisidor entendido habemos que estos dias passados à causa de ciertos robos que se facian en el feyo de femmy saluco (?) que es del doctor de Julien por unos quatro esclavos del dicho doctor con otros ladrones e bandidos que alli se recogen mando nuestro visorrey en esse Reyno al Capitan de la dicha tierra que trabajase en prenderlos todos, y diz que despues de haber prendido dos ò tres de ellos porque los otros siendo avisados se le fueron vos procedeis con censuras cerca del dicho capitan para que estos entreguen los dichos presos, diciendo que son del dicho doctor de Julien que es Official asalariado de esse Sancto Officio de la Inquisicion y que pertenece à vos el conoscimiento de los dichos ladrones, y para que creyesemos que esto fuesse asi se nos embiara traslado de las provisiones que vos disteis sobre esto. Tenemos no poco sentimiento que esse Sancto Officio de la Inquisicion querais ponerlo en defension de los ladrones lo que no procede de nuestra voluntad que si el doctor de Julien interviene en el vocar de los processos no por esso han de gozar de esempcion las personas que tiene en sus heredades de mal bibir asi que nuestra voluntad es y vos mandamos que luego revoqueis las dictas provisiones y mandamientos que el Sancto officio de la Inquisicion no se ha de entremeter de tales personas. Tambien diz que esto otro dia se echo un malfechor huyendo del Capitan de essa Ciudad en la cassa de esse Sancto Officio de la Inquisicion y siguiendolo los Officiales del dicho Capitan lo defendieron vuestros Officiales y mynistros mano armada. Esto da ocassion de escandolo y porque algun dia vos y vuestros Officiales seays poco acatados proveed que tales cossas no se fagan que no se podrian tolerar con paciencia, pues lo que se dice que se face en la Adduana por no pagar los derechos cossa es de muy mal exemplo. Todo es menester que se enmiende y no se faga desorden sino sera forcado que nuestro visorrey lo provea de una manera que assi gelo escribimos que los Officiales de tan Sancto Officio de la Inquisicion religiosamente han de bibir y quitarse de toda manera de escandalo y incombenientes y assi sera el Officio de la Santa Inquisicion mas honrrado y acatado.

Yo el Rey.—Calcena Secretario.

II.

Sicilian Instructions of Inquisitor-General Manrique, January 31, 1525.

(Archivo de Simancas, Inquisicion, Libro 933, p. 565).
(See p. 20).

Don Alonso Manrique, por la divina miseracion arzobispo de Sevilla, del consejo de sus Magestades, inquisidor apostolico general contra la heretica pravedad y apostasia en todos los sus reinos y señorios. A vos los reverendos inquisidores contra la heretica pravedad y apostasia en el reino de Sicilia y à los oficiales y ministros del oficio de la sancta inquisicion del dicho reino à quien lo de yuso en esta nuestra carta contenido toca y atañe y à cada uno y qualquiera de vos salud y bendicion. Sepades que ante nos en el consejo de la general inquisicion se ha agora visto y examinado el proceso de la visita que el venerable Benedicto Mercader maestro en sacra teologia hizo en este dicho sancto oficio por mandado y comision de nuestro muy sancto Padre Adriano Sexto de feliz recordacion siendo inquisidor general y ha parecido que por lo que conviene al servicio de Dios y de sus magestades y à la buena administracion de la justicia y por dar orden como el santo oficio se ejercite y haga con todo rectitud y brevedad que se deben guardar y cumplir las instrucciones siguientes por quanto por la dicha visita parece que aquellas hasta aqui no se han guardado y es cosa justa y debida que se guarden.

Primeramente la instruccion que manda que en las presiones de los que se mandaren prender concurran el alguacil para hacer y ejecutar su oficio y el notario de sequestros para hacer los inventarios de los bienes que se sequestran y deudas y acciones y escrituras que se hallan y el receptor para lo mismo por el interese que puede suceder al fisco y que con asistencia de todos tres, alguacil, notario de sequestros y receptor se hagan y firmen los inventarios y sequestros y firmados queden en poder del dicho notario de sequestros para hacer cargo dellos al dicho receptor en caso de condemnacion, la qual instruccion se guarde como en ella se contiene so pena de privacion de sus oficios.

Item, la instruccion que dispone que en el vender de los bienes confiscados concurran el receptor y notario de sequestros para que el uno los venda con las solemnidades y pregones que la instruccion manda y el otro haga cargo de los precios y plazos en que se venden so la dicha pena y en caso que ocurrieren necesidad que hayan de enviar otras personas en su lugar sea con parecer de los inquisidores y las tales personas sean de mucha confianza.

Item, la instruccion que manda que el juez de bienes confiscados y notario de su audiencia tengan libros en que asienten todas las condemnaciones de bienes que se hacen à instancia del receptor y sus procuradores para dar noticia dellos al notario de sequestros para que haga cargo dello al receptor y que los jueces de bienes y notarios de audiencias juran de ansi lo guardar y cumplir.

Item, la instruccion que manda que los bienes sequestrados, por las presiones de los que se mandan prender queden en poder de personas llanas y abonadas para acudir con ellos à quien los inquisidores mandaren y que hasta la distincion de la causa criminal y principal y condenacion del preso los receptores no tengan entrada en los bienes sequestrados so la pena de privacion de oficio y que vuelvan lo que asi entraren y ocuparen de los dichos bienes sequestrados con otro tanto para el oficio de la santa inquisicion.

Item, la instruccion que manda que por evitar dilaciones superfluas dentro de los quince dias de la presion de cada uno se hagan las tres amonestaciones caritativas y siendo negativos se presenten los acusaciones à los quince dias ò antes sobre lo qual se encarga la conciencia à los inquisidores.

Item, la instruccion que dispone que de quince en quince dias se visiten los presos para haber informacion de como son tractados y proveidos y curados en sus enfermedades.

Item, la instruccion que manda que en la camara del secreto donde estan las escrituras del crimen no entren sino solos los inquisidores y oficiales del secreto so pena de excomunion.

Item, la instruccion que manda que trabajen tres horas en la audiencia de mañana y otras tres à la tarde sobre lo qual se encarga la conciencia à los inquisidores para que asi lo hagan guardar y cumplir.

Item, por quanto parece que la instruccion del arca que habla cerca del depositarse el dinero confiscado que cobra el receptor no se guarda de dos ò tres años à esta parte y es cosa justa y necesaria que se guarde, mandamos que en todo caso sea guardada y cumplida so las penas en ella contenidas.

Item, que se guarden y cumplan de aqui adelante todas las otras Instrucciones del sancto oficio porque aquellas fueron hechas por los señores inquisidores generales con mucho consejo y acuerdo de letrados y en generales congregaciones para el bien y observacion de las inquisiciones particulares y que para mejor observacion dellas se lean aquellas dos veces en el año publicamente en el audiencia delante de todos los oficiales, la una vez por pascua de resurrecion y la otra por pascua de Navidad, y sobre esto encargamos las conciencias à los inquisidores.

Item, por quanto parece por el dicho proceso de la visita que por el receptor de los bienes confiscados se han vendido muchos esclavos reputados por cristianos que hobieron sido de condemnados ò reconciliados debiendo gozar de libertad y esto so color que no mostraban fé y testimonio de su conversion y bautismo, vos los inquisidores ò qualquiera de vos si asi es declarareis estos tales esclavos por libres y proveereis que sean puestos en libertad.

Item, porque parece y somos informado que el inquisidor Melchior Cervera ya defunto anduvo visitando por el reino y recibio muchas informaciones y testificaciones y es cosa justa y debida que aquellas se pongan en la camara del secreto para que se haya entera noticia de las penas de los que quebraron las carcelerias y de los bienes confiscados y mal llevados al tiempo de la inventariacion de los bienes hecha por los comisarios y factores y de otras cosas asi civiles como criminales, vos los dichos inquisidores ò qualquiera de vos proveereis que todas las dichas informaciones y testificaciones se recojan y se pongan en la camara del secreto, sino se hobiere ya cobrado para que se haya noticia de las dichas cosas y se provea en ello todo lo que fuere necesario y las que pertenecieren al oficio del receptor se le entreguen en presencia y por ante el escribano de sequestros.

Item, por quanto parece que las provisiones y letras del inquisidor general y del consejo que se embian à la dicha inquisicion no vienen algunas veces al secretario ni se alcanza à saber lo que se envia à mandar sino por discurso de tiempo mandamos que todas las dichas provisiones y cartas que hasta aqui se han despachado del inquisidor general y del consejo y de aqui adelante se despacharan se pongan en la camara del secreto para que de ellas se haya entera noticia y sean mejor guardadas y cumplidas.

Item, por quanto parece que hay algunos condenados à pena de galeras y otras penas las quales nunca se han ejecutado mandamos que vos los dichos inquisidores ò qualquiera de vos veais esto con diligencia y hagais justicia sobre lo qual os encargamos la conciencia.

Item, por quanto somos informado quel notario de los sequestros ha pedido muchas veces que se le de noticia de las penitencias impuestas y de las que dende en adelante se hobieren de imponer para tener cuenta y razon dellas y hacer cargo al receptor ò à quien las habia recebido ò recibiere y que nunca se ha hecho, mandamos que al escribano de sequestros se de noticia y razon de todas las penitencias pasadas.

Item, mandamos que todas las penitencias que de aqui adelante se impusieren se den al doctor Tristan Calvete el qual tenga razon de las dichas penitencias y mandamos à los inquisidores y à qualquiera dellos que pongan diligencia en cobrar las dichas penitencias y ponerlas en el arca del sancto oficio conforme à la justicia.

Item, porque parece que en la paga del quarto y quinto por las manifestaciones de bienes ocultos ha habido y hay abuso por los receptores no guardandose la provision que sobre esto està despachado, mandamos que aquella se guarde y que el dicho quarto y quinto no se pague à los denunciantes sino solo de bienes ocultos y que no hayan venido à noticia del receptor ni de otros oficiales de esa inquisicion y que los denunciantes no sean oficiales ò personas que por causa y razon del oficio hayan sabido y manifestado los dichos bienes, y mandamos que de aqui adelante no se de por manifestacion de bienes ocultos salvo la quinta parte de los bienes que se cobraren por la tal manifestacion.

Item, por quanto parece que el despensero de los presos tiene un mozo al qual se da de salario ocho tarines cada dia y de comer, vos los dichos inquisidores ò qualquiera de vos proveereis en esto lo que convenga de manera que no traya gastos superfluos.

Item, por quanto somos informado que el escribano de sequestros anduvo con el inquisidor Cervera en la visita de ese reino catorce meses fuera de la ciudad de Palermo y que en ese tiempo se han vendido muchos bienes y cobrado muchas deudas en la dicha ciudad y que no ha podido hallar razon cuenta de lo que se ha entrado y cobrado, mandamos que vos los dichos inquisidores ò qualquiera de vos averigueis brevemente con diligencia esto dando todo el favor que fuere menester al contador y escribano de sequestros.

Item, porque somos informado que en ese oficio se hacen muchos gastos que se podrian muy bien escusar y que los inquisidores dan los mandamientos para ello con mucha facilidad y es cosa justa y debida se provea esto, mandamos que vos los inquisidores ò qualquiera de vos os informeis destos gastos extraordinarios y proveais que de aqui adelante no se hagan gastos superfluos.

Item, porque parece que los presos de la carcel estan alguna vez mal proveidos de ropa de cama porque à los que son fuera de la ciudad no les curan de traer ropa y que seria bien que cuando el alguacil trae algun preso trugese ropa con èl de sus bienes para su cama, vos los dichos inquisidores ò qualquiera de vos provereis esto de manera que los presos sean bien proveidos y tratados.

Item, mandamos que los familiares deste santo oficio sean personas virtuosas, quietas, pacificas y abonadas y que el numero no sea superfluo porque no haya justa causa de quejas que lo mesmo està proveido en las otras inquisiciones.

Item, porque parece que por los notarios del secreto se han examinado algunos testigos del crimen sin presencia de los inquisidores ò de alguno dellos contra el tenor de la instruccion que esto prohibe mandamos que la dicha instruccion se guarde como en ella se contiene sobre lo qual encargamos la conciencia à los inquisidores y notarios del secreto salvo que fuere dificultoso ir alguno de los inquisidores à hacer el dicho examen en el qual caso el comisario juntamente con uno de los dichos notarios lo pueda hacer el qual comisario entonce de certificacion de la fe que se debe dar à los testigos que asi se examinaren.

Item, porque consta por el proceso de la dicha visita que à los oficiales y ministros dese sancto oficio le han hecho algunas resistencias è injurias las quales no han sido castigadas mandamos que el fiscal haga acerca desto sus instancias debidas y vos los inquisidores ò qualquiera de vos hagais justicia porque à los malhechores sea castigo y à los otros exemplo y los oficiales de aqui adelante no sean injuriados ni maltratados.

Item, por quanto parece que algunas veces los inquisidores no entienden personalmente en la ratificacion de los testigos y los comisarios no guardan el secreto mandamos que la ratificacion de los testigos se haga ante vos los inquisidores ò qualquiera de vos y que se guarde enteramente la instruccion que cerca desto habla ansi en el examen sumario como en las ratificaciones.

Item, porque parece que algunos llamandose comisarios sin tener comision ni poder del receptor han exigido y cobrado deudas debidas al fisco real en muchas partes asi en tiempo del receptor Obregon como de Garcia Cid y aunque algunos dellos vinieron à dar cuenta à los receptores otros no la han dado, mandamos que el inquisidor contador y escribano de sequestros que agora van proveidos averiguen esto con mucha diligencia y en todo provean mediante justicia.

Item, parece que al tiempo que vino en ese reino el ambajador moro de los Gelves el inquisidor Calvete hizo traer à la inquisicion un esclavito pequeño que los moros que vinieron con el dicho embajador le tenian hurtado para se lo volver en Berberia porque no le llevasen à pedimiento del dueño y tambien porque el mochacho diz que decia que queria ser cristiano y que ido deste reino el dicho ambajador entrego el dicho esclavito al fiscal de ese reino y no à la parte cuyo era aunque lo vino à pedir diversas vices. Porende mandamos que vos los dichos inquisidores ò qualquiera de vos proveais en esto lo que fuere de justicia de manera que el dicho esclavo se vuelva y de y entregue à cuyo es.

Item, parece que por parte de un Francisco Maynente preso por herege se hobo allegado para su defensa que los testigos fueron conspirados y conjurados contra èl por un Juan de Avisa y otros consortes suyos para lo qual nombro testigos y allende aquellos pidio que tambien se examinasen los nombrados por sus hijos y que yendo à entender uno de los inquisidores en la probanza desta conspiracion recibio en contradiccion del fiscal testigos nuevamento nombrados por los hijos è yernos del preso ò à un suegro suyo è à otros que continuamente con las armas en las manos han andado en defension del dicho Francisco

Mainente, y que en el examen los susodichos no fueron preguntados de deudos amistad ni de otras circumstancias necesarias de lugar y tiempo de manera que por esta via se ha embarazado esta causa y tornandose à desdecir algunos de los testigos. Porende mandamos que el fiscal haga sus pedimentos cerca desto ante los inquisidores y que ellos ò qualquiera dellos provean lo que fuere de justicia.

Item, por quanto parece que los reconciliados traen los habitos cubiertos por los ciudades y tierras donde moran, los inhabiles per condemnacion de padres y de abuelos traen armas, seda, oro, plata y usan de cosas que les son vedadas y prohibidas y que esto no se castiga y es en mucho deservicio de Dios y menosprecio de justicia mandamos que el fiscal haga sus pedimentos sobre esto y los inquisidores ò qualquiera dellos lo castiguen y provean mediante justicia.

Item, porque parece que el receptor se queja que el inquisidor Cervera en la visita que hizo por ese reino mando acudir con los aquileres de una casa à un Nadal Valaguer contra toda justicia y razon, la qual casa con otras bienes diz que estaban cedidos y traspasados à ese santo oficio por alcances que se ovieron hecho al dicho Nadal de haciendas cobradas en su tiempo y del receptor Obregon, mandamos que vos los inquisidores ò qualquiera de vos hagais brevemente justicia.

Item, porque parece que ha habido comunicacion de presos unos con otros por la mala guarda de las carceles y desto se siguen muchos inconvenientes al sancto oficio, mandamos que los inquisidores ò qualquiera de vos proveais cerca desto de remedio convenible.

Item, por quanto parece que al tiempo de la conmocion de ese reino muchos de los reconciliados por ese sancto oficio se quitaron los habitos penitenciales y despues aca no se los han vuelto los quales en mucho deservicio de Dios y grande daño de las animas de los dichos reconciliados, mandamos que vos los dichos inquisidores ò qualquiera de vos proveais que todos los dichos habitos se vuelvan à los dichos reconciliados para que los trayan publicamente y cumplan las sentencias que contra ellos fueron dadas mirando mucho que esto se haga en tiempo y de manera que por ello no se pueda seguir escandalo ni inconveniente alguno, que despues de vueltos se usara con los que cumplieren como deben sus penitencias de misericordia.

Item, por quanto parece que los inquisidores y otros oficiales de esa inquisicion han llevado algunos presentes contra la instruccion que esto prohibe, mandamos que de aqui adelante se guarde la dicha instruccion como en ella se contiene y lo que se ha llevado hasta aqui de presentes contra la dicha instruccion de confesos y litigantes se ha restituido à las partes que dieron los dichos presentes.

Item, porque somos informado que el inquisidor Melchior Cervera por descargo de su conciencia dejo en su ultimo testamento à ese santo oficio docientos ducados de oro, y es cosa justa que se cobren, mandamos que el receptor de los bienes confiscados no pague à el heredero del dicho Melchior Cervera de lo que se le debiere de su salario los dichos docientos ducados y si todo su salario fuese pagado se cobren por el dicho receptor ò contador de los bienes del dicho inquisidor Cervera.

Por ende mandamos à vos los dichos inquisidores y oficiales que agora sois ò por tiempo fueredes en el oficio de la santa inquisicion del dicho reino de Sicilia que veades las instrucciones y ordinaciones y cosas y capitulos susodichos y todas las otras instrucciones del dicho sancto oficio y cada uno de vos en lo que toca y atañe las guardeis y cumplais y hagais guardar y cumplir en todo y por todo segun que en ellas se contiene y contra el tenor y forma de lo en ellas y cada una dellas contenido no vayais ni paseis ni consintais ir ni pasar en tiempo alguno so las penas en los dichos capitulos é instrucciones contenidas sobre todo lo qual vos encargamos la conciencia, en testimonio de lo qual mandamos hacer la presente firmada de nuestro nombre refrendada del secretario y sellada con el sello deste sancto oficio.

Datum en la villa de Madrid à xxxi dias del mes de Enero del año del nascimiento de nuestro señor mil quinientos y veinte y cinco

Archiepiscopus Hispalensis.

De mandato Rmi. D. Archiepiscopi Hispalensis inquisitoris generalis

Joannes Garcia, secretarius.

Registrata in sancte inquisitionis quinto, f° clv.

III.

COMMISSION FOR THE ARREST OF HERETICS, ISSUED BY VICEROY RIBAGORZA, JANUARY 14, 1509.

(Chioccarello MSS., Tom. VIII).
(See p. 56).

Joannes de Aragonia Mag^{co} Viro, U. J. D. Antonio de Baldaxino regio fideli nobis carissimo, gratiam regiam et bonam voluntatem. Perche secondo avemo inteso ad esto si commette in aliquibus partibus Apuliæ certa eresia che lo venerdi Santo gl'uomini e donne di questi luoghi insieme con candele accese e dapoi di certa predica estinguono le candele e gl'uomini con le donne usano carnalmente taliter che usano li Padri colle figliuole ed altri colle sorelle, e questo en disservizio di nuestro Sig^{re} Dio e contra la fede nostra Cattolica. E volendo noi estirpare et radicitus abolire tal eresia e cose mal fatte e nefande ed ancora punire e castigare li tali eretici delinquenti. Pertanto a voi della fede, probità, perizia e scienza della quale molto confidamo, dicemo, ordinamo e comandamo quod præsentibus acceptis personaliter vi debbiate conferire in partibus Apuliæ vel in qualunque città, Terra, castello e luoghi del presente Regno, tanto demaniali quanto de Baroni ed Ecclesiastiche persone, dove parerà e sarà bisogno, e pigliar informazione esattamente di tutte le cose predette, e quelli trovarete colpabili pigliarete di persona e conducerete da noi, perche vista detta informazione possano quelli punirsi e castigarsi giusta loro demeriti, e se vi parerà dover annotare li beni di tali delinquenti, lo farete, e quelli pro tuitione Regiæ Curiæ ponerete in loco tuto, adeo che volendo quelli li possiamo avere, perche noi per tenore della presente circa præmissa per voi agenda et complenda vi commettemo e conferimo voces et vices Regias atque nostras plenumque posse et locum nostrum, e perche meglio possiate eseguire questa presente nostra commissione ordinamo e comandamo à tutti e singoli Prencipi, Duchi, Marchesi, Conti, Baroni, Lou^{rl} Regii ed altri officiali maggiori e minori ed altri qual siano sudditi della Cattolica Maiestà che circa l'eseguire per voi e complire delle cose predette non vi debbiano ponere ostaculo ne dare impaccio seu impedimento alcuno, immo vi dobbiano assistere e dare ogni ausilio, consilio, aiuto e favore opportuno, sempre che da voi saranno ricercati, e volemo vi debbiano provedere di stanza, letto e strama senza pagamento alcuno, e d'ogni altra cosa e ragione sotto pena della Regia disgrazia e di docati mille al R° fisco applicandi. Datum in Castro novo civitatis Neapolis, die 14 Januarii 1509. El Conde Lugart° General. V^t Montaltus R., V^t de Colle R., Dominus Locumt^s Gen^{lis} mandavit mihi Petro Lazaro de Exea. In Curiæ Locumtenentis 3° Comitis Ripacursiæ fol. 209 à t°.

IV.

PROMISE OF PHILIP II TO THE CITY OF NAPLES IN 1564.

(Chioccarello MSS., Tom. VIII).
(See p. 87).

Relazione fatta dal P. D. Paolo d'Arezzo alla Città di Napoli nel suo ritorno.

Quel che S. M. nell' espedirmi da lei mi comandò à me D. Paolo d'Arezzo, che Io dovessi far fede alla sua Fed^{ma} Città di Napoli della buona voluntà sua verso della Città e di tutto quel suo Regno di Napoli é come tutti l'ama grandemente e desidera ogni loro sodisfazione e la M. S. è pronta farli sempre nuove grazie e nuovi beneficii et in ogni occasione dimostrar l'amore e benignità sua, e la gratitudine dell' animo suo per la fedeltà la quale sempre hanno usata verso la M. S. e de suoi predecessori e per li continui e grandi servizii tanto in guerra quanto in pace, delli quali S. M. ne tiene memoria, aggradendoli e tenendoli in quel conto che si deve. E per quanto al particolare delle grazie che si hanno a S. M. domandate, quel che ha conosciuto esser utile benefizio e quiete della Città e Regno di Napoli di liberarli per sempre dall'Inquisizione ce l'ha concesso molto liberamente e benignamente, sperando che si portaranno piamente e cristianamente nelle cose della Religione e della S. Fede Catt^{ca} e cosi l'esorta tutti ad averne buona cura e diligenza. Ma in quanto a gli altri capi perche S. M. non vede che siano in beneficio loro, anzi potriano essere à loro stessi dannosi non l'ha parso poterli concedere in buona coscienza, ne però l'exclude del tutto ma si reserba ed averà buona e più matura considerazione e provederli più di spazio. Mi commise ancora ch'Io lo riferissi come desidera venire in questa città à visitare il Regno per mostrare à tutti l'amore e buona volontà che li porta, e così come in absenza ha conosciuto la fedeltà ed affezione di tutti per sua maggior consolazione e contento fruirla con la presenza e dal canto suo ancora dar tutta quella sodizfazione che può a così fedeli ed amorevoli vassalli, il che S. M. tiene intenzione di farlo colla prima occasione che dio benedetto gli darà.

Questo è quel tanto che S. M. mi comandò che da sua parte io dovesse riferire alla Città in testimonio ed esplicazione della benignità ed amor suo verso di questa Città e Regno di Napoli tutto il sopradetto l'ho visto con gli occhi e toccato con mano esser la pura verità.

El Rey.

Por quanto haviendose nos suplicado por parte de la nuestra ciudad y Regno de Napoles fuesemos servido declarar nuestra intencion cerca las cosas de heresia que alli succediere. Por ende por tenor de la presente deximos y declaramos no haver sido ni ser de nuestra mente ò intencion que en la dicha ciudad y Reyno se ponga la Inquisicion en la forma de España, sino que se proceda por la via ordinaria como esta aqui, y que assi se observara y complira con efecto en lo adelante, sin que en ello haya falta, en testimonio de lo qual mandamos dar la presente firmada de nuestra mano y sellado con nuestro sello secreto. En Madrid à diez dias de Marzo 1565. Yo el Rey.—V^t Figueroa R^s.—V^t Soto R^s.—V^t Vargas Secretarius.—Locus Sigilli.—Declaracion de que no se pondra en la Ciudad y Reyno de Napoles la Inquisicion en la forma de España.

Il duplicato di questa lettera fù rimessa da S. M. al Duca d'Alcala.

V.

APPLICATION TO THE VICEROY OF NAPLES FOR EXTRADITION, MARCH 6, 1610.

(Chioccarello MSS., Tom. VIII).
(See p. 91).

Illmo ed Ecc^{mo} Signore.

D. Fabio Orzolino dice à V. E. come si è necessario far notificare una citazione spedita in forma Bullæ dal S^{to} Officio contro l'Abbate Angelo e Carlo della Rocca. Supplica perciò V. E. per il Regio suo exequatur avendola da notificare in Regno ut Devotus et Reverendus Regius cappelanus major videat et referat. Constantius Reg^{s}. Provisum per S. Exc^{a}. Neapoli die 6 mensis Martii 1610. Vitalianus.

Illmo ed Ecc^{mo} Signore. Per parte del predetto supplicante mi è stato presentato il predetto memoriale con regia decretazione di V. E. di mia commissione. E volendo gl'ordini dell' E. V. eseguire e dell' esposto informarmi ho visto una provisione spedita da Monsignore Crecenzo Auditor Generale della Rota seu Camera Apostolica nella quale si narra che dovendo l'Abbate Angelo e Carlo della Rocca di Traetto, Diocesi di Gaeta ad esso supplicante docati ottant'otto in virtù di publico istrumento con l'obligazione camerale ed essendo per detto debito stati per cedoloni declarati per publici scomunicati ed avendono in detta scommunica persistito per un anno e più per il che si citano ad personaliter comparendum in detta corte Romana ed avanti il detto Auditore à dire la causa perchè non si devono dichiarare per insordescenti, come questo ed altro appare per detta provisione spedita in Roma per esecuzione publica della quale si suplica V. E. per il Regio exequatur. Per tanto visto e considerato il tutto, adhibito in ciò il parere del m° U. J. D. Gio. Geronimo Natale Avvogado Fiscale del R^{t} Patrimonio della Regia Camera della Summaria mia Auditore, sono di voto che l'E. V. puo restar servita per esecuzione della detta provisione di concedere ad esso supplicante il Regio Exequatur quo ad personas Ecclesiasticas tantum. E questo è quanto mi occorre riferire a V. E. —Da Casa in Napoli à di 7 Maggio 1610. De V. E. Servidor y Cappellan D. Gabriel Sanchez de Luna.—Jo. Hieronimus Natalis.

VI.

KING FERDINAND LIMITS SALARIES BY THE CONFISCATIONS, IN THE INQUISITION OF SARDINIA.

(Archivo de Simancas, Inquisicion, Libro III, fol. 308).
(See p. 114).

EL REY.

Bernardt Ros nuestro receptor de los bienes y facienda a nuestra camara e fisco confiscados e pertenecientes e que se confiscaran por el crimen de la heregia y apostasia en el Reino de Cerdeña, los salarios que en cada un año habeis de pagar al inquisidor y otros oficiales y ministros en el sancto oficio de la inquisicion en el dicho reino son los siguientes:

Al reverendo obispo del Alguer inquisidor . .	100 libras
A Micer Pedro de Contreras abogado en el crimen y judicatura de bienes	40
A Luis de Torres alguacil	30
A un escribano del secreto y judicatura de bienes y secrestos	30
A un portero e nuncio	10
A vos mesmo por receptor	100
A mossen Alonso de Ximeno procurador fiscal y canonigo de Callar	30

Los quales salarios ordinarios facen suma en universo trescientas quarenta libras barcelonesas las quales vos mandamos que les deis por sus tercios del año de qualesquier bienes y pecunias que sean confiscados y se confiscaren en la dicha inquisicion comenzando a contar a cada uno de ellas dende el dia que comenzara a servir sus oficios y dende adelante por tanto tiempo como cada uno servira su oficio y con restitucion de sus apocas de pago tan solamente, mandamos a la persona que vuestras cuentas oira y examinara que los dichos salarios segun dicho es vos pasen y admitan en quenta y descargo toda duda dificultad consulta y contradiccion cessantes. Queremos empero que si no hobiere bienes confiscados para pagar los dichos salarios que nos ni nuestra corte no seamos tenido ni obligado a los pagar antes queremos que no habiendo cumplimiento las dichas quantias se repartan entre los oficiales a sueldo por libra.

Datum en Valladolid a once de Septiembre de mil quinientos catorce.

Yo el Rey.—Calcena Secretario.

VII.

PHILIP II TO THE DUKE OF SESSA.
ABANDONING THE INTRODUCTION OF THE SPANISH INQUISITION IN MILAN.

(Archivio Civico Storico à S. Carpofaro in Milano. Armario A. Filza VII, N. 40).
(See p. 128).

Illmo Duque, Primo nuestro, Governador y Capitan General. Hanse rrecivido todas vuestras cartas hasta la ultima de xxiii del pasado y dexando de satisfaser a ellas para con el primero esta servira solamente para rresponder a lo de la Inquisicion, por ser negocio que no requiere delacion, quedando ese estado de la manera que nos screvis y lo avemos visto por las cartas que nos ha mostrado el obispo de Cuenca en conformidad de las vuestras. La dexceridad y buena manera con que os governastes para aquietar los animos de los desestado y estorvar que no embiasen aca embaxadores fue como convenia y se deve esperar de vuestra prudencia, y assi conformandonos con vuestro parecer damos orden al electo de Salerno que no parta de Trento y a Roma que cese la instancia y officio que se hazia con su Santidad para que mandase despachar la facultad, y vos con el buen modo que lo aveis començado hablareis a los desse estado dandoles a entender con las mejores palabras que vereis convenir que nuestra Intencion nunca fué ni es de hazer novedad en la forma de proceder del sancto officio sino solamente en la persona, para que con mas autoridad y teniendo mejor de comer se hiziese lo que convenia al servicio de Dios y bien de la Religion en tiempos tan infectos y peligrosos por la vezindad, y que assi pueden ser ciertos que en esto no avra novedad, quedando enteramente confiado que ellos por su parte como tan catholicos y zelosos del servicio de Dios y nuestro, siguiendose la forma y horden que hasta aqui se ha tenido haran lo que deven. Y todo os lo rremitionos como persona que estara sobrel negocio, os governeys en esto como mas vieredes convenir para escusar todo genero de Inconviniente y mala satisfacion. Y conforme a ello embiarcio (*sic*) luego essa carta al electo de Salerno y esotra despacho a Roma dando juntamente con el aviso al embaxador de lo que cerca desto se hiziese para que sepa como se avra de governar con su Santidad.—De Monçon a viii de Noviembre de M. D. lxiii.

El Senado nos ha scripto una carta sobre estos negocios. Dales ese aviso del Recivo y de lo que en ello se provee.—Yo el Rey.

J. Vargas.

VIII.

Quarantine Against Heretics.

(MSS. of Ambrosian Library, H. S. VI, 29).
(See p. 131).

DECRETI DELLA SACRA CONGREGAZIONE DEL SANTO OFFICIO DI ROMA CONTRO GLI HERETICI CHE VENGONO IN MILANO E SUO STATO.

Inquisitori Mediolani: Ut cum solitis conditionibus practicatis ante Bullam Gregorii XV permittat Rhetis et Helvetiis per aliquod dies manere Mediolani occasione mercaturæ et non aliter; invigilet tamen ne aliquid in fidem Catholicam machinentur.—19 Julii, 1625.

Alios tamen Hæreticos non permittat ibidem manere, datur tamen ei facultas concedendi Talibus licentias per aliquod breve tempus et certioret.—24 Junii, 1627.

Inquisitoribus Mediolani et Comi: Non inducant gravamina et novitates contra Helvetios et eorum Confœderatos Hæreticos Mediolanum accedentes, sed observant capitulationes antiquas.—5 Augusti, 1599.

Inquisitori Mediolani: Curet cum participatione Eminent^{ml} Archiepiscopi cum suavitate et paulatim tollere abusum commercii Mercatorum Catholicorum dictæ civitatis cum Hæreticis et adhibeat diligentiam ne denuo hujusmodi commercia introducantur.—10 Octobris, 1629.

Hæretici in Statu Mediolani non admittantur ab Inquisitoribus nisi sint ex Rhetis vel Helvetiis qui in eo habent commercium mercaturæ vigore Conventionum inter Regem Hispaniarum et ipsos factarum. Commercium litterarum inter Catholicos et Hæreticos non permittant nisi inter Confœderatos ratione mercaturæ. Mercium sarcinæ, vulgo *Balle*, si remanent Mediolani visitentur ab ipso Inquisitore an adsint libri Hæretici; si vero aliunde vehuntur fiat diligentia in loco ad quem ducuntur; si vero sint dolia librorum videatur ipsorum librorum lista, quæ si non exhibeatur non permittantur alio duci nisi visis libris et se intelligat Inquisitor Mediolani cum aliis Inquisitoribus civitatum ad quas deferuntur.—Inquisitori Mediolani 3 Julii, 1593.

Inquisitori Mediolani scriptum fuit ne permittat Ministros et Prædicantes Hæreticos accedere in hunc statum, sed quod alios Hæreticos Helvetios qui accedunt illuc pro Commercio observare faciat Capitulationes et alia ordinata cum declarationibus et moderationibus ultimo eis scriptis.—3 Decembris, 1599.

DECRETI CONTRO GL' ERETICI DIMORANTI IN VENEZIA E SUO STATO.

Nuntio Venetiarum scriptum fuit die duodecima Januarii, 1591, ut tractet cum Dominis Venetis quod nullo modo admitti debent in eorum Dominio Hæretici et Apostatæ a fide etiam conniventibus oculis.

Nuntio Venetiarum scriptum fuit die 23 Februarii, 1591 circa Hæreticos ultramontanos commorantes Venetiis in fundaco Germanorum habitum fuisse sermonem de prædictis cum Sanctissimo et ita concludit Epistola—

E perchè il ritenere ivi i nemici della Santa Fede ridonda in diservizio di Dio, e per esser quello un male contagiosissimo, bisogna che almeno in progresso di tempo causi grand' infezione in quell' Anime: ed il Commercio con quella nazione si puo conservare e continuare col mezzo d'altri mercanti Catolici e confidenti à cotesta Signoria, la Santità Sua ha ordinato che V. S. sempre le verra occasione, procuri colla sua prudenza e destrezza d'insinuare tutto ciò e metterlo in considerazione al Principe e a quei Signori acciocche si pensi di provedervi, e sua Santità ne deve parlare coll' Ambasciatore.

IX.

DECREE OF PIUS V, JUNE 6, 1566.

(Bulario de la Orden de Santiago, Libro III, fol. 91.—Archivo historico nacional de Madrid).
(See p. 132).

Die Jovis sexta mensis Junii, 1566, Sanctissimus in Christo pater D. N. D. Pius divina providentia Pius Quintus, in Congregatione officii Sanctæ Ro. universalis Inquisitionis, in throno majestatis suæ sedens, unacum illustrissimis et reverendissimis dominis Dominis Cardinalibus Inquisitoribus Generalibus, statuit, decrevit, ordinavit et mandavit ut negotia fidei omnibus et singulis aliis præferantur, cum fides sit substantia et fundamentum Christianæ religionis. Idcirco omnibus et singulis almæ Urbis ejusque districtus Gubernatori, Senatori, Vicario, Cameræ Apostolicæ auditoribus quibuscunque, Legatis, Vicelegatis, Gubernatoribus Provinciarum et Terrarum suæ Sanctitati et Sanctæ Romanæ Ecclesiæ mediate vel immediate subjectarum ac eorum locatenentibus, officialibus, barissellis aliisque ministris, necnon aliis locorum ordinariis cæterisque magistratibus, officialibus ac cujusvis conditionis et status hominibus in omnibus et singulis terris, oppidis, civitatibus ac in tota Republica Christiana existentibus, sub excommunicationis latæ sententiæ ac indignationis suæ Sanctitatis aliisque arbitrio suæ Sanctitatis ac illustriss, et reverendiss. D. D. Cardinalium Inquisitorum Generalium imponendis et exequendis pœnis, ut eisdem Cardinalibus Inquisitoribus hujusmodi ac eorum præceptis et mandatis in quibuscunque officium sanctæ Inquisitionis hujusmodi concernentibus pareant et obediant. Reges vero, Duces, Comites, Barones et quosvis alios Principes sæculares in Dei nomine rogavit ut eisdem Cardinalibus Inquisitoribus eorumque officialibus faveant auxiliumque præbeant, a suis magnatibus subditis auxilium præberi faciant in negotiis ad dictum officium spectantibus, necnon carceratos quoscunque pro quibusvis delictis et debitis etiam atrocibus, apud dictum Inquisitionis officium quomodolibet delatos vel denunciatos, suspensa aliorum criminum inferiorum cognitione, ad eosdem Cardinales vel Inquisitionis carceres, ibidemque ad criminis hæresis totaliter cognitionem et expeditionem retinendos, postea ad eosdem officiales pro aliorum criminum cognitione remittendos, sine mora transmittant. Instante magnifico Domino Pedro Belo procuratore fiscali officii Sanctæ Romanæ Universalis Inquisitionis.

X.

S. Carlo Borromeo's Memoranda for a Visitation.

(MSS. of the Ambrosian Library, Tomo V, F. 41 ed 177, Parte Inferiore, No. 76).
(See p. 133).

Ricordo di alcune cose delle quali principalmente s'a da far diligente inquisitione

Se nella patria sono heretici, sospetti di heresia, ricettatori et fautori di heretici, scandalosi nel parlare et chi abusà le parole della Scrittura.

Se si fanno conventicole ò ridotti di laici ne quali si parli delle cose della fede; se predichi e si disputi senza autorità di superiori Ecclesiastici.

Se vi è comertio di heretici ò sospetti et come si avertisse à quelle famiglie che praticano ne i paesi heretici ò per mercantia ò altro pretesto.

Se mandano i figlioli in Germania ò in altra provincia nelle parti sospette per imperar la lingua ò trafico ò per viver in Corti di Principi.

Di libri prohibiti ò scandalosi et che cura si tiene nel portare i libri nella patria et se s'avertischi bene à mercanti et à chi pratica ne paesi sospetti; se portano libri heretici ò sospetti dell' Inquisitione nelle librarie.

Come si governa l'offitio della Sta Inquisitione cioè di Vescovi et Inquisitori in quelle parti circa il tener ben purgato il paese da quella peste.

Se hanno qualche impedimento nell'offitio.

Se hanno il debito aiuto circa la essecutione da principi secolari, così gl'Inquisitori come li Vescovi nell'officio loro.

Di predicatori, che diligentia s'usi, acciò catholicamente predichino et che non disputino le cose controverse ma solamente in ogni occasione stabilischino la parte catholica, dichiarando bene et chiaramente il senso delle Scritture, et lasciando da parte li fondamenti delli heretici.

De Maestri di scuola come insegnano et che libri legono.

Se secondo il decreto del Consiglio Tridentino i Curati ammaestrano fanciulli nella dottrina Christiana.

Se vi sono superstitioni, divinationi et incanti et altre cose tali che vanno appresso all'heresie et molte volte sapiunt etiam manifestam heresim.

Se con quel honore che si deve sono tenute le sante relique.

* * * * * * * * * * *

Se vi sono pubblici peccatori, sprezzatori di commandamenti de la Chiesa, delle ceremonie, riti et traditioni et contemptori delle censure et giuditii Ecclesiastici.

* * * * * * * * * * *

Delli hebrei, se portano il segno, se conversano con Christiani con pericolo di corrutela dei costumi Christiani.

XI.

EXTRACT FROM EDICT OF NOVEMBER 10, 1571,
ISSUED BY THE INQUISITION OF MEXICO TO THE POPULATION OF NEW SPAIN EMBODYING THE OATH OF OBEDIENCE.

(From the MSS. of General Don Vicente Riva Palacio).
(See p. 203).

* * * Mandamos dar y dimos la presente por la cual vos ecshortamos, amonestamos y mandamos en virtud de santa obediencia y so pena de excomunion mayor, que del dia que esta nuestra carta fuere leida y notificada ó de ella supieredes en cualquier manera en adelante vos los susodichos y cada uno de vos como fieles y católicos cristianos, celadores de nuestra santa fé, verdaderos miembros de la Yglesia Católica cada y cuando y en cualquier lugar que os halláredes en cuanto en vos fuere favorecereis al dicho Santo Oficio, Oficiales y ministros de él, dandoles todo el favor y ayuda que os pidieren, y que no ayudareis ni favorecereis á los hereges enemigos de nuestra santa fé católica, antes como á lobos y perros rabiosos inficionadores de las animas cristianas y destruidores de la esposa divina del Señor que es la Yglesia católica, los perseguireis manifestandolos y no los encubrireis, y si lo contrario hicieredes, lo que Dios no quiera ni permita, incurrais y caigais en la ira é indignacion de Dios todo poderoso y de la Virgen Santa Maria su madre, y de los bienaventurados apostolos S. Pedro y S. Pablo y de todos los santos de la corte celestial, y venga sobre los inobedientes á esto las plagas y maldiciones que vinieron y descendieron sobre el Rey Faraon y los suyos por que resistieron á los mandamientos de Dios y la destruccion que vino sobre los de Sodoma y Gomorra que fueron abrasados, y la que vino sobre Coreb, Datan y Aviron que sorbió la tierra vivos por su inobediencia, y siempre esten endurecidos y en pecado y el diablo este á su mano derecha y su oracion sia siempre en pecado delante el acatamiento de Dios, sus dias sean pocos y su nombre y memoria se pierda en la tierra y sean arrojados de sus moradas en manos de sus enemigos y cuando sean juzgados salgan condenados del juicio divino con lucifer y Judas el traidor y sus hijos, queden huerfanos y mendicantes y no hallen quien bien les haga, y allende las otras penas y censuras en derechos establecidas contra los tales inobedientes al Santo Oficio y á los mandamientos apostólicos caegan é incurran en pena de escomunion mayor que nos por tales los declaramos en estos escriptos y por ellos y para mayor vigor y fuerza de lo susodicho mandamos que todas las personas que presentes estais de qualquier estado y condicion que sean alzeis las manos y jureis á Dios y á Santa Maria y á la señal de la Cruz y á las palabras de los cuatro santos evangelios que ante vuestros ojos teneis que de aqui adelante como verdaderos católicos y fieles cristianos y hijos de obediencia sereis en favor ayuda y defensa de la santa fé de nuestro S. Jesucristo y de su ley evangelica que tiene, predica, sigue y enseña la S. Madre Yglesia Católica Romana y de la S. Inquisicion, Oficiales y ministros de ella en cuanto en vos fuere con todas vuestras fuerzas y posibilidades sin impedirles ni embargarles publica ni secretamente, directe ni indirecte ni por cualquier exquisito color por vos ni por otra persona en cosa alguna tocante al dicho S. Oficio y ejecucion de él y que no favorecereis á los herejes, infamados y sospechosos del crimen de herejia y apostasia, ni á sus creyentes, favorecedores, receptadores ni defensores de ellos ni á los perturbadores ni impedidores del dicho Santo Oficio y de su libre y recto ejercicio, antes sereis en los perseguir, acusar, y denunciar á la S. Madre Yglesia y á nos los Ynquisidores y á nuestros sucesores como á sus ministros á quien por su Santidad y Sede Apostólica está reservado el conocimiento de las tales causas y que no lo encubrireis recibireis ni admitireis entre vosotros ni en vuestra familia, compañia servicio ni consejo, antes luego que de ello algo supieredes lo direis y si por ventura alguno de vos por ignorancia hiciere lo contrario cada y cuando que á vuestra noticia viniere ser las tales personas de la condicion susodicha luego los repelereis y alanzareis de vos y de cada uno de vos y nos dareis de ellos noticia y que para ejecucion y cumplimiento de lo susodicho y de cada una cosa y parte de ello dareis todo el favor y ayuda que os pidieren y fuere menester y cumplireis todo lo demas que en esta nuestra carta va dicho y declarado. Digan todos ansi lo prometemos y juramos. Si ansi lo hicierdes Dios nuestro S. Jesucristo cuja es esta causa os ayude en esto mundo en el cuerpo y en el otro en la alma donde mas habreis de durar, y si lo contrario hicieredes, lo que Dios no quiera, el os lo demande mal y caramente como á reveldes que á sabiendas juran su santo nombre en vano. Digan todos amen. En testimonio de lo cual mandamos dar y dimos la presente firmada de nuestro nombre, sellada con el sello del dicho Santo Oficio y refrendada por el Secretario de él. En la Cuidad de Mexico, 10 dias del mes de Noviembre de 1571. El Doctor Moya de Contreras. Por mandado del S. Inquisidor, Pedro de los Rios, Secretario.

XII.

CEDULA OF PHILIP II, AUGUST 16, 1570, REGULATING THE PRIVILEGES OF FAMILIARS IN NEW SPAIN.

(Biblioteca Nacional de Madrid, Seccion de MSS. X, 159, fol. 240).
(See p. 247).

EL REY, Nuestro Virrey y Capitan General de la Nueva España y Presidente de la Nuestra Audiencia Real que reside en la Ciudad de Mexico, Oidores de la dicha Audiencia, Presidente y Oidores de la Nuestra Audiencia Real que reside en la Ciudad de Santiago de la Provincia de Guatimala, é á los Nuestros Oydores, Alcaldes Mayores de la Nuestra Audiencia Real de la Nueva Galicia é qualesquier Nuestros Governadores, Corregidores y Alcaldes mayores é á otras justicias de todas las Ciudades, Villas y lugares de las Provincias de Nueva España, la Provincia de Nicaragua, asi de los Españoles como de los Indios Naturales, que al presente sois y por tiempo fueren, y á cada uno de vos á quien la presente ó su traslado autentico fuere mostrado y lo en ello contenido toca ó pudiere tocar en qualquiera manera, Salud y dileccion: Sabed que el Reverendisimo in Christo Padre Cardenal de Siguenza, Presidente del Nuestro Consejo é Inquisidor General Apostolico en Nuestros Reynos y Señorios con acuerdo de los del Nuestro Consejo de la General Inquisicion y consultado con Nos, entendiendo ser muy necesario y conveniente para el aumento de Nuestra Santa Fé y su conservacion, poner y asentar en esas dichas Provincias el Santo Oficio de la Inquisicion lo ha ordenado y proveido asi; y porque demas de los Inquisidores y Oficiales con su titulo y provision que han de residir y asistir en el dicho Santo Oficio es necesario que haya familiares como los ay en las otras Inquisiciones de estos Reynos de Castilla aviendose platicado sobre el numero de ellos y ansi mismo de los privilegios y exempciones que deven y han de gozar, consultado conmigo fue acordado que por ahora y hasta que otra cosa se provea, aya en la dicha Ciudad de Mexico, donde ha de residir y tener su asiento el dicho Santo Oficio, doze familiares, y en las Cabezas de Arzobispados y Obispados en cada una de las Ciudades dellos quatro familiares y en las demas Ciudades, Villas y Lugares de Españoles del distrito de la dicha Inquisicion, un familiar, y que los que hubieren de ser proveidos por tales familiares sean hombres pacificos y quales conviene para ministerio de dicho Oficio tan santo, y que los dichos familiares gozen de los privilegios de que gozan los familiares del Reino de Castilla, y que cerca del privilegio del fuero, en las causas criminales sean sus Juezes los Inquisidores quando los dichos Familiares sean Reos, excepto el Crimen *lese maiestatis humane* y en el Crimen nefando contra natura, y en el Crimen de levantamiento o comocion del Pueblo, y en el Crimen de Cartas de seguros nuestras, é de Revelion é inobediencia á Nuestros Mandamientos Reales, y en caso de aleve ó de fuerza de Muger ó robo della, ó de robador publico, ó de quebrantador de casa ó de Iglesia ó Monasterio, ó de quema de Campo ó de casa con dolo, y en otros delitos mayores que estos. Y tener resistencia ó desacato calificado contra Nuestras Justicias Reales, porque el conocimiento destos ni de las causas Criminales en que fueren actores los dichos familiares, ni en las Civiles en que fueren actores ó Reos no se han de entremeter los dichos Inquisidores ni tener Jurisdiccion alguna sobre los dichos familiares, sino que la Jurisdiccion en los dichos casos queda en los Juezes seglares. Item que los que tubieren oficios Reales publicos de los pueblos ó otros cargos seglares, y delinquieren in cosas tocantes a los dichos Oficios y cargos sean juzgados en los dichos delitos por las nuestras Justicias Seglares, pero en todas las otras causas Criminales en que los dichos Familiares fueren Reos que no sean de los dichos delitos y casos desuso exceptuados quede á los Inquisidores sobre los dichos Familiares la Jurisdiccion Criminal para que libremente procedan contra ellos y determinen sus causas como Juezes, que para ello tienen Nuestra Jurisdiccion para agora y adelante, y en los dichos casos en que los Inquisidores han de proceder pueda el Juez Seglar prender al Familiar delinquente con que luego le remita á los dichos Inquisidores que del delito hubieren de conocer, con la Informacion que hubiere tomado, lo qual se haga á costa del delinquente. Item, que cada y quando que algun familiar hubiere delinquido fuera de la dicha Ciudad de Mexico, donde como esta dicho ha de residir el Santo Oficio y fuese sentenciado por los Inquisidores, no pueda volver al lugar donde delinquio sin llevar testimonio de la sentencia que en su causa se dio y le presente ante la Justicia del lugar y la informacion del cumplimiento della, y para que no se exceda del dicho numero de Familiares que conforme á lo que declarado esta desuso ha de haver, los dichos Inquisidores guardaran lo que circa desto el dicho Inquisidor General y Consejo les han ordenado por sus instrucciones, y los dichos Inquisidores ternan cuidado que en el dicho su distrito se de al regimiento copia del numero de los Familiares que en cada una de las dichas Ciudades, Villas y Lugares de el á de haver para que los Governadores, Corregidores y las otras Justicias y regimientos lo entiendan y puedan saber y reclamar quando los Inquisidores excedieren del numero: y que asi mesmo se de la lista de los Familiares que en qualquier Gobernacion y Corregimiento se proveen para que los unos y los otros sepan como aquellos y no otros son los que han de tener por familiares, y que al tiempo que en lugar de aquellos familiares se proveyere otro los Inquisidores lo hagan saber al dicho Gobernador, Corregidor ó Justicia seglar en cuyo distrito se proveiere para que entienda que aquel ha de tener por familiar y no á otro en cuyo lugar se proveyere y para que si se supiere que no concurren en el tal proveido las dichas calidades puede advertir dello á los dichos Inquisidores y si fuere necesario al dicho Inquisidor General y Consejo para que lo provean. Por ende yo os mando que guardeis y hagais guardar y cumplir lo suso dicho en todo y por todo y que contra el tenor y forma dello no vayais, no paseis ni consentais ir ni pasar por ninguna causa, forma, ó razon que aya, y que cada uno de vos Juzgue y conosca en los casos que os quedan reservados y en los otros no os entremetais, que cese toda competencia de Jurisdiccion porque asi conviene al servicio de Dios Nuestro Señor y buena administracion de Justicia y esta mi voluntad, y de lo contrario nos tendriamos por deservidos. Fecha en Madrid, á 16 dias de el mes de Agosto de 1570 años.—Yo el Rey.

Por mandado de su Magestad, Geronimo Zurita.

XIII.

Sentence in Camara's Prosecution of the Inquisitors Estrada and Higuera.

(MSS. of David Fergusson Esqr.).
(See p. 263).

Ffallamos, attentos los autos y meritos de esta causa y lo demas que ver combino que devemos declarar y declaramos haver havido y haver lugar dicha querella y haverla probado el dicho Canonigo Doctor Don Juan de la Camara vien y cumplidamente segun le probar le combino damosla y pronunciamosla por bien probada, restituyendole en su antigua opinion y credito conformandonos en todo y por todo con la sentencia difinitiba dada y pronunciada á su favor en el quaderno segundo de estos auttos por dicho Sr Inq^r Don Bernave de la Higuera y Amarilla. Y que dichos Señores Inquisidores Dr Don Fran^{co} de Estrada y Escobedo y Liz^{do} Don Bernave de la Higuera y Amarilla no an probado cossa alguna que les pueda relebar de culpa grave. En cuia consecuencia devemos de declarar y declaramos havir cometido dichos Señores Inq^{res} grave culpa en dicha prision, secuestro y circunstancias de lo uno y otro cuia punicion se reserva para la determinacion de la visita pressente y cargos de ella. Y por lo que toca á la interesse de la parte querellante devemos de condenar y condenamos á dichos S^{res} Inq^{res} y á cada uno in solidum mancomunados en dos mill pesos de á ocho reales castellanos que den y paguen al dicho Canonigo Don Juan de la Camara, á el qual vuelva luego Don Juan Gonzalez de Castro vezino á el parezer de esta ziudad depositorio secuestrador que parece haver sido de los bienes de dicho Canonigo todos dichos vienes sin faltar cosa alguna segun el imbentario que dellos se hizo, pena de apremio, y casso que dicho depositario secuestrador deje de restituir dichos bienes ó parte de ellos ó algunos otros no se ayan depositario en el y no conste haverse buelto á dicho Canonigo todos los buelban y restituyan dichos Señores Inquisidores luego sin dilacion alguna, pena de mil pesos de dicha ley, en que assimismo les condenamos manconumados, y assimismo con la misma calidad de mancomunidad les condenamos en las costas de este caussa cuia thassacion en nos reserbamos. Y por esta nuestra sentencia difinitiba juzgando assi pronunciamos y mandamos en estos scriptos y por ellos.

Dr D. P^o Medina Rico.

XIV.

INQUISITORIAL EDICT AGAINST HIDALGO. MEXICO, JANUARY 26, 1817.

(From an original in my possession).
(See pp. 275, 281).

NOS LOS INQUISIDORES APOSTOLICOS, CONTRA LA HEretica Pravedad, y Apostasía en la Ciudad de México, Estados, y Provincias de esta Nueva España, Guatemala, Nicaragua, Islas Filipinas, sus Distritos, y Jurisdicciones, por Autoridad Apostolica, Real, y Ordinaria, &c.

A todas, y qualesquiera personas de qualquier Estado, grado, y condicion, preeminencia, ó dignidad que sean, exêntos, ó no exêntos, vecinos, y moradores, estantes, y habitantes en las Ciudades, Villas, y Lugares de este nuestro distrito, y á cada uno de Vos, Salud en nuestro Señor Jesucristo, que es verdadera salud, y á los nuestros mandamientos firmemente obedecer, y cumplir.

SABED: Que ha llegado á nuestras manos una Proclama del rebelde Cura de Dolores, que se titula: "Manifiesto, que el Señor Don Miguel ,,Hidalgo, y Costilla::::,, haze al Pueblo, y empieza: "Me veo en la ,,triste necesidad de satisfacer á las gentes; *y acaba*, sobre este basto ,,Continente.,, Sin lugar de impresion; pero sin duda la imprimió en Guadalaxara, y la publicó manuscrita en Valladolid en todas las Iglesias, y Conventos, aun de Monjas, despues de la derrota, que sufrió por las armas del Rey en Aculco. En ella vuelve á cubrirse con el velo de la vil hipocresia, protestando, que jamás se há apartado de la fé Católica, y pone por testigos á sus Feligreses de Dolores, y San Felipe, y al Exército, que comanda: testigos que para el Pueblo fiel, deben hacer la misma fé, que los ciegos citados para juzgar de los colores "¿Pero para qué, testigos, *prosigue en su capciosa Proclama*, ,,sobre un hecho, é imputacion, que ella misma manifiesta su falsedad? ,,Se me acusa, de que niego el infierno, y de que asiento, que algun ,,Pontifice de los Canonizados está en este lugar; ¿como se puede ,,concordar, que un Pontifice esté en el infierno, y negar al mismo ,,tiempo su exîstencia? Se me imputa, que sigo los perversos Dogmas ,,de Lutero, al mismo tiempo, que se me acusa, que niego la autentici- ,,dad de los Santos Libros: ¿Si Lutero deduce sus errores de estos ,,mismos Libros, que cree inspirados por Dios, como he de ser Luterano ,,si niego la autenticidad de estos Libros? ¿Os persuadiriais, Améri- ,,canos, que un Tribunal tan respetable, y cuyo instituto es el mas ,,Santo, se dexase arrastrar del amor al Paisanage, hasta prostituir ,,su honor, y reputacion?,, Mucho le escuece á este impío, que el Santo Oficio le haya manifestado en su propia figura á todo el Reyno, que por su fidelidad, y catolicismo llena de maldiciones á un monstruo, que abrigaba sin conocerle: pero quando copia para instruccion publica sus errores, no omite la contradiccion manifiesta entre ellos mismos; porque este es el caracter, y propiedad de todos los hereges, mientras no bajan à el último grado en la escala del precipicio, que es el Ateismo, y Materialismo, como le ha sucedido á éste impío; y así la contradiccion será suya, y respectiva á aquellos tiempos, en que fue Luterano, com- parados, ó contrahidos con los de su decidido Ateismo, y Materialismo, como se manifestará en la lectura publica de su causa fenecidos los terminos, que deben seguirse para condenarle en rebeldia. Satis- faccion, que no dá este Tribunal á su Manifiesto por que la merezca, síno para que este sofisma no alucine á los incautos, y vuelvan sobre sí los que hayan llegado á debilitar su opínion en favor del Santo Oficio, persuadiendose á que es capáz éste antemural de la Religion, y del Estado de valerse de la impostura, como quiere persuadir este Hipocrita, para degradar su opinion, y quitar por este medio, indigno de nuestra probidad y caracter Sacerdotal, la energia á su voz rebelde, y sediciosa, y para que conozcan de una vez, y teman todos los habitan- tes de este Reyno la justicia de Dios por los pecados públicos, empezada á manifestar en este azote, que han sufrido las Provincias, que este Atéo cruel, y deshonesto ha infestado con sus consejos, alucinando á tantos miserables, que ha hecho victimas del proyecto de trastornar el Trono, y la Religion, y declarandose el mas feroz enemigo de los que llama sus conciudadanos; pues parece que no quiere mas vidas que la suya poniendola en salvo con la fuga, y mirando con frialdad inaudita la mortandad de millares de infelices en las Cruces, en Aculco, Guanaxuato, Zamora, y Puente de Calderon. Obstinacion caracteris- tica de un Atéo, que no conoce, que el poder de Dios ha roto su arco tantas veces con una especie de prodigio visible respecto de los pocos fieles, que han perecido.

Son igualmente sediciosas y sanguinarias dos proclamas manuscritas; la una empieza *Hemos llegado á la época;* y acaba: *De un Patriota de Lagos:* La otra empieza, *¡Es posible Americanos!* y acaba: *será gratificado con quinientos pesos.* El objeto de ambas es el mismo que la del rebelde Hidalgo; y con ella se han quemado publicamente de orden del superior Gobierno por mano de Berdugo en la Plaza pública, y se han prohibido baxo de la pena de alta traicion por Bando publicado por el Excelentisimo Señor Virey de este Reyno, que ha excitado nuestro zelo para arrancarlas con las censuras correspondientes de vuestras manos. No necesitaban en realidad de especial prohibicion por estár comprendidas especificamente en nuestros anteriores Edictos particularmente en el de citacion en rebeldia al infame Hidalgo, publicado en trece de Octubre del año pasado como lo está igualmente el Bando que publicó el Licenciado Don Ignacio Antonio Rayon, su fecha en Tlalpujagua á 24 de Octubre proximo, en que convoca á todo Americano á la sedicion, llamando causa santa, justa, y religiosa esta escandalosa, atróz, y sanguinaria rebelion, proscribiendo á los Europeos, confiscando sus bienes, y dando nueva forma á la recaudacion de impuestos. En dicho Edicto de 13 de Octubre declaramos incursos en la pena de Excomunion mayor, de quinientos pesos, y en el crimen de fautoria sin excepcion á quantas personas aprueben la sedicion de Hidalgo, reciban sus Proclamas, mantengan su trato, y correspondencia, y le presten qualquiera genero de ayuda, ó favor, y á los que no denuncien, y obliguen á denunciar, á los que favorezcan sus ideas revolucionarias, y de qualquier modo las promuevan, y propaguen. En nuestro Edicto de 28 de Septiembre ultimo prohibimos baxo de las mismas penas qualquiera proclama, ya fuese del intruso Rey José, ó ya de qualquiera otro Español, ó Estrangero que inspirase desobediencia, independencia, y trastorno del Gobierno, renovando la fuerza de la regla 16 del Indice Expurgatorio, y de nuestros Edictos de 13 de Marzo de 1790, 27 de Agosto de 1808, 22 de Abril, y 16 de Junio de 1810: lo que se os hace presente por última y perentoria vez para quitaros las escusas, de que por nuevos no estais obligados á la denuncia, corriendo semejantes papeles incendiarios impunemente de mano en mano con peligro de la Patria, y de la Religion hasta que algun zeloso católico, y fiel vasallo los denuncia.

Y para la mas exâcta obserbancia, y cumplimiento de lo contenido en el Edicto General de Fé, en los anteriormente citados, y de los respetables encargos del Gobierno: Por el tenor del presente os exhôrtamos, requerimos y mandamos en virtud de Santa Obediencia, y só la pena de Excomunion mayor *latæ sentenciæ*, y pecuniaria á nuestro arbitrio, que desde el dia, que este nuestro Edicto fuere leido, y publicado ó de él supieredes de qualquiera manera, hasta seis dias siguientes (los quales os damos por tres terminos, y el ultimo perentorio) trahigais, exhibais, y presenteis las sobredichas Proclamas, y Bando, y qualquiera otro

Papel sedicioso impreso, ó manuscrito, ante Nos, ó ante los Comisarios del Santo Oficio fuera de esta Corte, denunciando à los que los tubieren, y ocultaren, y á las personas, que propaguen con proposiciones sediciosas, y seductivas el espiritu de Independencia, y Sedicion. En testimonio de lo qual mandamos dar, y dimos esta nuestra Carta firmada de nuestros nombres, sellada con el Sello del Santo Oficio, y refrendada de uno de los Secretarios del secreto de él. Dada en la Inquisicion de México á veinte y seis de Enero de mil ochocientos once.

Dr. D. *Bernardo de Prado,*
y Obejero.

Lic. D. *Isidoro Sainz de Alfaro,*
y Beaumont.

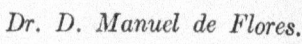

Dr. D. *Manuel de Flores.*

Nadie le quite, pena de excomunion mayor.
Por mandado del Santo Oficio
Dr. D. *José Antonio Aguirrezabal,*
Secretario.

XV.

SENTENCE OF JOSÉ MARÍA MORELOS BY THE INQUISITION OF MEXICO,
NOVEMBER 26, 1815.

(Archivo de Simancas, Inquisicion, Sala 39, Leg. 1473, fol. 30).
(See p. 296).

Dixeron conformes que se le haga auto publico de fé, en la sala de este tribunal el dia de mañana á las ocho, á que asistan los ministros y cien personas de las principales que señalará el señor Inquisidor decano. Que se declara al precitado presbitero José María Morelos, confitente diminuto malicioso y pertinaz: que se le declara herege formal negativo, despreciador, perturbador y perseguidor de la gerarquía eclesiastica, atentador y profanador de los santos sacramentos. Que es reo de Lesa Magestad Divina y Humana, Pontificia y Real y que asista al auto en forma de penitente inter misarum solemnia, con sotana corta, sin cuella ni ceñidor y con vela verde en su mano que ofrecera al sacerdote, concluida la misa, como tal herege y fautor de hereges desde que empezó la insurreccion, y como á enemigo cruel del Santo Oficio se le confiscan sus bienes con aplicacion á la Real camara y fisco de S. M. en los terminos que declarara el Tribunal y aunque merecedor de la degradacion y relajacion por los delitos cometidos del fuero y conocimiento del Santo Oficio, sin embargo por estar pronto á abjurar sus crasos y inveterados errores, se le condena, en el remoto é inesperado caso de que se le perdone la vida por el Excmo. Señor Virrey, Capitan General de esta Nueva España, á destierro perpetuo de ambas Americas, corte de Madrid y sitios reales, y á reclusion en carcel perpetua en uno de los Presidios de Africa, á disposicion del Excmo. é Ilustrisimo Señor Inquisidor General, se le depone de todo oficio y beneficio eclesiastico con inavilidad é irregularidad perpetua. Que á sus tres hijos aunque sacrilegos se les declara incursos en las penas de infamia y demás que imponen los canones y leyes á los descendientes de hereges, con arreglo á las instrucciones de este Santo Oficio. Que abjure de formali y sea absuelto de las excomuniones y censuras en que ha incurrido reservadas al Santo Oficio. Que haga una confesion general y sin omitir el Oficio Divino, rece los siete Psalmos Penitenciales los Viernes, y los Sabados una parte del Rosario durante su vida. Y que se fige su nombre, patria, religion y delitos en la Santa Iglesia Catedral de esta corte. Asi lo acordaron mandaron y firmaron. Doctor Flores—Doctor Monteagudo—Blaza—Campo—Madrid—D. Casiano de Chavarsi Secretario.

XVI.

Viceroy Villar's Petition for Absolution.

(Archivo nacional de Lima, Protocolo 228, Exp^{te} 5287[1]).
(See p. 379).

En la ciudad de los Reyes à 14 de Octubre de 1589 ante el Ynquisidor Lisenciado Ant° Gutierrez de Ulloa, estando en su audiencia de la mañana se presentò y leyò esta peticion.

El Virrey de este Reyno del Peru, D. Fernando de Torres y Portugal Conde del Villar, digo: que à mi noticia es venido que en este Santo Oficio se ha declarado por V. S^a que yo incurrì en ciertas Censuras de Excomunion por haber procedido criminalmente contra el Dr. Diego de Salinas y otras causas, y aunque à lo que puedo entender he tenido siempre seguridad y quietud de mi conciencia de no haber incurrido en ellas por no haber sido de mi intencion en ninguna de las causas que se han ofrecido hacer cosas por donde yo entendiese caia en la tal excomunion, creyendo que para proceder en los negocios y cosas sucedidas me competia derecho por razon de mi oficio y cargo y otras consideraciones. Pero entendido ahora que por V. S^a se ha declarado haber incurrido en la dicha excomunion, acudo à este Santo Oficio como obediente hijo de nuestra Santa Madre Iglesia para que V. S^a me de la absolucion, la cual pido y suplico se me conceda por aquella via y forma que hubiere lugar de derecho y mas y mejor convenga à la seguridad de mi conciencia que es justo yo tenga en todo tiempo, en especial habiendome de embarcar para España como con lisencia y por mandado del Rey nuestro Señor estoy para lo hacer con mucha brevedad.—El Virrey Conde del Villar.

En la Ciudad de los Reyes à 14 de Octubre de 1589 los Inquisidores Dr. Juan Ruiz de Prado y Lisenciado Antonio Gutierrez de Ulloa estando en su Audiencia de la tarde, habiendo visto esta dicha peticion dijeron que per cuanto por su parte de los dichos Ynquisidores se habia advertido diversas veces, asi por terceras personas como por escrito à su S^a del dicho Sr Virrey Conde del Villar que por las cosas que habia hecho contra el Santo Oficio y sus Ministros habia incurrido en las Censuras contenidas en el motupropio de nuestro muy Santo Padre Pio quinto y estaba excomulgado, y que el haber incurrido en ellas y en otras es tan claro que aunque no se hubiera advertido, estaba obli-

---

[1] I give the reference to the numbers in the archives prior to their dispersion in 1881.

gado à lo entender asi, porque todos entienden que incurren en ellas las personas que ponen impedimento directo ò indirecto al ejercicio del Santo Oficio de la Ynquisicion y su Libertad, y tratan mal con obras ò palabras de los Ynquisidores ù otros ministros de ella, en derogacion de su reputacion y autoridad, sin que en esto escuse ni pueda escusar la intencion por buena que sea, porque clara cosa es que no se atiende para incurrir en las Censuras sino solo à los hechos ò dichos esteriores, porque la Yglesia no juzga de las cosas asi ocultas, y habiendo sido las que el dicho Sr Visorrey ha hecho tan manifiestamente en perjuicio de la Ynquisicion y su libertad y autoridad en grande agravio y ofenza de las personas del Santo Oficio, como se ha visto en muchos casos, que por ser tan notorios no se refieren, las cuales cosas antes de la absolucion requieren satisfaccion condigna, especialmente lo que toca al notorio agravio que al dicho Dr Dionicio de Salinas Abogado de este Santo Oficio hizo su Señoria, en el tormento que le diò, pidiendo como el dicho Dr Salinas lo tiene pedido asi en este Santo Oficio.—Atento à lo cual los dichos Señores Ynquisidores amonestan à su Señoria del dicho Sr Visorrey que para que la absolucion por su Señoria pedida se le pueda dar y conseguirse el fruto de ella, ante todas cosas satisfaga en cuanto en si fuere al dicho Dr Salinas en la forma que mejor se pudiere, atendiendo en todo à la autoridad de su oficio, à la cual no se pretende derogar, sino hacerse lo que los dichos Ynquisidores estan obligados de derecho por aver como hay parte lesa que insta. Porque à lo que toca à la injuria y ofensa hecha al Santo Oficio, lo remiten (segun que lo tienen remitido) al Yll^{mo} Sr Cardenal Ynquisidor General y Señores del Consejo de la Santa general Ynquisicion, con todas las demas causas à esto tocantes, y que por ser cosa llana que el dicho Sr Viso Rey estando incurso en las dichas censuras por las dichas razones, y constar à los dichos Ynquisidores que habiendo sido advertido su Señoria no hacia diligencia alguna para salir de ellas, y que estaba à punto de embarcarse para España (viage tan peligroso como se sabe, especialmente en personas de edad) de nuevo se le enviò à advertir de palabra; y como todavia no hacia diligencia alguna, estandose siempre en las dichas Censuras, porque no fuese ligado en ellas, pareciò à los dichos Ynquisidores, movidos con celo de caridad para obligar à su Señoria à la seguridad de su conciencia, y que entendiese el peligro y riesgo de ella, declarar como declararon (como Ministros del derecho à quien competia el hacerlo) el haber su Señoria incurrido en las dichas Censuras; y acatando el respeto que se debe à su persona y oficio, se hizo la dicha declaracion en la sala de la Audiencia del Santo Oficio sin otros testigos mas que el presente Secretario, y de ello se diò noticia à su Señoria para el dicho efecto. En razon de lo cual como parece por la dicha peticion, pide su Señoria el beneficio de la absolucion en este Santo Oficio, la cual los dichos Señores Ynquisidores estan prestos de le dar en la forma que pueden y deben, conforme à derecho, haciendo su Señoria del Sr Virrey de su parte lo que esta obligado, conforme à lo dicho, sin que por esto pretendan obligar al dicho Sr Viso Rey à cumplir con las demas solemnidades que el derecho requiere en semejantes casos, atendiendo à la calidad de su persona y oficio como esta dicho; y asi lo proveyeron y firmaron.—El Dr Juan Ruiz de Prado.—El Lisenciado Antonio Gutierrez de Ulloa.—Antemi, Geronimo de Eugui Secretario.

INDEX.

ABUSES of Inq. of Sicily, 10, 13, 18, 19, 21, 30, 37, 41, 518
  of Sardinia, 117
  of Mexico, 251, 254
  of Peru, 335, 356, 375, 387, 435
  of New Granada, 473, 479, 487, 498
Accounts, statements of, refused by Inq. of Mexico, 216
  by Inq. of Peru, 342
  by Inq. of New Granada, 501
Acereta, Lorenza, case of, 461
Acqui, Bp. of, as inqr., 131
Acquittal, honors rendered in, 430, 437
Adrian, Card., endeavors to reform the Inq., 18
Agliata, Marino, case of, 34
Aguirre, Fermin de, case of, 396
Aguirre, Francisco de, case of, 322
Aillon, Nicolás de, a mystic, 405
Alaman, Lucas, prosecution of, 274
Alba, Viceroy, of Sicily, 29, 33
Alba, Viceroy, of Naples, 95
Albonesi, Tullio, his report as to Milan, 127, 129
Alburquerque, Duke of, on papal jurisdiction, 135
Alcavala, inqrs. subjected to, 215
Aldegato, Ambrosio, inqr. of Mantua, 133
Alguazils, number of, in Mexico, 252, 267
  sale of office of, 349
Alguazil mayor, office of, refused, 188
Alguazils, royal, arrest of, 252
Alcalá, Viceroy of Naples, 80
  claims confiscations, 84
  his instructions to Reggio, 89
  insists on exequatur, 90
Alexander VI, his bull of 1493, 191
Alienations of real estate, 14
Almendáriz, Bp. of Cuba, 475
Almoguera, Abp., his Instructions, 445
Alonso, Bartolomé, case of, 184
Altolaguirre, Felipe de, 367
Alva de Aliste, Viceroy, on confiscations, 219
  warned to favor Inq., 374
  complains of Inq., 381
Alvarez de Arellano, case of, 229

Alvarez, Duarte, case of, 155
Alvarez, Sebastian, burnt, 236
Amat y Yunient, Viceroy, complains of Inq., 381
America, New Christians forbidden access to, 193
Amusquíbar, Inqr., his alliance with Ilarduy, 352
  denounces his colleagues, 366, 410, 435
  disputes royal cédula, 388
  quarrels with Abp. Barroeta, 389
  his treatment of François Moyen, 442, 443
  is sole inqr., 571
Angelo da Cremona, inqr. of Milan, 124
Aniello, Tommaso, 73
Animali parlanti, gli, suppressed, 472
Antilles under Lima tribunal, 455
  under Cartagena tribunal, 457
Antioquia, sorcery in, 463
Antona, Franc. Ant., case of, 470
Apostasy, light penalty for, 439
Appeals only to Inq.-general, 21
  in the colonies, 203
Appointment, power of, in Peru, 330
Apulia, Waldenses of, 85, 524
Archives of Canary tribunal, 190
  of Mexican Tribunal, 288, 298
  of Philippine Tribunal, 317
  of Lima Tribunal, 320
Arciemboldo, Abp., his Edict of Faith, 123
Arechederra, Philippine Commissioner, 305, 306, 317
Arianza, Juan de, case of, 392
Armas, Joseph de, fiscal of Canaries, 150
Arenaza, visitador, 367
  his trading enterprise, 368, 369
  his troubles, 369
  his return and death, 371
  his services in earthquake, 372
  on the trials of Quietists, 410
Arms, licences to bear, 13
  privilege restricted, 32, 42
Army, foreigners in, 271
Arpide, Ant. de, his career, 375

(547)

548   INDEX

Arrests in Naples require royal exequatur, 56
  power of commissioners, 302, 303
Assassination excepted from *fuero*, 30
Assistenti of Inq., 132
Asti, Bp. of, as inqr., 131
Asylum, right of, claimed, 11, 254, 386
Atienza, Gomez de, 493
Atrato, navigation of river, 513
Atto di fede, in Palermo, 1724, 30
  in Naples, 1746, 104
Audience-chamber in Lima, 447
Audiencia, quarrels with Inq., 187, 269, 384, 396
Auto de fe, Mexican, of 1574, 205
  of 1646–1649, 229
  of 1659, 234
  of 1573 in Lima, 328
  of 1639, 425, 430
  of 1694, 405
  of 1736, 366, 410, 435
Aventrot, Jan, case of, 150
Ayacucho, battle of, 511
Ayuda de costa in Peru, 343
Azólares, Bp. of Canaries, 147, 162

BADAJOZ, Concordia of, 28
  Badaran, inqr., his quarrel with bp., 185
Banishment as punishment, 439
Bank of Lima, failure of, 428
Bankruptcies, frauds in, 41
Baños, Bp. of Santa Marta, 492
Banqueresme, Jacob, case of, 170
Baptism, cost of, in Sicily, 4
Barco de Centinera, his excesses, 336
Barnaba Capograsso, inqr. of Naples, 55, 64
Barroeta, Abp., his quarrels with Amusquíbar, 389
Beatas revelanderas in Canaries, 162
  in Mexico, 235
  in Peru, 396
Bedstead, censorship of, 266
Bello, Juan, his prosecution, 358
Belorado, Abp., appointed inqr. of Sicily, 6
  excommunicates magistrates, 8
  appointed inqr. of Naples, 54
Benavente, Francisco de, 336
Benavides, Bp. of Cartagena, 491, 493
  he goes to Rome, 497
Benedict XIV seeks to restore the Inq. in Naples, 107
Benevento, Jews of, persecuted, 53
Benjamin of Tudela on Neapolitan Jews, 49
Bernal, Alonso, inqr. of Sicily, 9
Bestiality, 244
Betanzos, Domingo de, inqr., 196

Bethencourt, Jean de, conquers Canaries, 139
Bibles, Spanish, sent to colonies, 267
Bigamy, frequency of, 206, 391
  powers of commissioner in, 302
Bishops, their quarrels with Inq., in Sicily, 35
  in Sardinia, 117
  in Mexico, 257
  in Peru, 325
  in New Granada, 473, 491
  their treatment by Inq., 182
  appointment of, for New World, 192
  their inquisitorial powers, 196
  their jurisdiction over Indians, 210
  their rapacity, 514
  (*See* also Inquisition, Episcopal).
Blasphemy in Peru, 391
  in New Granada, 465
Bohorques, Bp. of Oaxarca, 257
Bonelli, Giacomo, burnt, 80
Bonol, insurrection in, 307
Books, heretical, burnt in Naples, 70
  lists of, required in Mexico, 204
  prohibited, sale of, 265
  importation of, in Peru, 444, 446
Borbujo y Riba, inqr. of Canaries, 189, 190
Borromeo, Giulio Cesare, 124
Borromeo, San Carlo, his persecuting zeal, 124, 130, 132, 135, 532
  as inqr. of Milan, 131
  his mission to Mantua, 133
Bovino, Bp. of, and Apulian Waldenses, 85
Bowes, Ellen, case of, 106
Brasero in Mexico, 206
Brazil, influx of Portuguese from, 421
Brescia, Bp. of, as inqr., 131
Bribery of inqrs., 20, 487
  of Suprema, 367
Brujas, 167, 463
Bruñon de Vertiz, case of, 239
Bucchianico, Marquis of, 81, 82, 83
Buenos Ayres, bishopric erected, 337
  tribunal proposed, 339, 341
  solicitation in, 395
  influx of Portuguese, 421
Bugueiro, Abp. of Mexico, 257
Buil, Fray, as missionary, 191
Burnings in Canaries, 154
Bustamante, Andrés de, inqr. of Peru, 327

CABEZAS, Juan, Bp. of Cuba, 458
  Cáceres, Felipe de, case of, 324
Calabria, New Christians of, 52, 53
  persecution of Waldenses, 79
Calderon, inqr., his peculations, 351
  his property seized, 353

INDEX 549

Calderon, inqr., his scandals, 366
 his arrest, 368
 his release, 370
 end of his trial, 372
 condemns Quietists, 410
Calificadores in Mexico, 264
 prosecuted in Peru, 393
Calleja, Viceroy, suppresses Mexican Inq., 288
 invades its jurisdiction, 291
 executes Morelos, 297
Calvete, Tristan, inqr. of Sicily, 17, 18
Camara, Juan de la, case of, 259, 538
Camera reginale, districts of, 7, 8
Camera di Santa Chiara, 105
Campagna, Perrucio, burnt, 24
Campanella, Tommaso, case of, 93
Campeggio, Camillo, inqr. of Mantua, 133
Campos, Ant. de, case of, 392
Canaries, their conquest, 139
 (*See* Inquisition of Canaries).
Candioti, Teodoro, case of, 434
Cañete, Viceroy, complains of Inq., 380
Canonries for colonial tribunals, 216, 346, 501
 their value, 217, 506
Cantons, Catholic, relations with Milan, 129
Capasso, Niccolò, his report, 102
Caraccioli, Viceroy, on suppression of Inq., 44
Carafa, Abp., persecutes heretics, 87
Card tricks suspect of sorcery, 166
Cardenas, Bp. of Asuncion, 258
Cardona, Gabriel, inqr. of Sardinia, 109, 110, 111
Cardona, Ramon de, Viceroy of Naples, 58, 59
Cargoes, seizure of, 156, 169
Carlos II expels Inq. from Naples, 100
 on colonial subventions, 220
Carlos III controls the Inq. of Sicily, 42
 recovers Naples, 104
 suppresses its Inq., 107
 limits the *fuero*, 269, 388
 on pseudo-Catholic recruits, 271
 limits censorship, 445
 rebuilds Inq. of Cartagena, 468
Carmona, Jamariz, case of, 248
Carranza, Angela, case of, 400
Cartagena selected as seat of tribunal, 457
 bombarded in 1741, 468
 Jews allowed in, 469
 intellectual torpor, 470
 no clock there in 1648, 485
 its decline, 499
 expenditures on, 503
 revolutionary junta in 1810, 506
 tribunal expelled in 1812, 507

Cartagena, siege of 1815, 509
 recapture by revolutionists in 1821, 510
 its commerce in 1772, 513
 (*See* Inq. of New Granada).
Carvajal, Luis de, case of, 208
Casa de la misericordia, 438
Casannova, Angelo, kidnaps Cellaria, 134
Castaldo, Ant., on tumult of 1547, 77
Castañeto, Governor, his fate, 81
Castel Fuerte, Viceroy, 270, 386
Casti, his *Animali parlanti*, 472
Castillo, Santiago del, case of, 429
Castro, Ana de, case of, 435
Castro, Ant. de, inqr. of Lima, 364
Catalina de San Mateo, a *beata*, 162
Catholicism, pretended, risk of, 175
Cattle-brands, censorship of, 266
Cavendish, Thomas, his expedition, 415
Ceballos y la Cerda, Governor of Cartagena, 496
 his humiliation, 498
Cellarìa, Francisco, burnt in Rome, 134
Censorship in Naples, 84
 early, in Milan, 123
 in Canaries, 176
 in Mexico, 204, 264, 274
 in Peru, 444
 by the State, 445
 in New Granada, 470, 510
Cerezuela, inqr. of Lima, 319, 327
 suspends cases in Cuzco, 322
 on Indians and foreigners, 332
Ceruti, canon, tried for heresy, 133
Cervantes, Gaspar, proposed as inqr. for Milan, 125, 128
Cervantes, Juan de, his chaplaincy, 151
Cervantes, Pascual de, inqr. of Mexico, 201
Cervera, Melchor, inqr. of Sicily, 14, 15, 17
 his conscientious bequest, 20, 523
 unable to hang sanbenitos, 24
Cevallos, Gutiérrez de, inqr. of Lima, 365, 366
Chapter of Canaries, quarrels with Inq., 183, 186, 187
Charles VIII (France) baptizes Neapolitan Jews, 50
Charles V (Emp.) orders Sicilian Inq. restored, 16
 insists on the *fuero*, 20, 22
 suspends the *fuero*, 22
 restores the *fuero*, 24
 refuses redress of grievances, 26
 gives Malta to Knights of St. John, 45
 orders Inq. introduced in Naples, 70
 orders Naples to submit, 76
 expels Jews from Naples, 66
 his edict against Lutherans, 69

550 INDEX

Charles V (Emp.), his good-nature, 177
  appoints friars as bishops, 193
  permits New Christians to go to America, 194
  exempts Indians from Inq., 210
Charles VI controls Inq. of Sicily, 40
  limits the *fuero*, 41
  orders episcopal Inq., 102
  refuses entrance to Roman Inq., 103
Cheevers, Sarah, in Maltese Inq., 47
Chickens, throat-cutting of, 304
Children, exemption from confiscation, 21
  of heretics seized, 106, 136
China, episcopal Inq. in, 317
Chinchon, Viceroy, issues licences to leave Peru, 333
  on subdivision of district, 340
Chitterlings, privilege of, 255
Christ, image of, in audience-chamber, 447
Church, its development in Mexico, 193
Churches, sanbenitos in, 24, 188
Cid, Garcí, receiver of Sicily, 12, 15
Cid, Nicholas, case of, 135
Citations to Rome, 89
Claims against sequestrations, 428
Clavijo, Lope, Comr. of Santa Fe, 454
Claysen, Gaspar, case of, 154
Clement VII restricts travel in heretic lands, 137
Clement XII appoints Inq.-genl. of Sicily, 43
Clergy, character of, in colonies, 192, 514, 515
  of Peru complain of inqrs., 335, 356
Clerics, jurisdiction over, 35
Coca, use of, in sorcery, 391
Colombia, U. S. of, abolish Inq., 510
Colonial system, Spanish, 513
Commerce of the Colonies in hands of Conversos, 229, 425
  affected by persecution, 234, 428, 512
Commissioner of Roman Inq. in Naples, 92, 94, 96, 98, 99, 100
Commissioners, quarrels over troubles caused by, in Sicily, 35, 522
  troubles caused by, in Mexico, 248, 252, 254
  their limited functions, 301
  their duties in Peru, 334
  their tyranny, 335, 339
  of New Granada, 454
Commissions on confiscations, 19, 521
Communications in prison, 427, 430
Como, heretical infection in, 122
Competencias, 29
  suppressed by Carlos III, 43, 269
  in Canaries, 181
  in Mexico, 252, 267

Complaints of Palermo, 16
  of Sicilian Parliament, 13, 21, 22, 26
  of Neapolitans, 95, 99, 102, 104, 107
  of Viceroys, 255, 355, 379, 380
  of Council of Indies, 220, 256, 314, 345, 476, 478, 481, 484, 488, 503, 512
  of the clergy of Peru, 335, 356
  of governors of Cartagena, 473, 498
  of the Regular Orders, 474
  of the city of Cartagena, 480
  of the Junta de Guerra, 484
Complicidad grande of Peru, 426
Composition of Seville, 193
Concealment of resources, 216, 345, 501
Concordias, Sicilian, 28, 31, 37
  seven in Sardinia, 119
  of 1553 extended to Indies, 197, 247, 330
  of 1610, for Indies, 251
  of 1633, 218, 254, 267
Confession, deprivation of, for solicitation, 393, 394
Confiscations commence in Sicily, 7
  profits of, 12
  of contracts, 13, 21
  disorders in, 19, 521
  division of, 53, 134
  abolished and restored in Naples, 79, 99
  of Waldenses, 84
  as practised in Naples, 85
  in Sardinia, 112
  regulate salaries, 114, 528
  in Canaries, 156
  in Mexico, 213, 216, 219, 223, 232
  in Peru, 343, 347, 429
  in New Granada, 467, 501
  of heretic prisoners of war, 418
  entailed by reconciliation, 421
  influence of, 512
Conflicts of jurisdiction in Sicily, 25, 29, 31, 34, 37
  in Malta, 46
  in Sardinia, 110, 117, 118, 119
  in Milan, 125
  in Canaries, 180
  in Mexico, 245, 267
  in Philippines, 308
  in Peru, 381
  in New Granada, 473
Constitution, Mexican, condemned, 291, 294
Consulta de fe, in colonies, 203
Consulta magna on Sicilian Inq., 38
Contracts, confiscation of, 13, 21
Conversos, Jewish, in Sicily, 4
  forbidden to leave Sicily, 7, 26
  expelled from Naples, 62, 64
  forbidden to leave Canaries, 142
  not allowed in the Colonies, 193, 419

INDEX

551

Conversos control commerce of Colonies, 229, 425
Copernican system in New Granada, 471
Coquimbo, Dutch captured at, 418
Corcuera, Governor of Philippines, 309
Cordero, Antonio, case of, 426
Cornelius, William, case of, 205, 206, 207
Corral, Andrés, case of, 394
Corro Carrascal, inqr. of Cartagena, 488, 489
Cortájar, inqr. of Cartagena, 478, 479, 486
Cortés, Hern., asks for friars, 192
Cosenza, burnings at, 83
Creditors, claims of, allowed, 14, 21
Crime, immunity for, 28
  abrogated, 388
Crimes excepted from *fuero*, 31
Crockery subjected to censorship, 178
Croix, Marquis de, story of, 270
Crosses prohibited on profane objects, 265
Cruz, Bart. de la, case of, 394
Cruz, Fran. de la, case of, 396
Cruzada, the Santa, its jurisdiction, 385
Cuadros, Fran. Manuel de, case of, 241
Cuba, early bps. of, 195
  under Cartagena tribunal, 457
  Bp. of, on commissioners, 249
Cubelles, Bp. of Malta, his Inq., 45
Cueva, Claudio de la, his visitation, 150
Curses for not denouncing heretics, 534
Cuzco, episcopal Inq. in, 321, 322
  earthquake of 1784, 354

DAGOHOY, Francisco, his revolt, 308
Dealing with heretics raises suspicion, 130, 137
Debt, arbitrary collection of, 255
Debts, Inq. used to collect, 91, 362
Decadence of Inq. of Sicily, 42
  of Naples, 104
  of Sardinia, 119
  of Milan, 137
  of Canaries, 188
  of Mexico, 270
  of Lima, 447
  of Cartagena, 499
Defence disregarded, 230
Delation, training in, 160
Delays in trials, 237, 239, 410, 433, 443
  to be avoided, 519
Delgado, Rodríguez, inqr. of Lima, 352, 371
Demon, pact with, 166
Denunciations in Canaries, 142, 143, 147, 160
  caused by Edict of Faith, 227
  duty of, 202, 423

Denunciations, curses for neglecting, 534
Deputati of Naples, 100, 101, 102, 103, 104, 105, 107
Derechos del Hombre suppressed, 471
Deserters, military, in Philippines, 303
Deza, Abp. of Indies, 192
Díaz, Diego, burnt, 235
Discordia, in the colonies, 203
Discords, intestine, in Cartagena, 485, 488
Divination with sticks, 473
Domicile, inviolability of, 11, 254
Dominicans, slain in Mantua, 133
  missionaries to Indies, 192
  refute Copernicus, 471
Doria, Andrea, bombards Naples, 75
Dowries not to be confiscated, 14, 21
Drake, John, in Peru, 357, 415
Dutch, the, their attempt on Valdivia, 418
Duties, evasion of, in Sicily, 12, 517
Duzzina, Pietro, inqr. of Malta, 46

EARTHQUAKE of 1746, in Lima, 353, 370
Echarri, Secretary of Cartagena, 490, 499
Edict of Faith in Sicily, 7
  in Naples, 1695, 101
  in Milan, 123
  in Lombardy, 135
  in Canaries, 142
  in Mexico, 203, 204, 227, 290
  in the Philippines, 305
  in Peru, 328, 331
  episcopal in Mexico, 211
  against occult arts, 391
Edict of Grace in Sicily, 7
Edon, Adam, case of, 466
Effigies, burning of, 144, 149, 152, 155
Eguiluz, Paula de, case of, 464, 465
Elections, interference with forbidden, 254
Embezzlement in Lima tribunal, 340, 351
  in Cartagena tribunal, 487
Embusteras in Mexico, 235
  in Peru, 400
Emigration of conversos forbidden in Sicily, 7, 26
Encarnacion, María Josepha de la, 486
England, its treaty of 1604, 171
English factory in Sicily, its complaints, 41
  prisoners of war in Peru, 357, 414
Englishmen, treatment of, in Canaries, 153, 167, 172
  subject to censorship, 177
  in Mexican Inq., 205, 207
  changed treatment of, 448

552   INDEX

Enmity, gratification of, 161
Episcopal jurisdiction restored in Sicily, 43
Episcopal Inq. *See* Inq., episcopal.
Episcopate, inqrs. promoted to, 201
Erasmus on external observance, 69
Escalante, inqr. of Cartagena, 500
Esparza de Pantolosa, case of, 50
Espinal, Alonso de, a missionary, 192
Espontaneados, immunity for, 245
Estrada y Escobedo, inqr., 230, 263
Evans, Katharine, in Maltese Inq., 47
Evora, Rodrigo de, case of, 201
Excommunication of judges, 32, 34, 37
   of viceroys, 32, 377
   of inqrs., 185
   of insurgents *en masse*, 280
   restricted by Charles V, 42
   neglect of, is heresy, 91
   commissioners not empowered, 301
Exemptions of officials, 20, 22, 246
   from taxation, 215
   from military service, 263
Exequatur required for arrests, 90, 94
   formalities of, 91, 539
   Rome refuses to ask for it, 95, 99
Exile as punishment, 439
Expenses of Lima Inq., 350
   of Cartagena Inq., 503
Expulsion of Jews from Sicily, 3
   from Naples, 53, 62, 66
Extinction of Inq. of Sicily, 43
   of Naples, 106
   of Sardinia, 119
   of Milan, 137
   of Canaries, 190
   of Mexico, 298
   of Peru, 450
   of New Granada, 510
Extradition. *See* Exequatur.

*F*ABRICA *de Sevilla*, 225
Faith, propagation of, in New World, 191
Faith not to be kept as to heresy, 52
Fajardo, governor of Philippines, 310
Fallet, Pierre, case of, 306
False-witness punished in Rome, 91
Falsification of parish registers, 434
Familiars, their number in Sicily, 11, 13, 28, 31
   in Sardinia, 117
   in Canaries, 146
   in Mexico, 247, 536
   in Peru, 330
   in New Granada, 468
   their immunity, 27
   their excepted crimes, 31
   nobles not to serve as, 42
   regulations in Mexico, 247, 536

Familiars, illegal protection of, 251, 252
   their military service, 263
   deprived of *fuero*, 269, 388
Farmers of revenue, inqrs. as, 251
Fees in *visitas de navíos*, 267
Ferdinand of Aragon appoints Sicilian inqrs., 1
   expels Jews, 3
   reorganizes Sicilian Inq., 5
   enforces obedience to it, 8
   gift to Queen Germaine, 12
   explosion after his death, 14
   desires Inq. in Naples, 50
   orders payment of Pantolosa's bills, 51
   disregards Gonsalvo's pledge to Naples, 52
   expels Jews from Naples, 53
   commissions a papal inqr., 56
   attempts to introduce Spanish Inq., 57
   permits papal Inq., 64
   founds Inq. of Sardinia, 109
   supports its jurisdiction, 110
   his grants from confiscations, 112
   his kindliness, 113
   regulates salaries by confiscations, 114, 539
Ferdinando IV suppresses Sicilian Inq., 43
   allows no Inq. in Naples, 107
Feria, Viceroy, his struggle with Inq., 34
Fernando VI on pseudo-Catholic recruits, 271
   limits the fuero, 388
   sustains Amusquíbar, 389
Figueroa, Bp., his quarrel with Inq., 183
Figueroa, Governor of Cartagena, 489
Finances of Sicilian Inq., 9, 12, 19, 24, 26, 27, 39
   of Sardinian Inq., 109, 112, 114, 115, 116
   of Inq. of Canaries, 156
   of Inq. of Mexico, 212, 225, 288
   of Inq. of Peru, 342, 354
   of Inq. of New Granada, 460, 482, 487, 500
Fine inflicted on Naples, 76
Fines of officials, 28
   in Sicily, 8, 10, 19
   in Peru, 328, 329, 343
   in Cartagena, 461, 482, 493, 496
Finger-rings, censorship of, 266
Fishing-boat, selection of, by Inq., 184
Fiscal is equal of inquisitor, 365
Flemings, prosecution of, in Canaries, 171
Flores, Juan Gutiérrez, inqr. of Lima, 364
Flores, Manuel de, inqr. of Mexico, 289
   publishes Edict of Faith, 290
   tries José María Morelos, 291

Florida, attempts to establish Inq., 457
Fonseca, Pedro de, his office, 213
Fonte, Miguel, his assassination, 111
Foreigners, treatment of, in Canaries, 167
   in Peru, 332
   in army, danger from, 271
Fos, Pierre, case of, 413
Fragata de la Inquisicion, 92
Franciscan missionaries to Indies, 191
Francisco de San José, Fray, his sermons 307
Frauds in bankruptcies, 41
Frederic II, his forged decree, 1
Free-Masonry in Mexico, 274
Frenchmen in Mexico, their influence, 272
Fuensaldaña, Governor of Sinaloa, 249
Fuero of Inq. in Sicily, 10
   suspended and restored, 22, 24
   grants immunity to crime, 28, 30
   restricted by Charles VI, 41
   abuses of, in Naples, 100
   in the Colonies, 246
   abuses in Mexico, 248
   in Peru, 334, 382, 386
   limited by Carlos III, 269
   by Fernando VI, 388
Fúnez, Diego Ortiz, inqr. of Canaries, 145, 147, 149, 156, 162, 177, 181
Furniture, censorship of, 265

GACHUPINES, 280
Gage, Thomas, on Indian idolatry, 211
Gaitan, Andrés Juan, inqr. of Lima, 363, 364
Galleys, punishment of, 431
   for solicitation, 395
García de Arias, burnt, 236
García, Comr. of Cumaná, 454
Garfías, Isabel de, her convent, 151
Garza, Costanza, case of, 144
Gasco, Fray Alonso, case of, 396, 398
Gaspar, George, his burning, 153
Geltruda, burnt in 1724, 40
Germaine, Queen, gift to, 12
Gesuald, burnt for Lutheranism, 45
Ghislieri, Michele. See Pius V.
Gianbattista da Cremona, Inq.-genl. of Milan, 123
Giberti, Bp., overrides the exequatur, 99
   expelled from Naples, 100
Girgenti, Bp. of, his quarrel with Inq., 37
Giron, Governor of Cartagena, 475
Girard, Jacques, case of, 93
Gomera, departure of Columbus, 139
Gómez, Juan, *alumbrado*, 235

Gonsalvo de Córdova, his pledge to Naples, 52
Gonzaga, Guillelmo, Duke of Mantua, 133
Gozo, inqr., appointed for, 1
Gran Corte, conflicts with Inq., 29
Granero, Alonso, inqr. of Mexico, 201
Granvelle, Card., Viceroy of Naples, 88
Gregory XIII grants bps. jurisdiction over Indians, 210
Greek Christians, trials of, 240, 434
Grisons, their relations with Milan, 122, 129
   their territory violated, 135
Grosero, inqr., complains of bps., 36
Guadalupe, Our Lady of, 280
Guancavelica, mines of, 356, 359
Guerra de Latrás, inqr. of Cartagena, 488, 489
Guerro, Abp., on New Granada, 456
Guerrero, Abp. of Philippines, 309
Guigue, François, case of, 317
Guirior, Viceroy, on the clergy, 514
Gutiérrez de la Rosa, Bp., his quarrels, 185

HABITELLO, 83
Handkerchiefs, censorship of, 446
Havana, commissioner of, 249
   confiscations in, 501
Hawkins, Sir John, his men, 205, 207
Hawkins, Richard, his expedition, 416
Henríquez, Camilo, case of, 446
Henríquez, Manuel, case of, 433
Heresy, prevalence of, in Lombardy, 122
   of Indians, subject to bps., 210
   of popular sovereignty, 275
Heretics, dealings with, unlawful, 50
   their children seized, 106, 136
   relations with forbidden, 129, 130, 137
   kidnapping them, 134, 136
   foreign, in Canaries, 167
Hidalgo, Miguel, case of, 276
   edicts against him, 279, 281, 539
Hieronimo da Verona, his sermons, 15
Higuera y Amarilla, inqr., 230, 263
Hispañola, bishoprics in, 192
   case of Pedro de Leon, 195
Hollanders, cases of, in Canaries, 167
Holy See, effect of Spanish Inq. on, 128
Huerta, Gaspar de la, case of, 398
Hurtado, Fray Juan, on Indians, 209

IBANEZ, GASPAR, inqr. of Lima, 365, 366
Idolatry of Indians, 211
Ilarduy, receiver of Lima, 351, 352, 367
Ilarduy, inqr. of Cartagena, 468

Illuminism in Mexico, 235, 240
  in Philippines, 305
  in Peru, 406
Images, sacred, on profane objects, 265
Immaculate Conception in Philippines, 307
Immigration of Portuguese in Peru, 422
Immunity granted by *fuero*, 28, 30, 245, 249
Impostors, mystic, 235, 396
Independence of colonial tribunals, 203, 331
  oath of, required, 507
Index Librorum Prohibitorum in the colonies, 204
Indians, their readiness for conversion, 191
  their idolatry, 211
  exempt from Inq., 209, 332
  repartimientos of, 215
  sorcery among, 228
  judiciable for sorcery, 391
  offences against, 247
  failure of missions, 458, 514, 515
Indies, New Christians forbidden access to, 193, 419
  Concordia of 1553 extended to, 197, 247, 330
  Concordias of 1610 and 1633, 218, 251, 254, 267
  Council of, its complaints, 220, 255, 314, 345, 476, 477, 480, 484, 488, 503, 512
  inqrs. of, 195
Innocent XII defends Inq. of Naples, 100
Inquisition of Canaries, 139
  founded in 1505, 140
  dependent on Seville, 141
  activity of Inqr. Ximenes, 142
  prosecution of slaves, 144, 148, 149, 152, 159
  its suspension, 145
  its reorganization, 146
  its building, 146, 157
  visitations, 149
  active persecution, 152
  finances, 156
  Judaizers, 158
  trivial denunciations, 160
  beatas revelanderas, 162
  solicitation, 163
  sorcery, 165
  foreign heretics, 167
  censorship, 176
  conflicts of jurisdiction, 180
  suppression, 189, 190
Inquisition, episcopal, in Naples, 64, 66, 71, 78, 79, 84, 86, 92, 100, 102, 103, 104, 107
  in Sardinia, 117

Inquisition, episcopal, in Lombardy, 131, 135
  in the Canaries, 140, 145
  in Mexico, 195, 199, 210, 211, 289
  in the Philippines, 299
  in China, 317
  in Peru, 321, 325, 412
  in New Granada, 454, 510
Inquisition of Malta, 44
Inquisition of Mexico, 191
  exercised by bishops, 196
  established in 1571, 200
  its installation, 202
  its organization, 204
  auto of 1574, 205
    of 1596 and 1601, 207
  its activity, 209
  Indians exempt from, 209
  finances, 212
    early poverty, 213
    Indian *repartimientos*, 215
    concealment of confiscations, 216
    grant of prebends, 217
    dispute over subvention, 217 219, 223
    large confiscations, 219
    its sequestrations, 223
    its wealth, 225, 288
  cases in 1626, 226
  inactivity, 227, 240
  persecution of Judaizers, 229
  autos of 1646–1649, 219, 230
    of 1659, 234
  solicitation, 241, 271, 272
  conflicts of jurisdiction, 245
  concordia of 1610, 251
  competencias, 252
  concordia of 1633, 254
  quarrels with bishops, 257
  visitation of Medina Rico, 261
  military service, 263
  censorship, 264
  influence of Bourbon dynasty, 267
  decadence in 18th century, 270
  political activity, 272, 275
  last public auto in 1795, 273
  subordination to State, 275
  case of Miguel Hidalgo, 276
  suppression in 1813, 288
  revived in 1815, 290
  case of José María Morelos, 291
  final extinction, 297
  survival of fanaticism, 298
Inquisition of Milan, 121
  its early difficulties, 122
  prevalence of heresy, 123
  San Carlo Borromeo becomes Abp., 123
  Philip II proposes Spanish Inq., 125
  popular opposition, 126
  project abandoned, 128, 529

Inquisition of Milan, commerce with
    Switzerland, 129, 530
  episcopal Inq., 131
  suppressed by Maria Teresa, 137
Inquisition of Naples, 49
  Gonsalvo's pledge regarding it, 52
  disregarded by Ferdinand, 54
  papal Inq. active, 56, 64
  attempt to introduce Spanish Inq., 57
  popular opposition successful, 58
  exemption from Inq. claimed, 63
  refugees from Sicily, 63, 65
  papal Inq. accepted, 64
  its inertness, 65
  Charles V orders Inq. introduced, 70
  censorship introduced, 70, 84
  Inq. attempted indirectly, 71
  remonstrance of Piazze, 72
  popular rising and slaughter, 73
  envoys sent to Charles V, 74
  unsuccessful fighting, 75
  resistance abandoned, 76
  Roman Inq. introduced, 78
  its prisoners sent to Rome, 79, 88
  persecution of Waldenses, 79
  mixture of jurisdictions, 86
  popular hatred, 88
  exequatur required, 90, 94, 527
  popular spirit broken, 92
  papal commissioners admitted, 92
    assume inquisitorial powers, 94, 96, 98
    refuse to ask for exequatur, 95
  Roman Inq. established, 96
    its procedure, 97
  Inqr. Piazza expelled, 99
  Roman Inq. expelled, 100
  Edict of Faith in 1695, 101
  Roman Inq. returns, 102
  episcopal Inq. developed, 103
  suppressed by Carlo VII, 107
Inquisition of New Granada, 453
  under commissioners, 454
  demand for tribunal, 455
  extent of its district, 457
  endeavors to include Florida, 458
  tribunal founded in 1610, 460
  its royal subvention, 460
  early operations, 461
  sorcery and witchcraft, 462
  blasphemy, 465
  autos of 1622 and 1626, 466
  sack of Cartagena in 1697, 467
  decadence in 18th century, 468
  censorship, 470
  quarrels with the authorities, 473, 484
  visitation of Martin Real, 481
    of Medina Rico, 485
  quarrels continue, 488
    intestine, 485, 488, 490
  degradation of tribunal, 489
Inquisition of New Granada, quarrel
    with Bp. Benavides, 491
  arrogance and decadence, 498, 504
  poverty, 506, 509
  moves to Santa Marta in 1812, 507
  returns to Cartagena in 1815, 509
  abolished by United States of Colombia in 1821, 510
Inquisition of Peru, 319
  episcopal Inq., 321, 325
  Inq. established, 326
  auto of 1573, 328
  organization, 329
  extent of district, 333
  commissioners, 334
  subdivision proposed, 337
  finances, 342
    quarrels over subvention, 342, 344
    concealment of receipts, 342, 345, 348
    increasing income, 343
    suppression of canonries, 346
    gains from auto of 1639, 347
    from other sources, 349
    revenue and expenses, 350
    mismanagement and peculation, 351
    property at suppression, 354
  character of inqrs.—Cerezuela, Ulloa, 355
    Prado sent as visitador, 357
      his charges against Ulloa, 358
    Ulloa's sentence, 360
    he visits the district, 361
    Ordoñez, his greed, 362
    Verdugo, Gaitan, Mañozca, 363
    deplorable condition of tribunal, 364
  quarrels of inqrs., 366
  visitation of Arenaza, 368
  traffic in offices, 372
  quarrels with authorities, 373
  conflicts of jurisdiction, 381
  Fernando VI limits the *fuero*, 388
  quarrels with Abp. Barroeta, 389
  functions in matters of faith, 390
    bigamy, blasphemy, sorcery, 391
    propositions, 392
    solicitation, 393
    mystic impostors, 396
    Quietism, 406
    auto de fe of 1736, 410
    Protestantism, 412
    prisoners of war, 414
    Judaism, 419
      auto de fe of 1639, 425, 435, 438
    punishments, 437
  censorship, 444
  decadence and suppression, 447
  re-establishment, 448
  extinction, 450

556   INDEX

Inquisition of Peru, personnel and salaries, 451
  work accomplished, 451
Inquisition of Philippines, 299
  episcopal Inq., 299
  commissioner sent there, 300
    his functions, 301
  inactivity, 304
  censorship, 306
  conflicts of jurisdiction, 308
  imprisonment of Governor Salcedo, 311
  destruction of records, 317
Inquisition, Roman, organized, 70, 121
  burnings in Rome, 80, 88, 135
  introduced in Naples, 78
  sentences Waldenses, 83
  its prisoners sent to Rome, 87, 88, 91
  its arrests require exequatur, 89, 90
  used to collect debts, 91
  punishes false-witness, 91
  its regular service of vessels, 91
  commissioners established in Naples, 92
    assume to be inqrs., 94, 96, 98
  refuses to ask for exequatur, 95
  established in Naples, 96
  expelled in 1692, 100
  publishes Edict of Faith in 1695, 101
  is again introduced, 102
  Charles VI rejects it, 103
  objects to Spanish Inq., 125
  obstructs trade with heretics, 131
Inquisition of Sardinia, 109
  conflicts of jurisdiction, 110
  productive confiscations, 112
  two inqrs. tried, 114
  impoverishment, 114, 115, 116
  Charles V stimulates activity, 115
  its inefficiency, 116
  multiplication of officials, 117
  disappears under House of Savoy, 119
Inquisition of Sicily, 1
  its finances, 5, 9, 12, 19, 24, 27
  reorganized in 1500, 6
  a house provided, 7
  reorganized in 1510, 9
  activity in 1513, 12
  complaints of abuses, 13, 21, 22, 26
  reforms attempted, 13, 517
  suspended by rising in 1516, 15
  restored in 1519—its activity, 17
  Card. Adrian tries to reform it, 18
  Abp. Manrique also tries, 19, 518
  fuero of officials suspended, 22
  resistance to sanbenitos, 24
  continued activity, 24, 26, 27
  contests with secular authorities, 25, 29, 31, 34, 37
  number of familiars, 28
  claims obedience of its subjects, 33

Inquisition of Sicily, quarrels with bishops, 35
  activity in 17th century, 39
  under Savoy and Austria, 40
  under Carlos III, 42
  suppressed in 1782, 43
  statistics, 44
  wants evidence from Calabria, 52
  refugees in Naples, 63
  makes arrests in Calabria, 89
Inquisitors acquire bishoprics, 201
  of Peru, their character, 355
  of Cartagena, 473, 479, 485
Insane, punishment of, 38, 235, 236, 238, 239, 329, 397, 410, 420
Insanity procures exemption, 392
  case suspended for, 432
Installation of Mexican Inq., 202
  of Peruvian, 328
Instructions, Sicilian, 13, 18, 518
  special, for colonies, 203
Insurgents excommunicated *en masse*, 280
  their documents condemned, 291
Inviolability of officials' houses, 11, 254, 386, 517
Irazábal, auditor, his knavery, 352
Irregularities of procedure in Lima, 411, 436, 437
Irreverence, cases of, in Canaries, 161, 168, 178
Isabella of Castile conquers Canaries, 139
  her zeal for the faith in the Indies, 191

JANSENISM in China, 318
  Jesuits, drowning of, 168
    persecute Bp. Palafox, 258
    their expulsion from Mexico, 270
    their precautions against solicitation, 303
    their immunity, 305, 399
    their rule in Bonol, 308
    in Paraguay, 258
    persecution of Abp. Corcuera, 309
    incensed against Inq., 367
    favor visitor Arenaza, 369
    resent the trial of Ulloa, 411
    their superiority, 515
Jew held for ransom, 143
Jewelry, censorship of, 265
Jews of Sicily, persecution in 1474, 2
  expulsion in 1492, 3
  number of, in Naples, 49
  their compulsory baptism, 50
  expulsion from Naples, 53, 62, 64, 66
  persecution in 1571, 87
  allowed in Cartagena, 469
Jimeno, Sancho, 468

INDEX 557

Joanna II suppresses Jewish usury, 49
Juan Bautista de Cardenas, *alumbrado*, 240
Juan, Jorje, on Peruvian clergy, 514
Juana of Naples, her bills of exchange, 51
Juárez, Pedro, case of, 199
Judaism in Mexico, 207
  evidences of, 434
Judaizers in Sicily, 12, 22, 24, 27
  in Naples, 50, 64
  in Canaries, 142, 144, 158
  in the New World, 193
  in Mexico, 196, 226, 227, 228, 230, 235, 271
  one relaxed in 1792, 273
  in Philippines, 304
  in Peru, 327, 329, 337, 344, 419
  in New Granada, 455, 466, 469, 501
Judges, excommunication of, 32, 34, 37, 184, 187
  courtesy enjoined towards, 254
Julius II persecutes Jews of Benevento, 53
  opposes Spanish Inq. for Naples, 57, 61
Julius III, his bull on impeding Inq., 78
  abolishes confiscation in Naples, 79, 86
Jurisdiction over clerics, 36
  secular, over heresy in Naples, 66
  temporal, of Inq., 245
  profits of, 27
  restricted, 41, 269, 388
  suspended in Sicily, 22, 24
  in Mexico in 18th century, 268, 269
Jurisdictions, multiplied, in Spanish Colonies, 511

LABOR, enforced, of Indians, 215
La Guardia, Waldenses of, 81, 82, 83
Lamport, William, case of, 236
Lanzarote, bishopric founded in, 140
Las Casas, his inql. jurisdiction, 197
  on capacity of Indians, 211
Las Palmas captured by Dutch, 146
Lazaeta, inqr. of Cartagena, 467, 499, 500
Leniency for solicitation, 164, 243, 393, 395
  for sorcery, 439, 463
  for blasphemy, 465
Leon Colorado, case of, 169
Leon, Pedro de, case of, 195
Leon, Sancho de Herrera, case of, 160
Leon y Saravia, Governor of Philippines, 316
Leopoldo da S. Pasquale, case of, 107
Libra, value of, 6

Licences to bear arms, 13
  to read prohibited books, 178
  to visit heretic lands, 130, 136
  for sailing, 254
  to leave Canaries, 142
  to leave Mexico, 204
  to leave Peru, 333, 427
Lima, Inq. of, its records, 320
  council of 1583, 321
  (*See* Inquisition of Peru).
Limpieza required in Peru, 331
Lizardi, Fernández de, case of, 273
Llano Valdés, Francisco de, 478
Loaisa, Abp., holds auto de fe, 321
Lobaton, Juan and Martin, case of, 382
Loeb, Isidor, number of Sicilian Jews, 3
Lombardy, its relations with Switzerland, 121, 129
  precautions against foreign heretics, 129, 530
López de Aponte, case of, 235
López, Luis, S. J., case of, 396, 399
Los Tres Reyes, case of, 172
Louisiana Purchase, censorship in, 274
  Inq. attempted there, 459
Louis XII, his bargain with Ferdinand, 52
Loyola y Haro, Juan de, case of, 436
Lugardi, Enrico, revives Sicilian Inq., 1
Lujan, Felipe de, his proposition, 392
Lutheranism persecuted in Sicily, 24
  in Naples, 69
  dread of, in Colonies, 200

MALDONADO DE SILVA, case of, 423
Malta, inqr. appointed for, 1
  Inq. of, 44
Malvicino, Valerio, persecutes Waldenses, 81, 82, 84
Mancera, Viceroy, on expenses of Inq., 222
  complains of Inq., 255
  speculates on the Portuguese, 433
Mañozca, Juan de, inqr. of Lima, 364
  of Cartagena, 460
  his injustice, 461
  objects to prosecuting sorcery, 463
  complaints of him, 473
  transferred to Lima, 476
  is Abp. of Mexico, 257
Mañozca, Juan Saenz de, 230, 263
Manrique, Abp., his Sicilian Instructions, 19, 518
Manrique, Francisco, Comr. of Philippines, 300
Manso, Bp. Alfonso, as inqr., 195
Manso, Giacomo, inqr. of Sicily, 2
Mantua, Inq. enforced there, 133
Marcategui, Ant. de, case of, 385

Maria Teresa suppresses Inq. of Milan, 137
Marignano, Franciscan Guardian of, his escape, 124
Marin, Sancho, inqr. of Sardinia, 109
  transferred to Sicily, 5
Marinæus Siculus, his pension, 8
Martin, Diego, Governor of Buenos Ayres, 421
Martin de Valencia as inqr., 196
Matteo da Reggio, inqr. in Naples, 49
Mattos, Fran. Rodríguez, case of, 208
Mazza, Agostino, case of, 98
Media añata, 225
Medina, J. T., his works, 320
Medina Rico, his visitation in Cartagena, 485
  transferred to Mexico, 488
  his Mexican visitation, 230
  his arbitrary action, 255
  on persecution of Palafox, 258
  tries case of Juan de la Camara, 261
Melgarejo, Luisa, case of, 400
Melgarejo, Rodrigo Ortiz, case of, 394
Membretes, 228
Mendoza, Bp. of Popayan, 473
Mercader, Benito, visitor of Sicily, 19
Mercantile cases exempted from *fuero*, 41, 43
Merchants, heretic, residence of, 136
Messina receives the Inq., 17
Mexico, growth of the Church, 193
  sanbenitos in cathedral, 196
  apprehension of Protestants, 200
  (*See* Inq. of Mexico).
Mier, Gómez de, inqr. of Cartagena, 489, 490, 491
Mier Noriega y Guerra, case of, 297
Milan. *See* Inq. of Milan.
Military service of officials, 263, 357
Miró, Estevan, Governor of Louisiana, 459
Mission from Naples to Ferdinand, 60
  to Charles V, 74, 76
Missionaries to West Indies, 192
  character of, in Colonies, 319
Missions, unsuccess of, 514, 515
Modena, Bp. of, inqr. in Milan, 121
Moles, Antonio, as confiscator, 84
Molinism in Peru, 400
Moncada, Hugo de, Viceroy of Sicily, 14
Monge, D. Miguel, his book on Inq., 41
Monox, Edward, case of, 171
Montalto, Waldenses of, 81, 82
Monterey, Viceroy, defends the exequatur, 95
Monterey, Viceroy, warned to favor Inq., 374
Montesalto, Duchess of, 85
Montesclaros, Viceroy, complains of Inq., 380

Montoro, Bp., appointed inqr. of Sicily, 6
  of Naples, 57, 58
Montúfar, Abp., as inqr., 197
  his censorship, 264
Moorish slaves, cases of, 144, 145, 159
  forbidden to go to colonies, 194
Morals, censorship of, 446, 471
Morales, Padre, excites revolt, 308
Morejon, Catalina, 356
Morelos, José María, case of, 292
Moreno y Escandon, his report, 513
Moriscos in Canaries, 144, 145, 147, 160
Mormile, Cesare, 73, 74
Moro sailors, their pagan rites, 305
Mota, David de la, 469
Moya de Contreras, inqr. of Mexico, 200, 206
Moyen, François, case of, 439
Multiplicity of jurisdictions, 511
Múñoz, Diego, his censorship, 266
Murga, Bp. of Canaries, 146, 184
Murga, Governor of Cartagena, 476
Murgier, Jean Marie, case of, 272
Muros, Bp. of Canaries, as inqr., 140
Mussumelli, Count, case of, 29
Mutineers, naval, in Vera Cruz, 268
Mutis, José Celestino, case of, 471
Mystic impostors in Mexico, 235
  in Peru, 396

NAPLES, its conquest by Ferdinand, 53
  its municipal organization, 54
  tumult of 1547, 72
  English girl abducted in 1746, 106
  (*See* Inquisition of Naples).
Nava, Antonio, case of, 104
Negro slaves in Canaries, 148, 159
New Christians banished from Naples, 62, 64
  forbidden to leave Canaries, 142
  not allowed in the Colonies, 193, 419
New Granada, the earliest Spanish settlement, 453
  description of its people, 461
  revolution of 1810, 506
  its condition in 1772, 513
  (*See* Inquisition of New Granada).
New Mexico, Governor of, arrested, 256
Nicholas V sends inqr. to Naples, 49
Nobles as familiars, 28, 30, 32, 42
Nuevo Reino de Granada, 453
Number of Sicilian Jews, 3
  of familiars allowed, 13
  in Sicily, 28, 31
  in Sardinia, 117
  in Canaries, 146

Number of familiars in Mexico, 247, 536
  in Peru, 330
  in New Granada, 468

OATH of obedience to Inq., 11, 202, 534
  of independence in New Granada, 507
Oaxaca, Bp. of, penances Indians, 211
Obregon, Diego de, receiver of Sicily, 6, 9, 12
Occult arts, Edict of Faith against, 391
Ochino, Bernardino, 69, 70
Officials, crimes of, 14
  engage in trade, 21
  their exemptions, 22, 380
  their *fuero*, 22, 24, 245
  hostility towards them, 23, 26
  their excepted crimes, 31, 247, 330
  their abuses in Naples, 100
  in the Colonies, 251, 498
  multiplication in Sardinia, 117, 119
  royal safeguard for, 202
  their immunities, 246
  subordinated to State, 275
  not to receive commissions, 521
  not to receive presents, 523
Offices, traffic in, 372
Olivares, Viceroy, rebukes the Inq., 33
Olivitos, Angela, case of, 400
Onza of Sicily, 5
Opinions, political, prosecution for, 273
Orders, Religious, laxity in, 244, 515
  complain of Mañozca, 474
Ordóñez, Comr., arrests governor, 256
Ordóñez appointed inqr. of Lima, 360
  secures a legacy, 344
  his greed, 362
  made Abp. of Santafé, 363
  on solicitation, 394
Organization of Mexican Inq., 204, 289
  of Lima Inq., 350, 451
  of city of Naples, 54
Ortiz, Juan, inqr. of Cartagena, 479, 482, 486, 487
Ortíz, Tomas, as inqr., 196
Osuna, Viceroy, his obsequiousness, 93
Ottine of Naples, 55
Ovalle, Manuel de, S. J., 407, 410
Oviedo, Rodrigo de, 479, 484, 486, 487
Ozaeta, Pablo de, inqr. of Cartagena, 499, 500

PABLO DE SANTA MARIA, 423
  Pact with demon, 166
Padilla, José de, inqr. of Cartagena, 489, 490, 491
Padilla, Luis de, inqr. of Canaries, 144
Palacios, Andrés, 57, 60, 63

Palafox, Bp. Juan de, his persecution, 257
  his *Ejercicios devotos* suppressed, 471
Palermo, rising in 1511, 11
  complaints of Inq., 13
  rising in 1516, 15
  auto de fe of 1724, 40
Panamá, alguazil in, 331
  under Cartagena tribunal, 457
Pantelaria, inqr. appointed for, 1
Pantolosa the Neapolitan banker, 50
Panza, commissioner, 82, 86
Paolo d'Arezzo, mission to Philip II, 86, 525
Paolo Sarpi, on trade with heretics, 137
Papal Inq. in Naples controlled by viceroy, 56
Paraguay, Jesuits in, 258
Parliament of Naples in 1536, 66
  Sicilian, complaints of, 13, 21, 22, 26
Pascale, Giovan Luigi, burnt, 80
Pastry, sacred heads in, 266
Paternina, Commissioner of Philippines, 311
Paul III organizes Roman Inq., 70
  his relations with Naples, 76
  stimulates Inq. of Sardinia, 117
  stimulates persecution in Milan, 121
  forbids New Christians to go to America, 194
  on capacity of Indians, 210
Paul IV introduces Roman Inq. in Naples, 78
  restores confiscation, 79
  coerces Abp. of Sassari, 117
  degrades Bp. of Brescia, 122
  stimulates persecution in Milan, 123
Paul V intervenes in Sardinia, 118
Pay-roll of Neapolitan Inq., 57
  of Sardinian, 114
  of Mexican, 289
  of Peruvian, 350, 451
Payta, English descent on, 375
Pearls, confiscated, sent to Ferdinand, 112
Peculation in Inq. of Sicily, 19, 521
  in Inq. of Peru, 340, 351
  in Inq. of Cartagena, 487
Pedro de Córdova, a missionary, 192, 195
Pelayo, Nofre, case of, 51
Penitents, labor required of, 19
  their transportation, 234, 235
  pelting of, prohibited, 432, 438
Peña, Antonio de la, inqr. of Sicily, 2
Peñaranda, Viceroy, expels Piazza, 99
Peralta, inqr. of Mexico, 207, 208
Peralta, Governor, his arrest, 256
Pereira Castro, inqr. of Cartagena, 483, 485, 486, 487, 488
Pereyns, Simon, case of, 198

560   INDEX

Pérez, Manuel Bautista, case of, 431
Peru, episcopal inq. in, 197, 321
  royal rebuke of inqrs., 251
  irreverent use of crosses, 266
  its condition in 16th century, 319
    (See Inquisition of Peru).
Pestilence, atonement for, 143
Petronila de San Esteban, a beata, 163
Petronio, Bp., calls himself inqr., 94
Peyote, use of, in Mexico, 228
Philip II orders officials protected, 23
  restores the *fuero*, 25
  humiliates Viceroy Terranova, 25
  orders the Inq. aided, 26
  rebukes Viceroy Alba, 29
  makes concession to justice, 30
  his assurance to Naples, 86, 525
  asks aid for Sardinian Inq., 116
  proposes Spanish Inq. for Milan, 125
  abandons the project, 128, 529
  sustains Inq. of Canaries, 180
  zeal for the faith in the New World, 191
  forbids New Christians access to colonies, 194
  regulates familiars in colonies, 197, 247, 536
  fears Protestantism in Colonies, 200
  founds Inq. in Mexico, 203
  exempts Indians from Inq., 210
  his grant to Inq. of Mexico, 212
  suppresses episcopal Inq. in Philippines, 301
  founds Inq. of Peru, 326
  royal protection for officials, 374
  refuses tribunal to New Granada, 456
Philip III, his instructions for Sicily, 33
  his circular letter to viceroys, 35
  efforts to learn receipts, 216, 344
  issues Concordia of 1610, 251
  regulates competencias, 253
  excludes Bibles from colonies, 267
  royal protection for officials, 374
  his subvention for Cartagena tribunal, 460, 500
Philip IV orders the *via ordinaria*, 99
  enforces the exequatur, 95
  subjects inqrs. to *alcavala*, 215
  claims return of subvention, 220
  demands accounts from tribunals, 216, 221, 345, 348
  his gratification at autos, 233, 240
  regulates competencias, 253
  issues Concordia of 1633, 254
  on Philippine commissioners, 310
  proposes subdivision of Peru, 338
  on secret prison of Cartagena, 480
  on visitation of Martin Real, 481, 484
Philip V abandons Naples, 102
  orders foreigners expelled, 176
  rebukes Inq. of Canaries, 187

Philip V represses the Lima Inq., 384
Philippines, canonries in, 217
  solicitation in, 243, 302
    (See Inq. of Philippines).
Phillips, Miles, his account of auto of 1574, 205
Piazza, Bp., establishes a tribunal, 98
  is expelled, 99
Piazze of Naples, 54
Piélago, secretary, as office broker, 372
Pimienta, Governor of Cartagena, 499
Pinto, Paz, case of, 466
Piracy in Canaries, 168
Pius IV opposes Spanish Inq., 86
  agrees to it, for Milan, 125
Pius V objects to exequatur, 90
  as inqr. of Como, 122
  his decree as to Inq., 132, 531
  proposes Spanish Inq. for Venice, 132
  his quarrel with Mantua, 133
  his advice as to the Indies, 199
Pizarro, María, case of, 396
Placido di Sangro sent to Charles V, 74, 76, 77
Plata, Juan, case of, 242
Poblete, José Millan de, 313, 316
Pointis, Baron de, captures Cartagena, 467
Poisonings in Cartagena, 486
Political functions of Canary tribunal, 190
  of Mexican tribunal, 272, 275
Ponte y Andrade, inqr. of Lima, 365
Popular sovereignty a heresy, 275
Portorubio, Bp. of Malta, as inqr., 46
Portuguese Judaizers, 229
  complaints in Peru of, 337, 341, 421
  ordered to leave Peru, 433
  prosecuted in New Granada, 466
Poverty of Mexican Inq., 213
Prado sent as visitador to Peru, 357
  on commissioners, 335
  his charges against Ulloa, 358
  Ulloa's charges against him, 359
  his proposed reforms, 360
  prosecutes viceroy, 376
Pragmatic sanction of 1732, 42
Pralboino, Claudio, escapes burning, 123
Prebends for colonial tribunals, 216, 347, 501, 503, 504, 508
Precautions against heretics in Lombardy, 135, 530
Precedence in competencias, 253, 267
  in bull-fights, 254
Pre-emption forbidden, 251, 254
Printing-office, none in Cartagena, 470
Prison, secret, in Canaries, 157, 158
  confinement in, 480
  penitential, in Mexico, 214
Prisoners, cost of maintenance, 353
  care for them, 519, 521

INDEX

Prisoners, English, claimed by Inq., 357
  of war, trials of, in Peru, 414
  their rights respected, 418
Privileges of officials in Sicily, 10
  in the colonies, 245
Procedure of Roman Inq., 97
  of episcopal Inq., 105
Profits of jurisdiction, 28
Prohibited books, strictness as to, 274
  given to Archbishop, 289
  in Philippines, 306
Propagandism, Protestant, dread of, 200
Property, efforts to conceal, 427
Propositions, heretical, 392, 441, 455, 470
Protestantism, dread of, 200
Protestants, in Canaries, 167, 175
  in Mexico, 198, 205, 207, 208, 226
  in Peru, 321, 325
  in New Granada, 466
Punishment, capricious, in Lima, 437
Purchase of offices, 372

QUAKERESSES in Maltese Inq., 47
  Quarantine against heretics in Lombardy, 530
Quarrels with bishops, 35, 182, 257, 476, 491
  of inqrs., 355, 359, 363, 366, 479, 485, 488, 490
  with authorities, 373, 473, 484, 488
  financial, in Mexico, 212, 217
Quebrantamientos de escrituras de juego, 349
Queipo, Bp. of Mechoacan, 275, 290
Quemadero in Mexico, 206
Querétaro, censorship in, 266
Quevedo, Juan, Bp. of Cuba, 195
Quicksilver, distribution of, 255
Quietism of Juan de Valdés, 68
Quietists in Sardinia, 119
  in Peru, 406, 410
Quiñones, Dr., his confiscation, 343
Quiroga, Inq.-genl., his letter to Bp. Vera, 181
Quirós, Bernardo de, Inqr. of Cartagena, 489, 490, 491
Quito, Bp. Peña of, his legacy, 344

RANZANO, Bp., inqr. of Sicily, 2
  Real, Martin, his visitation, 348, 481, 483
Real estate, alienations of, 14
Rebeldía, 182
Rebiba, Scipione, in Naples, 78
Recalde, Fray Joseph, case of, 449
Receipts, statements of, refused, 216, 219, 345, 504

Receivership, dangers of, 111, 114
Reconciliation entails confiscation, 421
Records of the tribunals, 190, 288, 298, 317, 320
Recruits pretending Catholicism, 271
Reforms attempted in Sicily, 13, 18, 518
  proposed, in Peru, 360
Refugees from Sicily in Naples, 64, 65
Reggio, persecution in, 86
  arrests by Sicilian Inq., 89
Registers, parish, falsified, 434
  imperfect, 514
Relaxations in Canaries, 154
Remittances from Mexico, 219, 221, 224, 225
Renegades in Canaries, 160
Repartimientos of Indians, 215
Requisitions by Inq., 251, 252, 254
Resistance to sanbenitos, 24
Revolution, French, influence of, 272
Revolution of Mexico, its ferocity, 281
  of New Granada, 506
Reyes, Luisa de los, a *beata*, 304
Ribagorza, Viceroy, controls papal Inq., 56, 524
Ribera, Teodoro de, case of, 392
Riciullo, Bp., acts as inqr., 96
Rio de Janeiro, Portuguese arrested, 421
Rising of 1516 in Palermo, 15
  of 1547, in Naples, 72
Rivas, Gerónimo, case of, 375
Roda, Giacomo, inqr. of Sicily, 2
Rodríguez, Juan, his complaint, 266
Rodríguez, Rafael Gil, case of, 273
Roelas, Alonso de las, case of, 161
Rojas, José Ant., sentenced for liberalism, 273
Rome, citations to, 89
  prisoners sent there, 79
  burnings in, 80, 88, 135
Romero, the sisters, *embusteras*, 235, 239
Romo, Bartolo, alcaide, 367
Romualdo, Fra, burnt in 1724, 40

SAFEGUARD, royal, for officials, 202
  Sagro Monte della Pietà in Naples, 67
Sailors, foreign, prosecution of, 169
Sala reflexa, 387
Salaries of Sicilian tribunal, 6, 9
  of Sardinian tribunal, 109
  regulated by confiscations, 114, 528
  for Inq. of Naples, 57
  in Mexico, 212, 289
  in Peru, 350, 451
Salas y Pedroso, inqr. of Cartagena, 488, 489
Salar, Bp. of Manila, his Inq., 299
Salazar, Luis Rúiz de, case of, 152

562   INDEX

Salcedo, Governor of Philippines, his imprisonment, 311
Salcedo, inqr. of Cartagena, 460, 476
Salerno, Prince of, sent to Charles V, 74
Saldaña, Fray Juan de, case of, 242
Salice, Hercole, a heretic, 129
Salinas, Dr., 360, 376, 379
Salinas, Gregorio de, comr. in Vera Cruz, 268
Sanbenitos, opposition to, in Sicily, 15, 24, 523
  for Waldenses, 83
  discarded from churches in Canaries, 188
  burnt, 189
  in Mexican cathedral, 196, 226
  use made of them, 289
  of Morelos, 296
  of prisoners of war, 417
Sánchez, Miguel, case of, 113
Sanders, John, case of, 145, 168
San Lorenzo, Tribunale de, 55
San Sisto, Waldenses of, 81, 82, 83
Santa Clara, nuns of, at Cartagena, 491, 493
Santa Cruz, Domingo de, case of, 110
Santa Marta, Diego de, case of, 166
Santa Marta, see of, 453
  bishop of, 492, 493, 494
Santangel, Luis de, refuses Pantolosa's bills, 51
Santiago, commissioner of Chile, 346
Santo Domingo, subject to Lima, 333
  to Cartagena, 457
  Jews allowed in, 469
St. Augustine, attempts to found Inq. there, 458
St. John, Order of, in Malta, 45
Sardinia. *See* Inq. of Sardinia.
Sartolo, Bernardo, S. J., 405
Savoy, Sicilian Inq. under, 40
  obtains Sardinia, 119
Scrutinium Scripturarum, 423
Scourging in Mexico, 206
  in Peru, 431, 438
Sebastian, Inqr., attacked, 23
  his activity, 26
Secretaries of Suprema, payments to, 350
Secular jurisdiction over heresy in Naples, 56, 66, 524
Sedella, Ant. de, inqr. of Louisiana, 459
Seggi of Naples, 54
Sentence of Waldenses, 83
  of Morelos, 298
  of François Moyen, 443
Sentences not enforced, 20, 520
Sequestrations in Mexico, 223
  in Peru, 348, 429
  commerce destroyed by, 428
  not applied by commissioners, 301

Sequestrations not applicable to prisoners of war, 417
Servants of officials, their privileges, 31, 245, 474
Sessa, Duke of, Governor of Milan, 127, 128, 129
Seville, composition of, 193
  its jurisdiction over Canaries, 141
Sgalambro, Dr., inqr. of Sicily, 6, 8
Shaw, Robert, case of, 413
Sheep given to a Jew, 143
Ships, detention of, 252, 254, 333
Sickness, efforts to convert in, 175
Sinaloa, governor of, excommunicated, 249
Sixtus IV asks Inq. for Sicily, 1
Sixtus V places a commissioner in Naples, 92
Slavery, escape from, is apostasy, 149
Slaves, Christian, sold by Inq., 19, 520
  in Canaries, 144, 148, 149, 152, 159
  of officials, their immunity, 251, 474
  their exemption abrogated, 388
  false witness of, 437
  negro, in New Granada, 462
Snuff-boxes, censorship of, 178
Sobranis, Ana de, a beata, 183
Socaya, inqr. of Cartagena, 483
Solicitation in Canaries, 163
  in Mexico, 227, 228, 241, 271
  in Philippines, 302
  in Peru, 344, 393
Solis, José, case of, 407, 410
Soranzo Bp. of Brescia, case of, 122
Sorcery in Naples, 101
  in Canaries, 147, 148, 165
  in Mexico, 206, 228
  in Peru, 391, 439
  in New Granada, 462
Soto, Juan de, case of, 160
Spinelli, Abp., his Inq., 104
  forced to resign, 107
Spinello, lord of La Guardia, 80, 85
Stevenson, W. B., 373, 447
Stomeo, Giantonio, case of, 94
Stoning penitents prohibited, 432, 438
Suárez de Figueroa, inqr. of Cartagena, 495, 498
Subdivision of Peru proposed, 337
Subsidy, Sicilian, to Charles V, 22
Subvention, royal, of Mexican tribunal, 212, 216, 218, 220, 222
  of Lima tribunal, 342, 344, 347
  of Cartagena tribunal, 500, 501, 502
Sueldo, value of, 6
Superstitions in New Granada, 462
Superunda, Viceroy of Peru, 370, 387
Suppression of Sicilian Inq., 43
  of Neapolitan, 107
  of Sardinian, 119
  of Milanese, 137

Suppression of Canary Inq., 189
  of Mexican, 270, 288, 298
  of Peruvian, 354, 447
  of New Granadan, 507, 510
Suprema, its large receipts from Mexico, 219
  its duplicity and concealment, 219, 221, 223, 224, 348
  on Salcedo's arrest, 315
  relations with colonial tribunals, 331
  urges subdivision of Peru, 337
  payments to its secretaries, 350
  contributions to, from Cartagena, 502 505
  its demands for remittances, 513
Swiss, their relations with Milan, 129
Symbols, sacred, prohibited, 265
Syndics, Jesuit, in solicitation, 303
Syracuse, Bp. of, his quarrel with Inq., 36

TABALORO, CARLO, case of, 38
Tagal book, heresy in, 307
Tanner, John, case of, 173
Tanucci, Regent of Naples, 107
Tarragona, Abp. of, his bills of exchange, 51
Tattooing, censorship of, 266
Taxation, exemption from, in Mexico, 215
Tello de Sandoval, inqr. of Mexico, 197
Tenerife, foreigners in, 172, 175
Terracina, Domenico, 72
Terranova, Duke of, case of, 25
Terror aroused by Inq., 98
Tezcoco, cacique of, burnt, 196
Thimbles, crosses on, erased, 266
Toledo, Pedro de, Viceroy of Naples, 66
  urges introduction of Inq., 70
  bombards the city, 73
  his vindictive triumph, 76
Toledo, Viceroy of Peru, on condition of colony, 319
  gets rid of Aguirre, 323
  controls royal subvention, 342
  curbs the Inq., 374
Toleration proclaimed in Colombia, 510
Tormentors, 448
Toro, Pedro de, case of, 396, 398
Torquemada appoints inqr. for Sicily, 2
Torres, Comr. of Popayan, 454
Torture administered by physician, 142
  severity of, in Lima, 429
  implements of, 447
Trade forbidden to officials, 251, 254
  with heretics creates suspicion, 130, 136, 137
  danger of, in Canaries, 168
Traffic in offices, 372
Transportation of penitents, 234, 235

Travel in heretic lands, licence for, 130, 136, 137
Treaty of 1604 with England, 171
Trent, Council of, opposes Spanish Inq., 127
  on episcopal power over heresy, 211
Treviño, Tomás, his martyrdom, 233
Treviso, licences to travel required, 136
Tribaldos, Bart., first Canary inqr., 140
Tucuman, its conquest by Aguirre, 322
  solicitation in, 393, 394, 395
Tuscany, arrests require assent of ruler, 137
Tumult of 1516 in Palermo, 15
  of 1547 in Naples, 72

UBAU, PEDRO, case of, 353, 407, 410
Ulloa, Ant. Gut., inqr. of Peru, 355
  complaints against him, 356
  Prado's charges, 358
  his sentence, 360
  visits his district, 361
  his dismissal and death, 362
  prosecutes viceroy, 376, 544
Ulloa, Antonio de, on Peruvian clergy, 514
Ulloa, Francisco de, S. J., case of, 406, 410
Ulloa, Juan Fran. de, case of, 367
Ullos, Juan de, case of, 393
Unda, Diego de, inqr. of Peru, 352
  his property sequestrated, 352
  his confiscated jewels, 354
  his scandals, 366
  his arrest, 368
  his release and death, 370
  condemns Quietists, 410
Universities, compulsory degrees of, 252
University of Lima favors suppression, 449
Unnatural crime, 244
Urban VII suppresses canonries in Peru, 346
Urban VIII defends Fra Petronio, 95
  grants prebends to colonial tribunals, 216
Uriarte, Juan de, secretary, 479, 482, 486, 487, 488
Utrecht, treaty of, 40
Uzstáriz, Commissioner, his zeal, 305

VALERA, FRANCISCO, inqr. of Cartagena, 491
  his quarrel with Bp. Benavides, 492
  is transferred to Lima, 495
  his actions condemned, 365, 498
  insists on royal subvention, 503, 504
  as inqr. of Lima, 364

564   INDEX

Valera, Francisco, tries Angela Carranza, 400, 404
  his jubilation, 365
Valderrama, Francisco de, 356
Valdés la Vandera, 269
Valdés, Juan de, his influence, 67
  his disciples in Reggio, 86
Valdivia, Dutch attack on, 418
  as place of punishment, 438
Valtelline, foreign priests expelled, 136
  its territory violated, 135
Vandenbosch, Franz, case of, 170
Vanegas, Diego, case of, 361
Van Hoflaquen, Georg, case of, 170
Varas of alguazil, sale of, 224, 225, 349, 501
Vargas, Ant. de, case of his will, 387
Vazquez, Francisco, case of, 394
Vega, Viceroy, relations with Inq., 25
Velazco, Governor of Cartagena, his complaints, 473
Velazco, Juan Francisco, case of, 407, 410
Velazco, Viceroy, complains of Inq., 380
Vélez, Fray Andrés, case of, 399
Vélez, inqr. of Cartagena, 477
  transferred to Mexico, 478
Venadita, Viceroy, suppresses Mexican Inq., 298
Vendeja, inqr. of Cartagena, 499
Venice, its regulation of Inq., 132
  residence of foreign heretics, 531
Vera, Bp., his quarrel with Canary Inq., 181
Vera Cruz, mutineer sailors in, 268
Verdugo, Bp., on suppression of Inq., 189
Verdugo, Francisco, inqr. of Lima, 363
Vessels, service of, for Roman Inq., 91
  seizure of, 156, 169
Via ordinaria, 87, 90, 97, 99, 100, 102, 106, 526
Vicente, Juan, case of, 466
Vicente de Santa María as inqr., 196
Viceroyalty of New Granada, 453
Viceroys ordered to favor Inq., 35, 250, 374
  excommunication of, 32, 375
  not to be excommunicated, 252
Vico, Marquis of, case of, 90
Vienna, Sicilian Inq. subject to, 40
Viera y Clavijo, his history of Canaries, 180
Villadiego, Inqr. of Cartagena, 482, 483, 485, 486, 487
Villar, Viceroy, on clergy of Peru, 320
  banishes Catalina Morejon, 356
  his complaints of tribunal, 357
  his troubles with Inq., 374
  is excommunicated, 375
  is prosecuted, 376

Villar, his submission, 378, 544
  his appeal to Philip II, 379
  hands over prisoners of war, 414
Villareal, Abp. of Mexico, 257
Villaroel, Bp. of Chile, 346
Villaroel, Ant. Hernández, case of, 393
Visitas de navíos, in Canaries, 176, 179
  in Mexico, 266
  in Philippines, 304
Visitations of Canaries, 148, 149
  of Mexico, 261
  of Peru, 357, 367
  of Cartagena, 481, 485
  of districts of Peru, 332
Vitoria, Elena de, case of, 464, 465
Voz activa, officials deprived of, 14

WALDENSES in Calabria, 49
  eradicated, 79
  in Apulia, their fate, 85, 524
Wall-papers, censorship of, 446
Watches undergo censorship, 471
Wealth of Peruvian clergy, 515
White horse, parade of, 430, 437
Widows of officials, their privileges, 31, 42
Will case, quarrel over, 387
Wine, exportation of from Canaries, 156
Witchcraft in Canaries, 167
  in New Granada, 464
Witnesses' names, suppression of, 26, 97
Women, scourging of, 431, 438

XIMENES, CARD., his appointment of colonial inqrs., 195
Ximenes, Martin, inqr. of Canaries, 141, 142, 180
Xuquil, Indians of, their idolatry, 211

YÁÑEZ, GONZALO, case of, 248
  Yepes, Rodrigo de, case of, 248
Ynes de Tarifa, case of, 143
Yucatan, *visitas de navíos* in, 267

ZALDUEGUI, PEDRO, inqr. of Lima, 372
Zapata, Governor of Cartagena, 485
Zarate, Fray Francisco de, case of, 243
Zarate, Ortiz de, Inqr. of Cartagena, 494
Zayas, Bravo de, visitor of Canaries, 148, 161
Zuazo, Alonso de, on New Christians, 194
Zubieta, Pedro de, case of, 395
Zumárraga, Bp., burns cacique of Tezcoco, 196
Zuñiga, Viceroy, his subservience, 94
Zurita on Sicilian finances, 24

"The Greatest Historical Work yet Produced in America"

A HISTORY OF THE
INQUISITION OF SPAIN

BY

HENRY CHARLES LEA, LL.D.

In Four Volumes

"An achievement which places its author at the head of all American historical students now living. It makes him the peer of Motley, Prescott and Parkman, his only competitors in the past. To put the matter shortly Mr. Lea has produced a work on a subject of absorbing interest, which for many a long day to come must serve as an authority to European experts on the subject."—*New York Times.*

The *New York Tribune* describes the work as "an historical classic in which thoroughness, fairness and reserve are combined in a readable presentation of facts of universal interest."

"Dr. Lea has given the world of thoughtful students a work that will have a lasting place and a growing power in the right use of history. His works have found many readers in Europe, where the questions of Church and State are much more acute than in this country. Here scholars and the growing army of historical students and writers all unite to do honor to Doctor Lea as the foremost American historian, whose researches in an almost unknown field have shown how great a power he possesses of throwing new light on old facts and marshalling historical evidence so as to give the world a new picture of a far-distant past."—*Philadelphia Ledger.*

"Rarely has so significant an institution been so sanely and comprehensively studied, and rarely has the reader been placed in so good a position to observe its workings and draw his own conclusions from the evidence presented."—*The Nation.*

It is one of the most interesting problems in human history that Spain, whose brilliant achievements promised to make her as dominant in the world of letters as in military and naval enterprise, should, within the space of a couple of generations, have become the most uncultured land in Christendom. For this there must have been a cause and no other adequate one than the Inquisition has been discovered. In this work Dr. Lea makes clear the progress of its influence.

Complete in four 8vo volumes, cloth, gilt tops, the set, $10, net.

THE MACMILLAN COMPANY
PUBLISHERS

64-66 Fifth Avenue   New York

BY THE SAME AUTHOR

HISTORY OF THE
INQUISITION OF THE MIDDLE AGES

In Three Volumes

"To write of the Inquisition without bitterness, to bring the operations to calm analysis, to seek out its origin and reason for being in the conditions of the time, and to trace its influences—such is the task to which Dr. Lea brings the experience of a born investigator and the poise and dignity of a trained historian."—*New York Tribune.*

"There are some books which reveal the loftiest effort of a broad and earnest life; such a book springs from the highest aims, and will therefore be recognized not only as scientific, but as giving impulse to the intellectual action and aspiration of its epoch. Such a book is the 'History of the Inquisition of the Middle Ages,' by Henry Charles Lea."
—*Frankfurter Zeitung.*

Cloth, the set, $7.50, net.

A HISTORY OF
SACERDOTAL CELIBACY IN THE CHRISTIAN CHURCH

In Two Volumes, Third Edition, Revised

Of special interest to those who are watching a modern trend toward clerical ascetic celibacy. It aims to be an impartial statement of facts with references to the authority substantiating the statement.

Cloth, the set, $5, net.

THE MACMILLAN COMPANY
PUBLISHERS

64-66 Fifth Avenue   New York

Milton Keynes UK
Ingram Content Group UK Ltd.
UKHW041619250224
438379UK00008B/933